INTERNATIONAL ORGANIZATIONAL BEHAVIOR

Text, Cases, and Exercises

SECOND EDITION

INTERNATIONAL ORGANIZATIONAL BEHAVIOR
Text, Cases, and Exercises

Anne Marie Francesco
Hong Kong Baptist University

Barry Allen Gold
Lubin School of Business, Pace University

PEARSON
Prentice Hall

Upper Saddle River, New Jersey 07458

Library of Congress Cataloging-in-Publication Data

Francesco, Anne Marie.
    International organizational behavior: text, cases, and skills / Anne Marie Francesco,
Barry Allen Gold.—2nd ed.
        p. : ill. ; cm.
    Includes bibliographical references and index.
    ISBN 0–13–100879–X (pbk.)
    1. Organizational behavior.   2. International business enterprises.   I. Gold, Barry A.
II. Title.

HD58.7.F694 2005
658'.049—dc22

2004014881

Project Manager: Ashley Keim
Senior Acquisitions Editor: Jennifer Simon
Editor-in-Chief: Jeff Shelstad
Media Project Manager: Jessica Sabloff
Marketing Manager: Anke Braun
Marketing Assistant: Patrick Dansuzo
Managing Editor: John Roberts
Permissions Supervisor: Charles Morris
Manufacturing Buyer: Michelle Klein
Production Manager: Arnold Vila
Cover Design: Bruce Kenselaar
Cover Illustration: Hua Lee
Composition: Integra
Full-Service Project Management: Carlisle Communications
Printer/Binder: Hamilton

Credits and acknowledgments borrowed from other sources and reproduced, with permission, in this textbook appear on appropriate page within text.

Pearson Education LTD.
Pearson Education Singapore, Pte. Ltd
Pearson Education, Canada, Ltd
Pearson Education–Japan

Pearson Education Australia PTY, Limited
Pearson Education North Asia Ltd
Pearson Educación de Mexico, S.A. de C.V.
Pearson Education Malaysia, Pte. Ltd

10 9 8 7 6 5 4 3 2 1
ISBN 0–13–100879–X

This book is dedicated to the memory
of my father, Henry P. Francesco.
—Anne Marie Francesco

For Bonnie.
—Barry Allen Gold

Brief Contents

Contents

Preface

This book is a guide to the theories and practices necessary to understand international organizational behavior and to manage successfully in the global economy of the 21st century. The topics include anthropological theories that explain variations and similarities in human behavior across cultures, comparative perspectives of work motivation and leadership, as well as findings from research on practical issues such as how to select expatriates and techniques for managing culturally diverse virtual teams. The wide range of theories and applications that comprise international organizational behavior attest to the need for the broad intellectual preparation required for today's global managers.

Although international organizational behavior is a comparatively recent field, multinational corporations have navigated, with varying degrees of success, the complexities of different national cultures, languages, customs, and behaviors for several centuries. After World War II, however, with the acceleration of the growth of international business, some companies succeeded to a previously unimaginable extent in establishing a global presence and became synonymous with capitalism and globalization. Who hasn't seen the picture of a Coke machine in the jungle? Who doesn't have an opinion on McDonaldization? This book examines the effect of globalization on management theories and practices and debates whether there is convergence into a unitary global model of management and organization.

At the beginning of the 21st century even small business is becoming global. The likelihood that a small or medium-size business located anywhere now competes globally has increased because the Internet increases access and eliminates geographic distance. With geography less of a barrier and contact with other cultures increasingly common, understanding the implications of cultural differences and similarities is critical for all managers.

The experience of a small manufacturer of shelves for retail stores in Newark, New Jersey, is an example of how, because of the interconnectedness of the global economy, a local organization can suddenly need to understand other cultures. Paul Dunbach, the co-owner and CEO of Handy Manufacturing, Inc., explained his firm's immersion into the global economy.

> In November 2000, I received an e-mail from a manufacturer in China asking if I was interested in taking a look at their products. It was amazing how much they knew about the various types of retail shelves used in the United States. Even more amazing, the e-mail used the technical language of the industry and, to my total surprise, understood the needs and problems of my customers and me.
>
> I thought about the offer for a week and decided that I had nothing to lose so I had them ship me a sample.

The sample was very good. It was almost identical to the shelves I make in my factory. But incredibly, the difference was that even with shipping from China, the shelf cost me one-third less than I could manufacture it for in Newark, New Jersey.

This year we ordered 85% of our shelves from China; we only manufacture customized shelves that are usually odd sizes. In 2001 we had 300 workers, in 2003 we had about 100—next year we'll probably have 50.

If a customer asks, I tell them that our manufacturing facility is now in China. No one has ever mentioned anything more about it—even with the box clearly marked" "China." My customers are satisfied with the quality—even though sometimes I think it's a little shoddy—I can price my shelves competitively, and because of reduced expenses, I now have considerably more profit than before.

To manage this major organization change successfully, Dunbach had to learn quickly—as did the Chinese manufacturer to prepare to approach the U.S. market—how the Chinese communicate, negotiate, and relate to time. Most importantly, he had to determine if there was sufficient trust for the relationship to work. If product quality deteriorated, deliveries became unreliable, or prices increased unexpectedly, the relationship could become mired in conflict and possibly terminated, creating the need to locate a new supplier or, in the worst case, resume full production in the New Jersey factory. Before proceeding, some questions Dunbach thought about were:

- How will I communicate with the Chinese manufacturer?
- What negotiation tactics could I use to arrive at a fair price at the quality I need?
- What terms should I include in a contract? Do the Chinese understand the meaning of contracts in the same way as Americans?
- Would the Chinese manufacturer understand my concern with the timely delivery of products to customers?
- To what extent should I trust the Chinese company? How can I build trust and a long-term relationship?

International Organizational Behavior: Text, Cases, and Skills, 2/e provides theoretical perspectives to help identify these and other relevant questions when engaging in business across cultures. The text also contains possible answers to questions that managers confront when they enter the global economy.

▮▮▮ What's New in the Second Edition?

The second edition of *International Organizational Behavior: Text, Cases, and Skills* has been completely rewritten and contains a new chapter, significant new research in each chapter, several new "Culture at Work" vignettes that open each chapter, and updated examples of behavior in organizations. Highlights of material new to the second edition are:

- *New chapter:* Organizational Commitment, Organizational Justice, and Work-Family Interface

- *New topics:* Universal human behaviors, changes in global population mobility, the persistence of cultural values, the limits of cultural convergence, transnational teams, virtual teams, and network organizations.

- *New research:* The World Values Survey, Schwartz's Value Survey, Project GLOBE research on cross-cultural leadership, Transparency International's "Corruption Perceptions Index," research on managing diversity, and emerging perspectives on multicultural teams.

- *New cases:* There are 11 new cases that cover all areas of international organizational behavior including:
  - "Shell Oil in Nigeria" by Anne T. Lawrence
  - "Argentina Suites (II): 1996 to 1998" by Demian Hodari and Timothy R. Hinkin
  - "Fuquima Washing Machine Corporation" by Haihong Xu

- *New skill exercises:*
  - "Where Have You Been? An Exercise to Assess Your Exposure to the Rest of the World's People" by Paul Beamish
  - "Selected Intercultural Incidents" by S. Paul Verluyten
  - "Royal Flush: A Cross-Cultural Simulation" by Jessica Robinson, Tamu Lewars, La Shanda Perryman, Torla Crichlow, Kimberly Smith, and John Vignoe

- *New pedagogy:* Web sites at the end of every chapter provide Internet addresses for selected companies and content sites that students can access to learn more about important topics.

▪▪▪ Aims of the Text

The primary aim of the text is to provide students and instructors with an up-to-date introduction to the field of international organizational behavior and management. Understanding the functioning of Western European and American organizations has been an ongoing effort for most of the 20th century. In the 21st century it is important to understand how organizations function in a wide variety of cultures.

A second aim is to present the material as global rather than from a North American or Western European perspective. The second edition continues to move away from a purely Western conception of organizational behavior. Although significant new cross-cultural research has appeared since the first edition and is included in this edition, this remains difficult to accomplish for several reasons. First, much of the management and organizational literature—research, theory, and informed speculation—is either North American or Western European. In fact, American scholars dominate the field. Second, many countries view the West as a model for economic development, including the use of Western management principles, and often embrace them uncritically. In many instances, articles and cases written by indigenous writers about their cultures borrow extensively from American research and theory, making cultural variations difficult to detect. An example of the migration and intermingling of management ideas is that in 2003 Chinese professors translated the first edition of this book into Chinese because of Chinese interest in understanding other cultures to become more sophisticated and successful members of the World Trade Organization. Third, related to the last point, over the past twenty years, the distinction between Western and non-Western—particularly Asian—organization theory and management practice has blurred because of selective borrowing and the fusion of ideas and practices from East and West. Fourth, major parts of the globe—for example, Russia, China, and South Africa—are changing rapidly making it difficult to generate reliable knowledge and quickly dating what is known. Finally, the concept of modern organization in the United States as embodied in the corporation—which exerts a strong influence on other countries—is simultaneously undergoing temporary and fundamental changes. For example, in 2003 as a result of the business cycle, after a decade of exuberant growth, corporations in the United States downsized, consolidated through mergers, and in some cases well-established, formerly highly profitable companies struggled to survive. American business also experienced an historic crisis in corporate ethics that has influenced global business as well. At the same time, more enduring changes are that businesses continue to introduce technological innovations and globalize.

Another intention is to present a cultural perspective on organizational behavior and management. The emphasis on culture differs from other approaches because it views culture not only as important for understanding other societies and managing organizations, but as a major cause of much behavior in organizations. We discuss other causal variables of organizational behavior in this book—technology, strategy, size, and goals—as they relate to culture. Another variable, the organization's environment, is the national, and increasingly international, culture within which an organization operates. To a large extent, exploring this complex environment and its effects on organizations is the subject of this text.

The first edition, like most texts that focus on international management, emphasized the differences in behavior that culture creates. Although culture does produce fundamental differences in organizational behavior, the second edition contains recent research that concludes that a significant amount of behavior important for understanding organizations is similar across cultures. For example, research on leadership from Project GLOBE by Robert House and his 150 associates found that charismatic and transformational leadership is common to most cultures.

Another important issue is whether the forces of industrial development, economic growth, modernism, and post-modernism contribute to the convergence, persistence, or divergence of cultures and organizational behavior. Mauro Guillén's research suggests that cultures react similarly to globalization by attempting to act on what they perceive to be their competitive strengths instead of converging into one model of industrial society. Guillén's findings, along with data from the World Values Survey, challenge many of the assumptions of the homogenization of culture by globalization.

The text is selective in the theories and research it presents. There is no attempt to cover every organizational behavior or management theory or all research on the various topics. The theories and research selected primarily elucidate the cultural perspective.

Finally, an aim of this text is to provide material to improve student's interpersonal behavior concerning the cultural variations found in international organizations. The cases and skill exercises in the book serve to begin this complex lifelong learning journey. They highlight aspects of cultural variation, attempt to increase student sensitivity to culture, and provide an opportunity to analyze and experiment with new behaviors.

▪ ▪ ▪ Use of the Text

International Organizational Behavior: Text, Cases, and Skills, Second Edition, is a self-contained text for classes that focus on international or global aspects of management and organizational behavior. In addition to text, the book includes cases and skills. Readings and other supplementary material are available on the Web site www.prenhall.com/francescogold. This comprehensive approach provides instructors with an opportunity to choose from a variety of materials and to shape course content.

This text is appropriate for the following courses: Global Organizational Behavior, International Organizational Behavior, Organizational Behavior, Introduction to

Management, Global Management, International Management, and General Business. It assumes that students have taken an introductory course in management or organizational behavior. Because of the richness of material contained in the text, it is suitable for advanced undergraduate and MBA students.

▰▰▰ Organization of the Text

International Organizational Behavior: Text, Cases, and Skills, Second Edition, is more comprehensive than other international organizational behavior texts. Fourteen chapters cover the essential topics for understanding modern organizations from a global comparative perspective. Each chapter has these pedagogical features:

- **Learning Objectives:** A preview and guide to each chapter.
- **Culture at Work:** A vignette illustrating practical implications of the concepts in the text.
- **Key Concepts:** Definitions, concepts, and theories indicated in bold type.
- **Examples from Multiple Cultures:** Examples from a variety of cultures demonstrate how culture affects behavior in organizations.
- **Tables and Figures:** Tables and figures illustrate complex concepts and processes.
- **Convergence and Divergence:** A section that discusses forces creating similarities or differences in cultures worldwide.
- **Implications for Managers:** A section that outlines practical issues that managers in a global economy face now and in the future.
- **Summary:** A summary of each chapter's major points.
- **Discussion Questions:** Questions for use in classroom discussion or assignment.
- **Web Sites:** Internet sites and addresses that expand and enrich topics in the text.

▰▰▰ Text

In addition to chapters that cover standard topics such as motivation and leadership, several chapters expand the range of international organizational behavior. These topics are included because culture influences them, and they are critical for understanding international organizational behavior. These chapters are:

- Chapter 3: Ethics and Social Responsibility
- Chapter 8: International Human Resource Management
- Chapter 9: Organizational Commitment, Organizational Justice, and Work-Family Interface
- Chapter 10: Managing Diversity

▰▰▰ Cases

The cases in this book illustrate how culture influences behavior in realistic organization settings. The cases represent a variety of geographic regions and issues. A more important use of cases, however, is to assist students in the development of analytical skills; events in the case are not as important as the intellectual processes applied to examine critically the role of culture and other variables on organizational behavior.

Skill Exercises

The skill exercises demonstrate issues and problems in understanding cross-cultural meanings and interaction. When used in a college classroom, they often raise as many issues as they resolve. In most instances, they are designed to be used in one class period or less and require little, if any preclass preparation. The exercises accommodate any number of students.

Integrating Text, Cases, and Skill Exercises

Instead of locating the cases and skill exercises at the end of each chapter, the text consolidates cases in Section II and skills in Section III. This permits creative and flexible use because many of them address multiple topics. To aid the instructor, a chart indicating which cases and skill exercises can be used with each chapter is in the Instructor's Manual.

Teaching Support

Support materials for *International Organizational Behavior: Text, Cases, and Skills,* Second Edition, include an Instructor's Manual with Test Bank and PowerPoint slides. The Instructor's Manual portion contains the learning objectives, a summary of the chapter, and answers to end-of-chapter questions for each chapter. The Instructor's Manual also contains teaching notes for cases and exercises. PowerPoint slides for each chapter are also available.

Acknowledgments

This book involved many people beyond the authors. We thank Jennifer Simon and Jeff Shelstad of Prentice Hall for their contributions, encouragement, and patience in all phases of this project. Ashley Keim, also of Prentice Hall, and Ann Imhof of Carlisle Communications greatly expedited the final stages of putting the book into print.

Although the book has been thoroughly revised and updated, reviewers of the first edition have also influenced the second edition. We appreciate the contributions of Steven Cady, Bowling Green State University; Carol Carnevale, Empire State College; Joseph Cheng, University of Illinois; Paul Fadil, Valdosta State University; Erich Kerchler, Universitate Wien Austria; Wendy Klepetar, College of St. Benedict; Edwin Miller, University of Michigan; Cynthia Pavett, University of San Diego; Doug Ross, Towson University; Mikael Søndergaard, University of Aarhus; Frederick Ware, Valdosta State University; and Maryann Watson, University of Tampa.

We also thank colleagues and friends who provided feedback and suggestions for the second edition: Samuel Aryee, Hong Kong Baptist University; Randy Chiu, Hong Kong Baptist University; John B. Cullen, Washington State University; Janice Joplin, University of Texas El Paso; Chay Hoon Lee, Nanyang Technological University; Alick Kay, University of South Australia; Martha Maznevski, IMD; Hsu O'Keefe, Pace University; Mark F. Peterson, Florida Atlantic University; Roger Putzel, St. Michael's College; Jan Selmer, Hong Kong Baptist University; Margaret Shaffer, Hong Kong Baptist University; Michael C. Shaner, Saint Louis University; Mikael Søndergaard, University of Aarhus; David Thomas, Simon Fraser University: K. J. Tullis, University of Central Oklahoma; Richard J. Vorwerk, Governors State University; and Steven White, INSEAD.

We would like to acknowledge the many instructors who used the first edition for their constructive comments and suggestions for improving this edition. Of course, any deficiencies in the text are ours alone.

Gold once again deeply thanks his family, Bonnie, Lauren, and Ian for their love, support, and endurance in what often seemed to be an endless writing process. Gold would also like to thank and express appreciation to Dr. Ira Gouterman for his discriminating eye.

The authors, who are listed alphabetically, now understand the demands of revisiting a complex and dynamic subject and stand more appreciatively than before on the shoulders of giants.

C H A P T E R

The Management of International Organizational Behavior

Learning Objectives

After reading this chapter, you should be able to:

■ Define international organizational behavior.

■ Understand why it is important to study international organizational behavior.

■ Compare industrialization and culture as explanations for international organizational behavior.

■ Know the role of theory in the study of international organizational behavior.

■ Explain the benefits of the comparative perspective for studying international organizational behavior.

CULTURE AT WORK

Today or Mañana?

"The U.S. team members are driven by the exact dates on the schedule," explained Marianne Torrcelli, leader of an AT&T team working in Mexico and the United Kingdom. "The team members are disappointed and feel a sense of urgency when the schedule is not met. We believe that 'Time is Money' and missed dates equate to potential jeopardy in project completion, which results in lost revenue. To prevent this, the American AT&T team responds quickly to jeopardy situations, focuses on critical issues, engages additional resources, and works extensive overtime. The job takes priority over family."

"But in Mexico," Marianne observed, "as long as work items are being addressed—even if they are not on schedule—the U.S. team members feel comfortable that they will be completed at some point. The 'schedule' is not in jeopardy. We understand that in Mexico there isn't the sense of urgency that American AT&T team members feel when they miss critical task delivery times.

The 'mañana syndrome' is real. The Mexican team members have outstanding commitment and dedication to the project, but they place their family before work. The work can be done 'mañana.'"

"It's different in the U.K. There employees understand the concept 'schedule' the way Americans do. They also understand the need to complete tasks on time and that when a jeopardy situation occurs, the team needs to respond quickly. But the British team members maintain a balance between work and their personal lives. For example, they never work extensive overtime to resolve a critical issue. The U.S. expatriates, however, would work extensive overtime, putting work ahead of their personal lives."

Source: B.A. Gold

Organizations are becoming increasingly global. Multinational corporations formulate global strategies to expand into new markets, reduce their dependence on expensive labor, restructure into network or virtual organizations, and capitalize on innovative international financial arrangements. At the beginning of the 21st century, increasing numbers and types of organizations transcend geographic, economic, political, and cultural boundaries. Expectations are for the globalization of commerce to accelerate during the next decades.

At the same time, societies are irreversibly becoming global because **globalization** is "A social process in which the constraints of geography on social and cultural arrangements recede and in which people become increasingly aware that they are receding" (Waters 1995, p. 3). For example, during the past two decades the rapid growth of the Internet significantly facilitated cross-cultural communication, and heightened the awareness and interdependence of nations (Kogut 2003). But globalization is not a new phenomenon. Since 1795 trade globalization and the integration of the world-system has increased as the result of three waves of cross-cultural business contact (Chase-Dunn, Kawano, and Brewer 2000). These waves are not cyclical business patterns but are a trend toward increasing trade globalization explained, for the most part, by the dominance of Great Britain as the global power for the first wave of trade expansion, a rivalry among countries during the second wave, and dominance of the United States for the third wave (Chase-Dunn et al. 2000).

In addition to an acceleration of cross-cultural trade in the last decades of the 20th century and into the 21st century, a profound shift in consciousness occurred because globalization more immediately affected the daily lives of people around the world in diverse ways, such as the following:

- Corporations headquartered throughout the world became multinational and affected "local" employment practices.
- News organizations such as CNN began broadcasting international events in real-time.
- Job applicants competed with others from around the world.
- Workers in France, England, and the United States were unemployed because labor was cheaper in Mexico, Sri Lanka, Morocco, and China.
- Post-September 11, 2001, people throughout the world—but particularly citizens of the United States and Western Europe—were forced more than before to learn about other cultures to understand world events.

These trends continue to evolve.

Globalization is often powerful enough to affect corporations even though a company's philosophy and strategy resist certain aspects of it. For example, Levi Strauss & Co. embraced globalization in marketing its casual apparel throughout the world but resisted manufacturing globally. However, in the late 1990s, Levi reluctantly abandoned its policy of producing clothing primarily in United States manufacturing facilities and relocated most of its manufacturing offshore. "This is a painful but necessary business decision," said Philip Marineau, Levi's chief executive. "There is no question that we must move away from owned-and-operated plants in the U.S. to remain competitive in our industry" (Kaufman 2002, p. C2). The shift to inexpensive global labor markets occurred only after a precipitous drop in Levi's annual revenues. Global production violated a long-standing corporate social policy but became an economic necessity.

One implication of globalization for managers and their careers is that it is important to know how to manage culturally diverse, cross-cultural, and geographically dispersed organizations. Because the management of modern corporations is more than accounting and finance, business strategy, or site location, globalization requires managers to understand the behavior of people in organizations. Knowing how culture affects organizational behavior is essential. Some of the questions the global manager needs to answer are:

- Do all cultures have the same understanding of ethics?
- Are people in different cultures motivated in different ways?
- Are leadership styles the same in all cultures?
- How do different cultures manage diversity?
- Do all cultures negotiate business deals the same way?

Finally, increasing awareness of globalization through contact with and knowledge of different cultures should not be confused with the popular view—the McDonaldization of the globe—that the cultures of the world are relentlessly and inevitably becoming more similar. For example, although McDonald's uses the same management principles throughout the world (Royle 2000), the cultural meaning of McDonald's varies significantly in different societies. In some cultures McDonald's is regarded as an employer for temporary or marginalized workers while in others it is comparatively high-status work (Watson 1997). Indeed, much recent research, which we will discuss later in this chapter, indicates that cultural differences persist even as industrialization, modernization, and globalization proceed. What has changed is our awareness of other cultures and our consciousness of interconnected and interdependent social, cultural, political, and economic activities.

▪▪▪ What Is International Organizational Behavior?

International organizational behavior is the study of behavior in organizations around the world. In studying international organizational behavior, the influence of national culture on organizations is important because, "despite all of the discussion of globalization of the world economy and the so-called multinationalization of corporations, different societies continue to have distinctive organizational arrangements" (Fligstein and Freeland 1995, p. 33).

Even if globalization and multinational corporate structures eventually cause national cultures to become more alike, it is improbable that indistinguishable values will emerge across cultures to produce the same management techniques and organizational behavior. National values, attitudes, traditions, customs, and ideologies produce distinctive organization structures, cultures, and dynamics. To be successful, a manager in the global economy has to understand the effect of diverse cultures on organizational behavior.

Differences from Organizational Behavior in the United States

There are three reasons why organizational behavior theories developed in the United States, which produces a significant amount of the world's social science research, are different from international organizational behavior theories.

First, the study of organizational behavior in the United States is not sensitive to variations in national cultures (Hofstede 1993). Until recently, American researchers assumed that organizations existed within the culture of the United States or one that was similar—for example, Western Europe. Not all societies, however, adhere to capitalist economic principles or an ideology that emphasizes individualism, achievement, and equality. In fact, even capitalist societies other than the United States organize and manage differently as a result of culture. In addition, many U.S. theories receive either minimal or mixed support from data collected in the United States. It is unlikely, then, that these theories apply in other countries. One way to avoid the dominance of U.S. organizational theory is to develop theories in other cultures rather than merely test U.S. theories with international samples.

Second, the focus of studies conducted in the United States is usually individual roles and the functioning of groups. Although sociologists have studied organizations as entities, there are few studies that view organizations holistically as the product of a specific culture.

Finally, much U.S. organizational behavior research emulates natural science methods that emphasize narrow research questions, hypothesis testing, and quantifiable data. In contrast, culture is hard to quantify, and it is difficult to measure the multiple, often subtle ways that it influences behavior. An alternative approach to studying culture is using qualitative ethnographic techniques. This method produces rich, descriptive data presented in case studies that attempt to understand life from inside organizations. Often, despite the limitations of representativeness and researcher bias, these methods capture the meaning of culture more adequately than quantitative studies (Adler and Boyacigiller 1996).

Because of these limitations, the approach to international management and organizational behavior presented here extends the American model by using national culture as the organizational context and explanation. At the current time, however, while the American model remains important, its dominance as the lens for viewing the rest of the world is beginning to recede. Recent research increasingly uses a comparative approach with national culture as a central variable (Gannon and Newman 2002). For example, Project GLOBE (Javidan and House 2002), is a comparative study of leadership in 61 nations. Another recent development is the systematic comparative study of work across cultures from a sociological perspective (Cornfield and Hodson 2002). Qualitative studies that produce thick descriptions and interpretive understandings (Geertz 1973) of work places and the role of culture on organizational behavior are becoming more available (Bourdieu 2000; Burawoy, Krotov, and Lytkina 2000; Salzinger 2000). In addition, there is recognition that disciplines, for example psychology, should be inherently cross-cultural (Segall, Dasen, Berry, and Poortinga 1999). Finally, scholars view some of the effects of globalization as so extensive that, "Globalization poses a challenge to existing social scientific methods of inquiry and units of analysis by destabilizing the embeddedness of social relations in particular communities and places" (Gille and Riain 2002, p. 271).

■ ■ ■ Why Study International Organizational Behavior?

Competitive Advantage

One result of globalization is that organizations confront an external environment that is more complex, dynamic, and competitive. To succeed in the new economy, it is essential to have knowledge of other cultures and behavior in their organizations.

A practical aspect of studying global organizational behavior is understanding the nature of competition in the global marketplace. To remain competitive, companies must learn about the technologies, management practices, strategies, and product developments of firms around the globe as well as domestic rivals. This is particularly important with increased emphasis on international product quality, global finance, and the ability to purchase products from companies located anywhere.

A related reason to know about the activities of businesses throughout the world is to explore and evaluate prospects for collaboration with other companies. Increasingly, strategic alliances are common between competitors. For example, Mitsubishi, a Japanese company, has collaborated with Chrysler, an American firm, to create new automotive products, and the German luxury car company Daimler Benz merged with Chrysler. In some cases, such as the acquisition of United Kingdom–based Jaguar by the American Ford Motor Company, one firm purchases another in the same business, but the acquired firm retains distinctive cultural traditions that affect its business practices.

Learning about global organizational behavior can also facilitate borrowing ideas from other cultures to improve organization performance. Since the late 1970s, Great Britain and the United States have borrowed Japanese management techniques, including total quality control and just-in-time manufacturing (Oliver and Wilkinson 1992). On a larger scale, former Communist East European countries and China are eager to apply capitalist economic principles to improve their businesses and factories.

Finally, as a result of immigration in some countries and the use of temporary guest workers in others, multiculturalism in the workforce is increasing. The management of people with diverse cultural backgrounds improves when managers understand and apply organizational theories based on cultural explanations.

Organizational Analysis

The second reason to study international organizational behavior is that formal organizations are a major social structure in modern societies. The influence of organizations on daily life is pervasive, and their leaders have significant power. A systematic analysis of organizations is essential for interpreting the social control and economic production structures of advanced and developing societies.

Of course, many issues addressed in the academic study of organizations have implications for improvement of management theory and practice. Much of the research reported in this book had its origin in academic studies, but it also relates directly to the improvement of global management practices.

The Analysis of Culture

The third reason for studying international organizational behavior is intellectual curiosity about cultures other than one's own. Critical examination of management techniques across societies helps us understand how people interact and justify their relationships under conditions of power and resource inequalities.

In addition, knowledge of other cultures generates insights into one's own culture and behavior. Without systematic comparisons, it is difficult to appreciate how culture influences one's own behavior. This is because most of us believe that our culture is preferable—possibly superior—to other cultures. We only question our cultural assumptions when practices from other cultures appear to be strange, unethical, or more effective.

▬▬▬ Explaining International Organizational Behavior

The history of management and organizational behavior is marked by the development of increasingly sophisticated models of human behavior and more accurate explanations of social life. Early researchers focused on finding universals: What is the single most effective way to lead, motivate employees, or structure any organization? Typically, this research used mechanical models of individual and organizational behavior and ignored the influence of outside forces on behavior in organizations. Beginning in the 1960s, explanations of individual and organizational behavior evolved from single cause theories to models based on interaction among multiple variables. As the external environments of organizations became more turbulent, research focused more on the relationship between the organizations and their environments but usually excluded culture as a causal variable. Although recent research findings and theories usually emphasize that there is no single or "best" approach that applies to all management situations, there are still competing theories and debates over complex issues—for example, whether industrialization or culture exerts more influence on organizational structures and processes.

Industrialization

The industrialization argument is that the logic of industrialization—movement from animal and human to steam, electric, and petroleum energy sources for manufacturing—is a powerful economic force unaffected by culture (Harbison and Myers 1959). This view concludes that industrialization creates organizational structures and cultures that are fundamentally the same regardless of national culture.

Research has also identified influences on organizational behavior and structure as diverse as strategy (Chandler 1962), technology (Perrow 1967), size (Blau and Schoenherr 1971), and organizational ecology—the influence of the behavior of other organizations on the evolution of organizational types (Aldrich 1999; Hannan and Freeman 1989). Some of these studies support the industrialization thesis. For example, specific technologies are associated with particular organizational structures independent of other variables, as is large size, a measure of organization growth associated with increased complexity, which is an indicator of industrial and organization success.

Cultural Explanations

Recently, culture has been accepted as an explanation of organizational behavior. One reason is the increase in competitiveness of nations beginning in the 1980s. For example, the superior quality of Japanese automobiles prompted researchers and managers to ask: Is there something distinctive about Japanese national and organizational culture that contributes to high quality standards in the workplace?

A second reason is that business executives encounter different cultures in their contacts with people from other nations. It has become increasingly important to understand how members of other cultures behave. How should we communicate with them? Can we trust them? What leadership style do they think is effective?

How do they treat female executives? Answers to these questions require understanding the various external and internal cultural influences on organizations and how they interact.

Multiple Cultures

Nations and organizations have multiple cultures. National cultures have roots in ethnic identity, religion, social class, or some combination of these. Within nations, subcultures form on the basis of these variables and shape attitudes and values that affect behavior in organizations such as motivation, obedience to authority, and interpersonal relations. In organizations, subcultures develop from job specialization, departmentalization, friendship, and other factors.

External Culture

Until recently, organizational theorists viewed the boundary between organizations and external culture as rigid. New models of organizations conceptualize **external culture,** which includes multiple national and local cultures, as influencing internal organizational culture.

For example, social class, an external basis for distinctive cultures, seldom appears in organizational behavior studies conducted by management researchers in the United States. However, most research assumes that a managerial class controls organizations—but does not necessarily own them—and a social class of lower-level workers of various types requires management. A model of organizations sensitive to external culture would make these assumptions explicit, view them as problematic, and use them to explain behavior.

Internal Organizational Culture

Every organization creates a specific culture that influences its members' behavior in complex ways. **Internal organizational culture** is composed of artifacts, values, and basic assumptions that create meaning for organizational insiders and present it to individuals, groups, and other organizations outside the organization. Interest in organizational culture arises from the increase in global competition and recognition that the management of culture is central to successful organization change and for creating competitive advantages (Deal and Kennedy 1999; Kanter 2001; Schein 1992).

Limitations of Cultural Explanations

There are limits to the use of culture to explain organizational behavior. First, there are numerous definitions of culture; it is not entirely clear what composes either national or organizational culture. Related to this, many conceptualizations of culture originated in anthropological studies of "primitive" cultures, that in some cases no longer exist, and may not apply to industrial and post-industrial societies or complex organizations.

Second, culture, even when there is agreement on a definition, is a multifaceted concept that is difficult to measure. Compounding the problem, researchers often use forced-choice questionnaires developed in the West that impose predetermined categories instead of discovering indigenous concepts or developing theories grounded in data from a sample of organizations in diverse cultures. Culture is often specific to a society or organization and may contain nuances that inappropriate research methods fail to capture.

Third, it is possible to use culture as too comprehensive an explanation of organizational behavior. **Cultural determinism,** the position that all behavior is the product of culture, ignores economic, political, technological, and biological factors as plausible explanations. A counter argument to this criticism is that technology and the economy are products of culture. However, industrialization and related variables are complex processes that are distinct from culture and contribute to organizational behavior. In this book, culture is a key variable but not viewed as the exclusive cause of organizational behavior.

▪▪▪ Theory and International Organizational Behavior

Despite Kurt Lewin's aphorism, "Nothing is as practical as a good theory," (1945, p. 129) people often object to the prospect of learning theories. Their response is, "It's just a theory. It has *nothing* to do with what happens in the *real world*." Another frequent criticism of theory is that, "It all depends. Every situation is unique. It's *impossible* to make meaningful generalizations."

Real World Theory

Social science research identifies patterns of behavior, and descriptive theories explain events that occur in the real world. Supporting this statement, a recent study identified 73 organizational behavior theories—the vast majority were developed in the United States and attempts to locate theories from other countries produced very few—and surveyed management research experts who endorsed many of the theories as scientifically valid and useful for understanding and improving organizational behavior (Miner 2003). Theories also help researchers pose intellectually interesting and practical questions, assist with the arrangement of findings into meaningful patterns, and contribute to data analysis. More importantly, on occasion, a new theory either explains a previously unexplored area of organizational behavior or provides a more elegant or comprehensive explanation that replaces an earlier theory.

Normative and Descriptive Theory   Two types of theory are normative and descriptive. In organizational behavior and management, **normative theories** formulate the way organizations *ought* to function. An example of a normative theory is the view that a properly designed and managed organization does not experience internal conflict. The assumption is that conflict has negative influences on organizational effectiveness. But few organizations are conflict free. In fact, organizations without conflict may be harmonious, nonproductive places where few people care enough about the organization's goals to engage in conflict.

   Descriptive theories attempt to portray organizations realistically. From this perspective, if conflict exists in organizations and whether it hinders or advances the goals of an organization are matters for empirical investigation. If a pattern of conflict emerges in different types of organizations, it requires an explanation. Of course, findings from descriptive studies contribute to policies and practices intended to improve organizations.

   The difference between descriptive and normative theories has important implications for managers. For example, if a normative theory views conflict as a product of ineffective management, the objective is to eliminate it. However, if empirical research indicates that all organizations experience conflict, the issue is finding ways to manage it effectively.

Values   A related issue is the role of values in research. **Value judgments** are culturally biased assessments of behavior. It is pointless to pretend that people—even social scientists who profess to be objective—escape culture and it is natural to use one's own culture as the basis for comparison. However, researchers attempt to recognize values and perceptual biases that their culture and experience impose and attempt to reduce their influence on research. Two common forms of value judgment, ethnocentrism and culture shock, demonstrate these issues.

Ethnocentrism   **Ethnocentrism** is the belief that "one's own group is the center of everything, and all others are scaled and rated with reference to it" (Sumner 1906, p. 28). The Culture at Work vignette that opens this chapter illustrates the tendency to use one's own culture as the comparative and evaluative framework for behavior in other cultures. For Marianne Torrcelli, an American employee of AT&T, work is more a central life concern than it is for her British and Mexican co-workers. Marianne views the Mexicans as capable workers and accepts that they eventually perform their tasks but, nevertheless, appears to wish they were punctual like Americans. At the same time, Marianne recognizes that the Mexicans and British have different priorities in their relationship to work and family life than the American workers. Marianne believes her priorities are preferable while the other cultures' values are acceptable but nevertheless somewhat inferior.

Culture Shock   Behavior in cultures other than our own often appears to be exotic, harmful, irrational, or meaningless. **Culture shock,** an adverse or confused reaction to behavior in other cultures, challenges understandings between ourselves and others. What is "normal" behavior becomes problematic.

From a Western perspective, examples of culture shock encountered in organizations are forced child workers and prison labor—even though prison labor exists in the United States. A less dramatic example is pay differentials between executives and workers. Americans are surprised that Japanese executives receive only slightly more compensation than Japanese workers. Similarly, Japanese executives find it unusual that American executives often earn more than ten times the salary of workers. Another example is Americans visiting foreign countries and discovering that most of the world does not have American-style lavatories. This initial shock usually extends beyond the immediate experience to speculation about the foreign population's economic well-being and their lack of concern with appropriate hygiene.

▪▪▪ The Comparative Perspective

One way to reduce or eliminate ethnocentrism, culture shock, and other forms of culture bias is the **comparative method,** an intellectually sophisticated approach to describe and compare organizational behavior across multiple cultures. Although all empirical social research is in some way comparative—either through the use of statistical methods, implicit comparisons with pure cases, or experimental designs—international organizational behavior attempts to explicitly and systematically compare the effects of national culture on organizations (Ragin 1987). The comparative perspective can discover differences or similarities in behavior across cultures (Inkeles and Sasaki 1996; Javidan and House 2002; Punnett and Shenkar 1996; Segall et al. 1999).

Two Examples of the Comparative Perspective

Two recent studies illustrate the comparative method in international management and organizational behavior. The first study identifies changes in international finance that created similar types of organizations in three cultures; these changes resulted in specific organizational cultures in knowledge-intensive organizations. This study's theoretical framework expands the scope of research on organizations by identifying large-scale global trends shaping post-modern society and organizations.

The second study discovered differences in management philosophies and practices in four industrial societies. These findings were unexpected because the theoretical viewpoint of many researchers is that management in industrial nations is similar because of industrialization.

Both studies present extensive detailed data and complex theoretical arguments. The following are brief descriptions of some of their major themes.

Global Processes

Saskia Sassen's *The Global City* (1991) illustrates the discovery of similarities—convergence—across cultures produced by global economic activity. Sassen's thesis is that beginning in the 1980s, New York, London, and Tokyo have "undergone massive and *parallel* changes in their economic base, spatial organization, and social structure" (1991, p. 4). Control and power did not decentralize with the dispersion of business around the globe. Instead, New York, London, and Tokyo emerged as global cities and the control centers of the new global economy. This development affects organizations throughout the world because, according to Sassen, "Though large firms have increased their subcontracting to smaller firms, and many national firms in the newly industrializing countries have grown rapidly, this form of growth is ultimately part of a chain. Even industrial homeworkers in remote rural areas are now part of that chain" (1991, pp. 4–5).

Within the global cities are sections in which post-industrial production sites—knowledge industries—are concentrated. Knowledge industries specialize in financial and marketing services needed by complex organizations for running spatially dispersed networks of factories, offices, and service outlets.

One consequence of this is a division of the workforce into specialized high-salary work and low-wage support services. New organizational cultures arose that focus on financial knowledge and services. The same processes also reduced large segments of urban populations to marginal employment.

The similarity across cultures of these processes is observable only through the comparative method. Research on a single culture would not detect the simultaneous changes affecting the global economy and consequently, the social structure of cities and organizations.

Management Pluralism

Models of Management (1994) by Mauro Guillén is a comparative historical study of the United States, Great Britain, Germany, and Spain during the twentieth century. It demonstrates that these industrial societies adopted different paradigms of management philosophies and practices at different times: scientific management, the human relations school, and structural analysis.

Scientific management, based on the ideas of Frederick Taylor and others, was prevalent in the United States and Germany during the early part of the century, but was rejected as an ideology and practice in Great Britain and Spain.

The human relations movement, a reaction against scientific management, found favor in the United States, Great Britain, and Spain where it was consistent with social and political values. Germany, where social values did not support its practices, did not adopt it.

The last paradigm, structural analysis, is a critique of the search for "the one best way" to organize that was the driving force behind scientific management and the human relations school. Formulated and adopted with the creation of complex multinational organizations, it was in widespread use beginning in the 1960s in Great Britain, the United States, and Germany. Spain rejected it as an ideology and practice.

Guillén concludes that cultural factors influence the selection of management models, not only their scientific credibility or economic and technological factors. "Managers," Guillén writes, "in different countries adopted the three paradigms in selective ways during the twentieth century, depending on the problems they were facing and such institutional factors as their mentalities and training, the activities of professional groups, the role of the state, and the attitude of the workers" (1994, pp. 1–2).

In addition to the political and social factors that influenced managerial ideology and practice, Guillén found that religion—an important cultural element—also was significant in the adoption of a management model. Guillén writes:

> Catholicism has generally emphasized the community, self-actualization, paternalism, and organicism, while Protestantism has emphasized individualism, instrumentalism, independence, and contractualism. In Germany, Protestant management intellectuals generally supported the scientific management paradigm, while Catholic ones took sides with the human relations school. In Spain, the dominant Catholic background played a key role in the reception, adoption, and adaptation to local conditions of American ideas about human relations at work. In Britain, Christian humanist ideals similar to those proposed by the Roman Catholic Church prompted management intellectuals to accept human relations. In the United States, religion did not play a role either in the formulation or in the widespread adoption of the human relations paradigm. (1994, p. 297)

Guillén's research demonstrates two important issues. First, institutional arrangements, not only the type of economy, technology, or a particular definition of industrial efficiency, create ideologies that become guidelines for the way people manage organizations. One implication of Guillén's research is that national and organizational cultures influence the adoption of management paradigms and shape managers' and workers' behavior. Management philosophies and practices embody culture and contribute to determining aspects of work behaviors in nations and organizations.

Second, comparative analysis is a more productive way of understanding management and organizational behavior than single-culture studies. Without the systematic comparisons at the level of nation states, it is difficult to determine which variables affect the adoption of management models and the factors that cause them to change periodically. In addition, without comparisons, the misleading conclusion would be that all countries adopted the same managerial models at similar stages in economic development.

International Organizational Behavior in the 21st Century

Cultural Values in the 21st Century

At the beginning of the 21st century, cultural values impact the types of organizations that emerge, the behavior that takes place in them, how and in what directions they change, and the techniques to manage them. Demonstrating the importance of values, the World Values Survey, which draws on three waves of questionnaires from a sample of the global population, tracked modernization and cultural change and found that traditional values persist even during the process of globalization (Inglehart and Baker 2000). Although there has been significant value change during the past two decades, the researchers conclude that, "The impression that we are moving toward a uniform 'McWorld' is partly an illusion" (Inglehard and Baker 2000, p. 22). Instead, the data indicate that

> A history of Protestant or Orthodox or Islamic or Confucian traditions gives rise to cultural zones with distinctive value systems that persist after controlling for the effects of economic development. Economic development tends to push societies in a common direction, but rather than converging, they seem to move on parallel trajectories shaped by their cultural heritage. We doubt that the forces of modernization will produce a homogenized world culture in the foreseeable future. (Inglehart and Baker 2000, p. 49)

Similarly, Hofstede (2001, p. xx) concludes that "Time-series data show no convergence between countries but some worldwide or almost worldwide value shifts." A basic issue then is the role that culture plays in shaping organizations and organizational behavior and what types of changes are occurring in culture and values that can impact organizations.

Organizations Enter the 21st Century

As with national culture there has been an enormous amount of speculation that organizations are becoming increasingly similar in response to globalization. Again, the image of McDonaldization emerges as a powerful symbol of global pressures toward uniformity. But the reality is more complex and uncertain. In an assessment of the status of the firm at the beginning of the 21st century, Paul DiMaggio (2001, pp. 25–26) concludes that,

> The challenges to the twentieth-century model of the firm—to Weber's model of the bureaucratic enterprise and to the post-Marxian account of the systemic logic of advanced capitalism—have yielded a range of contradictory characterizations rather than a clarifying new synthesis. On the one hand, hierarchical bureaucracy is said to be yielding to more empowering and commitment-inducing systems of management. On the other, jobs and firms are becoming decoupled, with workers experiencing unprecedented career insecurity. At the same time that observers note a renewal of economic rivalry they also describe unprecedented forms of collaboration throughout the world's economies. Clearly the trends observers have discerned do not all point in the same direction, nor are contemporary corporations marching in lockstep along a single trajectory.

In a comparative study of management practices and the effects of modernization in Argentina, South Korea, and Spain, Guillén (2001, p. 3) concludes that "Countries and organizations do not gravitate toward a supposedly universal model of economic success and organizational form as they attempt to cope with globalization. Rather, the mutual awareness that globalization entails invites them to be different, namely, to use their unique economic, political, and social advantages as leverage in the global marketplace."

Convergence or Divergence?

If cultures are converging—that is, becoming more alike—there is little reason to study specific management practices and organizing principles. This echoes the logic of early management theorists in the United States who searched for the single most effective way to manage all types of business organizations. It is also the viewpoint of theorists who view industrialization and modernization as producing similar economic and organizational paradigms. If organizations throughout the world are similar, the same management techniques apply.

However, if cultures remain distinctive and basic values persist or are actually becoming more dissimilar—that is, there is a process of divergence—culture is an important factor in understanding and practicing management. This viewpoint suggests that it is urgent to become familiar with diverse cultures and develop culturally sensitive ways to manage organizations.

Forces for Convergence

Sassen's study indicates that globalization, which affects the economy and culture of cities, is a force for convergence. Major cities become centers of power and control in the global economy; part of the change in urban areas is the transformation of work. The primary negative consequence of this is concentrations of power and wealth that produce urban centers with two social classes, affluent knowledge workers and economically marginal support workers. The economic activities that produced globalization also affected the culture of cities and organizations.

Forces for Divergence

Guillén's study concludes that distinctive cultural elements influence the management of organizations. Unless globalization produces a uniform religion or other value system, there will continue to be differences in management philosophies and practices. These findings and interpretation support the divergence view.

Similarly, the findings of the World Values Survey indicate that values change but cultures persist. At first this appears to be an argument for divergence because cultures remain the same in important ways. However, it raises another issue: If distinctive cultures persist despite the forces of globalization, does it make sense to think in terms of the convergence or divergence of cultures as it affects management and organizational behavior? Should the study of cultures focus instead on unique configurations of values that endure and require in-depth analysis to improve cross-cultural management?

Implications for Managers

For international managers to perform successfully in the global economy, accurate information on how culture affects organizational behavior in different cultures is essential. Reliance on theories developed in one culture is not sufficient.

Managers also must distinguish between normative and descriptive theories. Normative theories can reinforce practices that "are fine in theory, but not in practice." The implication is that managers must evaluate theories by assessing if data support them.

Guillén's and Sassen's research has implications for managerial action. Guillén's findings imply that managers who work across cultures need to acquire an extensive knowledge of management practices different from their own. For example, not only do international managers from the United Kingdom have to adapt to the style of management in Spain, by implication they also have to understand the management practices of former Communist countries as well as other countries because there is significant variation in management ideologies even in industrial societies.

Sassen's study indicates that under certain conditions a particular type of work can be relatively unaffected by national cultural differences because the larger process of globalization creates pressures for standardization. For example, knowledge work in the financial industry requires rapid and accurate communication with other financial workers around the globe. Managers should understand that under specific conditions certain organizational behaviors escape the direct influence of national culture. Managing knowledge workers in a high technology environment requires techniques suitable for all knowledge workers. However, even as the financial industry becomes more similar across the globe, corporate cultures continue to vary.

SUMMARY ▪▪▪▪▪▪▪

International organizational behavior describes and explains behavior in organizations located in diverse national cultures. It differs from traditional organizational behavior as developed in the United States because it adds the dimension of national culture as an explanation.

Three reasons for studying international organizational behavior are to gain competitive advantage, to improve understanding of behavior in organizations and modern society, and to appreciate other cultures. Organizational and national cultures influence organizational behavior. Multiple cultures, including those based on ethnic identity, religion, and social class, affect behavior in organizations. However, there are limits to the use of culture as an explanation for organizational behavior. Technology, the organization's competitive environment, strategy, and size also account for organizational structure and behavior.

An objective of the study of international organizational behavior is to develop theories of behavior. Normative theory focuses on ways that organizations should operate and how people ought to behave. Descriptive theory attempts to objectively describe and analyze behavior without making judgments or prescriptions.

Ethnocentrism and culture shock can influence one's view of another culture, often negatively. Self-awareness in analyzing another culture reduces bias created by these processes. The comparative study of organizational behavior is a systematic method for reducing the entry of cultural values into the study of international organizational behavior. The comparative method often results in challenges to the implicit superiority of the investigator's own culture and social arrangements. Also, comparisons often result in unexpected findings. For example, Guillén's research concluded that industrial countries use different management philosophies and practices, not necessarily based on scientific reasons, but because of cultural factors such as religion.

While the process of globalization—particularly an increased awareness of other cultures—has progressed in various ways, the "McDonaldization" of culture into a homogeneous world culture has not occurred. Research documents that values change but that distinctive cultural characteristics persist and influence organizational behavior and management.

Finally, although much global organizational behavior research is comparative, additional research using systematic comparisons, especially studies of developing nations, will provide data for more comprehensive theories. In addition, these studies will contribute to understanding whether and how cultures and organizations in them are becoming more alike or different. This has implications for the management of international organizational behavior.

DISCUSSION QUESTIONS

1. Define and discuss international organizational behavior.
2. Why is international organizational behavior a subject that should be taught in business schools?
3. What role does research on organizations in the United States have on the study of organizations in other cultures?
4. Why is theory important for the study of international organizational behavior?
5. What is the comparative method?
6. What is an example of a business issue that could benefit from the approach of international management and organizational behavior?
7. Based on your understanding of globalization, are organizations around the world becoming more similar?
8. From your understanding of international management and organizational behavior, what personal goals do you expect to achieve by taking this class?

INTERNET SITES

Selected Companies in the Chapter

AT&T (http://www.att.com)
Levi Strauss & Co. (http://www.levistrauss.com)
McDonalds Corporation (http://mcdonalds.com)

Management of International Organizational Behavior Web Sites

The Globalization Web site (http://www.emory.edu/SOC/globalization). This site contains links to a variety of topics concerning globalization including debates, a glossary, theories, issues, books, organizations, news, and people.

Research Methods Knowledge Base (http://trochim.human.cornell.edu). To evaluate studies of international organizational behavior, it is useful to have a knowledge of the research methods provided on this site.

Paul Miesing's International Business (http://www.albany.edu/faculty/pm157/teaching/interbus/interbus.html). This site contains many links to Web sites of interest to international organizational behavior.

REFERENCES

Adler, N. J. and Boyacigiller, N. (1996). "Global Management and the 21st Century." In Punnett, B. and Shenkar, O. *Handbook for International Management Research.* Cambridge, MA: Blackwell Publishers.

Aldrich, H. E. (1999). *Organizations Evolving.* Thousand Oaks, CA: Sage.

Blau, P. M. and Schoenherr, R. A. (1971). *The Structure of Organizations.* New York: Basic Books.

Bourdieu, P. (2000). "Making the Economic Habitus: Algerian Workers Revisited." *Ethnography*, 1(1), 17–41.

Burawoy, M., Krotov, P., and Lytkina, T. (2000). "Involution and Destitution in Capitalist Russia." *Ethnography*, 1(1), 43–65.

Chandler, A. D. (1962). *Strategy and Structure.* Cambridge, MA: MIT Press.

Chase-Dunn, C., Kawano, Y., and Brewer, B. D. (2000). "Globalization Since 1795: Waves of Integration in the World-System." *American Sociological Review*, 65, 77–95.

Cornfield, D. B. and Hodson, R. (eds.) (2002). *Worlds of Work: Building an International Sociology of Work.* New York: Kluwer Academic/Plenum Publishers.

Deal, T. E. and Kennedy, A. A. (1999). *The New Corporate Cultures: Revitalizing the Workplace After Downsizing, Mergers, and Reengineering.* Cambridge, MA: Perseus.

DiMaggio, P. (ed.) (2001). *The Twenty-First-Century Firm: Changing Economic Organization in International Perspective.* Princeton, NJ: Princeton University Press.

Fligstein, N. and Freeland, R. (1995). "Theoretical and Comparative Perspectives on Corporate Organization." *Annual Review of Sociology*, 21–43. Palo Alto, CA: Annual Reviews.

Gannon, M. J. and Newman, K. L. (eds.) (2002). *Handbook of Cross-Cultural Management*. Malden, MA: Blackwell.

Geertz, C. (1973). *The Interpretation of Cultures: Selected Essays*. New York: Basic Books.

Gille, Z. and Riain, S. O. (2002). "Global Ethnography." *Annual Review of Sociology*, 271–295. Palo Alto, CA: Annual Reviews.

Guillén, M. F. *Models of Management: Work, Authority, and Organization in a Comparative Perspective*. (1994). Chicago: University of Chicago Press.

——. (2001). *The Limits of Convergence: Globalization and Organizational Change in Argentina, South Korea, and Spain*. Princeton: Princeton University Press.

Hannan, M. T. and Freeman, J. (1989). *Organizational Ecology*. Cambridge, MA: Harvard University Press.

Harbison, F. H. and Myers, C. A. (1959). *Management in the Industrial World: An International Study*. New York: McGraw-Hill.

Hofstede, G. (1993). "Cultural Constraints in Management Theories." *Academy of Management Executive*, 7(1), 81–94.

——. (2001). *Culture's Consequences: Comparing Values, Behaviors, Institutions, and Organizations Across Nations* 2d Ed. Thousand Oaks, CA: Sage.

Inglehart, R. and Baker, W. E. (2000). "Modernization, Cultural Change, and the Persistence of Traditional Values." *American Sociological Review*, 65, 19–51.

Inkeles, A. and Sasaki, M. (eds.) (1996). *Comparing Nations and Cultures: Readings in a Cross-Disciplinary Perspective*. Upper Saddle River, NJ: Prentice Hall.

Javidan, M. and House, R. J., (2002). "Leadership and Cultures Around the World: Findings from GLOBE: An Introduction to the Special Issue." *Journal of World Business*, 37(1), 1–2.

Kanter, R. B. (2001). *Evolve! Succeeding in the Digital Culture of Tomorrow*. Cambridge, MA: Harvard Business School Press.

Kaufman, L. (2002). "Levi Strauss to Close 6 U.S. Plants and Lay Off 3,300," *New York Times*, April 9, C2.

Kogut, B. (2003). *The Global Internet Economy*. Cambridge, MA: MIT Press.

Lewin, K. (1945). "The Research Center for Group Dynamics at Massachusetts Institute of Technology." *Sociometry*, 8, 126–135.

Miner, J. B. (2003). "The Rated Importance, Scientific Validity, and Practical Usefulness of Organizational Behavior Theories: A Quantitative Review." *Learning & Education*, 2(3), 250–268.

Oliver, N. and Wilkinson, B. (1992). *The Japanization of British Industry: New Developments in the 1990s*. Cambridge, MA: Blackwell.

Perrow, C. (1967). "A Framework for the Comparative Analysis of Organizations." *American Sociological Review*, 32, 194–208.

Punnett, B. J. and Shenkar, O. (1996). *Handbook for International Management Research*. Cambridge, MA: Blackwell Publishers.

Ragin, C. (1987). *The Comparative Method: Moving Beyond Qualitative and Quantitative Strategies*. Berkeley: University of California Press.

Royle, T. (2000). *Working for McDonald's in Europe: The Unequal Struggle*. New York: Routledge.

Salzinger, L. (2000). "Manufacturing Sexual Subjects: 'Harassment,' Desire and Discipline on a Maquiladora Shopfloor." *Ethnography*, 1(1), 67–92.

Sassen, S. (1991). *The Global City: New York, London, Tokyo*. Princeton, NJ: Princeton University Press.

Schein, E. H. (1992). *Organizational Culture and Leadership* 2d Ed. San Francisco: Jossey-Bass.

Segall, M. H., Dasen, P. R., Berry, J. W., and Poortinga, Y. H. (1999). *Human Behavior in Global Perspective: An Introduction to Cross-cultural Psychology* 2d Ed. Boston: Allyn and Bacon.

Sumner, W. G. (1906). *Folkways*. Boston, MA: Ginn.

Waters, M. (1995). *Globalization*. New York: Routledge.

Watson, J. (ed.) (1997). *Golden Arches East: McDonald's in East Asia*. Stanford, CA: Stanford University Press.

2

Culture and Organizational Behavior

Learning Objectives

After reading this chapter, you should be able to:

- Understand what culture is and the levels of culture.
- Explain how culture is learned.
- Understand the major frameworks for explaining the cultures of different societies.
- Discuss the importance of culture for understanding and managing organizational behavior.
- Discuss implications of the debate over cultural convergence versus divergence.

CULTURE AT WORK
It's Different, Or Is It?

"When someone retires or resigns at home, the office staff throws a party for that person. Here, the one who's leaving has to invite everyone and pay the bill!"

A Hong Kong computer programmer working in Australia

"When we go out for lunch we have to consider everyone's dietary requirements. The Indians usually don't eat beef and some are vegetarians. Some of the Chinese don't eat beef either. For the Malays, it's no pork. But Singapore is a multi-racial society and we're used to it."

A Singaporean explaining lunch plans to a visitor from the U.S.

"Every day he asks me, 'How are you?' How can I think of something different to say every time?"

A Hong Kong secretary who works for an Australian

> *"I was really surprised that it was so bureaucratic compared to China!"*
>
> A Mainland Chinese professor commenting about his new job in Singapore
>
> *Source:* A. M. Francesco

People from different countries often behave differently in organizations. Culture is a powerful way to explain individual and group variations in behavior. Models of culture provide a framework for understanding behavior encountered in business situations that initially appears odd, exotic, mysterious, or difficult to understand. As business becomes more international and global, sophisticated models for understanding cultures become a necessity. National culture affects, to some extent, much of management and organizational behavior.

The Culture at Work vignette illustrates that behaviors taken for granted in one culture may seem strange to someone from another culture. Even everyday events such as the manner of greeting or food preferences can be unfamiliar to people from different cultures.

▪▪▪ What Is Culture?

Culture can explain differences in business behavior and its meaning. To gain a deeper understanding of how culture influences organizational behavior, it is important to understand what culture is. At the most general level, **culture** is a way of life of a group of people. Researchers from diverse fields, including anthropology, psychology, sociology, political science, and management, have studied culture for a long time, but only recently have organizational scholars used culture to understand why people from different countries behave differently in organizations.

A narrow meaning of *culture* refers to the arts. A "cultured" society appreciates fine art, dance, drama, and intellectual discourse and develops institutions that support them such as museums, theaters, and schools. Although culture as used here does not exclude the arts, its meaning is much broader.

Defining Culture

A single definition of culture is not adequate because the concept is complex. Indeed, defining culture has become a study in itself. In 1952, researchers identified more than 160 definitions of culture (Kroeber and Kluckhohn 1952). Tylor proposed one of the earliest definitions as "that complex whole which includes knowledge, belief, art, morals, law, custom, and any other capabilities and habits acquired by man as a member of society" (1871, p. 1). Ferraro's more recent and simpler definition is "everything that people have, think, and do as members of society" (2002, p. 19). Definitions of culture encompass every aspect of human society including material artifacts, ideas, and interactions with other people. In other words, culture is a set of socially constructed meanings that shape the behavior of people in a particular society.

Levels of Culture

The analogy of an onion or an iceberg helps to conceptualize the different levels of culture (see Figure 2-1); certain aspects of culture are more apparent, just as the outer layers of an onion or the tip of an iceberg. These aspects are the **manifest culture** (Sathe

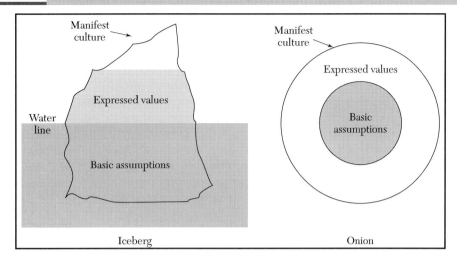

1985), containing easily observable elements such as behaviors, language, music, food, and technology. The manifest culture represents the first contact with a new culture, for example, people's speech, dress, interactions with each other, and possessions. Although the manifest level is easily accessible, it provides only a partial understanding of a particular culture. Observing the manifest culture does not necessarily reveal the meaning of a culture, but it could provide some important insights.

A deeper meaning of a culture develops from peeling away the outer layers of the onion or looking below the tip of the iceberg. The **expressed values level** represents how people in the culture explain the manifest level. In other words, it is the culture's own explanation of itself. For example, in the Chinese culture, leaving chopsticks sticking out from a bowl of rice is inappropriate because it looks similar to an offering made to one's ancestors. The expressed values level provides additional insight into a culture beyond the manifest level, but some aspects can still remain unclear.

The core of the onion or the submerged section of the iceberg represents the level of **basic assumptions.** These are the foundation of the culture: shared ideas and beliefs about the world and society as a whole that guide people's thoughts and actions. For example, in Hindu Indian society, people believe that true happiness only comes through spiritual enlightenment, not the possession of material wealth (Gannon 1994). Knowing the basic assumptions of a culture provides an understanding of the principles on which the other levels rest.

▪▪▪ How Is Culture Learned?

All of us learn a specific culture through a variety of experiences as we grow up. The most general learning mechanism, **enculturation,** is a nonintentional process that includes all of the learning available as the result of what is in an environment to be learned (Herskovits 1948). **Primary socialization,** which is a more intentional learning process than enculturation, occurs in the family and local community (Berger and Luckmann 1967). We learn appropriate age, gender, ethnic, and social class behavior from our families, friends, schools, and religious institutions, as well as from advertising and television. In some instances, instead of "normal" behavior, people acquire deviant or pathological behavior from role models who do not conform to the central values of the society. In both cases, culture is learned from the environment; it is not something we are born knowing.

People from one country usually behave differently from people who live in other countries because specific cultures are associated with geographic regions that typically correspond to countries. Complicating matters, social groups within a country may also have distinctive cultures or **subcultures** that develop because a group has an ethnic background, language, or religion that is different from the majority population. For example, in England, there is a subculture of ethnic Asian Indians, and in the United States there is an increasing presence of a Hispanic subculture.

Immigrant children growing up in a culture different from their parents' are subject to the influences of their parents' culture and the national culture. For example, the children of Chinese immigrants in the United States who represent a blend of their parents' native culture and American culture are often independent and individualistic like Americans yet posses the Chinese value of unquestioned respect for elders. In some cases, the values of the two cultures are in conflict.

The socialization process is usually not explicit. Parents try to teach their children "what-is-right" but they rarely consider that correct behavior is culturally determined or that they are intentionally reproducing their culture. Culture is so much a part of everyday life that trying to identify our own culture is often difficult. Because culture is "natural" to the members of a society, they experience it as the only way of doing things.

Another important type of socialization is **secondary socialization** (Berger and Luckmann 1967). Secondary socialization occurs after primary socialization and usually equips people with the knowledge, skills, and behavior to enact adult roles successfully, particularly family and occupational roles. In management and organizational behavior, a particular type of secondary socialization is organizational socialization that includes training and the influence of the informal and formal organizational cultures. This continuous process, which consists of formal and informal learning, affects work behavior in important ways including organizational motivation, reaction to planned organization change, career development, and to some extent, the acceptance of and ability to work with culturally diverse organization members.

▪▪▪ Frameworks for Examining Cultures

Because understanding a culture's basic assumptions is important for understanding the culture itself, researchers have developed frameworks to classify the cultures of the world. These frameworks are averages or norms of the value systems that compose a culture rather than exact descriptions. In other words, they represent approximate expected behavior in a culture. Obviously, not everyone in a particular culture behaves in the same way. In fact, there is often greater variation within single cultures than across cultures.

Kluckhohn and Strodtbeck's Variations in Values Orientations

American anthropologists Kluckhohn and Strodtbeck (1961) developed a framework of six dimensions to describe the values orientation of a culture (see Table 2-1). The **values orientations** represent how different societies cope with various issues or problems. In the Kluckhohn and Strodtbeck framework, a culture may favor one or more of the **variations** or approaches associated with a particular values orientation. In the following discussion, each of Kluckhohn and Strodtbeck's dimensions is identified along with how it influences organizational behavior.

TABLE 2-1 Kluckhohn and Strodtbeck's Variations in Values Orientations

Values Orientation	*Variations*		
Relation to Nature	Subjugation	Harmony	Mastery
Time Orientation	Past	Present	Future
Basic Human Nature	Evil	Neutral/Mixed	Good
Activity Orientation	Being	Containing/Controlling	Doing
Relationships among People	Individualistic	Group	Hierarchical
Space Orientation	Private	Mixed	Public

Adapted from Lane, H. W., DiStefano, J. J., and Maznevski, M. L. (1997). *International Management Behavior.* 3rd Ed. Cambridge, MA: Blackwell.

Relation to Nature

Kluckhohn and Strodtbeck consider how a culture copes with its **relation to nature** as varying among subjugation, harmony, or mastery. For example, the Inuit (Eskimo) culture of Canada, Russia, and the United States has a **subjugation orientation.** From the Inuit perspective, whatever happens to them is inevitable; they accept nature as it is rather than try to change it.

A culture that is in **harmony** with nature, such as the Chinese, attempts to orient behavior to coexist with nature. *Feng shui,* "wind water," is an example of this. The Chinese believe that elements of the environment constructed by humans need to be in harmony with nature; the orientation and layout of buildings affects the lives of those who live and work in them. In selecting or building new office space, a *feng shui* expert or geomancer's advice helps assess the *feng shui* of the location. When the *feng shui* is good, business should prosper. Table 2-2 presents examples of some of the basic principles of *feng shui.*

Mastery cultures—North America and Western Europe are examples—attempt to change aspects of the environment through technology when necessary or desirable. Land reclamation, air conditioned buildings, chemical fertilizer, and immunization against disease reflect this orientation. For example, after the discovery of oil at Prudhoe Bay, Alaska, engineers did not think that the severe climactic conditions were an insurmountable barrier to extracting it.

Some cultures—Canadian society is one example—demonstrate an almost equal preference for harmony and mastery in relation to nature (Maznevski and DiStefano 1997). Canadians accept the harsh winter weather of their geographic

TABLE 2-2 Examples of Basic *Feng Shui* Principles

- An ideal building site is on elevated ground with a hill or mountain behind to act as a protective shield and a slow-moving river or serene lake in the front.
- A poor location for a building is at a dead-end or blind alley or facing a Y- or T-junction.
- Entry doors into a home should not be too dark or too narrow.
- Windows should be able to receive fresh air and shield the residents from direct glare and heat.
- Good design results from balance.

Source: Adapted from Lip, E. (1986). *Feng Shui for the Home.* Torrance, CA: Heian International.

location but at the same time attempt to limit its harmful effects through a wide array of modern techniques.

Time Orientation

The **time orientation** dimension is a society's focus on the past, present, or future. A **past orientation** emphasizes tradition and using time-honored approaches. For example, Italians respect and value craftsmanship based on years of traditional practice, and an Italian organization treasures time-tested ways of making a product.

A **present-oriented** culture generally focuses on the short term. For example, in the United States, businesses evaluate employee performance yearly, managers look at financial results quarterly, and people are highly conscious of time.

A **future-oriented** society emphasizes the long term. For example, some large Japanese corporations hire employees for life and expect profitability from a venture only after several years of operation. Similarly, the Japanese often do things to benefit future generations.

Basic Human Nature

Basic human nature assesses a culture's belief in people as good, evil, or neutral/mixed. A society that understands people as mainly good is basically a trusting one. For example, in Japan, executives often trust each other and rely on verbal agreements for major business deals.

In a culture that believes that people are basically **evil,** there is a lack of trust. In making a business deal, a New Yorker, who often exhibits skepticism, is careful to guard against being cheated. He might have an attorney examine the terms of a contract and insist that every detail be in writing.

A society with a **mixed** or **neutral orientation** believes people are basically good, but, in some situations they behave in an evil manner; therefore it is important to be cautious to protect yourself. In many parts of Canada people display this ambivalence by having a legal contract accompany verbal business arrangements.

Activity Orientation

A culture's **activity orientation** is either doing, being, or containing/controlling. In a **doing** culture, emphasis is on action, achievement, and working. For example, in the United States, people are hard working and want recognition for their accomplishments. Motivation is primarily through increases in salary, promotions, and other forms of recognition.

A **being** country emphasizes enjoying life and working for the moment; people work to live rather than live to work. For example, in Mexico, businesspeople socialize and enjoy each other's company before discussing business.

Finally, a **containing/controlling** culture emphasizes rationality and logic. People restrain their desires to try to achieve a mind/body balance. As an example, the French approach to decision making emphasizes pragmatism, logic, and rationality.

Relationships among People

Relationships among people can be individualistic, group, or hierarchical. People in **individualistic** societies define themselves through personal characteristics and achievements. For example, in the United States, employees receive rewards for their own accomplishments, individuals have their own work goals, and managers often encourage competition.

In a **group-**oriented society, a positive relationship to the collective is important. People relate to and take responsibility for members of the family or community. Emphasis is on harmony, unity, and loyalty. For example, in Japan, organizational decisions are usually based on consensus, working from the lower levels and moving upward.

Hierarchical societies also value group relationships but emphasize the relative ranking of groups within an organization or society as a whole, making them more class conscious than group societies. For example, in India, as a result of the caste system, birth largely determines position in society, and people from certain castes are more likely to have higher- or lower-prestige jobs.

Space Orientation

The **space orientation** dimension indicates how people relate to the ownership of space. Is it public, private, or a mixture of the two? In a **public** society, space belongs to everyone. For example, Japanese companies arrange office space in an open plan with the desks of employees and supervisors in the same large room with no partitions. In a society that values **privacy,** such as the United States, employees think it is important to have their own space. Because privacy is highly valued, higher-status members of an organization often have larger, more private space. Finally, in a **mixed** society, views on space fall somewhere in the middle, and there is a combination of public and private spaces. For example, in Hong Kong, lower-level employees share a common work area while managers have private offices.

Hofstede's Dimensions of Cultural Values

Geert Hofstede's (1980, 2001) classic study of dimensions of cultural values focuses specifically on **work-related values.** Hofstede, a Dutch social psychologist, believes "that people carry 'mental programs' that are developed in the family in early childhood and reinforced in schools and organizations, and that these mental programs contain a component of national culture. They are most clearly expressed in the different values that predominate among people from different countries" (2001, p. xix).

The data used to develop Hofstede's theory came from IBM employee surveys conducted between 1967 and 1973 with over 116,000 employees in 72 countries participating. Hofstede identified four dimensions of values to explain the differences among cultures: individualism/collectivism, power distance, uncertainty avoidance, and masculinity/femininity. Using the average scores for each country, Hofstede developed national profiles to explain differences in work behaviors. Table 2-3 and Figure 2-2 present these profiles. Because the data were from employees in the same organization, these differences are more likely due to national culture than to differences in company cultures or practices.

Individualism/Collectivism

In **individualistic** countries, people have concern for themselves and their families, rather than others. The individual is important, and each person's rights are highly valued. Organization systems attempt to honor individual preference and choice, and an employee's evaluation and reward are based on individually agreed upon objectives. In the individualistically oriented United Kingdom, for example, individual initiative is important, and even when employees work as a team, they receive recognition for individual achievement.

TABLE 2-3 Hofstede's Dimensions of Cultural Values—Country Abbreviations

Country	Code		Country	Code
Argentina	ARG		Japan	JPN
Australia	AUL		Korea (S)	KOR
Austria	AUT		Malaysia	MOR
Belgium	BEL		Mexico	MEX
Brazil	BRA		Netherlands	NET
Canada	CAN		Norway	NOR
Chile	CHL		New Zealand	NZL
Colombia	COL		Pakistan	PAK
Costa Rica	COS		Panama	PAN
Denmark	DEN		Peru	PER
Ecuador	ECA		Philippines	PHI
Finland	FIN		Portugal	POR
France	FRA		South Africa	SAF
Great Britain	GBR		Salvador	SAL
Germany (West)	GER		Singapore	SIN
Greece	GRE		Spain	SPA
Guatemala	GUA		Sweden	SWE
Hong Kong	HOK		Switzerland	SWI
Indonesia	IDO		Taiwan	TAI
India	IND		Thailand	THA
Iran	IRA		Turkey	TUR
Ireland	IRE		Uruguay	URU
Israel	ISR		United States	USA
Italy	ITA		Venezuela	VEN
Jamaica	JAM		Yugoslavia	YUG

Source: Hofstede, G. (2001). *Culture's Consequences: Comparing Values, Behaviors, Institutions, and Organizations across Nations.* 2nd Ed. Thousand Oaks, CA: Sage. Reprinted by permission of Dr. Geert Hofstede.

Collectivistic cultures value the overall good of the group because the expectation is that people should subordinate their individual interests and needs for the benefit of the group. Because being part of the group is so important, there are very clear expectations of how people in the group should behave. Collectivists treat ingroup and outgroup members differently. An **ingroup** member is someone with whom a person has an affective relationship, usually a family member, friend, colleague, neighbor, or classmate. An **outgroup** member is a person with whom there is no recognized relationship, often a stranger. In collectivistic countries, such as Mexico, people look after each other in exchange for loyalty, emphasize belonging, and make group decisions (Oyserman, Coon, and Kemmelmeier 2002).

Power Distance

Power distance, which ranges from small to large, is the extent to which less powerful members of organizations accept the unequal distribution of power. A **small power distance** society is less comfortable with power differences such as class distinction or

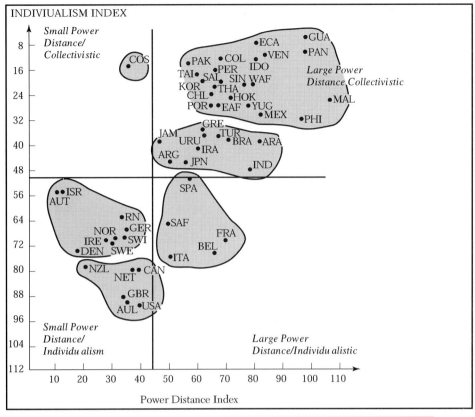

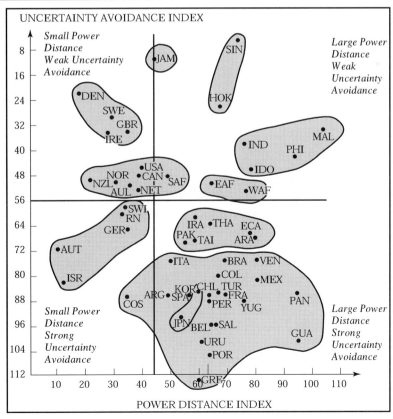

FIGURE 2-2 (*continued*)

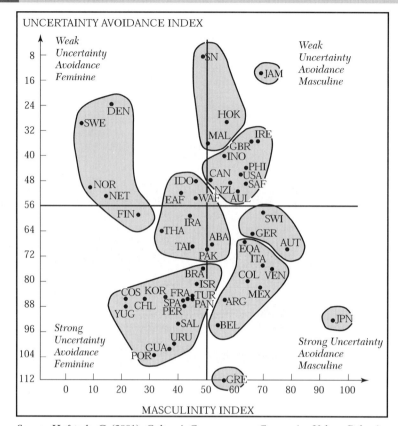

Source: Hofstede, G. (2001). *Culture's Consequences: Comparing Values, Behaviors, Institutions, and Organizations across Nations.* 2nd Ed. Thousand Oaks, CA: Sage, pp. 152, 217, 334. Reprinted by permission of Dr. Geert Hofstede.

organizational ranking than a large power distance culture. Rank differences are ignored in certain situations, for instance, when a subordinate complains to her boss's boss. It is positive for someone in a high-level position to treat those in lower-level positions as equals. In Denmark, a small power distance country, there is more participation in decision making and often a disregard of hierarchical level.

In a **large power distance** culture, differences among people with different ranks are accepted, and an individual's societal or organization position influences how he acts and how others treat him. A person in a high-level position treats those at lower levels with dignity, but the differences in rank are always clear. Delegating decision making implies incompetence because the rank of a manager's position requires him to make decisions himself. In a large power distance country such as Venezuela, managers tend to use an autocratic or paternalistic style, top managers make most decisions, and organizations have many layers of management.

Uncertainty Avoidance

Uncertainty avoidance, which ranges from strong to weak, indicates the preferred amount of structure. **Strong uncertainty avoidance** countries prefer more structure, resulting in explicit rules of behavior, either written or unwritten. These nations have strict laws with severe penalties for offenders, a high need for security, and great respect for experts. People are concerned about doing things correctly and are unlikely to start a new venture without very thorough research. For example, in a strong uncertainty avoidance country such as Greece, managers are risk-averse and, as a result, likely to work for the same company for a long time.

In contrast, **weak uncertainty avoidance** cultures favor unstructured situations. The culture is more flexible, people are more easy going, and a wide range of behaviors is acceptable. In the United States, where uncertainty avoidance is weak, individuals have strong feelings of personal competency, and entrepreneurial behavior is common and highly valued.

Masculinity/Femininity

In a **masculine** society, the "tough" values—including success, money, assertiveness, and competition—are dominant. There are often significant differences between men's and women's roles. The "masculine" label indicates that these tough values are almost universally associated with men's roles. Germany and Austria rank as highly masculine because they value earnings, recognition, advancement, and challenge. This type of society also encourages independent decision making.

Feminine cultures place importance on "tender" values such as personal relationships, care for others, the quality of life, and service. In these cultures, gender roles are less distinct and often equal. This dimension is called "feminine" because these traits are usually part of the female role. People in feminine Finland value cooperation, a friendly atmosphere, employment security, and group decision making.

The Chinese Value Survey

Because Hofstede's study presents a Western view of values, some researchers were concerned that his European values influenced his findings and theory. Consequently, Michael Harris Bond, a Canadian who lives and works in Hong Kong, and a group of Chinese colleagues developed a questionnaire reflecting Chinese cultural values. To prevent Western values from influencing the study, Chinese social scientists created the Chinese Value Survey (CVS) in Chinese (Chinese Culture Connection 1987), then translated it into other languages and administered it to students in 23 different countries on five continents including 20 countries in Hofstede's study.

Four dimensions of culture emerged from the study with three similar to Hofstede's dimensions of power distance, individualism/collectivism, and masculinity/femininity. The fourth dimension, however, represents Chinese values related to Confucianism. Originally called Confucian work dynamism, Hofstede later labeled it long-term/short-term orientation and included it as his fifth dimension.

Cultures high on **Confucian work dynamism**, or that are **long-term oriented**, have greater concern with the future and value thrift and persistence. These societies continuously consider how their current actions could influence future generations. In Hofstede's words, long-term orientation is "the extent to which a culture programs its members to accept delayed gratification of their material, social, and emotional needs" (2001, p. xx). In a long-term oriented country, such as Japan, companies take a far-sighted view of investments, and it is not necessary to show profits every year, but rather, progress toward a future goal is most important.

In countries low in Confucian work dynamism, or **short-term oriented**, values are oriented toward the past and present. There is respect for tradition and fulfilling social obligations is a concern, but the here and now is the most important. In the short-term oriented United States, for example, companies focus on quarterly and yearly profit results, and managers evaluate employee performance on a year-to-year basis.

Table 2-4 presents country scores for long-term and short-term orientation with their four Hofstede dimension scores.

TABLE 2-4 Cultural Dimension Scores

Country	Power Distance	Uncertainty Avoidance	Individualism/ Collectivism	Masculinity/ Femininity	Long-/Short-Term Orientation
	I	*I*	*I*	*I*	*I*
Argentina	49	86	46	56	
Australia	36	51	90	61	31
Austria	11	70	55	79	31
Bangladesh	80	60	20	55	40
Belgium	65	94	75	54	38
Brazil	69	76	38	49	65
Bulgaria	70	85	30	40	
Canada	39	48	80	52	23
Chile	63	86	23	28	
China	80	30	20	66	118
Colombia	67	80	13	64	
Costa Rica	35	86	15	21	
Czechia	57	74	58	57	13
Denmark	18	23	74	16	46
Ecuador	78	67	8	63	
Estonia	40	60	60	30	
Finland	33	59	63	26	41
France	68	86	71	43	39
Germany	35	65	67	66	31
Great Britain	35	35	89	66	25
Greece	60	112	35	57	
Guatemala	95	101	6	37	
Hong Kong	68	29	25	57	96
Hungary	46	82	80	88	50
Indonesia	78	48	14	46	
India	77	40	48	56	61
Iran	58	59	41	43	
Ireland	28	35	70	68	43
Israel	13	81	54	47	
Italy	50	75	76	70	34
Jamaica	45	13	39	68	
Japan	54	92	46	95	80
Korea (South)	60	85	18	39	75
Luxembourg	40	70	60	50	
Malaysia	104	36	26	50	
Malta	56	96	59	47	

■ ■ ■ ■ ■ ■ ■ ■ ■

(continued)

TABLE 2-4 *(continued)*

Country	Power Distance I	Uncertainty Avoidance I	Individualism/ Collectivism I	Masculinity/ Femininity I	Long-/Short-Term Orientation I
Mexico	81	82	30	69	
Morocco	70	68	46	53	
Netherlands	38	53	80	14	44
Norway	31	50	69	8	44
New Zealand	22	49	79	58	30
Pakistan	55	70	14	50	0
Panama	95	86	11	44	
Peru	64	87	16	42	
Philippines	94	44	32	64	19
Poland	68	93	60	64	32
Portugal	63	104	27	31	30
Romania	90	90	30	42	
Russia	93	95	39	36	
Salvador	66	94	19	40	
Singapore	74	8	20	48	48
Slovakia	104	51	52	110	38
South Africa	49	49	65	63	
Spain	57	86	51	42	19
Surinam	85	92	47	37	
Sweden	31	29	71	5	33
Switzerland	34	58	68	70	40
Taiwan	58	69	17	45	87
Thailand	64	64	20	34	56
Trinidad	47	55	16	58	
Turkey	66	85	37	45	
Uruguay	61	100	36	38	
United States	40	46	91	62	29
Venezuela	81	76	12	73	
Vietnam	70	30	20	40	80
Yugoslavia	76	88	27	21	
Regions:					
Arab countries	80	68	38	53	
East Africa	64	52	27	41	25
West Africa	77	54	20	46	16

Source: Adapted from Hofstede, G. (2001). *Culture's Consequences: Comparing Values, Behaviors, Institutions, and Organizations across Nations.* 2nd Ed. Thousand Oaks, CA: Sage, pp. 500, 502. Reprinted by permission of Dr. Geert Hofstede.

Schwartz's Value Survey

Shalom Schwartz, an Israeli psychologist, focuses on universal aspects of individual value content and structure (Schwartz 1992). Schwartz argues that values reflect the basic issues or problems societies confront in order to regulate social activities (Sagiv and Schwartz 2000). Schwartz's dimensions are based on three issues that confront all societies: (1) the nature of the relation or boundaries between the individual and the group, (2) how to guarantee responsible behavior, and (3) how to regulate the relation of people to the natural and social world.

In formulating his theory, Schwartz collected data over ten years from over 60,000 people in 63 countries on every inhabited continent (Sagiv and Schwartz 2000). Most of the subjects were schoolteachers and university students, but some were in other occupations. Based on these results, Schwartz derived three bipolar dimensions of culture that represent different solutions to the issues that confront societies. The dimensions are embeddedness versus autonomy, hierarchy versus egalitarianism, and mastery versus harmony. Usually, a society that emphasizes one end of a dimension will put less emphasis on the opposite end.

Figure 2-3 illustrates the model for schoolteachers from 57 countries. To identify a country's position on a particular value type, draw a line from the X in the middle of the plot that extends through the line to the arrow for that value type. Then, for any country, draw a perpendicular line from that country point to the line for the value type. The closer that country point is to the value type, the stronger the value is in that culture. For example, the embeddedness score for Bolivia is higher than for Poland, which is higher than Mexico's, while Switzerland and Greece have very low scores.

▪ ▪ ▪ ▪ ▪ ▪ ▪ ▪ ▪ ▪ ▪ ▪ **FIGURE 2-3** Dimensions of Schwartz's Value Theory

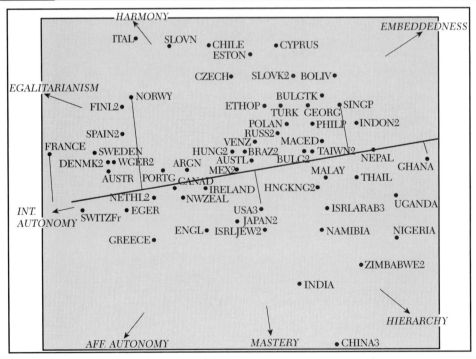

Source: Sagiv, L. and Schwartz, S. H. (2000). "A New Look at National Culture: Illustrative Applications to Role Stress and Managerial Behavior." In Ashkanasy, N. M., Wilderom, C. P. M., and Peterson, M. F. (eds.) *Handbook of Organizational Culture & Climate.* Thousand Oaks, CA: Sage, p. 423. Reprinted by permission of Sage Publications Inc.

Embeddedness Versus Autonomy

In **embedded** societies, people view others as inherently part of collectives. Meaning in life comes from social relationships, identification with the group, and participation in the group's shared way of life and goals. The important values for people include social order, respect for tradition, security, and wisdom. There is an emphasis on maintaining the status quo and preventing people from doing anything that might upset the group or the traditional order. In an embedded country, such as Indonesia, companies are like extended families, taking responsibility for all aspects of an employee's life and in return expecting the employee to contribute toward shared goals.

Autonomy cultures see individuals as autonomous, bounded entities who find meaning in their uniqueness. The society encourages people to express their internal attributes such as preferences, traits, feelings, and motives. There are two value types for autonomy. **Intellectual autonomy** means that people follow their own ideas and value curiosity, creativity, and open-mindedness. In France, which scores high on intellectual autonomy, people enjoy philosophical arguments and intellectual discussions that allow them to express their ideas. **Affective autonomy** focuses on individuals independently pursuing positive experiences that make them feel good, and value is put on pleasure and an exciting and varied life. Australians, who are high on affective autonomy, value quality of life, enjoy a healthy outdoor lifestyle, and engage in many different sports.

Hierarchy Versus Egalitarianism

A culture that values **hierarchy** uses a social system with clearly defined roles to make sure people behave responsibly. The unequal distribution of power, roles, and resources is legitimate, and people follow the rules and obligations that go along with their roles. A hierarchy society values social power, authority, humility, and wealth. In China, a hierarchy society, social power and wealth enhance a person's reputation.

In a country that emphasizes **egalitarianism,** people generally think of each other as moral equals sharing basic human interests. Members of the society go beyond their selfish interests and carry out voluntary behavior that promotes others' welfare. Important values are equality, social justice, responsibility, and honesty. The former West Germany, which emphasizes worker participation in organizational decision making, scored high on this value type.

Mastery Versus Harmony

A society with a **mastery** orientation encourages its members to master, change, and exploit the natural and social environment for personal or group goals. This type of culture values ambition, success, daring, and competence. Israel, which has many dynamic competitive companies, scores fairly high on this dimension.

The **harmony** value type emphasizes understanding and fitting in with the environment, rather than trying to change it. Important values are unity with nature, protecting the environment, and world peace. An example is Norway where people have a strong interest in protecting the environment.

Trompenaars' Dimensions of Culture

Fons Trompenaars (1993), a Dutch economist and management consultant, developed a framework to examine cultural differences using Kluckhohn and Strodtbeck's theory (1961) described previously, Hampden-Turner's dilemma theory (1983), and Parsons's pattern variables (1951). Over 14-years, Trompenaars collected data from over 46,000 managers representing more than 40 national cultures (Hampden-Turner and Trompenaars 2000).

Trompenaars describes national cultural diversity using six dimensions: universalism versus particularism, individualism versus communitarianism, specificity versus diffusion, achieved status versus ascribed status, inner direction versus outer direction, and sequential time versus synchronous time. As with Kluckhohn and Strodtbeck's framework, Trompenaars' dimensions represent how societies develop approaches to managing problems and difficult situations.

To measure a country's score on each dimension, Trompenaars used more than one question and depending on the question, country responses varied. Thus, it is difficult to construct an absolute categorization of countries on Trompenaars' dimensions.

Universalism Versus Particularism

In a **universal** culture, people believe the definition of goodness or truth applies to every situation, and they make judgments without regard to circumstance. A **particularist** society is more contingency oriented, believing that circumstances and relationships are more important in deciding what is right or good. Business contracts illustrate the differences between these two types. In a universalist culture such as the United States, lawyers are an essential part of most negotiations because they write a contract that defines a business relationship. The contract governs the relationship, and the parties refer to it when disputes arise. In a particularist country, such as China, a legal contract carries very little weight because the situation and the particular individuals involved define the relationship. The contract is a starting point, and the parties' behavior toward each other evolves as circumstances develop.

Individualism Versus Communitarianism

In an **individualistic** society, the focus is on self, personal freedom, and competitiveness. The society structures laws and rules to preserve the rights of the individual and to allow individual development and achievement. In individualistic Netherlands, employees receive recognition for their personal contributions and achievements at work.

A **communitarian** society emphasizes group membership, social responsibility, harmonious relationships, and cooperation. Belonging and contributing to a group are essential parts of the culture. In communitarian Japan, it is common for people not to reveal their personal preferences but to go along with the group for the sake of harmony.

Specificity Versus Diffusion

The **specificity versus diffusion** dimension focuses on the level of particularity or wholeness used by the culture to define different constructs. **Specific** countries tend to be objective and atomistic because they break things down into small parts. In their relationships, people usually have large public spaces and relatively smaller private spaces with the separation between spaces rigidly maintained. In **diffuse** cultures, the focus is on conceptual wholeness and relationships of all kinds are valued. People in diffuse cultures maintain a relatively smaller and more carefully guarded public space in their personal relationships.

In practice, people in a specific culture, such as the United States, tend to compartmentalize their public and private lives. Whereas it is easy to access someone in a work situation—public space—to conduct business, an American executive does not automatically allow a business associate to share his private life. In a diffuse culture, such as Spain, gaining access to an individual to transact business is more complicated because building a relationship precedes negotiating a deal. "Breaking into" the public space of a Spanish executive is initially more difficult, but once there, access to private or personal life often accompanies it.

Achieved Status Versus Ascribed Status

The **achieved status versus ascribed status** dimension describes how people in a culture gain power and status. An **achievement** society emphasizes attainment of position and influence through a demonstration of expertise. People in more powerful positions hold them because of their skills, knowledge, experience, and talents. Members of **ascriptive** cultures believe people are born into influence, and who you are, your potential, and your connections are all important. Those in power naturally have the right to be there because of their personal characteristics.

In achievement-oriented Australia, a person wins respect based on how well she performs in a position. Age, gender, and family background are not of major concern in making hiring or promotion decisions. An ascription-oriented society, such as Indonesia, generally places people in positions on the basis of who they are, and background, age, and gender are all important. Respect for senior members of an organization derives from who they are and their length of service.

Inner Direction Versus Outer Direction

Inner direction versus outer direction concerns the location of virtue. **Inner-directed** cultures conceive of virtue as being inside the individual and believe that conscience and convictions are internal. As a result, an individual, group, or organization can control a situation. In Canadian businesses, for example, there is often open discussion of conflicts and disagreements because confronting conflict is considered a means to control it. **Outer-directed** societies believe virtue is outside the person and located in nature and relationships. Individuals from outer-directed cultures are flexible and try to harmonize with the environment and focus on the "other." In Egypt, organizations manage conflict quietly over a longer period of time because this technique produces less stress.

Sequential Time Versus Synchronous Time

People in **sequential time** cultures do one thing at a time, make appointments and arrive on time, and generally stick to schedules. Organizations in sequential cultures such as England use detailed plans and evaluate performance every six months or annually based on meeting objectives by a certain date. In **synchronic time** countries, people do several activities simultaneously, the time for appointments is approximate, and interpersonal relationships are more important than schedules. The synchronic Mexicans often evaluate performance based on the whole person: looking at someone's history with the company, present accomplishments, and future potential. Rather than basing evaluations on objectives, they focus on the employee's personal aspirations and how these relate to the organization.

Hall's High- and Low-Context Cultural Framework

Edward T. Hall (1976), an American anthropologist, uses the concept of context to explain differences in communication styles among cultures. "**Context** is the information that surrounds an event; it is inextricably bound up with the meaning of that

TABLE 2-5 High- and Low-Context Countries

High-Context	Low-Context
China	Australia
Egypt	Canada
France	Denmark
Italy	England
Japan	Finland
Lebanon	Germany
Saudi Arabia	Norway
Spain	Switzerland
Syria	United States

event" (Hall and Hall 1989, p. 64). Cultures can be categorized on a scale from high- to low-context. "A **high-context** (HC) communication or message is one in which most of the information is either in the physical context or internalized in the person, while very little is in the coded, explicit, transmitted part of the message. A **low-context** (LC) communication is just the opposite; i.e., the mass of the information is vested in the explicit code" (Hall 1976, p. 79). Table 2-5 provides examples of high- and low-context countries.

In a high-context culture, such as Saudi Arabia, family, friends, co-workers and clients have close personal relationships and large information networks. Because of this, people know a lot about others within their networks; they do not require extensive background information. People in low-context cultures, such as Switzerland, separate their lives into different aspects, such as work and personal. Therefore, when interacting with others, they need to receive more detailed information.

In a high-context culture, people do not rely on language alone for communication. Tone of voice, timing, facial expression, and behaving in ways considered acceptable in the society are major means of expression. In contrast, a low-context culture depends on the use of words to convey meaning. Expressing complete, accurate meaning through appropriate word choice is important. The amount of information supplied in communicating is the key difference between the two types of culture.

Ronen and Shenkar's Country Clusters

Based on a number of earlier studies, Simcha Ronen and Oded Shenkar (1985) proposed clustering countries based on similarities in work values or goals. The map of the clusters (Figure 2-4) indicates the similarity of countries and clusters and level of economic development with countries that have higher GNP per capita closer to the center. Within each cluster, countries generally have similar work values, geographic location, language, and religion. The countries classified as independent did not clearly fit into any one of the eight clusters and are not similar to each other. Often they had higher levels of economic and technological development than their geographic neighbors.

Clustering is useful for both international managers and researchers (Ronen and Shenkar 1985). It gives managers a better understanding of similarities and differences between countries that can help them select the right employees for international

■ ■ ■ ■ ■ ■ ■ ■ ■ ■ ■ ■ **FIGURE 2-4** Ronen and Shenkar's Country Clusters

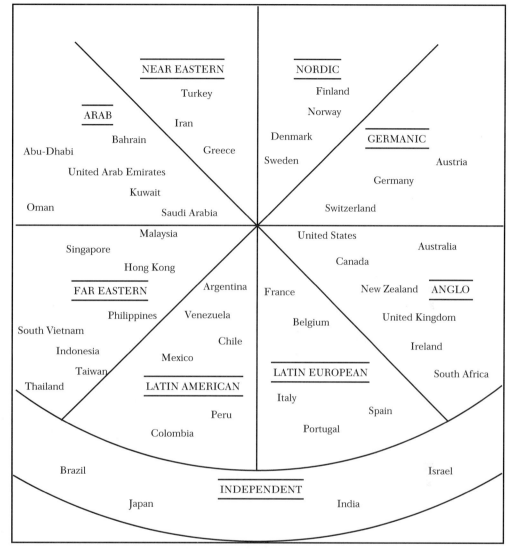

Source: From *Academy of Management Review* by Richard J. Klimoski. Copyright © 1985 by Academy of Management. Reproduced with permission of Academy of Management in the format Other Book via Copyright Clearance Center.

assignments, set up appropriate regional units, and anticipate how policies and procedures will operate in different places. Clustering also assists researchers by suggesting how results in one country may apply to others and by suggesting which variables could explain differences in goals and values.

The World Values Survey

The World Values Survey (WVS) is a long-term, large-scale study of sociocultural and political change that is investigating basic values and beliefs of people in more than 65 societies on all six inhabited continents, containing almost 80% of the world's population (World Values Survey 2003). Researchers from around the world are collecting data from a sample of at least 1,000 people in their own societies under the guidance of an international steering committee headed by American political scientist Ronald Inglehart. There have been four waves of data collection: 1981, 1990–1991, 1995–1996, and 1999–2001.

Data from the first three waves indicate that societal values relate to both economic development and cultural tradition (Inglehart and Baker 2000). The two most important dimensions of societal values according to the WVS are traditional versus secular-rational orientations toward authority and survival versus self-expression values.

Traditional Versus Secular-Rational Orientations toward Authority

Societies with a **traditional orientation toward authority** have values that reflect pre-industrial society and the centrality of the family. These values include the importance of God, the importance of obedience and religious faith over independence and determination, and views against abortion, euthanasia, and suicide. In addition, traditional cultures "emphasize social conformity rather than individualistic striving, believe in absolute standards of good and evil, support deference to authority, and have high levels of national pride and a nationalistic outlook" (Inglehart and Baker 2000, p. 25). Indicating a clear difference among cultures, the WVS found that "Societies with secular-rational values have the opposite preferences on all of these topics" (Inglehart and Baker 2000, p. 25).

Survival Versus Self-Expression Values

People from societies at the **survival** end of this dimension put priority on economic and physical security over self-expression and quality of life, are intolerant of homosexuality, and describe themselves as unhappy. These societies also have "low levels of subjective well-being, report relatively poor health, are low on interpersonal trust, relatively intolerant of out-groups, are low on support for gender equality, emphasize materialist values, have relatively high levels of faith in science and technology, are relatively low on environmental activism, and relatively favorable to authoritarian government" (Inglehart and Baker 2000, p. 28). Societies with high **self-expression values** tend to have the opposite preferences, for example, they are trusting and tolerant of others, politically active, happy, and put priority on self-expression and quality of life.

Figure 2-5 shows the location of 65 societies on a global cultural map of these two dimensions. An interesting pattern emerges. First, similar to the work of Ronen and Shenkar (1985), those societies with similar geographic location, language, and religion tend to have similar values. Second, there is a relationship between values and economic development. Lower-income countries are in the lower left quadrant, those with higher income in the upper right, and middle-income countries in the center. Thus, cultural heritage and economic development influence values.

The WVS also shows that there are generational differences in values that are greatest in societies with the highest life expectancies (Inglehart and Baker 2000). For example, in ex-Communist societies and advanced industrial democracies, younger people hold more secular-rational values than older people. In developing and low-income societies, the traditional value orientation is prevalent among both young and old. Ex-Communist societies and advanced industrial democracies also have the greatest generational differences on the survival/self-expression dimension, but for the advanced industrial democracies the differences are in the degree of self-expression. Both younger and older people have self-expression values, but the scores are higher for the young. The trend is in the same direction for the ex-Communist countries, but for these countries both young and old are on the survival side of the dimension. Even

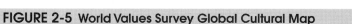

FIGURE 2-5 World Values Survey Global Cultural Map

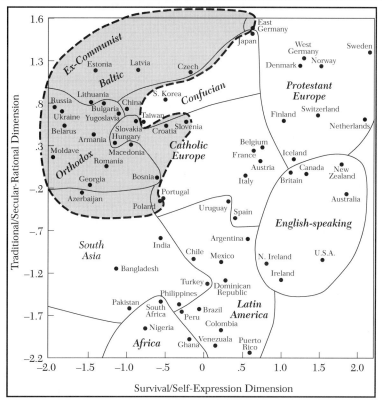

Source: Ronald Ingle and Wayne Baker, 2000, "Modernization, Cultural Change and the Persistence of Traditional Values," American Sociological Review, 2000, 65, (February), p. 29. Reprinted by permission.

though young people in the ex-Communist countries consider survival values as less important than older people, their scores are still lower than those in developing and low-income societies. In these two types of societies, there is relatively little generational difference, and these societies put greater value on survival.

It is important to note that a major finding from the WVS is that while there is significant change in values throughout the world, there is also evidence of the persistence of distinctive cultural traditions. Societies are changing in parallel rather than converging into a single set of values.

Cultural Metaphors

A different approach to understanding culture is the use of metaphors. American management scholar Martin Gannon (2001) identifies an important phenomenon, activity, or institution that members of a culture see as important as a metaphor for that culture. The metaphors are built upon the dimensions of Kluckhohn and Strodtbeck (1961), Hofstede (1980), and Hall (1976) and also include many other aspects of culture such as religion, public behavior, holidays and ceremonies, food and eating behavior, and rate of technological and cultural change. By understanding the metaphor, outsiders can describe and understand the essential features of a society.

The metaphors are framed in a four-stage model of cross-cultural understanding. The first stage considers process/goal orientation and degree of emotional expressiveness.

TABLE 2-6 Metaphors of Culture

Country	Metaphor
Brazil	the samba
England	the traditional British house
India	the dance of Shiva
Italy	the opera
Japan	the garden
Mexico	fiesta
Nigeria	the marketplace
Poland	the village church
Russia	the ballet
Saudi Arabia	Bedouin jewelry
Turkey	the coffeehouse
United States	football

Source: Gannon, M. J. (2001). *Understanding Global Cultures: Metaphorical Journeys through 23 Nations.* 2nd Ed. Thousand Oaks, CA: Sage. Reprinted by permission of Sage Publications Inc.

The second stage focuses on the link between economics and culture by looking at aspects of individualism/collectivism and power distance. The third stage examines other general cultural dimensions, and the fourth stage uses the metaphor to understand a culture. Using this model, Gannon discusses the history and culture of different countries and how the metaphor leads to greater understanding of each. Table 2-6 identifies some of the metaphors.

One example is the metaphor of American football for the United States. Americans typically belong to several groups or teams as part of their work and social life, and membership is often temporary. Although contributing to the team is an important value, rewards usually go to individuals. Gannon compares this behavior to the huddle in American football where team members decide what to do as a group. Then, all of them carry out their assignments and receive rewards for individual performance.

Universal Behaviors

The theories presented above focus on the role of values in forming and explaining society, culture, and consequently, individual behavior. Each theory assumes that values can be measured across cultures—usually as polar types, for example, individualism versus collectivism—and for purposes of comparison mean approximately the same thing in each culture. Other assumptions are that values translate fairly directly into behaviors and that without the presence of certain values, particular behaviors will not be found in the culture. In addition, clustering countries according to similar values, while acknowledging that countries share similar cultural elements, highlights the differences in values across cultures. Indeed, the implication drawn from most cultural frameworks, including those presented in this chapter, is that to manage successfully across cultures, international managers have to become familiar with significant, meaningful variations in cultures and behaviors. Whether intended or not, the emphasis is almost always on cultural differences.

An approach that challenges the assumption that human behavior is primarily determined by culture is American anthropologist Donald E. Brown's research on behavioral traits common to human beings (Brown 1991, 1999). Brown's list of 375 cultural universals that compose his concept of the "Universal People" contends that significant elements of human behavior are the same throughout societies, suggesting that similar biological and cognitive processes operate across cultures. For example, universal behaviors include conflict, cooking, decision making, marriage, and play. Universal concepts, attitudes, and values include ambivalence, beliefs about death, ethnocentrism, metaphor, and the concept of person. Focusing on behaviors found in organizations, every society creates a division of labor, plans for the future, overestimates objectivity of thought, and develops rituals. Psychologist Steven Pinker's assessment is that, "the sheer richness and detail in the rendering of the Universal People comes as a shock to any intuition that the mind is a blank slate or that cultures can vary without limit, and there is something on the list to refute almost any theory growing out of those intuitions" (Pinker 2002, p. 55).

Brown's list of human universals challenges but does not eliminate the role of culture as an explanation of behavior in societies and organizations. For example, even within a national culture, researchers have identified corporate cultures that vary significantly (Deal and Kennedy 1999; Schein 1992). Similarly, although genetics, economics, and the type of political regime in a country explain the level of happiness a population experiences, culture also contributes to explaining differences in happiness across nations (Inglehart and Klingemann 2000). Yet, supporting Brown's view, recent research demonstrates that important similarities exist in organizational behavior across cultures, for example, the finding from Project GLOBE that every society has a concept of and preference for transformational or charismatic leadership. Finally, according to Brown, every human society has the behavior "customary greeting." So, when we observe that when people greet in one society they rub noses while in others they hug, and some societies prefer handshakes, do we understand this behavior to be unique or universal?

Do the Cultural Frameworks Really Explain Cultural Differences?

Each cultural framework presented above attempts to explain general cultural differences among societies. Several build on and elaborate the work of others in an attempt to refine categories and concepts and to provide empirical support for complex theories. While none of the frameworks is absolutely correct or better than the others, ultimately what is important is how each perspective contributes to our understanding of why people from different cultures behave as they do.

A theoretical framework represents an average of people's behavior within a particular culture. Of course, there are always exceptions to the average, and sometimes particular behaviors common across a whole culture appear to be contrary to a theory's categorization. For example, at a recent conference, a Taiwanese scholar disagreed with the classification of Taiwan as collectivistic, asking, "Have you ever been in a traffic jam in Taipei? The individualistic behavior of the drivers certainly disproves Hofstede's classification!" Many countries classified as similar may view themselves as distinctive. For example, the American and the British cultures are classified similarly on many dimensions, to some extent because they share a common culture and language, but in many important ways their cultures are significantly different as the result of the specific social and historical events that create divergent meanings.

The use of different frameworks provides useful insights. For instance, where more than one framework uses a dimension in the same way and classifies a country similarly, reliability appears to be increased. For example, Hofstede, Trompenaars, and Kluckhohn and Strodtbeck all have a dimension focusing on relationships among people. The United States is considered highly individualistic in all three frameworks, giving more confidence in this classification. However, France varies from individualistic in the Hofstede model to collectivistic on Trompenaars' dimension to hierarchical in the Kluckhohn and Strodtbeck framework. What explains these differences? Is it because the definitions of the dimension vary? Is it due to differences in the samples of French respondents for the three models? These are some of the plausible explanations for the differences. Consequently, for foreigners approaching the French, what behavior to expect based on these cultural frameworks is not clear.

Research that applies the cultural dimensions to individual behavior finds that a range of differences on any dimension exists within the population of a single country (Brockner 2003). For example, because of individual differences, it is possible that a person from a country with strong uncertainty avoidance could have a lower score than someone from a weak uncertainty avoidance country. Therefore, it is important to remember that the country score for a particular dimension does not mean that everyone in that country holds the same value.

Cultural dimensions can also explain differences in individual people's behavior within the same country. Often these differences between individuals are more useful in predicting behavior than differences between countries. For example, research on the behavior of individualists and collectivists within a single country, such as China or the United States, has found meaningful differences between the two groups (Francesco and Chen in press; Wagner 1995). Also, research comparing people with individualistic and collectivistic orientations from different countries suggests that the individual differences are more important than the country differences (Earley 1993). We discuss some of these studies in other chapters.

However, a significant amount of research finds that although members of societies differ in many ways—age, gender, sexual orientation, skin color, occupation, income, and religion, among others—they nonetheless share fundamental values. For example, in the United States, which has a historically heterogeneous population that is becoming more diverse, the consensus around fundamental values and aspirations is so pronounced that sociologist Amitai Etzioni (2001) argues that the United States is "the monochrome society."

▪ ▪ ▪ How Culture Relates to Organizational Behavior

The cultural frameworks and other ways of thinking about culture help managers understand how culture relates to organizational behavior. Research on organizational behavior originated in the United States. Therefore, to a large extent, it continues to reflect American culture and values, such as the worth and uniqueness of the individual, the correctness of capitalism as an economic system, and the use of natural science methods to study human behavior. However, as the study of organizational behavior becomes increasingly widespread in other cultures and theories of comparative management become more sophisticated, more researchers are examining whether U.S. models of organizational behavior apply to other cultures.

An example is a study examining the relationship between the frameworks of Hofstede, Trompenaars, and Schwartz and how managers handled different work events in 47 countries (Smith, Peterson, and Schwartz 2002). The researchers identified eight events that managers in all the countries commonly handled—for example, a subordinate doing consistently good work or the need to introduce new departmental work procedures. Managers then had to indicate the sources of guidance that affected them in handling each event—for example, formal rules and procedures, superior, subordinates, or widespread beliefs about what is right. The sources of guidance reflected various cultural values from the three frameworks—for example, choosing superior as a source is indicative of high power distance. The most significant result was that managers in countries with values such as high power distance, collectivism, hierarchy, masculinity, and embeddedness relied more on vertical sources of guidance such as formal rules and procedures or advice from superiors. Managers in countries with low power distance, individualism, egalitarianism, femininity, and autonomy favored more participative forms of guidance such as ideas and opinions of subordinates. Overall, the findings indicate that cultural values can influence managerial behavior and that American models of management may not be universally appropriate.

These results suggest how values influence one aspect of international organizational behavior and have implications for international business practice. Unfortunately, multinationals often do not consider the impact of culture when doing business outside their home countries. For example, there are many documented failures of U.S. multinationals attempting to apply American management theories abroad. Because of this, both academics and business people want to understand why the failures occurred and what approaches are likely to be more successful. They recognize that U.S. theories are not universally applicable. In trying to understand how other countries differ from the United States, researchers examine the influence of variables such as government, the economy, language, technology, and geography.

It can be argued, however, that culture is the most useful variable for identifying and explaining differences in how people behave. The examples of cultural differences in this chapter strongly suggest that the application of American management and organizational behavior approaches is destined for failure when applied to cultures differing significantly from the United States. Consequently, throughout this book the frameworks for describing cultures are used to help us understand organizational behavior around the world.

The various frameworks and metaphors are useful for understanding one's own and others' cultures, but knowing the scores of a country on these frameworks or being able to identify an insightful metaphor will not make one an expert in that country's culture. Only through study of the history, traditions, and institutions of a culture, along with interaction with its people, can one achieve an in-depth understanding of a people's behaviors, values, and overall approach to life.

▪▪▪ Convergence or Divergence?

Forces for Convergence

As technology increases communication across cultures and countries become more closely linked through trade, information about other cultures becomes more available. Products are sold worldwide and in some cases marketed in the same way everywhere. Because of these and other changes, some might say that cultures are becoming more alike and that the study of culture is therefore irrelevant. At the surface level there may be truth to the idea of cultural convergence. For example, in virtually any country you can find someone eating a McDonald's hamburger while sitting in a Honda filled with Shell gasoline.

Forces for Divergence

A closer look at what seem to be similar culturally determined behaviors reveals many differences. A McDonald's hamburger in Moscow or Beijing is trendy and the cost is well above average; in Washington, D.C., eating at McDonald's is a mere convenience and one of the cheapest meals available. Christmas for many Italians is a family holiday with religious meaning whereas for many people in Hong Kong it is an occasion for fun among friends, time off work, commercial decorations, and no family obligations. Below the surface, cultures usually attach different meanings to what appear to be the same behaviors.

On another level, the effect of cultural differences can be clearly seen. Ethnic conflicts continue around the world and are often the result of attempts to maintain distinct cultural identities. In many cases the interventions of the United Nations or of peacekeeping countries fail to resolve the conflicts because the values underlying them are strong and persistent. Similarly, although there is a World Trade Organization, trade disputes continue and arguments over trade frequently reflect the cultural differences as well as the economic interests of the countries involved.

Culture, although not the only important variable, contributes significantly to explaining key differences in societal behavior. An appreciation of the role of culture in organizations creates a more sophisticated understanding of management and organizational behavior around the world.

▪▪▪ Implications for Managers

Understanding culture can equip you for the challenges of contemporary international business even if you never leave home. In an increasingly interdependent world, managers in every country must think globally. Even in a large market such as the United States, increasing numbers of domestic products face foreign competition at home. The new reality is that global competition exists for every product—and increasingly for services—in every market.

Another reason for studying culture is that in any country an organization's stakeholders—customers, competitors, suppliers, shareholders, and employees—could be from another culture. Worldwide, there are also increasing numbers of immigrant and guest workers who bring their own cultures to their jobs, and it is essential to integrate them into the existing workforce. Consequently, it is important to understand organizational stakeholders in order to serve them better and to manage successfully.

Even behavior that appears to be similar on the surface may have different meanings for different cultures. Recognizing the importance of cultural differences helps managers understand their international partners and competitors and ultimately to improve their managerial skills.

Finally, a basic framework for analyzing cultures enables managers to understand and evaluate changes in cultures that have implications for international organizational behavior. For example, global business requires some level of trust among those engaged in transactions even when written contracts exist. Trust is rapidly emerging as a transcultural value (Johnson and Cullen 2002) as well as an important value for understanding and managing behavior within organizations (Kramer 1999). For international managers, even though significant levels of conflict persist across cultures, it is important to create and manage enduring relationships built on trust. To do this, it is useful to know how different cultures regard trust in relationships with people from other cultures.

SUMMARY

There are many definitions of culture, but a useful and comprehensive one is "the way of life of a group of people." The levels of culture range from manifest to expressed values to basic assumptions. Understanding the deeper, less-apparent levels produces a more profound understanding of a culture. Culture is learned through enculturation as well as through primary and secondary socialization.

Cultural frameworks classify national cultures. The frameworks of Kluckhohn and Strodtbeck, Hofstede, the Chinese Value Survey, Schwartz, Trompenaars, and Hall, provide an initial understanding of different cultures by identifying important variables that explain behavior. Ronen and Shenkar's country clusters and the global map of the World Values Survey indicate similarities among countries based on geography, language, religion, and economic development. Gannon uses metaphors to give a more in-depth understanding of different cultures. Finally, Brown's human universals identify behaviors common to all societies, instead of how values differ across societies.

Organizational behavior theories developed in the United States may not apply elsewhere because of cultural differences. The debate over cultural convergence and divergence shows simultaneous trends in both directions.

The world is becoming increasingly more interdependent and better connected through improved communications technology, allowing managers access to more people and organizations. The implication for managers is that understanding diverse cultures as they affect organizational behavior is a critical management skill.

DISCUSSION QUESTIONS

1. What is culture? How is it useful in studying international organizational behavior?
2. Choose a familiar culture. Give examples of each of Sathe's three levels of culture.
3. Think about your own culture. How did the socialization process take place in your own life? Try to recall some of the behaviors and values you were taught early in life. How do these affect you now?
4. Using Hofstede's dimensions of cultural values, contrast two different cultures. What potential problems would people from these two cultures have in doing business with each other?
5. How did the results of the CVS complement the work of Hofstede?
6. Compare the cultural frameworks presented in this chapter. What are their similarities and differences? Do you like any better than the others? Why?
7. From your own experience, how do you think understanding culture can help you become a better manager?
8. Do you think that cultures are becoming more similar or more dissimilar? Why?

INTERNET SITES

Consortium for Culture and Generation Studies (CCGS) (http://spitswww.uvt.nl/web/iric/ccgs/). This is the Web site of the Consortium for Culture and Generation Studies, a European-based international, multidisciplinary network of social science university departments and research institutes that promotes the cross-cultural understanding of the relationship between culture and generations.

Culture and United Nations Educational, Scientific, and Cultural Organization (UNESCO) (http://www.unesco.org/culture/news/html_eng/index_en.shtml). This is one of the official Web sites of the United Nations Educational, Scientific, and Cultural Organization and includes information about topics such as tangible and intangible cultural heritage, cultural property protected by international law, and cultural events.

Culturelink Network (http://www.culturelink.org/). This Croatia-based site is a network for research and cooperation in cultural development and links to other cultural sites worldwide.

Institute for Research on Intercultural Cooperation (IRIC) (http://kubnw5.kub.nl/ web/iric/index2.htm). IRIC was founded in 1980 by Geert Hofstede and Bob Waisfisz and is now located at Tilburg University in the Netherlands. IRIC continues to do research on Hofstede's five cultural dimensions.

Welcome to Geert Hofstede's Homepage (http://kubnw5.kub.nl/web/iric/hofstede/ index.htm). Hofstede shares his past research and recent ideas at this Web site.

World Values Survey (http://wversusisr.umich.edu/). This official site of the WVS gives a full explanation of the research project, lists of related publications, and some recent findings.

REFERENCES ▐▐▐▐▐▐▐

Berger, P. and Luckmann, T. (1967). *The Social Construction of Reality.* New York: Doubleday.

Brockner, J. (2003). "Unpacking Country Effects: On the Need to Operationalize the Psychological Determinants of Cross-National Differences." In Kramer, R. M. and Staw, B. M. (eds.) *Research in Organizational Behavior*, 25, Oxford: Elsevier Press.   ·

Brown, D. E. (1991). *Human Universals.* New York: McGraw-Hill.

——. (1999). "Human Universals." In Wilson, R. A. and Keil, F. C. (eds.) *The MIT Encyclopedia of Cognitive Sciences.* Cambridge, MA: MIT Press.

Chinese Culture Connection (1987). "Chinese Values and the Search for Culture-Free Dimensions of Culture," *Journal of Cross-Cultural Psychology*, 15, 417–33.

Deal, T. E. and Kennedy, A. A. (1999). *The New Corporate Cultures: Revitalizing the Workplace after Downsizing, Mergers, and Reengineering.* Cambridge, MA: Perseus.

Earley, P. C. (1993). "East Meets West Meets Mideast: Further Explorations of Collectivistic and Individualistic Work Groups," *Academy of Management Journal*, 36 (2), 319–48.

Etzioni, A. (2001). *The Monochrome Society.* Princeton, NJ: Princeton University Press.

Ferraro, G. P. (2002). *The Cultural Dimension of International Business.* 4th Ed. Upper Saddle River, NJ: Prentice Hall.

Francesco, A. M. and Chen, Z. X. (2004). "Collectivism in Action: Its Moderating Effects on the Relationship between Organizational Commitment and Employee Performance in China," *Group and Organization Management* 29(4).

Gannon, M. J. (2001). *Understanding Global Cultures: Metaphorical Journeys through 23 Nations.* 2nd Ed. Thousand Oaks, CA: Sage.

—— and Associates (1994). *Understanding Global Cultures: Metaphorical Journeys through 17 Countries.* Thousand Oaks, CA: Sage.

Hall, E. T. (1976). *Beyond Culture.* Garden City, NY: Anchor Press/Doubleday.

—— and Hall, M. R. (1989). *Understanding Cultural Differences: German, French and American.* Yarmouth, ME: Intercultural Press.

Hampden-Turner, C. M. (1983). *Gentlemen & Tradesmen: The Values of Economic Catastrophe.* London: Routledge.

—— and Trompenaars, F. (2000). *Building Cross-Cultural Competence: How to Create Wealth from Conflicting Values.* New Haven, CT: Yale University Press.

Herskovits, M. (1948). *Man and His Works: The Science of Cultural Anthropology.* New York: Knopf.

Hofstede, G. (1980). *Culture's Consequences: International Differences in Work-Related Values.* Beverly Hills, CA: Sage.

——. (2001). *Culture's Consequences: Comparing Values, Behaviors, Institutions, and Organizations across Nations.* 2nd Ed. Thousand Oaks, CA: Sage.

Inglehart, R. and Baker, W. E. (2000). "Modernization, Cultural Change, and the Persistence of Traditional Values," *American Sociological Review*, 65 (February), 19–51.

—— and Klingemann, H. D. (2000). "Genes, Culture, Democracy, and Happiness." In Diener, E. and Suh, E. M. (eds.) *Culture and Subjective Well-Being.* Cambridge, MA: MIT Press.

Johnson, J. L. and Cullen, J. B. (2002). "Trust in Cross-Cultural Relationships." In Gannon, M. J. and Newman, K. L. (eds.) *Handbook of Cross-Cultural Management.* Malden, MA: Blackwell.

Kluckhohn, F. and Strodtbeck, F. L. (1961). *Variations in Value Orientations.* Evanston, IL: Peterson.

Kramer, R. M. (1999). "Trust and Distrust in Organizations: Emerging Perspectives, Enduring Questions," *Annual Review of Psychology*, 50, 569–98.

Kroeber, A. L. and Kluckhohn, F. (1952). "Culture: A Critical Review of Concepts and Definitions." *Peabody Museum Papers,* 47 (1). Cambridge, MA: Harvard University.

Lane, H. W., DiStefano, J. J., and Maznevski, M. L. (1997). *International Management Behavior.* 3rd Ed. Cambridge, MA: Blackwell.

Lip, E. (1986). *Feng Shui for the Home.* Torrance, CA: Heian International.

Maznevski, M. L. and DiStefano, J. J. (1997). "Culture and Its Impact on Management." Presented at the 4th International Organizational Behavior Teaching Conference, Hong Kong, January.

Oyserman, D., Coon, H. M., and Kemmelmeier, M. (2002). "Rethinking Individualism and Collectivism: Evaluation of Theoretical Assumptions and Meta-Analysis," *Psychological Bulletin*, 128(1), 3–72.

Parsons, T. (1951). *The Social System*. New York: The Free Press.

Pinker, S. (2002). *The Blank Slate: The Modern Denial of Human Nature*. New York: Viking.

Rockner, J. (2003). Unpacking country effects: On the need to operationalize the psychological determinants of cross-national differences. In R. M. Kramer & B. M. Staw (Eds.), Research in organizational behavior (Vol. 25, pp. 333–367). Oxford, UK: Elsevier Press.

Ronen, S. and Shenkar, O. (1985). "Clustering Countries on Attitudinal Dimensions: A Review and Synthesis," *Academy of Management Review*, 10(3), 435–54.

Sagiv, L. and Schwartz, S. H. (2000). "A New Look at National Culture: Illustrative Applications to Role Stress and Managerial Behavior." In Ashkanasy, N. M., Wilderom, C. P. M., and Peterson, M. F. (eds.) *Handbook of Organizational Culture & Climate*. Thousand Oaks, CA: Sage.

Sathe, V. (1985). *Culture and Related Corporate Realities*. Homewood, IL: Irwin.

Schein, E. H. (1992). *Organizational Culture and Leadership*. 2nd Ed. San Francisco: Jossey-Bass.

Schwartz, S. H. (1992). "Universals in the Content and Structure of Values: Theoretical Advances and Empirical Tests in 20 Countries." In Zanna, M. P. (ed.) *Advances in Experimental Social Psychology*, 25, 1–65.

Smith, P. B., Peterson, M. F., and Schwartz, S. H. (2002). "Cultural Values, Sources of Guidance, and Their Relevance to Managerial Behavior: A 47-Nation Study," *Journal of Cross-Cultural Psychology*, 33(2), 188–208.

Trompenaars, F. (1993). *Riding the Waves of Culture: Understanding Diversity in Global Business*. London: The Economist Books.

Tylor, E. (1871). *Origins of Culture*. New York: Harper & Row.

Wagner, J. A. III. (1995). "Studies of Individualism-Collectivism: Effects on Cooperation in Groups," *Academy of Management Journal*, 38(1), 152–72.

World Values Survey, "Introduction," [accessed July 24, 2003], available from http://wvs.isr.umich.edu/index.shtml

CHAPTER

3

Ethics and Social Responsibility

Learning Objectives

After reading this chapter, you should be able to:

■ Define ethics and understand the importance of ethical behavior for organizations.

■ Discuss four perspectives on ethics and arguments for ethical relativism and universalism.

■ Understand the efficiency and social responsibility perspectives of corporate social responsibility.

■ Know how ethics affect individual behavior in organizations.

■ Consider ways of scientifically studying organizational ethics.

■ Know methods for resolving cross-cultural ethical conflicts.

■ Analyze your ethics and how they affect your understanding of management and organizational behavior.

CULTURE AT WORK
Welcome to the World of Global Business Ethics

The ethical treachery of the world market places leaps from newspaper headlines almost daily.

- **Brazil's Prized Exports Rely on Slaves and Scorched Land** (*The New York Times,* March 25, 2002, p. 1)
- **Credit Card Theft Is Thriving Online as Global Market** (*The New York Times*, May 13, 2002, p. 1)
- **Report Says Software Piracy Is Rising Globally** (*The New York Times*, June 10, 2002, p. 3)
- **Bhopal Seethes, Pained and Poor 18 Years Later** (*The New York Times*, September 21, 2002)

At the same time that headlines point to the ethical and social breaches in the world of business, increasing numbers of corporations are formulating ethical and social responsibility policies. For example, Levi Strauss & Co's Web site (http://www.levistrauss.com) proclaims that:

> Our Global Sourcing and Operating Guidelines help us to select business partners who follow workplace standards and business practices that are consistent with our company's values. These requirements are applied to every contractor who manufactures or finishes products for Levi Strauss & Co. Trained inspectors closely audit and monitor compliance among approximately 600 cutting, sewing, and finishing contractors in more than 60 countries.

The Body Shop, which has become well known for its ethics and social responsibility, operates under the following principles (http://www.thebodyshop.com):

- We consider testing products or ingredients on animals to be morally and scientifically indefensible.
- We support small producer communities around the world who supply us with accessories and natural ingredients.
- We know that you're unique, and we'll always treat you like an individual. We like you just the way you are.
- We believe that it is the responsibility of every individual to actively support those who have human rights denied to them.
- We believe that a business has the responsibility to protect the environment in which it operates locally and globally.

Source: B. A. Gold

Ethics and social responsibility are major concerns in the global economy. One reason for the heightened awareness of moral issues is the notoriety of recent unethical business behavior. Examples include the scandals created in the United States by large mutinational corporations such as Enron, WorldCom, and Arthur Andersen; software piracy in China that continues even after the introduction of capitalist economic principles and China's membership in the World Trade Organization; multinational corporate bribery; the ruthlessness of the Russian Mafia during the 1990s and into the 21st century; and historic events with global consequences such as the destruction of the Brazilian rain forest. These events have increased concerns about the conduct of business throughout the world.

A second reason ethics and social responsibility are important is that as the global economy develops, diverse cultures come into contact. Dissimilar cultural assumptions, social norms, and societal values create conflicts that raise important ethical dilemmas, pose moral issues, and often force multinational corporations to address areas of social responsibility that they were previously able to ignore. These and other ethical issues in international organizational behavior and business, as well as research on ethics, remain an interest primarily in the United States and other Western democracies (Carroll 1999; Robertson 2002; Vogel 1992).

▪▪▪ What Are Ethics?

Ethics are moral standards, not governed by law, that focus on the human consequences of actions. Ethics often require behavior that meets higher standards than that established by law, including selfless behavior rather than calculated action intended to produce a tangible benefit. Ethics are sometimes in conflict with individual and corporate self-interest.

Ethics are a product of a society's culture that includes its traditions, customs, values, and norms. Members of a culture often take ethics for granted. They implicitly understand the requirements of relationships, duties, and obligations between people and groups and distinguish between their self-interests and the interests of others. When there is conflict between groups, it is usually because subcultures within a society have different ethical standards or significantly different interests. Under these conditions, the resolution of competing group interests becomes problematic. Similarly, when two or more countries interact, they often find that their ethics and understanding of social responsibility differ.

The Culture at Work examples of ethical and social responsibility issues suggest that there is a relationship between ethics and legality. An important distinction, however, is that ethics are complied with voluntarily as in the case of the Body Shop, whereas compliance with the law is often involuntary. In effect, when a company breaks a law, it is of no consequence unless detected and then enforced.

But in many instances, what is ethical and what is legal is not clear. An example is the ethical, moral, and legal behavior of industrializing nations toward intellectual property developed and copyrighted by companies in economically advanced countries. The following incident in China illustrates the complexity of the issues.

Pu Xanghua, a plump man given to nervous giggling, leaned back in the witness box as he was asked whether the factory he manages had illegally copied compact disks, several of which were displayed before him in the courtroom.

"It's been a long time," Mr. Pu said, trying to suppress a laugh. "Maybe we made some like this, but I don't remember."

The chief judge, Yang Jun, raised an eyebrow. Lawyers said later that under an agreement that had been worked out before the court session, Mr. Pu was supposed to admit wrong-doing in exchange for avoiding further prosecution. Now Mr. Pu was apparently thumbing his nose at the agreement.

For the foreign plaintiff, an association of music companies from the United States and elsewhere, represented by Mr. Steven Chang, a U.S. citizen, Mr. Pu's testimony in Shanghai Intermediate Court one recent morning was a sign that on top of all the many other frustrations in navigating China's evolving legal system the court was now unable to enforce its own decisions.

Only recently has it even become possible for a foreign company in China to take a local defendant to court and win. More than half the battle is simply getting into a courtroom, where proceedings are generally scripted to validate a decision that has already been made.

But if Chinese courts are inching toward greater fairness in disputes involving foreign companies, they are also becoming less able to control Chinese defendants. Fast-paced economic growth and receding regulation are making Chinese companies less accountable and harder to prosecute.

In the Shanghai case, the factory evaded any attempt at tough prosecution because Mr. Pu and other managers agreed to admit guilt, to produce previously withheld evidence and to promise not to copy any more CDs illegally. But the agreement turned out to be worthless.

After observing Mr. Pu's courtroom performance, Steven Chang, whose organization initiated the complaint, observed:

> "It's probably true that they didn't know much about the law when this case started. When I first visited their factory, they gave me a freshly copied CD as a gift. Can you believe it?" (Faison 1995, p. D1).

This example demonstrates the complex interaction among ethics, culture, and law. Different cultures and, within them, specific political regimes, have various understandings and interpretations of ethics and legality. Countries also control and punish unethical and illegal behavior in a variety of ways.

This example also suggests that cultures periodically redefine ethical and legal behavior. Advances in technology are difficult to keep pace with and often create ethical and legal problems for corporations. For example, many home computers now have compact disc (CD) burners that can duplicate CDs making copyright violation extremely easy. A larger problem for the international music industry is the ability of consumers to download music from the Internet to either CDs or MP3 files that make almost all music available to everyone with the requisite technology. Even though legal challenges resulted in the demise of Napster, an Internet-based free music sharing service, music swapping is epidemic on the Internet and eroding record company and artists' income. DVDs present manufacturers with the same problems because movies are increasingly pirated in major markets such as China where "industry executives and analysts say that in recent years piracy has become even more rampant, aided by the spread of the Internet, and computer technology that allow technology-savvy bootleggers to outrun the government's periodic crackdowns" (Buckley 2003, p. C9). Undoubtedly, whatever the next "hot" technology is will create similar challenges.

Is it illegal or unethical to download music from the Internet? You did not steal the music directly from the artist who created it or the company that produced and distributed it. Why should it be your concern? To untangle these complexities, it is useful to explore various ways of thinking about ethics.

▪▪▪ Four Perspectives on Ethics

Four perspectives for understanding ethics are the descriptive, conceptual, normative, and practical. The **practical** interests of the individual or group exploring ethical questions influence the appropriateness of each perspective.

The **descriptive approach** is the study of ethics using the methods and theories of social science. Researchers study the ethics of a particular society or corporation and explain their effect on behavior without making judgments concerning their correctness. For example, social scientists can ask executives in various industries to answer a questionnaire about their business practices. When compared across industries or nations, the data provide insights into behavior executives consider ethical.

The **conceptual approach** focuses on the meaning of key ideas in ethics such as obligation, justice, virtue, and responsibility. The emphasis is to refine definitions of important ethical concepts through philosophical analysis. This approach is useful for students of ethics including academics and members of the legal system.

The **normative approach** involves constructing arguments in defense of basic moral positions and prescribing correct ethical behavior. These arguments may rely on social science studies and conceptual clarification, but they focus primarily on the rationale for a particular position, often on the basis of logic as much as empirical evidence.

Finally, the **practical approach,** a variant of the normative perspective, involves developing a set of normative guidelines for resolving conflicts of interest to improve societal well-being (French and Granrose 1995). Because most organizations are concerned with achieving short- and long-term goals in a competitive environment, the utilitarianism of the practical approach makes it the most widely used by members of organizations.

▮▮▮ Ethical Relativism and Universalism

Who determines what is right or wrong? Ethical relativism and universalism are different views on whether a person or group should set ethical standards and to whom the standards apply.

Individual ethical relativism is the view that there is no absolute principle of right and wrong, good or bad, in any social situation. The individual persons in a particular situation determine what is right and wrong. In its extreme form, ethics are a personal judgment independent of societal norms and values.

Cultural ethical relativism is the doctrine that what is right or wrong, good or bad, depends on one's culture. If the values of a society support certain acts as ethical and morally correct, then they are acceptable behavior for that society. Extreme relativism can "condone slavery, torture, or even murder in a specific culture" (Robertson 2002, p. 363). The counter argument, **ethical universalism,** maintains that there are universal and objective ethical rules located deep within a culture, that also apply across societies. Examples are ideals such as "Treat people with respect," or "Do no harm." The relativist perspective views universalism as a form of ethical imperialism.

Moral philosophers usually reject ethical relativism because "despite differing practices and beliefs, people often do not disagree about ultimate moral standards" (Beauchamp and Bowie 1993, p. 9). For example, anthropological research demonstrates that behaviors in a wide variety of societies that appear to be unethical or immoral from a particular cultural perspective—usually Western culture—reflect similar ultimate values upon closer inspection.

Despite the strong arguments for ethical universalism, moral relativism has considerable appeal for multinational corporations. First, it is an attractive position when the business ethics of other cultures are difficult to understand and interpret. It avoids these problems because it permits a business to use its own ethical standards. A second, more compelling reason for accepting relativism, is reluctance to give competitive advantage to cultures that conduct business using different, often less stringent, moral and ethical standards. What, then, should be an organization's approach to ethics?

▮▮▮ The Social Responsibility of Corporations

Two fundamental perspectives of corporate ethical and social responsibility are the efficiency perspective and social responsibility theory. Scientific analysis cannot demonstrate the superiority of either theory because each contains different assumptions about the relationship between human action, economic principles, and desirable social outcomes.

The Efficiency Perspective

The **efficiency perspective** of corporate social responsibility argues that the obligation of business is to maximize profits for shareholders. Milton Friedman, a Nobel Prize winning economist, strongly endorses this position. According to Friedman,

> In a free-enterprise, private-property system, a corporate executive is an employee of the owners of the business. He has direct responsibility to his employers. That responsibility is to conduct the business in accordance with their desires, which generally will be to make as much money as possible while conforming to the basic rules of the society, both those embodied in law and those embodied in ethical custom.[1] (Friedman 1970, p. 32)

In this view, a corporation does not serve the interests of its owners by donating funds to charities. However, shareholders are free to support charitable causes or do whatever they want with their profits. Similarly, a corporation should not act to fulfill the needs of a particular segment of society, for example, by recycling packaging material to satisfy environmentalists, unless it creates profit for shareholders. In fact, from the efficiency perspective, managers should only recycle waste products if it results in profit.

Social responsibility is the function of government, not business. Businesspeople erroneously impose a tax on their customers, employees, and principals if they allocate profits for social programs. The government, however, can collect taxes and spend them on social programs.

From a cross-cultural perspective, the limitation of the efficiency perspective is that not all societies adhere to the free enterprise system. Political systems that intervene in the economy often alter the free exchange that occurs in competitive markets. Of course, even nominally free markets experience monetary intervention by central banks, monopolies, cartels, and tariffs. Since this perspective applies primarily to advanced capitalist economies, it is less useful for understanding management and organizational behavior in noncapitalist and emerging capitalist countries.

The Social Responsibility Perspective

Corporate social responsibility theory differs from the efficiency perspective

> by replacing the notion that managers have a duty to stockholders with the concept that managers bear a fiduciary relationship to stakeholders. Stakeholders are those groups who have a stake in or claim on the firm. [These] include suppliers, customers, employees, stockholders, and the local community, as well as management in its role as agent for these groups. (Evan and Freeman 1993, p. 76)

Along with recognizing multiple stakeholders, this theory regards stakeholder groups not as uninvolved actors, as efficiency theory does, but as active participants "in the future direction of the firm in which they have a stake" (Evan and Freeman 1993, p. 76). Another reason for including a variety of stakeholders in addition to shareholders is the argument that society—the stakeholders—grants corporations the right to exist.

Although stakeholder theory appears straightforward, there are practical problems with implementing it. First, it is difficult to identify an organization's stakeholders. For example, are unborn future generations stakeholders? If the answer is yes, who should represent them? Second, conflict often exists among stakeholders. Sources of

---

[1]"The Social Responsibility of Business is to Increase its Profits" by M. Friedman, *New York Times Magazine*, September 13, 1970. Copyright © 1970 Milton Friedman. Reprinted by permission.

stakeholder conflict are differential claims to participation in the corporation's activities and contention over the distribution of its outputs, particularly profits. Finally, it is uncertain that managers can adequately identify socially responsible actions.

By articulating two different understandings of the relationships among groups in society, the efficiency and stakeholder perspectives provide different orientations toward the ethical and social conduct of business. Multinational corporations, operating in diverse sociocultural environments, either formulate ethical and social policies within these frameworks or develop modifications based on particular circumstances. As globalization increases, with the result of increased scrutiny by more diverse outside groups, it is likely that corporations will evolve toward the stakeholder perspective.

The social responsibility perspective an organization adopts toward its environment affects, to some extent, the actions of individuals within the organization by specifying their obligations.

▪▪▪ Ethics and Individual Behavior

Individual employees act within an organizational context, including its value system, business philosophy, ethical codes, and business practices. These may not be congruent with employees' personal moral beliefs and ethics. Nonetheless, the organization influences its members' behavior in critical ways including relations with superiors, subordinates, customers, and competitors. To understand variation in individual persons' ethics, it is important to know the differences between universal and situational ethical theories.

A Theory of Moral Development

Lawrence Kohlberg, an American psychologist, takes a universal perspective in his theory of moral development. He posits six stages that form an invariant and universal sequence in individual development (Kohlberg 1976); people go through the same stages in the same sequence. It is possible, however, that a person could become "stuck" at one stage and fail to progress to the next. The six stages of Kohlberg's theory are:

- **Stage 1.** The "obedience and punishment" stage. The only criterion of right for a person at this stage of moral development is obedience to those in authority who have the power to punish.
- **Stage 2.** The "individualism and reciprocity" stage. What is right at this stage is the greatest good for the individual person making the decision. Often, to obtain the greatest good, a person enters into agreements with others and forms reciprocal relationships. However, these always have the motive of self-interest.
- **Stage 3.** The "interpersonal conformity" stage. The expectations of others, including friends, family members, and people in general, determine what is right for an individual.
- **Stage 4.** The "social system" or "law-and-order" stage. Morality is playing one's role in the social system, doing one's duty, and obeying rules.
- **Stage 5.** The "social contract" stage. Here, there is individual thinking on morality and less reliance on the society's recognized rules or duties. The principle of "the greatest good for the greatest number" is the criterion for right and wrong used by rational people.
- **Stage 6.** The stage of "universal ethical principles" is the highest stage. Moral decisions are made on the basis of principles selected freely by a person and that the individual is willing for everyone to live by.

Most American adults are fixated at Stage 4; they obey rules and fit into the social system, seeking to maintain it. From the perspective of management and organizational behavior, most organizations, not only bureaucracies, rely on and reinforce this level of moral reasoning.

Some American adults reach Stage 5. These people accept the idea that there are moral values or rights independent and prior to the actual laws of society. They see the rules and ethics of organizations as arbitrary constructions favoring one social group over another, rather than based on universal ethical principles.

Only a few individuals reach Stage 6. They believe in a higher set of ethical principles that go beyond what a society expects. They subscribe to "higher ethical laws beyond simple utilitarianism. People are to be treated as ends in themselves, not just as means to one's ends or even to the ends of a whole group or society" (French and Granrose 1995, p. 7). In other words, few people rise to a state of ethical awareness that involves viewing people as inherently valuable.

One criticism of Kohlberg's theory is that it is incomplete. A more profound type of social and political freedom than Stage 5 or 6, would become the seventh stage (Habermas 1979).

Another criticism concerns the extent to which the stages are invariant and universal. Although individuals experience moral evolution, elements of earlier stages persist into later stages. In this view, moral development is not a sequential unilinear process.

There are also several important criticisms of Kohlberg's theory from the perspective of culture. First, the stage model applies to masculine moral development but not to feminine moral development, which centers on the concept of "caring" (Gilligan 1982).

Second, concerning universalism, Kohlberg's theory may not apply to all cultures because of the wide variety of social, economic, and political conditions that shape values and behaviors. It is possible, however, that within a particular culture there may be universal stages of moral development.

Finally, for management and organizational behavior, a limitation is that organizational culture and corporate ethical policies influence group norms, individual attitudes, and organizational members' actions. This is particularly true when organizations encounter different ethical behavior outside their home countries. Under these conditions, organizations often challenge and redefine ethical behavior to accommodate the other culture.

These criticisms support arguments for ethical relativism. Gender, national culture, and organizational culture may contribute to notable differences in moral orientation and ethical development. Another approach is to view these variables as situational modifiers of Kohlberg's stage theory rather than as fundamentally challenging it or providing alternative theories.

Face and Ethical Behavior

A situational approach to ethical behavior is the concept of "**face.**" Usually identified as exclusively part of Asian culture, face is a social process found in many cultures, including Western societies. It is an ethical concept because face displays an individual's understanding of culturally defined moral codes as they apply to and maintain a particular social situation. Behavior that sustains the definition of the situation supports a person's face. Erving Goffman (1967, p. 5), an American sociologist, defines face as follows:

> The positive social value a person effectively claims for himself by the line others assume he has taken during a particular contact. Face is an image of self

delineated in terms of approved social attributes—albeit an image that others may share, as when a person makes a good showing for his profession or religion by making a good showing for himself.

However, face has a central importance in Asian cultures that is not present in Western cultures, but it is not a straightforward idea or an exactly proscribed behavior (Redding and Ng 1983). "Chinese people are the first to acknowledge the influence of 'face' in their lives, and yet even they have difficulty in setting out precisely how it works. Lu Xun, the famous Chinese writer, said of it:'It is all very well if you do not stop to think, but the more you think, the more confused you grow. There seems to be many kinds: each class in society has a different face' " (Tang and Ward 2003, p. 18). An approximate meaning of face in Asian cultures refers "to behavior that meets criteria of harmony, tolerance, and solidarity" (Mead 1994, p. 291). In addition, it differs from institutionalized rules found in organizations—for example, codes of ethics—because it is part of the general culture and internalized by individual persons. Finally, the Asian understanding of face reflects concern with social virtue instead of Western concerns with truth. This translates into a collectivist, high power distance cultural behavior in which "saving one's face and that of other group members—in particular the superior—is of central importance in highly integrated and authoritarian cultures" (Mead 1994, p. 291).

An example of face involves an Australian negotiating with a Taiwanese. At the end of the negotiation, rather than saying no to the Australian, the Taiwanese tells him that his company decided not to purchase any products. Actually, the Taiwanese decided to deal with another company, but to maintain harmony between himself and the Australian, he fabricates an excuse. For him, the ethical action is to maintain face. The Australian, however, will become incensed if he discovers the real reason. From his perspective, telling the truth, even if it is uncomfortable, is ethical behavior.

▪▪▪ Organizational Ethics

Ethical conflicts develop as a result of variations in ethical codes, moral standards, social values, and laws in different cultures. Complicating these issues is that not all organizations within a society adhere to the same ethics, morality, or respect for law. Of course, ethical relativism challenges the idea that these are ethical issues.

One way to examine ethical and social responsibility issues is to distinguish between those that are primarily internal to organizations and those that affect interactions between organizations. Frequently, when internal organizational issues raise ethical concerns, they eventually affect relations between organizations.

Internal Ethical Issues

Internal ethical issues primarily affect the conduct of organization members. These may include explicit policies and practices of organizations, laws in a particular place, or cultural values that prescribe certain behaviors, such as the following:

- **Discrimination.** Many societies give preference to members of certain groups. Race, ethnicity, age, gender, geographic region, and religion are variables used to discriminate. In some cultures, not being a native of the society is a basis for employment discrimination. Discrimination can be overt or covert and can determine hiring and promotion. It can also discourage group members from seeking certain types of employment or expecting career advancement.

- **Safety.** In many countries—both developing and developed—worker safety standards fail to provide adequate protection and create conditions that threaten workers' health. Unsafe working conditions, along with child and prison labor, are often part of a strategy to gain competitive advantage. They can also be a culturally based manifestation of indifference to human suffering.
- **Compensation.** Workers' wages vary considerably around the world. In many countries, a worker's annual salary may be what a person with a similar job in another country earns in a week. From the Western perspective, many developing nations pay incredibly low wages. However, because Western companies transplant their manufacturing facilities to low-wage countries, they reinforce this practice. It should also be noted that even in economically advanced societies, for example, the United States, "sweatshop" conditions still exist in urban areas with immigrant populations and in rural areas where employment opportunities are restricted or unions are unable to organize workers.
- **Child labor.** Many less-developed countries use child labor extensively. It raises questions similar to those of prison labor—which is also found in many developing nations—with the additional concern of corporate responsibility for establishing appropriate social welfare and educational institutions in a society.

Within a society, these practices may not only be legal but ethical. Only when cultures with different value systems object, do they become ethical issues. An example of change caused by ethical value conflict is the formation of a coalition of major Western European and American sporting goods manufacturers and child advocacy groups to combat the sale of soccer balls stitched by children in Pakistan.

Because of impoverishment, Pakistani parents in the Sialkot region of Punjab province force their children into soccer ball stitching as early as 6 years of age. According to one estimate, "Close to 10,000 Pakistani children under the age of 14 work up to 10 hours a day stitching the leather balls, often for the equivalent of $1.20 a day" (Greenhouse 1997, p. A12). In Western Europe and the United States, where children play with these soccer balls, child labor is illegal and unethical.

To avoid the experience of other efforts aimed at eliminating child labor that resulted in the unemployed children entering other occupations, including making bricks and prostitution, the coalition proposed to educate the children and to place parents and older siblings in jobs or provide small loans for them to start their own businesses.

Cross-Cultural Ethical Issues

With economic globalization, ethical issues increasingly affect the interaction of organizations across cultures, including the following:

- **Theft of intellectual property.** Not all countries honor copyrights and patents and many encourage piracy. This is a significant issue with the increased use of computer software, compact music discs, and other forms of proprietary information that are difficult to protect.
- **Bribery and corruption.** Two common forms of bribes are whitemail and lubrication bribes. **Whitemail** is a payment made to a person in power for favorable treatment that is illegal, or not warranted on an efficiency, economic benefit scale. **Lubrication bribes** are payments to facilitate, speed up, or expedite otherwise routine government approvals for things such as licenses or inspections.
- **Intentionally selling dangerous products.** Companies sometimes export products considered dangerous in their own country or not entirely appropriate for the

needs of the recipient culture. An example of the former is the sale of cigarettes in developing nations by multinational firms, often from nations such as the United States, that have public policies to discourage smoking. An example of the latter is the exportation of infant formula to countries where there is a high likelihood of improper and harmful use.

- **Environmental pollution.** Not all countries demonstrate concern for the natural environment, particularly because it is expensive to manufacture without polluting. Environmental degradation—such as toxic emissions from factories, radiation from nuclear power plants, and the destruction of vast forests—contributes to worldwide environmental problems.
- **Intentional misrepresentation in negotiations.** Bluffing, fraud, intimidation, and various other forms of deception may be acceptable negotiation tactics in some cultures yet considered unethical, or even illegal, in others.

The Interaction of Internal and Cross-Cultural Ethics

On occasion, internal ethical issues evolve into ethical and social responsibility concerns between organizations or countries. This occurs either because of a shift in corporate and public attitudes toward certain practices or exposure of hidden practices that were always objectionable. Examples include negative reactions to clothes imported from countries that use child or prison labor and the export of cigarettes to developing nations.

Some cases are extremely complex because they involve the use of products in ways other than intended. An example is the experience of H. B. Fuller in Central America. Fuller, a manufacturer of industrial glues, coatings, and paints located in St. Paul, Minnesota, prides itself on being a socially responsible company. Among its products is Resistol, a glue used for making shoes. For many years Resistol has been sniffed by children in Central America because it provides a temporary euphoria that relieves hunger and hopelessness. But Resistol's fumes are addictive and can cause brain damage and, in some cases, death.

Fuller has tried to stop Resistol's use as a drug by reducing the toxicity of the glue and putting restrictions on its sale in Honduras and Guatemala. It has not, however, followed other companies by adding mustard oil to the glue which, when sniffed, induces vomiting, not euphoria. The addition of mustard oil has greatly reduced sales.

Lawsuits have been filed against Fuller challenging its self-image and public perception as an ethical, socially responsible company (Henriques 1995). The ethical issue for Fuller is whether it should do more to prevent the abuse of its product, including withdrawing it from the market.

Can Fuller use scientific techniques to resolve its ethical dilemma?

■■■ Studying Ethics

Researchers use social science methods to study ethics in organizations. Participant observers, social scientists who assume organizational roles to study organizations, document how managers confront ethical dilemmas and adjust their behavior to them (Jackall 1988). Another approach is examining consequences of potentially compromised decision making. An example is a reconstruction of the ethical climate at the National Aeronautics and Space Administration (NASA) in the United States that led to the Challenger space shuttle disaster. Organizational culture and the bureaucratic process created the normalization of deviance; when a manufacturer produced a part that did not meet specifications, because of time pressures and social conformity, the integrity of the approval process was undermined (Vaughan 1996). Finally, researchers can use interviews or questionnaires to study managers' and other organization members' policies and practices concerning ethics.

Ethics in the United Kingdom and United States

Studies comparing the United Kingdom and the United States suggest that managers in both countries face similar management issues because they are almost the same on a number of cultural variables. For example, in Hofstede's (2001) framework they are similar in power distance, uncertainty avoidance, individualism, and masculinity. The United Kingdom and United States also share a common Anglo-Saxon heritage, system of law, economic system, and language.

Despite these similarities, a study of 813 U.K. and U.S. companies found important differences in their approaches to ethical issues (Robertson and Schlegelmilch 1993). First, U.K. companies are more likely to communicate ethics policies through senior executives, whereas U.S. companies rely more on their Human Resources and Legal departments. Second, U.S. firms consider most ethical issues more important than do their U.K. counterparts, particularly employee actions that may harm the firm. Third, U.K. managers consider external corporate stakeholders more important than do U.S. managers. Finally, with the exception of the right to privacy, U.K. firms are more protective of employee rights and more likely to specify policies forbidding employee conduct counter to the firm's interests.

In summary, although the basic value orientations of the two countries are similar, corporations vary in the emphasis of different aspects of ethics and how they manage them. If countries as similar as the United States and United Kingdom emphasize and manage ethics differently, more significant variation probably exists in countries that have extensive cultural differences.

Cross-Cultural Perceptions of Ethics

Beginning in 1995, Transparency International ranked the perception of unethical practices of corporations in countries around the world. According to Peter Eigen, Chairman of Transparency International, the 2001 Corruption Perceptions Index (CPI) indicates that "There is no end in sight to the misuse of power by those in public office—and corruption levels are perceived to be as high as ever in both the developed and developing worlds. There is a worldwide corruption crisis" (http://www.transparency.org).

The rankings of 91 countries on the CPI are presented in Table 3-1. These negative scores appeared before the Enron, Arthur Andersen, and Worldcom scandals. As indicated by the country rankings, some of the richest countries in the world—Finland, Denmark, New Zealand, Iceland, Singapore, and Sweden—scored 9 or higher out of 10 indicating very low levels of perceived corruption. However, 55 countries scored less than 5, indicating high levels of perceived corruption. Many of these countries are among the world's poorest, including Bolivia, Cameroon, Kenya, Indonesia, Uganda, Nigeria, and Bangladesh. The CPI also registers very high levels of perceived corruption in countries experiencing economic transition from communism, particularly those that were members of the former Soviet Union. For example, Romania, Kazakhstan, Uzbekistan, Russia, Ukraine, and Azerbaijan received scores of 3.0 or less.

What are the implications for international business ethics of the extensive differences in perceptions of corruption among countries? First, people conducting business across cultures should be aware that the understanding of corruption and levels

TABLE 3-1 Transparency International: The 2001 Corruption Perceptions Index

A CPI score ranges between 10 (highly clean) and 0 (highly corrupt).

Rank	Country	Score	Rank	Country	Score
1	Finland	9.9	42	Greece	4.2
2	Denmark	9.5		South Korea	4.2
3	New Zealand	9.4	44	Peru	4.1
4	Iceland	9.2		Poland	4.1
	Singapore	9.2	46	Brazil	4.0
6	Sweden	9.0		Bulgaria	3.9
7	Canada	8.9	47	Croatia	3.9
8	Netherlands	8.8		Czech Republic	3.9
9	Luxembourg	8.7	50	Colombia	3.8
10	Norway	8.6		Mexico	3.7
11	Australia	8.5	51	Panama	3.7
12	Switzerland	8.4		Slovak Republic	3.7
13	United Kingdom	8.3		Egypt	3.6
14	Hong Kong	7.9	54	El Salvador	3.6
15	Austria	7.8		Turkey	3.6
16	Israel	7.6	57	Argentina	3.5
	USA	7.6		China	3.5
18	Chile	7.5	59	Ghana	3.4
	Ireland	7.5		Latvia	3.4
20	Germany	7.4	61	Malawi	3.2
21	Japan	7.1		Thailand	3.2
22	Spain	7.0	63	Dominican Rep	3.1
23	France	6.7		Moldova	3.1
24	Belgium	6.6		Guatemala	2.9
25	Portugal	6.3	65	Philippines	2.9
26	Botswana	6.0		Senegal	2.9
27	Taiwan	5.9		Zimbabwe	2.9
28	Estonia	5.6	69	Romania	2.8
29	Italy	5.5		Venezuela	2.8
30	Namibia	5.4		Honduras	2.7
	Hungary	5.3	71	India	2.7
31	Trinidad & Tobago	5.3		Kazakhstan	2.7
	Tunisia	5.3		Uzbekistan	2.7
34	Slovenia	5.2	75	Vietnam	2.6
35	Uruguay	5.1		Zambia	2.6
36	Malaysia	5.0	77	Cote d'Ivoire	2.4
37	Jordan	4.9		Nicaragua	2.4
38	Lithuania	4.8		Ecuador	2.3
	South Africa	4.8		Cameroon	2.0
40	Costa Rica	4.5	79	Pakistan	2.3
	Mauritius	4.5		Russia	2.3

▪▪▪▪▪▪▪▪▪

(*continued*)

TABLE 3-1 (*continued*)

Rank	Country	Score	Rank	Country	Score
82	Tanzania	2.2	88	Indonesia	1.9
83	Ukraine	2.1	88	Uganda	1.9
	Azerbaijan	2.0	90	Nigeria	1.0
84	Bolivia		91	Bangladesh	0.4
	Kenya	2.0			

Source: Transparency International (http://www.transparency.org). Reprinted with permission.

of corrupt activity varies significantly across cultures. Second, the wide disparity in corruption levels suggests that cultures are likely to experience conflict over corporate ethics and business practices. Third, international managers need more information about specific forms of corruption that they may not be familiar with to improve their ability to manage ethics and social responsibility more effectively. This leads to consideration of ways to resolve ethical conflicts.

▮▮▮ Resolving Cross-Cultural Ethical Conflicts

Differences in values are the core of cross-cultural ethical conflicts because ethical value systems vary across cultures. When cultures come into contact, even when they are similar, there is the potential for conflict over what is right and wrong.

The U.S. Approach

In the United States, one method for regulating ethical conflict is to transform ethics into **laws.** Instead of voluntary compliance, there is a shift to mandatory compliance accompanied by formal punitive sanctions. An example is the Foreign Corrupt Practices Act (FCPA) of 1977 that was amended in 1988. The primary concern of the FCPA is the use of bribes by American firms to influence foreign executives to purchase their products. The FCPA makes it illegal for U.S. firms to offer bribes or otherwise corrupt the actions of foreign executives, politicians, or candidates for office. The penalties include fines and prison terms.

American firms often find ingenious ways to comply with the FCPA and yet achieve their objectives. An example is the strategy of the Chubb Corporation, an insurance company located in New Jersey. To enter the Chinese marketplace—a potentially huge insurance market—Chubb set up a $1 million program to teach insurance at a Shanghai university, naming as board members officials who can eventually grant Chubb its license to do business in China (Milbank and Brauchli 1995).

The Global Approach

The Organisation for Economic Co-operation and Development (OECD) is an international organization that helps governments tackle the economic, social, and government challenges of a globalized economy. On its Web page (http://www.oecd.org) the OECD asks, "Why has the OECD, along with other members of the international community, mobilised to fight corruption?" The reason is that "corruption respects no borders, knows no economic distinctions and infects all forms of government. In the long run, no country can afford the social, political or economic costs that corruption entails. The OECD takes a multidisciplinary approach in fighting corruption." The OECD

TABLE 3-2 Organisation for Economic Co-Operation and Development (OECD)	
Member Countries	
Australia	Korea
Austria	Luxembourg
Belgium	Mexico
Canada	Netherlands
Czech Republic	New Zealand
Denmark	Norway
European Communities	Poland
Finland	Portugal
France	Slovak Republic
Germany	Spain
Greece	Sweden
Hungary	Switzerland
Iceland	Turkey
Ireland	United Kingdom
Italy	United States
Japan	

views corruption in developing countries to be particularly harmful to their prospects for economic growth.

In November 1997, the 30 member countries of the OECD (Table 3-2) and five nonmember countries—Argentina, Brazil, Bulgaria, Chile, and the Slovak Republic—adopted a Convention on Combating Bribery of Foreign Public Officials in International Business Transactions. All signatories agreed to a coordinated effort to move toward national legislation making it a crime to bribe foreign public officials. The United States supported this agreement that targets the party that offers the bribe rather than the party accepting it, because many U.S. companies felt that they were at a disadvantage in complying with the Foreign Corrupt Practices Act as firms in other countries continued to use bribes.

In addition to the OECD, the Caux Round Table and the Conference Board have attempted to develop standards for global business ethics and social responsibility. The Caux Round Table, which includes business leaders from Europe, North America, and Japan, has proposed ethical positions such as "respect for rules," "respect for the environment," and ethical positions concerning the role of labor, for example, to provide jobs and compensation that improve workers' living conditions. The Conference Board, whose members are mainly from the United States, conducts surveys of companies throughout the world concerning issues such as the development and enforcement of codes of ethics.

Codes of Ethics

Another method for resolving ethical conflict is corporate **codes of ethics.** Although these are not laws, they codify behavior that is unacceptable under certain conditions. Organizations expect employees to adhere to the codes or suffer penalties ranging from reprimands to dismissal. In other words, ethical codes—involving issues as

TABLE 3-3 Highlights of the Coca-Cola Corporation's Code of Ethics

- Employees must follow the law wherever they are around the world.
- Employees must avoid conflicts of interest. Be aware of appearances.
- Financial records—both for internal activities and external transactions—must be timely and accurate.
- Company assets—including computers, materials, and work time—must not be used for personal benefit.
- Customers and suppliers must be dealt with fairly and at arm's length.
- Employees must never attempt to bribe or improperly influence a government official.
- Employees must safeguard the company's nonpublic information.
- Violations of the Code include asking other employees to violate the Code, not reporting a Code violation, or failing to cooperate in a Code investigation.
- Violating the Code will result in discipline. Discipline will vary depending on the circumstances and may include, alone or in combination, a letter of reprimand; demotion; loss of merit increase, bonus, or stock options; suspension; or even termination.
- Under the Code, certain actions require written approval by your Principal Manager. The Principal Manager is your Division President, Group President, Corporate function head, or the General Manager of your operating unit.
- For those who are themselves Principal Managers, written approvals must come from the General Counsel and Chief Financial Officer. Written approvals for executive officers and directors must come from the Board of Directors or its designated committee.
- If you have any questions about any situation, ask. Always ask.

This Code should help guide your conduct. But the Code cannot address every circumstance and isn't meant to; this is not a catalogue of workplace rules. You should be aware that the company has policies in such areas as fair competition, securities trading, workplace conduct, and environmental protection. Employees should consult the policies of The Coca-Cola Company in specific areas as they apply.

Source: From "The Coca Cola Company: The Code of Business Conduct" www.coca-cola.com.

diverse as sexual harassment, the use of company property, and giving or receiving gifts—reduce ambiguity by specifying appropriate behavior. Table 3-3 presents highlights from Coca-Cola's code of business conduct.

Resolving Ethical Issues

Laws and ethical codes do not cover all situations. To resolve problems raised by ethical relativism and universalism, managers facing ethical conflicts should consider the nature of the specific ethical situation. The response, according to Kohls and Buller (1994, p. 32), "depends on the centrality of values at stake, the degree of social consensus regarding the ethical issue, the decision-maker's ability to influence the outcome, and the level of urgency surrounding the situation."

Managers can take one of seven approaches for resolving ethical conflicts (Kohls and Buller 1994, p. 32).

1. **Avoiding.** One party simply chooses to ignore or not deal with the conflict.
2. **Forcing.** One party forces its will upon the other. Forcing is often used when one party is stronger than the other.
3. **Education-persuasion.** One party attempts to convert others to its position through providing information, reasoning, or appeals to emotion.

4. **Infiltration.** One party introduces its cultural values to another society hoping that an appealing idea will spread.
5. **Negotiation-compromise.** Both parties give up something to negotiate a settlement.
6. **Accommodation.** One party adapts to the ethics of the other.
7. **Collaboration-problem solving.** Both parties work together to achieve a mutually satisfying solution, a win-win outcome meeting the needs of both.

How does a manager select among these actions and is there a "correct" solution? First, they consider the **centrality of values.** Values form a continuum arranged from core values of universal concern and central to the ethical conduct of business to those on the periphery. Following the continuum idea, ethical decisions preserve core values and focus less attention on those in the periphery (Kohls and Buller 1994). Core values include freedom from torture, the right to nondiscriminatory treatment, the right to freedom of speech and association, and the right to political participation (Donaldson 1989; Donaldson and Dunfee 1999). Figure 3-1 presents a continuum of values from core to periphery based on Western preferences.

Second, a manager classifies values according to **home culture consensus.** An ethical decision maintains values widely shared by the home culture (Kohls and Buller 1994).

The third factor is the **influence** a manager has over the situation. There is a continuum from no ability to change the situation to complete control over the situation. When managers have no influence over the situation, they must accommodate to the other culture. If important values are involved, managers should take themselves out of the situation or not get involved (Kohls and Buller 1994).

▪▪▪▪▪▪▪▪▪▪▪▪ **FIGURE 3-1** Values: Core and Periphery

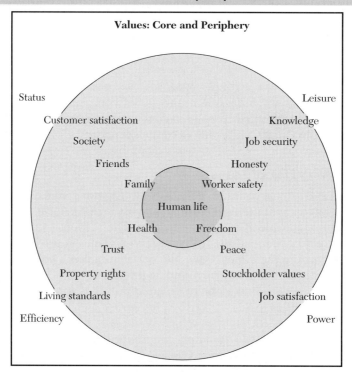

Source: Kohls, J. and Buller, P. (1994). "Resolving Cross-Cultural Ethical Conflict: Exploring Alternative Strategies." *Journal of Business Ethics,* 13, p. 33. Reprinted with kind permission of Kluwer Academic Publishers.

The final factor is **urgency.** How quickly or slowly something must be done influences the choice of conflict resolution strategy. Urgency limits the options to avoidance, forcing, or accommodation because infiltration, education, negotiation, and collaboration require extended time.

Ethics as a Competitive Advantage in Global Business

An emerging perspective on ethics in multinational business is that ethical behavior provides a competitive advantage (Buller and McEvoy 1999; Litz 1996). As a competitive tool, ethical capability is "an organization's ability to identify and respond effectively to ethical issues in a global context" (Buller and McEvoy 1999, p. 326). The elements of ethical capability are firm-specific including: (1) knowledge and skills to understand ethical frameworks and respond effectively to cross-cultural ethical situations; (2) leadership, teamwork, and organizational culture that facilitate ongoing dialogue and learning about global ethics; and (3) human resource systems and other organizational practices that acquire, develop, and sustain these capabilities (Buller and McEvoy 1999, p. 326).

Ethical capability resides in the three important organizational resources of perceiving interdependence, thinking ethically, and responding effectively (Litz 1996). Perceiving interdependence is recognition that a firm gains legitimacy by fulfilling diverse stakeholder needs. Ethical thinking is the result of organizational learning created from the interaction of diverse stakeholders and produces heightened sensitivity to ethical issues. Finally, responding effectively is "taking the appropriate ethical action in a timely manner" (Buller and McEvoy 1999, p. 328).

The alignment of strategic international human resource management with corporate strategy develops ethical capability. Human resource practices can create and sustain ethical capability through transformational leadership, enhancing organizational learning, and implementing specific human resource practices (Buller and McEvoy 1999). Specifically, transformational leadership initiates, articulates, and sustains an ethical vision for the corporation. Organizational learning requires that an organization learn from its international stakeholders concerning ethical practices. Specific human resource practices include an international code of ethics combined with appropriate mechanisms to implement the code which requires selection of culturally competent people, training in ethics, performance appraisal that incorporates ethical behavior, and rewards and recognition for ethical behavior.

It is important to sustain ethical competencies in multinational corporations. This requires continuous organization design which "is a process for identifying key tasks and modifying the reporting relationships, responsibilities, and coordinating mechanisms to accomplish those tasks" (Buller and McEvoy 1999, p. 336). Clear and consistent communication is also important for sustaining a shared vision of ethics in the multinational corporation. Last, the transformational organizational leader should create an ongoing capacity for change that includes audits of the ethical and cultural climate, a plan for continually improving ethical capability, overcoming resistance to change, and utilizing the resources necessary to develop and sustain ethical capability.

In summary, the idea that an organization can build and maintain ethical capability as a competitive advantage is related to trust emerging as a value among multinational corporations. In post-Communist Russia, ethical behavior in business is so unusual that the food company Wimm-Bill-Dann—the name is a transliteration of Wimbledon, the English tennis tournament—revealed in its initial public stock offering that one of its principal owners had spent nine years in prison, warning that his criminal record could hurt investors. This honest approach resulted in raising $161 million in the offering and made " 'transparency' and 'corporate governance' something of a fad, at least among the bigger and more profitable businesses" (Schmemann 2003, p. 1). Apparently, when everybody else is unethical and the expectation is that business will be unethical, being ethical pays—even if it only serves blatant self-interest.

▦ Convergence or Divergence?

With increasing globalization will pressures increase for standardization of ethics beyond the issue of bribery to facilitate interaction among organizations in different cultures? Will there be a set of mechanisms that permits diverse ethical codes to adjust to one another? Or, will ethics be a crazy quilt dependent on cultural preferences and individual corporate interests?

Forces for Convergence

As organizations modernize through bureaucratization, a bureaucratic ethic could replace local ethics based on religion, social values, and customs. For example, Jackall (1988) analyzed the ethics of an American corporation and argues that a bureaucratic ethic has replaced the Protestant ethic. In other words, an ethics of efficiency replaced the deeply held religious beliefs that originally provided businesses with their values. In addition to an increased bureaucratic ethic, as developing countries modernize and multinational companies expand, the regulation of knowledge workers—whose contribution to the economy is ideas—will probably influence ethical codes (Sassen 1991).

Another force for convergence is the emergence of international regulatory agencies, such as the OECD, that establish and enforce ethical standards targeted at multinational corporations (Frederick 1991). These standards, along with international trade agreements such as the World Trade Organization and the European Union, may eventually contribute to the replacement of culture-bound local moral and ethical norms.

Another factor increasing the similarity of ethical standards and social responsibility is the diffusion of capitalism worldwide. However, in the early years of the 21st century, the effects of capitalism are mixed. The tumultuous start, accompanied by the growth of organized crime and deterioration of traditional social controls in Russia and China, indicates that opportunistic amoral behavior flourished under the guise of capitalism. On the other hand, economic reforms in these countries have led to greater availability of consumer products, new business opportunities, and, for some, a higher standard of living. This combination of frontier capitalism and the creation of consumer demand may produce the ethical and cultural contradictions of American capitalism in the new capitalist countries (Bell 1976). For example, to manage the excesses of its experiment with capitalism, in 2002 Russia began examining Western models of law and ethics to develop a new legal code (Myers 2002).

Forces for Divergence

Religion is the most complex, deeply rooted, and persistent force for ethical divergence. Although there are significant areas of agreement on ethical practices among the world religions, perhaps the areas of disagreement are more important (Terpstra and David 1991). Indeed, since the September 11, 2001 attacks on the United States, the differences among world religions have become clearer to more people.

The treatment of women and their role in organizations provides an example of ethical conflict based in religion. In Muslim societies—as well as other cultures with fundamentalist interpretations of religious texts—women are the social inferiors of men. A typical conflict arises when a Western company assigns a female to work in a culture that does not recognize principles of gender equality and objects to dealing with a woman.

Another issue raised by religion is the definition of insiders and outsiders, those who believe in a religious doctrine as opposed to those who do not. This often results in ethical particularism, the view that insiders adhere to a superior set of ethics and moral behavior compared with outsiders (Nelson 1969).

National and ethnic cultures are reasserting themselves in a variety of ways. For example, armed conflicts continue around the globe to preserve a way of life based on religious and cultural identity. Because of nationalism and ethnic and cultural patterns, cultures are resistant to significant change and, in the early 21st century, have in some cases established themselves as major sources of international conflict (Huntington 1996).

Finally, countries have different economic systems and are at various stages of economic development. These may contribute to maintaining or creating different ethical standards. For example, developing countries frequently protest that it is unjust to hold them to the same environmental standards as developed countries because the expense impedes their economic development.

▭ Implications for Managers

Managers do not share the same ethical code and understanding of social responsibility. They also cannot assume that their own corporation's ethical conduct is superior. As a result, international managers need to develop a framework for evaluating ethical codes and determining their own ethics.

International managers must understand other societies' religion, values, culture, law, and ethics. What may be a shocking breach of ethics to a Western businessperson— child labor, a wage of pennies a day, or blatant gender discrimination—may be acceptable behavior in another culture. Knowing the behaviors and ethics of other cultures can help determine whether a course of action is appropriate. The suggestions in the chapter for resolving cross-cultural ethical conflict can also be useful.

Most scholars of international business ethics view the identification and resolution of ethical issues as difficult and complex. Because many ethical issues are emerging as new technologies develop, as new forms of organizational interdependence evolve, and as cultures come into contact, it is likely that precisely what ethical and legal behavior is will change. This implies that managers should keep informed concerning new developments in cross-cultural ethics and not assume that ethics are well defined and agreed upon and therefore nonproblematic.

SUMMARY ▭

Ethics and culture are intimately connected. Ethics translate abstract cultural values into rules and mutual understandings that govern everyday interactions. Ethical issues are important when there is conflict over what is proper conduct.

Four perspectives help us understand ethics: the descriptive, conceptual, normative, and practical. Ethical relativism and universalism are also important issues. Cultural relativism is the position that ethics vary with a specific culture. Universalism is the position that there are identifiable common ethics across cultures. Most philosophers argue for universalism as do influential theories such as Kohlberg's theory of moral development.

At the level of the organization, three prominent theories are the efficiency perspective, the stakeholder perspective, and the group social responsibility perspective. The efficiency perspective argues that managers' only ethical responsibility is to satisfy corporate stockholders. The social responsibility perspective suggests considering various stakeholders of a firm in decision making. Finally, the concept of face—found primarily in Asian cultures—is an ethic of individual responsibility to and for the group that incorporates situational elements.

Cross-cultural studies indicate that ethics and the management of ethics vary in different cultures. Transforming ethics into laws or developing international corporate ethical codes are two ways to regulate organizational ethics across cultures. Managers can deal with cross-cultural ethical conflicts through avoidance, forcing, education-persuasion, infiltration, negotiation-compromise, accommodation, and collaboration-problem solving.

In addition to enforcement through the FCPA and the OECD, the creation of international monitoring organizations, such as Transparency International, has brought the issue of corruption to the attention of considerably more people throughout the world. However, publication of corruption perceptions may not significantly reduce corruption because in some cultures what others view as corrupt is simply the way that people conduct business.

Ethical corporate behavior is a competitive advantage. This is particularly true during periods of ethical lapses by major corporations when even routine adherence to ethical standards appears to be exemplary.

Finally, there are various forces creating worldwide convergence of organizational ethics such as bureaucratization, professionalization, and the resurgence of capitalism. Forces for maintaining different ethical standards include religion, culture, economic systems, and varying stages of societal development. Managers can prepare for confronting cross-cultural ethical issues by understanding the societies in which they do business.

DISCUSSION QUESTIONS ▪ ▪ ▪ ▪ ▪ ▪ ▪

1. What are ethics?
2. How do ethics differ from law?
3. What role do culture and societal values play in creating ethics?
4. Are ethics in business situations relative or absolute?
5. How does the efficiency view differ from the stakeholder view of corporate social responsibility?
6. Does the concept of face apply to behavior in your university?
7. Why do ethics create conflict?
8. Under what conditions would education be a useful approach to resolving a cross-cultural ethical conflict?
9. Why is ethical behavior in business becoming a competitive tool?
10. In your opinion, as the global economy develops, will ethics and social responsibility become more similar or distinctive across cultures?
11. What are your views on the role of ethics in multinational organizations?

INTERNET SITES ▪ ▪ ▪ ▪ ▪ ▪ ▪

Selected Companies in the Chapter

Coca-Cola (http://wwww.coca-cola.com)
Levi Strauss & Co. (http://www.levistrauss.com)
The Body Shop (http://www.thebodyshop.com)

Ethics and Social Responsibility Sites

Amnesty International (http://www.amnesty.org). Amnesty International provides reports on human rights practices and abuses in 151 countries.

The Carnegie Council on Ethics and International Affairs (http://www.cceia.org). This is the Web site of the Carnegie Council on Ethics and International Affairs. It contains links to a variety of papers that discuss current issues in international business.

Greenpeace (http://www.greenpeace.org). Greenpeace is "an independent, campaigning organization which uses nonviolent, creative confrontation to expose global environmental problems, and to force the solutions which are essential to a green and peaceful future."

The International Labour Organization (http://www.ilo.org). The International Labour Organization provides data on labor conditions, human rights, and labor laws.

Transparency International (http://www.transparency.org). Transparency International monitors business ethics and corruption worldwide. It ranks the extent of corruption in each country in the world annually.

REFERENCES ▪▪▪▪▪▪▪

Beauchamp, T. and Bowie, N. (1993). *Ethical Theory and Business* 4th Ed. Upper Saddle River, NJ: Prentice Hall.

Bell, D. (1976). *The Cultural Contradictions of Capitalism.* New York: Basic Books.

Buckley, C. (2003). "Helped by Technology, Piracy of DVD's Runs Rampant in China," *New York Times*, August 18, C9.

Buller, P. F. and McEvoy, G. M. (1999). "Creating and Sustaining Ethical Capability in the Multi-national Corporation." *Journal of World Business*, 34(4), 326–43.

Carroll, A. B. (1999). "Corporate Social Responsibility." *Business and Society*, 38(3), 268–295.

Donaldson, T. (1989). *The Ethics of International Business.* New York: Oxford.

——and Dunfee, T. W. (1999). "When Ethics Travel: The Promise and Peril of Global Business Ethics." *California Management Review*, 41(4), 45–63.

Evan, W. and Freeman, R. (1993). "A Stakeholder Theory of the Modern Corporation: Kantian Capitalism." In Beauchamp, T. and Bowie, N. (eds.) *Ethical Theory and Business* 4th Ed. Upper Saddle River, NJ: Prentice Hall.

Faison, S. (1995). "Fighting Piracy and Frustration in China," *New York Times*, May 17, D1.

Frederick, W. (1991). "The Moral Authority of Transnational Corporate Codes." *Journal of Business Ethics*, 10.

French, W. and Granrose, J. (1995). *Practical Business Ethics.* Upper Saddle River, NJ: Prentice Hall.

Friedman, M. (1970). "The Social Responsibility of Business Is to Increase Its Profits," *New York Times Magazine*, September 13, 32–33, 122, 126.

Gilligan. C. (1982). *In a Different Voice: Psychological Theory and Women's Development.* Cambridge, MA: Harvard University Press.

Goffman, E. (1967). *Interaction Ritual: Essays in Face-to-Face Behavior.* Garden City, NY: Anchor Books.

Greenshouse, S. (1997). "Sporting Goods Concerns Agree to Combat Sale of Soccer Balls Made by Children," *New York Times*, February 14, A12.

Habermas, J. (1979). *Communication and the Evolution of Society.* Boston: Beason Press.

Henriques, D. (1995). "Black Mark for a 'Good Citizen,'" *New York Times*, November 26, 1, 11.

Hofstede, G. (2001). *Culture's Consequences: Comparing Values, Behaviors, Institutions, and Organizations Across Nations.* Thousand Oaks, CA: Sage.

Huntington, S. (1996). *The Clash of Civilizations and the Remaking of World Order.* New York: Simon & Schuster.

Jackall, R. (1988). *Moral Mazes: The World of Corporate Managers.* New York: Oxford University Press.

Kohlberg, L. (1976). "Moral Stages and Moralization, the Cognitive-developmental Approach." In Lickona, T. (ed.) *Moral Development and Behavior.* New York: Holt, Rinehart and Winston.

Kohls, J. and Buller, P. (1994). "Resolving Cross-cultural Ethical Conflict: Exploring Alternative Strategies." *Journal of Business Ethics*, 13, 31–38.

Litz, R. (1996). "A Resource-based View of the Socially Responsible Firm: Stakeholder Interdependence, Ethical Awareness, and Issue Responsiveness as Strategic Assets." *Journal of Business Ethics*, 15, 1355–63.

Mead, R. (1994). *International Management: Cross Cultural Dimensions.* Cambridge, MA: Blackwell.

Milbank, D. and Brauchli, M. (1995). "How U. S. Concerns Compete in Countries Where Bribes Flourish," *Wall Street Journal*, September 9, 1, 16.

Myers, S. L. (2002). "Russia Glances to the West for Its New Legal Code," *New York Times,* July 4, 1, A6.

Nelson, B. (1969). *The Idea of Usury: From Tribal Brotherhood to Universal Otherhood.* Chicago: University of Chicago Press.

Redding, S. and Ng, M. (1983). "The Role of 'Face' in the Organizational Perceptions of Chinese Managers." *International Studies of Management and Organization,* 13(3), 92–123.

Robertson, D. C. (2002). "Business Ethics Across Cultures." In Gannon, M. J. and Newman, K. L. (eds.) *The Blackwell Handbook of Cross-Cultural Management.* Malden, MA: Blackwell.

—— and Schlegelmilch, B. (1993). "Corporate Institutionalization of Ethics in the United States and Great Britain." *Journal of Business Ethics*, 12, 301–312.

Sassen, S. (1991). *The Global City.* Princeton, NJ: Princeton University Press.

Schmemann, S. (2003). "Some Russian Tycoons Resort to Honesty," *New York Times,* January 12, Section 4, 1.

Sundaram, A. and Black, J. (1995). *The International Business Environment.* Upper Saddle River, NJ: Prentice Hall.

Tang, J. and Ward, A. (2003). *The Changing Face of Chinese Management.* New York: Routledge.

Terpstra, V. and David, K. (1991). *The Cultural Environment of International Business.* Cincinnati: South-Western.

Transparency International (http:// www. transparency.org).

Vaughan, D. (1996). *The Challenger Launch Decision: Risky Technology, Culture, and Deviance at NASA.* Chicago: University of Chicago Press.

Vogel, D. (1992). "The Globalization of Business Ethics: Why America Remains Distinctive." *California Management Review,* 35, 1.

Communication

Learning Objectives

After reading this chapter, you should be able to:

■ Explain the basic communication process and define cross-cultural communication.

■ Understand how language affects communication and how different cultures use the four styles of verbal communication.

■ Discuss various types of nonverbal communication.

■ Identify major barriers to communicating cross-culturally.

■ Consider the advantages and disadvantages of virtual cross-cultural communication.

■ Enhance your cross-cultural communication skills.

CULTURE AT WORK

Virus-Free Communication

During the 2003 SARS (severe acute respiratory syndrome) outbreak, the World Health Organization advised travelers to avoid SARS affected areas that included Hong Kong, Guangdong, Beijing, Singapore, Toronto, and Taiwan. As a result, most organizations banned business travel to these regions while the advisory was in force. Yet, for Asians in particular, face-to-face communication is an essential part of doing business and not being able to meet was a challenge.

Wal-Mart, the largest American retailer, averaged 500 product development trips to China annually before the SARS outbreak. In order not to jeopardize business, they needed to find new ways to communicate. E-mail enabled the company to develop product specifications online while videoconferencing was the key to virtual meetings with suppliers.

The change in communication practices continued even after the lifting of the travel advisories. For Wal-Mart and other companies, the online approach was cost effective and reduced product turnaround time. The need to avoid face-to-face meetings may have a long-term impact on cultural communication practices. Eric Ryan, who used to travel to China every six weeks to make purchases for his American import-export company, found

---

that, "SARS has helped overcome a lot of the cultural taboos about not meeting face-to-face. It has allowed us to migrate in a culturally acceptable way to the Internet."

Source: Kahn, G. and Zimmerman, A. (2003). "Amid SARS, Wal-Mart Adjusts Buying," *The Asian Wall Street Journal,* May 29, A6. Reproduced with permission of Dow Jones & Co., Inc. in the format Other Book via Copyright Clearance Center.

Communication, particularly language, is central to culture and the management of organizational behavior. Without effective communication systems, organizations experience difficulty and even failure. However, it is challenging to achieve effective communication even within a single culture or organization. It becomes even more complex when people from multiple cultures and organizations need to interact. As the Culture at Work vignette illustrates, the rapid development of communication technology is having an impact on cross-cultural communication.

▮▮▮ What Is Communication?

The Communication Process

Communication is the process of transmitting thoughts or ideas from one person to another. The person who initiates the process is the **sender,** and the other person is the **receiver.** Figure 4-1 summarizes the communication process.

The communication process begins with the sender, who has a **thought** or idea to relay to another person. The sender expresses this thought in a form he believes the receiver will understand, whether verbal or nonverbal. Once the message is **encoded,** that is, expressed in an understandable format, it is then **transmitted** or sent via a medium such as voice, fax, memo, or e-mail. Once the receiver **receives** the message, he then **decodes** or interprets the meaning of the symbols used by the sender to **understand** or comprehend the meaning of the message. To the extent that the receiver's understanding and the sender's thought are the same, communication is effective. Although not an essential part of communication, the receiver can give the sender **feedback** indicating he has received and understood the message. The feedback process uses the same six steps, with the receiver and sender switching roles.

Noise caused by distortion and interruption often enters the communication process, for example, actual noise, such as traffic or other people talking, and technological problems, like a fax machine breaking down. More important sources of noise, however, are cultural and social differences between the sender and receiver that make it difficult for them to understand each other.

▮▮▮▮▮▮▮▮▮▮▮ **FIGURE 4-1** The Communication Process

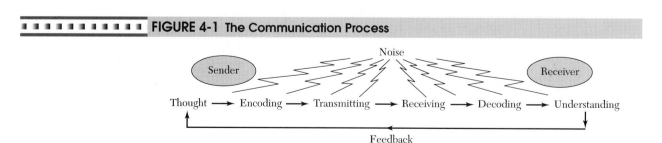

▊▊▊ Cross-Cultural Communication Differences

Cross-cultural communication occurs when people from more than one culture communicate with each other. This is more difficult than communication among people of the same culture. Noise develops due to differences in language, values, and attitudes, among other factors. The major differences in how people from different cultures communicate with each other are language usage, verbal style, and nonverbal communication.

Language Usage

The number of languages in the world is between 5,000 and 7,000 (Gibbs 2002) with Mandarin Chinese (Putonghua), English, Spanish, Hindi, and Arabic the five with the highest numbers of native speakers (Crystal 1997). English is the language spoken by the largest number of people (Crystal 1997) and has become the language of choice for international business and the Internet with about 75% of all Web sites using English (Gilsdorf 2002).

In Europe, many companies have adopted English as their official language both in order to establish their global image and to facilitate communication among managers and subsidiaries around the world. For example, Airbus, the aircraft manufacturer headquartered in France that includes aerospace companies from France, Britain, Germany, and Spain, chose English as its official language when it began more than 30 years ago. Although executives may choose to speak French, German, or Spanish if the majority at a meeting can do so, the minutes are always in English (Tagliabue 2002).

However, English as the language of business takes many forms, and an international manager must be prepared to communicate using a version of English that can be different from "Standard" (Gilsdorf 2002). For example, people from the United States and England both speak English, but the meaning of certain words is quite different, sometimes even opposite. One estimate suggests that American and British English speakers share 90% of their working vocabularies (Scott 2000) leaving ample room for misunderstanding. Americans call the storage compartment of the car, the "trunk"; the English call it the "boot." To get to the 50th floor, Americans take an "elevator," but the English use a "lift." When the English "table" an item in a meeting, they act on it immediately. When Americans "table" something, they expect to deal with it later! Table 4-1 gives further examples of differences between American and British English.

A more challenging situation is when native speakers of two different languages need to communicate. One or both may be able to speak a language that the other can understand, or they may require an interpreter. Complicating matters, words and concepts in one language may not have equivalents in another language. For example, the concept of *achievement* is almost impossible to translate into a language other than English (Hofstede 1980). The Chinese have many different terms for the single English word *dumpling*. In the Inuit Eskimo language, there are over 50 words for various types of snow (Deresky 1994). The precise meaning of *achievement* in the United States and the fine distinctions the Chinese give to dumplings and the Inuits to snow reflect their importance in those cultures.

Because of language and cultural differences, corporations must consider brand or product names when selling in international markets. Inadequate translations can result in a negative image for the product and company. An early translation of *Coca-Cola* into Chinese meant "bite the wax tadpole." Coca-Cola has since found and trademarked a new Chinese name that means "refreshing and delicious" (Warner 1996). The original brand name of a product can also create an unintended image in another language. The

TABLE 4-1 American Versus British English

When they say	Americans mean	British mean
Pavement	A hard road surface	A footpath or sidewalk
Pants	Trousers	Underpants
Tick off	To anger	To rebuke
Canceled check/Cancelled cheque	A check paid by the bank	A check that is stopped or voided
When they mean	**Americans say**	**British say**
To make arrangements for	Reserve	Book
To telephone	Call	Ring
Ongoing business	Trade	Custom
A detachable section of a check/cheque retained as a record	Check stub	Counterfoil

Source: Adapted from Scott, J. C. (2000). "Differences in American and British Vocabulary: Implications for International Business Communication." *Business Communication Quarterly,* 63(4), 32. Reprinted by permission of the Association for Business Communication.

Chinese "White Elephant" brand name conveys a positive meaning in Chinese but has a negative connotation in the United States. Table 4-2 lists additional international marketing blunders based on language differences.

Global corporations must also become aware of the impact of internal corporate communications sent to subsidiaries in the company's home language or translated into local languages. It is often difficult to convey the intended message.

In the process of preparing a European newsletter, articles were created in one European language to be translated into another by UK based translators. Very quickly it was realised a better job would be done by people whose mother tongue was that of the 'foreign' language. Even then, a draft outcome did not find universal favour in the company's plants around Europe. The translators had been out of the country too long and language had moved on. The most extreme example of this was a Czech translation that was returned with the comment that the language used was old Czech last used around the Second World War! At least this was better than the company's first attempt at corporate communication when the framed copy of the vision and values statement was returned from the Czech Republic with the comment from the local general manager that it was written in Russian and the Russians had left in 1989! (Holden 2001, p. 616)

TABLE 4-2 International Marketing Blunders

- The Chevrolet Nova car had trouble selling in Puerto Rico because it sounded like *no va* meaning "it doesn't go."
- A Finnish brewery found sales of Koff and Siff beers in the United States were slow because the names sounded unappealing in English.
- The soft drink Fresca was marketed in Mexico without a change of brand name. The company later discovered that *fresca* is slang for *lesbian* in Mexico.

Adapted from Ricks, D. A. (1983). *Big Business Blunders: Mistakes in Multinational Marketing.* Homewood, IL: Dow Jones-Irwin.

Even when translation is not necessary, managers must consider the impact of word choice and level of formality in their messages. For example, the new CEO of an American company sent an e-mail to all employees worldwide to try to establish rapport. Using American communication style, she addressed everyone by first name. Fortunately, managers in Germany, Italy, and Spain received drafts of the message and found the informal address to be offensive and inappropriate for their employees. They changed the salutation to the culturally acceptable formal style and avoided creating a negative impression of the new CEO (Holden 2001).

Verbal Communication Styles

Verbal communication styles are another way that cultures vary in their communication patterns. Gudykunst and Ting-Toomey (1988) identify four different verbal communication styles: direct versus indirect, elaborate versus succinct, personal versus contextual, and instrumental versus affective. "Verbal interaction styles reflect and embody the affective, moral, and aesthetic patterns of a culture" (Gudykunst and Ting-Toomey 1988, p. 100). The words used and the way they are put together tell much about a particular culture. Gudykunst and Ting-Toomey associate the four verbal styles with cultural characteristics by referring to Hofstede's (2001) dimensions of cultural values and Hall's (1976, 1983) high- and low-context culture descriptions.

The verbal styles are part of a culture. Often countries that speak the same language have similar cultures, but not always. Therefore, it is possible that speakers of the same language from different cultures employ different verbal styles. For example, East Indian English speakers use the contextual style, in contrast to the personal style of American or British English (Gudykunst and Ting-Toomey 1988). This presents a communication barrier that neither party may expect. Table 4-3 presents the major characteristics of the four verbal styles.

Direct Versus Indirect Style

The **direct versus indirect style** differs in the degree of explicitness of the verbal message. In the **direct style,** the speaker tries to convey her true feelings through the choice of words. In the **indirect style,** the speaker selects words to hide his real feelings. For example, North Americans using the direct style say, "No" or "I can't do that," if they are unable to make a particular deal. In contrast, a Korean speaker might say, "It might be possible," or "It's interesting in principle," rather than saying "no" directly.

The direct style is common in individualistic, low-context cultures, and the indirect style in collectivistic, high-context cultures. The direct style allows the individualist to express her own ideas clearly. The collectivist's orientation is to maintain group harmony and concern for the feelings of others.

Elaborate Versus Succinct Style

The second style is **elaborate versus succinct,** focusing on the quantity of talk with which people feel comfortable. There are three recognizable styles: the elaborate, the exacting, and the succinct. In the **elaborate style,** the quantity of talk is relatively high, description includes great detail, and there is often repetition. The use of metaphors, similes, and proverbs is frequent, many adjectives modify the same noun, and verbal elaboration and exaggeration are typical. People from Arabic countries use the elaborate style.

The emphasis in the **exacting style** is on precision and using the right amount of words to convey the desired meaning. The exacting style is typical in England,

TABLE 4-3 Major Characteristics of the Four Verbal Styles

Verbal Style	Variation	Major Characteristic	Cultures Where Found
Direct Versus Indirect	Direct	Message is more explicit.	Individualistic, low-context
	Indirect	Message is more implicit.	Collectivistic, high-context
Elaborate Versus Succinct	Elaborate	Quantity of talk is relatively high.	Moderate uncertainty avoidance, high-context
	Exacting	Quantity of talk is moderate.	Low uncertainty avoidance, low-context
	Succinct	Quantity of talk is relatively low.	High uncertainty avoidance, high-context
Personal Versus Contextual	Personal	Focus is on speaker, "personhood."	Low power distance, individualistic, low-context
	Contextual	Focus is on role of speaker, role relationships.	High power distance, collectivistic, high-context
Instrumental Versus Affective	Instrumental	Language is goal-oriented, sender-focused.	Individualistic, low-context
	Affective	Language is process-oriented, receiver-focused.	Collectivistic, high-context

Germany, and Sweden. In these cultures, it is important to use words in a clear manner, in just the right quantity, with just the meaning intended. Using too many words is considered exaggeration, and using too few words, ambiguous.

Finally, for the **succinct style,** people are comfortable with a relatively low quantity of talk. Understatements, pauses, and silence convey meaning. Individuals in China, Japan, Korea, and Thailand use the succinct style. Particularly in unfamiliar situations, they tend to use silence and understatement rather than using talk and risking a loss of face.

The elaborate style is found in moderate uncertainty avoidance, high-context cultures; the exacting style in low uncertainty avoidance, low-context cultures; and the succinct style in high uncertainty avoidance, high-context cultures.

Personal Versus Contextual Style
Personal versus contextual style is the third verbal communication style. In the **personal style,** the focus is on the speaker, and "meanings are expressed for the purpose of emphasizing 'personhood'" (Gudykunst and Ting-Toomey 1988, p. 109). In the **contextual style,** focus is on the "role" of the speaker, and "meanings are expressed for the purpose of emphasizing role relationships" (Gudykunst and Ting-Toomey 1988, p. 109).

North American English speakers use the personal style, addressing each other informally and directly on an equal basis. First names are common, and there is no special manner of addressing people of different status level or gender. In contrast, the Japanese speak in the contextual style; words reflect the role and hierarchical relationship of those in the conversation. The speaker must choose one of three different levels of language depending on his relationship to the receiver. For example, there are five different words for *you* in Japanese, the choice of which depends on the relative rank and status of the speaker and receiver (Gibson 1997). Even males and females use different vocabulary and ways of speaking.

People from low power distance, individualistic, low-context cultures such as Australia, Denmark, and Canada, speak in the personal verbal style. The contextual style is associated with high power distance, collectivistic, high-context cultures including Japan, India, Ghana, and Nigeria.

Instrumental Versus Affective Style

The last verbal style is the **instrumental versus affective**. In the **instrumental style,** the sender uses goal-oriented, sender-focused language. The **affective style** speaker is process-oriented and receiver-focused. People from Australia, for example, use the instrumental style. In speaking, the goal may be to persuade the listener, and the speaker develops the message with this in mind. In contrast, Puerto Ricans use the affective style, so that neither the speaker nor the receiver is put in an uncomfortable position. The speaker listens to and closely observes how the receiver reacts to the message. Often, meaning is expressed nonverbally or intuitively; what is not said could be just as important as what is said.

The instrumental style is common in individualistic, low-context cultures such as the United States, Denmark, and Switzerland. Collectivistic, high-context cultures, such as those in the Middle East, Latin America, and Asia, use the affective verbal style.

Because of differences in verbal styles, it can be very difficult to express one language's precise meaning in another language. Beyond that, someone speaking a second language, unless she is extremely fluent or very familiar with the culture of the second language, may attempt to speak the second language using the verbal style of her native language. This too makes communication more difficult. Table 4-4 lists the four verbal styles used in 10 countries.

Nonverbal Communication

Nonverbal communication includes the part of the message other than the words, such as facial expressions, gestures, and tone of voice (see Table 4-5). The verbal styles described previously may also include nonverbal aspects—for example, with the affective style. When people are not speaking their native language or are relying on an interpreter, it is likely that nonverbal aspects of communication take on greater meaning. Indeed, people often assume they can understand gestures even if they can't understand words. However, nonverbal meanings in different cultures vary tremendously. To be an effective communicator, it is important to know both the language and the nonverbal aspects.

Emotions

Emotional expression is one area where there seems to be universal agreement. Studies in cultures as diverse as Brazil, Sweden, Greece, Japan, the United States, and New Guinea show a high degree of agreement in recognizing the basic emotions of joy, sadness, and

TABLE 4-4 Verbal Styles Used in 10 Countries

Country	Direct Versus Indirect	Elaborate Versus Succinct	Personal Versus Contextual	Instrumental Versus Affective
Australia	Direct	Exacting	Personal	Instrumental
Canada	Direct	Exacting	Personal	Instrumental
Denmark	Direct	Exacting	Personal	Instrumental
Egypt	Indirect	Elaborate	Contextual	Affective
England	Direct	Exacting	Personal	Instrumental
Japan	Indirect	Succinct	Contextual	Affective
Korea	Indirect	Succinct	Contextual	Affective
Saudi Arabia	Indirect	Elaborate	Contextual	Affective
Sweden	Direct	Exacting	Personal	Instrumental
United States	Direct	Exacting	Personal	Instrumental

surprise (Gudykunst and Ting-Toomey 1988). However, why and when people in different cultures show these emotions differ. For example, in a culture low on power distance, such as Finland, people are uncomfortable with differences in rank and can become angry when they are present. In a high power distance country, such as Venezuela, rank differences are an acceptable part of the culture and do not cause anger in most people (Gudykunst and Ting-Toomey 1988). Because of the various causes of emotions in different cultures, cross-cultural communication can leave a person feeling he is "missing something" or that the other person is reacting inappropriately.

Kinesic Behavior

Kinesic behavior or **kinesics** is communication through body movements, including facial expression, gestures, and posture. For example, the smile usually indicates happiness or pleasure, but for Asians, it may also be a sign of embarrassment or discomfort (Samovar and Porter 1991). In the United States, maintaining eye contact is the sign of a good communicator; in the Middle East, it is an integral part of successful communication; but for the Chinese and Japanese, it may indicate distrust. Communication through eye contact and gaze is known as oculesics.

The meaning of gestures also varies significantly among countries. In Italy, Greece, and certain Latin American countries, the level of gesturing is so high that people

TABLE 4-5 Forms of Nonverbal Communication

Kinesics	Communication through body movements, including facial expression, gestures, and posture
Oculesics	Communication through eye contact and gaze
Haptics	Communication through the use of bodily contact
Proxemics	Communication through the use of space
Chronemics	Communication through use of time within a culture
Chromatics	Communication through the use of colors

appear to be speaking with their hands. In North America, the level of gesturing is moderate. Other than waving hello or good-bye, gestures with the elbow higher than the shoulder are rare. For Chinese and Japanese speakers, using gestures is less common; keeping hands and arms close to the body is the norm (Chaney and Martin 1995).

Greeting gestures also differ. In a business situation, North Americans shake hands, Japanese bow, and Middle Easterners of the same sex kiss on the cheek (Abbasi and Hollman 1993). In a cross-cultural situation, Japanese usually shake hands because they do not expect non-Japanese to be acquainted with the complex etiquette of bowing. Communicating through the use of bodily contact is called **haptics.**

The meaning of hand gestures varies in different countries too. The "V" for victory sign is common in the United States and England; it involves extending two fingers with the palm and fingers facing outward. However, in England reversing the gesture so that the palm and fingers face inward changes the meaning entirely so that it has an offensive connotation. Putting the thumb and forefinger together to form an "O" means "okay" in the United States, but "zero" or "worthless" in southern France. It stands for money in Japan and is an obscene gesture in Brazil (Chaney and Martin 1995; Hodgetts and Luthans 1994). In India, the side to side wave for hello that is common in many cultures usually means "no" or "go away" (Besher 1991).

Posture while standing or seated can also convey different meanings. The casual, sometimes slouching, standing or seating posture of people from the United States might be interpreted as rude or conveying a lack of interest by others. In the Middle East, crossing your legs or showing the sole of your shoe conveys to others the message that they are worthy of being stepped on and is highly insulting (Abbasi and Hollman 1993).

Proxemics

Proxemics is the use of space, either personal or office, to communicate. Hall (1966) believes that people control intimacy by using personal space to regulate sensory exposure. For example, in the United States, people use one of four zones (Hall 1966). Very close friends use the **intimate zone,** a distance of less than 18 inches (46 cm). The distance from 18 inches to about four feet (46 cm to 1.22 m), the **personal zone,** is for a close working situation or to give instructions. In most business situations, Americans use the **social zone,** a distance of four to 12 feet (1.22 to 3.66 m). The **public zone,** distances over 12 feet (over 3.66 m), is for infrequent formal occasions such as a speech.

The distances people feel comfortable with vary significantly by culture. South Americans, Southern and Eastern Europeans, and Middle Easterners prefer closer distances in communicating whereas Asians, North Europeans, and North Americans do not want to stand as close to others (Sussman and Rosenfeld 1982). These behaviors relate to a culture's overall tendency to be high contact or low contact. People in a **high-contact culture** like to stand close and touch each other. High-contact cultures usually are in warmer climates, have a greater interpersonal orientation, and are interpersonally "warm." Those from **low-contact cultures** prefer to stand further apart and touch infrequently. These cultures are often in cooler climate zones, and people there are task-oriented and interpersonally "cool" (Gudykunst and Ting-Toomey 1988).

Use of office space is another aspect of proxemics. Where an office is and the type and arrangement of the furniture communicate a nonverbal message. For example, in the United States, a senior executive usually occupies a large private corner office on an upper floor. The high floor, large size, and greater number of windows indicate the executive's prestige and status. In contrast, a high-level French manager sits in the middle of an office area because the central location allows him to monitor the activities of all the subordinates (Chaney and Martin 1995).

Chronemics

Chronemics reflect the use of time in a culture, and two dominant patterns are characteristic. In a culture with a **monochronic time schedule,** activities are linear and performed one at a time. Time is something people think of as a resource to control or waste, and as a result, time schedules and appointments assume great importance. Individualistic cultures such as in Northern Europe, Germany, and the United States generally have a monochronic time orientation. With a **polychronic time schedule,** people tend to do several things at the same time. Schedules are less important than personal involvement and the completion of transactions, and personal relationships have a higher priority than being "on time." The polychronic time orientation is common in collectivistic countries such as in Latin America and the Middle East (Gudykunst and Ting-Toomey 1988; Hall 1983).

The importance put on time also varies with culture. Those with monochronic time schedules generally emphasize time much more. For example, in Germany, a country with a monochronic time orientation, punctuality is extremely important, and being even a few minutes late for a business appointment is an insult. In polychronic Ecuador, business executives come to a meeting fifteen or twenty minutes late and still consider it "on time" (Morrison, Conaway, and Borden 1994).

Chromatics

Chromatics is communication through colors. The colors of clothing, products and packaging, or gifts send intended or unintended messages when communicating cross-culturally. For example, in Hong Kong, red signifies happiness or good luck. The traditional bridal dress is red, and at Chinese New Year lucky money is distributed in *hong bao*, red envelopes. Red packaging is common, particularly around the Chinese New Year. Men in Hong Kong, however, often avoid green because the Cantonese expression "He's wearing a green hat," means "His wife is cheating on him." In Chile, a gift of yellow roses conveys the message "I don't like you," while in the Czech Republic giving red roses indicates a romantic interest (Morrison et al. 1994).

How Cross-Cultural Communication Differences Affect the Communication Process

Language usage, verbal styles, and nonverbal communication affect the communication process at two points. The first point is when the sender encodes a thought. The choice of language, the verbal styles used, and the nonverbals expressed carry a meaning that the sender expects the receiver to understand. To the extent that the sender encodes her thought in a manner that the receiver can comprehend, the sender enhances the accuracy of her communication.

The second point where cross-cultural differences affect the communication process is when the receiver decodes and tries to understand the message. If the receiver is familiar with the sender, he can decode the language, verbal styles, and nonverbals and gain a better understanding of the message.

▪▪▪ Barriers to Cross-Cultural Communication

With the many verbal and nonverbal differences in communication, people from different cultures often misunderstand each other. Edward T. Hall observed that, "All human beings are captives of their culture" (Hall and Hall 1994, p. 3). People tend to interpret the words and actions of those from other cultures just as they would those of individuals from their home culture. This is a major barrier to cross-cultural understanding. Even after studying an unfamiliar culture in advance, once there, an individual still confronts the totality of a different communication approach that can include a different language, a different verbal style, and numerous different nonverbals. Along with these different approaches, variations in culture, perception, and experience also make communication difficult (Bell 1992).

Culture, Perception, and Experience

Culture becomes a barrier when people from two different cultures have different ways of reacting to the same situation. Throughout this book, the emphasis is on how cultural differences affect people's behavior. For example, if a Canadian manager asks his subordinates in Canada for ideas about a particular task, the subordinates would probably understand this as a positive message. They would think the manager has an interest in their ideas and wants to encourage participation. If this manager asks the same question while on assignment in India, however, the understanding of the message would be different. The subordinates would probably receive a negative message, believing the manager incompetent, as Indian subordinates expect their managers to know what they want subordinates to do.

Perception is an individual's personal view of the world. Whether it is correct or not, it is a person's definition of reality. In intercultural communication, a potential perceptual barrier is stereotyping. **Stereotyping** is a shortcut: Someone sees another person, categorizes her as a member of a particular group, and then assigns her the characteristics of that group. Stereotyped characteristics may be data based—for example, the cultural frameworks presented in this book—or learned from other sources. For example, a child hears his parents say that people from Country X are rigid and set in their ways and later holds this stereotype of Country X'ers.

Stereotyping acts as a barrier to communication when it sets up expectations that may be untrue. However, if a person is able to use a stereotype as an initial expectation of how someone from another culture might behave, it could be helpful. When the person actually meets someone from the other culture, then he needs to gain an understanding of this individual to make communication more effective. One study (Ratiu 1983) found that managers judged as "most internationally effective" could change their stereotypes as they learned more about the real people they were working with. Those considered "least internationally effective" failed to change their stereotypes even when the people they encountered acted differently.

Experience barriers arise due to differences in life events between two individuals. When two people are from different cultures, it is likely that their life experiences have varied in many ways. The type of homes, how they worship, their educational systems, what they eat, and how they spend their free time could all be different. Lacking a common body of experience is likely to make communication more difficult. For example, in the course of comparing the quality of students in Canada and the United States, one of the authors discovered that Canadian and U.S. universities attach different numerical scales to the letter grades given in courses. This knowledge provided the common experience needed to understand the situation correctly.

The experience of the expatriate manager in the following example illustrates how the three barriers of culture, perception, and experience all made understanding difficult.

> "When my husband, Asbjorn, was on his first African assignment, he realized that understanding the words in Burkina Faso was not enough. To

be effective in that country, expatriates need a good command of French and a respectable smattering of Moré, the principal African dialect. One day he was sitting on a large mat on the ground, meeting with a group of Mossi villagers. An older man spoke a short phrase in Moré and everyone nodded in agreement. Seeing Asbjorn's puzzled look, someone translated the phrase into French, thinking that might help. It turned out to be a parable, the gist of which was something like, 'the bird flew over.' Since the Mossi often employ parables and use them to capture the essence of what is occurring, Asbjorn's understanding of individual words was not enough; he needed an understanding of the cultural context as well." (Osland 1995, pp. 70–71)

How Culture, Perception, and Experience Affect the Communication Process

Differences in culture, perception, and experience influence the communication process by creating noise. The differences make it difficult for the sender and receiver to relate to each other interpersonally and also influence the encoding and decoding of the message. Without a common frame of reference, the sender and receiver have greater difficulty understanding one another. Even when people from the same culture are communicating, perception and experience can create barriers. With a cross-cultural situation, these barriers are usually greater.

Although the barriers to communication are analytically distinct, in the process of communication they simultaneously interact. Awareness of and sensitivity to these barriers is the first step in improving intercultural communication effectiveness.

⋅ Virtual Cross-Cultural Communication

As the opening vignette illustrates, virtual communication is becoming increasingly more important for global businesses. Fax and e-mail all but replace letters and memos sent by post or messenger, and more and more business meetings are via teleconferencing. E-commerce allows consumers to order goods online, and businesses can source raw materials or new products and services anywhere—all from a home or office computer. Globally, the Internet is changing the nature of business and communication (Kogut 2003).

E-mail accounts for 75 to 80% of virtual team communication. Because of the asynchronous nature of e-mail, compared to face-to-face meetings or telephone conversations, team participants who are not communicating in their native languages often find it easier to be effective. The sender can assure that the message is clear before sending it, and the receiver can take time to study the meaning and compose an appropriate response. Further, e-mail makes it more comfortable for people to ask questions without losing face (Grosse 2002).

However, virtual communication is not without problems. For example, an experiment had students from universities in different countries form virtual teams on the Internet to complete a case study in business strategy. One of the teams' major problems was that native speakers of English had difficulty communicating with non-native speakers. Since English was the language required for the final paper, the native English speakers felt it unfair to have to rewrite the contributions from the others (Simmers 1996). The objective of having people from different countries work together is to bring together more ideas and to develop synergies from the interaction of perspectives, but if language acts as a barrier, working in a multinational group becomes frustrating and counterproductive.

Enhancing Cross-Cultural Communication

Because many barriers to cross-cultural communication relate to differences in cultures, the first step for enhancing cross-cultural communication is an understanding of the other person's culture. The cultural frameworks provide a useful start. Some communication style differences relate directly to these cultural profiles. However, knowing that South Africans are individualists and Panamanians are collectivists is not enough. It is important to study details of the specific culture and learn about communication patterns such as verbal style and nonverbals. The more you know about the individual with whom you want to communicate, the more likely it is you can send a message that your receiver will understand.

Because cross-cultural communication often takes place with at least one of the parties speaking a non-native language or through an interpreter, using simple language and speaking slowly is helpful. Also, try to avoid colloquial expressions, slang, and technical terms that may be unfamiliar to the other party. A shorter sentence with a clear meaning is easier to understand than a longer sentence. As you become familiar with the other person, try to match his level of speech. If the other person is speaking too quickly or beyond your level of understanding, let him know. If your foreign language ability is not adequate, request an interpreter.

Repeating major points or summarizing is also helpful. Ask for feedback from time to time to make sure that each party understands the other. Merely asking a yes or no question for confirmation is not sufficient; in some cultures, such as Korea and Japan, a yes only indicates the other party is listening and not necessarily that she understands or agrees. Asking a question such as, "What is your view of this situation?" or "How do you feel about our proposal?" tests understanding and gives the important reaction of the other party.

Finally, underlying these suggestions, it is important in cross-cultural communication to express respect for other people and their cultures, to strive for equality by allowing all parties equal opportunity to express themselves, and to be flexible enough to handle the inevitable differences.

Convergence or Divergence?

Forces for Convergence

With the increasing sophistication of and more widespread access to communication technology, it is more common and much easier for people from different places to communicate. The increasing ease of communication is a force for convergence.

Another force for convergence is the widespread use of English, particularly for business communication. With more people speaking English than any other language, international managers can often communicate with each other without having to rely on interpreters.

As new words develop in technology and business, often in English, they become part of many languages, sometimes using the same sound as the English and sometimes using an equivalent meaning. For example, the Japanese have a distinct set of characters for foreign words used to make a Japanese "word" that sounds the same as the foreign word. The Chinese word for computer translates literally as "electric brain."

The extent to which words and concepts are similar in different languages also represents a force for convergence.

Forces for Divergence

The number of different languages spoken around the globe, however, represents a force for divergence. Even if people communicate in English, their levels of proficiency undoubtedly vary if they are not native speakers, and even native speakers from different places use different vocabulary.

The various barriers to cross-cultural communication discussed in this chapter also represent forces for divergence. Communication approaches vary significantly with culture, even when using the same language, and verbal style and nonverbal communication also have strong cultural influence.

Are communication approaches converging or diverging? There is evidence of both. As more people use a common language, there is pressure towards convergence. However, to the extent that culture retains or gains influence, there is movement towards divergence. Perhaps over time, as people's exposure to and interactions with each other increase, there will be a greater understanding of other cultures and more effective cross-cultural communication.

▪▪▪ Implications for Managers

Communication is a large part of every manager's job. By one estimate a typical manager spends as much as 80 percent of his day in communication activities (Greenberg 1996). As the worldwide trend toward increased global business continues and domestic labor forces in many countries become more diverse, the ability to communicate cross-culturally is critical.

Communication serves as the foundation for a relationship between individuals. If a manager is effective in expressing herself, the other aspects of managing international organizational behavior become easier. For example, effective leadership relies on communication skill, motivation depends on making subordinates understand job requirements and how their actions affect consequences, and organizational culture develops as a result of effective communication. Thus, by gaining a better understanding of cross-cultural communication and working to enhance cross-cultural communication skills, there may be an impact on many areas of behavior.

In analyzing where in the communication process barriers arise, most are due to problems with the sender encoding a thought, the receiver decoding a message to achieve understanding, or with noise affecting the overall communication process. This implies that managers need greater knowledge about their communication partners to help minimize these problems. A sensitivity to the possibility of different approaches to language, verbal styles, and nonverbals can lead to more accurate encoding and decoding. Being aware of differences in culture, perception, and experience can help to reduce noise and also enhance the encoding and decoding process.

In considering trends towards convergence or divergence in communication approaches, language is still a major force for divergence. Because of this, knowledge of other languages is an important skill for an international manager. English and Mandarin Chinese (Putonghua) are good choices of second languages, as these are the most commonly spoken worldwide. English is widely used in business, and with the continuing economic developments in China, it is likely that the use of Chinese for business communication will increase.

SUMMARY ▪▪▪▪▪▪▪

A variety of factors influence communication across cultures. The basic communication process of encoding and decoding is at the core of communication. Noise affects all aspects of communication and is a recurrent issue in effective communication. Also important are differences in language usage, verbal style, and nonverbal communication in different cultures. These differences represent major barriers to effective cross-cultural communication. Other barriers include culture, perception, and experience. As communication technology, particularly use of the Internet increases, there will be greater use of virtual communication, which provides both advantages and disadvantages over traditional forms. To enhance intercultural communication, it is important to understand other cultures and become sensitive to differences.

Another issue for managers to consider is whether approaches to communication are converging or diverging worldwide. Improved communication technology and widespread use of English, particularly in business situations, represent forces for convergence. Yet, the large number of languages spoken worldwide and the pervasive effects of culture on communication, even when using the same language, are strong forces for divergence.

Finally, because communication represents such an important part of a manager's job, an understanding of cross-cultural communication can lead to more effective management of international organizational behavior. By studying other languages and cultures and learning more about their communication partners, managers can become effective cross-cultural communicators.

DISCUSSION QUESTIONS ▪▪▪▪▪▪▪

1. Consider the basic communication model. At each point, discuss possible problems two individuals from different cultures may have in communicating with each other.
2. Think of your own experiences in communicating with individuals from another culture. What difficulties did you experience? What did you do to try to make yourself understood? How could you have handled the situation more effectively?
3. Using your own language, give examples of each variation of the four verbal styles.
4. In this chapter there are examples of nonverbals from different cultures. Think about your own culture. Give examples of each type of nonverbal communication.
5. Give an example of a stereotype. How could it act as barrier to effective communication? How could it be helpful?
6. "The Internet and e-mail are making it easier to communicate with people across cultures." Do you agree or disagree? Why?

INTERNET SITES ▪▪▪▪▪▪▪

Selected Companies in the Chapter

The Coca-Cola Company (http://www.cocacola.com/flashIndex1.html)
Wal-Mart (http://www.walmart.com/)

Communication Sites

American Communication Association (http://www.americancomm.org/index.html). This site has research findings and links to communication resources.

Association for Business Communication (http://www.businesscommunication.org/). This site has news about communication and the association.

Intercultural Communication Institute (http://www.intercultural.org/). The site offers a variety of resources relating to intercultural communication.

Intercultural Communication Homepage (http://www2.soc.hawaii.edu/css/dept/com/resources/intercultural/Intercultural.html). This site, prepared as part of a student's master's thesis, offers different resources for those who need to learn about intercultural communication for their future careers.

The Interculture Project (http://www.lancs.ac.uk/users/interculture/). This site has material relating to the intercultural experiences of U.K. students who have studied abroad.

International Association for Languages and Intercultural Communication (IALIC) (http://www.cf.ac.uk/encap/langcom/ialic/). The IALIC is an association of academics, practitioners, researchers, and students interested in living languages and intercultural understanding. The site has news and research about these topics.

Small World Research (http://smallworld.columbia.edu). This site invites you to participate in a research project at Columbia University that is trying to find out how closely connected people throughout the world are through the use of the Internet.

REFERENCES ■■■■■■■

Abbasi, S. M. and Hollman, K. W. (1993). "Business Success in the Middle East." *Management Decision*, 31(1), 55–9.

Bell, A. H. (1992). *Business Communication: Toward 2000*. Cincinnati, OH: South-Western.

Besher, A. (1991). *The Pacific Rim Almanac*. New York: Harper Collins.

Chaney, L. H. and Martin, J. S. (1995). *Intercultural Business Communication*. Upper Saddle River, NJ: Prentice Hall.

Crystal, D. (1997). *The Cambridge Encyclopedia of Language*. 2nd Ed. Cambridge, UK: Cambridge University Press.

Deresky, H. (1994). *International Management: Managing Across Borders and Cultures*. New York: Harper Collins.

Gibbs, W. W. (2002). "Saving Dying Languages," *Scientific American*, 287(2), 79–85.

Gibson, C. B. (1997). "Do You Hear What I Hear? A Framework for Reconciling Intercultural Communication Difficulties Arising from Cognitive Styles and Cultural Values." In Earley, P. C. and Erez, M. (eds.) *New Perspectives on International Industrial/Organizational Psychology*. San Francisco: New Lexington Press.

Gilsdorf, J. (2002). "Standard Englishers and World Englishes: Living with Polymorph Business Language." *The Journal of Business Communication*, 39(3), 364–78.

Greenberg, J. (1996). *Managing Behavior in Organizations*. Upper Saddle River, NJ: Prentice Hall.

Grosse, C. U. (2002). "Managing Communication within Virtual Intercultural Teams." *Business Communication Quarterly*, 65(4), 22–38.

Gudykunst, W. B. and Ting-Toomey, S. (1988). *Culture and Interpersonal Communication*. Newbury Park, CA: Sage.

Hall, E. T. (1966). *The Hidden Dimension*. New York: Doubleday.

——. (1976). *Beyond Culture*. New York: Doubleday.

——. (1983). *The Dance of Life*. New York: Doubleday.

—— and Hall, E. (1994). "How Cultures Collide." In Weaver, G. R. (ed.) *Culture, Communication, and Conflict: Readings in Intercultural Relations*. Needham Heights, MA: Ginn Press.

Hodgetts, R. M. and Luthans, F. (1994). *International Management*. 2nd Ed. New York: McGraw-Hill.

Hofstede, G. (2001). *Culture's Consequences: Comparing Values, Behaviors, Institutions, and Organizations Across Nations*. 2nd Ed. Thousand Oaks, CA: Sage.

——. (1980). "Motivation, Leadership, and Organization: Do American Theories Apply Abroad?" *Organizational Dynamics*, 9, 42–62.

Holden, R. (2001). "Managing People's Values and Perceptions in Multi-Cultural Organisations: The Experience of an HR Director." *Employee Relations*, 23(6), 614–26.

Kahn, G. and Zimmerman, A. (2003). "Amid SARS, Wal-Mart Adjusts Buying," *The Asian Wall Street Journal*, May 29, A6.

Kogut, B. (2003). *The Global Internet Economy*. Cambridge, MA: MIT Press.

Morrison, T., Conaway, W. A., and Borden, G. A. (1994) *Kiss, Bow, or Shake Hands: How to Do Business in Sixty Countries*. Holbrook, MA: Bob Adams.

Osland, J. S. (1995). *The Adventure of Working Abroad: Hero Tales from the Global Frontier*. San Francisco: Jossey-Bass.

Ratiu, I. (1983). "Thinking Internationally: A Comparison of How International Executives Learn." *International Studies of Management and Organization*, 13, 139–150.

Ricks, D. A. (1983). *Big Business Blunders: Mistakes in Multinational Marketing*. Homewood, IL: Dow Jones-Irwin.

Samovar, L. A. and Porter, R. E. (1991). *Communication between Cultures*. Belmont, CA: Wadsworth.

Scott, J. C. (2000). "Differences in American and British Vocabulary: Implications for International Business Communication." *Business Communication Quarterly,* 63(4) 27–39.

Simmers, C. (1996). "Internet in the Classroom: Case Analysis Across the Network: Across the Globe." Paper presented at the Tenth Annual Mid Atlantic Regional Organizational Behavior Teaching Conference, Philadelphia, PA, March 9.

Sussman, N. M. and Rosenfeld, H. M. (1982). "Influence of Culture, Language, and Sex on Conversational Distance." *Journal of Personality and Social Psychology*, 42, 66–74.

Tagliabue, J. (2002). "In Europe, Going Global Means, Alas, English," *The New York Times,* May 19, 15.

Warner, F. (1996) "Western Goods in Asia Lose Something in Translation," *The Asian Wall Street Journal Weekly*, February 12, 6.

5

Negotiation and Conflict Resolution

Learning Objectives

After reading this chapter, you should be able to:

■ Define negotiation and understand the basic negotiation process.

■ Explain how culture influences the negotiation process.

■ Consider the impact of situational factors and negotiating tactics on negotiation outcomes.

■ Analyze the differences between intracultural and cross-cultural negotiations.

■ Discuss the role of culture in the conflict resolution process.

■ Appreciate how approaches to conflict influence negotiation.

■ Identify ways to become a more effective cross-cultural negotiator.

CULTURE AT WORK

Ellie the Elephant vs. Geoffrey the Giraffe

Redgwoods Holdings Ltd., the owner of Reggie's Toy Store, legally registered the Toys "R" Us trademark during South Africa's apartheid regime. In post-apartheid South Africa, when trade embargoes vanished and the opportunity existed to participate more extensively in international trade, Redgwoods had to confront the possibility of a challenge to its trademark. The four Redgwoods Toys "R" Us stores were similar to the original Toys "R" Us chain in the United States except Redgwoods used Ellie the Elephant as its mascot instead of Geoffrey the Giraffe.

As expected, the U.S.-based Toys "R" Us objected to Redgwoods' use of its trademark. Rather than fighting in court, where they might have won, Redgwoods decided to negotiate with Toys "R" Us.

The result was a win-win solution. Redgwoods agreed to sell back the trademark to the U.S. company and simultaneously buy the rights to its use in South Africa. The South African government approved the deal in March 1996, making Redgwoods Toys "R" Us' seventh foreign franchisee.

Source: McNeil, D. G., Jr. (1996). "Restoring Their Good Names: U.S. Companies in Trademark Battles in South Africa," *The New York Times*, May 1, D1, D19.

In the global economy, companies increasingly do business outside their home countries. Because the majority of transactions involve two or more organizations deciding the terms of an agreement, cross-cultural negotiating is an important skill that occupies a great deal of an international manager's time.

Imagine the potential conflicts executives from the two companies in the Culture at Work vignette faced. Each company had a large stake in the outcome of the negotiation and wanted to make sure it received a fair deal. Yet it is likely that at the start of the negotiation, neither side had much information about the other. In addition, the United States and South Africa have different cultures, laws, and economic systems making it very challenging for the two sides to communicate and reach agreement. In this case, despite the difficulties created by cultural differences, both sides won.

IIII What Is Negotiation?

Negotiation is the process of bargaining between two or more parties to reach a solution that is mutually acceptable. Negotiating, either in a personal or work role, is something everyone does every day. The subject of the negotiation could be quite simple—two friends deciding whether to go to a movie or a football match—or it could be much more complex—companies from two different countries planning a joint venture. Negotiation is a communication process that traditionally involves a face-to-face meeting, but negotiations also take place by telephone, fax, e-mail, and letter.

IIII The Negotiation Process

The Goal

The overall goal of negotiation is to arrive at a solution acceptable to all parties involved. In some cultures, the optimum outcome is a **win-win solution** in which all parties achieve their objectives. In other cultures, negotiators think that they must **compromise** to reach agreement. That requires all parties to give up something and results in a **lose-lose** solution. In still other cultures, the goal of the negotiation is **win-lose;** one party receives all they want by forcing the other to concede defeat.

Negotiators can also consider **distributive outcomes** and **integrative agreements.** The idea of a distributive outcome is that the amount of resources available for negotiators to divide is fixed, which is consistent with a win-lose or lose-lose solution (Brett 2001). Under this assumption, negotiators compete to obtain as much as possible for themselves with little or no concern for the other party's outcomes. A distributive outcome refers to each individual party's gain at the end of the negotiation.

To achieve an integrative agreement, negotiators must transform fixed resources into something valued differently by each party, and then distribute the resources to the party that values them most (Brett 2001). An integrative outcome is consistent with a win-win solution and is often the approach recommended in American manuals on how to conduct successful negotiations (Brett 2001; Fisher and Ury 1981; Ury 1993). To achieve an integrative outcome, each party must have a clear understanding of the other's interests, preferences, and priorities (Brett 2000). An integrative agreement also refers to the sum of each party's gains at the end of the negotiation.

The Negotiation Process

The negotiation process consists of five steps: (1) preparation, (2) relationship building, (3) information exchange, (4) persuasion, and (5) agreement (Adler 1991; Deresky 1994). Throughout the process the thoughts and feelings of the negotiators influence what happens between them (Gelfand and McCusker 2002).

Preparation Stage

In the **preparation stage,** negotiators plan how to approach the actual negotiation and try to learn as much as possible about their negotiating partners. The negotiators need to understand their own position and anticipate the position of the other party through considering each party's objectives, needs, and interests (Ury 1993). This stage typically takes place at the home office before the face-to-face meeting.

Relationship Building Stage

The second stage, relationship building, starts when the parties begin their discussion, typically, at one of their offices or at a mutually acceptable neutral location. The objective of the **relationship building stage** is for the parties to get to know one another. This could involve a brief exchange of names and business cards or many days of conversation, dinners, and other forms of entertainment.

How much each party needs to know about the other depends to a great extent on culture—for example, Americans spend little time in the relationship building stage. Once the parties establish that they represent their respective companies, they move to the next stage of negotiation. However, for much of the world, this rapid progression is viewed as inappropriate, and even offensive. For example, Mexican negotiators usually prefer to spend time dining together and discussing topics not related to the negotiation. Thus, when foreigners travel to Mexico for a negotiation, their Mexican hosts often arrange visits to cultural sights that allow the visitors to learn more about Mexico and their Mexican partners. For the Mexican negotiators, getting acquainted with their negotiating partners is critical.

Another example is the importance of relationship building in China. A successful negotiator should begin this stage before the face-to-face negotiation. If a manager is seeking a new client, the manager can find a third party who has a good reputation with the prospective client and ask that third party to make the introduction and explain more about the prospective client's needs. Another approach is to try to build a positive company image before the negotiation begins, for example, with a charitable donation to the community where the client does business (Li and Labig 2001).

Information Exchange

Information exchange, the third stage, involves each party stating an initial position, usually in a formal presentation, followed by questions, answers, and discussion. The meaning of this stage varies depending on the negotiator's cultural background. Americans typically think this is the beginning of the "real" negotiation and expect each party to present relevant information followed by a logical discussion based on the presentation. A Mexican negotiator, in contrast, may be suspicious and indirect, presenting little substantive material (Deresky 1994). In negotiating with Mexicans, exploring issues informally and reaching some understanding with key individuals before the formal information exchange may be more beneficial (Fisher 1980).

Persuasion

The fourth stage of the negotiation process is **persuasion;** the parties try to convince their counterparts to accept their proposals. This might involve the parties consciously trying to work toward a mutually acceptable solution or one party using persuasive arguments to influence the other.

Agreement

The final stage of negotiation is **agreement** where the parties come to a mutually acceptable solution, and in the process, each may make concessions. Cultural variations exist at this stage as well. For example, U.S. negotiators prefer to negotiate in a linear fashion, deciding one issue at a time, and concluding with a binding legal contract. Russians view concessions as a sign of weakness and consequently make very few (Adler 1991), prefer to develop the final agreement at the end based on all the items (Pettibone 1990), and attach less meaning to the contract (Deresky 1994).

▪ ▪ ▪ How Culture Influences the Negotiation Process

Cultural variation exists at every stage of the negotiation process. Even the concept of the negotiation process itself varies across cultures as the following examples indicate.

Japanese culture highly values harmony. The Japanese typically make organizational decisions using the group consensus processes known as *nemawashi* and *ringi seido,* and the negotiation session functions as a ceremony to formalize a consensus decision previously reached. The Japanese prefer that the agreement not be too restrictive as it represents a beginning position. Emphasizing the tentativeness of negotiations, Japanese culture provides a mechanism for breaking a contract, *naniwabushi,* which allows a party to explain why he can not fulfill a contract and provides an honorable out if circumstances change (Chen 1995).

In contrast, Americans view the negotiation session as an opportunity for the parties involved to problem solve. Taking a factual approach, based on logic, they expect a give and take on various issues with compromises along the way (Glenn, Witmeyer, and Stevenson 1977). A legal contract confirms the agreement as an endpoint and deviations from it are causes for dispute and, in some cases, legal action.

The French also approach negotiation in a problem-solving mode. However, they think of negotiation more as an art and the negotiation table as a place "for searching out the solutions for which they have so carefully prepared. To them, the negotiation setting becomes more of a debating forum, with flexibility and accommodation simply for the sake of agreement less of an expectation" (Fisher 1980, p. 19).

These examples illustrate the wide cultural variation in the concept, understanding, and practice of negotiation and raise the issues of variation in interests, priorities, and strategies.

▪ ▪ ▪ Interests, Priorities, and Strategies

Culture influences the interests, priorities, and strategies of negotiators (Brett 2001). **Interests** reflect the underlying need or reason for a negotiator's position—for example, a manager is trying to expand global market share by introducing the company's products in a new country. **Priorities** indicate the importance of different alternatives—for example, the manager may put a higher priority on sales volume than profit. Finally, the **strategy** is the overall approach to negotiation that establishes the set of behaviors that the negotiator believes will lead to goal accomplishment.

Interests and Priorities

Cultural values often explain differences in interests and priorities (Brett 2001). For example, in a long-term oriented society, a company would be interested in establishing a presence in a new country, building market share, and creating a positive company image rather than short-term profitability. In contrast, a company from a short-term-oriented culture would only be interested in making money quickly, with the emphasis on maximizing profit in the short run. If these two companies were negotiating with each other, their cultural differences could make it difficult for them to understand why their interests and priorities were not the same. However, rather than one party trying to persuade the other to change, the negotiators can increase their opportunity for success if they integrate their differences (Brett 2000, 2001). In this example, the two parties would have to work toward an agreement with both short-term profitability and long-term market development.

Strategies

Culture also influences the choice of behaviors for pursuing different strategies (Brett 2001). In choosing a **confrontation strategy,** the degree of directness in communication is a concern. With a direct strategy, the negotiator clearly verbalizes concerns to the other party, whereas an indirect strategy either hints at similar concerns or expresses them nonverbally. **Motivation strategy** expresses the interests of the parties (Brett 2001). Whether the negotiator is interested in self, collective, or other interests influences the nature of the final agreement.

Influence strategy reflects the negotiator's use of power (Brett 2001). The negotiator might depend on the best alternative to a negotiated agreement **(BATNA)** (Fisher and Ury 1981; Ury 1993) as a power base. If the negotiator has an acceptable alternative available, the outcome of the negotiation is less important and this gives the negotiator more power. When the BATNA is unattractive, the negotiator is more dependent on the other party and therefore has less influence. An influence strategy could also use fairness standards, decision rules about what is fair including laws, contracts, precedents, or even social status or ideology (Brett 2001).

Information strategy can also be direct or indirect (Brett 2001). What information is disclosed and how it is conveyed will affect the type of agreement reached. Knowing about BATNAs, status, and fairness standards helps negotiators obtain more satisfactory outcomes. Most importantly, understanding both parties' interests and priorities can lead to an integrative agreement, where both parties feel that their needs are satisfied.

Cultural Influences on Strategy

Cultural characteristics influence negotiator behavior (see Table 5-1). For example, individualists pursue a strong self-interest motivation strategy by setting high goals for themselves (Brett and Okumura 1998) and often reject acceptable agreements that do not meet their self-interests (Brett 2000). In studies comparing American negotiators to negotiators in collectivist countries, Americans pursued more self-interested negotiation strategies compared to Japanese (Brett and Okumura 1998), Hong Kong Chinese (Tinsley and Pillutla 1997), and Greeks (Gelfand and Christakopoulou 1999). When individualists are accountable in a negotiation, that is, they have to justify their actions and will be evaluated and rewarded by those

TABLE 5-1 Culture and Negotiation Strategy

Cultural Characteristic	*Typical Behaviors*
Individualistic	Sets high personal goals Rejects acceptable but suboptimal agreements Has high self-interest, little concern for other parties' interests
Collectivistic	Cooperative with in-group members, willing to search for mutually satisfying agreement With out-group members, may be more competitive
Egalitarian	Refers to BATNA and other sources of power infrequently if negotiation is moving towards agreement Prefers to focus on issues, sharing information on priorities and interests, noting similarities and differences
Hierarchical	More likely to accept and use all types of power—status, BATNA, persuasion
Low-context	Prefers direct information sharing
High-context	Prefers indirect information sharing

Source: Brett, J. M. (2000). "Culture and Negotiation," *International Journal of Psychology,* 35, 97–104.

they represent, they behave more competitively and often produce inferior outcomes (Gelfand and Realo 1999).

Collectivists are likely to pursue more cooperative strategies if they are negotiating with an in-group member but may become more competitive if the other party is an out-group member (Brett 2000). When collectivists are accountable in a negotiation, they also behave more cooperatively (Gelfand and Realo 1999).

The egalitarian-hierarchical cultural dimension (Schwartz 1992) affects influence strategy because people from egalitarian cultures view power in a negotiation as deriving from information, particularly their own and their counterparts' BATNAs (Brett 2001). In contrast, people from hierarchical cultures are more likely to use power in a negotiation, which may derive from status, BATNA, or persuasion (Brett 2000). In a comparison of American and Japanese negotiators, the hierarchical Japanese were more concerned with power during the preparation for negotiations and did not consider BATNA as a source of power, as did the more egalitarian Americans (Brett and Okumura 1998). Finally, the Japanese made extensive use of influence tactics, whereas Americans used them relatively infrequently (Adair, Okumura, and Brett 2001).

Communication context influences confrontation and information strategies. People from low-context cultures are more likely to share information directly, whereas individuals from high-context societies use an indirect approach (Brett 2000). For example, low-context American negotiators used direct information to find out about their counterparts' preferences and priorities and were more willing to share information about themselves compared to high-context Japanese. The Japanese negotiators used indirect information exchange and inferred preferences and priorities from a series of offers and counteroffers that they made more frequently than American negotiators. Ultimately, although they used different strategies, both the Japanese and the Americans were able to arrive at integrative agreements (Adair et al. 2001).

▪▪▪ Situational Factors and Negotiating Tactics

The circumstances of the negotiation and the tactics used by the negotiating parties, such as geographical location, room arrangements, selection of negotiators, and time limits, are used to implement the negotiator's strategies and influence the success of the negotiation. Tactics include verbal aspects and nonverbal such as tone of voice, facial expressions, gestures, and body posture.

Situational Factors

Geographical Location

An important early decision negotiators make together is where they will meet. When people are working on opposite sides of the globe, the selection of a **geographical location** has implications for all parties. Generally, the choice is between the home location of one of the parties and a neutral location. Obviously, it is usually advantageous to conduct the negotiations in your home office because the home party does not incur extra expenses for travel and hotel, has greater access to information and advice, and lives in the comfort of home. In fact, when one or both of the parties are away from their home office, there is usually pressure to reach agreement more quickly as costs increase and managers expect the negotiators to finalize an agreement to justify the expense.

A neutral location is usually one equidistant from both parties—for example, North American and Asian negotiators meeting in Hawaii, or South American and European teams holding talks in New York. People from some countries have difficulty traveling abroad due to visa restrictions or financial constraints; others have a strong preference for conducting negotiations at home, for example, the Mainland Chinese (Chen 1995). This gives the Chinese the advantage of time since every day a foreigner is there is costly and stressful. A successful negotiator from Hong Kong claimed the secret of his success was to arrive in China, settle in, and appear that he was in no hurry to leave.

Room Arrangements

Another situational factor is **room arrangements,** the physical set-up of the negotiations. The shape of the table and where the negotiators sit can create greater competition or cooperation. For example, a rectangular or square table with the negotiating parties sitting on opposite sides leads to greater competition, whereas everyone sitting together at a round table usually creates a more cooperative climate.

Selection of Negotiators

The **selection of negotiators** concerns the number of people and which ones will represent a team. The number chosen often reflects the organization's national culture—for example, U.S. companies often send a small team or only a single individual to represent them because the American concern for efficiency views sending a large group as a waste of resources. The Japanese, in contrast, prefer a large group, and the size of their team can create an advantage by overwhelming the other side and allows them to have representatives from different areas within the company (Chen 1995).

The selection of a negotiator also reflects culture. For example, U.S. companies select negotiators based on position and competence; if the negotiation concerns a matter related to someone's position, that person is most likely to represent the company. Factors such as age, gender, or race are not important if an individual performs competently. In a Mexican organization, in contrast, personal qualities and social connections influence the selection of a negotiator (Fisher 1980).

Time Limits

Time limits are the real or presumed deadlines under which negotiating parties operate and the expected length of a negotiation varies with a culture's view of time. The United States, Switzerland, and Germany view time as a commodity and want to conduct negotiations as efficiently and quickly as possible. For other cultures, such as those in the Middle East or Asia, the time perspective is longer term, and the extended negotiation time helps build a long-term relationship.

If a negotiating team is away from home, their counterparts may discover how long they expect to stay by making hotel reservations or reconfirming their air tickets. Using this information to delay an agreement until close to the departure deadline makes the visitors anxious to grant concessions.

Verbal Tactics

Verbal tactics include spoken negotiating behaviors such as initial offer made, promises, threats, and recommendations. Negotiators can increase their profits by (1) asking more questions, (2) making fewer commitments before the final agreement stage, and (3) increasing the amount of the initial request, that is, seller asking for more and buyer offering less (Adler 1991).

Initial Offer

The **initial offer,** a beginning statement of intent made by each party, is one tactic influenced by culture. Chinese and Russian negotiators typically begin the negotiation with extreme initial offers (Adler 1991; Chen 1995) whereas negotiators from the United States and Sweden are more likely to make an initial offer closer to their actual expectation. (Adler 1991; Graham 1985). The Japanese typically do not like to make extreme offers, which they refer to as *banana no tataki uri,* the "banana sale approach," but they sometimes do so when negotiating with foreigners (Chen 1995).

Other Verbal Negotiating Behaviors

Other verbal negotiating behaviors include promises, threats, recommendations, warnings, rewards, punishments, normative appeals, commitments, self-disclosure, questions, and commands. A study comparing Americans, Brazilians, and Japanese found the verbal tactics of Americans and Japanese to be more similar than those used by Brazilians. For example, Brazilians make extensive use of much higher initial offers, fewer promises, fewer commitments, and more "no's" compared to American and Japanese negotiators (Graham 1985).

Nonverbal Tactics

Nonverbal tactics include negotiating behaviors other than the words used, for example, tone of voice, facial expressions, gestures, and body position. There is great variation in the nonverbal behaviors used by people from different cultures in daily conversation. These variations, as well as more specific behaviors relating to negotiating, make cross-cultural negotiation a challenge. Nonverbal behaviors often send a "louder" message than verbal behaviors, and people tend to interpret the behaviors of

TABLE 5-2 A Comparison of Nonverbal Negotiating Behaviors Used by Negotiators from Japan, the United States, and Brazil

Behavior (tactic)	Japanese	Americans	Brazilians
Silent periods (Number of periods greater than 10 seconds, per 30 minutes)	5.5	3.5	0
Conversational overlaps (Number per 10 minutes)	12.6	10.3	28.6
Facial gazing (Minutes of gazing per 10 minutes)	1.3	3.3	5.2
Touching (Not including handshaking, per 30 minutes)	0	0	4.7

Source: Adler, N. J. (1991). *International Dimensions of Organizational Behavior.* 2nd Ed. Boston: PWS-Kent, p. 210 based on Graham, J. L. (1985). "The Influence of Culture on Business Negotiations," *Journal of International Business Studies,* XVI, 81–96.

people from other cultures as having the same meaning that they have in their own culture. Negotiators who engage in indirect confrontation and information strategies typically use nonverbal tactics more extensively in negotiation. Table 5-2 gives examples of the nonverbal negotiating behaviors of negotiators from Japan, the United States, and Brazil.

Silence

As with verbal negotiating behavior, American and Japanese behaviors are more similar to each other than to the Brazilians'. The Japanese use of **silence,** an intentional period of nonresponsiveness, during negotiations, allows them to pause to reflect on what has been said, think about what should be said, or gain time if a problem arises (Chen 1995; Fisher 1980). Japanese consider this a normal part of conversation, yet an American or Brazilian may find it awkward or uncomfortable. In fact, people from the United States typically say something to break the silence after only a few seconds. In some cases, they interpret silence as rejection and offer further concessions to get the negotiation moving again.

Conversational Overlaps

Conversational overlaps occur when more than one person speaks at the same time. Interrupting or having two people speak at the same time is common, acceptable behavior for the Brazilians who prefer multiple events at one time, but Americans and Japanese consider it rude and usually stop if someone else starts to speak.

Facial Gazing

Facial gazing is looking at a counterpart's face, and eye contact is the most intense form of facial gazing. Reflecting the level of intimacy between two individuals, Brazilians use facial gazing extensively, Americans a moderate amount, and Japanese very little. The norm for a business situation such as a negotiation varies widely—for example, the polite Japanese directs his gaze somewhere around the neck or chest, rather than to the eyes (Goldman 1992) while Americans like to maintain eye contact but with less intensity than the Brazilians.

Touching

Touching behaviors, often an important aspect of negotiations, vary with cultures. The Japanese and American negotiators in the Table 5-2 example only touch via a handshake, whereas for Brazilians touching is a way to make the relationship closer, and they may interpret the lack of touching as rejection. Mexicans use physical contact to signal confidence, and Mexican men often use the *abrazo,* or hug, to indicate that a relationship is deepening (Fisher 1980).

▪▪▪ Differences Between Intra-Cultural and Cross-Cultural Negotiations

The dynamics of cross-cultural negotiation are different from intra-cultural negotiations. A comparison of Japanese, American, Francophone Canadian, and Anglophone Canadian negotiators found that all groups were different in the cross-cultural compared to the intra-cultural context (Adler and Graham 1989). The nature of these differences, however, varied significantly—for example, Francophone Canadians took a more cooperative approach to negotiating with Anglophone Canadians than with other Francophones, and Anglophone Canadians took longer and had lower joint profits when negotiating with Francophone Canadians. Japanese found American negotiators more attractive than other Japanese, even though they finished with lower profits. Americans did not act differently in the intercultural negotiation, but they experienced more satisfaction negotiating with the Japanese than with other Americans.

Another study comparing executives from the People's Republic of China and Canada found no differences in strategy in a cross-cultural situation (Tse, Francis, and Walls 1994). Managers from both countries used the same conflict resolution strategy, and the same underlying factors motivated them whether they were in an intra- or intercultural situation. However, executives from both countries preferred negotiating with Canadians rather than Chinese.

Focusing on outcomes, a study comparing Japanese and American intra-cultural and intercultural negotiations found that joint gains were lower in the intercultural situation (Adair et al. 2001; Brett and Okumura 1998). Same culture negotiators behaved in normative ways that were comfortable and effective in generating acceptable joint outcomes. However, in the intercultural situation, ineffective and frustrated communication resulted from different normative behaviors and made it difficult to attain strong integrative outcomes. The Japanese adapted more to the U.S. negotiating style, probably because of cultural and situational reasons. For example, Japanese value mutual understanding and adapting to their environment. In addition, they worked for Japanese companies in the United States and did the negotiation exercise there (Adair et al. 2001). However, even though the Japanese tried to adapt, the information sharing between the two parties was not effective, and both sides lacked motivation to achieve a mutually satisfying agreement (Adair et al. 2001). Interestingly, the intercultural negotiators were happier and more satisfied than the intra-cultural negotiators at the end of the negotiations (Brett and Okumura 1998).

These studies suggest that cross-cultural negotiations are more challenging than intra-cultural negotiations and are more satisfying to the negotiators. The experience of intercultural negotiating is different from negotiating within the same culture.

⚹⚹⚹ How Culture Influences Conflict Resolution

Negotiation is a communication process that resolves conflicts, as the parties begin with different positions from which they move to an agreement. The discussion of situational factors and verbal and nonverbal tactics in negotiating indicates that the approach to negotiation varies widely with culture. Similarly, culture influences the way that a society perceives conflict.

Intercultural communications expert, Stella Ting-Toomey, has developed a theory of culture and conflict that explains cultural differences using Hall's low- and high-context framework (Gudykunst and Ting-Toomey 1988; Hall 1976; Ting-Toomey 1985). People in low-context cultures think of conflict as **instrumental-oriented** and thus view the world in analytic, linear logic terms, separating issues from individuals. In a high-context culture, conflict is **expressive-oriented** because people do not separate the person from the issue. The consequence is that in low-context cultures, public disagreements are acceptable; individuals can have a conflict and still maintain a friendly relationship afterwards. But in the high-context culture, open disagreement and public confrontation are highly insulting, causing both parties involved to "lose face," and possibly ending their relationship (Gudykunst and Ting-Toomey 1988; Ting-Toomey 1985).

Why conflict develops in the two types of cultures also differs. Since the low-context culture is more individualistic, there is less specification of appropriate ways to behave, and conflict often arises because one party violates the other's expectations. In the high-context culture with more specific rules of behavior, conflict usually occurs when an individual violates cultural expectations.

Attitude towards conflict is the third aspect of the conflict situation. In the low-context culture, people are oriented toward action resulting in a direct, confrontational response to conflict with all parties desiring a quick resolution. In the high-context setting, the attitude towards conflict is evasive and nonconfrontational, leading to an indirect, inactive approach that often results in avoiding or ignoring the conflict.

The final aspect of the conflict situation is how the conflict evolves or the style used to manage the conflict. In low-context cultures, people prefer either a factual-inductive or axiomatic-deductive argument based on linear approaches to logic. The **factual-inductive style** uses relevant facts and moves towards a conclusion using inductive reasoning. The **axiomatic-deductive style** reasons from the general to the specific, establishing basic ideas from which implications are drawn. High-context cultures commonly use the **affective-intuitive style,** which relies on circumlocution or flowery speech to make an emotional appeal and ambiguity and understatement to diffuse conflict. Generally, people in low-context cultures have an intellectual view of conflict; those from high-context cultures see it from an emotional point of view. Table 5-3 summarizes the main ideas of Ting-Toomey's theory.

Two studies comparing a high- and low-context culture illustrate Ting-Toomey's model. Male business students in Hong Kong (high-context) and the United States

TABLE 5-3 Conflict Characteristics of Low- and High-Context Cultures

Key Questions	Low-Context Conflict	High-Context Conflict
Why	analytic, linear logic; instrumental-oriented; dichotomy between conflict and conflict parties	synthetic, spiral logic; expressive-oriented; integration of conflict and conflict parties
When	individualistic-oriented; low collective normative expectations; violations of individual expectations create conflict potentials	group-oriented; high collective normative expectations; violations of collective expectations create conflict potentials
What	revealment; direct, confrontational attitude; action and solution-oriented	concealment; indirect, nonconfrontational attitude; "face" and relationship-oriented
How	explicit communication codes; line-logic style: rational-factual rhetoric; open, direct strategies	implicit communication codes; point-logic style: intuitive-affective rhetoric; ambiguous, indirect strategies

Source: Ting-Toomey, S. (1985). "Toward a Theory of Conflict and Culture." In Gudykunst, W., Stewart, L., and Ting-Toomey, S. (eds.) *Communication, Culture, and Organizational Processes.* Beverly Hills, CA: Sage, p. 82. Reprinted by permission of Sage Publications.

(low-context) varied on how they handled conflict (Chiu and Kosinski 1994). The Hong Kong Chinese preferred avoidance and accommodation as ways of managing conflict whereas the Caucasian Americans chose direct methods of resolving conflict more frequently.

Another example of these differences is response to verbal insults. In a study comparing Chinese and North Americans (Bond, Wan, Leung, and Giacalone 1985), to avoid conflict, the Chinese advised an executive to speak separately to both the person who insulted someone and the target of the insult. The North Americans suggested that the executive hold a meeting with both parties present to resolve the conflict.

▪▪▪ How the Approach to Conflict Influences Negotiation

The way different cultures view conflict affects their approach to negotiation, particularly the differences between high- and low-context cultures. For example, basic differences exist between high- and low-context cultures in thinking patterns, individualistic versus collectivistic orientation, differing expectations, direct versus indirect attitude, and implicit versus explicit communication codes.

Negotiators from a high-context culture often behave in ways that appear harmonious on the surface because they express differences in opinion less directly and communicate real feelings through implicit language and nonverbal means. In high-context cultures, the identity of the negotiator is important, and the "persona" of the negotiator becomes integrated into how the negotiation is conducted. In contrast, negotiators from low-context cultures are open and direct, take an action orientation, and see negotiation as a problem-solving process. There is a clear difference between the negotiator as a person and the role of the negotiator in a negotiation.

These examples illustrate the major differences *between* negotiators from high- and low-context cultures. However, there are also differences *among* high- or low-context cultures. An earlier example in the chapter illustrates differences among negotiators from Japan, the United States, and Brazil. Japanese and Americans are more alike in their use of verbal and nonverbal negotiating behaviors than Brazilians. However, Brazil and Japan are both high-context cultures, and the United States is a low-context culture. Clearly, these differences reflect another aspect of cultural difference not represented by high- and low-context.

▪ ▪ ▪ How to Become a Better Cross-Cultural Negotiator

Substantial differences exist among cultures in the goals and behaviors associated with the negotiation process. How can an effective cross-cultural negotiator manage these? First, it is important to understand your negotiating partner. At the cultural level, a basic understanding of values, attitudes, and typical behaviors is very helpful. Many articles and books offer specific examples of how people negotiate in China, Mexico, France, Japan, the United States, and Russia (see Chen 1995; Fisher 1980; Goldman 1992; Shenkar and Ronen 1987).

When you are aware of culture and how it influences negotiating style, consider the specifics of your situation. Who is your negotiating counterpart—the organization and its representatives—and what experience do they have with your organization and your culture? Also think about your own and the other party's needs, interests, and possible goals. Finally, after you understand the background of your negotiating partner, you must consider how to handle the actual negotiation. Often, people do not behave the same way in a cross-cultural negotiation as in an intra-cultural negotiation. You might believe that doing what the natives do is the most effective approach, however, a foreigner trying to behave as a native may not be treated as a native and in fact may not be credible.

In a study of how Americans responded to Japanese and Korean businesspeople who attempted to adapt varying degrees of American behavior in a negotiation, a moderate adaptation of native behavior produced more successful outcomes than no adaptation or substantial adaptation (Francis 1991). Although these results are tentative, they suggest that neither totally following the approach of another culture nor totally ignoring the cultural differences is very effective.

Cross-cultural negotiation researcher Stephen Weiss (1994a, b) presents eight different culturally responsive strategies for cross-cultural negotiations. Each negotiator's familiarity with the counterpart's culture and the likelihood of explicitly coordinating the approaches determine the choice of strategy.

1. *Employ agent or advisor.*   When neither party is familiar with the other, a negotiator can hire an agent to represent him at the negotiation or an advisor to assist.
2. *Involve a mediator.*   This requires the two parties to agree on a third person to facilitate the negotiation and is also useful when neither party is familiar with the other's culture.
3. *Induce counterpart to follow one's own script.*   This is suitable if only the counterpart is familiar with the negotiator's culture and manner of negotiating. Then, the negotiator can try to induce the counterpart to follow the negotiator's approach.

4. *Adapt to the counterpart's script.* When each negotiator is moderately familiar with the other's culture, the negotiator can change some aspects of the usual negotiating approach to be more like the counterpart's.
5. *Coordinate adjustment of both parties.* Another strategy, appropriate when the two parties have moderate familiarity with each other's culture, is for the two to mutually coordinate how they will adjust to each other; in other words, they negotiate how they will negotiate.
6. *Embrace the counterpart's script.* One party can offer to completely follow the style of the other when only that party is very familiar with the other's culture.
7. *Improvise an approach.* When both parties are highly familiar with the counterpart's culture, they can improvise an approach, personalizing it and developing the approach as the negotiation unfolds.
8. *"Effect symphony."* This strategy, suitable when both negotiators have high familiarity with the other's culture, involves developing a synergistic approach in which the two parties cooperate to draw on the special capabilities of each negotiator.

In summary, there is an appropriate strategy whether the negotiators know very little about, or are entirely familiar with, the other party's culture and language.

Can someone totally adapt a negotiation strategy different from her own cultural style? Professional negotiators from Spain and Denmark received identical negotiation training from an American consulting firm specializing in communication and management (Grindsted 1994). The program goal was to train individuals to employ an appropriate negotiation style and to negotiate cooperatively. The training, administered in the home country and language of each group, was otherwise identical. Despite the same training, each group negotiated in culturally dissimilar ways. The Spanish group was more people-oriented compared to the Danish group who were more task-oriented. Although these two groups had the same training, their behavior continued to reflect their own cultures.

▮▮▮ Convergence or Divergence?

Forces for Convergence

As our knowledge and understanding of other cultures increase, some convergence in the approach to negotiation is likely to occur. For example, if two parties adopt the approach suggested by Weiss (1994a) and are explicit about how to handle their relative familiarity with the other's culture, this could provide a means for convergence. Also, if moderate adaptation proves to be more effective than complete or no adaptation, as in the study discussed previously (Francis 1991), cross-cultural negotiators may use more convergent approaches.

Forces for Divergence

People from various cultures retain a specific pattern of negotiation, even when trained in a different approach. Ingrained cultural patterns of behavior are difficult to change, and, even if people could totally match their behavior to that of another culture, the result may not be effective.

An additional source of divergence is the perception that a particular culture's negotiation style is more effective than that of other cultures'. If people from one culture believe that they are more effective negotiators, it is unlikely that they will change.

▪▪▪ Implications for Managers

Cross-cultural negotiations are an important part of the international manager's job, and understanding the dynamics of the negotiation process and the influence of culture can improve negotiating outcomes substantially. Although the evidence is not clear as to the differences between intra-cultural and cross-cultural negotiations, a moderate adaptation to the approach of the negotiating partner could be the most effective. The different strategies suggested by Weiss (1994a) are also helpful when considering which approach to take.

SUMMARY ▪▪▪▪▪▪▪

The basic negotiation process includes five steps: (1) preparation, (2) relationship building, (3) information exchange, (4) persuasion, and (5) agreement. Culture influences every step of this process as well as priorities, interests, strategies, situational factors, and negotiating tactics, both verbal and nonverbal. Location, room arrangements, choice of negotiators, and time limits can impact the final outcome for both parties. In comparing intra-cultural and cross-cultural negotiations, there is some evidence that people may behave differently depending on their negotiating partner. However, the nature of these differences is not clear.

High- and low-context cultures approach and manage conflict differently. Differences in conflict resolution style impact the approach to negotiation, but other cultural factors create differences between negotiators who are both from either a high- or low-context culture.

Increasing knowledge of your negotiating partner is a way to become a more effective cross-cultural negotiator. Learn as much as possible about the cultural background of both the people and the organization they represent. Also consider their approach to negotiation and specific concerns such as goals, needs, and interests. A moderate amount of adaptation to the other party's way of negotiating will probably lead to greater effectiveness. The two parties can also make their differences explicit and choose an appropriate means to negotiate based on each party's familiarity with the other's culture.

Negotiation approaches differ considerably because of culture. However, through greater understanding of these differences and by following suggestions for improving cross-cultural negotiations, there may be greater convergence in the future. Because international managers spend such a large amount of time negotiating, it is important to understand the negotiation process and how culture influences it.

DISCUSSION QUESTIONS ▪▪▪▪▪▪

1. Describe the steps in the negotiation process. For each step, give an example of how someone from your own culture might differ in comparison to someone from another culture.
2. How might cultural characteristics influence your choice of strategies in negotiation?
3. Situational factors and negotiating factors can have a strong impact on the ultimate outcome of a negotiation. How can you handle these to maximize your potential result?
4. Are you from a high-context or low-context culture? According to Ting-Toomey, how will this influence your approach to conflict? Do you agree or disagree? What are some characteristics of your culture that support your answer?
5. Identify another culture with which you have some familiarity. What differences would you expect to find between your approach and the other culture's approach to negotiation? Which differences are the most challenging? How would you attempt to handle these differences?
6. In negotiating with someone from another culture, which of the recommendations suggested do you think would be useful for you? Why? Can you think of other good advice to give those preparing for cross-cultural negotiations?

INTERNET SITES

Selected Company in the Chapter

Toys "R" Us (http://www1.toysrus.com/index.cfm?lb = 1)

Negotiation and Conflict Resolution Sites

Dispute Resolution Research Center, Northwestern University (http://www.kellogg.nwu.edu/research/drrc/index.htm). This site has information about the center's programs and research.

International Online Training Program on Intractable Conflict, Conflict Research Consortium, University of Colorado, Cultural Barriers to Effective Communication (http:// www. colorado. edu/conflict/peace/problem/cultrbar.htm). This site explains how culture and communication influence negotiation and provides links to examples of cross-cultural negotiation in different settings.

Interneg, Concordia University (Montreal), the University of Ottawa and Carleton University (Ottawa) (http://interneg.org/). This site has research and training material on negotiation including e-negotiation and negotiations in e-business.

United States Institute of Peace (http://www.usip.org/index.html). The Institute is an independent institution created by the U.S. Congress to promote the peaceful resolution of world conflicts. The site has information about their projects and educational resources.

REFERENCES

Adair, W. L., Okumura, T., and Brett, J. M. (2001). "Negotiation Behavior when Cultures Collide: The United States and Japan," *Journal of Applied Psychology*, 86, 371–85.

Adler, N. J. (1991). *International Dimensions of Organizational Behavior*. 2nd Ed. Boston: PWS-Kent.

—— and Graham, J. L. (1989). "Cross-Cultural Interaction: The International Comparison Fallacy?" *Journal of International Business Studies*, 20, 515–37.

Bond, M. H., Wan, K., Leung, K., and Giacalone, R. (1985). "How Are Responses to Verbal Insults Related to Cultural Collectivism and Power Distance?" *Journal of Cross-Cultural Psychology*, 16, 111–27.

Brett, J. M. (2000). "Culture and Negotiation," *International Journal of Psychology*, 35, 97–104.

——. (2001). *Negotiating Globally: How to Negotiate Deals, Resolve Disputes, and Make Decisions across Cultural Boundaries*. San Francisco: Jossey-Bass.

—— and Okumura, T. (1998). "Inter- and Intracultural Negotiation: U.S. and Japanese Negotiators," *Academy of Management Journal*, 41, 495–510.

Chen, M. (1995). *Asian Management Systems: Chinese, Japanese, and Korean Styles of Business*. New York: Routledge.

Chiu, R. K. and Kosinski, F. A. (1994). "Is Chinese Conflict-Handling Behavior Influenced by Chinese Values?" *Social Behavior and Personality*, 22, 81–90.

Deresky, H. (1994). *International Management: Managing Across Borders*. New York: HarperCollins.

Fisher, G. (1980). *International Negotiations: A Cross-Cultural Perspective*. Chicago: Intercultural Press.

Fisher, R. and Ury, W. (1981). *Getting to Yes: Negotiating Agreement without Giving In*. Boston: Houghton Mifflin.

Francis, J. N. P. (1991). "When in Rome? The Effects of Cultural Adaptation on Intercultural Business Negotiations," *Journal of International Business Studies*, 22, 403–28.

Gelfand, M. J. and Christakopoulou, S. (1999). "Culture and Negotiator Cognition: Judgment Accuracy and Negotiation Processes in Individualistic and Collectivistic Cultures," *Organizational Behavior and Human Decision Processes*, 79, 248–69.

—— and McCusker, C. (2002). "Metaphor and the Cultural Construction of Negotiation: A Paradigm for Research and Practice." In Gannon, M. J. and Newman, K. L. (eds.) *The Blackwell Handbook of Cross-Cultural Management*. Oxford: Blackwell.

—— and Realo, A. (1999). "Individualism-Collectivism and Accountability in Intergroup Negotiations," *Journal of Applied Psychology*, 84, 721–36.

Glenn, E. S., Witmeyer, D., and Stevenson, K. A. (1977). "Cultural Styles of Persuasion," *International Journal of Intercultural Relations*, 1, 52–66.

Goldman, A. (1992). "Intercultural Training of Japanese for U.S.-Japanese Interorganizational Communication," *International Journal of Intercultural Relations*, 16, 195–215.

Graham, J. L. (1985). "The Influence of Culture on the Process of Business Negotiations," *Journal of International Business Studies*, XVI, 81–96.

Grindsted, A. (1994). "The Impact of Cultural Styles on Negotiation: A Case Study of Spaniards and Danes," *IEEE Transactions on Professional Communication*, 37, 34–8.

Gudykunst, W. B. and Ting-Toomey, S. (1988). *Culture and Interpersonal Communication*. Newbury Park, CA: Sage.

Hall, E. T. (1976). *Beyond Culture*. New York: Doubleday.

Li, J. and Labig, C. E., Jr. (2001). "Negotiating with China: Exploratory Study of Relationship-Building," *Journal of Managerial Issues*, XIII, 345–59.

McNeil, D. G., Jr. (1996). "Restoring Their Good Names: U.S. Companies in Trademark Battles in South Africa," *The New York Times*, May 1, D1, D19.

Pettibone, P. J. (1990). "Negotiating a Joint Venture in the Soviet Union: How to Protect Your Interests," *Journal of Business Strategy*, November/December, 5–12.

Schwartz, S. H. (1992). "Universals in the Content and Structure of Values: Theoretical Advances and Empirical Tests in Two Countries." In Berkowitz, L. (ed.) *Advances in Experimental Social Psychology*. San Diego: Academic Press.

Shenkar, O. and Ronen, S. (1987). "The Cultural Context of Negotiations: The Implications of Chinese Interpersonal Norms," *The Journal of Applied Behavioral Science*, 23, 263–75.

Ting-Toomey, S. (1985). "Toward a Theory of Conflict and Culture." In Gudykunst, W., Stewart, L., and Ting-Toomey, S. (eds.) *Communication, Culture, and Organizational Processes*. Beverly Hills, CA: Sage.

Tinsley, C. H. and Pillutla, M. M. (1998). "Negotiating in the United States and Hong Kong," *Journal of International Business Studies*, 29, 711–28.

Tse, D. K., Francis, J., and Walls, J. (1994). "Cultural Differences in Conducting Intra-and Inter-Cultural Negotiations: A Sino-Canadian Comparison," *Journal of International Business Studies*, 25, 537–55.

Ury, W. (1993). *Getting Past No: Negotiating Your Way from Confrontation to Cooperation*. Rev. Ed. New York: Bantam.

Weiss, S. E. (1994a). "Negotiating with 'Romans' -Part 1," *Sloan Management Review*, Winter, 51–61.

——. (1994b), "Negotiating with 'Romans' -Part 2," *Sloan Management Review*, Spring, 85–99.

CHAPTER 6

Groups and Teams

Learning Objectives

After reading this chapter, you should be able to:

- Define groups and teams.
- Understand the elements of group structure.
- Know two models of group development.
- Discuss group processes including decision making and social loafing.
- Explain the differences between groups and teams.
- Appreciate the influences of differences in group and team composition on organizational behavior.
- Understand obstacles to effective work team functioning and ways to overcome them.
- Identify the characteristics of virtual teams.
- Know how groups function in different cultures.

CULTURE AT WORK

Are We Members?

Sally Barlow earned her MBA in 1999 and started working for the U.S. headquarters of a Japanese bank in New York City. She analyzed the financial statements of large international corporations for the commercial loan department. Sally's opinions greatly influenced the bank's decisions, which often involved loans of several hundred million dollars.

Sally's co-workers were Yoshi Kagami, a male Japanese analyst with the bank for five years in Japan and three years in the United States, and Sandra Marcus, an American MBA who had worked for the bank for almost three years. Although they never socialized after work, Sally and Sandra became friendly and often ate lunch together. Yoshi always ate with male Japanese employees.

One day at lunch, Sally told Sandra that she felt distrusted and regarded as a social inferior by her Japanese co-workers. "Sometimes I think even Yoshi looks at us that way," Sally said somewhat uncomfortably. Sandra responded, "Yes, I agree. In fact, I have a job interview at an American bank next week."

Source: B. A. Gold

Cultures view groups differently. For the Japanese, group orientation is an important part of national culture. In Japanese organizations participation in group decision making, *ringisei,* is a common practice. In the United States, which emphasizes individual achievement, corporations encourage participation in groups, but teamwork often conflicts with the ethic of individualism. In Israel, which has a socialist political tradition, cooperative work groups embody social ideals with the egalitarian ethic of the Kibbutz (Bar-Hayim and Berman 1991).

The cultural dimension of individualism-collectivism is important for explaining behavior in organizations, particularly the **roles** of individuals and groups (Hofstede 2001; Trompenaars and Hampden-Turner 1998). Individualism, a tendency for people to look primarily after their own interests rather than those of others, is characteristic of North American, Australian, and Western European societies. A collectivist value orientation, common in Asian, Eastern European, African, and Latin American cultures, emphasizes group welfare instead of individual self-interests. The orientation of the national culture—individualistic or collectivistic—affects the way groups function in organizations.

Understanding how groups and teams work is important because they are central to managing organizational behavior effectively. Groups and teams are part of all organizations and a primary tool for achieving an organization's goals. A central managerial task is to improve group and team performance.

▪▪▪ What Is a Group?

A **group** is "a plurality of individuals who are in contact with one another who take one another into account, and who are aware of some significant commonality" (Olmsted and Hare 1978, p. 11). Groups form as a result of mutual attraction or interests or because management assigns people to a group.

Group **size,** the number of individuals, is important because it influences communication and group dynamics. Groups range between two and approximately 20 members. Communication between two people in face-to-face contact is different from communication among 20 people which is more like a mass audience than a small group. Regarding group dynamics, while two people constitute a group, the addition of a third member creates opportunities for more complex interaction, for example, coalition formation.

Groups have common **goals** toward which their members work. Typically, groups work under conditions of a specific time frame and limited resources—for example, a two-week period and a budget for gathering and processing information to make a decision. Because of time constraints, resource scarcity, underdeveloped social skills, and other reasons, many groups are ineffective, and some fail to achieve their intended goals.

A **team,** which is a type of group, uses self-management techniques to achieve goals to which its members express high commitment. Teams and groups have a structure, a pattern of development, social processes, and decision-making styles that are affected to some extent by national and corporate cultures.

▪▪▪ Group Structure

Group structure creates patterns of interaction among members. Elements that compose structure are rules, norms, roles, and status. These are analytic concepts useful for understanding groups in all cultures. For example, all groups, regardless of cultural values, develop and maintain social norms. Similarly, most groups differentiate member status; typically, few members occupy high-status positions. Even groups designed to eliminate status eventually develop leadership positions.

Elements of Structure

Group structures form through administrative policies and rules or emerge during member interaction. Often, structure is a product of the interaction of management assignment and member preferences.

Rules and Norms

Rules specify expected behavior that the organization imposes on group members and can formally sanction disobedience. **Norms** differ from rules because they are informal, usually unstated, and taken for granted by group members. Norms are often more effective for regulating group behavior than rules because the group generates its own norms, often making administrative rules appear irrelevant. For example, a group can develop norms concerning punctuality that are different from the formal rules of the organization. A group could decide that punctuality is not important despite organizational rules that require it. However, the presence of group norms does not remove administrative constraints.

Roles

Roles are sets of norms that define behavior appropriate for and expected of various positions within a group. Every role in a group has a status. **Status** is the rank of the role in the hierarchy of the group. **Social power**—authority—is the ability to have others follow directives without question. There is a connection between status and social power. A person, who occupies a high-status position and performs the role in a way that the group approves, establishes power. It is possible, however, that inadequate role performance can fail to establish the voluntary approval that develops into support by a group. This decreases or eliminates the power of the role occupant and requires reestablishment of the legitimacy of the role.

Within an organization, group members often occupy multiple roles with different statuses. This creates **role conflict** because the demands of the various roles are incompatible. An example is conflict that managers experience between the roles of friend/colleague and supervisor/evaluator of subordinates.

Leaders and Followers

Two important roles are group leader and follower. Research on groups distinguishes between two types of leaders: task leaders and socioemotional leaders. The **task leader,** also labeled the *initiating leader,* focuses the group on goal achievement. Task leaders clarify goals, present information, ask other members for information, and evaluate the group's progress which is usually toward making a decision. In other words, the task leader's efforts aim directly toward specific outcomes.

The **socioemotional leader,** also known as the *relationship or maintenance leader,* focuses on the emotional and social aspects of a group. Socioemotional leaders encourage and praise others, resolve conflicts, and engage in behavior that facilitates the group's work. Overall, this leader role focuses on constructing and maintaining group cohesion.

The two leader roles are usually complementary in effective groups. Without a task leader, a work group risks evolving into a social club; the group focus becomes its members' sentiments and interpersonal relations instead of task achievement. Overemphasis on task leadership—when the leader makes important decisions without the participation of other members—results in members losing their sense of purpose. It is widely accepted that a balance between the two leadership styles is the most effective way to manage a group. However, it is likely that the emphasis on leadership type varies with national culture. For example, some cultures prefer autocratic leadership—an emphasis on task accomplishment and low participation in decision making—whereas others focus on group leaders as facilitators.

Followers, group members who do not have leadership roles, are important to understand. Although most research either ignores followers or assumes they support the leader and the group's goals, it is probable that the amount of subordinate participation and leader support varies with national and organizational culture. Hofstede's (2001) **power distance** variable suggests that national cultures low on power distance—those most likely to question the leader's actions—would be the least supportive followers, while cultures high on power distance would be the most supportive of a group leader's efforts.

Group roles often rotate among members. For example, the task leader role can shift when issues require a particular group member's expertise. However, in groups with cultures that prefer autocratic leadership, it is unlikely that a significant amount of leadership movement would occur. In groups that prefer democratic styles of leadership, the opportunities for various group members to occupy leadership roles is greater.

Similarly, members share or rotate the socioemotional leader role depending on the type of support behavior required. Autocratic group leadership reduces the visible function of the support leader role. This does not mean, however, that the leader fails to support the group, but instead acts alone to achieve what he perceives are its members' interests. Support roles increase in groups with democratic leadership and norms.

Formal and Informal Groups

Formal groups accomplish a particular goal or serve a specific purpose. In most instances, management appoints a leader, membership is mandatory, and rules govern behavior. This type of group reflects the idea that pooling resources for decision making is superior to individual effort.

Informal groups evolve naturally in organizations, often without the awareness or endorsement of management. People who work together in a functional area, across specializations, or as a result of frequent contact, form relationships based on similar experiences, common interests, and friendship. Informal groups vary in their contribution to an organization's goals. In some cases, informal groups contribute to goal achievement because their members cooperate on recognized tasks, for example, when they complete a committee assignment. In other cases, the group can undermine the achievement of official goals they view as invalid—for example, by collectively reducing production output. In either situation, the norms that develop are powerful, and informal groups exert significant social control over their members.

Informal subgroups often develop within a formal group and can exert considerable power. For example, they can form a voting block or, less overtly, influence a group's efforts by supporting its members for various roles. In addition, informal groups help their members make sense of the actions of management and protect member interests from what they perceive as unreasonable management demands.

A hypothesis is that culture contributes to managerial preferences for using either formal or informal groups. Cultures with high power distance are likely to use formal groups more than are cultures with low power distance. High power distance cultures often create barriers to informal group formation because the enforcement of rules and regulations prohibits interpersonal interaction. Low power distance cultures develop norms and have values that permit the development of informal groups but do not necessarily encourage their formation.

The situation is more complex in some cultures. High power distance collective societies, like China and Hong Kong, have many informal groups within organizations. Organizations achieve goals as a result of organization members belonging to powerful informal groups. In other words, despite the stated intention of formal decision-making groups, action often occurs through the use of *guanxi* or "connections."

Group Development: Two Models

The Five-Stage and Punctuated Equilibrium models of group development, like most research on groups, originated in the United States. Following a description of the two models, we discuss ways that cultural variations might influence them.

The Five-Stage Model

The **Five-Stage perspective** is the most well-known theory of group development. In this view, groups experience five distinct phases: forming, storming, norming, performing, and adjourning (Tuckman and Jensen 1977):

- *Forming.*   The initial phase of group development involves group members getting acquainted. This involves learning the traits, strengths, and behaviors of other members. Members also decide at this time whether participation in the group meets their needs. Finally, they also begin to identify group leadership.
- *Storming.*   After forming, the group confronts several important issues. First, the group has to establish its goals and priorities. The second issue involves structuring interaction among the members. A central concern is: Who will fulfill which roles?
- *Norming.*   During the norming stage, the group develops a set of rules and roles—implicitly or explicitly—that coordinate the group's activities and facilitate the accomplishment of its goals.
- *Performing.*   This stage is reached when the group understands its goals and roles and has developed rules that guide its performance. The group does most of its substantive work during this stage.
- *Adjourning.*   Once a group makes its decision, it often adjourns or disbands. Adjournment can occur because the allotted time for the group to make a decision expires, the issue the group was intended to address changed radically, the group failed to operate effectively or lost key members, or the group achieved its purpose and is no longer needed.

Groups often move back and forth between these stages as a result of conflict. With resolution of the conflict, sequential movement resumes. In other cases, an event such as a new member or a crisis can return the group to an earlier stage. Finally, the demarcation of stages is not clear or necessarily noticeable to group participants.

The Punctuated Equilibrium Model

Another theory of group development is the **Punctuated Equilibrium model** (Gersick 1988). Instead of a steady progression of stages, as in the Five-Stage model, the Punctuated Equilibrium model identifies two distinctly different modes of group functioning. In this model, the first meeting is important because it sets the climate for the group and establishes its leadership. An equilibrium period follows, characterized by routine group functioning. However, at the **midpoint** of the group's allotted time an abrupt change occurs. Recognition that the task has to be completed disrupts the equilibrium and creates a **revolutionary** change in the group's arrangements. The new arrangements shift, in effect, to a task orientation that results in project completion.

Research conducted in the United States supports this model of group development. However, a replication of Gersick's study, which is unusual in social science, found that as they develop, groups actually combine aspects of the Five-Stage and Punctuated Equilibrium models (Chang et al. 2003).

Culture and Group Development

Three variables that could affect these models in different cultures are power distance, individualism-collectivism, and orientation to time. For example, power distance can influence the level of participation in groups. In high power distance cultures there would be less follower participation than in low power distance cultures. This could reduce interaction between group leaders and followers and alter the developmental sequence by compressing the stages or eliminating the punctuation between periods of equilibrium and revolution because the leader has centralized power throughout the group's existence.

Individualism-collectivism affects group development because it influences the relationships among group members. An individualistic orientation encourages competition and conflict among members while the collectivistic orientation facilitates collaboration if members think of the group as an in-group. For example, in the Five-Stage model the storming stage would probably develop differently if group members willingly modify their opinions to conform to the group or aggressively defend individual positions. An extreme individualistic orientation could prevent a group from developing an effective work pattern and collectivists assigned to work with strangers are likely to be less cooperative.

If a culture views time as a scarce resource and sets rigorous deadlines, groups will probably develop differently than in cultures where time pressures are absent. For example, cultures less concerned with time may not set deadlines; the absence of time pressure could eliminate the midpoint and maintain equilibrium.

▪▪▪ Group Processes

A variety of social processes characterizes behavior in groups. Groups continuously experience some type of change as a result of member interaction. These processes sometimes transform group functioning as the Punctuated Equilibrium model suggests, or their cumulative effect could produce minor but meaningful changes.

Communication

Communication is central to groups because it is the major mechanism for achieving their goals. Culture affects **communication** in groups by shaping roles and statuses and the interactions among them. For example, culture influences group norms that govern who is permitted to talk, how much a member may talk, who may interrupt a conversation, and whether factual or emotional communication is viewed as persuasive. Communication in groups with low power distance differs from that in groups with high power distance values. Low power distance creates informal communication structures compared with formality in high power distance cultures. Finally, in high-context cultures, rules specify how members should communicate, which affects group interaction.

Group Culture

A group develops its own culture (Trice and Beyer 1993). The basis for **group culture** can be membership in a formal or informal group—for example, an occupation, union membership, ethnic or religious background, or membership in a department that provides common experiences. The distinctive cultures of groups form **subcultures** within organizations. Group culture and subcultures form and maintain themselves through shared symbols, ceremonies, rituals, and values. These become means for establishing a group's identity that differentiates it from other groups.

Strong group culture can affect groups in two ways: First, it can produce a highly cohesive group that works well together, either to achieve organizational goals or to establish goals that regulate the group output below the level expected by management (Mayo 1945), and second, strong group culture can result in conflict between groups over organizational resources such as personnel, technology, and finances. Some level of intergroup conflict is typical in organizations and can be a source of innovation; the absence of conflict among groups is often an indication that work groups have low levels of cohesiveness and competitiveness and are indifferent to organizational goals.

The culture of groups can change. New leadership, innovative technology, organization restructuring, and task reassignment can produce interpersonal tensions that change group culture. For example, the introduction of new technology challenges group member expertise producing changes in member status. New group norms and culture develop to realign group members with the new technology (Barley 1986).

Decision Making

A key function of groups is making decisions. **Group decisions** are useful for technical and organizational reasons. From a technical perspective, groups pool the skills, talents, and experiences of many people instead of relying on one decision maker. From an organizational perspective, group decision making—the active participation of many people—increases the likelihood of decision implementation.

Individual Versus Group Decision Making

Groups do not make all decisions because in many situations in organizations, individual managers or other employees make decisions by themselves. They then inform group members of the decision and expect them to implement it.

National and organizational cultures vary in the amount of decision making participation that organization members prefer and expect. In cultures with high power distance, that is, low expectations for influencing decision making, individual managerial decisions are acceptable; subordinates expect to "take orders" and implement them without question. However, in low power distance cultures that value the opinions of individuals, managers who continuously make decisions without consulting their subordinates frequently encounter resistance because group members think they should influence all phases of management, including decision making, instead of being restricted to implementation. An example is **codetermination** in Germany where worker representatives hold decision-making roles on corporate boards. Codetermination has permitted German industry to adjust effectively and peacefully to economic change (Thelen 1987).

But not all group decision making works as intended. Some group processes that appear desirable actually create conditions that result in misguided actions.

Groupthink

Groupthink is a group decision-making process that occurs when members of a highly cohesive group are unable to evaluate each other's inputs critically (Janis 1982).

Groupthink often results in less than optimal decisions, including decisions that lead to disasters. According to Janis (1982) symptoms of groupthink are as follows.

- *Illusions of invulnerability:* Members of the group overemphasize the strength of the group and feel that they are beyond criticism or attack. This symptom leads the group to approve risky actions about which individual members might have serious concerns.
- *Illusions of unanimity:* Group members accept consensus prematurely, without testing whether or not all members *truly* agree. Silence becomes mistaken for agreement.
- *Illusions of group morality:* Members of the group feel that the group is "right" and above reproach by outside critics. Thus, members feel no need to debate ethical issues.
- *Stereotyping of the "enemy" as weak, evil, or stupid:* Members do not realistically examine their competitors and oversimplify their motives. The stated aims of outside groups or anticipated reactions of outsiders are not considered.
- *Self-censorship by members:* Members refuse to communicate concerns to others because of fear of disturbing the consensus.
- *Mind-guarding:* Some members take responsibility to ensure that negative feedback does not reach influential group members.
- *Direct pressure:* In the unlikely event that a note of caution or concern is interjected, other members quickly respond with pressure to bring the deviant back into line.

Groupthink might be more prevalent in Southeast Asia than in other cultures (Leung 1992). Collectivistic-oriented cultures place group interests ahead of individual interests, and the influence of leaders on groups is stronger than in the West, as is obedience to hierarchical authority. As a result, it is difficult for individuals to express opposing views, and they eagerly conform to group standards. From the Asian point of view, this is not necessarily an undesirable process. However, in individualistic societies—as the original research demonstrated—groupthink is detrimental to group functioning and labeled as an organizational pathology.

Finally, "multicultural [groups and] teams find themselves less susceptible to groupthink because they are less likely to subconsciously limit their perspectives, ideas, conclusions, and decisions to that of the majority or team leadership" (Adler 1997, p. 137).

Participation and Social Loafing

Another important issue is member involvement in groups. Studies of social loafing—which originated in the United States—are one way to understand the effect of culture on group involvement. Social loafing "occurs when individuals decrease the amount of effort they put into a task—loaf—while doing that task with other people" (Northcraft and Neale 1994, p. 302; see Latane, Williams, and Harkins 1979).

Research has compared the effect of collectivistic and individualistic orientations on the presence and extent of social loafing (Earley 1989, 1993; Gabrenya, Latane, and Wang 1983). One study hypothesized that the composition of the group that a manager was in would affect the manager's level of participation (Earley 1993). If managers with collectivistic orientations worked in groups that shared their orientations, they would feel more efficacious—able to work well—alone and as a group member, than if they worked in a group with an individualist orientation. Managers with individualistic orientations "will anticipate more rewards and feel more efficacious, and thus perform better, while working alone than while working in an ingroup [people with the same values] or an outgroup [people with different values] context" (Earley 1993, pp. 324–325). In other words, in addition to an individual's cultural orientation, the value orientation of the work group they are part of effects social loafing.

This study collected data in the United States, a highly individualistic culture, the collectivistic People's Republic of China, and Israel, which also has a collectivistic value system. The results indicated that people's orientation toward individualism or collectivism was more important than the culture of the country they were from. The findings are that "collectivists have lower performance working alone or in an out-group than they do working in an in group" (Earley 1993, p. 341) and only work hard when they work in an in-group. The performance of individualists who thought they were working in an in-group or an out-group was lower than the performance of individualists working alone. In summary, social loafing applies to individualists who work in any type of group but only to collectivists who work in an out-group.

▪▪▪ Teams

Teams meet the needs of new types of organizations that require creativity, flexibility, and high levels of performance. Teams are similar to groups because they experience developmental stages, differentiate into roles, create norms, establish a culture, and have a communication structure.

How Teams Differ From Groups

Technically, a **team** is different from a group because it consists of "a small number of people with complementary skills who are committed to a common purpose, set of performance goals, and approach for which they hold themselves mutually accountable" (Katzenbach and Smith 1993, p. 112). Teams have more cohesiveness, more responsibility, and use member talents more effectively than do other groups. Weiss (1996, pp. 142–143) notes these specific differences:

- *Shared Leadership.*   Teams have shared leadership roles, whereas groups usually have a strong, focused leader.
- *Accountability.*   Teams have individual and mutual accountability, whereas groups are based mostly on individual accountability.
- *Purpose.*   Teams work toward a specific purpose, whereas a group's purpose is usually identical to the organization's mission.
- *Work Products.*   Teams deliver collective work products, whereas groups have individual work products.
- *Communication.*   Teams encourage open-ended discussion and active problem-solving meetings, whereas groups attempt to run meetings that are efficient.
- *Effectiveness.*   Teams measure performance by direct assessment of their collective work products, whereas groups measure effectiveness indirectly by their influence on others.
- *Work Style.*   Teams discuss, decide, and delegate but do the work together, whereas groups discuss, delegate and then do the work individually.

In addition to the differences between teams and groups, there are also issues concerning the function of teams in organizations and their composition. For example, teams can operate at various levels within an organization including the executive, middle management, and operations levels. An example of an operations level team is a total quality team whose approach to quality emphasizes continuous improvement instead of traditional bureaucratic post-production inspection.

▮▮▮ Group and Team Composition

The composition of groups and teams within organizations depends on the diversity of the national population. Multinational corporations are an important exception, however, because they consist of employees from countries with many different types of populations.

Types of Groups

Homogeneous cultures such as Japan and South Korea have little concern with group diversity. In Germany, where there is increasing **heterogeneity** in the workforce, diversity is becoming an issue because guest workers increasingly displace native workers. The United States has a heterogeneous population that will become more diverse in the future creating more demand for multicultural work groups.

In the global business environment, the types of groups are homogeneous groups, token groups, bicultural groups, and multicultural groups (Adler 2002, p. 139). A **homogeneous group** contains members who have similar backgrounds and generally understand events and the world more similarly than other types. A **token group** consists of members with the same background with the exception of one member who is different in some significant way. The token member probably interprets things differently from the other group members. **Bicultural groups** are those in which "two or more members represent each of two distinct cultures; for example, a fifty-fifty partnership between Peruvians and Bolivians, or a task force composed of Saudi Arabians and Jordanians, or a committee with seven Spanish and three Portuguese executives" (Adler 2002, p. 140). Finally, **multicultural groups** have members of three or more ethnic backgrounds—for example, a United Nations agency composed of representatives of as many as 15 to 20 cultures.

The composition of teams and groups—regardless of level within an organization—can range from monocultural to multicultural (Cox 1991). The managerial argument for using multicultural teams is that they are more innovative than monocultural teams because they incorporate diverse viewpoints into decision making (see Table 6-1). Also, because they reflect the composition of a society, rather than the preferences of a single group or a minority elite, they are more effective at understanding the needs and desires of customers. Finally, multicultural teams advance the social responsibility of firms by creating equal opportunity for all social groups.

However, there are also disadvantages to diversity in groups and teams within organizations (see Table 6-1). As noted previously, one possible advantage of diversity is that people with different value systems bring novel perspectives to a group, fostering creative problem solving. At the same time, however, the disadvantage is that group members may not trust each other and therefore fail to collaborate fully. Further, distrust may result in poor communication across subgroups that compose the group and create conflict or disorganization.

Research on Group Diversity

Research on diversity in organizations distinguishes between variables that are direct **observable attributes** of diversity—such as race, ethnic background, age, and gender—and less visible, or **underlying attributes,** such as education, technical abilities, functional background, tenure in the organization, socioeconomic background, personality characteristics, and values (Milliken and Martin 1996).

TABLE 6-1 Advantages and Disadvantages of Group Diversity

Advantages	Disadvantages
Diversity Permits Increased Creativity	***Diversity Causes Lack of Cohesion***
Wide range of perspectives	**Mistrust**
More and better ideas	Lower interpersonal attractiveness
Less groupthink	Inaccurate stereotyping
	More within-culture conversations
Diversity Forces Enhanced Concentration to Understand Others'	**Miscommunication**
Ideas	Slower speech: Nonnative speakers
Perspectives	and translation problems
Meanings	Less accuracy
Arguments	
	Stress
	More counterproductive behavior
	Less disagreement on content
	Tension
Increased Creativity Can Lead to Generating	***Lack of Cohesion Causes Inability to***
Better problem definitions	Validate ideas and people
More alternatives	Agree when agreement is needed
Better solutions	Gain consensus on decisions
Better decisions	Take concerted action
Teams Can Become	***Groups Can Become***
More effective	Less efficient
More productive	Less effective
	Less productive

Source: Adler, N. J. (2002). *International Dimensions of Organizational Behavior.* 3rd Ed. Cincinnati, OH: South-Western, p. 143. Reprinted with permission of South-Western, a division of Thomson Learning: www.thomsonrights.com.

The results of research on observable attributes—conducted mainly in the United States—are fairly consistent:

> In general, the more diverse a group is with respect to gender, race, or age, the higher its turnover rate (people leaving the group) and the more likely it is that dissimilar individuals will turn over and be absent . . .. Diversity may lead to discomfort for all members of a group, leading to lower integration within the group and a higher likelihood of turnover. There is also some evidence of negative affective reactions to observable differences on the part of supervisors—in that supervisors tend to perceive dissimilar subordinates less positively and tend to give them lower performance ratings. (Milliken and Martin 1996, p. 408)

Several studies suggest that diverse groups generate more alternatives in decision making and cooperation within the group. Research also finds that these benefits occur only when a diverse group has been intact for a period of time. However, member turnover may occur before groups reach a stage that takes advantage of diversity.

Research on groups composed of diverse nationalities in the Netherlands similarly found that individuals not of the majority nationality were less satisfied with their jobs than majority members (Verkuyten, de Jong, and Masson 1993). In a study conducted in Australia (Bochner and Hesketh 1994), minority members perceived more discrimination in the workplace but valued cultural diversity more highly than majority members.

Research on underlying attributes differs from studies of observable attributes because it usually focuses on top management teams rather than on lower-level participants. The research findings are as follows:

> Diversity along skill- or knowledge-based dimensions seems to have some positive cognitive outcomes for top management groups and project teams. One reason may be that diversity along these skill-based dimensions translates into a greater variety of perspectives being brought to bear on decisions and, thereby, increases the likelihood of creative and innovative solutions to problems. Also, problems such as those that a top management group deals with often require information input from a variety of functional areas within the organization. (Milliken and Martins 1996, p. 412)

There are also difficulties integrating diverse members into management groups, similar to those of lower-level groups, including the possibility of minority member turnover. Next, we examine the problems and prospects of teams in a single culture, transnational and global work teams, and virtual teams.

▪ ▪ ▪ Teams at Work

The Problems of Creating Single Culture Teams

Beginning in the 1960s and accelerating in the 1980s and 1990s, the use of work teams in the United States focused on quality circles as part of the Total Quality Management movement (Kirkman et al. 2002). Although many large companies have used teams and, according to their own accounts, have experienced success with them, few studies have documented and explained the actual processes by which traditional hierarchically arranged and coordinated work practices transform into team-based workplaces.

A recent study compared four paper mills in the United States where managers tried for ten years to create nontraditional work systems including self-directed teams and high-performance work systems (Vallas 2003). The objectives for creating work teams were for workers to assume responsibilities previously assigned to supervisors and for teams to create continuous improvement in the workplace.

Although there were a few cases of successful implementation, the attempt to change to work teams did not succeed. While management wanted to change the organization, and tried to take actions to create change, it failed to modify its traditional behavior and values to create a new organizational environment with "an overarching normative or moral framework within which workplace change might unfold" (Vallas 2003, p. 223). Instead, the persistence of an emphasis on scientific and technical rationality produced an anomic organizational culture—a lack of clear norms and values—that ultimately reinforced status distinctions between managers and workers and undermined attempts to create teams.

Another perspective on the failure to create change in the paper mills is that the inability of management to provide the normative climate for teams to develop was because management valued individual action, responsibility, and accountability. In addition, an obstacle to change is that the individualism of U.S. workers is difficult to transform into working in teams. Extensive reconstruction of the value system of the entire workplace would have to occur for teams to be successful, particularly because the intention was to replace traditional managerial activities and labor relations with self-managing teams.

Transnational Teams

Until recently, researchers paid little attention to the environment in which teams worked. The assumption was that the environment—including organizational and national cultures—either did not affect team performance or that environmental effects were obvious and did not require systematic study. With the use of cross-cultural teams and increasing transnational business, however, the environment has become a major variable for understanding and managing teams.

To understand multinational work teams, an important reconceptualization is that "a team is influenced by individual and team characteristics that lead to particular actions (and reactions) within a given social and work context" (Earley and Gibson 2002, p. 76). Even with this shift in emphasis, in many important ways, the characteristics of multinational work teams are similar to work teams composed of members of one culture. For example, as with single culture teams, multinational teams experience issues of individual identity, trust, expectations, respect and moral character, affect, confidence, and efficacy as well as social awareness. However, "the unique aspect of a multinational team not found in other types of work groups is that many of the underlying features of interpersonal interaction are not shared among group members" (Earley and Gibson 2002, p. 76). As a result, what would be commonly accepted and similarly understood behavior within a single culture becomes problematic to the extent that "even simple and preliminary forms of exchange require new thinking on the part of team members" (Earley and Gibson 2002, p. 76).

A reasonable expectation is that lack of common characteristics in a multinational work team could create significant obstacles for team development and goal attainment. But contrary to expectations, research on multinational work teams suggests that instead of hindering team functioning, the absence of a shared culture can

> provide a strong basis for initial interactions of sense-making and social construction that will provide a team with a basis for moving forward. That is, the weakness of not understanding is a potential strength if such a lack provides an excuse for a multinational work team to develop its own new and unique team culture. (Earley and Gibson 2002, pp. 76–77)

From this perspective, a new member, a situation that often creates problems for monocultural work teams, presents an opportunity to a multinational, multicultural team. The new member brings a potentially entirely new "'culture,' or style of acting, that is not understood by the existing members of the team" (Earley and Gibson 2002, p. 64). This requires reconstructing the social world of the team which can result in creative decision making and innovative solutions for previously intractable problems.

Field studies of multinational work teams support this perspective. The presence of multiple cultures, which at first appears to be a problem for team functioning, is actually a resource that group members have to examine and understand carefully. This process contributes to the team's development and by using the talents of members more effectively, enhances the group's goal attainment (Earley and Gibson 2002).

Managing Global Business Teams

There is evidence, however, that the creation of successful transnational and global teams is more complex than adjusting to or benefitting from the cultural diversity of the team members. A study of 70 global teams found that only 18% considered their performance "highly successful." The other 82% responded that they fell short of their intended goals and one-third of these teams rated their performance as largely unsuccessful (Govindarajan and Gupta 2001).

Obstacles to high performance in these global teams were similar to those found in domestic teams including misalignment of individual team members' goals, low levels of necessary knowledge and skills, and lack of clear team objectives. Of course, the global teams faced additional difficulties because of their inherent nature including members' differences in geography, language, and culture. Another important barrier attributable to the composition of global teams was a low level of trust among team members. Fortunately, managers can take several steps to reduce these barriers, the most basic of which are to "carefully craft the team's charter, composition and process" (Govindarajan and Gupta 2001, p. 65).

The global team's charter—its intended mission as specified by management—should be a clear agenda but is typically not discussed explicitly which often creates immediate problems for the team that frequently result in its demise. In addition to providing other benefits, a common understanding of the team's purpose avoids destructive conflict among its members.

Three important issues for selecting members are the balance of diversity, the size, and the leadership of the team. The extent of diversity is important because members come from diverse cultural and national backgrounds and often represent subsidiaries with different agendas as well as different functional units with different priorities and perspectives. Creating the correct amount of diversity also depends on whether the diversity is cognitive or behavioral. **Cognitive diversity** is "the differences in the substantive content of how members perceive the team's challenges and opportunities, options to be evaluated and optimal course of action" (Govindarajan and Gupta 2001, p. 67). An example is if the free Internet service model pioneered in the United Kingdom can transfer to countries that expect users to purchase Internet services. **Behavioral diversity** is the group members' "differences in language as well as culture-driven norms of behavior" (Govindarajan and Gupta 2001, p. 67). An example is the difficulty in communication created by different cultural norms, for example, how a group member decides to represent the group to outsiders.

The ideal team size is "one that can ensure the required knowledge and skill base with the smallest number of people" (Govindarajan and Gupta 2001, p. 67). A team that is too small is likely to lack necessary skills, but one that is too large often becomes dysfunctional. A solution is to create a core team and supplement it as needed with specific skills.

The final issue for team composition is leadership selection which, in addition, involves selecting an external coach and an internal sponsor. The primary consideration for selecting effective leaders is their ability to manage the organizational, linguistic, cultural, and the physical distances "that separate members, impede the development of trust and contribute to the misalignment of members' goals" (Govindarajan and Gupta 2001, p. 67). An external coach provides group process expertise and is particularly needed when the team experiences complex and challenging process issues, for example, conflict. Finally, a team sponsor "is typically a senior-level executive in the company who has a strong interest in the success of the team" (Govindarajan and Gupta 2001, p. 68).

An equally important aspect of creating an effective global business team is managing team process to enable team members to trust each other and communicate openly (Govindarajan and Gupta 2001, p. 68). In addition to finding ways to overcome language and culture barriers—for example, by company-sponsored training programs—a key issue is the establishment of norms, a focus on data-driven decisions, and the development of alternative solutions. Effective team process also contributes to the creation of trust and, as a result, to effective team functioning. Techniques for using process to create trust include face-to-face meetings, rotating and diffusing team leadership, linking rewards to team performance, and building social capital (Govindarajan and Gupta 2001).

Virtual Teams

The widespread use of technology and increasing globalization of corporations have created the opportunity and need for **virtual teams** which are "groups of geographically and/or organizationally dispersed coworkers that are assembled using a combination of telecommunications and information technologies to accomplish an organizational task" (Townsend, De Marie, and Hendrickson 1998, p. 7). Virtual teams provide benefits to organizations such as permitting access to the most qualified individuals for a particular job wherever they are located, enabling organizations to respond faster to competition, and creating flexibility for employees who can work at home. It is important to understand the characteristics of virtual teams and what distinguishes them from conventional teams, the types of virtual teams, and techniques to manage them successfully.

Virtual Team Characteristics

The composition and characteristics of virtual teams vary significantly. A virtual team could be composed of members from one culture and one country and be located in a relatively small geographic area. A radically different type of virtual team could have members from entirely different cultures that represent different countries and operate on a global scale. Of course, variations of these extreme types exist and the purpose of the team usually determines its composition.

Virtual teams are different than conventional teams because instead of team members being in face-to-face proximity, the members of a virtual team are usually separated by space, ranging from a short distance to the outer limits of cyberspace. Another important difference of virtual teams is that members are connected and communicate through technology such as e-mail, telephone, fax, videoconferencing, groupware, and project management software.

Types of Virtual Teams

Factors that form different types of virtual teams are temporal distribution, boundary spanning, life cycle, and member roles (Bell and Kozlowski 2002). **Temporal distribution** is the ability of virtual teams to cross the boundaries of time. Team members working in **distributed time** work on their own schedules—for example, a team with members in Los Angeles, Seoul, and Antwerp can work around the clock without the immediate participation of the other members. Working in **real-time** requires all members to interact simultaneously. In practice, the choice of "distributed or real time is dictated by the complexity of the tasks the team performs and the resulting workflow arrangements" (Bell and Kozlowski 2002, p. 24). In other words, the more interdependent the elements of a task, the more important it is for people to work on the task at the same time.

Boundary spanning means that virtual teams can also cross functional, organizational, and cultural boundaries. This flexibility enables virtual teams to access expert resources within and outside the organization, including consultants and even competitors. For example, people from different cultures can join a team fairly easily because, despite the differences in culture, they possess skills required for task completion. However, combining people with diverse languages, traditions, and cultural values makes working in and managing multicultural virtual teams difficult.

The **life cycle** of virtual teams varies. Because virtual teams exist to solve a particular problem, they usually disband after the task is completed, which creates fluid membership. When a task is comparatively easy "the need to develop cohesion and collaboration among team members is minimal and the degree of familiarity among team members is often not critical" (Bell and Kozlowski 2002, p. 28). Complex tasks require more cohesion among the group and usually a longer life cycle.

The final factor is **member roles,** which because of the flexibility of virtual teams, means that members usually experience multiple roles. The need to work quickly creates pressures for members to perform multiple tasks and hold various roles. Typically, the number of roles each member occupies varies with task complexity, with less complex tasks permitting more interchangeable roles because the skills required are not specialized.

Managing Virtual Teams

One implication of the differences from conventional groups is that virtual teams impede the traditional leadership functions of performance management and team development (Bell and Kozlowski 2002). Monitoring, coaching, mentoring, and other typical leadership functions require face-to-face interaction that is not part of virtual teams. Instead, a virtual team leader substitutes traditional management techniques by selecting members of virtual teams for their technical skills and prior virtual team experience, by providing clear direction and specific individual goals, and by establishing routines for the team. In addition, because of spatial dispersion, leaders have to monitor the environment to help the team make appropriate adjustments, for example, to new goals, or a new deadline. Finally, team leaders have to motivate team members to sustain their commitment to the team (Bell and Kozlowski 2002). Although leadership is required for virtual teams, the ideal is to create a self-managing team by distributing leadership functions to team members.

Virtual Teams and International Organizational Behavior

From the perspective of international organizational behavior, the more complex the task, the more spatially and temporally distributed, and the more culturally diverse the members, the more difficult it is to manage a virtual team. Cultural diversity, which will be increasingly common, adds to the complexity of managing virtual teams because different values, customs, and traditions require more leadership under conditions that reduce the ability to use direct leadership.

Finally, research on how virtual teams actually work indicates that they are as effective as conventional teams that experience face-to-face interaction. A study of a World Wide Web asynchronous computer conference system found that teams using sophisticated technology but geographically distributed—with most other conditions held constant—performed about the same as face-to-face teams. The only major difference was that though the two teams had similar levels of communication effectiveness, members of the face-to-face team had higher levels of satisfaction (Warkentin, Sayeed, and Hightower 1997). An important implication of virtual teams—particularly considering their effectiveness—is that they have the potential to fundamentally change what an organization is and consequently the management of organizations.

▮▮▮ Convergence or Divergence?

Forces for Convergence

An important trend over the past 20 years is that societies that have traditionally emphasized individualism are borrowing collectivistic, group-oriented management techniques, primarily from Japan. In the United States, for example, there is an emphasis on using groups for continuous improvement programs and in promoting autonomous work groups. However, not all organizations implement teams effectively. Nevertheless, one argument is that highly effective organizations in the United States blend individual and group orientations (Ouchi 1981).

Traditional collectivistic societies—for example, China—have become more individualistic by selectively introducing capitalist principles such as markets and profit. Although it is unlikely that selective borrowing between the East and West will produce a seamless blend, as complex cultural, political, social, and economic changes unfold, the result could be creative mixtures of individualism and collectivism.

Forces for Divergence

Creating effective multicultural teams requires more than combining people from different cultures in a group and expecting them to develop collaborative work styles by themselves. A force for divergence is that tensions among cultures may continue despite attempts to constructively manage them.

Another issue is that in organizations in heterogeneous societies, the perception may be that the use of multicultural teams is a threat to dominant groups. Because of reluctance to redistribute power, it may be difficult to move beyond tokenism and minimum compliance with legal requirements to the creative use of diverse teams. Of course, for similar reasons, homogeneous societies with autocratic leadership have no reason to use teams of any type.

▮▮▮ Implications for Managers

As new types of organizations emerge, groups and teams will become more important, particularly in organizations that operate in different cultures. Because of this, managers should become skilled at diagnosing, managing, and maintaining group performance.

Managing Groups

There are differences in managing monocultural and culturally diverse groups and teams. However, as groups and teams become more diverse, managers should avoid permitting nonfunctional performance criteria—such as religion or ethnic identity—to replace traits, skills, and talents that are important for a position. In other words, the objectives and goals of the organization should take precedence over, but not ignore, issues that affect the multicultural features of the work force (Adler 1997). To accomplish this, managers should emphasize a clear vision or superordinate goal, in an attempt to form a cohesive group. Without a clear, strong goal, the diversity of the group or team will produce multiple goals and evolve into competing subgroups.

Managers should attempt to create equal power among the members of a diverse group. If one subgroup gains more power through cultural dominance, the results could be nonparticipation by other members and destructive conflict. One way to manage this is to distribute authority according to ability to accomplish a task, rather than nonperformance-related criteria.

It is also important to avoid ethnocentrism—the assumption that one's own culture is superior to other cultures. Viewing one culture, particularly the manager's, as superior to other cultures, reduces the benefits of multicultural interaction. Group members should establish mutual respect for one another's cultures and recognize contributions of individuals based on expertise. Finally, because of group diversity, a manager has to provide more opportunities for feedback. According to Adler (1991, p. 141):

> Given the different perspectives present, culturally diverse teams have more trouble than homogeneous teams in collectively agreeing on what constitutes a good or bad idea or decision. . . . External feedback helps the group see itself as a team and serves the function of teaching the team to value its diversity, recognize the contributions made by each member, and trust its collective judgment.

In summary, it is important for managers to recognize the limits their own culture imposes for understanding the nature of groups in other cultures. Two important implications are that managers must learn how to diagnose group behavior that occurs in another culture and find ways to manage a group without unintentionally creating conditions that cause the group to develop norms that produce behavior contrary to the manager's intended results.

These implications for managers reflect the North American cultural preference for the rational, universalistic use of human resources to achieve organizational goals. Of course, there are other ways to use human resources that are valid from other cultural perspectives. For example, a manager could decide that only his blood relatives should make decisions because he distrusts nonkin experts. In a variety of cultures, a manager might believe that groups should not make decisions because they threaten her power; it is preferable to accumulate and maintain power even if the decisions are inferior.

The Future of Groups and Teams

One view of the role of groups and teams in the global context is that they are beginning to replace conventional organization structures and eventually will be the dominant form of organization. Instead of corporations and other types of hierarchies rooted in specific geographic locations, loosely knit, flexible groups and teams have an important place in capital intensive, high value-added, high technology companies that will probably increase (Reich 1991). These groups work on projects that require ideas, financing, and new combinations of people for specific short-term purposes. After project completion, the group disbands and its members re-form into new teams. However, this view may be too optimistic concerning the proliferation of teams because, as noted previously, single nation, multinational, and multicultural teams are not that easy to establish and manage. In addition, not all organizations require teams to attain their goals.

Finally, the use of teams will probably increase in cross-cultural negotiations. As issues facing organizations become more complex, teams of negotiators will be necessary because they can combine a variety of skills, exercise independent judgment, and self-manage. It is likely that these teams will be multicultural and serve as coordinating mechanisms for negotiating cultural and technical issues.

SUMMARY ▫▪▪▪▪▪▪

Groups and teams are an important part of organizations. Whether the values of a culture are individualistic or collectivistic affects the role of teams in organizations. Groups have different functions in collectivistic cultures than they do in individualistic cultures. For example, in Japan and Israel, groups are more important than individuals, but in the United States, individuals are more important than groups. Another important variable is the composition of groups and teams which can be either homogenous or heterogeneous, thereby creating different interaction patterns among members.

Managers need to understand how to diagnose groups and teams to be able to manage and improve their performance. Key elements of group structure are rules, norms, roles, and statuses. A central role in groups and teams is that of the leader who usually assumes either a task or socioemotional emphasis. The roles of followers are also important in groups.

Groups develop over time following either a rational linear progression or a Punctuated Equilibrium model of two distinct and almost unrelated phases. Another aspect of groups and teams is the processes that occur in them, including communication, culture formation, social loafing, and decision making. Some cultures view groupthink, a complex social process that affects decision making, as a pathology but other cultures consider it desirable.

Teams differ from groups because they share leadership, have more acceptance of goals, and are more accountable for their actions. An important issue is the composition of teams and groups and whether membership diversity is beneficial for performance. As globalization increases, it is likely that groups will become more multicultural.

In addition to becoming multicultural, groups and teams are frequently multinational, that is, they work with members located in different parts of the world. Virtual teams, which are usually but not necessarily geographically dispersed, may also include members from different cultures. Finally, managers have to understand the implications of the power of virtual teams to transform international organizational behavior and management.

DISCUSSION QUESTIONS ▪ ▪ ▪ ▪ ▪ ▪ ▪

1. What are the characteristics of a group?
2. How does the concept of individualism-collectivism contribute to understanding the way that culture affects the use of groups and teams?
3. Discuss the meaning of roles and status in groups. How are status and power related?
4. What is an informal group? Why is it important for managers to understand informal groups?
5. From your participation in groups, which model of group development—the Five-Stage perspective or the Punctuated Equilibrium model—explains the way that groups evolve over time in your country?
6. What are some techniques that can reduce the likelihood of a decision-making group experiencing groupthink?
7. How do groups differ from teams?
8. In your view, do the advantages outweigh the disadvantages of member diversity in groups and teams?
9. Examine the view that small groups of highly talented people acting as temporary systems will replace current pyramidal organizational structures. How probable is this scenario?
10. As the leader of a multicultural group, what actions could you take when the group forms to improve its long-term performance?
11. Do you think you could work in a virtual team? If yes, what aspects of a virtual team are most appealing to you?

INTERNET SITES ▪ ▪ ▪ ▪ ▪ ▪ ▪

Group and Team Sites

Group Dynamics (http://www.mapnp.org/library/grp_skll/theory/theory.htm). An introduction to topics in group dynamics, this Web page provides links to other sites with theoretical insights and practical advice for understanding and managing groups.

Total Quality Management (http://www.gslis.utexas.edu/~rpollock/tqm.html). This site contains links to sites that discuss various aspects of total quality management including the change processes required to increase organizational teamwork to improve product quality.

Virtual Teams (http://www.startwright.com/virtual.htm). This Web site contains numerous links to sites that present information on various topics about virtual teams including the MIT Center for Coordination Science and the Center for Virtual Organization and Commerce at Louisiana State University.

REFERENCES ▮▮▮▮▮▮▮

Adler, N. J. (2002). *International Dimensions of Organizational Behavior*. 4th Ed. Cincinnati, OH: South-Western.

Bar-Hayim, A. and Berman, G. (1991). "Ideology, Solidarity, and Work Values: The Case of the Histadrut Enterprises," *Human Relations*, 44(4), 357–70.

Barley, S. R. (1986). "Technology as an Occasion for Structuring: Evidence from Observations of CT Scanners and the Social Order of Radiology Departments," *Administrative Science Quarterly*, 78–108.

Bell, B. S. and Kozlowski, S. W. J. (2002). "A Typology of Virtual Teams: Implications for Effective Leadership," *Group & Organization Management*, 21(1), 14–49.

Bochner, S. and Hesketh., B. (1994). "Power Distance, Individualism/Collectivism, and Job-Related Attitudes in a Culturally Diverse Work Group," *Journal of Cross-Cultural Psychology*, 25, 233–257.

Chang, A., Bordia, P., and Duck, J. (2003). "Punctuated Equilibrium and Linear Progression: Toward a New Understanding of Group Development," *Academy of Management Journal*, 46(1), 106–17.

Cox, T. (1991). "The Multicultural Organization," *Academy of Management Executive*, May, 34–47.

Earley, P. C. (1989). "Social Loafing and Collectivism: A Comparison of the United States and the People's Republic of China," *Administrative Science Quarterly*, 34, 565–581.

———. (1993). "East Meets West Meets Mideast: Further Explorations of Collectivistic and Individualistic Work Groups," *Academy of Management Journal*, 36(2), 319–348.

——— and Gibson, C. B. (2002). *Multinational Work Teams: A New Perspective*. Mahwah, NJ: Erlbaum.

Gabrenya, W., Latane, B., and Wang, Y. (1983). "Social Loafing in Cross-Cultural Perspective," *Journal of Cross-Cultural Psychology*, 14(3), 368–384.

Gersick, C. J. G. (1988). "Time and Transition in Work Teams: Toward a New Model of Group Development," *Academy of Management Journal* 31, 9–41.

Govindarajan, V. and Gupta, A. K. (2001). "Building an Effective Global Business Team," *Sloan Management Review*, 42(2), 63–71

Hofstede, G. (2001). *Culture's Consequences: Comparing Values, Behaviors, Institutions, and Organizations Across Nations*. 2nd Ed. Thousand Oak, CA: Sage.

Jackson, S. and Ruderman, M. (eds.) (1996). *Diversity in Work Teams: Research Paradigms for a Changing Workplace*. American Psychological Association.

Janis, I. (1982). *Groupthink*. 2nd Ed. Boston, MA: Houghton-Mifflin.

Katzenbach, J. and Smith, D. (1993). "The Discipline of Teams," *Harvard Business Review*. March–April, 110–25.

Kirchmeyer, K. (1993). "Multicultural Task Groups: An Account of the Low Contribution Level of Minorities." *Small Group Research*, 24, February 1, 127–48.

Kirkman, B. L., Rosen, B., Gibson, E. B., Tesluk, P. E., and McPherson, S. O. (2002). "Five Challenges to Virtual Team Success: Lessons from Sabre, Inc.," *Academy of Management Executive*, 16(3), 67–78.

Latane, B., Williams, K. D., and Harkins, S. G. (1979). "Many Hands Make Light the Work: The Causes and Consequences of Social Loafing," *Journal of Personality and Social Psychology*, 37, 822–32.

Leung, K. (1992). "Groups and Social Relationships." In Westwood, R., *Organisational Behaviour: Southeast Asian Perspectives*. Hong Kong: Longman.

Mayo, E. (1945). *The Problems of an Industrial Civilization*. New York: Arno Press.

Milliken, F. and Martins, L. (1996). "Searching for Common Threads: Understanding the Multiple Effects of Diversity in Organizational Groups," *Academy of Management Review*, 21(2), 102–433.

Northcraft, G. B. and Neale, M. A. (1994). *Organizational Behavior: A Management Challenge*. Ft. Worth: Dryden Press.

Olmsted, M. and Hare, A. (1978). *The Small Group*. 2nd Ed. New York: Random House.

Ouchi, W. G. (1981). *Theory Z: How American Business Can Meet the Japanese Challenge*. New York: Avon.

Reich, R. B. (1991). *The Work of Nations: Preparing Ourselves for 21st-Century Capitalism*. New York: Alfred A. Knopf.

Thelen, K. (1987). "Codetermination and Industrial Adjustment in the German Steel Industry: A Comparative Interpretation," *California Management Review*, 3, 134–45.

Townsend, A. M., De Marie, S. M., and Hendrickson, A. R. (1998). "Virtual Teams Technology and the Workplace of the Future," *Academy of Management Executive*, 12, 17–29.

Trice, H. and Beyer, J. (1993). *The Cultures of Work Organizations*. Upper Saddle River, NJ: Prentice Hall.

Trompenaars, F. and Hampden-Turner, C. (1998). *Riding the Waves of Culture: Understanding Diversity in Global Business*. 2nd Ed. New York: McGraw-Hill.

Tuckman, B. and Jensen, M. (1977). "Stages of Small Group Development Revisited," *Group and Organization Studies*, 2, 419–427.

Vallas. S. P. (2003). "Why Teamwork Fails: Obstacles to Workplace Change in Four Manufacturing Plants," *American Sociological Review*, 68, 223–50.

Verkuyten, M., de Jong, W., and Masson, C. (1993). "Job Satisfaction Among Ethnic Minorities in the Netherlands," *Applied Psychology: An International Review*, 42, 171–89.

Wagner, J. (1995). "Studies of Individualism-Collectivism: Effects on Cooperation in Groups," *Academy of Management Journal*, 38, 152–72.

Warkentin, M. E., Sayeed, L., and Hightower, R. (1997). "Virtual Teams Versus Face-to-Face Teams: An Exploratory Study of a Web-based Conference System," *Decision Sciences*, 28(4), 975–87.

Weiss, J. (1996). *Managing Diversity, Cross-Cultural Dynamics, and Ethics*. Minneapolis/St. Paul: West.

CHAPTER 7

Motivation

Learning Objectives

After reading this chapter, you should be able to:

- Define and understand the nature of motivation.
- Explain major content and process theories of motivation and how culture influences their application.
- Discuss how culture influences rewards.
- Explain how the meaning of work in different countries influences motivation.
- Consider ways of developing cross-cultural motivation systems.

CULTURE AT WORK

Avon Anybody?

Eroildes C. Castro is on her way to work. Maneuvering her way around puddles in the unpaved streets or down the Amazon River in northern Brazil, the Avon saleswoman faces the hazards of poisonous water snakes, flesh-eating piranhas, and customers who do not pay. Although her monthly salary is often barely above US$110, Brazil's minimum wage, Avon's system of incentive prizes is clearly able to motivate Ms. Castro. An iron, a suitcase, and a plastic coffee cup set mean so much to her that Ms. Castro works despite the hardships.

   In Russia, when Avon calls, Svetlana Morosava is at the door. Ms. Morosova, who holds advanced degrees in mathematics and economics and has two small children, sold her first Avon products to other mothers at a children's playground in 1994. By 1996, she was an Avon manager, driving a company car and making US$2,000 a month, more than 15 times the national average salary. In addition to the material benefits, Ms. Morosova gains self-assurance and independence from her Avon position.

Sources: Brooke, J. (1995). "Who Braves Piranha Waters? Your Avon Lady! *The New York Times*, July 7, A4; Stanley, A. (1996). "New Face of Russian Capitalism: Avon and Mary Kay Create Opportunities for Women," *The New York Times*, August 14, D1, D16.

   What motivates people to work in different countries is not always the same. Organizations are beginning to realize that a reward an employee considers valuable in one culture may be meaningless or even insulting in another. As organizations globalize, the task of developing motivation systems to fit the values and preferences of workers in a variety of cultures is becoming more demanding.

Why do people work? Is it for money, sales prizes, and company cars? Is it the job itself that people find satisfying? Does culture influence the answers to these questions? For example, is a Brazilian more appreciative of sales prizes than a Russian?

▪▪▪ What Is Motivation?

One definition of **motivation** is the amount of effort that an individual puts into doing something. Motivation is also "a basic psychological process which explains why employees behave the way they do in the workplace" (Kanungo and Mendonca 1995, p. 16). Another view of motivation is "the willingness to exert high levels of effort toward organizational goals, conditioned by the effort's ability to satisfy some individual need" (Robbins 1996, p. 212).

Motivation is a key organizational concept. Organizations seek motivated employees, and view managers who have the ability to motivate others as successful. The majority of motivation theories, as with most organizational behavior research, originates within an American cultural context. In fact, when several of the theories were tested with non-Western subjects, they received only mixed support suggesting that these models do not identify variables or processes useful for understanding what motivates non-Americans (Hofstede 1980).

▪▪▪ American Motivation Theories and Their Applicability Outside the United States

Two types of motivation theories are content and process. **Content theories** focus on the "what," identifying factors that cause people to put effort into work. **Process theories** concern the "how," the steps an individual takes in putting forth effort.

Content Theories

Three major content theories are Maslow's Hierarchy of Needs, Herzberg's Motivation-Hygiene Theory, and McClelland's Needs Theory. This section presents a description of the basic ideas of each theory and a discussion of how the theory might apply in different cultures.

Maslow's Hierarchy of Needs

Maslow's Hierarchy of Needs (Maslow 1954) is a theory of general motivation developed in the United States in the 1950s. Abraham Maslow, an American psychologist, theorized that an individual would try to satisfy one category of needs at a time and that the hierarchical order of needs is the same for everyone.

Specifically, Maslow proposed five levels of needs:

- **Physiological needs** are the basic requirements for survival including air, food, water, and sex drives.
- **Safety and security needs** are shelter and protection from outside threat.
- **Affiliation needs** include affection, friendship, and belonging.
- **Esteem needs** focus on the need for respect, positive regard, status, and recognition from others.
- **Self-actualization needs** relate to developing one's full potential.

From the perspective of organizational behavior, employers could fulfill an employee's physiological needs by providing free or subsidized food. Safety and security needs could come in the form of job security and free or subsidized housing. Managers can meet subordinates' social needs through a team structure or various company sponsored social events. Fulfillment of self-esteem needs can occur when there is praise or recognition for performance. Finally, organizations can help employees self-actualize by assigning them meaningful, fulfilling work.

Money can satisfy any level of needs to some extent. For example, money can buy food or a house to fulfill lower-level needs, provide a feeling of self-worth to satisfy self-esteem needs, or make available the opportunity to pursue a hobby or further education to achieve higher-level needs.

According to Maslow, when a level of needs is satisfied, it no longer motivates behavior, and an individual moves to the next higher level which then motivates behavior. This progression continues and when an individual reaches the highest level of self-actualization, behavior is motivated indefinitely because in Maslow's view, no one could ever be totally self-actualized.

Although Maslow's theory has appeal in its simplicity and ease of application, "research has not been able to establish the validity of the need hierarchy itself" (Steers, Porter, and Bigley 1996, p. 15). Even in the United States, needs other than those identified by Maslow motivate people—for example, spiritual needs. People can also operate on more than one needs level simultaneously or may move to a lower level of needs if their life circumstances change (Alderfer 1969). For example, professionals who are suddenly "downsized" and unable to find work can find that their needs level changes from self-actualization to physiological or security needs.

In an international context, the circumstances and values of a particular culture influence the ordering and importance of needs. The values of individualism and collectivism can make the hierarchy more or less relevant. For example, if a culture is collectively oriented, the individualistic higher order needs of self-esteem and self-actualization could be irrelevant. Trompenaars writes (1993, pp. 65–66):

> Western theories of motivation have individuals growing out of early, and hence primitive, social needs into an individually resplendent self-actualization at the summit of the hierarchy. Needless to say, this does not achieve resonance the world over, however good a theory it may be for America and Northwest Europe. The Japanese notion of the highest good is harmonious relationships within and with the pattern of nature; the primary orientation is to other people and the natural world.

In cultures that are high on uncertainty avoidance, safety and security needs are likely to be most important. For example, in Japan, throughout their lives, people are highly motivated to compete for entrance into elite schools so that upon graduating, they can get jobs in large corporations that provide lifetime employment.

A masculine or feminine orientation, according to Hofstede's framework, can also influence the importance of different needs. In a feminine culture, such as Sweden or Finland, people value the traditionally feminine ideals such as quality of life and working relationships, so social needs dominate the motivation of workers over productivity (Adler 1997).

Economic and political circumstances also influence the importance of needs. For example, a study of Libyan managers after the 1973 Libyan People's Revolution, found that social needs were more fulfilled than security needs (Buera and Glueck 1979). Because the Revolution made Libyan managers more subject to dismissal, their security needs were less satisfied compared to non-Libyan managers working in the country. Maslow's theory would incorrectly predict that these managers could not focus on social needs until after they had fulfilled their security needs.

A more recent study comparing the work values and motives of managers from Britain and Zimbabwe suggested that Maslow's hierarchy should be reordered and redefined for Africans (Harvey, Carter, and Mudimu 2000). Specifically, the Zimbabwean managers put higher importance on security and self-esteem needs and less on accomplishment and friendship.

In conclusion, Maslow's hierarchy of needs theory is potentially useful for managers. It is clear, however, that the five needs in the order proposed by Maslow do not motivate everyone. Also, circumstances can cause an individual to return to a more basic needs level, and more than one needs level can be important at the same time. Despite these limitations, considering what needs are meaningful and in what order they might influence people in a particular culture can provide insight into how managers can motivate employees.

Herzberg's Motivation-Hygiene Theory

Herzberg developed his **Motivation-Hygiene Theory** (Herzberg 1968; Herzberg, Mausner, and Snyderman 1959) in the 1950s and 1960s and built on Maslow's theory. The premise of Herzberg's theory, often called **Two-Factor Theory,** is that satisfaction and dissatisfaction represent two separate dimensions rather than opposite ends of a single dimension. Working from this assumption, Herzberg questioned American engineers and accountants to determine which job factors caused them to feel satisfaction or dissatisfaction.

Herzberg believed that the resulting two factors, hygiene and motivation, have differential effects on motivation. The **hygiene factors,** also called extrinsic or context factors, are factors outside the job itself that influence the worker. They include company policy and administration, supervision, relationship with a supervisor, work conditions, salary, relationships with peers, and security. These factors are associated with dissatisfaction. If they are absent, a worker feels dissatisfied, but their presence only brings a person to a neutral state.

The **motivation factors,** also called intrinsic or content factors, are aspects of the job itself including achievement, recognition, interesting work, responsibility, advancement, and growth. The presence of these factors satisfies and motivates workers.

To apply his theory, Herzberg recommends **job enrichment.** In Herzberg's view, to motivate workers, a job has to include many motivation factors. Most likely, however, enriched jobs will only be motivating to employees in cultures with high individualism and low power distance such as the United States (Erez 1997). In fact, some American workers, mainly professional and semiprofessional, do respond well to job enrichment, supporting Herzberg's model of motivation. However, blue collar and farm workers often do not like having an enriched job and could experience reduced levels of satisfaction and motivation as a result. Thus, even in the culture in which it originated, the limitations of Herzberg's model are significant.

Research on Herzberg's model in New Zealand, which has similar scores to the United States on Hofstede's four cultural dimensions, did not support the model (Hines 1973). The factors of supervision and interpersonal relationships had a significant relationship with satisfaction and motivation for both middle managers and salaried employees.

Despite inconclusive results, Herzberg's theory is widely used by managers in the United States, Europe, Latin America, and the Pacific Rim (Gibson, Ivancevich, and

Donnelly 1994). Most likely this is because of its simplicity and the attractiveness of the basic concept, but different factors can produce satisfaction and motivation, with culture, and perhaps specific situations, influencing which factors (Adler 1997).

McClelland's Learned Needs Theory

A third content theory is **Learned Needs Theory** (McClelland 1966, 1985). American psychologist David McClelland proposed that three major needs influence people's behavior. These needs are not instinctive desires as in Maslow's theory, but learned. The learned needs, which help explain individual differences in motivation, are need for achievement, need for power, and need for affiliation.

Need for achievement is a concern for establishing and maintaining high levels of performance quality. Individuals with a high need for achievement want personal responsibility for their success or failure, like moderate risks, and prefer to receive immediate, concrete feedback on their performance. As a result, tasks that are too easy or too difficult do not appeal to them because they have less responsibility for the outcome.

Need for power is a concern for reputation, responsibility, influence, impact, and control over others. People high on this need prefer leadership positions and others usually rate them as effective leaders. In addition, individuals with a high need for power are usually good performers and have above-average attendance at work (Steers and Braunstein 1976).

Need for affiliation is a concern for establishing and maintaining social relationships. People who have a high need for affiliation like close, friendly relationships with others and prefer cooperative rather than competitive situations.

How do these needs relate to organizational behavior? Research indicates that individuals with a high need for achievement strive for personal success. They are often dynamic entrepreneurs but are not necessarily successful managers, because the achievement of others is not their concern. Jobs with responsibility, moderate challenge, and the opportunity to receive feedback motivate people with a high need for achievement. In contrast, successful managerial performance results from high power need and low affiliation need (McClelland and Burnham 1976).

Much of McClelland's work focuses on the need for achievement. McClelland theorizes that improving the level of need achievement among less economically successful groups would encourage the groups' economic development (McClelland 1966). McClelland and his colleagues developed a training course to increase need for achievement and instructed several groups with it, including executives in the United States and Mexico, underachieving high school boys, and businessmen in India. With the exception of one group in Mexico, those who received the training were more successful two years later than those who took another management course or no course. However, to continue the gains, the individuals had to work in an environment that supported achievement-oriented behavior. Subsequent research indicates that the business executives in India could not sustain the gains. Perhaps this was because of lack of social support for personal achievement in the culture (Misra and Kanungo 1994). This could also have been the reason that the course was not successful in Mexico. Both cultures have a group orientation, and the need for achievement is clearly an individualistic need.

Studies of actual and aspiring Russian entrepreneurs in the 1990s found a strong need for achievement (McCarthy, Puffer, and Shekshnia 1993; Tullar 1992). However,

Achievement, ambition, and initiative have been denigrated in Russia. People with a high need for achievement have been condemned for being individualistic, antisocial, and enemies of the people. Personal ambition has aroused feelings of envy, vindictiveness, and derision. And initiative has typically been received with indifference, at best, and punishment, at worst. Negative attitudes towards these characteristics are so deeply ingrained in the Russian psyche that many Russians who want to realize their ambitions feel pressure from two sources—public scorn and their own guilt from violating the values they were raised with. . . . If Russians seem reluctant to take initiative or be ambitious, they might respond positively to proposals that emphasize benefits to the collective or that reward individuals in ways that do not arouse feelings of envy. One should respect requests for not publicizing personal achievements, material possessions or privileges.[1] (Puffer 1993, p. 479).

In a study of Confucianism and needs in the People's Republic of China, MBA students in China scored lower than their North American counterparts in achievement, affiliation, change, cognitive structure, and impulsivity, and higher on autonomy and harm avoidance (Punnett 1995). It is possible that these needs affect the motivation of Chinese employees. For example, it might be more effective to put less emphasis on individual performance and short-term goals, to tie rewards to position and proper behavior, and to make rewards long term rather than immediate.

A comparison of employees and students in the United States, the Netherlands, Israel, Hungary, and Japan found that achievement motivation is associated with greater individualism (Sagie, Elizur, and Yamauchi 1996). However, this does not mean that collectivists have low motivation or are not interested in achievement; they are more interested in communal needs and may be motivated to achieve as members of a group or team, rather than by themselves.

Another concern with Learned Needs Theory is that the concept of achievement is difficult, if not impossible, to translate into languages other than English (Hofstede 1980). Hofstede found that countries that scored high on achievement need in McClelland's research were those that had weak uncertainty avoidance and high masculinity on his cultural dimensions. This combination, found only in countries in the Anglo-American group and some of their former colonies, includes Great Britain, the United States, Canada, New Zealand, Ireland, Hong Kong, Australia, India, South Africa, and the Philippines. Almost all of these countries use English as a primary language. Whether the concepts of achievement and need for achievement apply outside these countries is open to question.

Conclusions about the Content Theories

All of the content theories identify factors or needs related to motivation. By focusing on content, each theory restricts its explanation of motivation to a particular set of factors and explains how to motivate people using these factors. Because values across and within cultures are not universal, it is difficult to find a set of motivating needs or factors that applies to everyone, and therefore research results on the content models indicate a lack of conclusive support.

Does this mean that content theories are useless for understanding motivation? No. Their important contribution is to identify concepts useful for gaining a better understanding of motivation, and they are a valuable starting point for examining cultural and even individual differences in motivation. For example, managers can think about what, if any, hierarchies of needs exist for their employees, what factors motivate or dissatisfy them, and what major needs influence organizational behavior.

---

[1]Puffer, S. M. (1993). "A Riddle Wrapped in an Enigma: Demystifying Russian Managerial Motivation," *European Management Journal,* 11(4), p. 479.

Process Theories

Reinforcement or Learning Theory, Goal Setting Theory, Expectancy Theory, and Equity Theory are examples of process theories that, like content theories, developed in the United States. However, because they focus on *process* rather than content, these theories are more applicable in other countries. Process theories attempt to discover universal mechanisms to explain motivation. To apply these theories, managers can incorporate specific cultural and other factors into the models to adapt them to the individuals whom they wish to motivate.

Reinforcement Theory

The premise of **Reinforcement** or **Learning Theory** is that the environment determines people's behavior (Skinner 1971). As people grow from children into adults, what they learn is a result of the outcomes of their behavior. If individuals receive a reward or **reinforcement** for what they do, it is likely that they will repeat it. If no one acknowledges the behavior, a person could stop it. When people receive a negative outcome or **punishment** for their behavior, they usually stop doing it at the moment, but punishment does not guarantee that undesirable behavior will end.

Organizational behavior modification or OBMod is the application of Reinforcement Theory to motivating workers in organizations. A typical OBMod program involves a four-step process (Komaki, Coombs, and Schepman 1996).

1. Ensure that workers know the behaviors expected of them as part of the job.
2. Train observers and have them record the workers' correct and incorrect behaviors.
3. Reinforce workers who practice correct behaviors and provide corrective feedback.
4. Evaluate the effects of the program on behavior.

Many studies in the United States tested this approach, with the majority of them showing positive results. Behaviors that improved include performance, attendance and punctuality, safety and health related behaviors, and service to customers (Komaki et al. 1996).

One test of the applicability of OBMod outside the United States was a study of Russian textile workers (Welsh, Luthans, and Sommer 1993). Using a similar approach to an earlier study where OBMod improved performance in retail sales workers in the United States, the researchers trained Russian supervisors to give positive reinforcers—attention, praise, and positive feedback—to their workers when they observed them performing specific behaviors identified as leading to high-quality work outputs. The program was successful in producing a positive change in the workers' behavior. However, when the reinforcers were withdrawn, the positive behavior changes continued. The theory predicts that the positive behaviors should have eventually stopped.

Why the positive behaviors did not stop is unclear from the study. The authors suggest that co-workers provided social reinforcers that maintained the behaviors even after the supervisors formally stopped administering positive reinforcers. Because of the collective nature of Russian culture, approval from peers could be as rewarding, or even more rewarding, than from the supervisor. In other words, the positive behaviors might have continued because of positive reinforcers coming from a different source.

The ideas of Reinforcement Theory are simple, and the theory appears to be a convincing explanation for behavior. To apply it, managers must understand what is rewarding to the people they wish to motivate. At the organization level, managers can take into account reward preferences of the workforce. For example, if a Japanese company is establishing a subsidiary in the United States, the reward systems in the subsidiary must be more individualistic than in the home office to motivate American workers. In the vignette about the two Avon employees that begins this chapter, both material incentives and feelings of accomplishment function as reinforcers of performance.

Reinforcement Theory may not be a successful explanation of behavior in cultures where people do not perceive a connection between their own behavior and its consequences. For example, in the Middle East, many Muslims believe that whatever happens is God's will. Therefore, an OBMod program is likely to have no effect because people would consider rewards as what God had willed rather than a consequence of their own behavior.

Similarly, in societies such as Argentina and Uruguay, status derives from personal characteristics, ascription, rather than achievement. People believe high status deserves reward. It may be inappropriate to reward the performance of a lower-level worker directly; everyone associated with the successful performance should receive a reward in relation to her relative status. For example, in a sales situation, "The superior is by definition responsible for increased performance, so that relative status is unaffected by higher group sales. If rewards are to be increased, this must be done proportionately to ascribed status, not given to the person closest to the sale" (Trompenaars 1993, pp. 110–11).

When managers do give rewards to encourage performance, the rewards should be something an employee values. What an individual perceives as rewarding is subject to cultural influence. For example, praise and appreciation motivate members of family-dominated cultures such as Greece, Italy, Japan, Singapore, and South Korea more than money (Trompenaars 1993). Certain material rewards may also carry unexpected connotations—for example, in India, the reward of a cowhide leather wallet or key case with a corporate logo would be extremely offensive, as the cow is a sacred animal in the predominant Hindu religion.

Goal Setting Theory

Goal Setting Theory focuses on the effect that the setting of goals has on performance. Research on Goal Setting Theory, started in the late 1960s and conducted primarily in the United States, is largely supportive of the theory (Locke and Latham 1990; Pinder 1984). The theory is based on the idea that people are motivated by intentions to work toward a goal (Locke 1968). Researchers have found that performance increases when specific, rather than vague, goals are set. Setting a difficult but achievable goal generally leads to higher performance than setting an easy goal. In addition, feedback, especially that which comes from workers reviewing their own outputs, usually results in higher performance than no feedback does.

For Goal Setting Theory to work, an individual must be committed to the goal that is set. It does not matter whether a person participates in setting a goal or someone else assigns it, as long as there is commitment to it. However, people are usually more committed to goals they are involved in setting. A second condition for Goal Setting Theory is self-efficacy, a person's belief that he has the ability to do a particular task.

Studies of Goal Setting Theory comparing the United States with England and Israel indicate that culture can affect the goal setting process. For example, American workers in one study responded equally well to a goal setting program introduced by either a shop steward or a supervisor. However, the program initiated by the shop steward was more effective for a group of British workers (Earley 1986). Two studies with Israelis suggest that the effects of group participation in goal setting are stronger in a collective-participative culture (Erez 1986) and that participation in goal setting produces a stronger result in countries lower on power distance (Erez and Earley 1987).

Although the precise nature of the influence of culture on goal setting is unclear (Locke and Latham 1990), taking into account how values influence goal commitment could enhance the effects of the goal setting process. For example, in the studies just mentioned, the Israelis were higher on collectivism and lower on power distance than the Americans. Therefore, in the collective-participative culture of Israel, participating in goal setting produces a more favorable result because people are more committed to a goal they participate in setting. Relative to the Israelis, Americans have higher power distance and are more willing to commit to a goal set by a supervisor. Thus, in a higher power distance culture, employees are probably more willing to commit to a goal set by their supervisor, and direct participation may not be necessary or even desirable.

Because self-efficacy is also an important aspect of the goal setting process, cultural values that influence individual beliefs about personal ability to perform a task should also have an influence. For example, in China, a collectivistic country, it is often important to use *guanxi,* a special relationship, to accomplish certain tasks. As a result, if a person lacks *guanxi,* for a particular task, self-efficacy could be low regardless of personal talents or ability.

Expectancy Theory

The **Expectancy Theory** of motivation (Nadler and Lawler 1977; Porter and Lawler 1968; Steers et al. 1996; Vroom 1964) makes several important assumptions about people's behavior. First, behavior is a result of both personal and environmental factors. Second, people's decisions about whether to belong to an organization and how much effort to put into performing influence their behavior in organizations. Third, because of different needs, people seek different rewards from the organization. Finally, people decide how to behave based on beliefs about what leads to the most desirable outcomes.

Using these assumptions, researchers developed Expectancy Theory to describe how an individual decides how much effort to put into a task. Figure 7-1 presents one model of Expectancy Theory.

The process an individual follows in deciding how much effort to put into doing a particular behavior is dependent on several things. First, a person considers whether trying or making an effort could lead to successful performance. This is the **E→P expectancy,** effort leading to performance expectancy. If a person believes that trying can lead to success, she is more likely to put effort into a particular behavior.

Second, a person thinks about the likelihood that successful performance would lead to an outcome or reward. This is the **P→O expectancy,** performance leading to outcome expectancy. Associated with each outcome is a **valence,** the value of the reward to the individual receiving it. If a person feels that performance will be rewarded with a valued outcome, this will increase the amount of effort. If the person sees no connection between performance and outcome or the outcome is not desirable, she is less likely to exert effort.

Finally, a person considers **instrumentality,** the likelihood that a first-level outcome would lead to a second-level outcome. This means that an immediate reward could lead to further rewards; for example, if a supervisor praises an employee for a job well done, will the supervisor later give the employee a salary increase? If an immediate outcome can lead to something positive in the future, that also increases effort. The amount of effort a person expends then depends on how she evaluates each of the factors in the Expectancy model in relation to other possible choices of behavior.

Tests of the Expectancy model in the United States support some aspects, but there are also criticisms. One problem is that the model is difficult to test because researchers disagree on the measurement of variables in the model and question whether individuals consciously make choices the way the theory predicts. Although it appears to be

FIGURE 7-1 The Expectancy Model of Motivation

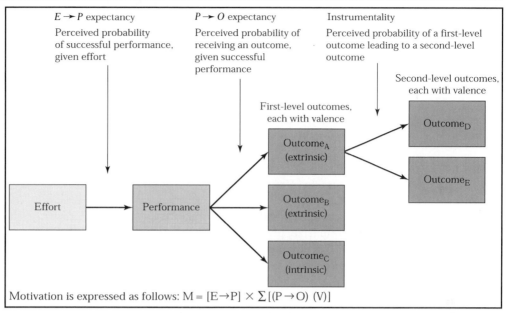

Motivation is expressed as follows: $M = [E \rightarrow P] \times \sum [(P \rightarrow O) (V)]$

Source: Nadler, D. A. and Lawler, E. E. (1977). "Motivation: A Diagnostic Approach." In Hackman, J. R., Lawler, E. E., and Porter, L. W. (eds.) *Perspectives on Behavior in Organizations.* New York: McGraw-Hill, p. 34.

complicated, Expectancy Theory does provide an understanding of motivation and is a basis for evaluating organizational reward policies and practices (Steers et al. 1996).

Even with its limitations, Expectancy Theory does explain the motivational processes of some people outside the United States, particularly those whose cultures emphasize internal attribution (Adler 1997). When people in a culture believe they can control the work environment and their own behavior, such as in the United States, England, and Canada, Expectancy Theory explains motivation to some extent. In cultures where people believe the work environment and their own behaviors are not completely under their control, such as in Brazil, Saudi Arabia, or China, an Expectancy model may not be totally applicable (Adler 1997). Finally, the theory has almost no applicability in Muslim countries where people think that many things that happen are beyond their control (Steers and Sánchez-Runde 2002).

Equity Theory

Equity Theory also developed in the United States (Adams 1963). The basic premise of the theory is that people try to balance their inputs and outcomes in relation to others. **Inputs** are what someone brings to a situation—for example, an employee's inputs include education, previous work experience, personality, and personal characteristics. **Outcomes** are what one takes from a situation—for example, pay, benefits, working conditions, co-worker relationships, and training opportunities.

Each person has his own perception of the value of these inputs and outcomes. Thus, a manager must consider how an employee values inputs and outcomes. For example, in Asia and the Middle East, workers usually accept objective inequity in order to maintain social harmony. However, from the worker's point of view, the situation is one of equity (Steers and Sánchez-Runde 2002).

Motivation results through the process of comparing one's own perceived outcomes to inputs ratio to the perceived ratio of a comparison other. When the individual's ratio is about equal to the comparison other's, equity is achieved, resulting in no motivation. However, if the two ratios are unequal, the person experiences a tension or discomfort that motivates him to try to bring the two ratios into perceived equity. In mathematical terms, equity exists when:

$$\frac{\text{Outcomes self}}{\text{Inputs self}} = \frac{\text{Outcomes other}}{\text{Inputs other}}$$

Inequity exists if the self ratio (the left side of the equation) is either less than or greater than the other ratio (the right side of the equation).

Equity Theory predicts a variety of possible means to reduce inequity including an individual distorting perceptions of the elements or changing the inputs or outcomes of the self or other. For example, if an individual perceives inequity due to his own outcomes being less than a comparison other's, the person may ask the supervisor for a raise.

Process Theories: Conclusions

To summarize, process theories are more effective than content theories in explaining motivational constructs that can apply both inside and outside the United States. However, just as with content theories, in applying these models outside of the United States, managers must consider the cultural differences between the United States and the other country. For example, cultural factors influence whether the basic assumptions in the models are met. Managers can also consider cultural variations to enhance the applicability of a particular model. Although the evidence is not conclusive, the ability of the process theories to achieve a deeper level of analysis and to allow for individual differences makes them more likely to fit people from a wider range of cultures.

Because rewards can have a great impact on motivation, the next section discusses how culture influences the choice of rewards.

▪▪▪ How Culture Influences Rewards

All motivation theories consider the effects of a reward or need fulfillment on behavior. Different cultural preferences influence the value of different rewards and affect motivational practices in organizations.

How Cultural Factors Influence the Value of Rewards

Western motivation models are culturally individualistic; applying them to a collectivistic culture is probably inappropriate. For example, a Japanese saying is, "The nail that sticks out gets hammered down" which means that no individual should stand out from the group. Giving an individual reward to a Japanese employee could embarrass the recipient and thus be demotivating. In some collectivistic societies, co-workers may actively try to prevent one employee from receiving disproportionately more than others in the group. For example, outstanding Balinese workers sometimes fear sorcery against them. In Papua New Guinea, a successful employee who dresses well risks being negatively labeled as a "Shoe-sock" for being nicely dressed, and in Hong Kong, an employee positively recognized by the boss could become a victim of a form of jealousy known as "red-eye" disease (Carr and MacLachlan 1997).

In high-context collectivistic cultures, there are often expected norms of behavior for particular situations. Offering rewards for individual behavior that runs counter to group norms is unlikely to have a positive influence on motivation. Thus, offering group-based rewards may be more effective—for example, Russians respond well to group rewards that focus on group benefits intended to reinforce the importance of teamwork (Elenkov 1998).

Hofstede's masculinity versus femininity dimension also suggests what could be rewarding for different societies. If a culture is masculine, people prefer to receive money, titles, or other materialistic or status-oriented rewards. In a feminine society, meaningful rewards are time off, improved benefits, or symbolic rewards.

In some countries, the perception of material items is as gifts rather than as rewards for performance. In China, for example, organizations often distribute food to all employees as holiday gifts. People in higher positions get more or superior quality items, but employees see no connection between their performance and the gifts.

Even within countries, a variety of factors influence the reward preferences of employees. For example, in the Bahamas, hotel workers ranked higher wages, good working conditions, appreciation and praise for work done, and interesting work as the top four of ten motivational factors (Charles and Marshall 1992). However, age, gender, education, organizational level, and tenure also influenced individual preferences with males and supervisors ranking higher wages as more important than females and nonsupervisors.

Employees in Taiwan also responded to benefits differentially based on their personal characteristics (Hong et al. 1995). Benefits that employees claimed had the most impact on their performance were year-end bonuses, dividends, pensions, holidays and leave, and working disease and damage compensation. However, there were many differences among groups based on gender, marital status, age, education, and position level. Single employees emphasized further education, career development, and flexible work time while married employees thought day care, dividends, child education subsidies, and pensions more important. Men emphasized entertainment, further education, loan, dividends, and laundry benefits compared to women who liked maternity leave, commuting subsidies, and flexible work time.

Organizational Reward Practices

Organizations often equate rewards with employee motivation. In difficult economic times when companies need to lay off staff or cut other costs, maintaining the loyalty and motivation of employees is even more important, and companies need to determine what their employees find rewarding.

During the 1990s dot.com boom, Asian companies often rewarded computer professionals with stock options. However, when the stock values dropped, such rewards were no longer motivating. Instead, in 2002, *Asia Computer Weekly*'s careers survey found health benefits and further education and training to be the most popular types of indirect bonus. Although information technology staff continue to appreciate cash, companies find that rewards such as a corporate gym, cafeteria, boat, holiday home, and concierge service appeal to their employees as well. One firm even provides its country managing director with a caddie at a golf club (Ng 2002).

In Europe, there is a trend toward more variable compensation and flexible benefits. Companies are making a larger percentage of pay contingent on performance and allowing employees to choose benefits that meet their needs. For example, an employee might choose to take less vacation in exchange for a bigger pension contribution. At accounting firm PricewaterhouseCoopers recognition is important too; outstanding employees can receive the "ABCD" (Above and Beyond the Call of Duty) reward that includes Eurostar train tickets and trips to health farms ("A Rewarding Strategy" 2002).

North American companies also use rewards to motivate employees. Because of the importance of giving meaningful rewards and the great diversity in the American workforce, stored-value reward cards, which allow the employee to select from incentives in stores, online or in catalogues, are becoming popular (Hutson 2002). Companies also develop rewards that are unique to their business. For example, FedEx holds a drawing to choose the name of an employee's child for each of its new airplanes, and the company flies the family to its headquarters in Memphis, Tennessee, for the plane's christening (Klaff 2003).

Finally, to some extent because of its nascent capitalist economy, hard currency motivates Russians. Companies can either provide cash awards or reward employees with consumer goods (Elenkov 1998).

▪▪▪ The Meaning of Work across Cultures

A major shortcoming of the motivation theories previously described is that they reflect 1950s and 1960s American culture. Even when tested in other cultures, it is not clear that the theories apply.

The Meaning of Work Study

The Meaning of Work (MOW) project examines basic concepts concerned with motivation and the meaning of work (England 1986; MOW International Research Team 1987). The study, designed and conducted by an international team of behavioral scientists, examines views of work in eight countries. The results, from a sample of approximately 15,000 workers in various occupations, strongly support the idea that the meaning of work is different in different countries. England and his colleagues define and assess the meaning of work using three key concepts:

- *Work Centrality.* The degree of general importance and value attributed to the role of working in one's life.
- *Societal Norms about Working.* Normative beliefs and expectations concerning specified rights and duties attached to working.
- *Work Goals.* Work goals and values sought and preferred by individuals in their working lives (England 1986).

Work Centrality

Questions on work centrality explore how important work is compared to other parts of a worker's life and to the worker's total life. Figure 7-2 presents the results for the eight countries on this measure.

The scores indicate a relatively great variation in the importance of work to people from different countries. The Japanese think of work as a very important part of their lives, whereas for the British, work has relatively less importance. An interesting finding is that in the eight countries studied, 86.1% of all individuals said they would continue to work even if they no longer had any financial need. Even in Britain, which had the lowest percentage, 68.9% said they would continue to work. In these eight countries with relatively developed economies, work is a major part of the average person's life. A different study of the meaning of work in Saudi Arabia found that 94% of respondents said they would continue to work even if they could live comfortably without doing so (Ali and Al-Shakhis 1989). This illustrates the importance of work in an Arab country.

FIGURE 7-2 Work Centrality Scores

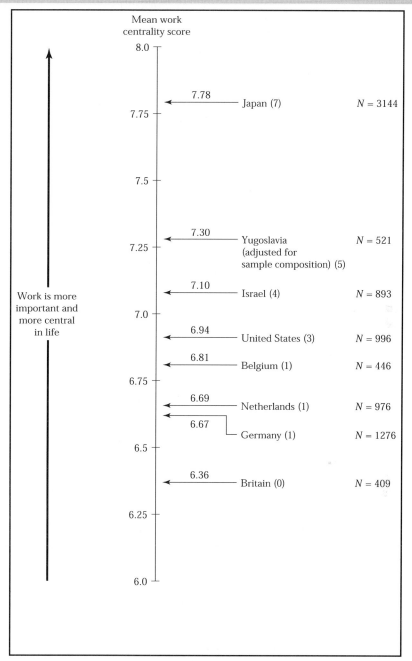

Source: MOW International Research Team (1987). *The Meaning of Work: An International Perspective.* London: Academic Press, p. 83.

Societal Norms toward Working

The second area the MOW Team investigated is societal norms toward working. They defined two norms and measured how people from the eight different countries responded to them. The **entitlement norm** "represents the underlying work rights of individuals and the work-related responsibility of organizations and society toward individuals. This norm included the notions that all members of society are entitled to meaningful and interesting work, proper training to obtain and continue in such work, and the right to participate in work/method decisions" (MOW International Research Team 1987, p. 94).

The **obligation norm** "represents the underlying duties of all individuals to society with respect to working. This norm included the notions that everyone has a duty to contribute to society by working, a duty to save for their own future, and the duty to value one's work, whatever its nature" (MOW International Research Team 1987, p. 94). Figure 7-3 presents the scores of the eight countries on the two types of norms.

A country with a higher obligation score supports the traditional work ethic more, whereas a country with a higher entitlement score is moving away from the traditional ethic. At the extremes, the United States and the Netherlands show the least balanced positions. The Netherlands has one of the highest entitlement scores and the lowest obligation score. This suggests that the Dutch put more emphasis on individual worker rights and agree less with the idea that everyone has a duty to work. In the United States, societal norms were opposite; Americans had one of the highest obligation scores but the lowest entitlement score. The traditional work ethic, at least as an ideal, is still strong in the United States.

Work Goals

The last area is the relative importance of work goals. Table 7-1 shows the importance of different work goals in the eight countries. None of the eight countries has the same relative ranking of work goals. However, for all countries, "Interesting Work" ranks in the first, second, or third position, and "Good Pay" ranks first, second, or third for six out of

▪▪▪▪▪▪▪▪▪▪▪▪ **FIGURE 7-3** Societal Norms Scores

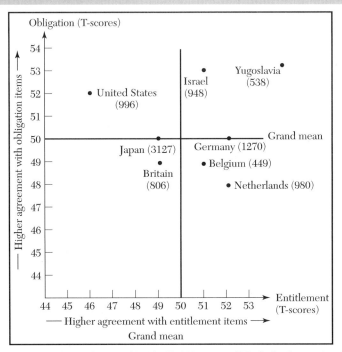

Source: MOW International Research Team (1987). *The Meaning of Work: An International Perspective.* London: Academic Press, p. 96.

TABLE 7-1 Importance of Work Goals

Work goals	Belgium (N = 446)		Germany (N = 1248)		Israel (N = 772)		Japan (N = 2897)		Netherlands (N = 967)		United States (N = 988)		Yugoslavia (N = 512)*		Britain (N = 742)	
Interesting work	8.25	1	7.26	3	6.75	1	7.38	2	7.59	2	7.41	1	7.47	2	8.02	1
Good pay	7.13	2	7.73	1	6.60	3	6.56	5	6.27	5	6.82	2	6.73	3	7.80	2
Good interpersonal relations	6.34	5	6.43	4	6.67	2	6.39	6	7.19	3	6.08	7	7.52	1	6.33	4
Good job security	6.80	3	7.57	2	5.22	10	6.71	4	5.68	7	6.30	3	5.21	9	7.12	3
A good match between you and your job	5.77	8	6.09	5	5.61	6	7.83	1	6.17	6	6.19	4	6.49	5	5.63	6
A lot of autonomy	6.56	4	5.66	8	6.00	4	6.89	3	7.61	1	5.79	8	5.42	8	4.69	10
Opportunity to learn	5.80	7	4.97	9	5.83	5	6.26	7	5.38	9	6.16	5	6.61	4	5.55	8
A lot of variety	5.96	6	5.71	6	4.89	11	5.05	9	6.86	4	6.10	6	5.62	7	5.62	7
Convenient work hours	4.71	9	5.71	6	5.53	7	5.46	8	5.59	8	5.25	9	5.01	10	6.11	5
Good physical working conditions	4.19	11	4.39	11	5.28	9	4.18	10	5.03	10	4.84	11	5.94	6	4.87	9
Good opportunity for upgrading or promotion	4.49	10	4.48	10	5.29	8	3.33	11	3.31	11	5.08	10	4.00	11	4.27	11

Countries

Left: Mean ranks.

Right: The rank of each work goal within a given country. Rank 1 is the *most* important work goal for a country and rank 11 is the *least* important work goal for a country.

*Combined target group data were used for Yugoslavia.

Source: MOW International Research Team (1987). *The Meaning of Work: An International Perspective.* London: Academic Press, p. 96.

the eight. At the opposite end, "Good Opportunity for Upgrading or Promotion" and "Good Physical Working Conditions" are among the three least important goals for most countries.

Recent surveys of the importance of work goals for Indian, Malaysian, and Thai managers reveal a slightly different picture (Chatterjee and Pearson 2000/1; Pearson and Kamolkasemsilp 2001). Both Indian and Thai managers ranked "Opportunity to Learn New Things" as their most important work goal followed by "Work That Is Liked and Interesting"/"Interesting Job." However, "A Good Salary"/"Salary" ranked ninth out of the 11 goals. "Good Opportunity for Promotion" was the most important goal for Malaysian managers, followed by "Opportunity to Learn New Things," but "Salary" only ranked fourth and "Interesting Job" fifth.

Applying the Meaning of Work Research

The meaning of work research can help managers better understand work motivation by providing knowledge of the relative importance and meaning of work in different countries. For example, looking at the work centrality scores, because of the greater importance of work to people in Japan compared with Germany, work itself may be more of a motivating factor in Japan. Therefore, it is not surprising that Germans work fewer hours than do the Japanese. In developing reward systems, managers should consider the importance of various work goals. For example, satisfying interpersonal relations are more important in Israel and the former Yugoslavia than they are in the United States and Japan, and salary may have less of an impact in India and Thailand than it does in Germany or the United Kingdom.

▪▪▪ Convergence or Divergence?

Forces for Convergence

With the popularity of U.S. business education among international managers throughout the world, there is a tendency to consider U.S. motivation theories as the best or only means for understanding motivational processes (Adler 1991). In addition, global corporations often try to develop consistent policies and practices across their subsidiaries for administrative efficiency and fairness to employees. Therefore, many of these organizations have motivational practices based on U.S. models. These two trends suggest a move toward convergence.

Forces for Divergence

The application of U.S. motivation theories is not effective across all cultures. Managers must develop organizational systems that are flexible enough to take into account the meaning of work and the relative value of rewards within the range of cultures where they operate. By developing an organization-wide approach that is adaptable, an organization should be able to simultaneously maintain consistency across locations and provide programs and rewards that motivate employees from many different cultural backgrounds.

▪▪▪ Implications for Managers

With the uncertainty surrounding the application of motivation theories developed in the United States to other countries, managers often find it difficult to choose an approach to motivating their subordinates. On the basis of current knowledge, the use of process theories appears to be more promising than content theories. The meaning of work and what people find rewarding varies with culture. In designing approaches to motivation, it is important for managers to take into account the cultural frameworks.

When developing a motivational system, managers should identify whether a culture is collectivistic or individualistic to determine if rewards should be given on a group or individual basis. Another factor, time orientation, influences whether setting deadlines would influence performance.

These examples present a few important differences in how culture affects approaches to motivation. Overall, managers need an understanding of the people who work for them to select an appropriate motivation system.

SUMMARY

Motivation is effort an individual puts into doing something. To understand motivation in an international context, it is important to learn about American theories and how they might be useful both in the United States and in other countries. Content theories of motivation, such as Maslow's Hierarchy of Needs, Herzberg's Motivation-Hygiene Theory, and McClelland's Needs Theory, describe the factors that cause people to put effort into their work. Although the precise factors suggested by the theories may not be correct across all societies, their basic frameworks serve as a starting point for understanding needs.

The process theories, including Reinforcement Theory, Goal Setting Theory, Expectancy Theory, and Equity Theory, focus on how someone becomes motivated. These theories, which aim at a deeper level of analysis than content theories, appear to be more promising both for the United States and other countries. However, cultural variables such as individualism or ascription may limit the applicability of some of the theories.

Because rewards are important in many theories and companies generally see rewards as motivating employees, it is important to select rewards that are culturally appropriate. Examples of trends in employee rewards and benefits in Asia, Europe, and the United States indicate employers are giving a wide range of rewards to motivate workers.

Research on the meaning of work in different countries provides further understanding of how to motivate people in different cultures. With insight into the meaning of work, managers can improve their understanding of work behaviors and attitudes in different cultures. Because of reliance on U.S. motivational approaches and global corporations' desires for consistent worldwide systems, there are trends toward convergence. However, because managers have difficulty applying U.S. models in other cultures, more local approaches to motivation could develop. Managers therefore need to develop flexible motivational systems that can be effective across different cultures.

DISCUSSION QUESTIONS

1. Why are content theories of motivation less likely to be applicable outside of the United States?
2. Select a country of your choice. What factors should a manager consider in developing a motivational system for this country?
3. What motivates you to work? How do your responses compare to examples of motivational preferences in other countries presented in the chapter?
4. What do you think about some of the new approaches to reward systems? What are some rewards that might be attractive for your culture in the future?
5. How does research on the meaning of work in different countries relate to the question of motivation?
6. If you had to design a global system of motivation for a large corporation, what would be some of your major concerns?

INTERNET SITES ▪ ▪ ▪ ▪ ▪ ▪ ▪

Selected Companies in the Chapter

Avon Products, Inc. (www.avon.com)
FedEx (www.fedex.com/us/about)
PricewaterhouseCoopers (www.pwc.com)

Motivation Sites

B. F. Skinner Foundation (www.bfskinner.org). The site has information about the work of B.F. Skinner and the role of contingencies in human behavior.

Herzberg Biography and Research, Business Library, The University of Western Ontario (www.lib.uwo.ca/business/herzberg.html). This site has biographical information about Frederick Herzberg and references to his research work.

Maslow Publications (www.maslow.com). This site has references to the books, articles, and personal papers of Abraham Maslow.

MOW International Research Center (http://allserv.rug.ac.be/~rclaes/MOW/). This is the site of the International Meaning of Work Research Center affiliated with the University Gent (Belgium).

REFERENCES ▪ ▪ ▪ ▪ ▪ ▪ ▪

Adams, J. (1963). "Toward an Understanding of Inequity," *Journal of Abnormal and Social Psychology*, 67, 422–36.

Adler, N. J. (1991). *International Dimensions of Organizational Behavior*. 2d Ed. Boston: PWS-Kent.

———. (1997). *International Dimensions of Organizational Behavior*. 3d Ed. Cincinnati, OH: South-Western College Publishing.

Alderfer, C. P. (1969). "An Empirical Test of a New Theory of Human Needs," *Organizational Behavior and Human Performance*, May, 142–75.

Ali, A. and Al-Shakhis, M. (1989). "The Meaning of Work in Saudi Arabia," *International Journal of Manpower*, 10(1), 26–32.

Brooke, J. (1995). "Who Braves Piranha Waters? Your Avon Lady!" *The New York Times*, July 7, A4.

Buera, A. and Glueck, W. F. (1979). "The Need Satisfaction of Managers in Libya," *Management International Review*, 19(1), 113–21.

Carr, S. C. and MacLachlan, M. (1997). "Motivational Gravity." In Munro, D., Schumaker, J. E., and Carr, S. C. (eds.) *Motivation and Culture*. New York: Routledge.

Charles, K. R. and Marshall, L. H. (1992). "Motivational Preferences of Caribbean Hotel Workers: An Exploratory Study," *International Journal of Contemporary Hospitality Management*, 4(3), 25–9.

Chatterjee, S. R. and Pearson, C. A. L. (2000/1). "Indian Managers in Transition: Orientations, Work Goals, Values and Ethics," *Management International Review*, 40, 81–95.

Earley, P. C. (1986). "Supervisors and Shop Stewards as Sources of Contextual Information in Goal Setting; A Comparison of the U.S. with England," *Journal of Applied Psychology*, 71, 111–8.

Elenkov, D. S. (1998). "Can American Management Concepts Work in Russia? A Cross-Cultural Comparative Study," *California Management Review*, 40(4), 133–56.

England, G. W. (1986). "National Work Meanings and Patterns—Constraints on Management Action," *European Management Journal*, 4, 176–84.

Erez, M. (1986). "The Congruence of Goal Setting Strategies with Socio-Cultural Values, and Its Effect on Performance," *Journal of Management*, 12, 585–92.

———. (1997). "A Culture-Based Model of Work Motivation." In Earley, P. C. and Erez, M. (eds.) *New Perspectives on International Industrial/ Organizational Psychology*. San Francisco: New Lexington Press.

——— and Earley, P. C. (1987). "Comparative Analysis of Goal-Setting Strategies across Cultures," *Journal of Applied Psychology*, 72, 658–65.

Gibson, J. L., Ivancevich, J. M., and Donnelly, J. H., Jr. (1994). *Organizations: Behavior, Structure, Processes*. Boston: Irwin.

Harvey, J., Carter, S., and Mudimu, G. (2000). "A Comparison of Work Values and Motives among Zimbabwean and British Managers," *Personnel Review*, 29(6), 723–42.

Herzberg, F. (1968). "One More Time: How Do You Motivate Employees?" *Harvard Business Review*, January–February, 53–62.

———, Mausner, B., and Snyderman, B. (1959). *The Motivation to Work*. New York: Wiley.

Hines, G. H. (1973). "Cross-Cultural Differences in Two-Factor Motivation Theory," *Journal of Applied Psychology*, 58(3), 375–7.

Hofstede, G. (1980). "Motivation, Leadership, and Organization: Do American Theories Apply Abroad?" *Organizational Dynamics*, 9, 42–62.

Hong, J. C., Yang, S. D., Wang, L. J., Chiou, E. F., et al. (1995). "Impact of Employee Benefits on Work Motivation and Productivity," *International Journal of Career Management*, 7(6), 10–14.

Hutson, D. A. (2002). "Shopping for Incentives," *Compensation and Benefits Review,* March/April, 75–9.

Kanungo, R. N. and Mendonca, M. (1994). "Introduction: Motivational Models for Developing Societies." In Kanungo, R. N. and Mendonca, M. (eds.) *Work Motivation: Models for Developing Countries.* New Delhi: Sage.

Komaki, J. L., Coombs, T., and Schepman, S. (1996). "Motivational Implications of Reinforcement Theory." In Steers, R. M., Porter, L. W., and Bigley, G. A. (eds.) *Motivation and Leadership at Work.* 6th Ed. New York: McGraw-Hill.

Klaff, L. G. (2003). "Getting Happy with the Rewards King," *Workforce,* April, 46–50.

Locke, E. A. (1968). "Toward a Theory of Task Motivation and Incentives," *Organizational Behavior and Human Performance*, 3, 157–89.

—— and Latham, G. P. (1990). *A Theory of Goal Setting and Task Performance.* Upper Saddle River, NJ: Prentice Hall.

Maslow, A. (1954). *Motivation and Personality.* New York: Harper & Row.

McCarthy, D. J., Puffer, S. M., and Shekshnia, S. V. (1993). "The Resurgence of an Entrepreneurial Class in Russia," *Journal of Management Inquiry*, 2(2), 125–37.

McClelland, D. C. (1966). "That Urge to Achieve," *THINK Magazine.*

——. (1985). *Human Motivation.* Glenview, IL: Scott, Foresman.

—— and Burnham, D. H. (1976). "Power Is the Great Motivator," *Harvard Business Review*, March–April, 100–10.

Misra, S. and Kanungo, R. N. (1994). "Bases of Work Motivation in Developing Societies: A Framework for Performance Management." In Kanungo, R. N. and Mendonca, M. (eds.) *Work Motivation: Models for Developing Countries.* New Delhi: Sage.

MOW International Research Team (1987). *The Meaning of Work: An International Perspective.* London: Academic Press.

Nadler, D. A. and Lawler, E. E., (1977). "Motivation: A Diagnostic Approach." In Hackman, J. R., Lawler, E. E., and Porter, L. W. (eds.) *Perspectives on Behavior in Organizations.* New York: McGraw-Hill.

Ng, Q. (2002)." "Cash Is King, but Health Benefits Are Also Welcome," *Asia Computer Weekly,* October 28, 1.

Pearson, C. and Kamolkasemsilp, K. (2001). "Managerial Work Goals: A Study with Malaysian and Thailand Managers," *International Journal of Management,* 18(4), 412–20.

Pinder, C. C. (1984). *Work Motivation.* Glenview, IL: Scott, Foresman.

Porter, L. W. and Lawler, E. E., III. (1968). *Managerial Attitudes and Performance.* Homewood, IL: Irwin.

Puffer, S. M. (1993). "A Riddle Wrapped in an Enigma: Demystifying Russian Managerial Motivation," *European Management Journal*, 11(4), 473–80.

Punnett, B. J. (1995). "Preliminary Considerations of Confucianism and Needs in the PRC," *Journal of Asia-Pacific Business*, 1, 25–42.

"A Rewarding Strategy," (2002). *Business Europe,* April 17, 3.

Robbins, S. P. (1996). *Organizational Behavior: Concepts, Controversies, and Applications.* 7th Ed. Upper Saddle River, NJ: Prentice Hall.

Sagie, A., Elizur, D., and Yamauchi, H. (1996). "The Structure and Strength of Achievement Motivation: A Cross-Cultural Comparison," *Journal of Organizational Behavior,* 17, 431–44.

Skinner, B. F. (1971). *Contingencies of Reinforcement.* East Norwalk, CT: Appleton-Century-Crofts.

Stanley, A. (1996). "New Face of Russian Capitalism: Avon and Mary Kay Create Opportunities for Women," *The New York Times,* August 14, D1, D16.

Steers, R. M. and Braunstein, D. N. (1976). "Behaviorally Based Measure of Manifest Needs in Work Settings," *Journal of Vocational Behavior,* 9, 251–66.

——, Porter, L. W., and Bigley, G. A. (eds.) (1996). *Motivation and Leadership at Work.* 6th Ed. New York: McGraw-Hill.

—— and Sánchez-Runde, C. J. (2002). "Culture, Motivation, and Work Behavior." In Gannon, M. J. and Newman, K. L. (eds.) *The Blackwell Handbook of Cross-Cultural Management.* Oxford: Blackwell.

Trompenaars, F. (1993). *Riding the Waves of Culture: Understanding Diversity in Global Business.* London: The Economist Books.

Tullar, W. L. (1992). "Cultural Transformation: Democratization and Russian Entrepreneurial Motives." Paper presented at the Academy of Management meetings, Las Vegas, cited in Puffer, S. M. (1993). "A Riddle Wrapped in an Enigma: Demystifying Russian Managerial Motivation," *European Management Journal*, 1(4), 473–80.

Welsh, D. H. B., Luthans, F., and Sommer, S. M. (1993). "Organizational Behavior Modification Goes to Russia: Replicating an Experimental Analysis across Cultures and Tasks," *Journal of Organizational Behavior Management*, 13, 15–35.

Vroom, V. H. (1964). *Work and Motivation.* New York: Wiley.

CHAPTER 8

International Human Resource Management

Learning Objectives

After reading this chapter, you should be able to:

■ Define international human resource management (IHRM).

■ Understand how corporate strategy influences IHRM.

■ Explain the major IHRM functions: recruitment and selection, training and development, performance evaluation, compensation and benefits, and labor relations.

■ Discuss additional special concerns of managing expatriate employees.

CULTURE AT WORK

Salaryman and Freeter

Japan's long recession is changing traditional human resource practices. Until recently, large Japanese companies—Sony, Hitachi, Sumitomo—hired large groups of new employees each year. University graduates, particularly men, would easily find lifetime employment as "salarymen." Many of them lived together in a company dormitory and were encouraged to marry other employees to intensify the importance of the company in their lives. The average salaryman was extremely loyal to the company and often worked long hours.

Today, the salaryman's children are likely to be "freeters." A freeter—taking the "free" from English and the "ter" from the German "arbeiter," meaning worker—is usually 20-something, works short-term jobs, and otherwise enjoys life. Freeters usually live at home and rely on their parents to cook their meals and do the laundry. Freeters may skip work when it gets boring or quit altogether to take a long vacation.

Sources: Brooke, J. (2001). "Young Japanese Breaking Old Salaryman's Bonds," *The New York Times International*, October 16, A3; Dillon, L. S. (1990). "The Occidental Tourist," *Training and Development Journal*, 44, 72–80.

Organizations have different approaches to managing employees. How they find employees, pay, train, and promote them varies with culture. These issues are more complex when companies are global because they usually attempt to treat their employees equitably, yet in a culturally appropriate manner. In addition, organizations often send employees to assignments outside their home countries, creating special concerns for the organization and these employees.

The Culture at Work vignette contrasts the impact of the traditional Japanese culture that values close links between the lives of employees and employer with an emerging culture that emphasizes personal freedom. The human resource management practices for the salaryman, which create loyalty and stability, reflect the collective, strong uncertainty avoidance, future-oriented Japanese culture. Freeters reject the lifestyle of their parents' generation and value individualism more. The very different requirements for employing salarymen or freeters illustrates the need for organizations to be responsive to changes even within a single culture. How cultures and organizations in them treat employees is the focus of international human resource management.

▪▪▪ What Is International Human Resource Management?

The field of **international human resource management (IHRM)** includes three major areas:

1. the management of human resources in global corporations
2. the management of expatriate employees
3. the comparison of human resource management (HRM) practices in a variety of different countries

IHRM is responsible for all aspects of employee administration including recruiting and selecting employees, providing orientation and training, evaluating performance, administering a compensation system, and handling other aspects of labor relations. Operating an organization in different countries that employs citizens of different nationalities can be quite complex.

A major part of IHRM is managing **expatriates,** employees who work outside their home countries. The company takes greater responsibility for expatriates than domestic workers because of the circumstances of their work. International human resource (IHR) managers might help prepare expatriates to live in another country, find them housing, or arrange for the company to pay their taxes.

When managing human resources, a global organization uses a consistent policy across countries, treats each country as unique, or something in between. Factors influencing this decision are corporate strategy, the mix of countries where subsidiaries are located, and laws affecting HRM practices in these countries. The IHR manager needs to be familiar with local HRM laws and practices to make the correct decision.

HRM laws, regulations, and practices may influence a company's decision on where to locate a subsidiary. Prevailing wage rates, employee benefits required by law, and ease of dismissing employees can make one country more attractive than another. For example, in the Netherlands, companies must pay employees who lose their jobs unemployment benefits equal to 70% of their salaries for up to two and one-half years (Wiersma 1996). In France, the legal workweek is 35 hours and workers are limited to nine hours of overtime per week. In contrast, Middle Eastern countries generally allow a workweek of 42 to 48 hours (Duane 2001). Such differences require companies to think carefully about how legal requirements will influence their operation and potential profitability.

▪▪▪ International Corporate Strategy and IHRM

The approach to IHRM often reflects an organization's international corporate strategy. IHR managers participate in the international strategic planning process, but usually in a limited way (Bird and Beechler 1995; Briscoe 1995; Miller, Beechler, Bhatt, and Nath 1986). However, "HR managers can and should provide essential advice and input at every step of the traditional strategic management process" (Briscoe 1995, p. 33). A more effective strategy results if a broader range of organizational units participates in its development. Regardless of the extent of their involvement in developing international corporate strategy, it influences IHR managers. An organization's overall corporate strategy usually determines the approach to managing and staffing subsidiaries.

Approaches to Managing and Staffing Subsidiaries

There are four major approaches to managing and staffing subsidiaries (Dowling, Schuler, and Welch 1994; Phatak 1995). These reflect how the organization develops its human resource policies and the preferred type of employee for different positions.

1. **Ethnocentric.** The home country approach prevails. Headquarters makes key decisions, employees from the home country hold important jobs, and the subsidiaries follow home country HRM practices.
2. **Polycentric.** Each subsidiary manages on a local basis. A local employee heads a subsidiary, because headquarters managers may not have adequate local knowledge, but promotion from a foreign subsidiary to headquarters is rare. Subsidiaries usually develop HRM practices locally.
3. **Regiocentric.** This is similar to the polycentric approach, but regional groups of subsidiaries reflecting the organization's strategy and structure function as a unit. There is some degree of autonomy in regional decision making, and promotions are possible within the region but rare from the region to headquarters. Subsidiaries within a region develop a common set of HRM practices.
4. **Geocentric or global.** Using a worldwide integrated business strategy, the organization manages and staffs on a global basis. Nationality is not a major factor in promotion decisions. HRM practices develop with input from headquarters and subsidiaries and are generally consistent across locations.

In the ethnocentric approach, the cultural values and business practices of the home country are dominant. Headquarters develops a managing and staffing approach and consistently applies it throughout the world. Companies following the ethnocentric approach assume the home country approach is best and that employees from other parts of the world can and should follow it. Managers from headquarters develop practices and hold key positions in the subsidiaries to ensure consistency.

The polycentric approach is in direct opposition. The assumption is that each country is different and that the subsidiaries in each country should develop locally appropriate practices under the supervision of local managers. The regiocentric approach is similar except that the "local" unit is a region rather than a country.

With the geocentric approach, organizations try to combine the best from headquarters and the subsidiaries to develop consistent worldwide practices. Competency rather than nationality determines manager selection.

Organizations taking either an ethnocentric or geocentric approach have fairly consistent practices worldwide. Those taking a polycentric or regiocentric approach have variation in practice based on location.

Choosing an Approach to IHRM

Overall international corporate strategy determines the choice of the four approaches to IHRM. However, the following six factors also influence the approach to IHRM (Brewster 2002; Fisher, Schoenfeldt, and Shaw 1993):

1. **Political and legal concerns.** A subsidiary in a foreign country is subject to local law. Some laws impact directly on HRM policy. For example, some countries limit the number of expatriates a foreign company may employ, precluding an ethnocentric approach. In other countries, foreign companies qualify for tax incentives if they hire and provide training for locals. This may predispose the company towards a polycentric approach.

2. **Level of development in foreign locations.** Some locations may lack adequate numbers of local people with appropriate levels of managerial and technical skills, requiring an organization to bring in expatriates. This makes an ethnocentric approach more likely. The availability of a talented workforce allows a company to select any approach.

3. **Technology and the nature of the product.** This factor relates to the two previous items. With the use of highly sophisticated manufacturing technology or the need for high quality standards, headquarters employees help ensure consistency, thereby necessitating an ethnocentric approach. Modifying the basic product to appeal to local or regional markets calls for managers who know the local situation. Here, a polycentric or regiocentric approach makes more sense.

4. **Organizational life cycle.** The organization's stage of internationalization or the product's stage in the life cycle can influence the approach to IHRM. For example, when an organization first ventures into international business, it often takes an ethnocentric approach. As the organization expands internationally, management may treat subsidiaries as additions to the corporation with management by locals, a polycentric approach. As the firm continues to grow, increased productivity and cost control become more important. At this stage, the company could take a regiocentric or geocentric approach. In the final stage, the company views its operations as global and the approach to HR should be global as well.

5. **Age and history of the subsidiary.** Long established subsidiaries may take on the characteristics of the host country where they are located. It may be difficult for a company to globalize these operations. In contrast, a greenfield operation is easier to integrate.

6. **Organizational and national cultural differences.** The cultures of the headquarters and subsidiaries influence the approach. Some organizations and countries prefer the ethnocentric approach. For example, the Japanese are more likely than either Americans or Europeans to use headquarters managers in subsidiaries (Tung 1988). A second issue is the number and makeup of cultures in foreign subsidiaries. If the number and extent of cultural differences among the subsidiaries become too great, instituting a geocentric policy may be difficult.

Choosing an approach to IHRM is complex. If an organization integrates human resources practices into its overall strategy, it is likely to be more successful. However, HRM, more than any other function, is likely to reflect local practice (Rosenzweig and Nohria 1994). American management researchers consider consistency between corporate level strategy and the HR practices of subsidiaries to be important (Bird and Beechler 1995). In contrast, Europeans emphasize the strategic role of HRM less. European HR managers may have to follow the dictates of top management giving them less control and autonomy than their American counterparts. However, there is usually more government support for the labor market giving the manager more choices (Fisher et al. 1993).

Cost is also a factor in choosing an approach to IHRM. A localized approach is less expensive because the head office does not need to monitor and coordinate activities in the subsidiaries. Companies that follow a more consistent approach worldwide incur more cost but will achieve a more standardized approach worldwide, and different subsidiaries can learn from each other (Brewster 2002). Even within one organization, there may be more localization of some HR functions and less of others. For example, pay scales for local employees are almost always set locally whereas programs to develop global organization leaders need to be centrally managed (Brewster 2002).

▮▮▮ Major IHRM Functions

IHRM has responsibility for the five functional areas discussed in this section: recruitment and selection, training and development, performance evaluation, compensation and benefits, and labor relations. Because expatriate employees often receive different treatment than other employees, a discussion of additional issues involved in managing expatriates follows this section.

Recruitment and Selection

Recruitment and selection are the processes through which an organization takes in new members. **Recruitment** involves attracting a pool of qualified applicants for the positions available. **Selection** requires choosing from this pool the candidate whose qualifications most closely match the job requirements.

Classifying Employees

Traditionally, employees in international organizations are classified as one of three types:

1. **Parent Country National (PCN).** The employee's nationality is the same as the organization's—for example a French citizen working for a French company in Algeria.
2. **Host Country National (HCN).** The employee's nationality is the same as the location of the subsidiary—for example, an Algerian citizen working for a French company in Algeria.
3. **Third Country National (TCN).** The employee's nationality is different from both the organization's and the subsidiary's—for example, an Italian citizen working for a French company in Algeria.

However, as IHRM staffing becomes increasingly more complex, these classifications do not cover all employees (Briscoe 1995). For example, within the European Union (EU), citizens of member countries can work in other member countries without a work permit. Therefore, how to classify a German citizen working for a Spanish company in Spain is not clear. Is this person a PCN, HCN, or TCN? Classification may seem unimportant, but in many organizations, an employee's classification determines compensation, benefits, and opportunities for promotion.

How Managing and Staffing Approaches Influence Recruitment and Selection

In an international organization, the managing and staffing approach strongly influences the type of employee the company hires. In a company with an ethnocentric approach, PCNs usually staff important positions at headquarters and subsidiaries. With a polycentric approach, HCNs generally work in foreign subsidiaries while PCNs manage headquarters positions. In the regiocentric approach, both PCNs and managers from the region—either HCNs or TCNs—staff regional headquarters positions while HCNs primarily staff local subsidiaries. Finally, an organization with a geocentric approach chooses the most suitable person for a position, regardless of type.

In its approach to recruitment and selection, an organization considers both headquarters practices and those prevalent in the countries of its subsidiaries. Local culture always influences recruitment and selection practices, and in some countries, local laws require a specific approach. For example, in international manufacturing and processing facilities in Mexico, known as *maquiladoras,* companies recruit with a sign announcing job openings outside the facility or by employees introducing family members who are looking for jobs (Teagarden et al. 1995). In Greece, organizations seek applicants through a government-run Employment Office since private employment agencies are illegal (Duane 2001).

Selecting the Right Candidate

In choosing the right candidate, a balance between internal corporate consistency and sensitivity to local labor practices is a goal. Different cultures emphasize different attributes in the selection process depending on whether they use achievement or ascriptive criteria. When making a hiring decision, people in an achievement-oriented country consider skills, knowledge, and talents. Although "connections" can help, companies generally only hire those with the required qualifications. In an ascriptive culture, age, gender, personal relationships, and family background are important, and an organization selects someone whose personal characteristics fit the job. Individualism and collectivism also influence selection. Although individualist countries generally prefer to use selection testing for hiring (Ramamoorthy and Carroll 1998), some collectivist countries such as China, Indonesia, and South Korea also consider testing important (Huo, Huang, and Napier 2002).

Some countries have laws prohibiting discrimination against certain groups in hiring, promotion, and compensation. In the United States, for example, it is illegal to make hiring decisions based on race, gender, color, national origin, religion, age (over 40), disability, pregnancy, and in some locales, sexual orientation. In choosing a candidate to hire, employers cannot ask questions relating to these personal characteristics.

In countries where laws regarding hiring practices are limited or nonexistent, an employer may ask any questions or seek candidates with certain personal characteristics. For example, in Japan, some large companies looking for new management trainees only consider recent male graduates from elite universities.

Companies taking a global approach to strategy may have difficulty integrating subsidiary practices that vary due to the level of government regulation. One global approach, developed by Artise (1995), begins with a basic selection system appropriate for the company's operating system. Using the basic selection system, the organization then makes modifications to adapt it to the various cultures where the company does business. Artise suggests choosing applicants based on competency, motivation, and fit with the company. He recommends a Job Model to characterize a position on five aspects: results achievable, priorities, obstacles, environment, and management style. The goal is to find the optimum match between the Job Model and applicant qualifications.

Artise also suggests modifying the basic process of selection for cultural differences. For example, after a Korean applicant responds, "the interviewer should allow for a three- to four-second silent gap to take place, remaining focused on the applicant and displaying a subtle pleasant smile. [This is to allow] a nonverbal *reading* of the other's intentions" [known as *nunchi*] (Artise 1995, p. 92).

Artise's proposal for a global system is based on an achievement orientation. Matching applicant qualifications with the needs of the job is the classic approach to selection developed in North America. A North American company's managers might consider this system sufficiently global to implement worldwide. A Japanese company, conversely, might feel it places too much stress on qualifications and not enough on personal characteristics. Because the Japanese recruit for a general position within the company rather than a specific job, creating a Job Model is irrelevant.

Training and Development

The **training and development** function includes planned individual learning, organization development, and career development. It is a recognized professional field known as **human resource development (HRD).** At the international level, HRD professionals are responsible for training and development of employees located in subsidiaries around the world, specialized training to prepare expatriates for assignments abroad, and development of a special group of globally minded managers.

Delivery of Programs Worldwide

The delivery of international HRD programs is either centralized or decentralized (Marquardt and Engel 1993). With a centralized approach that fits the ethnocentric model, training originates at headquarters and corporate trainers travel to subsidiaries, sometimes making adaptations to fit the local situation. A geocentric approach is also centralized, but the training develops through input from both headquarters and subsidiary staff. Trainers from various positions in the headquarters or subsidiaries could travel to any other corporate location. In a decentralized approach, training is on a local or regional basis, following a polycentric or regiocentric model.

In decentralized training, the cultural backgrounds of the trainers and trainees are usually similar; local people develop training materials and techniques for use in their own area. If the organization takes a centralized approach, the trainers still need to make appropriate adaptations to the local culture, and consider the cultures of both the trainers and the trainees.

To maximize training effectiveness, it is important to take into account how trainees learn most effectively, as cultural factors have a strong impact on training practices in different parts of the world. For example, in North America, where power distance is small, the relationship between the trainer and trainees tends toward equality. The trainer and trainees use first names, and the trainees feel free to challenge or question the trainer. In Malaysia, where power distance is large, a trainer receives greater respect—students use his surname and title—and treat him as an undisputable expert.

A study of graduate students in Britain and China confirms the impact of power distance on the role relations between tutor and student that is similar to the trainer–trainee relationship (Spencer-Oatey 1997). Chinese students perceive a greater power differential between themselves and their tutors than do British students. However, the Chinese students also feel closer to their tutors which may be due to the more paternal role of leaders in China.

Table 8-1 outlines the effect of culture on training practices in four parts of the world: the United States and Canada, East Asia, the Middle East and North Africa, and Latin America. Although the table describes the regions in broad, general terms, it provides

TABLE 8-1 The Impact of Culture on Training and Development Practices

	U.S.A./Canada	*East Asia*	*Middle East/North Africa*	*Latin America*
HRD Roles	Trainer and trainee as equals; trainees can and do challenge trainer, trainer can be informal and casual.	Trainees have great respect for trainer who should behave, dress, and relate in a highly professional, formal manner.	Trainer highly respected, trainees want respect and friendly relationship, formality is important.	Preference for a decisive, clear, charismatic leader as trainer, trainees like to be identified with and loyal to a successful leader.
Analysis and Design	Trainer determines objectives with input from trainees and their managers, trainees openly state needs and want to achieve success through learning.	Trainer should know what trainees need, admitting needs might represent loss of face to trainees.	Difficult to identify needs since it is improper to speak of others' faults, design must include time for socializing, relationship building, and prayers.	Difficult to get trainees to expose weaknesses and faults, design should include time for socializing.
Development and Delivery	Programs should be practical and relevant using a variety of methodologies with lecturing time limited.	Materials should be orderly, well organized and unambiguous, trainees most accustomed to lecture, note taking, and limited questioning.	Need adequate opportunity for trainer and trainees to interact, rely on oral rather than written demonstrations of knowledge acquired, avoid paper exercises and role playing.	Educational system relies on lecture and more theoretical emphasis, training should be delivered in local language.
Administration and Environment	Hold training in comfortable, economical location, trainee selection based on perceived needs of organization and individual.	Quality of program may be judged based on quality of location and training materials, ceremonies with dignitaries, certificates, plaques, and speeches taken as signs of value of program.	The learning process should be permeated with flourishes and ceremonies, program should not be scheduled during Ramadan, the month of fasting.	Value and importance judged by location, which dignitaries invited for the ceremonies, and academic affiliation of trainer, time is flexible: beginning or ending at a certain time not important.

▪▪▪▪▪▪▪▪▪▪

Source: Marquardt, M. and Engel, D.bW. (1993). *Global Human Resource Development.* Upper Saddle River, NJ: Prentice Hall, 25–32. Adapted by permission of Pearson Education, Inc., Upper Saddle River, NJ.

insight into the major differences. An effective trainer must learn the specifics of the country and culture of the trainees to select the most effective approach.

Developing Globally Minded Managers

As global competition intensifies, it is increasingly important for successful companies to have a group of managers with a global perspective. A study of American multinationals indicates that companies whose CEOs have international assignment experience are better performers. Performance is even stronger when the top management team also has international experience and when the company has an extensive global strategy. However, the number of CEOs who have extensive international or global experience is small (Carpenter, Sanders, and Gregersen 2001).

Companies must identify managers with global potential and provide them various training and development opportunities. For example, having one or more international assignments, working on cross-national teams and projects, and learning other languages and cultures contribute to making a manager more globally minded. In addition, an organization should include in this group both PCNs and employees from other countries.

Performance Evaluation

Performance evaluation is the systematic appraisal of employees' performance within the organization. In Western multinational corporations, performance appraisals, typically done annually, include a standardized evaluation form, and the company often requires supervisors to discuss the results of the appraisals with each employee.

Performance evaluation is challenging for any organization. In the U.S. context, its purposes are to provide information for organizational decisions such as promotions and salary increases, and to give feedback to employees to help them develop and improve. In other countries, the purposes may be completely different. For example, in Korea, the aim is for the employee and supervisor to develop a relationship (Cascio 1998).

At the international level, the complexity is greater because the organization must evaluate employees from different countries working in different subsidiaries. The need for consistency across subsidiaries for performance comparisons conflicts with the need to consider the cultural background of employees to make the evaluation meaningful. For example, collectivists may not like the type of formal appraisal system that is common in most Western multinationals (Ramamoorthy and Carroll 1998) because they may feel that individually based evaluations interfere with team spirit (Milliman et al. 1998).

The communication style in some countries may also influence performance evaluation (Audia and Tams 2002). Since collectivists value harmony, direct feedback could be damaging, creating a negative self-image and undermining an employee's loyalty to the organization. In Russia, for example, it is preferable to give feedback indirectly; a third person, trusted by both the supervisor and the employee, can deliver the feedback or the supervisor may withdraw favors to indicate displeasure. Russians also like group-based feedback with input from peers and customers (Elenkov 1998). In Mexico an individual's public image is important, and public criticism of an employee might cause him to leave (de Forest 1994). Consequently, the delivery of a balanced performance review including both strengths and weaknesses requires tact and delicacy. In Korea, managers deliver criticism in a subtle and indirect way—often verbally—and it may take a manager as long as five years after joining a company to learn how he is doing (Cascio 1998).

As with other functions, the approach to performance evaluation depends on the organization's overall HRM strategy. A company with an ethnocentric approach is likely to use the performance evaluation process developed in its headquarters for all its subsidiaries. Some companies translate evaluation forms into local languages whereas others use the original language everywhere. An enterprise with a polycentric or regiocentric approach develops local procedures within each country or region. Finally, a company with a geocentric approach uses the same performance evaluation system worldwide, but it has universal applicability. Developing a global system is the most challenging.

One example of a global approach is the performance measurement system developed by Sonoco Products, a global supplier of industrial and consumer packaging that employs over 16,000 people in 32 countries (Wellins and Rioux 2001). The objective of the system is for managers to understand the link between their own performance and organizational goals. To successfully implement the program, the company trains executives to manage their own performance and development.

Compensation and Benefits

The **compensation and benefits** function develops and administers the salary system and other forms of remuneration such as vacation and sick pay, health insurance, and pension funds. In developing an international system of compensation and benefits, an organization has two primary concerns. The first is comparability (Briscoe 1995). An effective compensation system assigns salaries to employees that are internally comparable and competitive within the marketplace. For example, the salary of a senior manager is usually higher than that of a supervisor, and each position should receive an amount within the local market range. The international organization must also consider the salaries of people who may transfer from other locations.

Cost is the second major concern (Dowling et al. 1994). Organizations strive to minimize all expenses, and payroll is one of the largest. Labor costs vary widely by country, and companies often locate subsidiaries in countries that have lower wage rates than at home. Table 8-2 compares wages for production workers in selected countries.

TABLE 8-2 Hourly Compensation Costs for Production Workers in Manufacturing in U.S. Dollars – 2001

Australia	$13.15	Japan	$19.59
Brazil	$3.02	Korea	$8.09
Canada	$15.64	Mexico	$2.34
Finland	$19.94	Netherlands	$19.29
France	$15.88	Singapore	$7.77
Hong Kong	$5.96	Spain	$10.88
Germany	$22.86	Taiwan	$5.70
Ireland	$13.28	UK	$16.14
Italy	$13.76	USA	$20.32

Source: U.S. Department of Labor, Bureau of Labor Statistics, "International Comparisons of Hourly Compensation Costs for Production Workers in Manufacturing, 1975–2001," accessed June 5, 2003, ftp://ftp.bls.gov/pub/special.requests/ForeignLabor/supptab.txt

Setting Compensation and Benefit Levels

Compensation and benefits reflect local labor market conditions even when an organization takes an ethnocentric or geocentric approach. The availability of qualified local people to fill positions, prevailing wage rates, the use of expatriates, and local laws interact to influence the level of compensation and benefits. For example, if there are few applicants available for positions, the remuneration for those positions generally increases. To reduce expenses, the IHR manager might then consider bringing in an expatriate.

A company usually develops a policy, which could apply globally, to offer salaries and benefits representing a specific market level. For example, a large successful multinational that emphasizes the quality of its products and employees may have a global policy to pay the highest wages everywhere it operates. Another company could offer top salaries in the country where it does research and development yet pay average wages in the country where it manufactures.

Culture may influence the value that people in different societies put on various compensation and benefit practices. For example, more masculine countries make less use of flexible benefit programs and are less likely to provide workplace childcare, opportunities for career breaks, or maternity leave (Schuler and Rogovsky 1998). Using culture as a guide, companies may develop more effective approaches for their subsidiaries (Hempel 1998). Table 8-3 suggests how cultural characteristics may influence desirability of different practices.

Labor Relations

The **labor relations function** identifies and defines the roles of management and workers in the workplace. The concept of labor relations varies greatly in different

TABLE 8-3 Offering Culturally Consistent Compensation and Benefit Practices

Cultural Characteristics	*Preferred Practices*
High uncertainty avoidance	More certainty in compensation systems (Seniority- or skill-based), centralized bureaucratized pension system with many controls and protections
Low uncertainty avoidance	Defined contribution pension plan with flexible plan implementation
High power distance	Separate pension plans for different levels of employees
Low power distance	Same type of pension plan/health coverage offered to all employees
Feminine	"Family friendly" policies and other benefits to enhance quality of work life
Individualistic	Individual incentive compensation systems, flexible benefits programs
Individualistic, low power distance, low uncertainty avoidance	Stock options, stock-ownership plans

▪ ▪ ▪ ▪ ▪ ▪ ▪ ▪

Sources: Hempel, P. S. (1998). "Designing Multinational Benefits Programs: The Role of National Culture," *Journal of World Business*, 33, 277–94.; Schuler, R.S. and Rogovsky, N. (1998). "Understanding Compensation Practice Variations across Firms: The Impact of National Culture," *Journal of International Business Studies*, 29, 159–77.

parts of the world. In the United States, for example, labor relations are often a formal relationship, sometimes antagonistic, between labor and management defined by a union contract. In Japan, the relationship between management and unions is cooperative, and management often appoints union leaders (Hodgetts and Luthans 1994).

In many countries the government regulates labor relations practices. Consequently, in this function more than other HRM functions, an organization may have to be polycentric. However, even though labor relations are local-level issues, it is good corporate strategy to coordinate labor relations policy across subsidiaries (Dowling et al. 1994).

Union Organization

Although some unions are "international," in fact, most unions are organized at the local, company, regional (within country), or national level. There is no multinational union that allows a global corporation to negotiate terms for its employees worldwide. However, some unions are developing multicountry regional offices that handle issues related to regional trading blocs such as the European Union (Briscoe 1995). Nevertheless, the right to negotiate and the right to strike remain at the national level in Europe, and because of the history and tradition in different countries, it may be difficult for one union to represent all Europeans (Wahl 2002).

Union Membership

The number of workers within a country who are union members varies significantly around the world (see Table 8-4). In addition, the union membership figures may not represent the unions' relative power. For example, **union density,** the percentage of all employed people in a country who belong to a union, is higher in Western Europe than

TABLE 8-4 Union Density Figures for Selected Countries

Country	Union Membership (as a percentage of total paid employees)	Year
Australia	28%	1998
Canada	30%	1999
China	90%	2000
Colombia	7%	1996
Germany	26%	1998
Hong Kong	22%	1999
Iceland	89%	2000
India	26%	1997
Japan	22%	2000
Norway	71%	2000
Slovakia	60%	1999
South Korea	12%	2000
Turkey	57%	2000
United States	14%	2001

Source: ILO Bureau of Statistics (unpublished) data compiled from Official National Statistical Publications

in the United States. However, the laws in most Western European countries do not require employers to conduct collective bargaining with unions, thus greatly diminishing the unions' power (Duane 2001).

▪▪▪ Best IHRM Practices Project

In 1990, a team of North American researchers led by Mary Ann von Glinow planned a long-term, large-scale study to identify "best international HRM practices" under a variety of conditions (Geringer, Frayne, and Milliman 2002). The research examines whether practices are context free, context specific, or context dependent. **Context free** practices apply to any country or company. **Context specific** indicates the practice could apply in companies or countries that are similar. Finally, **context dependent** approaches are only effective in certain countries or companies.

The researchers wanted to find out how often certain practices were used, how effective they were, what types of organizations used what types of practices, and how context factors such as business strategy, national culture, or external environment influence the effectiveness of different practices. From 1991 to 1998, 37 scholars from around the world collected data from companies in ten different locations including Australia, Canada, China, Indonesia, Japan, Latin America (Costa Rica, Guatemala, Panama, Nicaragua, and Venezuela), Mexico, South Korea, Taiwan, and the United States (Geringer et al. 2002; Lowe, Milliman, De Cieri, and Dowling 2002).

Table 8-5 summarizes the major findings.

TABLE 8-5 Trends in International Human Resource Management Practices across Selected Countries and Regions - Findings from the Best International Human Resource Management Practices Project

Practice	*Universals Derived ETICS "Best Practices"**	*Regional or Country Clusters*	*Country Specific*
COMPENSATION	Pay incentives should not comprise too much of an employee's compensation package. Compensation should be based on individual job performance. There should be a reduced emphasis on seniority. Benefits should comprise an important part of a compensation package.	Seniority-based pay, pay based on group/ team or organizational goals, and pay based on future goals—all are used to a larger extent in the Asian and Latin countries now.	United States and Canada had less use of pay incentives than expected. China and Taiwan had above-average use of pay incentives, and wanted more based on individual contributions.

▪▪▪▪▪▪▪▪▪

(continued)

TABLE 8-5 (cont.)

Practice	Universals Derived ETICS "Best Practices"	Regional or Country Clusters	Country Specific
SELECTION	"Getting along with others," and "Fit with the Corporate Values" signals a shift in selection from "West meets East."	Selection practices were remarkably similar among the Anglo countries. Specifically, job interview, technical skill, and work experience are the most important selection criteria. How well the person fits the company's values replaces work experience as one of the top selection criteria for future selection practices. Selection practices are quite similar in Korea, Japan, and Taiwan. Specifically, proven work experience is de-emphasized as a selection practice in these countries. In the Anglo and Latin American countries, allowing subordinates to express themselves is perceived as an important future appraisal practice.	In Japan, a heavy emphasis is placed on a person's potential (thus hiring new graduates) and his/her ability to get along with others. A relatively low weight was given to job-related skills, and experience as a selection criterion. In Korea, employment tests are considered crucial and are used to a large extent as a selection tool, as well as hiring new graduates. Koreans de-emphasize experience. In Taiwan, the job interview is considered the most important criterion in the selection process.
PERFORMANCE APPRAISAL	In all countries, the "should-be" scores were higher on every purpose, suggesting that the purposes of PA have fallen short in every country. All countries indicated that a greater emphasis be placed on development and documentation in future PA practices. In particular, recognizing subordinates, evaluating their goal achievement, planning their development activities, and (ways to) improving their performance are considered the most important appraisal practices for the future.	In contrast, in the Asian countries expression is used to a low extent, particularly in Korea. In the Latin American countries, the administrative purposes of performance appraisal are considered important in future practice.	In Taiwan, the administrative purposes of performance appraisal are considered important in future practice.

TABLE 8-5 (cont.)

Practice	Universals Derived ETICS "Best Practices"	Regional or Country Clusters	Country Specific
T&D	In most countries, T&D practices are used to improve employees' technical skills. There is a growing trend toward using T&D for team building and "soft management practices."	In the Anglo countries, the softer T&D practices such as team building, understanding business practices and corporate culture, and the proactive T&D practices such as preparation for future assignment and cross-training are used moderately; however, a significant increase in these practices is desired. In the Latin countries, an increase in the extent to which all T&D practices are used is desired. In the Asian countries, most T&D practices are used moderately and are consistently considered satisfactory.	In Mexico, T&D as a reward to employees is considered a highly desirable practice. In the United States and Korea, preparing employees for future job assignments is used to a lesser extent. United States is using outsourcing more. In Japan, remedying past performance is used to a small extent, however, a significant increase in this practice is desired. In Korea, team building is used extensively and emphasized in all T&D practices.
RELATION TO BUSINESS STRATEGY	Across most countries, the HRM practices most closely linked to organizational capability are training and development and performance appraisal.	In the Asian countries, linkages were indicated between both low cost and differentiation strategies and HRM practices.	In Mexico, no linkages were indicated between organizational capability and HRM practices.
STATUS OF HRM FUNCTION			In Japan and Taiwan few linkages were indicated between organizational capability and HRM practices. Status of HRM was highest in Australia and lowest in Indonesia.

▪▪▪▪▪▪▪▪▪

Source: Von Glinow, M. A., Drost, E. A., and Teagarden, M. B. (2002). "Converging on IHRM Best Practices: Lessons Learned from a Globally Distributed Consortium on Theory and Practice," *Human Resource Management*, 41, pp. 133–5.
*Derived etics are practices that are "universal" within the set of cultures surveyed.

▪▪▪ Managing Expatriates

Organizations that employ PCNs and TCNs must deal with the complexities of employing and moving people outside of their home countries. Employing expatriates, although it may be a good business decision, is expensive. Because of the additional compensation required, an expatriate's remuneration package could be two to three times base salary (Parker and Janush 2001). Consequently, successfully managing all aspects of expatriate HRM is extremely important.

Expatriate Failure Rates

Because of the great expense involved in employing expatriates, it is important that they be successful once in the foreign assignment. Researchers define **failures** as expatriates who do not remain abroad for the duration of their assignment. Another problem is "**brownouts,**" managers who finish their assignments, but do so ineffectively. An expatriate returning early may cost a company $200,000 to $1.2 million. There are also additional costs to the organization such as damaged reputation or lost business (Black, Gregersen, Mendenhall, and Stroh 1999).

Differences in Failure Rates

The success rates of expatriates from different countries vary. In a large-scale comparative study of companies from the United States, Western Europe, and Japan, human resource administrators reported the expatriate failure rates in their organizations, including those who had to be recalled to the home country or dismissed because they couldn't function in the foreign assignment (Tung 1988). For U.S. companies, the percentage rates varied from less than 10% to as high as 40% with most companies responding in the 10–20% range. Most Western European firms were below 5% with very few companies reaching as high as 15%. The Japanese had the lowest failure rates with a large majority at less than 5%, and no company reporting higher than 15%.

For all groups, the failure rate correlated with the rigor of selection and training procedures, but the reasons for failure varied. American and Western European expatriates generally failed because of lack of social abilities or problems with their families. The number one reason was failure of the spouse to adjust. For the Japanese, the major reason for failure was the expatriate's inability to cope with larger responsibilities.

A study of Japanese expatriates living in Hong Kong and Taiwan concluded that Japanese failure rates may be as high as those found in the U.S. companies. The major reason for failure was family-related problems caused by the children's education or the spouse's social life (Fukuda and Chu 1994).

These two studies collected information on failure rates from HR managers within the companies. Self-reports indicate that Japanese expatriates experience greater difficulty adjusting and consider themselves less effective than American expatriates (Stening and Hammer 1992). A more recent study of expatriates from the U. K. reports a failure rate of 8.62% based on expatriate self-report while the 36 companies they worked for report failure rates between 0 and 18% (Forster 1997).

Men and women also have different failure rates. Of 686 major North American multinationals surveyed, only 3% had women expatriates, but 97% of the women reported a successful assignment (Adler 1994). However, Western male and female expatriates, mostly from Europe and the United States, working in Hong Kong were equally well adjusted generally, but females adjusted better at work and in handling interpersonal relationships while males had better psychological adjustment (Selmer and Leung 2003).

These studies suggest that companies must improve their approach to selection and training. Possible solutions include more attention to selection, training, assistance in cultural adjustment, evaluation, compensation, and cultural reentry for expatriates.

Selection of Expatriates

Successful expatriates have to perform their jobs and simultaneously adjust to a new cultural environment; this requires technical and managerial skills along with social and coping skills. Ultimately, expatriates must do their jobs competently, learn to live comfortably in a new culture, and ensure that their families adapt as well.

Western European and Japanese multinationals emphasize the need for two types of skills: technical competence and the ability to acclimate quickly to a new cultural environment. In North American corporations, in spite of research showing the importance of both skills, technical competence is often the only criterion for an expatriate position (Dowling et al. 1994; Mendenhall, Dunbar, and Oddou 1987; Tung 1988). In fact, when choosing candidates for overseas assignments, many companies lack an international staffing plan and rely on less valid selection techniques, for example, unstructured interviews and supervisor references. Ironically, this results in selecting expatriates who are successful in their home cultures but who may not have the skills needed for success in another culture (Mendenhall et al. 2002).

In many cases, behaviors that are successful at home may not work abroad. American managers working in Hong Kong exhibited the same behaviors that were successful in the United States, but these behaviors did not match those of successful Hong Kong Chinese managers. For the Hong Kong Chinese managers, there was no relation between successful job performance and any of the behaviors on a standard U.S. measure of managerial behavior. For the American managers in Hong Kong, only "integration," maintaining a closely knit organization and resolving intermember conflicts, related to success (Black and Porter 1991).

Logically, previous experience abroad should be an accurate indicator of success for an expatriate assignment. However, research is inconclusive with some studies reporting that previous experience relates to cross-cultural adjustment while others show no effect or even a negative impact on adjustment and effectiveness (Mendenhall et al. 2002). One study suggests that only experience in the same location can influence sociocultural adjustment and therefore every new expatriate assignment in a different location requires "starting over" (Selmer 2002).

Expatriate Training

As discussed earlier, expatriates are more successful when their organizations train them to prepare for their life and work abroad. However, many expatriates, particularly those from North America, receive little or no training prior to their new assignments (Briscoe 1995; Dowling et al. 1994; Tung 1988). Those who receive training usually only take a course for a week or less that includes an area briefing or language training. Finally, companies rarely offer cross-cultural skills training or training for family members (Mendenhall et al. 2002).

The most important aspect of expatriate training is **cross-cultural training (CCT)**. CCT prepares an expatriate to live and work in a different culture since coping with a new environment is much more challenging than dealing with a new job. A variety of training methodologies is available for CCT. Table 8-6 outlines some of the popular ones and gives a brief description of each.

TABLE 8-6 Cross-Cultural Training (CCT) Methods

• Cultural Briefings	Explain the major aspects of the host country culture, including customs, traditions, everyday behaviors.
• Area Briefings	Explain the history, geography, economy, politics, and other general information about the host country and region.
• Cases	Portray a real-life situation in business or personal life to illustrate some aspect of living or working in the host culture.
• Role Playing	Allows the trainee to act out a situation that he or she might face living or working in the host country.
• Culture Assimilator	Provides a written set of situations that the trainee might encounter living or working in the host country. Trainee selects one from a set of responses to the situation and is given feedback on if it is appropriate and why.
• Field Experiences	Provide an opportunity for the trainee to go to the host country or another unfamiliar culture to experience living and working there for a short time.

An organization can choose an appropriate CCT method based on three situational factors of the expatriate's assignment: culture novelty, degree of interaction with host country nationals, and job novelty (Black and Mendenhall 1989).

Culture novelty is the degree of difference between the new culture and the expatriate's home culture. A method for measuring this is comparing the two cultures on a cultural framework such as Hofstede's or Trompenaars'. Differences in language represent another aspect of culture novelty. The need to speak a language that is very different from the expatriate's native language is indicative of higher culture novelty. Finally, the expatriate's previous experience with the culture is important. For example, a Chinese-American assigned to Taiwan might experience less culture novelty than an Italian-American.

The degree of interaction with host country nationals refers to how often and at what level the expatriate communicates with locals. The central issues are the frequency, importance, and nature of communication. Finally, job novelty depends on the new job demands including expectations, job constraints, and job choices, particularly the degree of autonomy.

Culture novelty is the most strongly weighted, because adjusting to a new culture is more challenging than adjustments to the other two factors. With greater culture novelty, more need to interact with host country nationals, and greater job novelty, the need to have more rigorous CCT increases. Figure 8-1 illustrates how the situational factors affect the selection of a CCT method.

American expatriates who receive rigorous CCT both predeparture and postarrival feel that they adjust to the new culture and become proficient in their new jobs more quickly. The expatriates with the highest levels of CCT also experience greater job satisfaction (Eschbach, Parker, and Stoeberl 2001).

Cross-Cultural Adjustment

Moving to a new country is interesting but can also be stressful. The level of stress involved in relocation can create as high as a 90% chance for a health breakdown if the expatriate does not adjust quickly (Coyle 1988). Expatriates and their families need time to become familiar with their new environment and to become comfortable living there. When they arrive, the newness of the experience is exciting, but a few months

∎∎∎∎∎∎∎∎∎∎∎∎ **FIGURE 8-1** How Situational Factors Influence the Selection of a CCT Method

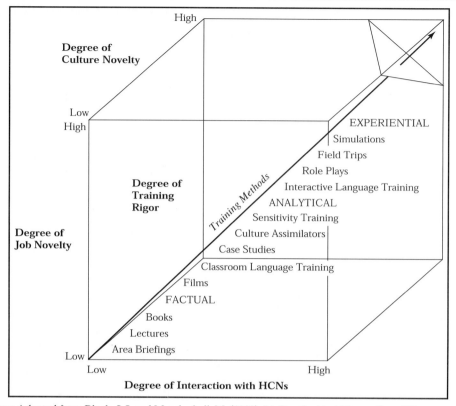

Source: Adapted from Black, J. S. and Mendenhall, M. (1989). "A Practical but Theory-Based Framework for Selecting Cross-Cultural Training Methods," *Human Resource Management,* 28(4), 511–39.

later, after more experience with the culture, expatriates may begin to feel frustrated or confused. This feeling is "culture shock." As expatriates get comfortable and understand more about the culture, usually three to six months after arrival, the culture shock will wear off, and they will experience a more normal feeling (Adler 1997). Figure 8-2 diagrams the culture shock cycle.

∎∎∎∎∎∎∎∎∎∎∎∎ **FIGURE 8-2** Culture Shock Cycle

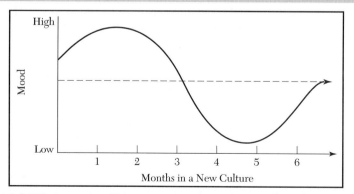

Source: Adler, N. J. (1997). *International Dimensions of Organizational Behavior.* 3d Ed. Cincinnati, OH: South-Western College Publishing, p. 238. Reprinted with permission of South-Western, a division of Thomson Learning: www.thomsonrights.com.

Expatriates must adjust to a new work situation, interactions with locals, and a new general environment (Black and Gregersen 1991). A company can facilitate the adjustment by providing training for expatriates and their families before and during the assignment (Black and Mendenhall 1990), making job requirements clear, and arranging the predecessor to orient the expatriate (Black and Gregersen 1991). It is also helpful if a company can make arrangements for housing before arrival, have support staff available in the foreign location, and provide assistance in dealing with foreign government matters such as visas and work permits (Shaffer, Harrison, Gilley, and Luk 2001).

Although it seems logical that expatriates who adjust well should perform effectively, this may not always be true. In some cases, people who have difficulty adjusting and experience the most culture shock may be the most effective performers. Paradoxically, the traits that result in superior expatriate task performance, such as perceptual skills and interpersonal sensitivity to others, also contribute to making cultural adjustment stressful (Thomas 1998).

Expatriate Evaluation

The performance evaluation of expatriate managers is particularly difficult. The job abroad may include much more than what it does at home. A manager often steps into the role of counselor, trainer, troubleshooter, or diplomat in addition to the assigned job responsibilities. With the need for adapting to a new culture, a different way of doing business, and often a new language, many factors influence an expatriate evaluation.

For senior expatriate managers, part of the evaluation often includes the financial performance of the subsidiary. Many factors outside the manager's control, such as local tax rates, currency rate fluctuations, or local labor laws, affect an organization's financial performance in a particular location. For example, an American expatriate working in Chile was able to stop a strike that would have closed his plant for months. At the same time, due to exchange rate fluctuations, the subsidiary experienced a significant downturn in sales. When evaluating this manager, headquarters decided to ignore his achievement of averting the strike and instead focused on the sales data giving him a slightly better than average rating (Oddou and Mendenhall 1995). In this situation, the home office did not fairly weigh all the external factors.

One study of American multinational companies found that perceived accuracy of expatriate performance appraisals is higher: (1) when companies use standardized evaluation forms that are customized for the local situation, (2) when the appraisals are conducted once or twice a year, (3) when the rater is geographically closer to the ratee, and (4) when there is a balance of raters from within and outside the host country. However, not many companies actually follow these practices, perhaps because they require more time and resources than the procedures they use (Gregersen, Hite, and Black 1996).

Expatriate Compensation

The cost of relocating and compensating expatriates for living outside their home countries generally makes them much more expensive than hiring locals and therefore influences the number of expatriates an organization employs. Table 8-7 illustrates the costs involved in sending an American expatriate for an assignment in London, Brussels, Tokyo, and Riyadh.

Compensation Approaches

An organization's general compensation policy influences expatriate compensation. Three common approaches are a home-based policy, a host-based policy, and a region-based

TABLE 8-7 Typical U.S. Expatriate Remuneration Package*

	London	*Brussels*	*Tokyo*	*Riyadh*
Cash Premiums and Allowances	$12,540 (28.5%)	$37,625 (30.1%)	$45,080 (19.6%)	$62,700 (33.0%)
Relocation Assistance	8,888 (20.2%)	24,875 (19.9%)	53,750 (28.8%)	25,650 (18.5%)
Itemized Reimbursements (benefits-in-kind)	8,184 (18.6%)	18,750 (15.0%)	41,880 (18.2%)	39,330 (20.7%)
*Taxation***	*14,888 (32.7%)*	*43,750 (35.0%)*	*91,310 (39.7%)*	*62,320 (32.8%)*
Total Annual Incremental Cost	$44,000 (100%)	$125,000 (100%)	$230,000 (100%)	$190,000 (100%)
Total Three-Year Incremental Cost	132,000	375,000	690,000	570,000
Total Three-Year Cost (incremental plus base)	432,000	675,000	990,000	870,000

*Based on total additional expatriate costs for M + 2 (school-age children) earning a base salary of $100,000 working abroad for three years.
**Could be substantially less, depending upon taxability of certain allowances.
Source: Parker, G. and Janush, E. S. (2001). "Developing Expatriate Remuneration Packages," *Employee Benefits Journal,* 26(2), p. 4. All rights reserved.

policy (Dowling et al. 1994). With a home-based policy, employees' compensation follows the scale of their home countries. For example, a German and a Canadian working in the same position in Thailand receive a salary based on their pay in Germany and Canada. Although the result is salary inequity, if the assignment abroad is not long, the expatriate may still use colleagues at home for comparison. With longer assignments, however, expatriates from countries with lower pay scales may feel they are being treated unfairly.

The host-based policy sets salaries at the level of the host country with benefits usually similar to the home country. This is attractive to employees relocated to an area with higher salaries than their home countries. However, if the assignment is short term, returning home to a lower salary could be difficult.

Finally, region determines the third approach to compensation. For employees working outside their home countries, compensation reflects whether their relocation is within their home region or in another region. With this approach, an assignment closer to home, that is, within the region, receives compensation at a lower rate than one further away which is outside the region.

Special Compensation and Benefits

Expatriates usually receive extra compensation for the inconvenience of living abroad. Large companies often also pay additional benefits to their expatriate employees to motivate and provide a comfortable life for them abroad. These benefits include an overseas premium, housing allowance, cost of living allowance, moving expenses, tuition for dependent education, home leave, and tax reimbursement payments. Table 8-8 describes these.

The amount paid depends on the company, employee nationality, and location of the assignment. Established policies for expatriate compensation exist in many large multinational corporations. In other companies, expatriate compensation and benefits are ad hoc and dependent on the negotiating ability of the expatriate.

There may also be differences in the types and costs of benefits expatriates receive in different places. For example, in India, expatriates typically receive a rest

TABLE 8-8 Typical Expatriate Benefits	
• Overseas Premium	Additional percentage of base salary (usually 10 percent) paid to compensate for inconvenience of living abroad
• Housing Allowance	Provision of comfortable housing for free or at a rate similar to what the expatriate would incur at home
• Cost of Living Allowance (COLA)	Payment of additional amount to cover extra costs to allow expatriate to live in the same manner as they did at home
• Moving Expenses	Expatriate and family transportation and goods shipment to and from assignment location
• Tuition for Dependent Education	Reimbursement for expatriate's children to receive a home country education, for example, private school in the assignment location or boarding school back home
• Home Leave	Expatriate and family transportation and time off to return home
• Tax Reimbursement Payments	Reimbursement for any additional taxes payable by expatriate as a result of living abroad

and recreation allowance that covers the cost of a family vacation to a neighboring country twice a year in addition to normal vacation time. In Indonesia, rent for expatriate housing ranges from US$2,000 to $5,000 per month, but the company must pay three years in advance (Watson Wyatt Data Services 2002).

Expatriate Reentry

After expatriates complete their assignments and return home, they must adjust in the same way as when going abroad as the work, people, and general environment are no longer familiar. Expatriates may worry about career development or feel that the company does not value their overseas experiences. Often, expatriates, their families, and their company are unprepared to deal with this disorientation, known as **"reverse culture shock."**

The expatriate gains valuable information and experience from an international assignment, but for many organizations this is lost because of failure to successfully manage expatriate reentry. By one estimate, about 25% of returning expatriates leave the company within a year after returning (Black, Gregersen, and Mendenhall 1992) with some American and European companies losing as many as 55% of their returning expatriates after three years (Black et al. 1999). Companies may have trouble finding a suitable job for a returning expatriate, and this has become even more difficult with recent corporate downsizing (Mendenhall et al. 2002).

Many expatriates are dissatisfied with the way their companies integrate overseas assignments into career planning. They think that their companies are not doing enough long-term career planning and fail to give expatriates enough support while they are abroad (Stahl, Miller, and Tung 2002). Nevertheless, expatriates are generally happy with their overseas assignments (Stahl et al. 2002; Tung 1998).

The new concept emerging from the experiences of expatriates is the "boundary-less career." Expatriates value their international assignments because they can develop valuable skills. However, if their own companies do not offer them attractive opportunities for career advancement, they are prepared to change companies to find better prospects (Stahl et al. 2002).

Organizations must do more to avoid the loss of valued repatriates. Planning the reentry before the assignment begins can ease the transition of returning expatriates (Chowanec and Newstrom 1991). The organization can also assign mentors to maintain contact with expatriates throughout their assignments, keeping them up to date on events in the company at home. As the return date gets closer, the mentor can look for a suitable reentry position for the expatriate and provide a realistic reentry preview. The company can also plan to include the expatriate in short-term projects at head-quarters during home leave. Finally, the organization can provide some of the same supports that it supplied upon going abroad, for example, a reorientation program or help with moving and children's education (Chowanec and Newstrom 1991; Mendenhall et al. 2002).

▪▪▪ Changes in Global Mobility

The expatriate experience described in this chapter may become less common in the future. A survey of 175 companies from all regions of the globe reports that new types of cross-border employee transfers are becoming popular (Cendant Mobility 2002). The companies in the survey employ 3.4 million people, and more than 200,000 are globally mobile. The HR managers from these companies indicate that 44% of cross-border transfers involve relocation from one country to another for a year or longer, but they expect this number to decline.

HR managers believe that short-term relocations—from six months to a year—extended business travel, and cross-border moves that assign an employee to permanent local status will increase. The reasons for these changes include demand for project work, mergers and divestitures, new operations, and restructuring.

The most important objectives for cross-border transfers are to transfer skills and knowledge and to develop and manage global competencies. The HR managers expect the second reason to take on even more importance in the future.

▪▪▪ Convergence or Divergence?

Forces for Convergence

Are IHRM practices across countries converging or diverging? Large global companies are striving to develop international human resource management systems that have consistent applicability in a wide variety of countries. Organizations of every nationality face similar problems in trying to manage a workforce spanning many countries and cultures. As HRM becomes increasingly recognized as a field that can impact profits, even smaller companies try to professionalize their approach to managing their human resources. These systems have similar goals and often share similar principles.

Forces for Divergence

Even with the move toward more consistency and professionalism, there is increasing sensitivity to local cultural and legal differences. Although many companies would like to use "cutting edge" HRM practices, there is growing recognition that these practices cannot be imported wholesale into a country. As a result, unique techniques and practices developed for different areas are becoming common.

▪▪▪ Implications for Managers

Every international manager has responsibility for effectively managing human resources. Although an organization may employ professional HR managers, the line manager is ultimately responsible for selecting competent people, training them, assessing their performance, and compensating them fairly. The discussion in this chapter provides some insight into the complexities of these issues.

From another perspective, it is also helpful to understand IHRM as it potentially has a personal impact on every international manager. Understanding the dynamics of an international assignment and how it may influence career development is useful for every current and aspiring international manager.

SUMMARY ▪▪▪▪▪▪▪

International human resource management focuses on the management of human resources on a global basis. An organization's corporate strategy on globalization strongly impacts the approach it takes to IHRM. The approach to IHRM in turn influences implementation of the major IHRM functions of recruitment and selection, training and development, performance evaluation, compensation and benefits, and labor relations. Companies taking an ethnocentric approach attempt to impose their home country methods on their subsidiaries. Polycentric or regiocentric approaches follow local practices. Finally, a geocentric or global approach develops practices for worldwide use.

One of the major concerns of IHR managers is managing expatriate employees. Because they must function effectively in a foreign work and living situation, they receive different treatment than other employees. In choosing expatriates, a company must consider both technical and interpersonal abilities. Successful expatriates receive appropriate training to prepare them to live and work abroad. To motivate them in their assignment, compensation and benefits to expatriates must also be attractive. Changes in global mobility suggest that the expatriate experience may change in the future.

In considering whether approaches to IHRM are converging or diverging worldwide, there is evidence of both. Large global corporations prefer consistent worldwide systems and smaller companies usually seek more professional IHRM. However, with the variety of local cultures and laws that exist across subsidiaries, the IHR manager must be ready to adapt.

Finally, since international managers have the ultimate responsibility for managing human resources, they must be aware of the complexities involved. It is also useful to understand IHRM for personal career development.

DISCUSSION QUESTIONS ▪▪▪▪▪▪▪

1. Why is international human resource management more complex than managing human resources in one country?
2. What is an expatriate? Why is employing an expatriate different from employing a host country national (HCN)?
3. How does the overall strategy an organization takes to managing international business affect its human resource strategy?
4. What are some of the differences in training practices in different parts of the world? Explain these differences using one or more of the cultural frameworks.

5. How does culture influence the performance evaluation process? How can companies assure that their employees are fairly evaluated?

6. How do you feel about an international career? Would you like to work as an expatriate? Why or why not?

7. What trends may influence the employment of expatriates in the future?

INTERNET SITES ▪▪▪▪▪▪▪

Selected Companies in the Chapter

Cendant Mobility (www.cendantmobility.com)
Sonoco (www.sonoco.com)
Watson Wyatt Worldwide (www.watsonwyatt.com)

International Human Resource Sites

International Labour Organization (www.ilo.org/). This site has news and information about international labor issues.

SHRM Global Forum (www.shrmglobal.org/). This site is managed by the Society for Human Resource Management and provides news and information to global HR professionals.

U.S. Department of Labor (www.dol.gov/). This site provides news, labor statistics, and other information about labor issues.

REFERENCES ▪▪▪▪▪▪▪

Adler, N. J. (1994). "Competitive Frontiers: Women Managing across Borders." In Adler, N. J. and Izraeli, D. N. (eds.) *Competitive Frontiers: Women Managers in a Global Economy.* Cambridge, MA: Blackwell.

———. (1997). *International Dimensions of Organizational Behavior.* 3d Ed. Cincinnati, OH: South-Western College Publishing.

Artise, J. (1995). "Selection, Coaching, and Evaluation of Employees in International Subsidiaries." In Shenkar, O. (ed.) *Global Perspectives of Human Resource Management.* Upper Saddle River, NJ: Prentice Hall.

Audia, P. G. and Tams, S. (2002). "Goal Setting, Performance Appraisal, and Feedback across Cultures." In Gannon, M. J. and Newman, K. L. (eds.) *The Blackwell Handbook of Cross-Cultural Management.* Oxford: Blackwell.

Bird, A. and Beechler, S. (1995). "The Link between Business Strategy and International Human Resource Management Practices." In Mendenhall, M. and Oddou, G. (eds.) *Readings and Cases in International Human Resource Management.* 2d Ed. Cincinnati, OH: South-Western.

Black, J. S. and Gregersen, H. B. (1991). "Antecedents to Cross-Cultural Adjustment for Expatriates in Pacific Rim Assignments," *Human Relations,* 44, 497–515.

———, ———, and Mendenhall, M. E. (1992). "Toward a Theoretical Framework of Repatriation Adjustment," *Journal of International Business Studies,* 23, 737–60.

———, ———, ———, and Stroh, L. H. (1999). *Globalizing People through International Assignments.* New York: Addison-Wesley, Longman.

——— and Mendenhall, M. (1989). "A Practical but Theory-Based Framework for Selecting Cross-Cultural Training Methods," *Human Resource Management,* 28, 511–39.

——— and ——— (1990). "Cross-Cultural Training Effectiveness: A Review and a Theoretical Framework for Future Research," *Academy of Management Review,* 15, 113–36.

——— and Porter, L. W. (1991). "Managerial Behaviors and Job Performance: A Successful Manager in Los Angeles May not Succeed in Hong Kong," *Journal of International Business Studies,* 22, 99–113.

Brewster, C. (2002). "Human Resource Practices in Multinationals." In Gannon, M. J. and Newman, K. L. (eds.) *The Blackwell Handbook of Cross-Cultural Management.* Oxford: Blackwell.

Briscoe, D. R. (1995). *International Human Resource Management.* Upper Saddle River, NJ: Prentice Hall.

Brooke, J. (2001). "Young Japanese Breaking Old Salaryman's Bonds," *The New York Times International,* October 16, A3.

Carpenter, M. A., Sanders, W. G., and Gregersen, H. B. (2001). "Bundling Human Capital with Organizational Context: The Impact of International Assignment Experience on Multinational Firm Performance and CEO Pay," *Academy of Management Journal,* 44, 493–511.

Cascio, W. F. (1998). "Commentary: The Theory of Vertical and Horizontal Individualism and Collectivism: Implications for International Human Resource Management." In Cheng, J. L. C. and Peterson, R. B.

(eds.) *Advances in International Comparative Management*, Vol. 12. Stamford, CT: JAI Press.

Cendant Mobility (2002). *Cendant Mobility's 2002 Worldwide Benchmark Study: New Approaches to Global Mobility.* Bethesda, MD: Cendant Mobility.

Chowanec, G. D. and Newstrom, C. N. (1991). "The Strategic Management of International Human Resources," *Business Quarterly*, 56, 65–70.

Coyle, W. (1988). *On the Move: Minimizing the Stress and Maximizing the Benefit of Relocation.* Sydney: Hampden.

de Forest, M. E. (1994). "Thinking of a Plant in Mexico?" *Academy of Management Executive*, 8, 33–40.

Dillon, L. S. (1990). "The Occidental Tourist," *Training and Development Journal*, 44, 72–80.

Dowling, P. J., Schuler, R. S., and Welch, D. E. (1994). *International Dimensions of Human Resource Management*, 2d Ed. Belmont, CA: Wadsworth.

Duane, M. J. (2001). *Policies and Practices in Global Human Resource Systems.* Westport, CT: Quorum.

Elenkov, D. S. (1998). "Can American Management Concepts Work in Russia? A Cross-Cultural Comparative Study," *California Management Review*, 40(4), 133–57.

Eschbach, D. M., Parker, G. E., and Stoeberl, P. A. (2001). "American Repatriate Employees' Retrospective Assessments of the Effects of Cross-Cultural Training on Their Adaptation to International Assignments," *International Journal of Human Resource Management*, 12, 270–87.

Fisher, C. D., Schoenfeldt, L. F., and Shaw, J. B. (1993). *Human Resource Management*, 2d Ed. Boston: Houghton-Mifflin.

Forster, N. (1997). "The Persistent Myth of High Expatriate Failure Rates: A Reappraisal," *International Journal of Human Resource Management*, 8, 414–33.

Fukuda, K. J. and Chu, P. (1994). "Wrestling with Expatriate Family Problems: Japanese Experience in East Asia," *International Studies of Management and Organization*, 24, 36–47.

Geringer, J. M., Frayne, C. A., and Milliman, J. F. (2002). "In Search of 'Best Practices' in International Human Resource Management: Research Design and Methodology," *Human Resource Management*, 41, 5–30

Gregersen, H. B., Hite, J. M., and Black, J. S. (1996). "Expatriate Performance Appraisal in U.S. Multinational Firms," *Journal of International Business Studies*, 27, 711–38.

Hempel, P. S. (1998). "Designing Multinational Benefits Programs: The Role of National Culture," *Journal of World Business*, 33, 277–94.

Hodgetts, R. M. and Luthans, F. (1994). *International Management*, 2d Ed. New York: McGraw-Hill.

Huo, Y. P., Huang, H. J., and Napier, N. K. (2002). "Divergence or Convergence: A Cross-National Comparison of Personnel Selection Practices," *Human Resource Management*, 41, 31–44.

ILO Bureau of Statistics (unpublished) data compiled from Official National Statistical Publication.

Lowe, K. B., Milliman, J., De Cieri, H., and Dowling, P. J. (2002). "International Compensation Practices: A Ten-Country Comparative Analysis," *Human Resource Management*, 41, 45–66.

Marquardt, M. and Engel, D. W. (1993). *Global Human Resource Development.* Upper Saddle River, NJ: Prentice Hall.

Mendenhall, M. E., Dunbar, E., and Oddou, G. (1987). "Expatriate Selection, Training and Career-Pathing: A Review and a Critique," *Human Resource Planning*, 26, 331–45.

——, Kühlmann, T. M., Stahl, G. K., and Osland, J. S. (2002). "Employee Development and Expatriate Assignments." In Gannon, M. J. and Newman, K. L. (eds.) *The Blackwell Handbook of Cross-Cultural Management.* Oxford: Blackwell.

Miller, E. L., Beechler, S., Bhatt, B., and Nath, R. (1991). "The Relationship between the Global Strategic Planning Process and the Human Resource Management Function." In Mendenhall, M. and Oddou, G. (eds.) *Readings and Cases in International Human Resource Management.* Boston: PWS-Kent.

Milliman, J., Nason, S., Gallagher, E., Huo, P., Von Glinow, M. A., and Lowe, K. B. (1998). "The Impact of National Culture on Human Resource Management Practices: The Case of Performance Appraisal." In Cheng, J. L. C. and Peterson, R. B. (eds.) *Advances in International Comparative Management*, Vol. 12. Stamford, CT: JAI Press.

Oddou, G. and Mendenhall, M. (1995). "Expatriate Performance Appraisal: Problems and Solutions." In Mendenhall, M. and Oddou, G. (eds.) *Readings and Cases in International Human Resource Management.* 2d Ed. Cincinnati, OH: South-Western.

Parker, G. and Janush, E. S. (2001). "Developing Expatriate Remuneration Packages," *Employee Benefits Journal*, 26(2), 3–5.

Phatak, A. V. (1995). *International Dimensions of Management.* 4th Ed. Cincinnati, OH: South-Western.

Ramamoorthy, N. and Carroll, S. J. (1998). "Individualism/Collectivism Orientations and Reactions toward Alternative Human Resource Management Practices," *Human Relations*, 51, 571–88.

Rosenzweig, P. M. and Nohria, N. (1994). "Influences on Human Resource Management Practices in Multinational Corporations," *Journal of International Business Studies*, 25, 229–51.

Schuler, R. S., and Rogovsky, N. (1998). "Understanding Compensation Practice Variations across Firms: The Impact of National Culture," *Journal of International Business Studies*, 29, 159–77.

Selmer, J. (2002). "Practice Makes Perfect? International Experience and Expatriate Adjustment," *Management International Review, 42,* 71–87.

—— and Leung, A. S. M. (2003). "International Adjustment of Female vs. Male Business Expatriates," *International Journal of Human Resource Management,* 14(7), 1117–31.

Shaffer, M. A., Harrison, D. A., Gilley, K. M., and Luk, D. M. (2001). "Struggling for Balance Amid Turbulence on International Assignments: Work-Family Conflict, Support and Commitment," *Journal of Management, 27,* 99–121.

Spencer-Oatey, H. (1997). "Unequal Relationships in High and Low Power Distance Societies: A Comparative Study of Tutor-Student Role Relations in Britain and China," *Journal of Cross-Cultural Psychology,* 28, 284–302.

Stahl, G. K., Miller, E. L., and Tung, R. L. (2002). "Toward the Boundaryless Career: A Closer Look at the Expatriate Career Concept and Perceived Implications of an International Assignment," *Journal of World Business,* 37, 216–27.

Stening, B. W. and Hammer, M. R. (1992). "Cultural Baggage and the Adaptation of Expatriate American and Japanese Managers," *Management International Review,* 32, 77–89.

Teagarden, M. B., Von Glinow, M. A., Butler, M. C., and Drost, E. (1995). "The Best Practices Learning Curve: Human Resource Management in Mexico's Maquiladora Industry." In Shenkar, O. (ed.) *Global Perspectives of Human Resource Management.* Upper Saddle River, NJ: Prentice Hall.

Thomas, D. C. (1998). "The Expatriate Experience: A Critical Review and Synthesis." In Cheng, J. L. C. and Peterson, R. B. (eds.) *Advances in International Comparative Management,* Vol. 12. Stamford, CT: JAI Press.

Tung, R. L. (1988). *The New Expatriates: Managing Human Resources Abroad.* Cambridge, MA: Ballinger.

Tung, R. L. (1998). "American Expatriates Abroad: From Neophytes to Cosmopolitans," *Journal of World Business,* 33, 125–44.

U.S. Department of Labor, Bureau of Labor Statistics, "International Comparisons of Hourly Compensation Costs for Production Workers in Manufacturing, 1975–2001," accessed June 5, 2003, ftp://ftp.bls.gov/pub/special.requests/ForeignLabor/supptab.txt

Von Glinow, M. A., Drost, E. A., and Teagarden, M. B. (2002). "Converging on IHRM Best Practices: Lessons Learned from a Globally Distributed Consortium on Theory and Practice," *Human Resource Management,* 41, 123–40.

Wahl, A. (2002). "European Labor: Social Dialogue, Social Pacts, or a Social Europe?" *Monthly Review,* 54(2), 45–55.

Watson Wyatt Data Services (2002). *2002/03 Benefits Report Asia Pacific.* Hong Kong: Watson Wyatt Worldwide.

Wellins, R. and Rioux, S. (2001). "Solving the Global HR Puzzle," *Workspan,* February, 26–9.

Wiersma, U. J. (1996). "Human Resource Management Practices in the Netherlands: An Exploratory Study," BRC Papers on Cross-Cultural Management, Hong Kong Baptist University, Series no. CCMP 96006, April.

9

Organizational Commitment, Organizational Justice, and Work-Family Interface

Learning Objectives

After reading this chapter, you should be able to:

■ Compare the three types of organizational commitment and how each influences employee work behavior.

■ Describe how culture influences commitment.

■ Understand the three types of organizational justice and how culture influences each type.

■ Explain how perceptions of justice influence organizational behavior.

■ Discuss the dynamics of the work and family interface and the impact of culture.

■ Consider the role of organizations in helping employees manage work-family interface.

CULTURE AT WORK

"I think probably none of us here are living a balanced life. Number one, I think we don't spend enough time with our families. This is a very big issue for me. Because I want to try to spend as much time as possible with my family, especially since my kid is very young, only one and a half years old. And quite often I talk to my wife, I say, 'Look I travel all the time. When I'm traveling, I miss all these minutes and seconds and hours of my kid in the different stages. And these are the things that you can never buy with money.' It seems that we are in the middle of a kind of scenario. If you want to get further ahead, you probably would live a non-stop life. If you stop here, you would get behind. So it is sometimes quite difficult

> to make a decision about what to do next. Right now I think life can be number one. I give the priority to my family; this is on top of my priorities. Two is try, of course, to do my [MBA] program as well as I possibly can, and three, try to minimize my traveling as much as possible, which quite often I fail to do. . . . So anyway, if I want to make any improvement, I just want to find a more efficient way to do my work and spend more time with the family."
>
> A Shanghai manager's opinions about work and family.
>
> *Source:* A. M. Francesco

International managers increasingly have to understand and manage issues that a few years ago were not important in many workplaces. The worldwide movement toward a market economy and its accompanying work ethic, along with the processes of globalization, have created new conditions in organizations in many cultures. For example, it is unlikely that the Chinese manager in the Culture at Work vignette would have expressed concern about balancing work and family life prior to the introduction of elements of a market economy in China and the changes in work that they created.

Three issues that have recently become more prominent in global organizations are organizational commitment, organizational justice, and work and family interface. Although all of these issues are fundamental to the relationship between employer and employee, it is only in the past few years that managers and researchers began to consider how culture may influence them. The way an organization deals with commitment, justice, and work and family interface will affect that company's image and overall competitiveness.

Organizational commitment is important because organizations seek to attract and retain effective workers in order to compete globally. Research indicates that an organization strategy that creates commitment in employees can lead to competitive advantage and financial success (Mowday 1998). Organizational justice is important because the perception and reality of unfair treatment often lead to reduced effort and inferior work outcomes within an organization and can produce negative feelings that influence intercultural business relationships. Finally, work and family interface is increasingly a concern because, as with commitment and justice, how an organization deals with a worker's life outside the organization influences its ability to attract and retain the most competent employees. Recognizing how the two major life roles of work and family influence each other and what role organizations should play in reducing conflict between them is becoming even more important as globalization progresses.

▪▪▪ Organizational Commitment

Organizational commitment, an employee's attachment to a particular organization, is important because it affects employees remaining with an organization and other positive employee behaviors (Allen and Meyer 1996). There are three different types of commitment. Employees have **affective commitment** when they identify and become involved with the organization and feel an emotional attachment to it. When employees experience affective commitment, they work for a company because they like it and want to be part of it. Those with **continuance commitment** remain in an organization because they realize that they will lose something if they leave—for example, they may give up retirement benefits if they resign. Employees with continuance commitment stay with an employer

TABLE 9-1 Employee Feelings Related to Three Types of Organizational Commitment

Type of Commitment	*Representative Feelings*
Affective	I would be very happy to spend the rest of my career with this organization. I feel a strong sense of belonging to my organization. This organization has a great deal of personal meaning for me.
Continuance	Too much of my life would be disrupted if I decided I wanted to leave my organization now. I feel that I have too few options to consider leaving this organization. If I had not already put so much of myself into this organization, I might consider working elsewhere.
Normative	Even if it were to my advantage, I do not feel it would be right to leave my organization now. I would feel guilty if I left this organization now. I would not leave my organization right now because I have a sense of obligation to the people in it.

Source: Adapted from Meyer, J. P., Allen, N. J., and Smith, C. A. (1993). "Commitment to Organizations and Occupations: Extension and Test of a Three-Component Conception," *Journal of Applied Psychology, 78,* 538–551.

because they feel they have to do so. Finally, people with **normative commitment** feel a sense of obligation to remain with a firm and believe that employees should be loyal to their employer. These employees stay because they feel they should. Table 9-1 illustrates the type of feelings expressed by people who have each type of commitment.

How Organizational Commitment Develops

Because each type of commitment is distinct, each develops from different sources (Allen and Meyer 1996). Table 9-2 presents some of these sources.

Employees develop affective commitment when they feel comfortable and competent working in the organization. For example, a receptive management or a dependable organization makes a person feel at ease working in a company and can create affective commitment (Allen and Meyer 1990). Employees feel competent when the company gives them a challenging job, a difficult but attainable goal, and feedback about how they are performing, which then leads to affective commitment. Factors

TABLE 9-2 Sources of Organizational Commitment

Affective Commitment	*Continuance Commitment*	*Normative Commitment*
Personal Characteristics	Personal Characteristics	Personal Characteristics
Work Experiences	Job Alternatives Available	Socialization Experiences
	Employee Investments in the Organization	Organization Investments in the Employee

Source: Adapted from Meyer, J. P., Stanley, D. J., Herscovitch, L., and Topolnytsky, L. (2002). "Affective, Continuance, and Normative Commitment to the Organization: A Meta-Analysis of Antecedents, Correlates, and Consequences," *Journal of Vocational Behavior, 61,* p. 22.

relating to employees' work experience influence their affective commitment the most (Meyer, Stanley, Herscovitch, and Topolnytsky 2002). For example, when employees believe that the organization cares about their welfare, they develop affective commitment. Treating employees fairly and providing strong leadership are two things companies can do to show their concern (Meyer et al. 2002).

The comments of employees working for Engle Homes, a highly respected American construction company, illustrate these ideas. One employee commented that "The focus on improvement and positive recognition are the attitudes of choice at Engle, as opposed to finger pointing and finding fault." Another said, "Our managers make us feel like we can walk on air." (O'Toole, Stromberg, Haynes, and McCune 2002, p. 56).

People build continuance commitment as they realize that they have a substantial investment in the company where they work or there are limited opportunities to work elsewhere. This happens when workers feel they have to stay with an organization because they would lose too much if they leave or they have no other reasonable job choices. For example, when the job market is weak (Allen and Meyer 1990) or when it is difficult for employees to transfer their skills and education to other jobs (Meyer et al. 2002), continuance commitment is higher.

Finally, employees develop normative commitment as part of the primary socialization process. The feeling of obligation to the organization comes from family experiences with employment such as parents' attitudes, cultural values such as how much loyalty one should have to an organization, and personal experiences that make people feel they "owe something" to the organization (Allen and Meyer 1996). For example, if a company pays the tuition for an employee's MBA program, this can lead to normative commitment. The employee may feel that she should stay with the company, even though there is no contract keeping her there.

Personal factors also influence commitment. Older people and those who have been with an organization or in the same position longer are more likely to have higher levels of all types of commitment (Meyer et al. 2002). For example, a person who works for a company a long time is more likely to develop continuance commitment than someone who just started a job.

How Organizational Commitment Influences Employee Behavior

Commitment influences employee behaviors that are important to both the organization and to the employee (Meyer et al. 2002). Table 9-3 gives some examples of these. One reason that organizations are concerned with the organizational commitment of their employees is because commitment influences job performance. Workers with higher affective and normative commitment generally perform better, but those with higher continuance commitment have lower job performance (Meyer et al. 2002). This is because when people like the organization where they work, it has a positive impact on performance. However, if employees only stay with a company because they have no other choices, they lack interest and may do only the minimum necessary to keep the job.

Commitment also relates to **organizational citizenship behavior (OCB),** things that an employee does for the organization that are not formally part of the job, for example, helping new colleagues find their way around the company. People who have higher affective and normative commitment are likely to do more OCB, but continuance commitment seems to have no impact (Meyer et al. 2002). Employees with high affective or normative commitment want to do things to help the organization, even if they are not required. However, someone with continuance commitment only stays because no attractive alternatives are available and consequently may be unwilling to do anything extra.

TABLE 9-3 How Organizational Commitment Influences Employee Work Behaviors		
Affective Commitment	*Continuance Commitment*	*Normative Commitment*
Lower Turnover Intention and Actual Turnover	Lower Turnover Intention and Actual Turnover	Lower Turnover Intention and Actual Turnover
Higher Job Performance and OCB	Lower Job Performance, No Impact on OCB	Higher Job Performance and OCB
Higher Attendance Rate	No Impact on Attendance Rate	No Impact on Attendance Rate
Lower Stress and Work-Family Conflict	Higher Stress and Work-Family Conflict	No Impact on Work-Family Conflict

Source: Adapted from Meyer, J. P., Stanley, D. J., Herscovitch, L., and Topolnytsky, L. (2002). "Affective, Continuance, and Normative Commitment to the Organization: A Meta-Analysis of Antecedents, Correlates, and Consequences," *Journal of Vocational Behavior,* 61, 20–52.

One of the most serious problems created by lack of commitment is employee turnover. When commitment is low, employees think about leaving their jobs or leave (Allen and Meyer 1996). When employees look for a new job, they either find something and quit or discover that nothing attractive is available. When a valued employee leaves, this creates both a financial and psychological loss; the company must spend money to recruit, select, and train someone new, and other employees may become demoralized.

Another important issue is that employees who are frustrated because they can't leave may emotionally or mentally withdraw. As a result, they may be absent from work more often or reduce the enthusiasm and effort put into the job (Russ and McNeilly 1995).

In addition to the impact on organizational performance, commitment can also affect an employee's personal health and well-being (Meyer et al. 2002). People with higher affective commitment have less stress and less work-family conflict, but those with continuance commitment experience the opposite. The positive feelings towards the organization that come with affective commitment can help to lower stress and conflict levels, but the opposite occurs when a person feels forced to stay with a company.

The example of Royal Dutch Shell, a global energy company, illustrates how organization policies affect organizational commitment, which then influences employee performance. Shell was a highly successful organization throughout the 1970s and '80s and into the '90s. However, by the 1990s, top management was unable to create a positive vision for the future, the company persisted in developing a business strategy using an outdated approach, and changes in human resource management policies indicated a lack of concern for employees (Boyle 2002). These factors combined to have a negative impact on employees' organizational commitment and resulted in poor performance. In 1998, Shell had the worst results in its history which had a strong impact on management. With the help of consultants, Shell's management restructured the organization and introduced new policies that helped to rebuild organizational commitment. By 2000, profits had improved, and Royal Dutch Shell was moving in a positive direction.

Culture and Organizational Commitment

Research on organizational commitment focused mostly on employees in North America until the 1990s. At that time, because of increasing globalization and international managers' need to understand employee attitudes in various parts of the world, researchers moved to an "international phase" (Boyacigiller and Adler 1991). Although the number of studies conducted outside of North America is still small, researchers have identified some topics where findings are universal and others where culture matters.

How employees develop commitment and its influence on behavior seem to be the same in countries outside of North America. For example, managers in 15 European and Canadian affiliates of an American multinational company had higher affective commitment when they had a wide job scope, a good understanding of how to do their jobs, good pay, and opportunities for promotion (Palich, Hom, and Griffeth 1995). Another study of employees from 12 countries in the translation department of the European Commission indicates that low levels of affective or continuance commitment led employees from all countries to want to quit (Vandenberghe, Stinglhamber, Bentein, and Delhaise 2001). Table 9-4 gives examples of other studies that show results similar to those in North America.

Culture can also influence commitment. For example, American employees' individual levels of power distance, uncertainty avoidance, and individualism/collectivism affected their degree of organizational commitment (Clugston, Howell, and Dorfman 2000). People with larger power distance had higher continuance and normative commitment. Because larger power distance makes people feel more dependent and perceive fewer alternatives, this creates higher continuance commitment. Power distance can also create a sense of obligation where employees feel they must be loyal to the organization, leading to normative commitment. Employees with strong uncertainty avoidance had high continuance commitment. They may consider the security of the job, what they have invested in it, and worry about getting a new job. Finally, collectivists had higher levels of normative commitment, suggesting that they feel an obligation to the organization and treat it as an in-group.

In the Middle East, a strong **Islamic work ethic,** the view that life without work is meaningless and work is an obligation, can enhance organizational commitment (Yousef 2000, 2001). For people with a high Islamic work ethic, the value of work

---

TABLE 9-4 Examples of Studies of Organizational Commitment Outside of North America

Country	*Results*
India	Salespersons had higher commitment when they were clear about their job requirements and when they had considerate supervisors.[1]
China	Employees with higher affective commitment had higher job performance, OCB, and job satisfaction and lower intention to quit the job.[2]
United Arab Emirates	Employees who were unclear about how to do their jobs had lower affective and normative commitment.[3]

▪▪▪▪▪▪▪▪▪

Sources: [1] Agarwal, S., DeCarlo, T. E., and Vyas, S. B. (1999). "Leadership Behavior and Organizational Commitment: A Comparative Study of American and Indian Salespersons," *Journal of International Business Studies,* 30(4), 727–43.

[2] Chen, Z. X. and Francesco, A. M. (2003). "The Relationship between the Three Components of Commitment and Employee Performance in China," *Journal of Vocational Behavior,* 62, 490–510; Cheng, Y. and Stockdale, M. S. (2003). "The Validity of the Three-Component Model of Organizational Commitment in a Chinese Context," *Journal of Vocational Behavior,* 62, 465–89.

[3] Yousef, D. A. (2002). "Job Satisfaction as a Mediator of the Relationship between Role Stressors and Organizational Commitment: A Study from an Arabic Cultural Perspective," *Journal of Managerial Psychology,* 17(4), 250–66.

comes from the positive intentions of the worker, not the results actually achieved on the job. In the United Arab Emirates, people with a higher Islamic work ethic had higher levels of all forms of commitment.

In Taiwan, Chinese employees' commitment to their supervisor as well as to the organization is important (Cheng, Jiang, and Riley 2003). When employees were committed to the supervisor, they had better job performance, but organizational commitment did not influence performance. When employees did have high organizational commitment, it led to high supervisor commitment, which then brought about higher levels of OCB. Because of the emphasis on personal relationships in collectivistic Chinese society, the commitment to one's supervisor can be more important than commitment to the organization.

The influence of Chinese culture is also important for workers from China and Hong Kong (Wong, Wong, Hui, and Law 2001). The impact of organizational commitment on job satisfaction and intention to leave the job is greater than in Western countries. Because of the value put on relationships, loyalty, and mutual commitment, developing organizational commitment is more important in Chinese societies.

▪▪▪ Organizational Justice

Organizational justice focuses on perceptions of fair treatment within an organization. As organizations continue to globalize and workforces become more diverse, an understanding of how different cultures view justice is important. Because justice is important to people, when they believe that an organization is treating them unfairly, they are likely to respond in a negative way. The result can be lower performance, stealing, absenteeism, quitting, protests, and lawsuits against their employers (Leung and Stephan 2001). When doing business across cultures, perceptions of injustice can lead to conflict, mistrust, anger, stress, dissatisfaction, and less effective interpersonal relationships. Most employees believe that fair procedures lead to favorable outcomes and provide feedback about their status within a group (Ambrose 2002).

Societies develop rules of justice to guide their population. The result is that cultures have **norms of justice,** behaviors the society accepts as fair (Leung and Stephan 2001). What people believe to be fair depends on general norms and values, and these vary with culture (Greenberg 2001).

Three types of justice are: distributive, procedural, and retributive (Leung and Stephan 2001). **Distributive justice** considers the fairness of reward distribution. **Procedural justice** examines the fairness of processes for making organizational decisions about outcomes, and **retributive justice** looks at the fairness of punishments given to those who commit infractions.

Distributive Justice

Employees in all societies are concerned about whether the organizations they work for distribute rewards fairly, but ideas about what is fair vary greatly. For example, in the Japanese language, there is no word for "fair," and consequently the Japanese judge distributive justice very differently than people in Western countries (Greenberg 2001). In making a decision about the fairness of reward distribution people consider (1) the rewards they and others receive, (2) what behaviors deserve rewards, and (3) the reward distribution process (Leung and Stephan 2001).

Making Comparisons

One aspect of judging fairness is how an individual's rewards compare to those received by others. Equity Theory (Adams 1963) suggests that it is likely that people will compare themselves to similar people, and that the "other"—the comparison group—may change over time. For example, in 1996 local Chinese managers working in international joint ventures did not judge the much higher salaries received by expatriate managers in the same company to be unfair because they compared their salaries to those of local employees working in other companies, rather than to the expatriates (Leung, Smith, Wang, and Sun 1996). However, a few years later, a similar study had different results (Leung, Wang, and Smith 2001). After working with the expatriate managers for a longer time, the local managers saw their own level of skills and knowledge as similar to the expatriates'. As a result, the Chinese managers used the expatriates as their comparison group and judged the high expatriate salaries as very unfair.

People also make comparisons to "everybody" or "people in general," or compare themselves to groups who are dissimilar which are the basic processes of the **status-value approach** (Berger, Zelditch, Anderson, and Cohen 1972). For example, a minority group may use the majority group as its comparison. Minority group members are often treated less well than the majority so this comparison usually results in the minority group member perceiving injustice. A person from a culture with low power distance or egalitarian values is more likely to use the status value approach (Leung and Stephan 2001).

Evaluating Inputs

Another aspect of evaluating fairness is consideration of what deserves a reward. As with Equity Theory (Adams 1963), an individual weighs the relative inputs and outcomes of the self versus a comparison other. Cultural values can influence this evaluation—for example, ascriptive societies view personal characteristics such as age, gender, and family background as relevant inputs. In contrast, achievement-oriented countries look at education, work experience, and skills. Collectivists value loyalty and commitment to the group, so in collectivistic societies seniority is a valued input, but individualists think that performance is more important (Leung and Stephan 2001).

Allocating the Rewards

The final aspect used to judge distributive justice is how rewards are allocated. One method is according to the **equity norm** defined by Equity Theory that an outcome to input ratio should be relatively equal for every employee. A second approach is an **equality norm** where each employee receives the same outcomes regardless of inputs. Finally, a **need norm** means that each employee receives outcomes according to personal need.

Collectivistic cultures prefer an equality norm, in contrast to individualistic cultures, that favor an equity norm (Chen 1995; Erez 1997). This is because the equality norm allows collectivistic societies to maintain interpersonal harmony, whereas the equity norm gives individualists the opportunity to achieve. In individualistic countries, organizations typically give performance-based rewards using individual merit-based incentive plans. In contrast, cooperation and teamwork are more important in collectivist countries (Erez 1997).

Procedural Justice

There is less cross-cultural research on procedural justice, but many of the underlying elements that lead people to think a procedure is fair are universal (Greenberg

2001). For example, a comparison of electronics workers in Lithuania and the United States found that the Lithuanians perceived their organizations to use far fewer merit-based practices than did the American workers (Pearce, Bigley, and Branyiczki 1998). Although the companies in Lithuania did not use these practices often, when they did, it positively influenced the Lithuanian employees' perceptions of procedural justice. American workers also associated merit-based practices with justice. In both countries, when employees thought that procedures were fair, they had higher organizational commitment and greater trust in their co-workers. In the collectivistic, particularistic ascription-oriented culture of Lithuania, managers are more likely to make decisions based on relationships and circumstances, rather than applying uniform rules based on merit. However, the Lithuanian workers still view this kind of approach to be unfair.

Two characteristics of organizations influence justice perceptions. The first is **structural,** focusing on whether the rules and policies of the organization lead to fair evaluation (Pearce et al. 1998). The second is **relational** or **interpersonal,** which considers whether the way the organization treats employees conveys respect and supports positive social relationships. For example, people usually believe that having a **voice** over outcomes, an opportunity to express their opinions, is a fair procedure. When employees can give their views, they feel that they can influence outcomes and that the organization respects and values people (Lind and Tyler 1988). Thus, voice provides both aspects of procedural justice. People across cultures also consider objectivity, clarity, and openness in judging fairness (Greenberg 2001).

When British retailer Marks & Spencer remodeled their food halls in 2002, they also changed their management practices (Mills 2003). The new policy of allowing customer assistants to have a voice brought about many interesting ideas. As a result, the company improved service to customers, increased sales, and improved their organizational culture:

> . . . once ideas started to flow, senior management didn't block any of them. This single factor had the greatest impact on the initiative's success. For example, Scott and Olaf, in Cafe Revive, introduced newspapers, bigger meal portions, a wider range of choice in the children's menu and distributed top-up tea/coffee vouchers when queues developed. Leon brought in children from a special needs school to hear Hallowe'en Stories. Beverley and Theresa knew customers liked food tasting but got frustrated when they couldn't find the product. So they commandeered a fridge, stocked it with product and placed it next to the food tasting. Sales doubled. (Mills 2003, p. 62)

Originally, procedural justice research focused on structural aspects, specifically conflict resolution procedures and approaches to conflict (Leung and Stephan 2001; Pearce et al. 1998). Individualists prefer direct procedures in which they control the process, but they like an impartial third party to decide the outcome. For example, in the United States legal system, parties that disagree give evidence and arguments in front of a judge and jury. The disagreeing parties decide how to argue their cases, usually with the advice of an attorney, and the judge and jury decide the outcome. Collectivists, in contrast, prefer to decide disputes using less direct methods such as mediation, negotiation, or use of a third party in order to maintain harmonious relationships.

Another aspect of procedural justice, **interactional justice,** focuses on the interpersonal aspect. Across cultures, people expect respectful, dignified treatment and an opportunity to give their opinions (Leung and Stephan 2001). However, what people believe to be respectful and dignified, and to what extent they should be able to express their opinions, varies with culture. For example, since the Japanese value interpersonal relationships and harmony, they are more likely to offer apologies and excuses to create an impression of fairness whereas Americans are more direct and try to justify their actions (Greenberg 2001).

Retributive Justice

Retributive justice involves questions about whether those who break rules and do harm are responsible for their actions and whether they deserve punishment (Hogan and Emler 1981). In judgments about fairness, people consider who has committed the act, in what context, and what the outcomes are (Leung and Stephan 2001). Individualists are more likely to hold an individual personally responsible for doing something wrong, but collectivists consider social forces and external circumstances and are less likely to make such a judgment. Because of these differences, collectivists are more lenient about giving punishment. For example, in the United States, which is individualistic, law experts and university students blamed criminal behavior on personality, drug abuse, and family problems, but in Korea, which is collectivistic, students saw situational and societal factors as responsible. (Na and Loftus 1998). The Koreans also thought the punishment should be more lenient than the Americans did.

How Justice Perceptions Influence Organizational Behavior

When employees judge a situation as unjust, it often leads to various negative outcomes for an organization. Those who believe they have been treated unfairly could become angry, disappointed, or resentful, or they might quit or put less effort into work (Leung and Stephan 2001). When organizations treat employees fairly, the reverse is true—greater job satisfaction, more commitment to the organization, and other positive outcomes. For example, an important reason that companies are judged as the best employers in Asia is because their employees feel that they are paid fairly (Casio 2002).

Although similar reactions to justice occur in all societies, culture often influences the magnitude or nature of the reactions. Power distance is one cultural dimension that can affect reactions to justice. For example, bank employees in Hong Kong and the United States who felt that distributive and procedural justice were high had better job performance, greater job satisfaction, and less absenteeism (Lam, Schaubroeck, and Aryee 2002). This relationship was even stronger for employees with lower power distance scores, and most of these were in the United States. Because those with high power distance accept differences in rank, they also are more willing to accept differences in treatment. However, overall they appreciate and respond well to both distributive and procedural justice.

Culture also influences the impact of voice. When employees from low power distance countries such as Germany and the United States had little opportunity to express their opinions, it led to negative work outcomes (Brockner et al. 2001). However, in high power distance cultures, such as Hong Kong and Mexico, having the chance to express opinions was less important. Even within one country, China, employees with lower power distance scores were more satisfied with their jobs and committed to the organization, and less likely to leave when the company allowed them to participate. People respond positively to voice across cultures, but the lack of voice is more acceptable to individuals with higher power distance scores.

▪▪▪ Work and Family Interface

Work and family interface focuses on how aspects of life at work and at home influence each other and the impact of that influence on the individual. For most adults, work and family are the two most important aspects of life (Mortimer, Lorence, and Kumka 1986), yet often, the activities in one domain interfere with those in the other creating **work-family conflict.** Because a person's time and energy are limited, and demands in one domain drain resources available for the other, conflict is created that negatively impacts work, family, and individual outcomes (Frone, Russell, and Cooper 1992). For example, an important business trip on a child's graduation day creates a stressful situation. However, in some cases the experience, skills, and opportunities from one domain make it easier to participate in the other, creating **work-family facilitation** (Frone 2003). For example, a parent can share personal work experiences at a child's school career day.

As with other organizational behavior topics, research on work and family interface focuses mainly on Americans. In the early 1990s this started to change, and in the following decade more studies focused on work and family issues in other countries. Two trends that are universally relevant influence work and family interface (Watanabe, Takahashi, and Minami 1997). The first is gender inequality that exists to some extent in all societies. Because women are traditionally responsible for taking care of home and family, these responsibilities are likely to interfere with women's work role. For men, the traditional breadwinners, the direction is the opposite because their work responsibilities interfere with family obligations. The second trend is a movement away from traditional roles toward more gender neutrality. Because more women are entering the workforce around the world, their needs are changing, and they increasingly expect their husbands to be equally involved in both domains. Table 9-5 presents comments from managers and professionals in five countries that illustrate these trends (Shaffer, Francesco, Joplin, and Lau 2004).

Several models try to explain the connections between family and work. The **spillover model** suggests that satisfaction at work spills over into satisfaction at home and conversely dissatisfaction at work can create problems at home (Champoux 1978). The **compensatory model,** on the other hand, says that dissatisfaction in one domain can be made up in the other—for example, a worker might try to enjoy a day out with her family to forget about problems at work. Research indicates that these and other models are valid, and it is possible that any of them could be correct for certain people in specific situations at particular times (Watanabe et al. 1997). However, since no one model is clearly correct, we present specific examples of sources and outcomes of conflict and facilitation.

Sources of Conflict and Facilitation

Various factors within the work and family domains can lead to conflict or facilitation. Demands from either domain that are incompatible create conflict. One major demand is time (Greenhaus and Beutell 1985). For example, the need to work long hours or to spend a long time commuting to work means that less time is available to the family, and a sick child or parent can interfere with going to work. Another type of demand is organizational expectations such as the need to participate in social or professional activities to advance a career. The family can also have expectations, such as a mother must be at home when her children return from school. Other sources of conflict can be job insecurity (Larson, Wilson, and Beley 1994) or need for more family

TABLE 9-5 Gender Role Expectations of Managers and Professionals in Five Countries – Selected Comments	
China	"In most families, I think women are expected to do more housework than men. But I think that Shanghai probably is one of the very, very few cities, if not the only city, where women get the most respect. If you travel outside of Shanghai, in many places you will hear people talking about Shanghainese men. Oh, these Shanghai men, they are the slaves of their wives. In Shanghai, I think the men respect the women the most, more than men in other cities do."
Hong Kong	"Roles are changing in Hong Kong. The family job is becoming a part of the job of males; previously it was the job of females. Now, some men go back home to cook because they like to enjoy their family life."
Mexico	"Mexican culture makes you feel pressured. There's a lot of pressure for men because the Mexican culture is 'macho.' But that culture is beginning to change. We are starting to erase that culture. Women are gaining positions."
Singapore	"I think the bulk of the responsibility falls on the woman. I think that internal conflict is greater for the woman. The man has a support, the moral support of the wife, and I think that in Singapore, priority is given to the man's career. The woman is the one expected to quit her job and become a housewife if anything happens, if the child is sick or something. It is always the wife whose career will be sacrificed first."
United States	"In terms of gender expectations, I would say that for men it's bringing home the big paycheck. That's not saying it's right or anything, but that's kind of the expectation. A lot of guys still have that ego. They saw their father as the principal breadwinner growing up, so they think that's what they have to do."

▪ ▪ ▪ ▪ ▪ ▪ ▪ ▪

Source: Shaffer, M. A., Francesco, A. M., Joplin, J. R. W., and Lau, T. (2004, July) Reconciling Life roles: A cross-cultural model of work-family interface and life balance. Presented at the Academy of International Business Annual Conference, Stockholm, Sweden. Reprinted by permission of the authors.

income (Oppenheimer 1982). All of these issues, but particularly stress over keeping a job, can influence interactions with family members.

Although there is little research on the sources of facilitation, researchers have identified some factors. When friends, family, and co-workers are supportive about work demands or when employees have the opportunity to make decisions at work, this creates facilitation. Having family-related social support—for example, a relative who can stay with children if the parents need to work late also leads to facilitation (Grzywacz and Marks 2000).

Outcomes of Conflict and Facilitation

When employees experience work and family conflict, it often leads to negative outcomes for themselves and the organization. (Frone 2003). For example, work-family conflict can make family members unhappy (Carlson and Kacmar 2000). Employees also miss work, come late, or perform poorly due to family-related causes (Frone, Yardley, and Markel 1997). Work-family conflict can also result in job dissatisfaction (Carlson and Kacmar 2000) or have a negative impact on psychological and physiological health (Frone, Russell, and Barnes 1996).

On the other hand, work-family facilitation can lead to role satisfaction (Tiedje et al. 1990) or positively influence mental health (Grzywacz 2000). A combination of high facilitation with low work-family conflict leads to optimal mental health (Grzywacz and Bass 2003).

Work-Family Interface in Different Cultures

Work-family interface is a relevant issue for employees and organizations across societies. However, the dynamics of the interface can vary with the cultural dimensions of masculinity/femininity and individualism/collectivism having the most influence.

Masculinity/Femininity

The masculinity/femininity dimension influences work-family interface and creates different situations for men and women in different cultures. Feminine societies expect males and females to have more equal roles. In contrast, masculine societies expect men to be more aggressive and to take a dominant role as the breadwinner in the family, while they think women should be more passive, focusing on the role of mother and homemaker (Shaffer et al. 2004).

Men and women in Finland experience similar levels of work-family conflict (Kinnunen and Mauno 1998). Family characteristics such as the number of children living at home cause conflict for both men and women. However, there are some gender differences. Poor relationships with a supervisor create work-family conflict for women, but a high level of education and many children living at home lead to this type of conflict for men. Because Finland is a feminine society that emphasizes gender equality, men and women experience many aspects of work-family interface similarly. Since the expectation for men in Finland is to spend time with their families, they may feel guilty if they neglect the family because of work, leading to work-family conflict.

Employed mothers and fathers in India experience higher levels of facilitation than conflict (Aryee, Srinivas, and Tan in press). However, there are many gender differences in the sources and outcomes of work-family conflict and facilitation. For example, having too much work leads to work-family conflict for many women and having too many parental responsibilities leads to lower facilitation. In a masculine country such as India with traditional gender role expectations, it can be more difficult for women to separate the work and family domains. In contrast, job involvement leads to facilitation for men. When men successfully carry out their traditional role, it can have a positive impact.

In China, traditional gender roles also influence men and women's experience of the work-family interface (Choi and Chen 2003). Women feel stronger family demands than men, which creates more life stress for them. Although men and women have similar work demands, men experience more stress. In Hong Kong, traditional Chinese values are also strong and women feel more conflict from the family, and men experience more from work (Fu and Shaffer 2001). Because Chinese societies expect women to take greater responsibility for the family and men to focus on earning money, the source of stress or conflict is different for men and women.

Masculinity/femininity also influences whether the job demands of a spouse create stress (Westman 2004). In masculine cultures such as Russia, the husband's job demands often create stress in the wife but not the opposite. However, in societies with greater gender equality such as Finland and the United States, either party could suffer stress as a result of a spouse's job demands. These differences could be due to the different roles for men and women in these two types of societies.

Individualism/Collectivism

Individualism and collectivism influence behavioral preference and choice. Individualists are motivated by their own preferences, and they choose their goals over those of others, whereas collectivists are motivated by the norms and duties of their in-group, and they put the group's goals ahead of their own (Triandis 1995). In individualistic countries, women and men have a greater choice of acceptable behavior, and following a nontraditional gender role creates less conflict (Shaffer et al. 2004). In collectivistic cultures, people must follow the group, and women generally find themselves subordinate to men (Triandis 1995).

A study comparing Americans and Chinese found that family demand, such as the need to do housework and take care of children, had a greater impact on work-family conflict in the United States than in China. However, work demand, such as heavy workload and deadlines, had greater impact on work-family conflict in China (Yang, Chen, Choi, and Zou 2000). In the United States, which is predominantly individualistic, people view overwork as selfish—sacrificing family for personal career development. In contrast, the collectivistic Chinese view overwork as a sacrifice for the family's benefit.

A 15-country study of work-family stress also shows the influence of individualism/collectivism on work-family interface (Spector et al. 2003). In the Anglo countries of Australia, Canada, England, New Zealand, and the United States, which are generally individualistic, people who work more hours experience greater work-family pressure. In the collectivistic regions of China (China, Hong Kong, and Taiwan) and Latin America (Argentina, Brazil, Colombia, Ecuador, Mexico, Peru, and Uruguay), there is no connection between hours worked and work-family pressure.

Organizational Responses to Work and Family Issues

Since work and family issues affect employee well-being and organizational outcomes, what can organizations do to assure that they get the best performance from their employees? Two approaches are helpful. One is to develop a positive working environment where supervisors and co-workers provide social support. The second is to offer benefits or practices that can reduce or prevent stress (Shaffer et al. in press). For example, employed parents in Hong Kong had higher organizational commitment and were less likely to want to leave their companies when they were happy with the supervisor's work-family support and work schedule flexibility (Aryee, Luk, and Stone 1998).

Social support from supervisors and co-workers helps employees handle the strain of work-family conflict (Schwartz 1994). On the other hand, an unsympathetic supervisor is a major source of work-family problems (Galinsky and Stein 1990). Employee stress can be reduced when a boss allows an employee to work a flexible schedule or offers kind words when a family problem occurs. For example, employees in Hong Kong who felt that they had organization support were less likely to experience work-family conflict (Foley, Ngo, and Lui 2003).

Organizations can also offer programs and practices such as telecommuting/teleworking, flextime, part-time work, job sharing, employer supported child- and eldercare, and maternity, paternity, and family leave that help employees cope with potential work and family conflicts (Hochschild 1997). For example, flextime can reduce the stress experienced by working parents (Fredriksen-Goldsen and Scharlach 2001). In Hong Kong, women had higher affective commitment when their companies offered supportive programs such as job sharing, flexible work hours, on-site childcare, and enhanced maternity benefits (Chiu and Ng 1999).

In Europe, the actual use of telecommuting/teleworking relates to power distance and uncertainty avoidance (Peters and den Dulk 2003). Countries where power distance is small and uncertainty avoidance weak have more teleworkers. For example, telework is widespread in northern European countries that have this cultural profile, including Scandinavia, the Netherlands, and the United Kingdom. Southern European countries, such as Italy, Spain, and Greece, have the opposite cultural profile on these two dimensions and less widespread use of telework. Finally, countries like Austria and Germany with small power distance and strong uncertainty avoidance are in the middle. These differences may be because people in high power distance and high uncertainty avoidance cultures prefer to supervise work directly, rather than allow employees to work more independently at home.

For employees, having family-friendly policies along with the ability and willingness to use them, is important. For example, in the United States, when the informal culture was not supportive, employees did not take advantage of available benefits (Thompson, Beauvais, and Lyness 1999). For managers and professionals from 20 European countries, greater national gender equality in a country led to organizations having more supportive work-family cultures and more flexible work arrangements, which made it easier for employees to balance work and family responsibilities (Lyness and Kropf 2003). For expatriates working in these European countries, the gender equality of the organization's home country influenced the availability of benefits, but the host country's gender equality affected the organization supportiveness and the employees' ability to balance work and family.

In another study comparing work-family policies in computer companies in India and the United States, employees in both countries complained that supervisors were often unwilling or unable to structure work to accommodate a flexible schedule (Poster 2002). In addition, in India, inadequate infrastructure interfered with employees' access to flextime. Because of the location of the factory, it was almost impossible for employees to get there on time. Also, frequent interruptions of water and electricity limited employees' ability to work at home.

Finally, when organizations provide social support and family-friendly practices and policies, how does this affect corporate performance? A study of the 100 Best Firms for Working Mothers listed in *Working Mothers* magazine between 1995 and 2002 shows that helping employees deal with work and family issues pays off (Cascio and Young 2004). The stock performance of these 100 companies was better than the Standard & Poor's 500 and Russell 3000 stock indices during that time period. Someone who bought the stock of the 100 Best Companies in 1995 and held it until 2002 would have achieved a 120% higher return than the average of the two stock indices.

▪▪▪ Convergence or Divergence?

Forces for Convergence

The importance to organizations of organizational commitment, justice, and work-family interface is a force for convergence. Since all three of these issues relate to important work outcomes, including financial success, companies must consider how to create a positive working environment with regard to these relationships. For each issue, certain elements of the model appear to be culturally universal, and this can help organizations develop global systems that ultimately attract and retain high-quality employees.

Another source for convergence is the diffusion of human resource management policies that address these issues. As global corporations bring new approaches to managing employees to other parts of the world, these practices will become more familiar and acceptable, and other organizations may realize their value. For example, employees appreciate organizational practices that they consider fair, even when such practices are not common in their countries.

Forces for Divergence

Although each of the issues has many aspects that apply across societies, there are cultural variations that managers need to consider when applying organizational systems in different locations. International managers will also discover differences in the way that managers and employees react to these issues across countries.

▪▪▪ Implications for Managers

Managers should consider the impact of organizational commitment, justice, and work-family interface on their own employees. Since each of these can have a strong influence on employee outcomes that are relevant to an organization, managers have to think about how their approaches to leadership can positively affect these outcomes.

Organizational commitment creates positive outcomes such as lower turnover and improved performance across cultures. There also are commonalties in how commitment develops. Generally, managers can enhance employee commitment by providing a positive working environment, a clear understanding of how to perform a job, good pay, and promotion opportunities. In collectivist societies, such as China and Hong Kong, the influence of organizational commitment may be quite strong since interpersonal relationships are so important.

Positive outcomes also result when employees believe that the organization is treating them justly. In fact, fair rules and procedures and respect for employees create perceptions of justice. However, international managers should understand that people from different cultures have different ideas about what is fair. The appropriateness of how rewards are distributed, on what basis employee-related decisions are made, and the choice of rewards and punishment are all interpreted differently in different societies.

Work-family interface is also relevant across cultures. There is evidence that companies that help employees manage work-family issues have better corporate performance. Providing more flexible work schedules, employer supported child- and eldercare, and maternity, paternity, and family leave can help employees avoid potential work-family conflict. Culture influences the dynamics of work-family interface, and international managers should be sensitive to variations.

SUMMARY ▪ ▪ ▪ ▪ ▪ ▪ ▪

Organizational commitment, organizational justice, and work-family interface are issues that are becoming increasingly important for international managers. These processes influence important work outcomes, and organizations need to create a work environment that maximizes the positive outcomes related to each. This will help organizations attract and retain the high-quality employees needed to compete in the global environment.

The three types of commitment, affective, continuance, and normative, have different antecedents and outcomes. Many of these are the same across cultures, but there are also cultural differences. Power distance, uncertainty avoidance, and individualism/collectivism can influence the levels of the different types of commitment. The Islamic work ethic also can create higher levels of commitment. Research on commitment in Chinese societies suggests that the role of relationships is important and that commitment to the supervisor can affect commitment to the organization.

The three different types of justice, distributive, procedural, and retributive, focus on the fairness of different aspects of the organizational reward system. In judging distributive justice, employees compare their own rewards to those received by others, evaluate their inputs and those of other employees, and select the basis on which to allocate the rewards. In evaluating procedural justice, employees look at objectivity, clarity, and openness. They also consider having a voice over outcomes as fair. In appraising interactional justice, an aspect of procedural justice, people universally expect respectful, dignified treatment and an opportunity to express their opinions. Finally, in judging retributive justice, employees consider who is responsible, in what context, and what the outcomes are. There is significant cultural variation in making all of these judgments. When employees believe the organization is treating them fairly, they have positive psychological and behavioral reactions. Culture often influences the magnitude and nature of these reactions.

Since work and family are the two most important aspects of life for most adults, the interface between them has become an important organizational issue. The influence between the domains can either be negative, conflict, or positive, facilitation. Each has different sources and outcomes. The cultural dimensions of masculinity/femininity and individualism/collectivism have the most influence on work-family interface. Social support from co-workers and supervisors along with organizational benefits and practices that reduce or prevent stress help employees better manage work-family interface. These two approaches can lead to positive work outcomes for employees and improved stock performance for the company.

DISCUSSION QUESTIONS ▮▮▮▮▮▮

1. Think about your own work experiences. What makes you feel committed to an organization?
2. What kinds of things can an organization in your country do to enhance employees' organizational commitment?
3. When evaluating distributive justice, employees consider the value of inputs to the job made by themselves and others. In your country what types of inputs do people consider more valuable? How does this relate to your culture?
4. Not much is known about the sources of work-family facilitation. What sources do you think would be worthwhile for researchers to investigate?
5. How much responsibility should an organization take for helping its employees manage work and family interface? How does culture influence your opinion?

INTERNET SITES ▮▮▮▮▮▮

Selected Companies in the Chapter

Engle Homes (www.englehomes.com)
Marks & Spencer (www2.marksandspencer.com/thecompany)
Royal Dutch Shell (www.shell.com)

Organizational Commitment, Organizational Justice, and Work-Family Interface Sites

Australian Institute of Family Studies (http://www.aifs.gov.au). The Institute, established by the Australian Government, promotes the identification and understanding of factors affecting marital and family stability in Australia.

Berger Institute for Work, Family, and Children (http://berger.research.claremontmckenna.edu). The Berger Institute at Claremont McKenna College is an interdisciplinary research institute that aims to advance knowledge about the interactions between work and family through education, dissemination, research, and communication.

The European Observatory on the Social Situation, Demography, and Family (http://europa.eu.int/comm/employment_social/eoss). The site presents news and research findings from the European Union.

Families and Work Institute (www.familiesandwork.org). The Families and Work Institute does research on work-life issues and concerns confronting workers and employers in order to inform decision-makers in government, business, communities, and families.

Organizational Justice and Workplace Bias Research Lab (http://s.psych.uiuc.edu/ research/Justice/). The site includes research on justice and bias done by the Lab at the University of Illinois at Urbana-Champaign.

REFERENCES ▐▌▐▌▐▌▐▌▐▌▐▌▐▌

Adams, J. (1963). "Toward an Understanding of Inequity," *Journal of Abnormal and Social Psychology, 67,* 422–36.

Agarwal, S., DeCarlo, T. E., and Vyas, S. B. (1999). "Leadership Behavior and Organizational Commitment: A Comparative Study of American and Indian Salespersons," *Journal of International Business Studies,* 30(4), 727–43.

Allen, N. J. and Meyer, J. P. (1990). "The Measurement and Antecedents of Affective, Continuance, and Normative Commitment to the Organization," *Journal of Occupational Psychology,* 63, 1–18.

—— and —— (1996). "Affective, Continuance, and Normative Commitment to the Organization: An Examination of Construct Validity," *Journal of Vocational Behavior,* 49, 252–76.

Ambrose, M. L. (2002). "Contemporary Justice Research: A New Look at Familiar Questions," *Organizational Behavior and Human Decision Processes,* 89(1), 803–12.

Aryee, S. (1992). "Antecedents and Outcomes of Work-Family Conflict among Married Professional Women: Evidence from Singapore," *Human Relations,* 45(8), 813–37.

——, Luk, V., and Stone, R. (1998). "Family-Responsive Variables and Retention-Relevant Outcomes among Employed Parents," *Human Relations,* 51(1), 73–87.

——, Srinivas, E. S., and Tan, H. H. (in press). "Rhythms of Life: Antecedents and Outcomes of Work-Family Balance in Employed Parents," *Journal of Applied Psychology.*

Berger, J., Zelditch, M., Anderson, B., and Cohen, B. P. (1972). "Structural Aspects of Distributive Justice: A Status-Value Formulation." In Berger, J., Zelditch, M., and Anderson, B. (eds.) *Sociological Theories in Progress,* Vol. 2. Boston: Houghton-Mifflin.

Boyacigiller, N. A. and Adler, N. J. (1991). "The Parochial Dinosaur: Organizational Science in a Global Context," *Academy of Management Review,* 16, 262–90.

Boyle, E. (2002). "A Critical Appraisal of the Performance of Royal Dutch Shell as a Learning Organisation in the 1990s," *The Learning Organization,* 9(1), 6–18.

Brockner, J., Ackerman G., Greenberg, J., Gelfand, M. J., Francesco, A. M., Chen, Z. X., Leung, K., Bierbrauer, G., Gomez, C., Kirkman, B. L., and Shapiro, D. (2001).

"Culture and Procedural Justice: The Influence of Power Distance on Reactions to Voice," *Journal of Experimental Social Psychology,* 37, 300–15.

Carlson, D. S. and Kacmar, K. M. (2000). "Work-Family Conflict in the Organization: Do Life Role Values Make a Difference?" *Journal of Management,* 26, 1031–54.

Cascio, W. F. (2002). *Responsible Restructuring: Creative and Profitable Alternatives in Layoffs.* San Francisco: Berrett-Koehler.

—— and Young, C. E. (2004). "Work-Family Balance: Does the Market Reward Firms that Respect It?" In Halpern, D. F. and Murphy, S. (eds.) *Changing the Metaphor: From Work-Family Balance to Work-Family Synthesis.* Mahwah, NJ: Erlbaum.

Champoux, J. E. (1978). "Perceptions of Work and Nonwork: A Reexamination of the Compensatory and Spillover Models," *Sociology of Work and Occupations,* 5, 402–22.

Chen, C. C. (1995). "New Trends in Rewards Allocation Preferences: A Sino-U.S. Comparison," *The Academy of Management Journal,* 38(2), 408–28.

Chen, Z. X. and Francesco, A. M. (2003). "The Relationship between the Three Components of Commitment and Employee Performance in China," *Journal of Vocational Behavior,* 62, 490–510.

Cheng, B. S., Jiang, D. Y., and Riley, J. H. (2003). "Organizational Commitment, Supervisory Commitment, and Employee Outcomes in the Chinese Context: Proximal Hypothesis or Global Hypothesis?" *Journal of Organizational Behavior,* 24, 313–34.

Cheng, Y. and Stockdale, M. S. (2003). "The Validity of the Three-Component Model of Organizational Commitment in a Chinese Context," *Journal of Vocational Behavior,* 62, 465–89.

Chiu, W. C. K. and Ng, C. W. (1999). "Women-Friendly HRM and Organizational Commitment: A Study among Women and Men of Organizations in Hong Kong," *Journal of Occupational and Organizational Psychology,* 72, 485–502.

Choi, J. and Chen, C. C. (2003). "The Role of Gender in the Life Stress of Chinese Employees: Women Tired from Housework and Men Tired from Work." Presented at the Annual Meeting of the Academy of Management, Seattle, August.

Clugston, M., Howell, J. P., and Dorfman, P. W. (2000). "Does Cultural Socialization Predict Multiple Bases and Foci of Commitment?" *Journal of Management,* 26(1), 5–30.

Erez, M. (1997). "A Culture-Based Model of Work Motivation." In Earley, P. C. and Erez, M. (eds.) *New Perspectives on International Industrial/Organizational Psychology.* San Francisco: New Lexington Press.

Foley, S., Ngo, H. Y., Lui, S. (2003). "An Investigation of the Main and Moderating Effects of Gender and Perceived Organizational Support on the Relationship between Work Stressors and Work-Family Conflict." Presented at the Annual Meeting of the Academy of Management, Seattle, August.

Fredriksen-Goldsen, K. I. and Scharlach, A. E. (2001). *Families and Work: New Directions in the Twenty-First Century.* New York: Oxford University Press.

Frone, M. R. (2003). "Work-Family Balance." In Quick, J. C. and Tetrick, L. E. (eds.) *Handbook of Occupational Health Psychology.* Washington, DC: American Psychological Association.

——, Russell, M., and Barnes, G. M. (1996). "Work-Family Conflict, Gender, and Health-Related Outcomes: A Study of Employed Parents in Two Community Samples," *Journal of Occupational Health Psychology*, 1, 57–69.

——, ——, and Cooper, M. L. (1992). "Antecedents and Outcomes of Work-Family Conflict: Testing a Model of the Work-Family Interface," *Journal of Applied Psychology,* 77, 65–78.

——, Yardley, J. K., and Markel, K. S. (1997). "Developing and Testing an Integrative Model of the Work-Family Interface," *Journal of Vocational Behavior,* 50, 145–67.

Fu, C. and Shaffer, M. (2001). "The Tug of Work and Family: Direct and Indirect Domain-Specific Determinants of Work-Family Conflict," *Personnel Review,* 30, 502–22.

Galinsky, E. and Stein, P. (1990). "The Impact of Human Resource Policies on Employers," *Journal of Family Issues,* 11, 368–83.

Greenberg, J. (2001). "Studying Organizational Justice," *The International Journal of Conflict Management,* 12(4), 365–75.

Greenhaus, J. H. and Beutell, N. J. (1985). "Sources of Conflict between Work and Family Roles," *Academy of Management Review,* 10(1), 76–88.

Grzywacz, J. G. (2000). "Work-Family Spillover and Health during Midlife: Is Managing Conflict Everything?" *American Journal of Health Promotion,* 14, 236–43.

—— and Bass, B. L. (2003). "Work, Family, and Mental Health: Testing Different Models of Work-Family Fit," *Journal of Marriage and Family,* 65, 248–62.

—— and Marks, N. F. (2000). "Reconceptualizing the Work-Family Interface: An Ecological Perspective on the Correlates of Positive and Negative Spillover between Work and Family," *Journal of Occupational Health Psychology,* 5, 111–26.

Hochschild, A. (1997). *The Time Bind: When Work Becomes Home and Home Becomes Work.* New York, NY: Henry Holt.

Hogan, R. and Emler, N. P. (1981). "Retributive Justice." In Lerner, M. J. and Lerner, S. C. (eds.) *The Justice Motive in Social Behavior.* New York: Academic Press.

James, K. (1993). "The Social Context of Organizational Justice: Cultural, Intergroup, and Structural Effects on Justice Behaviors and Perceptions." In Cropanzano, R. (ed.) *Justice in the Workplace.* Hillsdale, NJ: Erlbaum.

Kinnunen, U. and Mauno, S. (1998). "Antecedents and Outcomes of Work-Family Conflict among Employed Women and Men in Finland," *Human Relations,* 51, 157–77.

Lam, S. S. K., Schaubroeck, J., and Aryee, S. (2002). "Relationship between Organizational Justice and Employee Work Outcomes: A Cross-National Study," *Journal of Organizational Behavior*, 23, 1–18.

Larson, J. H., Wilson, S. M., and Beley, R. (1994). "The Impact of Job Insecurity on Marital and Family Relationships," *Family Relations,* 43, 138–43.

Leung, K. (1997). "Negotiation and Reward Allocations across Cultures." In Earley, P. C. and Erez, M. (eds.) *New Perspectives on International Industrial/Organizational Psychology.* San Francisco: Jossey-Bass.

——, Smith, P. B., Wang, Z. M., and Sun, H. F. (1996). "Job Satisfaction in Joint Venture Hotels in China: An Organizational Justice Analysis," *Journal of International Business Studies,* 27, 947–62.

—— and Stephan, W. G. (2001). "Social Justice from a Cultural Perspective." In Matsumoto, D. (ed.) *The Handbook of Culture & Psychology.* Oxford: Oxford University Press.

——, Wang, Z. M., and Smith, P. B. (2001). "Job Attitudes and Organizational Justice in Joint Venture Hotels in China: The Role of Expatriate Managers," *International Journal of Human Resource Management,* 12(6), 926–45.

Lind, E. A. and Tyler, T. R. (1988). *The Social Psychology of Procedural Justice.* New York: Plenum Press.

Lyness, K. S. and Kropf, M. B. (2003). "The Relationships of National Gender Equality and Organizational Support with Work-Family Balance: A Study of European Managers." Presented at the Annual Meeting of the Academy of Management, Seattle, August.

Meyer, J. P., Allen, N. J., and Smith, C. A. (1993). "Commitment to Organizations and Occupations: Extension and Test of a Three-Component Conception," *Journal of Applied Psychology, 78,* 538–51.

———, Stanley, D. J., Herscovitch, L., and Topolnytsky, L. (2002). "Affective, Continuance, and Normative Commitment to the Organization: A Meta-analysis of Antecedents, Correlates, and Consequences," *Journal of Vocational Behavior, 61,* 20–52.

Mills, N. (2003). "A Fun Factory Delivers," *Grocer,* August 23, 62.

Mortimer, J. T., Lorence, J., Kumka, D. S. (1986). *Work, Family and Personality: Transition to Adulthood.* Norwood, NJ: Ablex.

Mowday, R. T. (1998). "Reflections on the Study and Relevance of Organizational Commitment," *Human Resource Management Review,* 8(4), 387–401.

Na, E. Y. and Loftus, E. F. (1998). "Attitudes towards Law and Prisoners, Conservative Authoritarianism, Attribution, and Internal-External Locus of Control: Korean and American Law Students and Undergraduates," *Journal of Cross-Cultural Psychology,* 29(5), 595–615.

Oppenheimer, V. K. (1982). *Work and the Family: A Study in Social Demography.* New York: Academic Press.

O'Toole, P. L., Stromberg, M., Haynes, M., and McCune, H. (2002). "One Hundred and One Best Companies' Best Practices," *Professional Builder,* 67(6), 54–65.

Palich, L. E., Hom, P. W., and Griffeth, R. W. (1995). "Managing in the International Context: Testing Cultural Generality of Sources of Commitment to Multinational Enterprises," *Journal of Management,* 21(4), 671–90.

Pearce, J. L., Bigley, G. A., and Branyiczki, I. (1998). "Procedural Justice as Modernism: Placing Industrial/Organisational Psychology in Context," *Applied Psychology: An International Review,* 47(3), 371–96.

Peters, P. and den Dulk, L. (2003). "Cross-Cultural Differences in Managers' Support for Home-Based Telework: A Theoretical Elaboration," *International Journal of Cross Cultural Management,* 3(3), 329–46.

Poster, W. R. (2002). "Work-Family Policies in Global Corporations: Lessons from High-Tech Companies in India and the United States," Unpublished manuscript. Department of Sociology, University of Illinois at Urbana-Champaign, February.

Russ, F. A. and McNeilly, K. M. (1995). "Links among Satisfaction, Commitment, and Turnover Intentions: The Moderating Effect of Experience, Gender, and Performance," *Journal of Business Research,* 34, 57–65.

Schwartz, D. (1994). *An Examination of the Impact of Family-Friendly Policies on the Glass Ceiling.* New York: Families and Work Institute.

Shaffer, M. A., Francesco, A. M., Joplin, J. R. W., and Lau, T. (in press). "Easing the Pain: A Cross-Cultural Study of Support Resources and Their Influence on Work-Family Conflict." In Poelmans, S. (ed.) *Work and Family: An International Research Perspective.* Mahwah, NJ: Erlbaum.

———, ———, ———, and ———. (2004). Reconciling Life Roles: A Cross-Cultural Model of Work-Family Interface and Life Balance. Presented at the Academy of International Business Annual Conference, Stockholm, Sweden. July.

Spector, P. E., Cooper, C. L., Poelmans, S., Allen, T. D., O'Driscoll, M., Sanchez, J. I., Siu, O. L., Dewe, P., Hart, P., Lu, L., Renault de Moraes, L. F., Ostrognay, G. M., Sparks, K., Wong, P., and Yu, S. (2003). "A Cross-National Comparative Study of Work/Family Stressors, Working Hours, and Well-Being: China and Latin America vs. the Anglo World." Presented at the Annual Meeting of the Society for Industrial and Organizational Psychology, Orlando, FL, April.

Thompson, C. A., Beauvais, L. L., and Lyness, K. S. (1999). "When Work-Family Benefits Are Not Enough: The Influence of Work-Family Culture on Benefit Utilization, Organizational Attachment, and Work-Family Conflict," *Journal of Vocational Behavior,* 54, 392–415.

Tiedje, L. B., Wortman, C. B., Downey, G., Emmons, C., Biernat, M., and Lang, E. (1990). "Women with Multiple Roles: Role Compatibility Perceptions, Satisfaction, and Mental Health," *Journal of Marriage and the Family,* 52, 63–72.

Triandis, H. C. (1995). *Individualism and Collectivism.* Boulder, CO: Westview Press.

Vandenberghe, C., Stinglhamber, F., Bentein, K., and Delhaise, T. (2001). "An Examination of the Cross-Cultural Validity of a Multidimensional Model of Commitment in Europe," *Journal of Cross-Cultural Psychology,* 32(3), 322–47.

Watanabe, S., Takahashi, K. and Minami, T. (1997). "The Emerging Role of Diversity and Work-Family Values in a Global Context." In Earley, P. C. and Erez, M. (eds.) *New Perspectives on International Industrial/Organizational Psychology.* San Francisco: New Lexington Press.

Westman, M. (in press). "Cross-Cultural Differences in Crossover Research." In Poelmans, S. (ed.) *Work and Family: An International Research Perspective.* Mahwah, NJ: Erlbaum.

Wong, C. S., Wong, Y. T., Hui, C., and Law, K. (2001). "The Significant Role of Chinese Employees' Organizational Commitment: Implications for

Managing Employees in Chinese Societies," *Journal of World Business,* 36(3), 326–40.

Yang, N., Chen, C. C., Choi, J., and Zou, Y. (2000). "Sources of Work-Family Conflict: A Sino-U.S. Comparison of the Effects of Work and Family Demands," *Academy of Management Journal,* 43, 113–23.

Yousef, D. A. (2000). "Organizational Commitment as a Mediator of the Relationship between Islamic Work Ethic and Attitudes toward Organizational Change," *Human Relations,* 53(4), 513–37.

—— (2002). "Job Satisfaction as a Mediator of the Relationship between Role Stressors and Organizational Commitment: A Study from an Arabic Cultural Perspective," *Journal of Managerial Psychology,* 17(4), 250–66.

10

Managing Diversity

Learning Objectives

After reading this chapter, you should be able to:

- Define diversity.
- Understand how different cultures view diversity.
- Explain Cox's model of the multicultural organization.
- Discuss various ways of managing diversity in organizations.
- Describe unintended results of managing diversity.
- Consider how managing diversity can be a competitive advantage.

CULTURE AT WORK

Learning Diversity from a Foreign Acquisition

In the late 1980s, to cut costs in its battle against a hostile takeover, U.S. based Pillsbury closed its Affirmative Action Department. A short time later, Grand Metropolitan, a British firm, acquired Pillsbury, including its well-known brands Burger King, Green Giant, and Häagen-Dazs.

The new owners believed that in the United States multiculturalism could benefit Pillsbury. Grand Metropolitan reinstated the Affirmative Action Department renaming it the "culture diversity" function. *Diversity* was defined as meeting the needs of women and African-Americans.

After reinstituting the department, top management attended a series of lectures emphasizing the business value of diversity. As a result, Pillsbury introduced a reward structure that awarded bonuses to senior managers for encouraging diversity. Within six months there was a serious commitment to diversity by Pillsbury. In fact, the definition of diversity expanded to include working style, age, education, and sexual preference.

The commitment to diversity in the United States and the program's success encouraged Grand Metropolitan's headquarters in the United Kingdom to implement similar programs. Eventually, the company made managing diversity a priority throughout its global operations.

Source: Herriot, P. and Pemberton, C. (1995). *Competitive Advantage through Diversity: Organizational Learning from Difference.* London: Sage.

As organizations globalize and employ people in other countries they have to search for effective ways to manage people with different cultures. At the same time, organizations in many countries are experiencing increased diversity in their domestic employees as labor forces become more diverse as a result of immigration, social movements, political events, and population trends. Examples of increasing diversity are:

- Although the United States has always been a country of immigrants, minority group members have made up 40% of new additions to the labor force since 1998. This trend is expected to continue until at least 2008 (Campbell 2003).
- In the last 20 years, the proportion of working women has increased in all Organization for Economic Cooperation and Development (OECD) countries. In Denmark and Sweden, almost as many women as men are employed OECD (2002).
- As a result of the changes in governments in Eastern Europe, many people moved to Western Europe, particularly Germany, to seek greater economic opportunities.
- Saudi Arabian organizations employ 7.5 million foreign workers, a number equal to 40% of the indigenous population (Janardhan 2003).
- Hong Kong's rising standard of living has led to the importation of a substantial population of Filipino and Indonesian domestic helpers.
- Japanese companies in the United States find managing their diverse American employees to be complex and perplexing.

With increasing diversity across the globe, as well as the greater internationalization of corporations, managers need to understand diversity and how to manage it. From the perspective of international organizational behavior, however, the management of diversity remains an emerging issue because many cultures are not yet diverse, others are gradually becoming diverse, and still others do not acknowledge diversity as a social or organizational issue. Further, many domestic and international organizations are just beginning to manage diversity or don't consider it at all. Adler (2002, p. 248) observes that

> Few global companies have reached the stage at which they consistently value diversity, whether cross-cultural or male/female, and can readily leverage it to their advantage. Equally daunting, few women have, as yet, had the opportunity to consistently use all of their strengths in the service of senior-level leadership. The majority of leaders, both male and female, remain constrained within styles of leadership more restricting than those needed for the twenty-first century. Evolution toward more synergistic approaches, by both organizations and individuals, will be enhanced and accelerated by a more open discussion of the nature of diversity and a deeper understanding of the assumptions embedded in our leadership processes.

In addition, data from the World Values Survey indicate that the deepest cultural difference between Western cultures and the Islamic world is the role of women in society (Inglehart and Norris 2003a). Western cultures are moving toward gender equality, whereas Islamic cultures have entirely different views concerning divorce, abortion, and gender equality in general. Finally, gender inequality persists, although to a lesser extent than between the West and Islam, in cultures throughout the world (Inglehart and Norris 2003b).

▪▪▪ What Is Diversity?

Diversity is a range of differences that includes gender, race, ethnicity, and age, which are characteristics that are usually apparent from looking at someone. It also includes differences that are not visible such as education, professional background, functional area of expertise, sexual preference, and religion. These differences are important because they affect how individuals behave within an organization. Employees who belong to the same group often have similar patterns of behavior. As an organization becomes more diverse, differences among groups often become more pronounced raising questions about how to manage diversity effectively.

Research on managing diversity developed from studies of equal employment opportunity that focused on discrimination that significantly hindered the assimilation of women and minority groups into the mainstream workforce. Decades later research emphasized the "celebration" or valuing of differences. The most recent focus is on the "business case" for diversity, the view that managing diversity successfully is a business necessity (Kochan et al. 2003). Lew Platt, the former CEO of Hewlett Packard commented:

> I see three main points to make the business case for diversity:
>
> **1.** A talent shortage that requires us to seek out and use the full capabilities of our employees.
> **2.** The need to be like our customers, including the need to understand and communicate with them in terms that reflect their concerns.
> **3.** Diverse teams produce better results. (Kochan et al. 2003, p. 5)

There are various definitions of managing diversity and multiple viewpoints on how it contributes to an organization, but most management researchers agree on the following points (Kandola 1995). First, effective management of diversity and differences between people adds value to a company. Second, diversity includes all types of differences, not only the obvious physical differences such as gender or ethnicity. Third, organizational culture and working environment issues are important concerns of managing diversity. One contemporary view of diversity is that:

> Managing diversity, if it has an overriding image, is that of an organization as a mosaic. The differences come together to create a whole organization, in much the same way as the single pieces of a mosaic come together to create an image. The differences are acknowledged, accepted and have a place in the whole structure (Kandola 1995, p. 132).

Another metaphor for diversity is the salad bowl: In the same sense as the mosaic, the concept is that each individual has a unique contribution to make in an organization. When diverse backgrounds and talents combine in an organization, they produce a synergistic effect.

The dimensions of diversity and how different nations or organizations identify the different groups represented within them vary significantly. For some, gender and racioethnicity constitute diversity while for others, a greater array of variables is important.

▪▪▪ How Different Cultures View Diversity

The way a country views diversity depends on the cultural values of the people, the range of differences in the population, and attitudes toward these differences. Some countries, such as the United States, have a long history of dealing with people who are different, and as a highly individualistic country, the United States values these differences. Other countries, such as Japan, have been isolated from other cultures for centuries, and today are still relatively homogeneous. As collectivists, the Japanese prefer conformity and are more comfortable with in-group members. The next section presents views of diversity in the United States, Canada, Japan, and Germany.

The United States

In the United States, there is a fundamental tradition of valuing equality and equal opportunity. Although relationships among members of different racial and ethnic groups have not always been harmonious—and are not today—law, social, and corporate policy over the past 50 years have made numerous attempts to address equity and diversity issues.

In the 1960s, attempts to manage diversity grew out of the need to comply with various laws that provide **equal employment opportunity.** These laws prohibit employment discrimination on the bases of race, gender, ethnicity, religion, color, age, disability, pregnancy, national origin, and citizenship status. There are also **affirmative action** laws that attempt to correct past systemic discrimination against women and minorities. Table 10-1 lists some of these laws. Their objective is to employ adequate numbers of women and minorities and to treat all groups of employees in a nondiscriminatory way.

In the late 1970s and throughout the 1980s, organizations realized that merely filling quotas to comply with the law was not an effective way to manage the workforce. In response, companies developed organizational cultures that were more supportive of diverse employees and offered training programs on valuing diversity. This expanded the concept of diversity beyond race and gender to include a wider range of differences (Kochan et al. 2003).

An example of this approach is the Valuing Differences program instituted by the Digital Equipment Corporation (DEC) in the mid-1970s that focused on the need for people with different backgrounds to talk about their differences. Discussion groups called Core Groups included men and women of all ethnic backgrounds and races, representing all levels of the organization. The program evolved, and in 1985, Digital made Valuing Differences a company function and included it in DEC's written policy. Within a short time, employees at DEC realized that by recognizing and appreciating each other's differences, they could work most effectively with each other (Mandell and Kohler-Gray 1990). Eventually, the Core Groups discussed similarities as well as differences among employees (Dass and Parker 1999).

By the 1990s, multiculturalism and valuing diversity were well established in American businesses. Organizations then became concerned with the actual impact of diversity, the "business case," that assumes that a diverse workforce should be more effective (Kochan et al. 2003). At the same time, managing diversity became more strategic. For example, in a large financial services firm all senior managers must manage a formal diversity plan and link diversity to education, recruiting, succession planning, career development, and business growth. The firm also has a company-wide Diversity Council headed by the CEO (Kochan et al. 2003).

Another view of diversity is in management education. The United States-based AACSB International (The Association to Advance Collegiate Schools of Business), the international accrediting agency for business schools, requires schools to demonstrate diversity in their business programs as part of the accreditation process. The

TABLE 10-1 Major U.S. Federal Laws and Regulations Affecting Equal Employment Opportunity

Law	Coverage
Equal Pay Act of 1963	Prohibits gender-based pay differentials for equal work.
Title VII, 1964 Civil Rights Act (as amended in 1972)	Prohibits job discrimination in employment based on race, color, religion, gender, or national origin.
Executive Order 11246 (1965)	Requires contractors and subcontractors performing work on federal or federally assisted projects to prepare and implement affirmative action plans for minorities and women, persons with disabilities, and veterans.
Age Discrimination in Employment Act of 1967–(ADEA)	Prohibits age discrimination in any terms and conditions of employment, including areas such as hiring, promotion, termination, leaves of absence, and compensation. Protects individuals age 40 and over.
Rehabilitation Act of 1973	Prohibits contractors and subcontractors of federal projects from discriminating against applicants and/or employees who are physically or mentally disabled, if qualified to perform the job. This statute also requires the contractor to take affirmative action in the employment and advancement of individuals with disabilities.
The Vietnam Era Veterans Readjustment Assistance Act of 1972 and 1974	Requires government contractors and subcontractors to take affirmative action with respect to certain classes of veterans (of the Vietnam Era and Special Disabled Veterans).
The Immigration Reform and Control Act of 1986 (IRCA)	Prohibits employers from discriminating against persons authorized to work in the U.S. with respect to hiring or termination from employment because of national origin or citizenship status. IRCA makes it illegal for an employer knowingly to hire an alien who is not authorized to work in the U.S. All new hires must prove their identity and eligibility to work in the U.S.
Americans with Disabilities Act of 1990, Title I (ADA)	Prohibits employers from discriminating against qualified applicants and employees with disabilities in regard to any employment practices or terms, conditions, and privileges of employment.
Civil Rights Act of 1991	Focuses on burdens of proof and remedies in cases of discrimination based on race, color, religion, gender, age, disability (under the ADA), and/or national origin. The Act grants to plaintiffs the right to a jury trial and makes available compensatory and punitive damages (capped at $300,000).

Source: Adapted from Fernandez, J. P. (with M. Barr) (1993). *The Diversity Advantage: How American Business Can Out-perform Japanese and European Companies in the Global Marketplace.* New York: Lexington, pp. 314–6. Reprinted by permission.

rationale is that diverse people and ideas enhance management education, and business programs should include multiple viewpoints to prepare students for careers in a global context (AACSB International 2003).

The study, management, and legislation of diversity continue to develop in the United States. Despite the legal basis for equality in the United States Constitution and recent civil rights and equal opportunity legislation, the overwhelming evidence indicates that within organizations individuals from different groups continue to experience discrimination (Cox 1993). Although 40% of Americans no longer believe affirmative action programs are needed to achieve workplace diversity, the number of race-based discrimination claims filed with the Equal Employment Opportunity Commission reached a seven-year high in 2002 (Armour 2003). Opportunities for women and minorities have improved considerably since the early 1960s, but many organizations make minimal efforts to manage diversity and some still resist complying with the law (Allard 2002).

Canada

Although Canada is adjacent to the United States, the history of managing diversity there is very different. Unlike the United States, where federal laws apply to all organizations, Canadian federal employment law only regulates certain industries, including broadcasting, telecommunications, banking, railroads, airlines, shipping, other interprovincial transportation, uranium mining, and government owned corporations. Businesses in other industries are subject only to the laws of the province where they operate—for example, Ontario and Quebec have pay equity laws (Mentzer 2002).

The Canadian Human Rights Act of 1977 applies only to the regulated industries and prohibits discrimination on the basis of race, gender, and certain other grounds. The Act forbids both direct discrimination, such as refusing to hire women for certain jobs, and indirect discrimination, for example, sexual harassment. The act also mandates that males and females must receive equal pay for work that is the same or equally important and difficult. The Canadian Human Rights Commission adjudicates complaints relating to the law and in severe cases orders hiring quotas (Mentzer 2002).

The Canadian Employment Equity Acts of 1986 and 1995 encourage covered employers to proactively fight discrimination against women and minority employees. The Act includes women, native peoples, people with disabilities, and visible minorities including those of black, Asian, Arab, Pacific Islander, and Latin American ancestry. The 1986 Act required companies to report to the federal government, which then assessed their performance. However, there were no financial penalties, and the government relied on persuasion and embarrassment for compliance. The 1995 Act mandated fines of up to C$50,000 for companies not meeting their targets, but they are rarely issued (Mentzer 2002).

Although Canadian legislation is not as extensive as in the United States, companies there also manage diversity, and some have developed comprehensive programs. For example, the Royal Bank of Canada (RBC) has won numerous awards for its diversity management programs (RBC Financial Group 2003). RBC offers an extensive support program for employees including flexible work arrangements, maternity and parental leave, and workplace accommodation. In order to accommodate employees with disabilities, the RBC has created a central fund so individual managers do not need to include such expenses in their budgets (Young 2000). Jason, a paraplegic sales and service representative, comments on his experience at the bank (RBC Financial Group 2003):

> Due to my disability, constant sitting does affect me physically. RBC has allowed me to modify my work schedule, which allows me to give my body a break. Also, RBC has made me feel comfortable from the very first day. RBC understands some of the physical difficulties and barriers that I face such as easy access through doors, which they have made easier.
>
> RBC's commitment to hiring and retaining people with disabilities is greatly reflected in my business group. From the onset we worked together. RBC assessed my workplace needs to ensure the work environment was acceptable for me to get around and work properly and efficiently. Both of us have benefited from this relationship. RBC's efforts in creating an accommodating work environment have enabled me to make a significant contribution to this organization, which has given me a greater sense of self worth.[1]

Japan

The view of diversity in Japan is quite different than in the United States or Canada. Japan had little contact with the rest of the world until the mid-1800s (Fernandez 1993). As a small isolated island nation, it was important for individuals to work together to provide the necessities to survive. Today the population of Japan is relatively homogeneous with the vast majority ethnic Japanese along with small numbers of ethnic Koreans and Chinese, some of whom have lived in Japan for generations, and tiny populations of expatriates and foreign students.

Japanese culture is extremely group-oriented with acceptable behavior clearly defined. In Japanese society, an individual knows how to behave based on age, gender, and position and deviation is subject to sanction. Behaviors that deviate from appropriate norms are subject to sanction.

The Japanese have a distinctive management style that contributed to the worldwide success of Japanese business and the rapid development of the Japanese economy in the latter part of the twentieth century. The management system, intertwined with Japanese culture, incorporates practices brought from abroad, such as quality circles, into the Japanese way of managing.

Characteristics of the Japanese management system include managerial autonomy, rigid hierarchical organizations, consensus decision making, lifetime employment, promotion based on seniority, and relative equity in compensation between management and workers (Chen 1995). However, the Japanese recession that began in the early 1990s and continued into the early 21st century along with changes in Japanese society, have created the need for new organizational forms and practices that borrow from the West (Abegglen and Stalk 1995; Chen 1995; Durlabhji and Marks 1993; Pascale and Athos 1981; Whitehill 1991).

In large corporations in Japan the level of a position is related to the age and gender of the incumbent with older males holding the most senior positions. Retirement has been age 55 to 60, and the number of women in managerial positions has been extremely limited.

In 2001, women made up 40.4% of the labor force in Japan yet 40% of these were part-timers ("Some 40 Pct of Japan's Working Women Part-Timers" 2002). In large

---

[1] From "Employee Testimonial by Jason a Sales and Service Representative for RBC Financial Group on disability workplace accommodations" on RBC website, www.rbc.com.

companies and government, women occupy only 2% to 3% of managerial positions, but more opportunities are available in foreign companies, particularly in financial services, that are generally not attractive to top male university graduates (Jameson 2001). Over the last 20 years, more women entered the workforce than men, and 70% of working women are married. The long recession has benefited female workers as companies hire them to reduce labor costs (Jameson 2001).

In 1986 an equal opportunity law went into effect throughout Japan prohibiting discrimination against women in new employee training, retirement, and dismissal. It also lifted some restrictions against night work and overtime for women. However, the law merely *encouraged* equal opportunity in recruiting, hiring, and promoting (Fernandez 1993), and the sole enforcement mechanism was "administrative guidance" (Steinhoff and Tanaka 1994).

As a result of the law, companies developed a two-track system. At the time of initial hiring, women choose between a traditional woman's job and a career position supposedly equivalent to those offered permanent male employees (Steinhoff and Tanaka 1994). Although this opened new opportunities for women and led to higher female career aspirations, only a very small percentage choose the managerial track, and their employers often discourage them from staying on it (Liu and Boyle 2001).

The 1999 revision of the Equal Employment Opportunity Law brought an end to restrictions on women's work such as no shift work after 10 p.m. and overtime limits of six hours per week. Employers are also no longer allowed to specify certain jobs as being for men or women (Thornton 1999). The new law allows the government to investigate disputes at the employees' request and to warn companies that do not deal with sexual harassment complaints and even name them publicly as a punishment (Amaha 1999).

The Japanese maintain a highly restrictive immigration policy, yet have a birthrate of only 1.3 per woman and a population that will begin shrinking in 2005 (Zielenziger 2002). Although at present diversity in domestic organizations is unimportant or even irrelevant, these factors combined with a long-term labor shortage, suggest that the Japanese may need a more diversified workforce with respect to age, gender, and possibly foreign workers. Outside the country, Japanese companies constitute some of the major forces in global markets. As their experience with subsidiaries outside of Japan demonstrates, the Japanese need to think about ways to manage diversity on a worldwide basis.

Germany

Germany has another view of diversity. Although the majority of German residents is ethnically German, there is a history of "**guest workers**" from abroad in the former West Germany that began after World War II when there was a shortage of men to rebuild the war devastated economy. German industries recruited workers primarily from southern Europe and northern Africa including Turkey, Greece, Yugoslavia, Italy, Spain, Portugal, Morocco, and Tunisia. The intention was that guest workers would eventually return to their home countries, but the foreign worker population in Germany increased tremendously over a 40-year period, from 80,000 in the mid-1950s to 2.6 million in the mid-1990s. In 1992, guest workers constituted almost 12% of all wage and salary workers (Fernandez 1993).

As the economic and political situation in Europe changed, so did the attitude toward foreign workers. "Foreigners at first were not considered threatening but somewhat magical and very exotic. By 1964, however, an anti-Turkish image emerged. . . . Resentment and prejudices against Turks have increased since then, leading to violent and even deadly attacks" (Fernandez 1993, p. 167).

With the change of governments throughout Eastern Europe and the reunification of East and West Germany in October 1990, the situation for guest workers grew more complex. Germany's liberal asylum laws and generous provisions for social services made the country a magnet for many from the former Communist states of Eastern Europe. The number of asylum seekers increased rapidly in the early 1990s to half a million in 1992, and by the end of the year Germany changed its asylum laws. Asylum seekers from bordering countries and countries that did not practice political persecution could not enter Germany and could only appeal from abroad (Fernandez 1993).

The enormous costs of integrating the former East Germany and the influx of asylum seekers coupled with the lackluster economy of the early 1990s created a climate of resentment against foreign workers. Although many Germans prefer that guest workers return home, they perform essential jobs in garbage collection, janitorial services, and the hospitality industry that Germans avoid (Fernandez 1993).

By 2002, Germans were showing increasing tolerance towards Turks who accounted for 20% of the population in some parts of large cities (Garcea 2002a). Many who first came to Germany as guest workers, now own and manage their own businesses and over 50,000 Turks live in Berlin (Garcea 2002c).

The treatment of working women is also evolving. In the former West Germany, approximately half of working aged women were in the labor force compared to over 80% in the former East Germany. With the change in the economic system in East Germany in the early 1990s came massive unemployment. Women, who made up more than 60% of the unemployed, felt the impact of unemployment more strongly (Berthoin Antal and Krebsbach-Gnath 1994; Wiedemeyer, Beywl, and Helmstadter 1993).

Although women were widely present in the labor force in the former East and West Germanys, they received on average one-third less pay than men, were concentrated in relatively few industries, and were far less likely than men to be managers, particularly at a senior level. The constitution of the Federal Republic of Germany recognizes the equal rights of men and women and additional laws passed in the 1980s require equal opportunity and the development of equal opportunity positions throughout public administration. The private sector voluntarily uses similar policies (Berthoin Antal and Krebsbach-Gnath 1994).

Although the law required the government to take measures to increase the recruitment, promotion, and training of women, there were no sanctions for failure to comply. During the reunification process, both in the public and private sectors, the equal opportunity guidelines and standard practices that had been used in West Germany were not applied in East Germany resulting in "significant gender bias in the decisions to keep, fire, or recruit staff in both the public and private sectors, and that bias [was expected to] have far-reaching consequences" (Berthoin Antal and Krebsbach-Gnath 1994, p. 218).

In 2001, Germany's female labor force participation rate was 64.4% (OECD 2003). Although German society expects women to be wives and mothers, employment is becoming a more acceptable option. In the past, the three K's, *Kinder, Küche, und Kirche* (Children, Cooking, and Church), explained women's role, but today the third K has come to stand for *Karriere* (Career) (Gracea 2002b).

As a member of the European Union (EU), Germany recognizes the six core dimensions of diversity that were established in article 13 of the Treaty of Amsterdam in 1997. They are gender, race or ethnic origin, age, disability, sexual orientation, and religious or personal beliefs (Gracea, 2002b; Stuber 2002). The EU adopted a Declaration on Cultural Diversity in 2000 outlining how diversity can be expressed, sustained, and enabled, and in the same year, the EU also established guidelines for the Community Initiative EQUAL, a program of transnational cooperation to fight discrimination and inequalities in the labor market (Simons 2002).

Since the reunification of Germany in 1990, the dynamics of diversity have changed and continue to evolve. With a low birthrate, it is likely that in the future Germany will have to make continued and, most likely, greater utilization of women and foreign workers to sustain its economy.

The examples of the United States, Canada, Japan, and Germany illustrate how different cultures view diversity. The workforce in many countries continues to increase in diversity as more businesses are going into international markets, creating the need to manage a wider variety of employees, customers, and suppliers. The result is academic research on issues related to diversity and organizational action to develop programs and practices to deal with diversity.

Cox's Model of the Multicultural Organization

A model of diversity developed by Taylor Cox (1991, 1993) identifies six dimensions to analyze an organization's capability for effectively integrating culturally diverse employees. Table 10-2 presents these dimensions and their definitions.

Based on how an organization treats these six dimensions, Cox classifies it as one of three organizational types: monolithic, plural, or multicultural. Table 10-3 presents the characteristics of these organizations.

The Monolithic Organization

The **monolithic** organization includes predominately the same type of people. Individuals who are different from the majority often work only in a limited number of positions or departments. Because people with different backgrounds do not hold positions throughout the organization, to survive, minority group members usually follow the organizational norms set by the majority. Members of the minority culture usually

TABLE 10-2 Six Dimensions to Analyze Organizational Capability for Effective Integration of Culturally Diverse Employees

Dimension	*Definition*
1. Acculturation	Modes by which two groups adapt to each other and resolve cultural differences
2. Structural Integration	Cultural profiles of organization members including hiring, job-placement, and job status profiles
3. Informal Integration	Inclusion of minority-culture members in informal networks and activities outside of normal working hours
4. Cultural Bias	Prejudice and discrimination
5. Organizational Identification	Feelings of belonging, loyalty, and commitment to the organization
6. Inter-group Conflict	Friction, tension, and power struggles between cultural groups

Source: Cox, T., Jr. (1991). "The Multicultural Organization," *Academy of Management Executive*, 5(2), p. 35. Reproduced with permission of Academy of Management in the format Other Book via Copyright Clearance Center

TABLE 10-3 Characteristics of Cox's Three Organizational Types

Dimension of Integration	Monolithic	Plural	Multicultural
Form of Acculturation	Assimilation	Assimilation	Pluralism
Degree of Structural Integration	Minimal	Partial	Full
Integration into Informal Organization	Virtually none	Limited	Full
Degree of Cultural Bias	Both prejudice and discrimination against minority-culture groups are prevalent	Progress on both prejudice and discrimination but both continue to exist especially institutional discrimination	Both prejudice and discrimination are eliminated
Levels of Organizational Identification*	Large majority-minority gap	Medium to large majority-minority gap	No majority-minority gap
Degree of Intergroup Conflict	Low	High	Low

*Defined as difference between organizational identification levels between minorities and majorities.

Source: Cox, T., Jr. (1991). "The Multicultural Organization," *Academy of Management Executive,* 5(2), 45–56. Reproduced with permission of Academy of Management in the format Other Book via Copyright Clearance Center

do not participate in many informal activities, and the majority group is unlikely to adopt minority-culture norms. Intergroup conflict is relatively low because the organization is almost homogeneous, however, discrimination and prejudice are common.

Most large Japanese companies are monolithic. The majority of people working in them are Japanese men, and the few women are primarily concentrated in lower-level and part-time positions. An important part of Japanese work culture involves socializing with co-workers after work, usually at male-oriented bars and small restaurants. Although it is increasingly becoming more acceptable for women to join these informal after-work activities, married women with home and family responsibilities do not have adequate time, and many are uncomfortable participating in such activities (Steinhoff and Tanaka 1994).

Because of the dominance of men, conflict between men and women in Japanese organizations is low. As a result of their inferior status, women receive less favorable treatment than men, but in complying with organization norms and cultural values, do little to change their treatment.

The Plural Organization

The **plural organization** is the second type. It includes a wider variety of people, and management makes a greater effort to include people who differ from the majority. Structural integration is more extensive than in the monolithic organization because the number of minority group members is usually greater. However, representation of minority group members at different levels or in different functions is infrequent.

Minority group members are more involved in informal activities, and prejudice and discrimination are less than in the monolithic organization. However, the level of conflict among different groups tends to be high.

Many large firms in the United States are plural. These companies emphasize an affirmative action approach to managing diversity. They have programs to promote equal opportunity or affirmative action, for example, recruitment and selection procedures to ensure equal access to jobs or special training programs to benefit women and minority members. As a result, many large American companies have the same proportion of minority employees as in the population, but there are few women and minority managers. Because of special programs, and in some cases preference for hiring and promoting women and minority group members, some Caucasian men in the United States object to affirmative action programs. This is one reason for group conflict.

The Multicultural Organization

The third type of organization is **multicultural.** This type overcomes the problems of the plural organization, and rather than just having a diverse set of employees, diversity is valued. One characteristic of the multicultural organization is pluralism; majority and minority group members adopt some of the norms of the other. In addition, in the multicultural organization members of different groups hold positions throughout the organization and participate fully in informal activities. There is no prejudice or discrimination, all employees identify equally with the organization, and conflicts among groups are minimal. Some companies with systemic programs and a long-term commitment to managing diversity fit the multicultural type.

▪ ▪ ▪ How Organizations Manage Diversity

Organizations manage diversity in a variety of ways. To illustrate one approach this section presents a comprehensive model for an organizational level diversity program and several examples of techniques to implement it.

An Organizational Level Approach

Contemporary organizational structures may not be appropriate for managing diversity (Kandola 1995). However, eight factors that are important for creating a new type of organization that can manage diversity are:

1. Organizational vision. An organizational statement of why diversity is important, a general policy on diversity and how to use it, and the expected benefits. Over 70% of Fortune 500 companies have diversity programs including a mission statement and definition of diversity (Digh 1998).

2. Top management commitment. Top management must set an example for others to follow and allocate the necessary resources to implement the vision. An interesting example is Peter deRoo, founder of Baobab Catering, a Belgian company that specializes in multicultural cuisine and employs political refugees. De Roo's personal experience working in Cambodian refugee camps has led to a strong personal commitment to equal opportunity at Baobab (Claes 2002).

3. Auditing and assessment of needs. The organization collects data to ensure that different groups receive the same treatment. For example, an organization could determine the number of minority group employees at various levels and in different areas of the company or administer an attitude survey to collect information on how members of different groups feel they are being treated. A firm can discover potential problem areas with these techniques. An unexpected diversity issue arose at a company leadership conference of the American School Food Service Association when cafeteria workers in elementary schools reported that they were treated with less respect than workers in high schools. In addition, workers in satellite kitchens felt they were at a disadvantage compared to those in the school district's central kitchens (Digh 1998). The location of work is not an obvious diversity category but discrimination can take many forms.

4. Clarity of objectives. Based on the results of the audit and assessment, management can set clear objectives relating to diversity and tie these to overall business objectives. It is important that managing diversity be seen as essential to the overall success of the business. At the Australian bank Westpac, managers need to meet both quarterly financial goals and equal employment targets (Kramer 1998).

5. Clear accountability. Members of the organization should be responsible for carrying out diversity objectives. Allowing employees to participate in objective setting is one way of ensuring an understanding of and commitment to the goals. All involved should have an understanding of the policies and strategies. For example, United States-based Sun Microsystems used five focus groups to collect data to assist in recruiting, hiring, and developing employees with particular backgrounds (Dass and Parker 1999).

6. Effective communication. Effective communication must exist within and outside the organization; everyone needs to know the organization's diversity initiatives. An example is European SaraLee DE's. *The Diversity Challenge*, a 12 page brochure about diversity for both internal and external distribution (Stuber 2002).

7. Coordination of activity. An individual or group coordinates the implementation of the diversity strategy. Part of this coordinating effort involves seeking information about new diversity initiatives from all sources. For example, the Victoria Police in Australia developed a new position, Manager, Equity and Diversity Unit, to oversee their Diversity Awareness Program (Sinclair 2000).

8. Evaluation. Evaluation of the overall diversity strategy, as well as individual actions, should occur periodically. Data collected in the auditing and assessment of needs provide a starting point against which to compare the program outcomes. In Australia, Esso conducted a culture audit to see whether employees complied with the six corporate core values and to assess the effectiveness of people management. With data from the audit, managers developed priority areas for action (Kramer 1998).

By following this strategy, an organization can be more successful in implementing diversity initiatives (Kandola 1995).

Techniques for Managing Diversity

To implement an organizational level approach to managing diversity, companies need to undertake specific activities such as those in the previous examples. Popular techniques include training programs, core groups, multicultural teams, and using senior managers to oversee diversity programs.

Diversity Training

A widely used technique is **diversity training.** Training could range from a single session designed to raise levels of awareness and sensitivity to diversity issues to a long-term continuous program that focuses on various aspects of managing diversity. For example, at a Tyson Food plant in the U.S., supervisors attended sessions to help them understand how Hispanics' cultural values differed from those in the mainstream American culture. Motorola's more extensive program offers an entire range of courses including diversity as a competitive advantage, the spirit of diversity, transition to diversity, sexual harassment and diversity management, and diversity awareness and interviewing (Dass and Parker 1999).

Core Groups

Core groups consist of a number of employees from different cultural backgrounds who meet regularly to discuss their attitudes, feelings, and beliefs about cultural differences and how they influence work behavior. The group provides an opportunity for individuals to speak frankly about their differences, and over time, they usually become more comfortable in dealing with diversity issues. Cox believes that the core group "is one of the most powerful tools available for organization change work related to managing diversity" (1993, p. 260). The DEC program discussed earlier is an example of this type.

Multicultural Teams

Multicultural teams contain workers from different cultural groups who learn how to maximize their effectiveness by taking full advantage of their differences. An example of this approach is British Petroleum's European finance center in Brussels, Belgium, where the staff comes from more than a dozen countries. The objectives of the program include, (1) making team members aware of cultural differences and how they influence various aspects of the organization; (2) assisting members in becoming more aware of their differences and how they can work with other team members; (3) improving communication among team members and with others at the finance center; (4) creating a set of work rules for the team; and (5) developing a shared team vision (Fernandez 1993).

Senior Managers of Diversity

In many organizations, the management of diversity is so important that the corporation creates a senior management position responsible for all diversity initiatives. This position demonstrates the company's commitment and ensures that its efforts are genuine. A Conference Board survey of 131 companies found that 60% had diversity positions at the director or vice president level (Dass and Parker 1999).

Other Approaches

Other approaches used by corporations include recruitment and selection programs that focus on hiring individuals who value diversity, compensation and reward programs tied to achieving diversity goals, language training, mentoring programs, cultural advisory groups, and corporate social activities that celebrate diversity (Cox 1993; Fernandez 1993).

▪▪▪ Unintended Results of Managing Diversity

So far, this chapter presents a positive view of managing diversity, suggesting that organizations of the future need to be multicultural and that including members of all groups leads to more positive organizational outcomes. Evidence indicates, however, that in some situations, managing diversity has had unintended negative consequences (Nemetz and Christensen 1996; Thomas and Ely 1996). For example, when organizations develop special programs to encourage women and minorities, majority males often feel discriminated against. Another unintended outcome is that affirmative action programs that give preferential treatment to certain groups may stigmatize individuals from those groups if others think that their qualifications are substandard and their positions are unearned. Similarly, management that recruits increased numbers of women and minorities, yet fails to appreciate and reward their contributions, can engender tension throughout the organization.

Organizations that make a commitment to managing diversity must also realize the effect of other influences on employees' attitudes and behavior (Nemetz and Christensen 1996). Their family and friends, religion, education, profession, and other factors shape people's views on managing diversity. Therefore, an organization must recognize that the impact of managing diversity programs may be limited because of competing influences.

▪▪▪ Managing Diversity for Competitive Advantage

As the workforce becomes increasingly more diverse worldwide, organizations that manage diversity effectively may develop a competitive advantage (Cox and Blake 1991; Mandell and Kohler-Gray 1990). In addition to social responsibility benefits, there are six areas where companies can gain competitive advantage from managing diversity well: (1) cost, (2) resource acquisition, (3) marketing, (4) creativity, (5) problem solving, and (6) organizational flexibility (Cox and Blake 1991).

Managing diversity well can create cost savings for organizations because people who are dissatisfied with their jobs are more likely to be absent or leave the organization. In the United States, women and minorities are likely to have higher absenteeism and turnover rates than white males (Cox 1996; Cox and Blake 1991) that might result from dissatisfaction with a firm's treatment. On the positive side, pregnant workers in the United States have greater organizational commitment to organizations judged to be "family friendly" (Francesco and Thompson 1996). Since there is a cost associated with absenteeism and turnover, reducing them translates into cost savings for the employer.

Failure to manage diversity successfully in countries that have equal employment opportunity laws can also be expensive. For example, in 1993, Shoney's, a family-style restaurant chain in the United States, paid US$134.5 million to settle a class action suit claiming that the company had discriminated against African Americans (Gaiter 1996).

The resource acquisition benefit comes when an organization develops a reputation as a good place for all kinds of people to work. As women and minorities become a larger percentage of the workforce in many countries, the ability to attract the most talented of these groups is becoming increasingly important.

Managing diversity effectively also improves a corporation's marketing because as products and services become available to increasingly diversified domestic and global markets, a diverse set of employees can provide insight into the most advantageous approaches to these markets. Consumers from diverse groups may also prefer to buy from companies that value diversity.

Improved creativity and innovation is another potential result of having diverse groups and teams in an organization. A variety of viewpoints stimulates creativity and higher-quality solutions to problems. A heterogeneous group can produce more creative solutions to complex or innovative problems. Positive outcomes result when the group is able to manage its differences. Understanding the background of each member and giving each an equal opportunity to participate can help facilitate the process.

The final potential advantage is organizational flexibility. As the organization welcomes a diverse set of individuals and the different viewpoints they bring, it is likely to become more open and adaptable to new ideas and changing environments.

The potential advantages of managing diversity effectively are substantial, but what are the actual benefits? A 2001 survey of 121 human resource professionals from *Fortune* magazine's "1000 Top Companies" and "100 Top Companies To Work For" found that 91% believed that diversity initiatives positively affect the company's competitive advantage, 79% said that diversity improves corporate culture, 77% that it improves employee recruitment, and 52% that it improves client relations. Negative outcomes were that 57% thought that diversity initiatives raised expectations for actions that might not be met, 38% were concerned with cost, and 30% with significant staff time spent managing diversity (Society for Human Resource Management 2001).

While opinions are important, there are very few studies of the actual impact of diversity on business performance. One study compared companies recognized by the U.S. Department of Labor for exemplary affirmative action programs to those that paid to settle discrimination lawsuits (Wright, Ferris, Hiller, and Kroll 1995). The stock of the award winning companies went up after the announcement of their awards whereas the stock of those who had to pay damages went down after public disclosure of the results of the lawsuits.

Another study collected in-depth data on the impact of racial and gender diversity on business performance in four large American organizations with a longstanding commitment to managing diversity (Kochan et al. 2003). The results showed that the well-developed programs had few positive or negative effects on corporate performance. In addition to case studies, the researchers interviewed members of more than 20 large, well-known, highly regarded firms about the state of diversity practices. They suggest managers can do the following:

1. *Modify the business case for diversity.*   Diversity is neither inevitably good nor bad for an organization. To be successful, companies need a sustained systemic approach and a long-term commitment to managing diversity. Companies that invest resources to take advantage of diversity opportunities should perform better than those that do not.

2. *Look beyond the business case.*   Although managing diversity may not influence company performance, it is a labor market reality and an American value and social expectation. Therefore, managers should try to build an organizational culture, human resource practices, and group process skills to make diversity into a positive result for individuals, groups, and the organization.

▪▪▪ Convergence or Divergence?

Forces for Convergence

Managing diversity in organizations is gradually becoming a concern for more companies throughout the world. With increasing multiculturalism as well as more involvement in international markets, there is a growing need to more effectively manage diversity.

Organizations have a wide variety of approaches to managing diversity domestically, and in some cases these extend to global operations. For example, in the Culture at Work vignette at the beginning of this chapter, when Grand Metropolitan, a British company, acquired the American food company Pillsbury, it reinstated and expanded the former Affirmative Action Department and made it into the "culture diversity" function. Later, Grand Metropolitan's management brought this concept back to its headquarters in the United Kingdom, and the company made the decision to manage diversity from a corporate multinational perspective.

As companies continue to internationalize and populations become more mobile, it is possible that a wider variety of groups will exist in the work force of countries such as Japan. Even now, Japanese companies have subsidiaries around the world and must manage a diverse workforce. As diversity within organizations worldwide increases, approaches to managing diversity could become similar.

Forces for Divergence

In some countries with relatively homogenous populations, the idea of managing diversity seems unimportant or irrelevant. In others, traditional workplace norms could perpetuate differential treatment of certain groups. With positions of power based on gender and age and no movement towards diverse representation, societies will not recognize the need to manage diversity.

▪▪▪ Implications for Managers

With the simultaneous trends toward globalization and domestic multiculturalism, an increasingly important part of an international manager's job is managing a diverse workforce. Understanding the impact of diversity within an organization and knowing how to efficiently utilize the diversity are valuable skills.

It is also important for international managers to realize that different cultures view diversity differently and that countries with diverse populations have different approaches to diversity. In some, members of diverse groups maintain a degree of separation, preferring to associate with members of their own groups and keeping their own traditions while in others, they freely interact. In countries where diversity is limited, there may be no societal guidelines for working with people who are different. Effective international managers must understand how the cultures they work in treat diversity and the potential impact of diversity on them.

SUMMARY ▪▪▪▪▪▪▪

The concept of managing diversity is gradually developing worldwide. As a result of changing demographics in many countries, domestic labor forces are increasingly more diverse. There are also increasingly greater numbers of businesses entering international markets. As a result of these changes, employee diversity requires more management to increase organizational effectiveness.

Cox's (1993) model of the multicultural organization analyzes an organization's capability to effectively integrate culturally diverse employees. There are three organizational types: the monolithic, plural, and multicultural. Although most organizations throughout the world fit the monolithic or plural type, in the future there will be greater need for companies, particularly those that are global, to be multicultural. In using an organization level approach to move a company towards the multicultural organizational type, managers can take a systemic approach that encompasses different activities.

Managing diversity can sometimes have unintended results. An organization might create negative attitudes in the majority if they view management as unfairly accommodating minorities. Organizations must also realize the multiple influences on employees' attitudes and behaviors as they establish diversity programs.

Managing diversity effectively can potentially be a competitive advantage for organizations. However, having a diversity program, even one that is highly regarded, does not necessarily influence business performance.

The concept of managing diversity is becoming increasingly common, particularly in global corporations that have employees from around the world. However, in some parts of the world, the issue of diversity is unimportant or irrelevant. With changing demographics and greater internationalization of businesses worldwide, the need for managing diversity will spread and could lead to greater convergence.

An effective international manager needs to develop skills for understanding and managing diversity. Since different cultures have various approaches to diversity, it is important to understand these approaches and the potential impact they could have on the manager.

DISCUSSION QUESTIONS ▪▪▪▪▪▪▪

1. How does your community define diversity? Your country? How are people who differ from the majority treated at work?
2. Select an organization with which you are familiar. (If you don't work, it could be your school, church, student, or community organization.) Using Cox's organizational types, how would you classify this organization? What do you think would be the most effective type for this organization now? In the future? Why?
3. What approaches do organizations use to manage diversity? Give an example from your personal experience or one that you have read about in another source. How effective is the approach taken in your example?
4. As a manager of a work group that has members from different backgrounds, what can you do to maximize the team's effectiveness?
5. Select a country of the world (your own or another). How does this country's view of diversity compare to those of the United States, Canada, Japan, and Germany?

INTERNET SITES ▪▪▪▪▪▪▪

Selected Companies in the Chapter

Baobab Catering (www.baobabcatering.be)
Hewlett-Packard Company (www.hp.com)
The Pillsbury Company (www.pillsbury.com)
RBC Financial Group, Diversity (www.rbc.com/uniquecareers/diversity)
Westpac Banking Corporation
(www.westpac.com.au/internet/publish.nsf/Content/WI+HomePage)

Diversity Sites

American Association for Affirmative Action (www.affirmativeaction.org). This is the site of an association of professionals managing affirmative action, equal opportunity, diversity, and other human resource programs.

American Institute for Managing Diversity (aimd.org/nonprofit/aimd). This is the site of AIMD, a national, nonprofit diversity think tank created for the purpose of advancing the field of diversity management.

EURopean Employment Services (http://europa.eu.int/eures). This is the public employment services Web site for the European Union.

Paths to Equal Opportunity, Government of Ontario—Ministry of Citizenship (www.equal opportunity.on.ca/). This site has extensive resources and information for business and service providers on workplace diversity and creating accessibility for people with disabilities.

University of Maryland, Diversity Database (www.inform.umd.edu/EdRes/Topic/Diversity/). The database includes multicultural and diversity resources.

REFERENCES ▪▪▪▪▪▪

AACSB International. (2003). *Eligibility Standards and Procedures for Business Accreditation.* St. Louis, MO: AACSB International.

Abegglen, J. and Stalk, G., Jr. (1991). *Kaisha, the Japanese Corporation.* New York: Basic Books.

Adler, N. J. (2002). "Women Joining Men as Global Leaders in the New Economy." In Gannon, M. J. and Newman, K. L. (eds.) *The Blackwell Handbook of Cross-Cultural Management.* Oxford: Blackwell.

Allard, M. J. (2002). "Theoretical Underpinnings of Diversity." In Harvey, C. P. and Allard, M. J. (eds.) *Understanding and Managing Diversity: Readings, Cases, and Exercises.* 2d Ed. Upper Saddle River, NJ: Prentice Hall.

Amaha, E. (1999). "Blazing a Trail," *Far Eastern Economic Review,* July 1, 34.

Armour, S. "Debate Revived on Workplace Diversity: New Research Casts Doubt on Financial Benefits," *USA Today,* [accessed July 22, 2003], available from http://www.shrm.org/hrnews_published/CMS_005 120.asp#P-12_0.

Berthoin Antal, A. and Krebsbach-Gnath, C. (1994). "Women in Management in Germany: East, West, and Reunited." In Adler, N. J. and Izraeli, D. N. (eds.) *Competitive Frontiers: Women Managers in a Global Economy.* Cambridge: Blackwell Publishers, 606–23.

Campbell, T. (2003). "Diversity in Depth," *HR Magazine,* March, 152.

Chen, M. (1995). *Asian Management Systems: Chinese, Japanese and Korean Styles of Business.* New York: Routledge.

Claes, M. T. (2002). "Equal Opportunities for Women and Men in the European Union: The Case of E-Quality in Belgium." In Simons, G. F. (ed.) *Eurodiversity: A Business Guide to Managing Differences.* Amsterdam: Butterworth-Heinemann.

Cox, T., Jr. (1993). *Cultural Diversity in Organizations: Theory, Research & Practice.* San Francisco: Berrett-Koehler.

——. (1991). "The Multicultural Organization," *Academy of Management Executive,* 5(2), 34–47.

—— and Blake, S. (1991). "Managing Cultural Diversity: Implications for Organizational Competitiveness," *Academy of Management Executive,* 5(3), 45–56.

Dass, P. and Parker, B. (1999). "Strategies for Managing Human Resource Diversity: From Resistance to

Learning," *The Academy of Management Executive,* 13(2), 68–80.

Digh, P. (1998). "Coming to Terms with Diversity," *HRMagazine,* November, 117–20.

Durlabhji, S. and Marks, N. E. (eds.) *Japanese Business: Cultural Perspective.* Albany, NY: SUNY Press.

Fernandez, J. P. (with M. Barr) (1993). *The Diversity Advantage: How American Business Can Out-perform Japanese and European Companies in the Global Marketplace.* New York: Lexington.

Francesco, A. M. and Thompson, C. A. (1996). "Pregnant Working Women: An Unrecognized Diversity Challenge." Presented at the Annual Meeting of the American Psychological Association, Toronto, Canada.

Gaiter, D. J. (1996). "Eating Crow: How Shoney's, Belted by a Lawsuit, Found the Path to Diversity," *Wall Street Journal,* April 16, A1, A6.

Garcea, E. A. A. (2002a). "Current Crises, Fears, Fantasies, and Foreseeable Futures." In Simons, G. F. (ed.) *Eurodiversity: A Business Guide to Managing Differences.* Amsterdam: Butterworth-Heinemann.

Garcea, E. A. A. (2002b). "The Legacy of the Past: How National and Regional Differences Continue to Effect Trade, Cooperation, Politics, and Relationships." In Simons, G. F. (ed.) *Eurodiversity: A Business Guide to Managing Differences.* Amsterdam: Butterworth-Heinemann.

Garcea, E. A. A. (2002c). "Managing Diversity to Create Marketable Value Added from Difference." In Simons, G. F. (ed.) *Eurodiversity: A Business Guide to Managing Differences.* Amsterdam: Butterworth-Heinemann.

Herriot, P. and Pemberton, C. (1995). *Competitive Advantage through Diversity: Organizational Learning from Difference.* London: Sage.

Inglehart, R. and Norris, P. (2003a). "The True Clash of Civilizations," *Foreign Policy,* March/April, 67–74.

—— and ——. (2003b). *Rising Tide: Gender Equality and Cultural Change around the World.* New York: Cambridge University Press.

Jameson, S. (2001). "Liberation Limbo," *Asian Business,* January, 64.

Janardhan, N. (2003). "Labor-Saudi Arabia: Foreigners Limited as Joblessness Grows," *Global Information Network,* February 5, 1.

Kandola, R. (1995). "Managing Diversity: New Broom or Old Hat?" *International Review of Industrial and Organizational Psychology*, 10, 131–67.

Kochan, T., Bezrukova, K., Ely, R., Jackson, S., Joshi, A., Jehn, K., Leonard, J., Levine, D., and Thomas, D. (2003). "The Effects of Diversity on Business Performance: Report of the Diversity Research Network," *Human Resource Management*, 42(1), 3–21.

Kramer, R. (1998). "Managing Diversity: Beyond Affirmative Action in Australia," *Women in Management Review*, 13(4), 133–42.

Liu, D. X. and Boyle, E. H. (2001). "Making the Case: The Women's Convention and Equal Employment Opportunity in Japan," *International Journal of Comparative Sociology*, 42(4), 389–404.

"Lower-Paid Women," (2002). *Organisation for Economic Cooperation and Development. The OECD Observer*, August, 64.

Mandell, B. and Kohler-Gray, S. (1990). "Management Development that Values Diversity," *Personnel*, March, 41–7.

Mentzer, M. S. (2002). "How Canada Promotes Workplace Diversity." In Harvey, C. P. and Allard, M. J. (eds.) *Understanding and Managing Diversity: Readings, Cases, and Exercises*. 2d Ed. Upper Saddle River, NJ: Prentice Hall.

Nemetz, P. L. and Christensen, S. L. (1996). "The Challenge of Cultural Diversity: Harnessing a Diversity of Views to Understand Multiculturalism," *The Academy of Management Review*, 21, 434–62.

OECD, Organisation for Economic Co-Operation and Development, "Frequently Asked Statistical Tables," [accessed July 20, 2003], available from http://www.oecd.org/document/15/0,2340, en_2649_201185_1873295_1_1_1_1,00.html.

Pascale, R. and Athos, A. (1981). *The Art of Japanese Management*. New York: Warner Books.

RBC Financial Group, "Diversity," [accessed July 20, 2003], available from http://www.rbc.com/uniquecareers/ diversity/index.html.

Simons, G. F. (ed.) (2002). *Eurodiversity: A Business Guide to Managing Differences*. Amsterdam: Butterworth-Heinemann.

Sinclair, A. (2000). "Women within Diversity: Risks and Possibilities," *Women in Management Review*, 15(5/6), 237–46.

Society for Human Resource Management, "Diversity Initiatives Help Keep A Competitive Edge," June 4, 2001, [accessed July 22, 2003], available from http://www.shrm.org/press_published/ CMS_000671.asp.

"Some 40 Pct of Japan's Working Women Part-Timers," (2002). *Jiji Press English News Service*, March 27, 1.

Steinhoff, P. G. and Tanaka, K. (1994). "Women Managers in Japan." In Adler, N. J. and Israeli, D. N. (eds.) *Competitive Frontiers: Women Managers in a Global Economy*. Cambridge: Blackwell Publishers.

Stuber, M. (2002). "Corporate Best Practice: What Some European Organizations are Doing Well to Manage Culture and Diversity." In Simons, G. F. (ed.) *Eurodiversity: A Business Guide to Managing Differences*. Amsterdam: Butterworth-Heinemann.

Thomas, D. A. and Ely, R. J. (1996). "Making Differences Matter: A New Paradigm for Managing Diversity," *Harvard Business Review*, September–October, 79–90.

Thornton, E. (1999). "Make Way for Women with Welding Guns," *Business Week*, April 19, 54.

Whitehill, A. M. (1991). *Japanese Management: Tradition and Transition*. New York: Routledge.

Wiedemeyer, M., Beywl, W., and Helmstadter, W. (1993). "Employment Promotion Companies in Eastern Germany: Emergency Measures or a Basis for Structural Reform?" *International Labour Review*, 132, 605–21.

Wright, P., Ferris, S. P., Hiller, J. S., and Kroll, M. (1995). "Competitiveness through Management of Diversity: Effects on Stock Price Valuation," *Academy of Management Journal*, 38(1), 272–87.

Young, L. (2000). "Leveraging Diversity at Royal Bank Financial Group," *Canadian HR Reporter*, 13(6), 9.

Zielenziger, M. (2002). "Fewer Births, Marriages Threaten Japan's Future," *Knight Ridder Tribune Business News*, December 30, 1.

CHAPTER 11

Leadership

Learning Objectives

After reading this chapter, you should be able to:

- Define leadership.
- Understand the relationship between culture and leadership.
- Discuss the theory of leader legitimacy and its practical importance.
- Describe typical leadership patterns in different cultures.
- Understand the implications of Project GLOBE for cross-cultural leadership.
- Identify issues that affect women becoming leaders in various cultures.
- Consider ways that leadership is becoming more similar or different because of changes in organizations worldwide.

CULTURE AT WORK

Machismo!

Working in the banana plantations in Central America is difficult. The scorching sun and oppressive humidity make the ten hour days seem endless. Pay is low and the food is terrible. Sanitation is inadequate; diarrhea is common. Yet the men who harvest the banana crop each cut tons of bananas every day.

Ernesto was a field foreman. His job was to make the men work hard—he "pushed" them to keep production high. To make money, labor costs had to be kept low and productivity high. Often the men would gripe among themselves that Ernesto was too demanding.

One day, Manuel, a new, young, hard-working field hand, complained to Ernesto that he was pushing him too hard. The older workers looked on in silence. Ernesto told Manuel that if he wanted to keep his job he should do as told.

Later in the day, Manuel again complained to Ernesto. This time the exchange was more intense and Ernesto told Manuel not to complain again or he would fire him.

Manuel swung his machete at Ernesto. Instead of ducking, Ernesto blocked the blow with his hand. With blood gushing from a deep wound, Ernesto pinned Manuel to the ground. Two workers helped subdue and remove Manuel.

> At his retirement party, 21 years later, Ernesto's long time co-foreman, Armando, recounted this story to the assembled friends. He told them—barely able to suppress a tense laugh—that after that incident no one ever challenged Ernesto's authority again.
>
> *Source:* B. A. Gold

Cultural values and norms shape and support organizational leadership. Without the compliance of organizational members—their acceptance of socially constructed assumptions, values, and behaviors—leaders cannot maintain authority. With the support of followers, leaders can manage the resources required for the achievement of organizational and societal goals.

While social values support a particular style of leadership, a successful leader interprets and translates the culture's value system, in the process modifying it, to achieve organizational efficiency and effectiveness. For example, formulating corporate strategies, developing new products and markets, managing the organization's culture, and initiating change, engage leaders in simultaneous support from and change of the culture. National and organizational cultures affect the leader and the leader affects the cultures. How culture affects leadership and how leaders and managers can adapt their behavior to particular cultures are key issues in international organizational behavior and global management.

▮▮▮ What Is Leadership?

Defining leadership is not straightforward, especially in a cross-cultural context. One difficulty is that not all cultures have the term *leader*. The closest equivalent in Japanese, Chinese, and Korean to leader is similar to *coach* in English (Trice and Beyer 1993). *Headship* captures the nature of the authority role in familial organizations, which are prevalent in Asian cultures (Westwood and Chan 1992). In the German language, there is "no word exactly corresponding to the meaning of the term *manager* in English. Present-day Germans also avoid using the German word for leader (*fuhrer*) because of its association with Hitler" (Trice and Beyer 1993, p. 254). Of course, the variety of terms used in different cultures does not mean leadership is absent, but rather the nuances indicate that different cultures vary in their understandings and expectations of authority roles.

Another difficulty is that in cultures where the leader is an important role in organizations, it has multiple scientific definitions (Bass 1990) and diverse meanings in everyday life. Consider the subtle differences used in the United States to distinguish leadership roles and responsibilities. Terms for leader include *boss, administrator, head honcho, supervisor, director, manager, mentor, coach, executive, head, chief, master*, and *chairperson*. In addition, in the United States, distinctions in titles such as *assistant vice president, vice president, executive vice president, senior vice president*, and *president* have a great deal of meaning. Not all cultures recognize such fine distinctions or view leadership as so important. Nevertheless, management scholars accept that "leadership" has, with some qualifications, meaning beyond the United States and is useful for studying leadership across cultures (Peterson and Hunt 1997).

The concept of power distance (Hofstede 2001) captures an important element of "leadership." Power distance is the willingness of less powerful members of organizations to accept the unequal distribution of power. Of course, a central characteristic of modern organizations is the separation of roles and responsibilities between leaders and followers. However, some cultures—as we shall see later in this chapter—emphasize power differences more than others.

A definition of **leadership** is "the influential increment over and above mechanical compliance with the routine directives of the organization" (Katz and Kahn 1978, p. 528). This definition captures the essence of the distinction between the leader and other organizational roles. Without an increment over mechanical compliance, instead of leadership, administrative or management functions occur. Leadership focuses on creativity, vision, and long-term organizational development, whereas management deals with routine operations. Before discussing leadership theories, we present variables that affect cross-cultural leadership.

▪▪▪ Culture and Leadership

National Culture

National culture influences leadership. Deeply held values regarding the rights and duties of citizens form the core of national culture and constitute a worldview. These values, codified in documents such as constitutions, laws, and ethical codes, proscribe and control behavior. Like other aspects of culture, they are taken for granted by the members of a society as the correct, and perhaps, only, way to act.

The ideals expressed in a worldview frequently fail to be attained, and, on occasion, are violated. Most societies have mechanisms for identifying and punishing deviation. In the case of leadership, if the leader violates core values—for example, engaging in immoral or illegal activities—he can lose his authority over subordinates and risks removal from the leadership position. Leadership derives from and represents socially constructed legal, moral, and ethical obligations.

The relationship between national cultural values and actual behavior in organizations is complex. For example, in many Western cultures women are increasingly encouraged to become organizational leaders and managers, and the concept of equal pay for equal work receives wide support. However, even in the United States where employment laws mandate equal treatment for men and women, a "glass ceiling" effect exists. This is a set of subtle barriers that conflict with cultural ideals and often function to prevent women from achieving the highest levels of management (Northcraft and Neale 1994). In Japanese companies in the United States, the glass ceiling takes a different form; non-Japanese workers often experience barriers to promotion.

Political Culture

The values of the political system of a country affect organizational leadership. Political structures usually reflect central national cultural values including ideas about the most appropriate and effective type of leadership. Countries with democratic political values and systems of government, such as the United Kingdom and United States, prefer participative leadership in the workplace, a key element in the human relations school of management theory (Guillén 1994). Countries that have had autocratic political regimes and limited experience with democracy, such as Spain, have low expectations for worker participation in organizational decision making and use nonparticipatory management philosophies, typically some form of scientific management (Guillén 1994).

Organizational Culture

Leaders influence organizational culture and often attempt to create, maintain, or change it to improve the performance of an organization (Trice and Beyer 1993). One widely accepted view is that managing organizational culture is a leader's major contribution to an organization (Schein 1985). But the relationship between leadership and organizational culture is not necessarily that direct and is the focus of much recent research.

Not only do leaders create, maintain, and on occasion change organizational culture, but at the same time, culture places constraints on leaders and shapes their behavior. For example, in an organization with a culture that values participatory decision making, a leader who prefers centralized decision making has difficulty being effective. Similarly, an organizational culture that values stability and continuity resists attempts to change it unless there is a prolonged deterioration in performance.

In summary, national, political, and organizational cultures vary across societies and affect leadership in multiple ways. Management scholars have recently conducted empirical research into the influence of these variables on leadership behavior which this chapter will present. However, although there is increasing research concerning which leadership behaviors are universal and which are products of a specific culture, it remains difficult to determine the precise interaction among the levels of culture—which in some cases are unconscious or too complex to measure adequately—as they influence leadership (Dorfman 1996).

Leadership, Culture, and Organizational Change

Daimler-Benz AG's initial efforts to become a global company demonstrate the interaction of leadership, national, political, and organizational culture. In 1993 Daimler-Benz, a major German corporation that manufactures luxury automobiles, lost money for the first time since World War II. Part of the reason for the loss was a recession in 1992–93 and a belated response to increased global competition.

To return to profitability, Edzard Reuter, Chief Executive of Daimler-Benz, initiated major changes at the company. Significant union concessions included reducing the workforce by 20%, and it disposed of unprofitable businesses and old-line managers. In addition, management decided that Mercedes Benz would manufacture automobiles outside Germany to increase its global presence.

The scope of the changes was so significant that "from the shop floor to the boardroom, it imposed an unfamiliar new creed: Change or die"(Gumbel and Choi 1995, p. A10). These rapid changes occurred despite difficulty firing workers, labor representation on the board of directors, and the glacial speed of change in Germany. Explaining the changes, a senior executive observed, "We simply want to become less German" (Gumbel and Choi 1995, p. A10). To create movement toward a global presence, the changes required the corporation's leaders to specify a new vision for the organization's future, restructure the organization, and create a new organizational culture within a national and organizational culture that resisted change. As a result of the changes, Daimler-Benz was profitable by early 1995 and, to accelerate its globalization, a few years later merged with Chrysler.

The experience at Daimler-Benz illustrates the complexities of effective leadership. The changes at Daimler were not proactive but implemented after the organization experienced intense competition from Japanese automobile manufacturers. But even under conditions of duress—a threat to long-term survival—change was not easy. For example, Reuter had to circumvent long-established national and corporate culture to create a new corporate culture oriented toward the demands of the global economy. In implementing innovations, Reuter had the difficult job of changing the culture that supported his authority without alienating customary sources of support.

Organizational leadership is a difficult, demanding set of behaviors. It is a product of an organizational culture that, periodically, challenges the culture by exploring and implementing new management methods to make organizations responsive to changing economic and social conditions.

Leadership Theories

Theories Developed in the United States

Since World War II, there have been over 3,500 studies of leadership, the majority conducted by social scientists in the United States (Bass 1990). Important leadership theories formulated in the United States are trait theory, Theory X and Y, the Ohio State and University of Michigan behavioral theories, Managerial Grid theory, situational, contingency, and Path Goal theory. Although the conceptual framework of each theory is different, the objective of most is to understand the level of participation required to create follower motivation and compliance or, under conditions in which participation is neither appropriate or effective, to specify other methods to achieve specific goals. For example, several recent theories postulate that in certain situations, a leader's use of power over subordinates is necessary to improve effort because participation is ineffective.

Limitations of U.S. Theories

Despite their intuitive appeal, widespread dissemination by consultants, and use by business people, U.S. theories have received either very little or inconclusive support from research with data collected in the United States. As a result, "The field has rushed from one fad to the next, but the actual pace of theory development has been quite slow" (Yukl 2002, p. 423). Of course, lack of support in the culture that produced a theory reduces the probability that the theory can explain behavior in other cultures. There are several reasons for this. First, it is difficult to demonstrate empirical support for most social science theory. Second, these theories and the studies designed to test them reflect American values and the context of American business for the past half-century. For instance, only recently have American businesses had to contend with issues such as a diverse domestic workforce and the need to manage in a global economy. Therefore, it is premature to assume that American leadership theories have universal application.

Theory X and Y

Rather than discuss the strengths and weaknesses of each leadership theory mentioned previously, Douglas McGregor's Theory X and Y illustrates some of the limitations of American theories, particularly their culture boundedness.

McGregor's thesis is that leadership and management styles vary according to assumptions about human nature. McGregor's theory is based on the insight that leadership is

> . . . the result of management's conception of the nature of its task and all the policies and practices which are constructed to implement this conception. The way a business is managed determines to a very large extent what people are perceived to have "potential" and how they develop. . . . The blunt fact is

that we are a long way from realizing the potential represented by the human resources we now recruit into industry. (1960, p. iv)

According to McGregor, Theory X is a set of assumptions that people prefer to avoid hard work and therefore require constant direction and supervision. Theory Y assumptions are more optimistic and view workers as self-motivated and capable of undertaking complex work with little direct supervision under the proper conditions. The task of management under these assumptions is to trust workers more and provide opportunities for workers to flourish.

The assumptions of Theory X and Y correspond to Kluckhohn and Strodtbeck's basic human nature dimension. Theory X managers believe people are primarily evil and Theory Y managers view people as basically good.

Although McGregor's theory is a seminal contribution to management theory, it is unclear that it accurately explains leader behavior in the United States or other cultures. For instance, not all cultures view human nature as consisting of either exclusively positive or negative qualities. The Kluckhohn and Strodtbeck framework suggests that some cultures have a more complex or mixed view of human nature. People exhibit a variety of work characteristics, some consistent with Theory X and others similar to Theory Y assumptions. The complexity of human nature and multiple orientations toward work are apparent even in the United States and will probably become more varied as its population becomes more diverse.

One leadership style that a culture with contradictory norms and values produces is **ambivalent leadership** (Merton 1970). Ambivalence—alternation between opposite values and behaviors—is not the product of an inadequate understanding of human nature, but rather consists of difficulty acting in a consistent, coherent way in response to the diverse, sometimes conflicting, values of a complex, heterogeneous, society.

With minor modification, McGregor's theory reflects the ambivalence of modern societies and organizations. Instead of viewing Theory X and Y as mutually exclusive, human behavior and organizations are now understood to be composed of elements of both X and Y. Leaders experience inconsistent sets of organizational norms producing contradictory behavior.

McGregor's Theory Y also assumes that collaboration between leaders and followers is more productive than an adversarial, controlling relationship. This leadership style is consistent with a low power distance orientation. In high power distance cultures, however, participative leaders may appear incompetent because the expectation is to lead by displaying expertise, power, or other dominating behaviors rather than including subordinates in decision making. Additionally, collaboration and cooperation are components of a distinctly American ideology that fits the requirements of an industrialized democratic society, rather than an inherent aspect of human nature. Similarly, not all societies value achievement and self-development.

Cultural Assumptions of Leaders about Workers

One way to view the consequences of assumptions leaders and workers develop is to examine labor relations in various countries. Labor relations reflect key assumptions about human nature, for example, whether workers are lazy and untrustworthy or able to take initiative and work autonomously.

Labor relations in Europe are substantially different than in the United States. In most European countries, labor relations are political and based on greater social class distinctions between workers and management or ownership. Also, the government takes a more direct role in regulating labor and management and in responsibility for worker social security concerns. Finally, because of the long history of unions there is a higher degree of acceptance and integration of them into the economy than in the United States (Briscoe 1995).

In Japan, labor relations are different from those in the United States and Europe. Each firm organizes and usually controls a union. For example, the head of the union could be a middle manager appointed by the company. Other labor management practices including lifetime employment, seniority-based promotions, and firm performance-based bonuses "were developed as a response to a very militant union action after the end of World War II. Largely because of their successes, today's Japanese unions tend to be quite responsible in negotiations, they abide by their contracts, and strikes are quite rare" (Briscoe 1995, p. 163).

In South America there is yet another relationship between management and labor. There is a "close relationship between the unions and government, with the result that many rights and benefits for workers have been codified in law" (Briscoe 1995, p. 163). Codification reduces the potential for adversarial relationships between the parties and provides a framework for cooperation.

This brief survey of labor relations demonstrates that assumptions that govern interaction between management and lower-level participants vary considerably in different cultures. The presence of unions and laws governing labor relations is consistent with Theory X assumptions that workers require close monitoring and strict enforcement of rules. It also reflects worker wariness of management that requires institutionalized arrangements to control the power of organizations.

Although McGregor and other American theorists identified important issues, serious limitations in American leadership theories remain, indicating that their generalization to other cultures without adjustments is unwarranted (Bass 1990; Yukl 2002). Before presenting recent comparative studies, we briefly present two leadership theories from non-Western societies. In both theories, culture influences assumptions about human nature and the relationship between leaders and followers.

Leadership Theories Developed in Non-Western Societies

Two non-Western leadership theories are PM theory developed by Misumi (1985) in Japan and NT theory based on research conducted by Sinha (1980, 1995) in India.

PM Leadership Theory PM leadership theory identifies two functions that leaders in any situation either need to provide directly or in some other way (Misumi 1985). P is the performance function and has to do with task accomplishment, and M is the maintenance function that creates and sustains good relations among workers engaged in the task. The theory states that the P and M functions are not independent but complement one another. This means that "the effectiveness of a leader who places substantial emphasis on both the P and M functions is said to be greater than could be predicted by simply summing the known effects of a leader who is high on P and one who is high on M" (Smith and Peterson 2002, p. 227). More importantly, leaders who display equal amounts of P and M "do so in a holistic, interwoven way, consistent with the high context nature of Japanese society. In other words, the theory itself has characteristics of the culture in which it was developed" (Gannon and Newman 2002, p. 188).

PM theory also argues that leadership functions in different ways from situation to situation, dependent on elements of the culture in which leadership takes place and specific contexts within a culture. This aspect of PM theory receives support from research in Japanese organizations with leaders high on P and M rated the most effective. Research in Hong Kong, the United Kingdom, and the United States also supports it with the largest difference between P and M occurring in the United States. Finally, despite the observation that the theory reflects Japanese culture, and that equal amounts of P and M are often the most effective, the research support from other cultures endorses Misumi's view that "leader behaviors have no objective and generalized meaning; they acquire meaning through the context in which they occur" (Smith and Peterson 2002, p. 228).

NT Leadership Theory   Like Misumi's PM theory, Sinha's NT theory (1980, 1995), developed in India, focuses on two dimensions of effective leader behavior, Nurturance (N) and Task (T).

> Sinha observed that within the relatively hierarchical context of India, leaders often emphasize task aspects of leadership and neglect any form of nurturant or supportive behaviors. Indeed, some studies show that autocratic supervision is preferred by subordinates in India. However, Sinha's research revealed that Indian leaders in a range of organizations were in fact more effective when they were able to foster greater participation by subordinates. This was accomplished through a gradual process of nurturing subordinates toward the taking of greater responsibility. (Smith and Peterson 2002, p. 229)

The preferred leadership style provides Nurturant and Task behaviors simultaneously, creating a type of distinctive paternalistic leadership. This theory has received some support from research conducted in countries with high collectivistic orientations.

The Differences in Leadership Theories

Western social theorists—particularly Max Weber and Kurt Lewin—as well as Western positivist social science methods, influenced the development of PM theory. In addition, the focus on two characteristics of leader behavior in the PM and NT theories is similar to the focus on task and maintenance functions found in leadership theories developed in the United States. However, the difference between the PM and NT leadership theories and those developed in the United States is that the cultural context is conceptualized as part of the theories. In the case of American theories, there is no explicit attempt to incorporate culture as a variable, but most theories reflect the assumptions that American culture is individualistic and characterized by low power distance. The PM and NT theories differ from theories developed in the United States that view leadership as fundamentally the same across cultural contexts.

These theories offer different perspectives than U.S. theories and provide insights into the differences in leaders across cultures; however, they have had little impact on how multinational managers think about leadership. It is important to note that the limitations in generalization of Western leadership theories to other cultures also apply to non-Western theories. Next, we discuss leader legitimacy and how it interacts with culture.

▪▪▪ Types of Leadership Legitimacy

Weber's Theory of Leadership

Max Weber, a German sociologist who died in 1920 but whose theories continue to influence social research, developed a comparative framework for understanding the legitimacy of leaders. Weber, along with most other major social theorists, wanted to understand the conditions required for the establishment of legitimate authority (Zelditch 2001). In historical and cross-cultural investigations, Weber identified three social bases of leader legitimacy: traditional, rational, and charismatic authority.

- **Traditional authority** "rests on an established belief in the sanctity of immemorial traditions and the legitimacy of the status of those exercising authority under them" (Weber 1947, p. 328).
- **Rational authority** "rests on a belief in the legality of patterns of normative rules and the right of those elevated to authority under such rules to issue commands" (Weber 1947, p. 328).
- **Charismatic authority** is based "on devotion to the specific and exceptional sanctity, heroism or exemplary character of an individual person, and of the normative patterns or order revealed or ordained by him" (Weber 1947, p. 328).

These types of authority exist in cultures throughout the world. Often, however, one type is more prevalent in a society than others. For example, traditional authority patterns are characteristic of Asian societies where senior males, a patriarchy, provide organizational leadership.

Legal authority underpins bureaucratic organizations (Weber 1947). Bureaucracy is the administrative structure of government agencies, schools, businesses, and other organizations throughout the world. Despite the negative connotations of bureaucracy—for example, red tape, unnecessarily elaborate hierarchy, and lack of creativity—it is the model of modern rational organizations. Bureaucracy is very efficient and effective when used in organizations that perform predictable, routine tasks (Perrow 1986).

Charismatic authority, which according to Weber occurs infrequently, can erupt in all societies, regardless of the dominant type of authority. The intense conviction of followers that the leader possesses special gifts or talents supports the charismatic leader. Charismatic authority creates radical change in a society or organization and the change that results can be either positive or negative.

Charismatic leadership is the most appropriate type for leaders in developing countries because their primary goal is to produce social change (Kanungo and Mendonca 1996). Other types of leadership—for example, those that encourage employee participation—seek to maintain society and organizations or help them adjust gradually to changing circumstances. These types of leadership are more appropriate for developed nations with established institutions and organizations.

Although it is possible to characterize a society as having a predominant type of authority structure, there are often multiple sources of leadership legitimacy. For example, in the United States and other societies with advanced economies, it is common practice that an organization's leaders, along with all other employees, are subject to rationally constructed rules. These include codified personnel polices, financial practices, and organizational structure. But, at the same time, in the United States as in developing countries, many family-owned-and-operated businesses use a form of traditional authority. For example, in a family business, instead of selecting personnel on qualifications—a rational method—personal characteristics such as family membership are more important. In Trompenaars' cultural framework, this is the difference between achievement and ascription.

Finally, charismatic leaders emerge periodically in both rational and traditional organizational settings. Charismatic leaders break established patterns that create dramatic departures from "business as usual." For example, in 1979 Lee Iacocca, then the chairman of the Chrysler Corporation, rescued it from bankruptcy by persuading the United States government to guarantee loans to the failing corporation. Iacocca's surprising success was a radical departure from past practice because the federal government never intervened so extensively in the finances of a private corporation. Moreover, the government's rescue of Chrysler took place within the context of widespread acceptance of fundamental tenets of capitalism that viewed bankruptcy as a normal, even beneficial outcome, of a highly competitive economy.

Leadership and Ethics

Legitimate leadership is moral. Leaders, like occupants of other social roles, represent themselves to others as sincere. In modern societies, of course, leaders often use impression management to present themselves in a more positive way than might actually be the reality.

Leaders set the moral and ethical standards for an organization. If they are not what they claim and discrepancies between their intentions and actions are substantial, organization members are likely to challenge their authority. Because this has become fairly common, many leaders find their legitimacy challenged and need to continually reestablish their authority. Being elected prime minister of England is one thing; maintaining the authority to exercise power in the role is another.

Rational authority has less of an ethical obligation than traditional and charismatic authority, but leadership based on rational authority nonetheless has legal and ethical requirements to meet. Unlike traditional and charismatic authority, it does not uphold long-established traditions that preserve a culture's way of life or provoke social change that creates significant uncertainty. Rational authority derives legitimacy from efficient administration that distills ethical and moral issues into rules. It is ethical when it enforces rules and does not disobey laws.

Transformational Leadership

A concept related to charismatic authority is **transformational leadership** (Burns 1978). Transformational leadership is a more commonly found type of leadership than charisma, especially in contemporary business organizations. The transformational leader acts as a teacher, role model, and inspirational figure to create conditions under which subordinates enthusiastically contribute to the organization (Bass 1985). In addition, transformational leaders focus on the nonroutine aspects of an organization, including establishing a vision for the organization's future, making decisions with long-term consequences, creating an organizational culture, and initiating and managing change (Kotter 1990).

In high power distance societies, the use of transformational leadership faces limitations because leader and follower expectations and behaviors are significantly different. The assumptions of these cultures do not promote intermingling of leadership and subordinate roles. Under such circumstances, a leader empowering subordinates, rather than directing them, is unlikely.

Leadership and Meaning

An important element of leadership, particularly charismatic and transformational, is that leaders create **symbolic meaning systems** for organizational participants (Trice and Beyer 1993). A meaning system constructs into a coherent pattern selective interpretations of societal and organizational traditions, customs, rituals, and artifacts that contribute to organizational culture. The leader interprets and shapes the larger culture to the needs of the organization. Its products are particular ways of doing things in organizations in different cultures and often a distinctive organizational identity.

From the perspective of international organizational behavior "while there are general leadership functions, the meaning of specific actions is culturally contingent" (Smith and Peterson 2002, p. 221). A meaning system creates *the* Japanese, *the* British, and *the* South African way of doing things. It also produces the specific identity of a corporation within a national culture. For example, the meaning system embodied in organizational culture distinguishes NEC from Sony in Japan, IBM from Apple in the United States, and BMW from DaimlerChrysler in Germany.

The Culture at Work vignette is an example of a single act that captures the meaning of leadership in a particular culture and organizational setting. Agricultural labor in Central America requires toughness, endurance, and courage. The leader created legitimacy by confronting worker disobedience directly with the possibility of physical harm. A single act symbolized the qualities of a leader and epitomized a core value of the organizational culture. Even in a culture that views leadership as a display of machismo, not everyone is willing to risk bodily harm to establish his credentials. But a successful leader does and reinforces the values of the larger culture and the organization.

▪▪▪ Leadership in Two Cultures

Overseas Chinese cultures, where age and family relationships are of central importance for leadership, illustrate leadership and organization based on a mixture of cultural traditions and contemporary business practices. Leadership in France provides a portrait of a culture in which there is interaction between traditional and rational authority.

Overseas Chinese Leadership

In Chinese culture, the legitimacy of a leader derives from patrimonial loyalty, which according to Weber's typology, is a traditional form of authority. Peter Drucker, writing about the business activities of overseas Chinese—ethnic Chinese living outside Mainland China—captures the essence of this leadership style:

> Outwardly, these new multinational groups look exactly like other businesses. But they function drastically differently, as a clan. The Japanese, it has often been said, owe their success to their ability to run the modern corporation as a family. The overseas Chinese owe their success to their ability to run their family as a modern corporation.
>
> All the plant managers in the Manila group [a branch of a multinational corporation], for example, are related to the founder—and to each other—by blood or marriage.
>
> "We wouldn't dream of going into a new business," the chief operating officer told me, "if we did not have a relative available to run it." He, himself, is Dutch, but he is married to the founder's niece. When he joined the group the founder said to him: "I don't care how many concubines or mistresses you have. But on the day on which my niece and you separate or file for divorce you can look for another job."
>
> The word of the founder-CEO is law. But his authority far more resembles that of a Confucian head of the house (or Scottish Highland chieftain of yore) than that of the head of a business. He is expected to base his decisions on the best interests of the clan and to manage so as to guarantee the clan's survival and prosperity. What holds the multinationals together is neither ownership nor legal contract. It is mutual trust and the mutual obligations inherent in clan membership. (1994, p. 20)

Mainland Chinese business practices are changing rapidly as the result of economic policies introduced in the 1980s that include capitalist principles—for example, the idea of profit, private enterprise, and market forces. These changes could influence the overseas Chinese. In fact, in 21st-century China, variation in leadership ranges from managerial practices based on traditional values, continuation of key elements of the communist industrial system, and modern capitalist management (Tang and Ward 2003). However, despite the possibility of change, "Private business in China, as with business in overseas Chinese communities, remains very much a family affair" (Tang and Ward 2003, p. 5). Traditional cultures and leadership preferences are slow to change even under pressure to modernize, and continuity with the past remains a central value. Thus, despite considerable pressure to change, the overseas Chinese leadership style continues the tradition of patriarchy in modern global organizations.

French Administrative Leadership

The French, like the Chinese, accept the unequal distribution of power and centralization of decision making. Another theme in French organizations is an emphasis on uncertainty avoidance which is characteristic of organizations in which "familial relationships are. . . very much in evidence, specifically paternalistic ones" (Sorge 1993, p. 69). At the same time, another element found in France is a fairly strong belief in individualism that creates a "constant tension between the demand for strong authority, and individualistic assertion against it" (Sorge 1993, p. 71).

Embedded in formal organizations are characteristics that protect individuality through conformity with rules and regulations. "Whereas the Anglo-Saxon individualist tries to do his or her 'own thing' and considers hierarchy a dirty word, the French individualist tries to achieve a perfection within a protective niche provided by a stable organization" (Sorge 1993, p. 72). In other words, French culture, which highly values equality, is consistent with bureaucratic rationality.

Comparative studies of European organizations have found that French organizations usually have more levels of hierarchy, along with more lateral segmentation into departments and work groups. Also, staff and line responsibilities are clearer in France than in Britain or Germany. Directly concerning leadership,

> the hierarchy is more top-heavy in France, with between 1 1/2 and 2 times as many supervisors and managers as in German organizations. The lowest level of the industrial production hierarchy is more separate from the workers, enjoys more disciplinary authority, and is counted among the white-collar employees, whereas the equivalent in Germany has blue-collar status and less disciplinary authority. Spans of control at different levels in France are usually smaller, indicating the possibility of tighter supervision. (Sorge 1993, p. 75)

Compared with German organizations, there are also more nonmanagerial white-collar specialists in either administrative or technical functions. This proliferation of roles along with written rules, instructions, and communications is the result of the high uncertainty avoidance orientation of the French.

At the top of the hierarchy is the chairman of the board. The chairman's leadership style is typically "paternalistic and charismatic, in the manner of the great generals and field marshals" (Sorge 1993, p. 78). Between the top leaders and the workers is a large group of managers or cadres. Although this system does result in certain inefficiencies, it provides reliable uniformity of operation, not a pathological bureaucracy.

With increased globalization there is evidence that this pattern, while still prevalent in many French organizations, is beginning to change. In a 2002 interview, Christian Pierret, the French Secretary of State for Industry from 1997 to 2002, observed that French organizations are becoming more flexible and competitive and that, " . . . it is in smaller businesses that hierarchical structures are most deeply ingrained and permanent, while larger companies are more participative." (Deneire and Segalla 2002, p. 28) In other words, for many French companies paternalistic, hierarchical relations remain central elements of leadership, but French multinational corporations are increasingly decentralizing.

Observations on Two Cultures

The Chinese and the French, as with most cultures, are not easy to compare. Nevertheless, they both have paternalistic elements in their leadership—a traditional basis of legitimacy found in many societies—with a significant difference. While Chinese culture retains traditional male forms of leadership coupled with familialism, the French have developed a merit system for employment within bureaucracies, rather than relying on age or kinship.

This variation reflects a different cultural heritage. The French pattern developed from the nation building and revolutionary ideas of the eighteenth century, particularly the ideals of fraternity and equality. The Chinese leadership style retains traditional male control over institutions that characterized the dynastic regimes throughout China's history. Cultural and historical influences on leadership informed a recent comparative study of leadership with data collected from a large sample of countries with different cultures.

▪ ▪ ▪ Project GLOBE: A Large-Scale Cross-Cultural Study of Leadership

Project GLOBE (Global Leadership and Organizational Behavior Effectiveness) is a major long-term multiphase, multimethod research project to study cross-cultural leadership differences and similarities among countries (Javidan and House 2002). Project GLOBE's 150 researchers, located in universities around the world, collected data from 15,000 middle managers from 875 organizations in the financial services, food services, and telecommunications industries in 61 nations. The fundamental research questions are:

- Are there leader behaviors, attributes, and organizational practices that are universally accepted and effective across cultures?
- Are there leader behaviors, attributes, and organizational practices that are accepted and effective in only some cultures?
- How do attributes of societal and organizational cultures affect the kinds of leader behaviors and organizational practices that are accepted and effective?
- What is the effect of violating cultural norms relevant to leadership and organizational practices?
- What is the relative standing of each of the cultures studied on each of the nine core dimensions of culture?
- Can the universal and culture-specific aspects of leader behaviors, attributes, and organizational practices be explained in terms of an underlying theory that accounts for systematic differences across cultures (House, Javidan, Hanges, and Dorfman 2002, p. 4)?

The GLOBE project definition of leadership is *the ability of an individual to influence, motivate, and enable others to contribute toward the effectiveness and success of the organizations of which they are members* (House et al. 2002, p. 5). Starting with 23 leadership styles, the researchers eventually identified the following six global leader behavior dimensions:

1. The *transformational-charismatic* leader is decisive, performance-oriented, a visionary, an inspiration to subordinates, and is willing to sacrifice for the organization.
2. The *team-oriented* style characterizes a leader who is an integrator, diplomatic, benevolent, and has a collaborative attitude about the team.
3. The *self-protective* leader is self-centered, status conscious, conflictual, procedural, and a face saver.
4. The *participative* leader is a delegator and encourages subordinate participation in decisions.
5. The *humane* style leader is characterized by modesty and a compassionate orientation.
6. *Autonomous* leaders are individualistic, independent, autonomous, and unique.

The GLOBE project defines culture as "shared motives, values, beliefs, identities, and interpretations or meanings of significant events that result from common experiences of members of collectives and are transmitted across age generations" (House et al. 2002, p. 5). Project GLOBE uses nine cultural dimensions. The first six dimensions had their origins in the dimensions of culture identified by Hofstede (1980) and include (1) uncertainty avoidance; (2) power distance; (3) societal collectivism; (4) in-group collectivism; (5) gender egalitarianism; and (6) assertiveness. Dimension (7), *future orientation*, is from Kluckhohn and Strodtbeck's framework and (8) *performance orientation,* is similar to McClelland's concept of *need for achievement* while (9) *humane orientation* is similar to his *need for affiliation.* Definitions of the nine dimensions of culture studied by Project GLOBE are:

1. *Uncertainty Avoidance* is the extent to which members of an organization or society strive to avoid uncertainty by reliance on social norms, rituals, and bureaucratic practices to alleviate the unpredictability of future events.
2. *Power Distance* is the degree to which members of an organization or society expect and agree that power should be unequally shared.
3. *Collectivism I: Societal Collectivism* reflects the degree to which organizational and societal institutional practices encourage and reward collective distribution of resources and collective action.
4. *Collectivism II: In-Group Collectivism* reflects the degree to which individuals express pride, loyalty, and cohesiveness in their organizations or families.
5. *Gender Egalitarianism* is the extent to which an organization or a society minimizes gender role differences and gender discrimination.
6. *Assertiveness* is the degree to which individuals in organizations or societies are assertive, confrontational, and aggressive in social relationships.
7. *Future Orientation* is the degree to which individuals in organizations or societies engage in future-oriented behaviors such as planning, investing in the future, and delaying gratification.
8. *Performance Orientation* refers to the extent to which an organization or society encourages and rewards group members for performance improvement and excellence.
9. *Humane Orientation* is the degree to which individuals in organizations or societies encourage and reward individuals for being fair, altruistic, friendly, generous, caring, and kind to others. (House et al. 2002, pp. 5–6)

To measure each dimension, questionnaire items distinguished what a respondent thinks of *as is* in organizations and what *should be*. Parallel questions asked respondents about what actually *is* in society and what they think *should be* in society.

The Country Clusters

Clustering societies provides a way to examine similarities and differences across societies. Project GLOBE divided the 61 countries in its sample into 10 clusters (Gupta Hanges, and Dorfman 2002). Table 11-1 presents the country clusters.

TABLE 11-1 Project GLOBE Societal Cluster Classification

Anglo Cultures
England
Australia
South Africa (White Sample)
Canada
New Zealand
Ireland
USA

Latin Europe
Israel
Italy
Portugal
Spain
France
Switzerland (French Speaking)

Nordic Europe
Finland
Sweden
Denmark

Germanic Europe
Austria
Switzerland
The Netherlands
Germany (Former East)
Germany (Former West)

Eastern Europe
Hungary
Russia
Kazakhstan
Albania
Poland
Greece
Slovenia
Georgia

Latin America
Costa Rica
Venezuela
Ecuador
Mexico
El Salvador
Colombia
Guatemala
Bolivia
Brazil
Argentina

Sub-Sahara Africa
Namibia
Zambia
Zimbabwe
South Africa (Black Sample)
Nigeria

Arab Cultures
Qatar
Morocco
Turkey
Egypt
Kuwait

Southern Asia
India
Indonesia
Philippines
Malaysia
Thailand
Iran

Confucian Asia
Taiwan
Singapore
Hong Kong
South Korea
China
Japan

Source: Gupta, V., Hanges, P. J., and Dorfman, P. (2002). "Cultural Clusters: Methodology and Findings," *Journal of World Business*, 37(1), p. 13. © 2002 with permission from Elsevier.

Findings in Four Cultural Clusters

This section presents selected research findings from four country clusters identified in Project GLOBE—the southern Asia, Anglo, Arabic, and Latin European clusters. To provide context for interpreting the survey data, the Project GLOBE reports provide detailed demographic, economic, historical, and religious data for each cluster. However, the focus here is on the findings concerning the cultural values and leadership patterns based on data collected from a sample of middle managers who reported the cultural practices and values of their countries and the effectiveness of alternative leader behaviors.

The Southern Asia Cluster

Countries in the southern Asia cluster are India, Indonesia, Philippines, Malaysia, Thailand, and Iran. Of the nine dimensions of societal practices, group collectivism, power distance, and humane orientation rated high. Gender egalitarianism rated low with the other cultural dimensions in the mid range. "The cluster is distinguished as highly group oriented, humane, male dominated, and hierarchical" (Gupta et al. 2002, p. 20).

On societal values, this cluster rates high on performance orientation, future orientation, group collectivism, and humane orientation. It scores very low on power distance. "In comparing the societal practices and values, the managers from this cluster prefer their countries as a whole to be more performance and future oriented, and more assertive. They desire a higher level of structure in their societies, but a lower level of male domination and power differentiation" (Gupta et al. 2002, p. 21).

Concerning leadership, transformational-charismatic and team-oriented leadership rated highest for the most effective models for achieving outstanding results in southern Asia. This means that the most effective leaders are visionary, inspirational, decisive, performance-oriented, and willing to make personal sacrifices. Leaders who are team building, collaborative, and diplomatic are also highly valued.

Humane and participative leadership rate as effective in this cluster. Autonomous leadership has an average score, and self-protective leaders scored the lowest suggesting that "whether or not leaders are self-centered, status conscious, face-saver, and procedural has no positive or negative effect on effectiveness" (Gupta et al. 2002, p. 24).

These leadership preferences are explained by this cluster's high power distance and family-oriented culture that expects leaders to act as patriarchs while maintaining the team and family orientation of organizations.

The Anglo Cluster

The Anglo cluster comprises Australia, Canada, England, Ireland, New Zealand, South Africa (white sample), and the United States. The scores of these countries on the nine cultural societal practices were at the mid range for all dimensions except for a high score on power distance and a low score on gender egalitarianism.

Concerning societal values—how things should be rather than are—this cluster scores high on performance orientation, humane orientation, family collectivism (collectivism II), and future orientation. The managers gave low scores to power distance and mid-range scores to all other dimensions.

Leadership scores were highest for the charismatic, team-oriented, and participative styles. Humane leadership also scored relatively high and autonomous and self-protective leadership relatively low. The GLOBE researchers observed that:

> An important conclusion for these results, and consistent with the culture findings, is the emphasis placed on participative leadership as a means to facilitate effective leadership. As the countries in this cluster are relatively individualistic in cultural orientation, and all are democracies, people place great emphasis on their freedom and being able to have their say. It is therefore very important for a leader to recognize this, to induce all relevant parties in the decision making process, to delegate responsibility, and not to try to lead uncompromisingly from the top. (Ashkanasy, Tevor-Roberts, and Earnshaw 2002, p. 370).

The Arabic Cluster

The Arabic cluster consists of Egypt, Morocco, Turkey, Kuwait, and Qatar. Societal practices for this cluster indicate high ratings on in-group and family collectivism and power distance and low on future orientation and gender egalitarianism (Kabasakal and Bodur 2002). Uncertainty avoidance, institutional collectivism, humane orientation, performance orientation, and assertiveness are in the mid range. In societal values this cluster rates high on future orientation, performance orientation, humane orientation, group and family collectivism, institutional collectivism (collectivism I), and uncertainty avoidance. Low ratings are for power distance, assertiveness, and gender egalitarianism.

Leadership scores were highest for team-oriented and charismatic followed by participative and humane styles which respondents understood to have a slight influence on effective leadership. Self-protective and autonomous styles received low scores, and the managers reported them to have a slight negative influence on effective leadership.

The Latin European Cluster

The Latin European cluster of countries includes Spain, Portugal, Italy, French Switzerland, France, and Israel. This cluster's scores on societal practices are high on power distance and relatively high on group and family collectivism. Gender egalitarianism had the lowest score with future orientation slightly higher. The other dimensions—humane orientation, uncertainty avoidance, and assertiveness—are at the mid point.

For the societal values, this cluster rates high on performance orientation, group collectivism, future orientation, and humane orientation with a very low score on power distance. These scores are similar to the averages in the 61 countries. For leadership, charismatic, team-oriented, and participative leadership rate as the most effective leadership attributes. Low scoring behaviors are humane leadership, followed by autonomous and self-protective leadership.

What Do The Project GLOBE Findings Mean?

The most important implication of Project GLOBE for global managers is that because each culture varies, the actual leadership and leadership preferences of each culture vary. This indicates that an approach to leadership based on cultural values and differences in leader behavior should inform the global manager's selection of leaders for specific international assignments. It also suggests that international managers should interact with managers from other cultures in ways that correspond with the preferred leadership style of the specific country. For example, an implication for managers from the findings of the Arabic cluster is that "foreigners should demonstrate their capabilities and competencies and at the same time be ready to allocate time for building trust in order to maintain business in the Arabic cluster" (Kabasakal and Bodur 2002, p. 52). In the Anglo cluster, it is important for managers to know that individualism is the actual practice but there is a desire to be more collectivistic. Similarly, while gender inequality is the norm, there is a desire to promote gender equality that is consistent with a meritocratic approach to managing people (Ashkanasy et al. 2002).

Another important finding from Project GLOBE is that across cultures there is strong and universal endorsement of charismatic-transformational leadership (Den Hartog et al. 1999). This suggests that despite important cultural differences, most populations have similar understandings and expectations of leaders—at least as understood from the perceptions of middle-level managers. This contradictory finding—that despite cultural differences there is a universal preference for a particular type of leadership—is also ironic because it is difficult for most managers, including those in the top ranks of organizations, to either become or display the traits of charismatic-transformational leaders.

Women as Leaders

Project GLOBE also found that most country clusters have relatively low scores on gender egalitarianism. In many parts of the world, including the Anglo cluster which is the most advanced economically, women occupy a secondary role compared to men, particularly in leadership positions in organizations. However, the Eastern European cluster—Albania, Georgia, Greece, Hungary, Kazakhstan, Poland, Russia, and Slovenia—is relatively high on gender egalitarianism compared with other clusters. The World Values Survey also documents the persistence of gender inequality in most cultures and the difficulty women experience moving into leadership roles (Inglehart and Norris 2003), as do studies of women in specific cultures (Hollway and Mukurasi 1994; Siemienska 1994; Steinhoff and Tanaka 1994).

Findings from a study that used Project GLOBE data to examine the perception of organizational culture and women's advancement in organizations found

> that characteristics of organizational culture typically associated with women are related to opportunities for women in management. In particular, organizational cultural practices reflecting high humane orientation, high gender equity, high performance orientation, and low power distance are related to women's advancement in organizations. Further, organizational values, emphasizing high humane orientation and high gender equity are also related to women's advancement. Relatively speaking, the results . . . suggest that organizational culture practices may be more strongly related to women's advancement in organizations than organizational cultural values. (Bajdo and Dickson 2002, pp. 409–410)

The distinction between organizational culture *practices* and organizational *values* is important because it suggests that although organizations reflect the values of the larger culture, they may develop internal practices that recognize the contribution of women on the basis of merit. Although the extent of the difference in organizational practices and values is not known, the existence of variation between them illustrates that in some ways, management practice is more pragmatic and egalitarian than either societal or organizational values.

Finally, the rational and humane use of human resources argues that societies should permit women to develop to their fullest potential. While many cultures disagree with this position, and the rise of fundamentalist religion reinforces the traditional role of women (Inglehart and Norris 2003), the participation of women in managerial positions worldwide is likely to increase as modernization and globalization progresses. Another factor influencing prospects for more gender equality is that multinational corporations usually select the most talented people for management positions (Adler 2002).

■ ■ ■ Convergence or Divergence?

Are there cultural trends and business issues common among nations creating pressures for one style of leadership in organizations? Or will various types of leadership continue and multiply as more cultures participate in global commerce? Will global organizations impose their leadership style throughout their operations, adapt to local preferences, or develop new styles of leadership?

Forces for Convergence

Project GLOBE found that there is significant convergence of leadership in organizations because in most countries in the study there is a preference for charismatic and transformational leadership. This could reflect a universal human desire for authority figures to provide meaning and direction to human activity.

Related to Project GLOBE's findings, another force for change toward a universal leader style is global corporations. General Electric (GE) illustrates the impact that a global organization can have on changing leadership in other cultures. To restructure from an international to a global corporation, GE's former Chairman Jack Welch, a transformational leader, initiated an extensive organizational change process to revolutionize the way GE did business. "A primary motivation for GE's transformation is the need for speed" (Tichy and Sherman 1993, pp. 20–21) which requires new types of leadership based on this philosophy:

> Until employees accept personal responsibility for their work, they need supervision, which Welch regards as a waste of time. So whenever possible, GE tries to eliminate supervisory positions, giving people more power to control their own work. Such responsibility can transform the relationship of workers to their employer: Instead of behaving like children who follow their parents' orders, employees interact with their bosses as adults and peers. (Tichy and Sherman 1993, p.21)

For leadership of its global operations, GE's strategy was to develop executives with "global brains" and "the ability to understand and respect the national and ethnic biases of others, and to feel comfortable anywhere in the world" (Tichy and Sherman 1993, p. 227).

Forces for Divergence

Despite the widespread preference for charismatic and transformational leadership, a force for divergence is the resistance of national cultures to new styles of leadership. An example is Bernard Liautaud, a 34-year-old French entrepreneur with an MBA from Stanford University, who started a software company modeled after the Silicon Valley, California way of running a business. In 1990 the company began with $1 million venture capital and by late 1996 the company was worth almost $1 billion. This extraordinary growth was uncharacteristic in France.

Liautaud, who became a highly visible businessman, told the President of France that the key to business success was to "Promote a shareholding culture: Think global, think marketing, reduce taxes" (Cohen 1997, p. 1). But the President made no changes to the heavily regulated economy. When Liautaud's company's "shares fell recently because of delays in a new software program, there were some smug' 'I told you so's' from the Paris establishment" (Cohen 1997, p. 1).

Liataud transplanted a new leadership style to his company, yet many people in France view global entrepreneurship as a threat to their economy and national identity and prefer to retain traditional leadership styles. As discussed previously, however, there is evidence that France is moving toward embracing the implications of globalization.

▪▪▪ Implications for Managers

Understanding leadership is important for managers, even if they are not at the executive level, because all managers perform leadership functions (Sayles 1993). Culture influences the legitimacy of a leader or manager and certain types of cultures accept a particular leadership style, for example, paternalism, that other cultures either reject or accept with difficulty. In a cross-cultural situation, a manager has the choice of either imposing a leadership style on subordinates with different cultures or adapting her leadership style to the culture. However, it is possible that the culture of a country is so different from a leader's own culture that neither option is viable. Under conditions where cultural differences are extensive, it may be more effective to use indigenous managers rather than those from a corporate headquarters whose culture does not fit the situation. It is important then for managers to carefully assess cultures other than their own to determine those aspects they can change in a particular situation and which are immutable.

A final implication is that when a considerable amount of organizational change is desirable—and possibly in routine situations as well— either a charismatic or transformational leadership style is appropriate. In addition, this type of leadership is often useful in developing countries even if it is inconsistent with explicit cultural preferences. However, an obvious difficulty with charismatic and transformational leadership is that very few managers have the leadership qualities and skills to create, maintain, and sustain charismatic authority.

SUMMARY ▪ ▪ ▪ ▪ ▪ ▪ ▪

The role of leadership in an organization is complex. Leadership has many definitions because it has multiple meanings to members of organizations. Also, the meaning of leadership varies across cultures. Basically, however, leadership involves power distance, which varies with national culture and political culture.

Most leadership theories developed in the United States have limitations when applied to other cultures. McGregor's Theory X and Theory Y illustrate these limitations but also suggest that the research questions asked by American scholars have applicability to various cultures. Leadership theories developed in other cultures, for example, PM Theory from Japan and NT Theory from India, reflect key universal issues in leadership theory but adapt it to specific cultures. Weber's typology of traditional, charismatic, and rational authority provides a set of concepts for examining leadership across cultures.

The major patterns of leadership in two societies illustrate Weber's typology. In overseas Chinese societies, traditional patriarchal leadership patterns combine with familialism. French leadership is also patriarchal but relies less on kin relations and extensively on bureaucratic principles. It is gradually changing, because of pressure from globalization, toward less patriarchal decentralized authority.

Project GLOBE is a major contribution to the study of cross-cultural patterns of leadership. An important finding is that most cultures have a preference for charismatic and transformational leadership. Another finding is that significant inequality in leadership opportunities exists on the basis of gender throughout the world. While some societies are striving toward gender equality, others persist in maintaining traditional gender roles.

Forces for convergence are the spread of leadership styles of multinational and global organizations. Forces for divergence include attempts to preserve culturally specific leadership styles. International managers need to understand leadership because they often perform leadership functions even at nonexecutive levels. Knowing which leadership approaches are appropriate in different situations helps a manager become more effective.

DISCUSSION QUESTIONS ▪ ▪ ▪ ▪ ▪ ▪ ▪

1. Why is leadership important for organizations?
2. In what ways does culture affect leadership?
3. What are some of the limitations of American leadership theories for understanding cross-cultural leadership?
4. Why is the concept of legitimacy important for understanding leadership?
5. How does large-scale research such as Project GLOBE help us understand cross-cultural leadership?
6. What are some of the contributions of charismatic and transformational leaders to organizations?
7. What role do ethics play in effective leadership?
8. What leadership behavior should an international manager use in a culture different from her own?
9. Discuss leaders who you are familiar with from two different cultures. How does culture affect their leadership style?

INTERNET SITES ▪ ▪ ▪ ▪ ▪ ▪ ▪

Selected Companies in the Chapter

General Electric Company (http://ge.com/en)
DaimlerChrysler (www.daimlerchrysler.de)

Leadership Sites

Project GLOBE (www.haskayne.ucalgary.ca/GLOBE/Public). This site provides information on Project GLOBE including its history and recent publications.

Leader Values (www.leader-values.com). This site provides links to many sources on leadership and includes self-assessments for leadership skills and other useful material.

The James MacGregor Burns Academy of Leadership (www.academy.umd.edu/ILA/links). James MacGregor Burns wrote *Leadership* (Harper and Row 1978), an influential study of leadership that first differentiated transforming leadership and transactional leadership. This site has links to a wide array of leadership sites.

REFERENCES ▪▪▪▪▪▪

Adler, N. J. (2002). "Women Joining Men as Global Leaders in the New Economy," In Gannon, M. J. and Newman, K. L. (eds.) *Handbook of Cross-Cultural Management*. Malden, MA: Blackwell.

—— and Izraeli, D. (eds.) (1994). *Competitive Frontiers: Women Managers in a Global Economy*. Cambridge, MA: Blackwell.

Ashkanasy, N. M., Tevor-Roberts, E., and Earnshaw, L. (2002). "The Anglo Cluster: Legacy of the British Empire," *Journal of World Business*, 37(1), 28–39.

Bajdo, L. M. and Dickson, M. W. (2000). "Perceptions of Organizational Culture and Women's Advancement in Organizations: A Cross-Cultural Examination," *Sex Roles*, 45(5/6), 399–414.

Bass, B. (1985). *Leadership and Performance Beyond Expectations*. New York: The Free Press.

——. (1990). *Bass & Stogdill's Handbook of Leadership: Theory, Research, and Managerial Application*. 3d Ed. New York: Free Press.

Blunt, P. Jones, M., and Richards, D. (eds.) (1993). *Managing Organisations in Africa: Readings, Cases, and Exercises*. New York: Walter de Gruyter.

Briscoe, D. (1995). *International Human Resource Management*. Upper Saddle River, NJ: Prentice Hall.

Burns, J. (1978). *Leadership*. New York: Harper & Row.

Cohen, R. (1997). "For France, Sagging Self-Image and Esprit," *New York Times*, February 11, 1 & 6.

Den Hartog, D. N., House, R. J., Hanges, P. J., Ruiz-Quintanilla, S. A., and Dorman, P. W. (1999). "Culture Specific and Cross Culturally Generalizable Implicit Leadership Theories: Are Attributes of Charismatic/ Transformational Leadership Universally Endorsed?" *Leadership Quarterly*, 10(2), 219–256.

Deneire, M. and Segalla, M. (2002). "Mr. Chistian Pierrret, Secretary of State for Industry (1997–2002), on French Perspectives on Organizational Leadership and Management," *Academy of Management Executive*, 16(4), 25–30.

Dorfman, P. (1996). "International and Cross-Cultural Leadership." In Punnett, B. and Shenkar, O. (eds.) *Handbook for International Management Research*. Cambridge, MA: Blackwell Publishers.

Drucker, P. (1994). "The New Superpower: The Overseas Chinese," *The Wall Street Journal*, December 20.

DuBrin, A. (1995). *Leadership: Research Findings, Practice, and Skills*. Boston: Houghton Mifflin.

Gannon, M. J. and Newman, K. L. (2002). *Handbook of Cross-Cultural Management*. Malden, MA: Blackwell.

Guillén, M. (1994). *Models of Management: Work, Authority, and Organization in a Comparative Perspective*. Chicago: University of Chicago Press.

Gumbel, P. and Choi, A. (1995). "Germany Making Comeback, With Daimler in the Lead," *Wall Street Journal*, April, 7, A10.

Gupta, V., Hanges, P. J., and Dorfman, P. (2002). "Cultural Clusters: Methodology and Findings," *Journal of World Business*, 37(1), 11–15.

Hickson, D. (ed.) (1993). *Management in Western Europe: Society, Culture and Organization in Twelve Nations*. New York: Walter de Gruyter.

Hofstede, G. (1980). *Culture's Consequences: International Differences in Work-Related Values*. London: Sage.

——. (2001). *Culture's Consequences: Comparing Values, Behaviors, Institutions, and Organizations Across Nations*. 2d ed. Thousand Oaks, CA: Sage.

Hollway, W. and Mukurasi, L. (1994). "Women Managers in the Tanzanian Civil Service," In Adler, N. and Izraeli, D.(eds.) *Competitive Frontiers: Women Managers in a Global Economy*. Cambridge, MA: Blackwell.

House, R. J. and Mitchell, T. R. (1974). "Path-goal Theory of Leadership," *Contemporary Business*, 3 (Fall), 81–98.

——, Javidan, M., Hanges, P., and Dorfman, P. (2002). "Understanding Cultures and Implicit Leadership Theories Across the Globe: An Introduction to Project GLOBE," *Journal of World Business*, 37(1), 3–10.

—— and Podsakoff, P. (1994). "Leadership Effectiveness: Past Perspectives and Future Directions for Research, " In J. Greenberg (ed.) *Organizational Behavior*. Hillsdale, NJ: Lawrence Erlbaum.

Inglehart, R. and Norris, P. (2003). *Rising Tide: Gender Equality and Cultural Change Around the World*. Cambridge UK: Cambridge University Press.

Jesuino, J. D. (2002). "Latin Europe Cluster: From South to North," *Journal of World Business*, 37(1), 81–89.

Javidan, M. and House, R. J. (2002). "Leadership and Cultures Around the World: Findings from GLOBE: An Introduction to the Special Issue," *Journal of World Business*, 37(1), 1–2.

Kabasakal, H. and Bodur, M. (2002). "Arabic Cluster: A Bridge Between East and West," *Journal of World Business*, 37(1), 40–54.

Katz, D. and Kahn, R. (1978). *The Social Psychology of Organizations*. 2d Ed. New York: John Wiley.

Kotter, J. (1990). *A Force For Change: How Leadership Differs From Management*. New York: The Free Press.

McGregor, D. (1960). *The Human Side of Enterprise*. New York: McGraw-Hill.

Mead, R. (1994). *International Management: Cross Cultural Dimensions*. Cambridge, MA: Blackwell.

Merton, R. (1970). "The Ambivalence of Organizational Leaders," In J. Oates, Jr. (ed.) *The Contradictions of Leadership*. New York: Appleton-Crofts.

Misumi, J. (1985). *The Behavioral Science of Leadership: An Interdisciplinary Japanese Research Program*. Ann Arbor, MI: University of Michigan Press.

Northcraft, G. and Neale, M. (1994). *Organizational Behavior: A Management Challenge*. 2d Ed. Fort Worth, TX: The Dryden Press.

Oliver, N. and Wilkinson, B. (1992). *The Japanization of British Industry: New Developments in the 1990s*. 2d Ed. Oxford, UK: Blackwell.

Ouchi, W. (1981). *Theory Z: How American Business Can Meet the Japanese Challenge*. New York: Avon Books.

Pavett, C. and Morris, T. (1995). "Management Styles Within a Multinational Corporation: A Five Country Comparative Study," *Human Relations*, 48(10), 171–190.

Perrow, C. (1986). *Complex Organizations: A Critical Essay*. 3d Ed. New York: Random House.

Peterson, M. F. and Hunt, J. G. (1997). "International Perspectives on International Leadership," *Leadership Quarterly*, 8(3), 203–32.

Phatak, A. (1995). *International Dimensions of Management*. 4th Ed. Cincinnati, OH: South-Western.

Sayles, L. (1993). *The Working Leader: The Triumph of High Performance Over Conventional Management Principles*. New York: The Free Press.

Schein, E. (1985). *Organizational Culture and Leadership*. San Francisco: Jossey-Bass.

Siemienska, R. (1994). "Women Managers in Poland: In Transition from Communism to Democracy," In Adler, N. and Izraeli, D. (eds.). *Competitive Frontiers: Women Managers in a Global Economy*. Cambridge, MA: Blackwell.

Sinha, J. P. B. (1980). *The Nurturant Task Leader*. New Delhi: Concept.

——. (1995). *The Cultural Context of Leadership and Power*. New Delhi: Sage.

Smith, P. B. and Peterson, M. F. (2002). "Cross-Cultural Leadership," In Gannon, M. J. and Newman, K. L. (eds.) *Handbook of Cross-Cultural Management*. Malden, MA: Blackwell.

Sorge, A. (1993). "Management in France," In Hickson, D. (ed.) *Management in Western Europe: Society, Culture, and Organization in Twelve Nations*. New York: Walter de Gruyter.

Steinhoff, P. and Tanaka, K. (1994). "Women Managers in Japan," In Adler, N. and Izraeli, D. (eds.). *Competitive Frontiers: Women Managers in a Global Economy*. Cambridge, MA: Blackwell.

Tang, J. and Ward, A. (2003). *The Changing Face of Chinese Management*. New York: Routledge.

Tichy, N. and Sherman, S. (1993). *Control Your Destiny or Someone Else Will: Lessons in Mastering Change—The Principles Jack Welch Is Using to Revolutionize General Electric*. New York: Harper Collins.

Trice, H. and Beyer, J. (1993). *The Cultures of Work Organizations*. Upper Saddle River, NJ: Prentice Hall.

Weber, M. (1947). *The Theory of Social and Economic Organization*. New York: The Free Press.

Westwood, R. and Chan, A. (1992). "Headship and Leadership," In Westwood, R. (ed.) *Organisational Behaviour: Southeast Asian Perspectives*. Hong Kong: Longman.

Yukl, G. (2002). *Leadership in Organizations*. 5th Ed. Upper Saddle River, NJ: Prentice Hall.

Zelditch, M. (2001). "Theories of Legitimacy," In Jost, J. T., and Major, B. (eds.) *The Psychology of Legitimacy: Emerging Perspectives on Ideology, Justice, and Intergroup Relations*. New York: Cambridge University Press.

Organization Structure

Learning Objectives

After reading this chapter, you should be able to:

- Define organizational structure and understand the elements that compose it.
- Know how bureaucracies and other types of organizations are structured.
- Appreciate the structure and role of family businesses in international business.
- Know how national culture affects various types of organization structure.
- Have an awareness of emerging types of organizational structures in the global economy.

CULTURE AT WORK

To Restructure or Not to Restructure? That, Is the Question

Four MBA students in New York City made a class presentation on corporate downsizing. Wall Street, where many in the class worked, was consolidating its operations departments with firings, and major corporations were laying off thousands of people.

In a class of 30, four students had been "rightsized" and seven others worked in firms that either had, or were going to restructure, by eliminating middle managers. Downsizing affected their employment opportunities, job security, career paths, and to some extent, their confidence in the future.

During the presentation, the students expressed some personal anxiety but accepted periodic restructuring as part of corporate America. To them it was necessary to have "lean and mean" management and a proactive approach to change to survive increasing domestic and global competition.

In the discussion after the presentation, a student from Germany said, "We have similar problems with excess workers in Germany." The class looked in his direction with expressions of mild irritation that he had merely repeated the presentation.

"But," he continued, "we deal with it somewhat differently. Instead of laying people off, we share work so that people don't suffer as much. Also, it's done with the long-term view that the economy will improve in a few months or

---

years. At some point they will get their jobs back. We don't understand why you Americans are so short-term oriented and ready to fire people."

The Americans questioned the German student about the strength of unions in Germany and their role in advocating work sharing. After heated discussion, they concluded that unions and socialist political parties influenced avoiding layoffs and convinced themselves that an impersonal organizational logic dictated the restructuring of U.S. corporations. It was, they decided, a question of good business practice, and social welfare policy should not influence business decisions.

Source: B. A. Gold

Organization structures vary considerably. Some multinational corporations have hundreds of thousands of employees dispersed throughout the world, dozens of managerial levels, independent business units, and extensive research and development departments. Other multinational corporations have only several thousand employees, few managerial levels, no independent business units, and minimal research and development. There are also family-owned businesses in most societies that vary in their organization structure, ranging from small corner grocery stores to billion-dollar transnational conglomerates.

Culture influences organizational structure in many ways. Because of different social values, the structure of a Korean multinational corporation, which has many of the characteristics of a family business, differs from those found in Japan, Greece, Argentina, South Africa, or the United States. The Culture at Work vignette demonstrates that culture affects how people think about organizational structure and consequently, their actions: One culture views structure as determined by impersonal, rational market forces, whereas the other culture views structure as directly linked to the fates of individuals and the product of social policy choices.

▪▪▪ What Is Organization Structure?

Organization structure is the arrangement of positions in an organization that are intentionally designed to accomplish its goals. The basic components of structure are **complexity, centralization,** and **formalization.** Before discussing them, we present the open systems perspective of organizations because properties in an organization's environment influence variations in the components of structure.

The System Perspective of Organizations

Organizations are **open systems** that interact with their environment rather than exist independently of surrounding influences. Organizations continuously require inputs from the environment in the form of raw materials, human resources, finance, and ideas. After the inputs are transformed through a variety of processes, an organization returns output to the environment in the form of products, services, and knowledge (Katz and Kahn 1978).

One important element in the organization's environment is the values of the national culture. Values influence a wide array of behaviors in organizations—for example, what is moral or legal, hiring practices, and preferences concerning the type and use of authority.

Another key component of an organization's environment is other organizations. These include raw material suppliers, competitors, regulatory agencies, and customers.

An important aspect of the relationships among organizations that affects structure is the diffusion of management theories and practices. Contact with other organizations—usually in the same industry—influences organization structure because of a desire to emulate successful management theories and practices (Abrahamson 1996).

Another feature of structure is that management can change it to adapt to an organization's environment. An example is the change in the structure of the Coca-Cola Company. Because it sells products around the world, for many years Coke was symbolic of the global company. It was not until January 1996, however, that Coke changed its organizational structure to reflect its global presence.

Now, the Coca-Cola Company could adopt the song "We Are the World" as its corporate motto.

> The $10 billion company announced a basic shift in its world view yesterday, eliminating the very concept of a "domestic" and "international" Coca-Cola beverage business in the administrative structure of its worldwide operations.
>
> Coca-Cola downgraded its United States business to be just part of one business unit among the six Coke has for its global regions. Analysts said that move was a first for any major consumer products company, but agreed that it could be imitated.[1] (Collins 1996, p. 35).

In the discussion of multinational organization structures later in this chapter, we present the various types of organizational structures from which companies like Coke can select.

▪▪▪ Elements of Structure

One approach to understanding organization structure is to examine variables that compose it. The extent of complexity, centralization, and formalization of every organization reflects its structure.

Complexity

Complexity is the extent to which an organization has subparts. Three important components of complexity are: horizontal differentiation; vertical or hierarchical differentiation; and spatial dispersion.

Horizontal differentiation is the way that tasks performed by the organization are subdivided (Hall 1996). There are two ways to divide organizational tasks. The first type of job specialization is the **micro division of tasks,** breaking jobs into their smallest components that individuals can perform well with low levels of education and training. An example is automobile assembly lines, which fragment and simplify work. The second is division of labor using highly trained specialists who have extensive responsibilities in performing a complex task—for example, medical doctors who do open-heart surgery. The larger the number of different positions across the organization, the higher the level of horizontal differentiation.

Vertical or **hierarchical differentiation** is the number of levels in an organization. A measure of vertical differentiation is the number of levels between the highest and lowest position in an organization. The assumption is that the higher the level, the greater the authority of the position. Some organizations have few levels and others have dozens; more levels indicates greater differentiation.

---

[1]From "Coke Drops 'Domestic' and Goes One World" by Glenn Collins, *The New York Times*, January 13, 1996. Copyright © 1996 by The New York Times Co. Reprinted with permission.

The final component of complexity is **spatial dispersion,** a form of horizontal and vertical differentiation. The activities of an organization can be in one place or in different locations on either the basis of power centers, that is, hierarchy, or specialization. An example of spatial dispersion based on specialization is a corporation headquartered in Mexico with factories in Honduras, Brazil, and Canada that manufacture products customized for local markets. Regarding the location of authority, management can decide to replicate the power structure at each location, resulting in **decentralization,** or concentrate it at headquarters.

Centralization

Centralization focuses on the decision-making authority of members of an organization. When a few people make decisions—usually those at the top—an organization is centralized. When many people, including lower-level participants, contribute to or make decisions, organizational decentralization increases. Decentralization is measured by the percent of important decisions made by lower-level members; the more broad based decision making is, the greater the decentralization.

Formalization

Formalization is the extent to which rules, policies, and procedures govern organization members' behavior. The more extensive the documentation and regulation of appropriate behavior, the more formalized the organization. Theoretically, rules can specify all actions in an organization. It is possible that an organization has no formal rules or policies. Typically, organizations operate between these extremes.

Patterns

These variables often form specific patterns. Typically, centralized organizations also contain high formalization and specialization based on a micro division of labor. This is characteristic of **mechanistic** or bureaucratic organizations. Decentralized organizations often have low formalization and specialization based on depth of knowledge. This type of organization is an **organic structure** (Burns and Stalker 1961).

▪▪▪ Explaining Structure: The Contingency Perspective

Through logical argument, inductive and deductive theories, and empirical research, management scholars and sociologists have argued that one variable explains more of the structural aspects of organizations than others. These explanations—**determinist theories**—range from technology as the primary causal variable of structure (Perrow 1967) to strategy (Chandler 1962) and size (Blau and Schoenherr 1971).

Most organizational studies conducted in the United States identify one best way to structure organizations and manage them. Even **contingency theories,** the perspective that there are multiple causes that produce different types of structures, limit variables that affect structure to a small number that are controllable by management such as types of coordination (Lawrence and Lorsch 1967) or the task structure of the organization (Thompson 1967).

In addition, most research in the United States and Western Europe views organization structure as **culture-free**—that is, consisting of universal causes (Child 1974; Hickson, Hinings, McMillan, and Schwitter 1974). In this view, the logic of formal organization is independent of values found in different cultures. It does not deny variations in values, but views them as irrelevant because technology, strategy, size, and other variables apply across cultures as explanations for organization structure.

An alternative argument is that culture is the major determinant of whether a specific management philosophy and organizational structure will be prevalent in a society (DiMaggio 2001; Trompenaars and Hampton-Turner 1998). The values and assumptions of a culture determine preferences for the arrangement of positions in organizations. Proponents of this view argue that cultural and managerial choices influence organization structures rather than deterministic processes such as industrialization, mechanization, and bureaucratization.

The position taken here is that culture is an important variable but not the only explanation of organization structure; multiple factors influence and cause organization structure. However, the focus will be on the contribution of culture to structure.

Culture and Organization Structure

Research on Japanese automobile plants in the United States tested the prediction of organizational theory that the environment of the United States would make Japanese practices, such as team-based management and just-in-time supplier relationships, difficult to transfer (Florida and Kenney 1991). The research found that transplanted Japanese factories successfully implemented these practices. This suggests that cultural values—ways of structuring work—are strong enough to persist in the value system of another society.

A study that compared 14 matched English and Indian manufacturing firms in a variety of industries explored the contingency and universal—that is, culture-free—approaches to explaining organization structure (Tayeb 1987). The English and Indian organizations were similar in terms of centralization, joint decision making, specialization, and number of hierarchical levels. Key areas in which there were differences were delegation, formalization, use of job descriptions, and the direction of communication.

The universalistic theory explains the similarities in the organizations. However, different *means* achieved the similarities. For example, both groups of organizations had centralized decisions. In the English sample, however, managers consulted with lower-level employees and delegated to them before making a final decision. In the Indian sample, there was comparatively little discussion of decisions with lower-level workers. Tayeb (1987, p. 257) concluded that:

> Contingency theory and the culture-free thesis gained moderate support . . . but the model they suggest is inadequate and cannot explain the many differences between the Indian and English organizations which were also found. These differences appear to be more consistent with the general characteristics of the societies in which these organizations operate, and their employees' cultural traits.

An interesting example of the effects of culture on organization structure is the Swedish automobile industry. Instead of assembly line production made famous by Henry Ford and refined by U.S. automobile companies, the Swedish automotive industry has experimented with a variety of structures largely determined by their value system, not the requirements of efficient production.

A distinctive feature of Swedish automobile production—for example at Saab—is "reflective production" (Ellegard et al. 1992). Some characteristics of reflective production that differ from assembly line production structures are:

- The view of assembly work is from a wide context on the shopfloor. It must include not only the assembly itself, but also the preceding phases (i.e., controlling the materials, structuring the materials and tools, and the subsequent phases (i.e., final inspection), and if necessary, adjustment and further inspection). The vertical division of labor is also affected in that assembly workers take over certain administrative tasks. This new concept of assembly work calls for the workers' own reflections.

- In reflective production, the assembly work itself becomes intellectualized and thereby meaningful. The work teams are able to rebalance their own work.
- Established empirical knowledge of grouping and restructuring work tasks is also a basic precondition for the realization of efficient and humane production systems (Ellegard et al. 1992, pp. 121–122).

From the perspective of organization structure, reflective production blurs traditional distinctions of horizontal and vertical differentiation and adds an intellectual, or "reflective" component, to assembly work. Workers understand the entire manufacturing process and contribute to its structure. Swedish culture values work as an intellectual, humane activity, and the structure of reflective production fulfills these values more than standard assembly line structures that predetermine microtasks and reduce workers to appendages of machines.

Finally, conducting an historical study of the management philosophies and practices of the United States, Great Britain, Germany, and Spain, Guillén (1994) discovered variation according to each nation's value system. Cultural values—including religion—influence the management and structure of organizations in these countries.

In summary, these and other empirical studies suggest that differences in cultural values contribute to variation in organizational structure.

Organization Structure, Culture, and Organization Behavior Revisited

There are three views of how organization structure affects organizational behavior. The first view, which is consistent with the studies already discussed, is that cultural values affect organization structure, which then influences organizational behavior.

An alternative view, **structuralism,** is that organization structure influences—even determines—values. This position claims that, "the structures of objective social positions among which people are distributed exert more fundamental influences on social life than do cultural values and norms, including ultimately the prevailing values and norms" (Blau 1977, p. x).

A third view is that organizational behavior is the product of the interaction of structure and values. National cultural values and corporate culture interact with structural variables. In other words, a dialectical process among national culture, organizational culture, and structure creates constraints and opportunities for behavior in organizations.

▪▪▪ Types of Organization Structure

Another approach to understanding organization structure is to construct models of different types of organizations instead of isolating specific variables such as complexity, centralization, and formalization.

Bureaucracy

In a classic typology, Max Weber (1946) identified the following characteristics of **bureaucracy:**

- *Each position has fixed official duties.* Job descriptions exist for each position that create a high degree of specialization in a small number of comparatively routine tasks.

- *Impersonal rules and regulations govern conduct.*   Impersonal—not intentionally abrasive behavior—ensures that each case the bureaucracy deals with receives the same treatment.
- *Effort is coordinated through a hierarchy of levels of authority.*   The assumption of this arrangement is that the higher the position, the more expertise the position holder possesses.
- *Written communication and files maintain order and reliability.*   A bureaucracy documents all transactions; this establishes records that create accountability.
- *Employment is a full-time occupation for members of the organization.* Members of the organization are "professionals"; their primary occupational focus is the tasks of their position.
- *Superiors make appointments to offices.*   Appointments to positions depend on appropriate skills.
- *Merit determines promotion.*   Those most qualified—as demonstrated through a written examination or other method—are promoted.

Weber viewed bureaucracy as the product of historical progression toward rational administration because, compared to other ways of organizing, bureaucracy was efficient and effective. For example, in patrimonial administration, legitimate authority derived from a male leader. Regardless of knowledge or ability, only members of the patriarch's clan could occupy positions. In many contemporary societies, some variations of this type of organization still exist, usually in family businesses as discussed subsequently.

Because it is a major form of organization, there are many studies of bureaucracy. One approach examines the extent to which bureaucracy actually achieves rational administration. In fact, organizational researchers discovered many departures from rationality or the **dysfunctions** of bureaucracy. For example, a central insight is that the strict adherence to rules for situations that are not standard or "typical" cases often produces results that are contrary to the goals of the organization. This rigid behavior exemplifies the bureaucratic personality (Merton 1968).

Other studies focus on the relationship of elements such as hierarchy and centralization of power, the effects of size on organizations, and how bureaucracies develop and change. Many of these research findings are counterintuitive. For example, after a review of studies on the relationship between size and centralization, Blau and Meyer (1987, p. 100) conclude:

> Almost all the empirical research on organizations . . . suggests that stereotypes of large organizations as excessively bureaucratic are misleading. To be sure, structural differentiation increases with size, but the rate of increase in numbers of organizational units and in levels of hierarchy actually decreases with size. Administrative overhead, measured by ratios of either administrators to production workers or supervisory to nonsupervisory personnel, also decreases with size. And large, multitier organizations, particularly those whose personnel rules are most formalized, tend to be the most decentralized, in that decisions are delegated to levels below top management. Altogether, bureaucratic controls seem to be less intensive in large organizations than in small ones.

Not all cultures or subcultures view rational administration as desirable. For example, one objective of family businesses is intergenerational transfer and control of the business. Whether this behavior is rational or not depends on cultural assumptions and values. Most societies, however, regardless of their values, have some approximation of bureaucratic organization in business and the public sector because, even with inevitable dysfunctions, it is efficient and effective for administering routine, repetitive tasks. For example, McDonald's, despite frequent criticism on social, cultural, and political grounds, is a major global company primarily because it is a highly efficient and effective bureaucracy.

Simple Structure

Simple structure is characteristic of new or small organizations. There is little need for elaborate coordination because the organization is not complex; top management supervises through direct supervision. There is also centralization in top management with employees exerting little independent decision making or influence. The organization's goals are those of its top manager, who is frequently also its owner. This type of organization is typical of entrepreneurial activity in its early stages and of small family businesses.

Organic Structure

Organic structure is the opposite of bureaucracy. Bureaucracy is a rigid, often dysfunctional type of organization, whereas organic structures are flexible, change oriented, and foster creativity. The following are features of organic structures:

- Knowledge and ability determine participation in decision making and problem solving rather than position titles.
- Decision making is decentralized, and there is an attempt to involve lower-level participants in decision making whenever possible.
- Communication channels operate vertically and horizontally. In other words, information is shared throughout the organization including across areas of expertise and status.

One type of organic structure is the **matrix.** In matrix structures, instead of a bureaucratic authority structure with employees accountable to a supervisor, an employee reports to more than one supervisor. For example, an engineer can report to the head of a functional area and a project manager when developing a product or project. Of course, it is more complex than either a simple structure or a bureaucracy and has the potential for creating conflict among the supervisors. Nevertheless, many cultures use matrix structures including the United Kingdom, the United States, and Germany. Other cultures prefer the principle of a single supervisor—unitary chain of command—particularly the French.

Multiple Structures

Many organizations have **multiple structures** (Hall 1996). Hospitals and universities are complex structures that contain both bureaucratic administration and more organic or professional structures. In addition to requiring more coordination, these types of organizations often experience conflict as a result of the coexistence of different structures. For example, doctors, who work in a professional bureaucracy with some of the characteristics of organic structures, are often in conflict with nurses, who work in a fairly bureaucratic mode.

▄▄▄ Structural Variations

Although bureaucracy and organic structures are common organizational types throughout the world, some organizations modify them by incorporating selected elements of each. One widespread type of organization, family business, takes a variety of forms and demonstrates the impact of culture on organization structure.

Family Business

Family business is a major form of organizational structure throughout the world. Even in economically advanced societies, family businesses are a large segment of the economy. Features of family businesses that distinguish them from non-family-owned-and-operated corporate structures follow:

- The composition of the governance and management structures—the organizational elite—are primarily family members. In other words, ascription—who you are—is a more important criterion for employment than achievement.
- There is usually distrust of nonkin employees and outsiders. However, it is possible that nonkin employees can become trusted, particularly when they demonstrate long-term loyalty.
- There are often difficulties with leadership succession. The issue is usually conflict over selecting a child or other relative to succeed the founder or current head. This illustrates one of the nonrational qualities and weaknesses of family businesses.
- The business can suffer from family member lack of expertise. If, for example, no family member is an attorney or accountant, the advice of professionals could be evaluated as untrustworthy.
- Business decision making is often on the basis of kin requirements, instead of "rationality." There is a preference for affective relationships, characterized by personal obligations over calculated, nonpersonal decision making.
- In family firms, paternalism is the typical management style. This creates centralization of authority in the male leader. Family respect for the patriarch often creates conservative, risk-averse behavior, including reluctance to use external financing as a source for expansion.

The following example illustrates conditions typical of family businesses:

[Corporate] growth strategies in India also relate to family structure. There, family objectives such as creating employment for family members are a strong impetus for forming a business. Recently, an American businessman suggested to his Indian joint venture partner that the latter use a standard market-portfolio model (a la Boston Consulting Group) to plan his business expansion. His partner refused to invest unequally in the five existing businesses because each business was managed by a son. Unequal investment would cause family discord. Even in firms where some of the board of directors are not family members, the norm of family consensus can be very strong. Family owner-managers often hold private council before submitting plans to the Board. (Terpstra and David 1991, p. 172).

Within the constraints of these characteristics, family businesses take various forms. Some are small and local, whereas others develop into dispersed multinational conglomerates. For example, in the 1990s, the Garza Sada family of Mexico controlled

Grupo Industrial Alfa, Mexico's largest conglomerate with interests in steel, petro-chemicals, and food (Carroll 1995).

Chinese Family Business

Overseas and Mainland **Chinese family businesses** (CFBs) present an interesting example of family business structure. The structure of overseas CFBs is usually either a small business that includes only family members or is controlled by family members but also employs nonfamily members and operates as a clan or extended family, which permits it to grow considerably larger than businesses restricted to family members.

The ideology of CFBs centers on patrimonialism, which, in practice means pater-nalism, hierarchy, mutual obligation, responsibility, familialism, personalism, and con-nections (Chen 1995). Related to this—as in family businesses in other cultures—is a close relationship between power and ownership. The product of this combination is autocratic leadership and a personalistic style of management. These features result in organizations that include a key role for the owners in management, keep the organi-zation small, and promote factionalism.

The small size of CFBs limits them to simple structures that usually restrict them to focus on only one aspect of a business—for example, production, sales, or service (Chen 1995). This creates a situation in which "all employees are expected to be involved in the main products or the services of the company, which directly create profits" (Chen 1995, p. 87). Another feature is that CFBs do not have systematic sets of rules, systems, or roles. This also creates a low level of specialization, and workers can be assigned to any task "at the whim of the business owners" (Chen 1995, p. 87). The result is an informal organization in which the owner has extensive power that he often uses arbitrarily and abusively.

Within this framework—a lack of formal structure and rules—personal relationships and "feelings about other people are likely to take precedence over more objectively defined concerns such as organizational efficiency" (Chen 1995, p. 87). This creates a situation in which cliques form as a substitute for formal structure. One consequence of clique formation based on personal loyalties is that intergroup contests frequently escalate into disruptive conflicts.

In Mainland China, although for many years the government officially prohibited family businesses, they continued to exist and currently operate under the auspices of policies intended to modernize the economy (Tang and Ward 2003). In fact, private enterprise in China, when agriculture under the control of individual farmers is included, accounts for almost one half of China's gross domestic product (International Finance Corporation 2000). From the perspective of organizational structure, similar to overseas CFBs, Mainland CFBs, instead of becoming more complex and formal as they increase in size, "tend to retain the informality that char-acterizes [the early] stage of business as they grow and mature. This has a number of benefits in the Chinese context, although it is not entirely without cost" (Tang and Ward 2003, pp. 110–111).

A key benefit is that the family retains ownership and control. However, once a company grows beyond a certain point and distant relatives become employees, issues of trust and loyalty that the family business benefits from become more of a problem because the distant relatives have little hope of owning the business and are widely viewed as idle spendthrifts.

Many features of both overseas and Mainland CFBs are also present in family businesses in other cultures. For example, a recurring theme in the CFB is factionalism and conflict that occurs over issues such as ownership, control, career development, and particularly, over succession. These conflicts are inherent in families and occur between parents and children, among children, between nuclear and extended family members, and between family members and nonfamily members (Levinson 1971).

In the next section we discuss structures that are family businesses at their core but develop into enormous conglomerates as the result of government intervention and values different from those typically found in family businesses.

National Structural Variations

In addition to family businesses and their diverse structures, there are cultural variations in the governance of business that affect organizational structure. Two forms that are substantially different from corporate governance in the West are the Japanese *keiretsu* and the Korean *chaebol*. They have origins in, and still have characteristics of, family firms, which not only affect their governance, but to some extent, also influence the microstructure of work and interpersonal relationships. They are of additional importance because they have played a critical role in the rapid economic development of Japan and Korea (Lincoln, Gerlach, and Ahmadjian 1996).

Japanese *Keiretsu*

The origins of the Japanese *keiretsu* are family-owned federations of firms, *zaibatsu*, that existed prior to World War II. Reorganized after the war into the looser *keirestu,* they are complex interfirm networks that combine market exchange and noneconomic social relations. To facilitate control and coordination, each member firm of a *keiretsu* owns a small part—up to 20%—of the stock of the other firms in the group. "The group is usually in a large number of industries, and at the core of the group is often a bank. Very few shares of the firm trade on open equity markets. Since investment is internally generated, it is usually oriented to long-run gains and holding market share" (Fligstein and Freeland 1995, p. 38).

In addition to a bank, *keiretsu* usually include a *soga shosha*, a general trading company that supports the *keiretsu* by coordinating the companies within the group by buying and selling services, providing information, and maintaining information networks within the *keiretsu.* This aspect of Japanese business structure is unique to Asian culture. Other countries, including Korea, Mexico, and Brazil have started organizations similar to *soga shosha,* with Korea the only one experiencing success.

The effect of *keiretsu* on the performance of Japanese firms is considerable. According to Lincoln, Gerlach, and Takahashi (1992, p. 561):

> Once castigated as atavistic "feudal" structures imperiling the full modernization of an ascendant economy, *keiretsu* networks, like other institutions in Japanese economic life, are increasingly credited with conferring a key competitive advantage on Japan. For their member firms, *keiretsu* networks reduce costs and risk, facilitate communication, ensure trust and reliability, and provide insulation from outside competition.

Korean *Chaebols*

Large conglomerates or financial cliques known as *chaebols* dominate the South Korean economy. The definition of a *chaebol* is "a business group consisting of large companies which are owned and managed by family members or relatives in many diversified business areas" (Yoo and Lee 1987, p. 97). Examples of *chaebols* are corporations such as Hyundai, Samsung, LG Group, Hanjin, and Daewoo.

Since the end of the Korean War, the government has played a large and active role in the investment patterns of the *chaebols*. As a result, unlike in the United States and other countries, private financial markets play almost no role in the growth of the South Korean economy. Most financing comes from government-controlled banks, enabling the government to decide which *chaebols* receive money for expansion. In return for favorable treatment, the *chaebols* make large contributions to politicians.

The family ownership and diversified business operations of *chaebols* are similar to the former Japanese *zaibatsus*. An important feature of *chaebols* that differs from Japanese *keiretsu* is that founders are more active in management; in Japan there are more nonfamily managers. As a result, the founder's business philosophy influences the management style of *chaebols*.

In summary, "Korean firms are large, integrated, and diversified, yet under the control of a small number of families with strong ties to government" (Fligstein and Freeland 1995, p. 39).

▪▪▪ Emerging Structures in the Global Economy

The globalization of the economy has created new types of organizational structures that attempt to use human resources more efficiently, manage increasing levels of complexity, and become more responsive to changes in their environment.

Boundaryless Organizations

One new structure, the **boundaryless organization,** breaks the traditional demarcations of authority, political, communication, and task specialization found in bureaucracies and other organizational structures. Features of a boundaryless organization include a widespread use of project teams, interfunctional teams, networks, and similar structural mechanisms, thus reducing boundaries that typically separate organizational functions and hierarchical levels. In addition, boundaryless organizations form strategic alliances with suppliers, customers, and in some cases, with competitors (Hirschhorn and Gilmore 1992). The purpose of the blurring of internal and external boundaries is to be more responsive to changes in a dynamic global economy.

Of course, even in a boundaryless corporation, there is an authority structure as well as task and political boundaries. However, these boundaries are flexible and have no resemblance to the rigid horizontal and vertical dimensions of traditional organizations. In its extreme form, the boundaryless organization is a horizontal structure organized around basic processes such as new product development, sales, and customer support instead of traditional functional areas.

In boundaryless organizations a key management challenge is to socialize and train organization members to encourage new forms of behavior and prevent returning to the segmenting effects of the bureaucratic mentality.

Multinational, Global, International, and Transnational Structures

A characteristic of many corporations is that they are not located within the geographical boundaries of one country. In addition, these corporate structures are complex because they usually produce multiple products and services and have large numbers of employees.

Multinational firms focus on a strategy that is primarily country oriented and locally responsive. Decentralization is a key feature of these organizational

TABLE 12-1 Organizational Characteristics of Multinational, Global, International, and Transnational Firms

Organizational Characteristics	Multinational	Global	International	Transnational
Configuration of assets and capabilities	Decentralized and nationally self-sufficient	Centralized and globally scaled	Sources of core competencies centralized, others decentralized	Dispersed, interdependent, and specialized
Role of overseas operations	Sensing and exploiting local opportunities	Implementing parent company strategies	Adapting and leveraging parent company competencies	Differentiated contributions by national units to integrated worldwide operations
Development and diffusion of knowledge	Knowledge developed and retained within each unit	Knowledge developed and retained at the center	Knowledge developed at the center and transferred to overseas units	Knowledge developed jointly and shared worldwide

▪ ▪ ▪ ▪ ▪ ▪ ▪ ▪

Source: Bartlett, A. and Ghosal, S. (1991). *Managing Across Borders: The Transnational Solution.* Boston: Harvard Business School Press, p. 65. Copyright © 1989 by the Harvard Business School Publishing Corporation, all rights reserved.

structures. In contrast, **global** companies are centralized and follow a strategy built on global-scale cost advantage. **International** firms develop products and innovations in their domestic market and then transport them to foreign affiliates where the products and technologies are adapted to local needs. These companies are centralized and sequential. Table 12-1 presents the organizational characteristics of these types of firms.

The **transnational** firm differs from these types in that it avoids dichotomous structures such as product- or geography-based, centralized or decentralized, independent or dependent (Bartlett and Ghosal 1989). Alternatively, it attempts to achieve solutions tailored to specific situations, and differentiated structures replace systemwide structures. For example, some businesses within a corporation might require a worldwide centralized structure, whereas others should adapt to local conditions and decentralize to take advantage of local manufacturing and marketing.

This type of organizational structure creates high levels of interdependence among countries and cultures. Bartlett and Ghoshal (1989, p. 60) write:

> The transnational centralizes some resources at home, some abroad, and distributes yet others among its many national operations. The result is a complex configuration of assets and capabilities that are distributed, yet specialized. Furthermore, the company integrates the dispersed resources through strong interdependencies . . . The British subsidiary may depend on France for one range of products, while the French depend on the British for others. Some of these interdependencies are automatic outcomes of the configuration of assets and resources. Frequently, however, they are specifically designed to build self-enforcing cooperation among interdependent units.

Heterarchy

Heterarchy is a type of multinational organization that utilizes aspects of markets and hierarchies to interweave a multiplicity of organizing principles. Market principles are situations in which economic activities between unrelated parties use explicit contracts or prices as the primary mechanism to coordinate their activities. Each party does what is in their best interest for each transaction. Hierarchy involves transactions between parties related to one another—for example, through ownership or implicit contracts, such as between employers and employees and when coordination exists through vertical authority relations.

According to Hedlund (1986, p. 20),

> The heterarchical MNC [multinational corporation] differs from the standard geocentric [a single headquarters] one in terms of strategy and in terms of [the direction of the relationship between strategy and] structure. *Strategically,* the main dividing line is between exploiting competitive advantages derived from a home country base on the one hand, and actively seeking advantages originating in the global spread of the firm. . . . When it comes to the *structure* of the enterprise and the process of managing it . . . the idea of structure determining strategy [rather than the other way around] . . . is a fundamental one for the heterarchical MNC. Rather than identifying properties of the industry in which it competes and then adapting its structure to the demands thus established, the [heterarchical] MNC first defines its structural properties and then looks for strategic options following from these properties.

In this type of organizational structure, instead of reliance on traditional hierarchy—where ideas, technology, and people originate from the geographical center of the organization—managers design the multinational structure so that ideas, products, technology, and other functions and processes, can originate from any element in the system. The following are the basic features of this new type of MNC (Hedlund 1986; Vernon, Wells, and Rangan 1996):

- The heterarchical multinational enterprise has multiple centers, each with competence in one or another business, product, or function. Resource diffusion exists within the network of affiliates, and the assumption is that ideas can come from any country.
- Subsidiary managers play strategic roles, not just within their own units but within the enterprise as a whole. This dilutes the notion of "headquarters."
- Thinking and decision making are not restricted to the center; every part of the enterprise can participate. In this manner, there is tightening of the feedback loop between action and thought.
- Integration is achieved primarily through normative control and only secondarily through coercive or bureaucratic means. Socialization and "corporate culture" become more important.
- In contrast to a matrix, a heterarchy recognizes that organizations can be built along more than two dimensions. Thus, research and development could be organized one way, production a second, and marketing a third.
- Finally, managers have flexibility in the selection of governance modes. A subsidiary may purchase components from it or sell its production externally. Similarly, coalitions with other firms and actors may be frequent in the heterarchical multinational enterprise.

Because of the ability of this new form to "find solutions that promote constructive organizational reflexivity, or the ability to redefine and recombine resources" (Stark 2001, p. 75), heterarchy is found increasingly in postsocialist states as they transition to market economies. Finally, from the perspective of culture, to some extent heterarchy treats each culture equally or ignores cultural differences; there is no headquarters, ideas flow from all divisions, and corporate culture replaces national culture as a control mechanism.

Network Organizations

Although there is debate over the extent to which they are replacing traditional organizational structures, network organizations are increasingly common throughout the world (DiMaggio 2001). Because they are more informally organized than typical 20th-century organizations, particularly bureaucracy, networks are characteristic of emerging 21st-century organizational structures that are flexible and adaptive to continuously changing environments. Identifying a basic shift in organization structure that occurred in the West in the 1990s that, in effect, provided the groundwork for the structures of the 21st century, Walter Powell (2001, p. 35) writes:

> This new logic of organizing involves changes in the standard recipes for jobs, organizations, and industries. The new architecture is of a work world in which jobs disappear and projects ascend, and design and production become simultaneous processes rather than orderly sequential steps. The boundaries of many firms have become so porous that to focus on boundaries means only to see trees in a forest of interorganizational relations. The core competence of a firm . . . is based on knowledge production and building a sustainable advantage that can be leveraged across products and services, thus enmeshing firms in all manner of different relationships and markets that were traditionally called industries. Power, to be sure, remains crucial, but it is employed to enhance reach and access and to compete in high-speed learning races. These new innovations are inherently fragile because they are premised on obtaining deeper engagement and participation from "core" employees and more collaboration and mutual involvement among ostensible competitors. But employees toil in a context of greater labor market volatility and interfirm cooperation coexists with rivalry among competing networks.

Network organizations may also be a response to the decline of the nation state and the inability of the nation state to continue to provide the legal frameworks on which more traditional organizational structures such as bureaucracy have been legitimized (Tilly 2001). In this view, the nation state was an historical anomaly with a comparatively short life—a few centuries—and the network is a response to the fragile condition of the state. Instead of a new type of organization structure, network organizations are a return to a previous solution that responds to widespread economic uncertainty and political instability. Charles Tilly (2001, p. 203) observes that:

> Partly as a consequence of alterations in firms and states, the late twentieth century is witnessing expansion of people's efforts to create trustworthy solidarity within networks defined chiefly by shared religion, ethnicity, locality, or cultural preference. People are again trying strenuously to shield such networks from disruptive intervention by governments and economic organizations—except where those networks control their own governments and economic organizations. Finally and inevitably, interactions among economic structures,

governmental organizations, and trust networks are shifting in ways that forecast significantly different qualities of life during the twenty-first century.

▫▫▫ Convergence or Divergence?

Forces for Convergence

Two organizational structures that exist in most societies are bureaucracy and patrimony. Most societies have government agencies and private corporations that are bureaucratic in principle and practice. Hierarchy, a microdivision of labor, the concept of position or office, and appointment and promotion on merit are widely accepted principles. Of course, compromises to these principles occur with nepotism and various practices based on custom and tradition rather than rational administrative or economic calculation.

Similarly, the presence in most societies of family ownership and management of business organizations suggests that patrimony is still widespread. It is likely that these organization arrangements persist because they are effective in achieving valued outputs and are consistent with cultural values, legal structure of corporations, and practices in many societies. An argument then is that there are and will remain similarities in organizational structures across societies (Kraakman 2001).

At the same time, however, pressures are increasing to replace or supplement many traditional organizational structures with networks that permit flexibility and foster innovation. Usually these are organizations that are capital intensive, knowledge based, and technology driven. These new types of organization structures create pressures toward convergence, as do standard forms of multinational organizations. To a great extent, however, whether organizational structures become more similar depends on the extent to which organizational environments converge.

Forces for Divergence

Factors producing divergence are the stage of economic development of a country, variations in relationships between political and industrial sectors, cultural values, and competitive pressures that result in new forms of organization. Regarding competitive pressures, organization structure—such as the use of teams, relations with suppliers, the use of technology—are important ingredients in gaining strategic advantage. In other words, there are important strategic reasons for the development and maintenance of distinctive organization structures (Guillén 2001).

▫▫▫ Implications for Managers

Organizational structure is a competitive tool in international business. Downsizing, the reduction of middle-level managers and other workers, that is one of several adjustments to global competitive pressures, has created the possibility that elaborate hierarchies are no longer necessary, and that flexible organizational structures are replacing them. But at the same time that many American corporations are reducing the scale of organizations to become more flexible, although it may be a limited phenomenon, the Koreans and particularly the Chinese, are creating large, complex organizations.

As noted previously, not all corporations have impersonal rules and professional relationships—bureaucratic principles—but often rely on the insights of strong authority figures and affective relationships. A key issue for global managers is the ability to understand and, in some cases, manage unfamiliar structures in unfamiliar cultures.

An alternative approach is to manage as though structure is irrelevant. This is similar to the culture-free or universalistic perspective: all that matters is individual relationships. The limitation of this approach is that organizational structures shape employee behavior. To understand workers' behavior, a manager must understand the structure they work in.

Yet another issue for managers is to learn how to operate in network organizations. These either have no hierarchies or minimal vertical differentiation and patterns substantially different than traditional vertical differentiation into a microdivision of labor. In addition, the spatial dispersion and often temporary nature of network organizations, requires adaptation to extreme levels of flexibility.

SUMMARY

Organization structures vary within industries, between industries, and across cultures. One of the determinants of organization structure is culture, particularly social values concerning the nature of work, the rational use of resources, the desired quality of interpersonal relationships, and the social welfare of a society. A counter argument is that there are universal organization structures that are determined by noncultural variables such as technology, size, strategy, and the organization's competitive environment. In this view, culture plays little, if any, role in determining organization structure.

Key variables for understanding organization structures are complexity, centralization, and formalization. Depending on their arrangement, these variables produce various forms of organization. Some commonly found types of organization structures are simple structure, bureaucracy, matrix, and family businesses. Culturally distinct structures are Japanese *keiretsu* and Korean *chaebols*. In recent years new forms of global structures have emerged including boundaryless organizations, networks, and heterarchies.

Some factors—for example, transnational corporations and networks—are creating similar organization structures throughout the globe. At the same time, other factors such as national culture produce distinctive structural arrangements. An example is the Swedish automotive industry, which over many years, has attempted to find ways to assemble high-quality cars without sacrificing the human aspects of work to the technical efficiency requirements of the traditional assembly line.

Finally, managers can choose to manage in a way that is sensitive to variations in organizational structure or to approach every organization as though structural variations do not affect interpersonal relationships. In some instances, however, such as the family business structure, it is difficult to avoid the implications of culture on structural arrangements.

DISCUSSION QUESTIONS

1. What is organization structure?
2. What variables contribute to creating organizational structure?
3. Discuss the rationale for including culture as a determinant of organizational structure.
4. How does a matrix organization differ from a bureaucracy? When would it be appropriate to use a matrix structure?
5. What are the characteristics of a family business?
6. In what way does the *keiretsu* form of organization differ from the macrolevel organizational structures found in the United States?
7. What features distinguish new and emerging organizational structures from established ones?
8. Why should a manager have knowledge of organizational structures in different cultures?

INTERNET SITES ▪ ▪ ▪ ▪ ▪ ▪ ▪

Selected Companies in the Chapter

Coca-Cola (www.coca-cola.com)
Saab (www.saab.com)
Samsung (www.samsung.com)

Organizational Structure Sites

Virtual organizations (www.virtual-organization.net). This is the site of an electronic journal devoted to research on virtual organizations.

David Stark (www.sociology.columbia.edu/people/index.html?professors/dcs36/index.html) and (www.santafe.edu/sfi/publications/Bulletins/bulletinFall99/features/organizationDiversity.html). David Stark is a professor of sociology at Columbia University. One of his areas of research is organizational structures in post-socialist countries, particularly Hungary. Several interesting papers on heterarchy are available on this site.

Max Weber (www.faculty.rsu.edu/~felwell/Theorists/Weber/Whome.htm). Weber is one of the most influential social scientists of the twentieth century. His analysis of bureaucracy is one of the classic statements about organization structure.

REFERENCES ▪ ▪ ▪ ▪ ▪ ▪ ▪

Abrahamson, E. (1996). "Management Fashion," *Academy of Management Review*, 21(1), 254–285.

Bartlett, C. and Ghosal, S. (1989). *Managing Across Borders: The Transnational Solution.* Boston: Harvard Business School Press.

Blau, P. M. (1977). *Inequality and Heterogeneity: A Primitive Theory of Social Structure*. New York: The Free Press.

—— and Meyer, M. (1987). *Bureaucracy in Modern Society*. New York: Random House.

—— and Schoenherr, R. (1971). *The Structure of Organizations*. New York: Basic Books.

Burns, T. and Stalker, G. (1961). *The Management of Innovation*. London: Tavistock Publications.

Carroll, P. (1995). "Garza Sadas Build an Unrivaled Latin Empire," *The Wall Street Journal*. December 11, A9.

Chandler, A. (1962). *Strategy and Structure.* Cambridge, MA: MIT Press.

Chen, M. (1995). *Asian Management Systems: Chinese, Japanese and Korean Styles of Business.* New York: Routledge.

Child, J. (1974). "What Determines Organizational Performance? The Universals vs. the It-All-Depends," *Organizational Dynamics,* Summer, 2–18.

Collins, G. (1996). "Coke Drops 'Domestic' and Goes One World," *New York Times,* January 13, 35.

DiMaggio, P. (2001). *The Twenty-First-Century Firm: Changing Economic Organization in International Perspective*. Princeton, NJ: Princeton University Press.

Ellegard, K., Jonsson, D., Enstrom, T., Johansson, M., Medbo, L., and Johansson, B. (1992). "Reflective Production in the Final Assembly of Motor Vehicles: An Emerging Swedish Challenge," *International Journal of Operations & Production Management,* 12(7/8), 117–133.

Fligstein, N. and Freeland, R. (1995). "Theoretical and Comparative Perspectives on Corporate Organization," *Annual Review of Sociology,*: 21–43. Palo Alto, CA: Annual Reviews.

Florida, R. and Kenney, M. (1991). "Transplanted Organizations: The Transfer of Japanese Industrial Organization to the U.S.," *American Sociological Review* 56, 381–398.

Guillén, M. F. (1994). *Models of Management: Work, Authority, and Organization in a Comparative Perspective.* Chicago: University of Chicago Press.

——. (2001). *The Limits of Convergence: Globalization and Organizational Change in Argentina, South Korea, and Spain.* Princeton, NJ: Princeton University Press.

Hall, R. (1996). *Organizations: Structures, Processes, and Outcomes.* Upper Saddle River, NJ: Prentice Hall.

Hedlund, G. (1986). "The Hypermodern MNC: A Heterarchy?" *Human Resource Management*, 25(1), 9–25.

Hickson, D., Hinings, C., McMillan, D., and Schwitter, J. (1974). "The Culture-Free Context of Organization Structure: A Tri-National Comparison," *Sociology,* 8, 59–80.

Hirschhorn, L. and Gilmore, T. (1992). "The New Boundaries of the 'Boundaryless' Company," *Harvard Business Review*, 70(3), 104–115.

International Finance Corporation (2000). *China's Emerging Private Enterprises: Prospects for the New Century*. Washington, DC: International Finance Corporation.

Katz, D. and Kahn, R. (1978). *The Social Psychology of Organizations*. Revised Ed. New York: John Wiley and Sons.

Kraakman, R. (2001). "The Durability of the Corporate Form." In DiMaggio, P. (ed.) *The Twenty-First-Century Firm: Changing Economic Organization in International Perspective*. Princeton, NJ: Princeton University Press.

Lawrence, P. and Lorsch, J. (1967). *Organization and Environment*. Cambridge, MA: Harvard University Press.

Levinson, H. (1971). "Conflicts That Plague Family Businesses," *Harvard Business Review,* March–April, 90–98.

Lincoln, J. (1989). "Employee Work Attitudes and Management Practice in the U.S. and Japan: Evidence from a Large Comparative Survey," *California Management Review*, 32(1), 89–106.

Lincoln, J., Gerlach, M., and Ahmadjian, C. (1996). "*Keiretsu* Networks and Corporate Performance in Japan," *American Sociological Review*, 61(1), 67–88.

Lincoln, J. Gerlach, M., and Takahashi, P. (1992). "*Keiretsu* Networks in the Japanese Economy: A Dyad Analysis of Intercorporate Ties," *American Sociological Review*, 57(5), 561–585.

Merton, R. K. (1968). *Social Theory and Social Structure* Enlarged Ed. New York: Free Press.

Oliver, N. and Wilkinson, B. (1992). *The Japanization of British Industry*. Cambridge, MA: Blackwell.

Perrow, C. (1967). "A Framework for the Comparative Analysis of Organizations," *American Sociological Review*, 26, 688–99.

Powell, W. W. (2001). "The Capitalist Firm in the Twenty-First Century: Emerging Patterns in Western Enterprise." In DiMaggio, P. (ed.) *The Twenty-First-Century Firm: Changing Economic Organization in International Perspective*. Princeton, NJ: Princeton University Press.

Stark, D. (2001). "Ambiguous Assets for Uncertain Environments: Heterarchy in Postsocialist Firms." In DiMaggio, P. (ed.) *The Twenty-First-Century Firm: Changing Economic Organization in International Perspective*. Princeton, NJ: Princeton University Press.

Tang, J. and Ward, A. (2003). *The Changing Face of Chinese Management*. London: Routledge.

Tayeb, M. (1987). "Contingency Theory and Culture: A Study of Matched English and Indian Manufacturing Firms," *Organization Studies*, 8(3), 241–261.

Terpstra, V. and David, K. (1991). *The Cultural Environment of International Business*. 3d Ed. Cincinnati: South-Western.

Tilly, C. (2001). "Welcome to the Seventeenth Century." In DiMaggio, P. (ed.). *The Twenty-First-Century Firm: Changing Economic Organization in International Perspective*. Princeton, NJ: Princeton University Press.

Thompson, J. (1967). *Organizations in Action*. New York: McGraw-Hill.

Trompenaars, F. and Hampton-Turner, C. (1998). *Riding the Waves of Culture: Understanding Diversity in Global Business*. New York: McGraw Hill.

Vernon, R., Wells, L., and Rangan, S. (1996). *The Manager in the International Economy*. Upper Saddle River, NJ: Prentice Hall.

Weber, M. (1946). *Essays in Sociology*. New York: Oxford University Press.

Yoo, S., and Lee, S. (1987). "Management Style and Practice of Korean Chaebols," *California Management Review*, 24(4), 95–109.

CHAPTER 13

Organizational Culture

Learning Objectives

After reading this chapter, you should be able to:

- Define organizational culture and know why it is important.
- Distinguish among organizational, national, and global culture and understand the relationships among them.
- Evaluate the culture-free approach to understanding organizational culture.
- Identify levels of organizational culture.
- Know what organizational culture does.
- Discuss the cultural dimensions and typology approaches to understanding organizational culture.
- Understand how organizational culture can be managed.

CULTURE AT WORK
Old Age Benefits

The server took our order for two shrimp tempura and one assorted sushi. The conversation turned to our experiences as university professors. Our lunch guest, a professor from a German university, started the conversation. "I have been in the School of Business Administration, Department of Public Administration at the University of Mannheim for eight years. Before that I was an Associate Professor at the Free University of Berlin. I received my doctorate from the University of Erlangen-Nurnberg in 1967. I'm fifty-seven years old. My research interests are how public bureaucracies can become more efficient."

My American colleague asked: "Why did you tell us your age? In the United States we would never tell people how old we are."

The German professor explained: "In Germany age determines seniority. As I get older, I get more benefits: a larger office, more administrative support, and more research assistants. This way the distribution of resources is very clear and done fairly."

Source: B. A. Gold

Organizations, like nations, have cultures. Different organizations may have the same objectives—to make DVD players or to provide financial services, for example—but variations in organizational culture differentiate how they pursue these goals. For example, the culture of one financial services company promotes innovation and risk taking, while another firm's culture emphasizes reliability and customer service.

Research into how organizational culture influences organizational behavior has increased dramatically (Cooper, Cartwright, and Earley 2001). The primary reason for interest in organizational culture is that it contributes to the success of many companies. For example, in the automobile industry, Japanese organizational culture, which reflects major themes from Japanese national culture, became an important factor for explaining the superior workmanship and quality in Japanese cars compared with American cars (Cole 1990). Indeed, since the 1980s the role of organizational culture in the automobile industry and its relationship to quality have become so prominent and widely accepted that in June 2003 General Motors (GM) placed advertisements in major publications titled "The Road to Redemption." The ad in the June 8, 2003, issue of the *New York Times Magazine* proclaimed,

> GM presents an overnight success story, a decade in the making.
>
> Ten years ago, we had a choice. We could keep looking in the rearview mirror, or out at the road ahead.
>
> It was the easiest decision we ever made.
>
> The hard part meant breaking out of our own bureaucratic gridlock. Learning some humbling lessons from our competitors. And instilling a true culture of quality in every division, in every department, in every corner of the company.
>
> Today, with quality at the core of our values, we're building the best cars and trucks in our history. GM is now challenging the automotive world in fuel efficiency, advanced emissions controls, styling and design, and manufacturing productivity.
>
> It didn't start yesterday. And it doesn't happen overnight. But last year we launched over twenty new models on the way to posting our second straight year of market share gains. And a whole lot of you rediscovered that an American car can be a great car.
>
> The road to redemption has no finish line. But it does have a corner.
>
> And it's fair to say we've turned it.

General Motors, one of the world's premier corporations, felt compelled by global competition to change its organizational culture to produce higher quality products. In its decision to admit its former quality deficiencies, GM contributed significantly to reasserting the importance of corporate culture as a central concept for understanding organizational behavior and managing change in organizations. From the perspective of international organizational behavior, GM's statement emphasizes that corporate culture, while different from but influenced by national culture, varies across organizations and cultures and is a competitive tool.

▮▮▮ What Is Organizational Culture?

Organizational culture is a pattern of basic assumptions—invented, discovered, or developed by a given group as it learns to cope with its problems of external adaptation and internal integration—that has worked well enough to be considered valid and, therefore, to be taught to new members as the correct way to perceive, think, and feel in relation to those problems. (Schein 1985, p. 9)

Like societal culture, members of an organization often take for granted organizational culture, which is actually a product of secondary socialization (Schutz 1967). It is the "natural" way of understanding the business world and taking action. Because of this, it is difficult for members of an organization to appreciate the impact of corporate culture on their behavior. Similarly, an outsider—such as a foreign businessperson, consultant, or researcher—usually experiences difficulty discovering the basic assumptions that form an unfamiliar organization's culture.

▪▪▪ National and Global Culture

National Culture

National culture, like organizational culture, provides basic assumptions that legitimate and guide behavior. Although they operate in similar ways, many management researchers view the relationship between national and corporate culture as complex (Trice and Beyer 1993).

Other theorists see little, if any, relationship between national and corporate culture and argue that a "logic of industrialization" (Harbison and Myers 1959, p. 117) affects all organizations the same way. In this view, one outcome of economic development, along with modern technology, is to produce organizational cultures and structures that are similar and independent of national culture.

Although the argument is different from the industrialization theory, one study demonstrates that Japanese automobile companies successfully transplanted their organizational cultures and structures to the United States (Florida and Kenney 1991). The environment—national and corporate culture in the United States—did not affect Japanese firms' ability to establish their business practices in a different culture. This study provides support for the view that organizational culture and structure form and operate independently of local or national culture.

An alternative perspective is that national culture and other elements in an organization's environment, determine, to some extent, internal organizational culture. For example, Martin writes,

> It is misleading to deny the influence of the environment on the content of cultures in organizations. The implication, of course, is that *we cannot understand what goes on inside an organizational culture without understanding what exists outside the boundary.* (1992, p. 113)

Precisely how national culture affects organizational culture is not yet totally clear. It is possible that in some cultures—for example, theocracies, which intertwine religion, politics, and culture—the influence on organizational cultures is substantial. In contrast, in secular cultures, which separate religion from other spheres of life, it is possible that the effect on organizational culture is less or takes a different form.

Global Culture

Globalization, increasing awareness of activities in other parts of the world, also affects organizational culture. First, in the global economy many competitors are no longer local or national but global; shoe manufacturers in São Paulo and New York City compete with those in Shanghai for sales worldwide. The extension of the organization's environment creates heightened awareness of innovations, cost competition, and consequently pressure to respond to the organizational practices of international competitors. For example, American industries have borrowed practices, such as just-in-time inventory control and quality circles, that were exclusively part of Japanese corporate culture.

A second global cultural force is communication. Mass media, particularly global advertising, news broadcasts—for example, CNN—and the Internet are mechanisms for the diffusion of deep-rooted enduring social practices that reflect democratic values along with transient consumer preferences. Modern communication also connects manufacturers, merchants, financiers, and consumers more than ever. An important example is the growth of Internet transactions both among businesses as well as between businesses and consumers.

A third element of globalization is the educational systems of economically advanced countries. Higher education and university-based research transfer management ideas and business values globally. Elementary and secondary education are also influential because advanced industrial countries monitor the education their students receive in comparison to other nations (Bracey 1996). This often results in curricular reforms particularly in mathematics, technology, and science education.

Finally, multinational corporations contribute to shaping organizational culture on a global basis through the development and diffusion of their corporate cultures. The management philosophy of McDonald's restaurants in Russia and IKEA's corporate culture, discussed in the next section, illustrate this process.

▪▪▪ Understanding Organizational Culture

One way to understand an organization's culture is to ask people how they get work done in an organization. Moscow State University Professor Oleg Vikhanskii interviewed Glen Steeves, the manager of the first McDonald's to open in Moscow, to discover how McDonald's adjusted to Russian society which had never experienced a fast food restaurant (Puffer 1992).

Vikhanskii asked: "Do you use the same systems and procedures as in other McDonald's restaurants around the world?" Steeves replied:

> Absolutely. The training systems and all the procedures used here are exactly the same as what we use in Canada, Japan, England, or Spain. The procedures are the same as the ones we use everywhere around the world.
>
> Vikhanskii: But Russians' behavior is different from Americans', isn't it? Steeves: I disagree with that. I remember the orientation sessions. People ranged from eighteen to fifty-five years old. Until they started talking, I thought I was back in Canada: they looked the same, they interacted the same, they were smiling, and they had a good time. Our employees take to McDonald's with a passion. They're very proud of what they're doing. What's more, they're very proud of the exciting opportunities.
>
> Have we had to do anything different here because of different attitudes and behavior? No. We applied the same principles here in Moscow as we would in Canada. We have the same training program, and we evaluate employees the same way. We use the same motivational techniques to make it interesting for them. For example, we have crew meetings every three months. This creates a sense of family, a sense of belonging to a specific company. Last summer, for example, we rented one of the large liners on the Moscow River and took them for a cruise. We had a big party with dinner, dancing, and entertainment, and George Cohan [Vice Chairman of Moscow McDonald's and

President and founder of McDonald's Restaurants of Canada] came and talked with the crew members.

Vikhanskii: Can you mention some differences in Russians' attitudes and behaviors? Steeves: We do a great deal of job screening as well as intensive interviewing. We believe we get the best people. Moreover, the training process, motivational system, and reward system certainly prevent attitude and behavior problems from arising in the restaurant. Employees' performance is reviewed every three months in terms of what they do well and how they can improve their performance.

Every month we have some sort of activity going on that makes working here different and special. For instance, we have large parties and dances on a regular basis. We also had a Halloween dance, even though it is not typically practiced in Moscow. The Canadians and the Russian crew members decorated the restaurant, and we all wore costumes and danced. It was just as we would have done in Canada. As George Cohan likes to say, it was a form of cultural exchange between Canadians and Russians.

I have nothing but great respect for the employees. What they do is tremendous. They are working in the busiest restaurant in the world in which there is no end to the line of customers. One of the things that customers mention is not only the quality of the food, but also the quality of the service. On opening day one of our Soviet partners turned to George Cohan and asked, "Where did you get those people?" George Cohan answered, "We got them right here."[1] (Puffer 1992, pp. 279–280)

This interview demonstrates that McDonald's has a strong organizational culture that it developed over many years as the correct, and in its view, the only way to run a business. It applies its organizational culture throughout the world with great success. Indeed, it appears to never cross Steeves' mind that Russians may be different from Canadian, Japanese, or English workers. To him, all national cultures fit McDonald's understanding of effective work practices and organizational culture (see Royle 2000).

McDonald's corporate philosophy illustrates the **culture-free approach** to global management and organizational behavior. Basically, it states that because of technology, policies, rules, organizational structure, and other variables that contribute to efficiency and effectiveness, the role of national culture in shaping organizational behavior, and therefore the need to understand it, is irrelevant for managing succesfully.

An interview with Pavel Ivanov, an assistant manager of the Moscow McDonald's when it opened, suggests, however, that national culture does affect the behavior of McDonald's Russian employees. According to Ivanov, who is now a U.S. citizen, there are distinct differences between McDonald's in Russia and in the United States. For Russians, employment at McDonald's was high status because it offered steady work, comparatively high wages, opportunity for promotion, and free meals. These features not only made a job at McDonald's attractive but difficult to obtain and keep.

In contrast, in the United States, McDonald's is often an employer of last resort. Students and senior citizens take part-time positions and earn minimum wage until a job with better working conditions, pay, and opportunity becomes available. American culture denigrates employment in fast food restaurants with the result that many such restaurants perpetually search for employees.

According to Ivanov, the result of these different cultural orientations is that the service, cleanliness, and quality of food were superior in the Moscow McDonald's

---

[1]Excerpts from Interview between Professor Oleg Vikhansky and Glen Stteves regarding the opening

restaurants compared to those in the United States. This suggests that national culture does affect organizational culture. It is possible, however, that the novelty of McDonald's in Russia could contribute to these differences; as McDonald's becomes more familiar and the Russian economy strengthens, conditions such as those found in the United States could develop.

IKEA, the Swedish furniture company, like McDonald's, has a strong global brand identity and operates 150 stores in 20 countries including China, Iceland, Israel, and Slovakia. It has 70,000 workers and annual sales over 11 billion euros. It started in 1943 as a one-man mail order company in the small farming village of Smaland in the southern part of Sweden and similar to McDonald's, perfected a domestic business model. To grow, because the population of Sweden is small, IKEA exported the model to other countries and has not changed significantly since (Kling and Goteman 2003).

IKEA became distinctive and successful because it turned retailing upside down. Instead of locating small boutique stores in a city as furniture companies traditionally did, IKEA developed huge stores at the outskirts of cities. More importantly, IKEA pioneered the "do-it-yourself" concept of furniture; customers purchase furniture from IKEA's warehouse, then have to transport and assemble it.

In a 2003 interview, IKEA CEO Anders Dahlvig said of IKEA's organizational culture that:

> It's a very informal type of culture. It's based on a few values that have their roots in Smalandish or Swedish culture. Things like informality, cost consciousness, and a very humble and "down to earth" approach. Also letting people have responsibilities. So there are a number of core values and intentions that we always describe in communication and training. For IKEA it has always been one very important part of our culture. We think that the organizational or company culture is important for the business and in some ways for industrial investors. We do give it a lot of attention in terms of marketing and sales as well as development, training, and recruitment. (Kling and Goteman 2003, p. 35)

When asked if different countries or markets had different IKEA corporate culture values, Dahlvig answered:

> Of course there are differences. It has less to do with differences of the national boundaries and different countries. It has more to do with individuals. So there can be big variations between one store and another. Those can actually be bigger than between countries. It has more to do with how the individual managers are. That really influences the culture. Emphasis on culture has to be a fair part of the recruitment phase so that when you recruit someone into the company, this is understood and evaluated when choosing a person. Then as you go along, I would say it's something that has to be a part of the improvement. If you see that a certain behavior is rewarded, which is one way to streamline, the individual can say "These values are not for me" and leave the company. There is no right or wrong, only a question of wanting to be there or not. Do you like to be there or don't you? (Kling and Goteman 2003, p. 35)

In response to a question about the role of values in IKEA's corporate culture, Dahlvig answered,

> I think it's more a question of individuals being different. Certain characteristics may be stronger in some countries, but to see it as a pattern—no. It has never been a problem in the sense that we have not been able to find a manager

in Germany, for example, because Germans are so and so. That has never been the case. (Kling and Goteman 2003, p. 35)

Summarizing the relationship between national and organizational culture, and to some extent explaining the different approaches to the management of organizational culture by McDonald's and IKEA, Trice and Beyer (1993, p. 339) write:

> Neither managers nor researchers can assume that practices from one country will be automatically acceptable in another; at the same time, there are powerful forces within organizations emanating from the logic of organizing and the technologies employed to produce goods and services that undoubtedly pattern behaviors and perhaps some values and beliefs in similar ways across nations and geographical regions. In effect, organizations are culture free in some respects, but culture bound in many others.

Culture—organizational and national—is only one variable for explaining behavior in organizations. Other variables are strategy, size, power, technology, and the noncultural elements of the external environment—for example, political and economic events (see Hodge, Anthony, and Gales 1996). Both McDonald's and IKEA are low technology businesses that sell standardized products through impersonal short-term interactions with customers. Despite these important similarities, the companies have different managerial orientations toward organizational culture.

National cultures distinguish a McDonald's in Moscow from one in Bombay or Brooklyn, or in Saudi Arabia where McDonald's have separate sections for women and children. But McDonald's management does not recognize national cultural differences in its management style and organizational culture which leads it to impose uniformity. In contrast, IKEA experiences and permits a variety of organizational cultures—indeed IKEA's CEO thinks of individual managers as architects of their own organizational cultures—and views them as a natural part of the business and not something that should be uniform across national cultures. However, as indicated in Dahlvig's interview, the employee selection process, corporate socialization, and standardized technology used in IKEA stores throughout the world, exert pressure toward creating a uniform corporate culture.

To explore the role of organizational culture further, we discuss levels of culture in the next section.

▪ ▪ ▪ Levels of Organizational Culture

An image of organizational culture, like national culture, is an iceberg, with some elements above water and others submerged. Elements above water are visible and usually easier to understand than those below water which, while difficult to observe, are often more important for understanding a culture because they comprise its foundation. In addition, elements above water are more amenable to change while the submerged elements are more likely to be resistant and slow to change.

Several differences between national and organizational culture modify the iceberg metaphor. First, organizational culture is less comprehensive than national culture; the range of values and underlying assumptions of organizations are narrower. Second, organizational culture is more self-contained than national culture; management philosophy, strategy, and goals provide organizational boundaries even though elements of national culture influence it. Finally, organizational culture is manageable whereas national culture is not. For example, the selection, training, socialization, and reward structure for employees restricts the variability of its members and constructs a comprehensive set of values and norms that management controls.

As a result, the submerged and visible elements of organizational culture are less likely to be unknown or in conflict, than they would be in national culture. This does not mean, however, that no submerged elements exist, but rather that the line between the submerged and visible elements is extremely porous. For analytical purposes, however, it is useful to separate organizational culture into four levels: artifacts, espoused values, actual values, and basic underlying assumptions (Schein 1990).

Artifacts

Artifacts, the most visible and observable elements of organizational culture, are the concrete aspects of an organization that symbolize its culture. These include material aspects of the organization such as its architecture, physical layout, and decoration.

A second type of artifact is slogans, organizational stories, myths, corporate heroes, rites, rituals, and ceremonies. The organization's members, clients, and general public construct and interpret them. Often, these groups interpret artifacts differently, and multiple meanings of them arise within and outside the organization (Martin 1992).

Many theorists view artifacts as the least representative of the actual culture of an organization. Because it is not difficult to interpret them—although some may be intentionally false or misleading—they are shallow compared with actual values and basic assumptions. Another perspective, however, is that artifacts interact with "deeper" cultural traits in complex ways.

The Culture at Work vignette illustrates an organization ritual—enacted by a rule—and the difficulty interpreting it. Age determines a professor's resources in German universities. Older academics receive larger offices, additional research assistants, and a more generous budget than their younger colleagues. What does this mean? Do the infirmities of old age suggest that older faculty members need more assistance? Does advanced age indicate wisdom and that older faculty use resources more wisely than their younger colleagues? Is it a reward for longevity? Or, is it a bureaucratic device that bypasses the sometimes nasty politics of resource allocation?

Espoused Values

Espoused values are the public values and principles that the organization's leaders announce it intends to achieve. They include mission statements, goals, and ideals. It is possible, of course, that espoused values are not the actual values manifested in organizational behavior. For example, most government officials espouse the value of service to the people who put them in office. Occasionally, however, political figures act on a different set of values and use the government agencies they control to enrich themselves or advance the agenda of interest groups, rather than to benefit their constituents.

Actual Values

When independent, observable behavior validates espoused values, they attain the status of **actual values.** If an organization espouses to have high levels of worker participation in decision making, it should demonstrate that workers actually contribute to decisions. Enacted espoused values reflect the basic underlying assumptions—the deepest level of culture—and also contribute, to some extent, to the construction of artifacts.

Basic Underlying Assumptions

Basic underlying assumptions are unconscious beliefs and values that structure feelings, perceptions, thoughts, and actions that members of a culture view as the only correct understanding of life. Basic assumptions develop through the complex processes of enculturation that include primary and secondary socialization, and result in a specific orientation toward diverse social conventions and understandings of time, space, nature, and human relations. Unlike espoused values, the basic assumptions do not require validation because they are articles of faith.

Generally, while an organization may have basic assumptions and values different from the national culture, the deep structure of national culture makes it unlikely that the organization modifies them extensively. In most instances, corporate culture emphasizes or exaggerates major national cultural themes. Therefore, within a society, basic underlying organizational assumptions and values are relatively similar. An example is that in Japan a fundamental assumption of most corporate cultures is group allegiance. In comparison, in the United States, the values that support an ethic of individual achievement are usually unquestioned.

Identifying and understanding basic assumptions is difficult. Ironically, foreign observers often generate insights into the meaning of the assumptions and values of a culture that are more insightful than native participants. For example, de Tocqueville (2000) in the mid-nineteenth century and Varenne (1977) more than a century later, both French intellectuals, produced some of the most astute observations of the basic values and behaviors of Americans. This may be due, in part, to the sensitivity of outsiders to cultural differences and the inability of insiders to recognize and question their assumptions systematically.

Similarly, concerning organizations, an independent consultant or researcher—an outsider—who does not share the basic assumptions of the organization is likely to understand its value system more accurately than do its members. However, outsiders whose national culture is the same as the organization's experience limitations; they share the assumptions of the national culture in which the organization functions.

During periods of organizational change, however, underlying assumptions become more problematic and visible even to the organization's members. In the organizational change process—particularly a response to external forces—the new values are often the subject of debate and conflict before they become part of a new organizational culture.

Subcultures

The cultures of organizations are not unitary. Whereas basic assumptions permeate an organization, alternative assumptions that either supplement or replace some common assumptions form organizational subcultures. **Subcultures,** shared meanings created and maintained by groups within an organization, reflect the division of labor, including departments, professional expertise, union membership, and position status. Also contributing to subculture formation are age, gender, race, ethnic background, religion, and national culture.

Subcultures contain their own rituals and ceremonies that have distinct meaning for their members and create in-group identification. As informal groups within an organization, subcultures often challenge and conflict with the organization-wide culture. An example is workers who identify with their department or occupation rather than with the entire organization and act to enhance their department at the expense of others.

▪▪▪ What Organizational Culture Does

The Functions of Culture

Organizational culture produces functional behaviors that contribute to organizational goal achievement. It also is a source of dysfunctional behaviors that have adverse effects on organizational success (Robbins 1996).

An important **function of organizational culture** is to distinguish an organization from other organizations and its general environment by providing it with an **external identity.** In a similar way, culture provides an identity for organization members; it locates them within an organizational and occupational structure that is recognizable to themselves and others. Culture also creates a **sense of commitment** to a social entity greater than one's self-interest.

Culture is also a source of **high reliability** in organizations. According to Weick (1987, p. 113):

> a system which values stories, storytellers, and storytelling will be more reliable than a system that derogates these substitutes for trial and error. A system that values stories and storytelling is potentially more reliable because people know more about their system, know more of the potential errors that might occur, and they are more confident that they can handle those errors that do occur because they know that other people have already handled similar errors.

Culture also provides members with an **interpretive scheme,** or way to make sense of the arrangements of positions and activities in an organization (Weick 1995). It acts as a perceptual filter, embodied in stories and myths, that creates meaning of routine, frequently experienced events, as well as unique situations.

Finally, culture is a **social control mechanism.** Through culture—particularly a strong, effective culture—the organization defines the reality that organization members experience. It socializes new members into a particular way of doing things and periodically resocializes its long-term members. For example, organizational rites and ceremonies reward and reinforce desired behavior as well as demonstrate and legitimate the organizational power structure.

The Dysfunctions of Culture

The major **dysfunction**—negative outcome—of organizational culture is that it can create **barriers to change.** A strong organizational culture provides members with an explicit set of behaviors that have worked well in the past. Of course, the expectation is that these behaviors will be effective in the future. Paradoxically, a strong culture can produce rigidity in the organization, preventing appropriate modifications to new conditions.

For example, the International Business Machine Corporation (IBM), which developed a strong corporate culture, became hostage to it. IBM had specially designed notebooks for "taking notes at IBM meetings, with spaces at the bottom of each page for two witnesses to sign off" (Hays 1995, p. 1). This practice grew out of the culture of efficiency but symbolizes the extent to which IBM's culture became absorbed in trivial rules instead of cultivating innovation and change.

Of course, an organizational culture that resists change is not a problem in national cultures that value a time orientation toward the past and seek stability rather than change. A strong, change-resistant culture is also not a central issue for organizations that operate in stable environments that require repetitive, predictable, reliable performance.

Another dysfunction of culture is that it can create **conflict within the organization.** As noted previously, subcultures often emerge in organizations. Subcultures may become so cohesive that they develop values that are distinctive enough to separate the subgroup from the rest of the organization. For example, a research and development department may be oriented toward conducting basic research, a professional value orientation, ignoring the development of new products the organization can manufacture.

Another type of dysfunctional behavior is that subcultures can change at different rates than other units in the organization. This results in reduced internal coordination that adversely affects external relations. For instance, an information technologies department can introduce computer systems that are beyond the skills of average employees. Even with training, workers can resist the new technology or experience a long learning period. Related to this, change-oriented subcultures can experience conflict with subcultures that do not value change. This prevents them from exploring novel solutions for organizational problems.

Organizational cultures can also clash when two companies merge. DaimlerChrysler, the result of the initially equal merger between Daimler Benz, the German luxury auto manufacturer, and Chrysler, one of the "Big Three" American auto companies, ran into difficulties soon after the merger was completed. Part of the problem was difficulty blending the strong cultures of each company. Even after several years, Jurgen Schrempp, DaimlerChrysler's Chief Executive, was actively working to find ways to integrate the two cultures. One barrier was that Daimler was reluctant to divulge its technology secrets to Chrysler (Boudette 2003).

Finally, as a result of globalization, organizational cultures can become a "cultural Tower of Babel" (Deal and Kennedy 1999) because many organizations have not learned to manage the different cultures represented by their employees in domestic and international locations. Cultural differences such as language and orientation toward work often produce conflict. In addition, even slight variations in cultures often accelerate the erosion of previously stable organizational cultures caused by downsizing, mergers, and other rapid organization changes that disrupt or prevent the development of cohesive organizational cultures.

▐▐▐ Analyzing Organizational Culture

Two methods for analyzing organizational culture are to examine the dimensions of an organization's culture within the context of the general culture and to develop an organizational culture typology.

Dimensions of Organizational Culture

Dimensions of national culture are also useful for analyzing organizational culture. Adapting Kluckhohn and Strodtbeck's framework to organizational culture, Schein (1990, 1992) identifies the following dimensions: (1) the organization's relationship to its environment, (2) the nature of human activity, (3) the nature of reality and truth, (4) the nature of time, (5) the nature of human nature, (6) the nature of human relationships, and (7) homogeneity versus diversity.

Each dimension has associated questions (see Table 13-1). For example, the relationship of the organization to its environment emerges through questioning members about whether the organization perceives itself as dominant, submissive, or harmonizing in relation to its environment. Similarly, for the dimension of time, relevant questions concern organizational orientation toward the past, present, and future.

TABLE 13-1 Some Underlying Dimensions of Organizational Culture

Dimension	*Questions to be answered*
1. The organization's relationship to its environment	Does the organization perceive itself to be dominant, submissive, harmonizing, searching out a niche?
2. The nature of human activity	Is the "correct" way for humans to behave to be dominant/proactive, harmonizing, or passive/fatalistic?
3. The nature of reality and truth	How do we define what is true and what is not true; and how is truth ultimately determined, both in the physical and social world?
4. The nature of time	What is our basic orientation in terms of past, present, and future, and what kinds of time units are most relevant for the conduct of daily affairs?
5. The nature of human nature	Are humans basically good, neutral, or evil, and is human nature perfectible or fixed?
6. The nature of human relationships	What is the "correct" way for people to relate to each other, to distribute power and affection? Is life competitive or cooperative? Is the best way to organize society on the basis of individualism or groupism? Is the best authority system autocratic/paternalistic or collegial/participative?
7. Homogeneity versus diversity	Is the group best off if it is highly diverse or if it is highly homogeneous? Should individuals in a group be encouraged to innovate or conform?

Source: Table adapted from Schein, E. H. (1985). *Organizational Culture and Leadership*. San Francisco: Jossey-Bass, p. 86.

The dimensions have different values because answers to the questions vary within and across cultures. Organizational cultures within a country are likely to vary less than those across countries. Subsidiaries of multinational and global corporations experience variation based on the cultures of countries where they operate.

The result is a paradigm or configuration that specifies patterns among the dimensions and explains how the organization's culture affects behavior in the organization. It also provides a way to understand the influences of the organization on its external environment and the environment's influences on the organizational culture.

A Cross-Cultural Typology

Another approach to understanding organizational culture is to identify specific types of organizational cultures in different countries. This strategy assumes that "differences between national cultures help determine the type of corporate culture 'chosen'" (Trompenaars 1994, p. 152), rather than variations in technology, economic systems, or other factors. It differs from Schein's approach in that it (1) focuses more on internal organizational variables—for example, the authority system; (2) develops only four organizational culture types; and (3) links the types to specific national cultures.

According to Trompenaars and Hampton-Turner (1998), organizational cultures are one of four analytical types: family, Eiffel Tower, guided missile, and incubator. Table 13-2 presents the variables and characteristics of each type.

TABLE 13-2 Characteristics of Trompenaars and Hampton-Turner's Four Corporate Cultures

Variables	Family	Eiffel Tower	Guided Missile	Incubator
Relationships between employees	Diffuse relationships to organic whole to which one is bonded	Specific role in mechanical system of required interactions	Specific tasks in cybernetic system targeted upon shared objectives	Diffuse, spontaneous relationships growing out of shared creative process
Attitude towards authority	Status is ascribed to parent figures who are close and powerful	Status is ascribed to superior roles which are distant yet powerful	Status is achieved by project group members who contribute to targeted goal	Status is achieved by individuals exemplifying creativity and growth
Ways of thinking and learning	Intuitive, holistic, lateral, and error-correcting	Logical, analytical, vertical, and rationally efficient	Problem centered, professional, practical, cross-disciplinary	Process oriented, creative, adhoc, inspirational
Attitudes towards people	Family members	Human resources	Specialists and experts	Co-creators
Ways of Changing	"Father" changes course	Change rules and procedures	Shift aim as target moves	Improvise and attune
Ways of motivating and rewarding	Intrinsic satisfaction in being loved and respected	Promotion to greater position, larger role	Pay or credit for performance and problems solved	Participating in the process of creating new realities
Management style	Management by subjectives	Management by job description	Management by objectives	Management by enthusiasm
Criticism and conflict resolution	Turn other cheek, save others' faces, do not lose power game	Criticism is accusation of irrationalism unless there are procedures to arbitrate conflicts	Constructive task-related only, then admit error fast and correct	Must improve creative idea, not negate it

Source: Table from Trompenaars, F. and Hampton-Turner, C. (1999). *Riding the Waves of Culture: Understanding Diversity in Global Business.* 2d Ed. New York: McGraw-Hill, pp. 161–183.

Family Culture

Family organizational culture emphasizes personal, face-to-face relationships. It is hierarchical with an authority structure based on power differentials commonly experienced between parents and children. According to Trompenaars and Hampton-Turner

> The result is a power-oriented corporate culture in which the leader is regarded as a caring parent who knows better than his subordinates what should be done and what is good for them. Rather than being threatening, this type of power is essentially intimate and benign. The work of the corporation in this type of culture is usually carried forward in an atmosphere that in many respects mimics the home. (1998, p. 163)

The Japanese create a family organizational culture in many of their corporations. Other cultures with similar arrangements are in nations that industrialized relatively late, creating a rapid transition from feudalism to industrialism. France, Belgium, India, Greece, Italy, Singapore, South Korea, Japan, and Spain are examples of nations that prefer family corporate cultures (Trompenaars 1994; Trompenaars and Hampton-Turner 1998).

Eiffel Tower Culture

Eiffel Tower culture is a classic bureaucratic structure. It emphasizes a division of labor and coordination through a hierarchy of authority and relies on planning to accomplish its goals. Trompenaars and Hampton-Turner distinguish it from the family culture, where the authority structure is diffuse, based on the observation:

> Each higher level has a clear and demonstrable function holding together the levels beneath it. You obey the boss because it is his or her role to instruct you. The rational purpose of the corporation is conveyed to you through him. He has legal authority to tell you what to do, and your contract of service, overtly or implicitly, obliges you to work according to his instructions. If you and other subordinates did not do so, the system could not function. (1998, p. 171)

A central characteristic of this organization is replacement of individual human qualities with the idea of a **social role,** a position governed by impersonal rules and norms. The source of status is the role, not personal attributes. Change in a bureaucratic organization occurs with changes in the roles and rules. Because reorganization threatens the established culture, change usually meets with resistance. Employees become comfortable with the roles they occupy and the authority of their position. New roles and norms create the possibility of reduced status and norms that circumscribe behavior in unwelcome ways—for example, by increasing accountability for performance by readjusting hierarchical relations. In Trompenaars' view, the Eiffel Tower type is characteristic of corporate cultures in Denmark, the Netherlands, and Germany.

Guided Missile Culture

Guided missile culture differs from the family and Eiffel Tower cultures because it is egalitarian. However, it is impersonal and task oriented, resembling the Eiffel Tower culture. "Indeed," write Trompenaars and Hampton-Turner,

> . . . the guided missile culture is rather like the Eiffel Tower in flight. But while the rationale of the Eiffel Tower culture is means, the guided missile has a rationale of ends. Everything must be done to persevere in your strategic intent and reach your target.

The guided missile culture is oriented to tasks, typically undertaken by teams or project groups. It differs from the role culture in that the jobs of members are not fixed in advance. They must do whatever it takes to complete a task, and what is needed is often unclear and may have to be discovered. (1998, p. 177)

This culture is egalitarian because it employs experts in technical fields. Experts work on projects together rather than take directives from superiors. Technical expertise reduces emotional elements in the culture, producing a bureaucratic culture based on knowledge rather than position, as in the Eiffel Tower, or on emotional ties, as in the family culture. Guided missile culture flourishes in the United States, Canada, and the United Kingdom.

Incubator Culture

The **incubator culture** is radically different from the other cultures; it attempts to minimize organizational structure and culture. It develops with this mind-set: "If organizations are to be tolerated at all, they should be there to serve as incubators for self-expression and self-fulfillment" (Trompenaars and Hampton-Turner 1998, p. 179). Minimal organizational structure facilitates a culture that is egalitarian, personal, and highly creative. In most cases, incubator cultures are in knowledge and science industries such as computer software development firms. This type of organizational culture is prevalent in Silicon Valley, California, and on Route 128 near Boston in the United States, and in Sweden where automobile manufacturing systems create a culture to enhance the intellectual and physical conditions of work.

These four cultures are ideal types—mental constructs that represent "pure" organizational cultures. In reality, most societies contain mixtures of them. For example, in Canada, the United Kingdom, and the United States, which Trompenaars and Hampton-Turner characterize as Guided Missile–types, many organizations have family or incubator cultures. In addition, many organizations contain multiple culture types within them, for example, a guided missile and an incubator culture. Usually, however, one type characterizes the entire organization more than the others.

▪ ▪ ▪ Managing and Changing Organizational Culture

Leadership and Organizational Culture

Can leaders manage organizational culture? The answer depends on whom you ask. Edgar Schein, an influential theorist of organizational culture, maintains that the central role of an organizational leader is to create, manage, and when necessary, destroy an organization's culture (Schein 1985). The destruction of culture is necessary to create organizational change by establishing a new culture. This view suggests that organizational cultures are rational, manageable entities.

Another answer is that, "the part that leadership plays in organizational cultures has not been systematically explored" (Trice and Beyer 1993, p. 255). Many models of organizational culture and the role of leadership in managing are anecdotal and prescriptive instead of based on scientific investigation. Consequently, it is not known if organizational culture can be managed effectively.

A third response is that organizational cultures contain significant amounts of **nonrational elements,** behavior not grounded in empirical data or distorted to serve a particular group's interests. These include destructive or negative emotions, erroneous beliefs, and idiosyncratic interpretations of the organization's past, present, and future. They often result in smoldering resentments and prolonged overt conflicts at the individual, group, and organizational levels.

Nonrational elements of organizational culture can be dysfunctional by impeding goal attainment. For example, during periods of organizational innovation, they are often barriers to change. Leaders are frequently unable to shape or otherwise control nonrational and other aspects of organizational culture.

Elements of Culture Leaders Can Change

Even if the leader is not central to creating and managing organizational culture, a leader can affect organizational culture in a variety of ways. For example, a leader can change the selection criteria for people to become organization members. This could involve raising the educational level of new entrants, selecting people more or less representative of the population in terms of race, ethnicity, age, and gender, or hiring only the leader's friends and relatives.

Similarly, a leader can change the socialization of organizational members including reformulating training programs and introducing new managerial philosophies and values. For example, in industrialized countries in recent years, new hires and existing employees attend workshops to improve their contributions to product and service quality. Also, movement toward decentralized organizations that emphasize worker empowerment represent a shift in managerial philosophy that influences organizational culture.

Leaders can also change the meaning of work in an organizational culture. Their interpretations of ceremonies, rituals, stories, and organizational heroes can fit new circumstances and provide new meanings to adapt an organization to changing external environments. An example is IBM's dress code change. IBM built a reputation of corporate efficiency symbolized by its employees' dark, three-piece business suits. This image became dysfunctional in the early 1990s when it became apparent that IBM had failed to adapt to a rapidly changing global business environment. It symbolized rigidity and inability to change rather than its intended message. In an attempt to change the corporate culture, IBM introduced more casual dress for its employees that symbolized its desire to be flexible and in touch with the times.

Even by using sophisticated managerial tools, a leader may not be able to change the underlying assumptions of an organization. Most organizational theorists conclude that it is difficult to change the deeper levels of organizational culture (Hofstede 2001; Deal and Kennedy 1999; Hofstede, Neuijen, Ohayv, and Sanders 1990). Most prominently, Schien, who as previously noted, was originally optimistic about a leader's ability to create deep changes in organizational culture—including continuous organizational learning—has recently expressed reservations concerning the ability of organizations to learn and change in fundamental ways (Coutu 2002). For example, changing from a risk-averse to a risk-seeking organizational culture is extremely difficult, particularly if the national culture is not supportive. Similarly, in an ascriptive national culture with hiring and promotion based on close interpersonal relationships, it would be difficult to change to an achievement-based organizational culture. As these examples suggest, because important societal values shape organizational culture and become basic assumptions that are unconscious, it is difficult to raise them to a level of consciousness to initiate the organization change process. It is even more difficult to implement and sustain significant change when challenges to basic assumptions are part of the change process.

It is clear, however, that leaders can change the artifacts or surface manifestations of organizational culture. Changes at this level include developing new corporate images—including logos, buildings, and dress codes—the elimination of corporate status symbols such as parking spaces reserved for executives, and promoting renewed attention to customers.

International managers can manage foreign subsidiaries to accommodate local organizational cultures or change them by attempting to establish the headquarters' organizational culture. As noted previously, Japanese automobile companies have successfully transplanted their organizational culture to manufacturing facilities in the United States (Florida and Kenney 1991).

Instead of directly changing organizational culture, an alternative approach is to create culture change by changing organizational structure. By rearranging positions within an organization, for example, increasing or decreasing the levels in a hierarchy, elements of organizational culture change. However, change often occurs in an organization's structural arrangements but fails to change its culture or individual worker behavior (Elmore, Peterson, and McCarthey 1996).

In summary, managers can change organizational culture by using an array of techniques along with general secondary socialization processes. But planned organizational culture change—like any type of change—encounters resistance and implementation difficulties that often produce unintended consequences.

▪▪▪ Convergence or Divergence?

Forces for Convergence

There are social, economic, and technological forces that have been present for decades that tend to produce similar organizational cultures throughout the world. The most powerful factor is industrialization. Along with technological innovations, bureaucratic administration usually accompanies industrialization. Bureaucratization creates a distinctive organizational culture characterized by an emphasis on standardization of performance. It also contains several dysfunctions, however, including inability to adapt to changing conditions and an inflexible hierarchy. But some theorists argue that the hierarchic structure of bureaucracy is not dysfunctional and that the benefits of bureaucracy are underappreciated (Jaques 1990).

Another factor contributing to convergence is organizational strategies for managing culture. Hoecklin (1995) identified four ways multinational corporations can manage cultural differences: (1) build a strong corporate culture internationally, (2) develop a common technical or professional culture worldwide, (3) rely on strong financial or planning systems, and (4) leave each corporate culture alone.

Of the four strategies, the first two are likely to produce policies and rules encouraging uniform cultures. The third one, strong financial or planning systems, could also affect culture if these systems extend beyond the organization's technical production. In summary, with the growth of multinational corporations, it is likely that organizations themselves will produce pressures toward the convergence of organizational cultures.

Forces for Divergence

One force for divergence is the use of organizational culture as a competitive tool. Many companies attempt to create unique cultures that foster innovation, competitiveness, or a relationship with customers that distinguishes them from their competitors (Guillén 2001).

A second force creating divergence is national culture. This manifests itself in the emergence of preferences for doing things in specific, culturally expressive ways (Guillén 2001). An example is the collectivist culture of the Israeli kibbutz that attempts to create an egalitarian work environment (Bar-Hayim and Berman 1991). Another example is the Japanese cultural preference for group orientation that Western cultures experience difficulty adapting (Ouchi, 1981). A final example is experimentation with humanistic work designs in the Swedish automobile industry that have not diffused to other cultures (Ellegard et al. 1992).

Implications for Managers

International managers should be as familiar with different organizational cultures as they are with differences in national cultures. They cannot assume that organizational cultures in other countries are the same as the culture of their organization. Consequently, they must analyze organizational cultures to be able to coordinate activities with them or change them.

Managers must understand what levels of organizational culture they can influence. For example, it is unlikely that international managers can change the basic assumptions of an organizational culture in a national culture that is significantly different from their own. However, it is possible that they can change and manage culture at the artifact level.

Managers also must know how an organization's culture can influence them. For example, organizational culture can affect managers by either supporting or undermining management initiatives. Cultures with values different from a manager's are unlikely to be supportive and require appropriate adjustments.

SUMMARY

Organizational culture is an important factor shaping behavior in organizations. An alternative viewpoint is that culture plays a small role in determining the functioning of an organization and that processes such as industrialization are universal and cut across cultures. Another viewpoint is that organizational culture is not unique but closely related to national culture because organizational boundaries do not prevent the values and behavior of the surrounding culture from influencing it.

Organizational culture exists on several levels in organizations, ranging from observable artifacts to difficult-to-detect basic assumptions. These features construct a culture that can either be functional or dysfunctional for the organization.

One approach to understanding organizational culture is a typology such as Trompenaars and Hampton-Turner's family, Eiffel Tower, guided missile, and incubator cultures. They suggest that certain types of organizational culture develop more predominately in different national cultures.

Although there is little agreement as to what extent culture is manageable, organizational leaders can influence the entrance and socialization of new members, and interpret stories and rituals important to the organization. These are key components of culture creation and maintenance. The leader can also change the organization's culture by attempting to reframe the underlying assumptions.

The prospect of organizational cultures becoming more alike or dissimilar depends on the evolution of national cultures. Movement toward more homogeneous national cultures—which to many observers of business trends appears unlikely—would probably result in similar organizational cultures.

It is important for managers to understand organizational culture in order to coordinate activities within the organization. Managers also should know how organizational culture influences their behavior.

DISCUSSION QUESTIONS ▪▪▪▪▪▪▪

1. Define organizational culture.
2. What is the relationship among organizational, national, and global cultures?
3. Why are basic assumptions considered by many theorists to be the deepest level of organizational culture?
4. Discuss the argument that organizations are culture-free.
5. Could you use Trompenaars and Hampton-Turner's typology of organizational cultures to analyze organizations in your country? If yes, how?
6. Is it possible to prevent some of the dysfunctional aspects of organizational culture, such as resistance to change, from occurring?
7. What are some of the elements of organizational culture that a leader can change?
8. In your view, are the cultures of organizations becoming more alike, staying about the same, or under pressure to become distinctive from each other? Why?

INTERNET SITES ▪▪▪▪▪▪▪

Selected Companies in the Chapter

General Motors (www.gm.com)
International Business Machines (www.ibm.com/us)
IKEA (www.ikea.com)

Organizational Culture Sites

Organizational Culture (www.mapnp.org/library/org_thry/culture/culture.htm). This site contains definitions, types of culture, and links to numerous organizational culture sites.

Corporate Culture Diagnosis (www2.inc.com/leadership_and_strategy/advice/23312.html). This site is a 15-question survey designed to help you diagnose and understand your school or corporate culture. When you are done with the survey, think about how useful a survey is compared with direct observation of an organizational culture.

NDMA Management Consultants (www.ndma.com/products/cu/cu.htm). This Web page takes an extremely practical approach to organizational culture. It claims that "Culture in action teaches the specific behaviors that are expected of everyone in the organization."

REFERENCES ▪▪▪▪▪▪▪

Bar-Hayim, A. and Berman, G. (1991). "Ideology, Solidarity, and Work Values: The Case of the Histadrut Enterprises," *Human Relations*. 44(4), 357–370.

Boudette, N. E. (2003). "At DaimlerChrysler, a New Push to Make its Units Work Together," *Wall Street Journal*, March 12, 1.

Bracey, G. (1996). "International Comparisons and the Condition of American Education," *Educational Researcher*, 25(1), 5–11.

Cole, R. (1990). "U.S. Quality Improvement in the Auto Industry: Close but No Cigar," *California Management Review*, 32, 4.

Cooper, C. L., Cartwright, S., and Earley, P. C. (eds.) (2001). *The International Handbook of*
Organizational Culture and Climate. West Sussex, England: John Wiley & Sons.

Coutu, D, L. (2002). "The Anxiety of Learning," *Harvard Business Review,* March, 2–8.

Deal, T. E. and Kennedy, A. A. (1999). *The New Corporate Cultures: Revitalizing the Workplace after Downsizing, Mergers, and Reengineering.* Cambridge, MA: Perseus.

Ellegard, K., Jonsson, D., Enstrom, T., Johansson, M., Medbo, L., Johansson, B. (1992). "Reflective Production in the Final Assembly of Motor Vehicles: An Emerging Swedish Challenge," *International Journal of Operations & Production Management.* 12(7/8), 117–33.

Elmore, R., Peterson, P., and McCarthey, S. (1996). *Restructuring in the Classroom: Teaching, Learning, & School Organization*. San Francisco: Jossey-Bass.

Florida, R. and Kenney, M. (1991). "Transplanted Organizations: The Transfer of Japanese Industrial Organization to the U.S.," *American Sociological Review*, 56: 381–98.

Guillén, M. F. (2001). *The Limits of Convergence: Globalization and Organizational Change in Argentina, South Korea, and Spain*. Princeton, NJ: Princeton University Press.

Harbison, F. and Myers, C. (1959). *Management in the Industrial World: An International Study*. New York: McGraw-Hill.

Hays, L. (1995). "Manzi Quits at IBM and His Many Critics Are Not at All Surprised," *Wall Street Journal*, 1.

Hodge, B., Anthony, W., and Gales, L. (1996). *Organization Theory: A Strategy Approach*. Upper Saddle River, NJ: Prentice Hall.

Hoecklin, L. (1995). *Managing Cultural Differences: Strategies for Competitive Advantage*. Reading, MA: Addison-Wesley.

Hofstede, G. (2001). *Culture's Consequences: Comparing Values, Behaviors, Institutions, and Organizations Across Nations*. 2d Ed. Thousand Oaks, CA: Sage.

——, Neuijen, B., Ohayv, D., and Sanders, G. (1990). "Measuring Organizational Cultures: A Qualitative and Quantitative Study Across Twenty Cases," *Administrative Science Quarterly*, 35.

Jaques, E. (1990). "In Praise of Hierarchy," *Harvard Business Review*. January–February.

Kling, K. and Goteman, I. (2003). "IKEA CEO Anders Dahlvig on International Growth and IKEA's Unique Corporate Culture and Brand Identity," *Academy of Management Executive*, 17(1), 31–7.

Martin, J. (1992). *Cultures in Organizations: Three Perspectives*. New York: Oxford University Press.

Puffer, S. (ed.) (1992). *The Russian Management Revolution: Preparing Managers for the Market Economy*. Armonk, NY: Sharpe.

Robbins, S. (1996). *Organizational Behavior: Concepts, Controversies, Applications*. Upper Saddle River, NJ: Prentice Hall.

Royle, T. (2000). *Working for McDonald's in Europe: The Unequal Struggle?* New York: Routledge.

Schein, E. (1985). *Organizational Culture and Leadership*. San Francisco: Jossey-Bass.

——. (1990). "Organizational Culture," *American Psychologist*, 45(2), 109–19.

——. (1992) *Organizational Culture and Leadership*, 2d Ed. San Francisco: Jossey-Bass.

Schutz, A. (1967). *The Problem of Social Reality*. The Hague: Martinus Nijhoff.

Tocqueville, A. (2000). *Democracy in America*. Chicago: University of Chicago Press.

Trice, H. and Beyer, J. (1993). *The Cultures of Work Organizations*. Upper Saddle River, NJ: Prentice Hall.

Trompenaars, F. (1994). *Riding the Waves of Culture: Understanding Cultural Diversity in Global Business*. New York: Irwin.

—— and Hampden-Turner, C. (1998). *Riding the Waves of Culture: Understanding Cultural Diversity in Global Business*. 2d Ed. New York: McGraw-Hill.

Varenne, H. (1977). *Americans Together: Structured Diversity in a Midwestern Town*. New York: Teachers College Press.

Weick, K. (1987). "Organizational Culture as a Source of High Reliability," *California Management Review*, 29(2), 112–27.

—— (1995). *Sensemaking in Organizations*. Thousand Oaks, CA: Sage Publications.

CHAPTER 14

Organizational Change

Learning Objectives

After reading this chapter, you should be able to:

■ Define organizational change and understand why managing organizational change is an important part of international management.

■ Understand the individual, group, and structural levels of change.

■ Know what internal and external factors influence organizational change.

■ Explain the role of national and organizational culture on organizational stability and change.

■ Understand the processes involved in planned organizational change, including sources of resistance to change and ways to overcome them.

■ Understand how macro level theories of organizational change influence the management of change.

CULTURE AT WORK

Another Change?

In November 1995, the 33 members of Jani Hanson's contract compliance department at AT & T had to fill out a form asking them to supply their individual job history, current job responsibilities, and a justification for retaining their jobs. For Jani and her coworkers—along with other AT & T workers across the United States—it was the first step in the planned reduction of 40,000 employees. A few months earlier, AT & T's CEO had announced one of the largest corporate restructurings in history. In the next year, AT & T would split into three separate companies to become more competitive in the global economy.

For Jani it was a stressful time. When she graduated from college six years earlier, she considered herself extremely lucky to get a job at AT & T. It was a cutting-edge company with a sophisticated corporate culture, and she expected long-term employment there. But as she filled out the employment history form—after eight different jobs within the company in six years—she found herself becoming anxious. Jani enjoyed her job and considered AT & T a good employer. She wanted to stay with the company in New Jersey. Also, she and her boyfriend were thinking about getting married and buying a condominium.

> In January 1996 Jani's supervisor told her that she still had a job with AT & T—in Chicago. Relocating was difficult but better than unemployment; the restructuring terminated one-third of her department. Jani, reflecting on her experience, concluded, "I have a job—at least until the next restructuring."
>
> *Source:* B. A. Gold

Organizations throughout the world are undergoing rapid changes. Recent large-scale changes include the increased globalization of corporations and privatization of industries in former communist countries. Other recent changes, though less dramatic than the fall of communism, have had significant implications for organizations, including the ubiquity of e-mail and the Internet, international quality standards, network forms of organization, and increasing levels of collaboration between business organizations that were formerly competitors. Organization change is so prevalent that the management of change has become a major part of every international manager's responsibilities.

But initiating, managing, and sustaining large-scale organization change is not easy. The dot-com phenomenon that greeted the 21st century illustrates vividly the difficulty of changing organizations and sustaining change. The dot-com explosion was initiated by the convergence of multiple communication technologies followed by a rapid implosion that was caused in part by overcapacity, inadequate management, and, ironically, the inability to create organization change fast enough to adapt to environmental challenges. Whatever the cause, the dot-com bubble may be a temporary set back, not the failure of a new form of organization. However, despite the predictions of many management analysts, brick-and-mortar organizations did not collapse from the onslaught of Internet-facilitated virtual commerce (Hamel 2000; Kanter 2001). Whatever the eventual impact the Internet has on organizations, it is a change that affects organizations throughout the world because it transcends national boundaries (Kogut 2003).

Reflecting the uncertainty of the future impact of the Internet on organizations, management research provides significantly different views of the current state of organizations (DiMaggio 2001). While some researchers think that organizations have changed from rigid hierarchies that stifle workers into flexible structures that empower employees, others view organizations as becoming more hierarchical and reducing workers to performing work on a temporary contract arrangement. Because of the multiple changes occurring simultaneously, it is difficult to discern a single trend. A few years ago it appeared that the Internet would replace many traditional forms of organization in an historic shift. A few years later, it is clear that multiple types of organizations exist throughout the world and will probably persist for a long time. The implication of this is that an array of organization types is available that existing organizations could either intentionally change to, or through selection processes evolve toward (Aldrich 1999; Burke 2002; DiMaggio 2001; Kogut 2003; Pettigrew and Fenton 2000; Vallas 2003).

To manage change effectively, it is necessary to understand the influences of societal and organizational culture on organizations. For example, some cultures and organizations have an orientation toward the future and adapt fairly easily to change—under some circumstances they may be proactive toward change—whereas other cultures and organizations seek to preserve traditional behavior and actively resist change.

While the focus of this chapter is the influence of culture on organization change, issues other than culture affect change. Do organizations change as a result of changes in their environments? Does change occur because organizations have life-cycles? Or, do they change in rationally planned ways under the guidance of managers?

▪▪▪ What Is Organizational Change?

Planned organizational change reconfigures components of an organization to increase efficiency and effectiveness. Change typically occurs at the individual, group, or organization level, and each level usually, but not necessarily, initiates change as the result of the reformulation of organizational goals. Because organizations are systems—the various components of an organization interact—change in one area affects other areas to some extent, including unanticipated outcomes. However, organization structure change influences group and individual change more than changes in individuals and groups affect the organization structure.

Individual Change

Individual change occurs when the behavior of a person is different as a result of new information, training, experience, or rearrangement of an organization's structure. The Culture at Work vignette illustrates individual change created by structural change. AT & T, like many other large companies, changed frequently, creating continuous uncertainty for employees. As a result, Jani's attitude toward the corporation changed, and she felt less secure in her job and consequently less company loyalty. In addition, Jani and other AT & T employees experienced change as individuals because their roles, including job descriptions and responsibilities, were different after the organization restructured.

Group Change

Group change can take several forms including new leadership, increased or diminished cohesiveness, and transition into a team. One type of group change is development through either a series of rational stages, for example, forming, storming, norming, performing, adjourning (Tuckman and Jensen 1977) or one rapid, dramatic change or punctuation (Gersick 1988). An example of planned group change is the introduction of a continuous quality improvement program such as Total Quality Management (TQM). To implement TQM successfully, a group changes into a team, shares responsibility and accountability, and learns how to initiate, manage, and sustain its own change process when necessary.

Structural Change

Organization structure change is the deliberate rearrangement of the positions, departments, or other major units of an organization. For example, over the next decades many firms in the People's Republic of China plan to become multinational conglomerates. To accomplish this, private firms and large state-owned monopolies are forming groups that share senior management. These large groups, often headed by former government officials, receive preferential access to financing, stock market listings, and government-regulated areas of industry and trade (Kahn 1995; Tang and Ward 2003). Large size increases the power of an organization's management.

Senior Chinese managers believe that these changes will enable them to compete more effectively in the global marketplace. At the same time that the Chinese initiated these structural changes, many Western companies are restructuring through downsizing and decentralization to become more competitive. The management theory that supports the change to smaller organizations is that large-scale conglomerates are not able to respond rapidly to changing market conditions.

Recent experiences of the German telephone company provide an example of the reasons for and difficulties of organizational level change. Germany, renowned for its manufacturing excellence, never developed the business practice of responsiveness to customers. Deutsche Telekom AG, the German telephone monopoly, typically kept people waiting for years to have a phone installed, and its customers learned to accept inferior service (Steinmetz 1995).

To change this situation, the German government privatized the phone company to improve it through competition. To create change, the company hired an industry outsider, Ron Sommer, formerly of the Sony Corporation. In addition to upgrading the system's equipment, Sommer eliminated one-quarter of the workforce and, through improved training, attempted to refocus the remaining employees more directly on customers (Steinmetz 1995).

These basic changes were not easy to accomplish. In addition to extensive government regulations—for example, telephone lines had to be laid underground, not hung from poles—the employees were government workers and each was entitled to a 35 1/2 hour workweek and a six-week annual vacation. These and other employment conditions made it difficult to increase worker productivity and control costs.

Although Sommer succeeded in creating some changes, he was not able to transform Deutsche Telecom from a state monopoly into a global communication giant. In July 2002, under pressure from German Chancellor Gerhard Schroder, who feared that Deutsche Telekom's plummeting share price would adversely affect his reelection, Ron Sommer resigned. At the same time, the telecommunications industry throughout the world experienced severe financial difficulties due to overexpansion, overcapacity, changes in cellular telephones, and aggressive competition within and across national borders. In 2002 Deutsche Telekom posted a loss of 24.6 billion euros, the biggest corporate loss in Europe's history (Eakin 2003).

These examples demonstrate that change occurs at various organizational levels and that a variety of factors initiate and influence the change process. They also demonstrate that change is usually a long-term, complex, and often failure prone process.

▪▪▪ Sources of Organizational Change

Two sources of organizational change are internal and external factors. They interact with the national culture, organizational culture, management philosophy, and organization structure to produce either minor adjustments or major changes in individual roles, group performance, or the entire organization.

Internal Change Factors

Internal change factors are an organization's technical production system, political processes, and culture (Tichy 1983). At times these factors exert strong and direct pressures for change. At other times, when the organization is in equilibrium, internal factors maintain organizational stability but retain the potential for creating change.

Technical Production Processes

Sources of change in the **technical production system,** which involves core transformation processes, include the following:

- *Production.* These include problems such as high personnel turnover, inadequate training, coordination difficulties between organizational units, high rates of waste, and downtime because of machinery malfunctions.
- *New technologies.* The introduction of a new technology can change patterns of behavior within an organization. In addition to displacing workers and requiring retraining, a new technology can rearrange the organization's power structure. For example, workers skilled in a new technology often acquire higher status.
- *Quality.* Many variables contribute to the quality of a product—including materials, design, and assembly—making quality problems difficult to detect and possibly located throughout the organization.

Political Processes

Sources of change in the organization's **political processes,** the distribution of power, include the following:

- *New organizational goals.* New goals realign the organization's resources and produce a series of changes throughout the organization, including increasing the power of groups whose interests the new goals represent.
- *Conflict.* Interpersonal and intergroup conflict either results in diversion of energy from organizational goals or creates pressure for change.
- *New leadership.* The primary purpose of a new leader is to create change (Gersick 1991). This is more likely when the organization is confronting crises or severe problems and when the new leader is from outside the organization.

Organizational Culture

In the organization's symbolic system, or **culture,** sources of change include the following:

- *Values.* The organization's values—a central element in its culture—can become a source of strain and conflict if they are no longer appropriate for the organization's goals.
- *Norms.* The unwritten, but widely understood and powerful informal "rules" of the organization, become a source of change if they are inconsistent with the organization's goals.
- *New member socialization.* New members are a source of change because they create departures from past practice. Organizations are not able to reproduce themselves without some unintended change because of imperfect socialization of new members that results in deviations from desired behavior.

The Role of Internal Change Variables

Some internal change factors produce incremental pressures for change that are not apparent until they accumulate into significant problems. Contributing to this is the tendency to avoid or delay change on the basis of the belief that problems will self-correct. The result is that change often occurs under urgent conditions.

In other instances, the diagnosis of a problem is correct and timely, but a solution is not apparent or available. Also, a problem may be unique, the organization could be unable to formulate a solution, or multiple variables interact, creating unmanageable complexity.

An example of the complexity of internal change is the adoption of new technologies. Although it appears that new technology is a neutral element that should not significantly affect an organization beyond improving efficiency, many studies demonstrate that it can affect the nature of work (Zuboff 1985) and the social relations among workers (Barley 1986).

External Change Variables

External sources of change are events in the environment that are usually beyond the organization's control. They can affect the organization immediately, influence other elements in its environment that then affect it, or impact it in the future. With increased awareness of events in other countries and the globalization of the economy, even external events far removed from an organization's immediate environment, are important sources of change. The distinction between immediate and general environments is becoming difficult to maintain as globalization increases.

The Immediate Environment

Some important external forces in an organization's **immediate environment,** influences with which it is continually in contact, that create pressures for change are the following:

- *Domestic competition.*   Most organizations have competitors that require some form of monitoring and response.
- *Population trends.*   Demographic factors that affect the workforce include birth rate, age, gender, race, ethnicity, religion, and culture. To some extent, immigration and population control policies affect how these variables create change.
- *Social trends.*   Consumer preferences, increases in two-wage earner families, divorce rates, crime rates, education levels, and urbanization are some social trends that affect organizations.
- *Government actions.*   National and local governments affect organizations by either reducing or increasing their regulation of areas such as taxation, labor laws, and the environment.

The General Environment

Sources of change in an organization's general environment, which extends beyond its immediate environment and expands as globalization progresses, are the following:

- *Foreign competition.*   The globalization of business intensifies the nature of competition; competitors can be located anywhere in the world. This is also true of the flow of capital, information, and knowledge.
- *Social movements.*   Recent examples of social movements—organized citizen protest groups—intended to exert influence on governments and organizations, are campaigns to end child and prison labor, feminism, and the environmental or "green" movement.
- *Political-economic movements.*   These are organized attempts to influence the distribution of economic resources through legislation or other forms of regulation. Examples are the North American Free Trade Agreement, the European Union, and the World Trade Organization. Agreements such as these formulate policies that reduce trade barriers and may result in the relocation of factories across national borders.
- *Technology.*   New technologies that affect business organizations include improvements in communication, computerization, and automation. These can be developed in one country but in a relatively short time affect businesses everywhere.

- *Professionalization.* The growth of expertise impacts organization change because as occupational knowledge bases improve, they become more influential in the way organizations operate. Increasingly, knowledge workers such as computer programmers and investment bankers are transnational.
- *Culture contact.* Globalization has increased familiarity with other cultures' management techniques—for example, the influence of Japanese management practices on non-Japanese corporations and the diffusion of American business practices and capitalism throughout the world.

The Role of External Change Variables

Organizational theories such as **population ecology** (Hannan and Freeman 1989) and to some extent, **institutional theory** (Scott 1995) and **evolutionary theory** (Aldrich 1999), view the primary source of change as external and largely beyond the control of management (Burke 2002). For example, similar to natural selection in biology, population ecology views the environment as selecting those types of organizational forms that survive. From this perspective, organizations do not adapt; instead, certain types fail and new types emerge to replace them. An implication for the management of organizations is that instead of being proactive through attempts to change the organization's environment, management is reactive and, in most instances, finds it difficult to adapt to the new environment. An example of this perspective is Carroll and Hannan's (1995, p. xi) observation:

> When the ecological perspective on organizations initially appeared in the mid-1970s, critics . . . were quick to claim that it was a theory applicable only to small organizations. Large and powerful organizations such as General Motors, IBM, and the Bank of America could control their environments and therefore were immune from selection processes. . . . Less than twenty years later, the speciousness of these claims jumps off the page, as many previously dominant firms have failed or are in the process of doing so. History abounds with examples of fallen organizations that once seemed unassailable.

A somewhat different perspective that draws on evolutionary theory views organizations as more able to adapt to environmental changes (Aldrich 1999). This model emphasizes that organizations experience variation of behaviors and practices in their environments, select behaviors from the environment, and retain the selected behaviors that management perceives will improve the survival of the organization.

As the globalization of the economy progresses, the environments in which organizations exist will become increasingly more complex and difficult to understand, let alone control. Demands on management to adapt or radically change organizations to new circumstances will probably increase.

Change Variables and Culture

Regardless of whether external or internal variables initiate organization change, an important issue is whether for change to be successful, the members of an organization have to change their values before behavior can change or if only behavior change—that is, values remain intact—is sufficient (Burke 2002). For international organizational behavior, the relationship of value and behavior change is important because of the emphasis on the role of different values in different cultures. More importantly, the role of values and behavior in change is critical because of the assumption that values influence, if not directly cause, behavior.

It is possible, however, that the relationship between values and behavior varies with cultures and that in some cultures individuals can change behavior without changing their values. For example, salespeople learn over time to express certain values in their behavior such as being friendly and courteous to customers, while they can retain personal values that do not value customers highly and, in fact, mistrust their motives.

The argument for the power of structural change is that when organization structures change, behavior changes, whether or not individuals' values change. In other words, change is more likely to occur when behavior changes because value change is very difficult to create, manage, and sustain over time (Burke 2002). Externally generated change is more likely to create structural and consequently behavioral change.

Whatever role they play in change, internal and external variables exist in the context of national and organizational culture. They simultaneously influence culture and are influenced by it; their impact on organizations could be direct but is often mediated by culture. Important issues then are how national cultures respond to change and what change strategies can be used in particular cultures. In the next section we discuss some ways that national culture influences the organizational change process.

▪ ▪ ▪ National Culture and Organization Change

Cultures vary in their receptivity to change. Some cultures change slowly and actively resist change—even to the point of attempting to prevent outside influences—because they value traditional behavior. Other cultures embrace change, but on occasion, significant segments of their population attempt to reestablish traditional values and behavior and view progress as a threat (Hunter 1996). Yet other cultures are ambivalent toward change and simultaneously embrace, resist, and fear it.

Time Orientation

One way to understand a culture's relationship to change is its orientation toward time (Trompenaars and Hampton-Turner 1998). Some cultures are **past oriented,** view tradition and history as important, and interpret the present through the lens of ancient principles, customs, and texts. Other cultures are **present oriented** and focus on the moment. For these societies, history is relatively unimportant, and the future is not of great concern. Finally, some cultures are **future oriented** and emphasize planning and future achievements. In these societies, progress is a central theme, the fate of future generations is a concern, and there is belief that rational thought can guide human action (Nisbet 1980).

Traditional cultures with a past orientation resist change while cultures with a present orientation display either ambivalence or reluctant acceptance of the new. Cultures with a future orientation tend to view change as desirable and, to some extent, inevitable.

Resistance to Change

Even present- and future-oriented societies experience resistance to change. To some extent, for all cultures, resistance to change is attributable to the uncertainty associated with change, including the awareness that change does not always lead to improvement and may produce unintended consequences (Merton 1936) or reverse results with negative outcomes (Sieber 1981).

Evolutionary psychologists argue that human beings are constrained by a genetic structure that limits human ability to change (Nicholson 1998). For example, from the perspective of evolutionary psychology, human beings "seek superiority or security in hierarchical systems" (Nicholson 1998, p. 142) that makes it difficult to change to non-hierarchical organizations. The implication for organization change is that managers should "recognize that hierarchy is forever and that people will establish status distinctions even if the organization tries to remove them" (Nicholson 1998, p. 142).

It is important for managers to understand the sources of resistance to change—and the possible biological limits to human change—so they can anticipate, reduce, or accept them. Tradition, habit, resource limitations, threats to power and influence, and fear of the unknown are forms of resistance to change found to some extent in all societies.

Tradition

Tradition is a preference for acting based on custom and precedent. The most compelling reason for adherence to tradition—including the influence of religion—is that the practices it prescribes have worked sufficiently well to warrant continuing them. Indeed, if the environment changes very little over a long time, tradition may not be an impediment to change because there is no reason for the organization to change. However, changes in an organization's external environment can create problems if the organization persists with traditional behavior. In the early years of the 21st century relatively little remains static, creating pressures for change in many different types of tradition-bound organizations. At the same time, however, even under conditions of extensive change, key elements of cultures persist and preserve traditions (Hofstede 2001; Inglehart and Baker 2000).

Habit

Habit differs from tradition, because all organizations, whether they revere traditions or not, establish, engage in, and to some extent reproduce, habitual behaviors. Much of what an organization does is habitual because it forms regular, stable patterns of events over time that are taken for granted and become mindless actions, "overlearned routines triggered by simple categories and coarse attributions of causality" (Weick 1987, p. 8).

Resource Limitations

Another barrier to change is **resource limitations.** Societies and organizations within them have varying levels of resources—human, financial, and intellectual. From a comparative perspective, organizations in advanced industrial economies generally have more resources for supporting change than organizations in developing countries. Of course, within countries the availability of resources varies with the history and success of an individual organization. For example, in the United States, Microsoft has more ability to finance and manage change than a small family-owned company.

Power and Influence

Threats to **power** and **influence** are frequently barriers to change. Change in an organization can involve both anticipated and unanticipated alterations in the power and influence structure. Those with power could inadvertently find that they have participated in a change that decreases their power and increases the power of others. The introduction of a new technology—for example, personal computers—could shift power toward computer programmers and away from senior executives who are unfamiliar with cutting edge technology. This redistribution of power could result in senior managers exploring ways to impede additional change to maintain or increase their diminished power base.

Fear of the Unknown

Another barrier to change is **fear of the unknown.** Even if the proposed change has clear benefits, participants in the change may experience concern over not knowing their future situation. An example is a promotion that brings more responsibility and enhanced compensation. Although it is positive, the person receiving the promotion may experience uncertainty over his ability to achieve a high level of performance with new coworkers, an increased number of subordinates, and more demanding work.

Of course, a change that could result in potentially harmful results or possible negative outcomes increases reasons to fear the unknown. Examples of such changes include corporate downsizing, transfer to a distant organization subunit, a new boss, and a hostile takeover.

Values

Hofstede's (2001) dimensions of culture provide a way to categorize national levels of resistance to change. In Table 14-1 countries with the strongest resistance to change, as measured by high power distance, low individualism, and high uncertainty avoidance, include most of Latin America, Portugal, and the former Yugoslavia. Countries most accepting of change have low power distance, high individualism, and low uncertainty avoidance and include the United Kingdom, the United States, Sweden, Finland, Norway, and the Netherlands. Harzing and Hofstede (1996, p. 315) write:

> Summarizing the assumed influence of the various cultural dimensions on resistance to change we suggest that both power distance and uncertainty avoidance increase the resistance to change, while individualism reduced it. We did not find clear indications for a relationship with masculinity.

TABLE 14-1 Resistance to Change in Different Clusters of Countries

	Dimension Scores			
Resistance Level	*PD*	*ID*	*UA*	*Country Clusters*
4 (strongest)	high	low	high	most of Latin America, Portugal, Korea, the former Yugoslavia
3 (strong)	med	med	high	Japan
	high	high	high	Belgium, France
	high	med	high	Spain, Argentina, Brazil, Greece, Turkey, Arab countries
	high	low	med	Indonesia, Thailand, Taiwan, Iran, Pakistan, African countries
2 (medium)	high	low	low	Philippines, Malaysia, India,
	low	med	high	Austria, Israel
	med	high	med	Italy, Germany, Switzerland, South Africa
1 (weak)	med	low	low	Singapore, Hong Kong, Jamaica
0 (weakest)	low	high	low	Anglo countries, Nordic countries, Netherlands

PD-power distance; ID-individualism; UA-uncertainty avoidance

Source: Excerpts and table from Harzing, A. and Hofstede, G. (1996). "Planned Change in Organizations: The Influence of National Culture." In Bamberger, P. and Erez, M. (eds.) *Research in the Sociology of Organizations: Cross-Cultural Analysis of Organizations,* Greenwich, CT: JAI Press, pp. 315, 316, and 327. Copyright © 1996, with permission from Elsevier.

Regarding Korea, Japan, and Taiwan, Harzing and Hofstede (1996, p. 316) note that their location on the values dimensions is counterintuitive. They write:

> These three countries are very innovative, and innovation certainly requires change. So one would expect these countries to show up in the weak resistance-to-change clusters. . . . A partial explanation for this contradiction can be found by introducing the . . . fifth dimension, long-term orientation. [1]

Long-term orientation includes values such as persistence that explain the growth of these economies.

▪▪▪ Organizational Culture and Change

The resistance to change of national culture is not identical to resistance to change in organizations. While Harzing and Hofstede's schema is useful for explaining resistance to change at the societal level, it neglects the possibility that within a society, diverse industries and different types of organizations experience more or less resistance. In other words, even though the values of a society appear to be uniform, subsystems within a society often have different values. For example, a technology firm in a high resistance to change society is unlikely to have the same level of resistance as the society. However, it may not be as change oriented as a similar firm in a society that is receptive to change.

Another limitation to focusing exclusively on values is that, as discussed previously, a wide array of internal and external factors interact with culture to create organizational change. Managing change involves more than understanding values.

Managing Change

There are many approaches to managing organizational change (Burke 2002; Guillén 2001; Pettigrew and Fenton 2000). For example, one view is that the leadership of an organization should initiate change (Tichy and Sherman 1993). An alternative view is that top-down change fails because lower-level employees, who are closest to customers, are the most knowledgeable about what requires change (Beer, Eisenstat, and Spector 1990). Disagreement also exists about which components of an organization to change and in what ways. For example, to improve efficiency, should a company increase or decrease the number of job specializations? Or should management invest in new technology and employee training?

Organization Development

Organization development (OD), a type of planned organization change, is an attempt to apply social science research and theories to create more "rational" organizations (Burke 1982). OD tries to improve organizational efficiency and effectiveness, create organizational "health," and build capacity for continuous change. Top management usually initiates an OD project and has to participate in the change for it to be successful. OD practitioners often use collaborative strategies to involve the various groups and individuals that are part of the change. For example, in diagnosing an organization, with the assistance of all relevant groups, OD seeks to understand both the problems an organization experiences and their causes. After the diagnosis, the OD expert works with members of the organization to create a vision of the future organization. Typical interventions target improving diverse areas such as leadership, team functioning, decision making,

---

[1] Reprinted from Research in *The Sociology of Organizations* by Bamberger et al, "Planned Change in organizations: The Influence of National Culture" by A. W. Harzik et al, Copyright © 1996, with permission from Elsevier.

communication, and organization structure. Ironically, if the changes are successful, they can result in the redistribution of power in an organization; although top management initiates and participates in OD, it may not benefit from it if the changes are too extensive.

OD interventions have been successful in a variety of cultures, including developing nations, with comparatively minor adjustments to the specific culture where the intervention occurs (Golembiewski 1987). However, some data suggest that the assumptions and values of OD are specific to the United States and not congruent with values in other advanced economies such as France (Amado, Faucheux, and Laurent 1991).

Lewin's Model of Change

A widely used model of planned organizational change is Kurt Lewin's (1951) three-stage process of unfreezing, movement, and refreezing. In the version presented here, we add a diagnosis phase to the beginning and renewal as the last phase.

• *Phase 1: Diagnosis.* At the beginning of planned organizational change, it is essential to accurately understand what requires change. During diagnosis and other phases of change, two possible approaches are (1) a doctor-patient relationship where the patient—the organization—provides information for the doctor—an OD consultant or other expert—who alone determines the type of "illness" and its cure and (2) a collaboration involving as many participants as possible throughout the change process. Diagnosis involves identifying the problem, isolating its primary causes, and developing an appropriate and effective solution. Of course, not all problems are self-evident. For example, the cause of employee discontent can be extremely difficult for management to unearth; an outside consultant might have to survey groups of employees, analyze the data, and then work with selected groups to understand it. Similarly, locating the major cause of a problem is also difficult because there are often multiple causes, some "hidden" deep within the organization's history or culture. Finally, there are many potential solutions to a problem. Are dissatisfied employees motivated by more money, better working conditions, or increased responsibility? Or should highly motivated individuals replace workers who perform poorly? Organizational problems typically exist in the organization's purpose, structure, reward system, technology, interpersonal relationships, leadership, and environment. Problems causing pressures for change can exist in several areas simultaneously. Because organizations are complex systems, a problem in one area usually affects other areas—but sometimes indirectly.

• *Phase 2: Unfreezing.* As with diagnosis, this phase is preparatory to change. Increasing recognition of the need for change develops along with the definition of organizational problems. The objectives are to overcome resistance to change, formulate an implementation plan, and identify ways to measure the outcomes of the change. For OD to succeed, the diagnosis must be understood and accepted by the individuals and groups involved in the change.

• *Phase 3: Movement.* The task of this phase is implementing recommendations for change. Managers often believe if the diagnosis was correct and the unfreezing phase was successful, implementation should be comparatively easy because organization members simply must follow plans. In many instances, however, even well-developed plans are not easy to execute (Gold and Miles 1981) and fail either permanently or temporarily (Gold 1999).

A **change agent** is usually an outside expert, but sometimes an employee, who consults with an organization for a specific change project. In addition to participating in all stages of the change process, a change agent often facilitates the movement phase by resolving conflicts and guiding the organization when it either intentionally or unintentionally deviates from its plans.

- *Phase 4: Refreezing.* Refreezing is the institutionalization of changes implemented in the movement phase. The changes are now part of everyday life in the organization. An aspect of institutionalization is measuring the effects of the changes. Key questions following refreezing are: Did the changes accomplish the goals identified in the diagnosis phase? As a result of the change, were there any unanticipated outcomes?

- *Phase 5: Renewal.* The final stage, organizational renewal, includes processes in which management and other members engage after refreezing to determine if and when the organization requires additional planned change. After an organization has successfully changed, it is likely that either its environment or internal conditions will change again. Instead of waiting for a crisis to develop, producing the need for major change, an organization can change incrementally.

Managing Resistance to Change

Resistance to change in organizations is similar to resistance in cultures. As discussed previously, tradition, habit, limited resources, shifts in power and influence, fear of the unknown, and values affect receptivity to change. With few exceptions, some form of resistance to change is common in organizations because groups in an organization have different interests. One group could perceive certain actions as benefiting itself and the organization, whereas another group can interpret those same actions as ill conceived and potentially harmful to the organization.

To overcome resistance to change, Lewin's theory suggests that it is more effective for change agents to remove barriers than to emphasize reasons supporting change. Kotter and Schlesinger (1979) identify five ways to manage resistance to planned organizational change:

- *Education and communication.* Organization members often fail to understand the type and benefits of change and resist what they do not understand. Communication explaining the nature of anticipated change often reduces resistance or at least notifies people of what to expect.
- *Participation and involvement.* Consultation, collaboration, and other forms of joint decision making in the design of change increase understanding, support, and enthusiasm for the change. This strategy reduces resistance, increases commitment, and improves the likelihood of implementation.
- *Negotiation and agreement.* Organization members who support the change and those who oppose it negotiate various aspects of the change to achieve an acceptable change program and workable implementation plan. There is an exchange of concessions for cooperation.
- *Manipulation and co-optation.* When the initiators of change have more power than those who oppose the change and the opponents have little bargaining power, the use of formal authority and power can gain compliance. Changes in policies and rules and, if necessary, personnel transfers or terminations, remove barriers and induce others to change.
- *Coercion.* When the need for change is urgent—that is, the organization is in crisis—opposition becomes irrelevant, and formal power and authority unilaterally implement the change.

The Interaction of National and Organizational Cultures

The success of a change program, as well as approaches to overcoming resistance, vary with the complexity and scope of behavior that an organization attempts to change, the change techniques it uses, as well as national and organizational culture.

National Culture

One approach to selecting change strategies for different cultures is to determine the extent to which values resist change and fitting a change strategy to them. Harzing and Hofstede (1996) propose change strategies based on Kotter and Schlesinger's models for the groups of countries, which we present in Table 14-2.

Countries with high power distance, low individualism, high masculinity, and high uncertainty avoidance require a change strategy that emphasizes power or coercion. Countries in this category are Colombia, Equador, Venezuela, and Mexico. At the other end of the scale, countries with low power distance, high individualism, and low uncertainty avoidance need consultative, participative change strategies. These countries include the United Kingdom, the United States, Australia, Sweden, Denmark, Finland, and the Netherlands.

In Asian organizations "where authoritarian ways are still firmly in place, proposed changes are usually implemented unilaterally by those in authority, and resistance, if any at all, is seldom overt. To be sure, some Asian managers may go through the motions of explaining the rationale for a change, but this is usually done *ex post*—that is, after the change has already been adopted" (Poblador 1992, p. 396). Change in these cultures involves strategies based on power, manipulation, and some persuasion.

Organizational Culture

Not all organizations, however, have the same values as the national culture. It seems likely, therefore, that certain organizational cultures will be more receptive to change. A hypothesis is that the more technologically and knowledge-oriented an

TABLE 14-2 Change Strategies for Different Groups of Countries

| Change Strategy | Dimension Scores | | | | Country Clusters |
	PD	ID	MA	UA	
5 (power)	high	low	high	high	Colombia, Equador, Venezuela, Mexico
4 (power, manipulation/ persuasion)	high	low	med	high	rest of Latin America, Spain, Portugal, former Yugoslavia, Greece, Turkey, Arab countries, Korea
3 (manipulation/ persuasion)	med	med	high	high	Japan
	high	high	med	high	Belgium, France
	high	low	med	low	Indonesia, Thailand, Taiwan, Iran, Pakistan, African countries
	high	low	med	low	Philippines, Malaysia, India
	med	low	high	low	Singapore, Hong Kong, Jamaica
2 (manipulation/ persuasion, consultation)	low	med	med	high	Austria, Israel
	med	high	high	med	Italy, Germany, Switzerland, South Africa
1(consultation, participation)	low	high	high	low	Anglo countries
	low	high	low	low	Nordic countries, Netherlands

PD-power distance; ID-individualism; MA-masculinity; UA-uncertainty avoidance
Source: Adapted from Harzing, A.W. and Hofstede, G. (1996)."Planned Change in Organizations: The Influence of National Culture." In Bamberger, P. and Erez, M. (eds.) *Research in The Sociology of Organizations: Cross-Cultural Analysis of Organizations.* Greenwich, CT: JAI Press, p. 327. Copyright © 1996, with permission from Elsevier.

organization, the less likely it is to resist change despite existing in and possessing change-resistant national culture variables. This does not suggest that national culture plays no role in change, but that specific corporate cultures modify it.

From another perspective, although in the Harzing and Hofstede (1996) model the culture of the United States is very low on resistance to change and the change strategy inferred is a mixture of consultation and participation, there are organizational cultures in American industries that would not be responsive to these techniques. For these companies, manipulation, persuasion, and possibly coercion, would be more effective change strategies. Examples are retail outlets, fast-food restaurants, and other bureaucratically organized industries. There is also substantial evidence that large segments of American public education have organizational cultures resistant to change (Sarason 1996), although it is unlikely that manipulation or coercion would be effective change strategies for schools.

Another issue is that certain types of studies produce more detail and nuance in describing and analyzing an organization's culture. For example, Kim (1992, p. 217), who conducted an ethnographic study of a Korean company, writes:

> My study has led me to conclude that the culture of Poongsan [the company's name] cannot be dichotomized in terms of polar concepts, as if they were mutually exclusive and exhaustive. Rather, the traditional and modern cultures coexist in Poongsan's organizational culture. For the present, at least, the behavior patterns of Poongsan industrial workers seem to be marked not by convergence but by contrasting dual ethics, the traditional and the modern.
>
> As for the precise balance between tradition and modernity in the organizational culture of Poongsan, it is difficult to discern or assess the ranges of the two cultures for each employee and manager. The balance differs from issue to issue, and from one individual to another. The self-interest of managers and workers leads them to respond to each situation selectively, choosing between two contrasting ethics at each time.

Dichotomies, ambivalence, conflict, and contradictions in an organization's culture that affect the acceptance of change often escape detection in large-scale survey research. The detailed study of a single organization reveals the complexity of organizational culture and suggests that it is not fully congruent with national culture. An important implication of the Korean study is that to manage change successfully, those initiating and implementing it must thoroughly understand the richness and complexity of an organizational culture and not assume that it reflects the dominant values of the national culture.

▪▪▪ Macro-Organizational Change Theories

A **macrolevel typology** of organizational change provides a larger framework for understanding the processes of organizational change described previously. For example, although culture plays a significant role in reactions toward and the management of change, macrolevel theories identify processes that create change independent of national culture and, to some extent, managerial action. We describe four macro-organizational change theories: life-cycle, teleological, dialectical, and evolutionary theory (Van de Ven and Poole 1995), in the following sections.

Life-Cycle Theory

Life-cycle theory borrows concepts from fields as diverse as biology, child development, and moral development. The central view of life-cycle theory is that

> the developing entity has within it an underlying form, logic, program, or code that regulates the process of change and moves the entity from a given point of departure toward a subsequent end that is prefigured in the present state. (Van de Ven and Poole 1995, p. 515)

A form that is originally primitive becomes more developed and complex over the course of the life cycle. In addition, the progression over the life cycle follows a single sequence of stages, is cumulative, and "each stage of development is seen as a necessary precursor of succeeding stages" (Van de Ven and Poole 1995, p. 515). Life-cycle theory views organizational development as driven by something similar to a genetic code within the developing organization. The implication of this theory for the management of change is that organizations have developmental patterns that managers have to recognize and adapt to.

Teleological Theory

Teleological theory relies on the philosophical doctrine that a purpose or goal is the final cause for guiding the movement of an organization. It assumes that "the entity is purposeful and adaptive; by itself or in interaction with others, the entity constructs an envisioned end state, takes action to reach it, and monitors the progress" (Van de Ven and Poole 1995, p. 516).

Teleological theory differs from life-cycle theory because it does not prescribe a sequence of stages of organizational development. With its emphasis on goal achievement, this theory underlies much managerial and organizational behavior theory. The perspective is that management is proactive and exerts considerable control through strategy, planning, and decision making.

Dialectical Theory

Another approach to understanding development and change in organizations is **dialectical theory.** In dialectical theory,

> stability and change are explained by reference to the balance of power between opposing entities. Struggles and accommodations that maintain the status quo between oppositions produce stability. Change occurs when these opposing values, forces, or events gain sufficient power to confront and engage the status quo. (Van de Ven and Poole 1995, p. 517)

The product of conflict—the struggle between thesis and antithesis—is a synthesis. The synthesis can become the thesis of a new conflict that starts the dialectical process again. Change is the product of conflict in historical forces. These forces are beyond managerial control—for example, the dynamics of capitalist economies or the ideology of socialism. In this sense, dialectical theory is similar to population ecology theory because both view external variables as major determinants of organizational behavior.

Evolutionary Theory

Evolutionary theory borrows key ideas from biological evolutionary theory and views change as proceeding

> through a continuous cycle of variation, selection, and retention. Variations, the creations of novel forms of organizations, are often viewed to emerge by blind or random change; they just happen. Selection of organizations occurs principally through the competition for scarce resources, and the environment selects entities that best fit the resource base of an environmental niche. (Van de Ven and Poole 1995, p. 518)

Two types of evolution are continuous or **gradual evolution** and **punctuated equilibrium.** Punctuated equilibrium is the argument that evolution is not gradual but instead characterized by long periods of organizational stability or equilibrium punctuated by short periods of intense, fundamental change that create discontinuities (Romanelli and Tushman 1994). It is possible to manage transitions from one stage to another—for example, by intentionally creating a punctuation that transforms the organization.

Cultural Implications of Macrochange Theories

From the cultural perspective, these theories are useful for analyzing organizational change in societies with different cultural orientations. Life-cycle theory can describe the organizational change processes of past-oriented societies since even tradition-bound organizations experience birth, growth, and decline. For example, family businesses are often traditional in their outlook toward change but, nonetheless, experience change as a result of maturational processes; the founding members eventually leave the business and change usually occurs when their children assume ownership and management responsibilities.

Punctuated equilibrium theory can explain the type of change experienced by organizations in present- and future-oriented societies that produces turbulent environments resulting in evolutionary discontinuities. An example is the change organizations experienced in former Communist countries. Instead of the Soviet government operating them, many Russian corporations found themselves suddenly thrust into private ownership with the expectation of operating efficiently enough to generate profits. Another example is the global computer industry, which periodically experiences revolutionary change because of new technology and the development of innovative software.

▪ ▪ ▪ Convergence or Divergence?

Forces for Convergence

The major forces for organizational change throughout the world are pressures on nations and corporations to be competitive. The limitations of pyramidal organizations—with chains of command, rules, and regulations—that focus on producing large quantities of standardized products, are increasingly evident as national economies and geographic boundaries become less important (Reich 1991). Replacing rigid structures are flexible, temporary teams of knowledge workers who act as free-floating quasi-entrepreneurs whose mission is to create change.

Even if organizations fail to transform into flexible forms such as networks or webs, other pressures for change include attempts to standardize product quality across nations, the diffusion of advanced management techniques, and the transfer of technological innovations.

Forces for Divergence

Casting doubt on convergence, emerging nations often have difficulty eliminating stages of development and instead evolve gradually through economic and organizational stages. Even though acculturation, the transfer of elements of one culture to another, has probably accelerated, problems remain with diffusion of organizational innovations. For example, Japanese quality control techniques transferred imperfectly to the automobile industry in the United States (Cole 1990).

In addition, culture and local conditions may act as barriers to change and continue to influence management and organizational behavior. The appeal of national, regional, religious, ethnic, and other variables that provide distinct cultural identities may increase, fragmenting the global economy in significant ways, creating resistance to change rather than propelling organizations toward similar changes. From this perspective, the global economy may eventually integrate as a result of trade interdependencies but the probability remains low of change toward a unitary corporate culture and structure (Guillén 2001).

Implications for Managers

The primary implication for managers is that culture influences organizational change. National and organizational cultures play a role in determining when management perceives a need for change, what change is appropriate, the nature of resistance to change, and the success of planned change.

An international manager must assess each of these areas when formulating a change program. Although all cultures resist change to some extent, it is likely that cultures with reverence for tradition will either not perceive the need for change or strenuously resist it. One strategy under these conditions is replacement of local managers with local or expatriate managers who accept the rationale for change. Another option is extensive retraining programs for indigenous managers and lower-level employees. Yet another approach is a combination of structural rearrangements and new technology that requires minimal voluntary value change but alters roles, interaction, and ultimately, worker behavior and values.

Along with the influence of culture, the international manager must be aware of internal and external forces for change and how specific cultures respond to them. Finally, it is also important for managers to understand the larger processes that affect organization change, such as social evolution and economic development, within the context of limitations they impose on planned change as well as the opportunities created.

SUMMARY

Organization change is an important topic for managers because a substantial part of their job requires the formulation and implementation of planned organization change. Affecting all managers and workers is the increasing amount of change produced by the internationalization and globalization of organizations. Instead of managing primarily local external and internal pressures for change, managers now have to contend with forces for change from many parts of the world that have the potential to change an organization.

Organization change occurs at the level of individuals, groups, and organization structure. The most significant change is structural because it affects the other levels. Forces for change are internal and external. Internal variables include the technical production process, political processes, and the organization's culture. External forces are population and social trends, political-economic movements, social movements, technology, competition, professionalization, and culture contact.

National culture influences organization change because cultures respond differently to change. The time orientation of cultures can be past, present, or future oriented. In addition, various factors create resistance to change such as tradition, habit, resource limitations, power and influence, fear of the unknown, and values.

Lewin's theory for managing change, organization development, and macrochange theories are useful for managers to understand the dynamics of change. It is also important for managers to understand methods for overcoming resistance to change, including education and communication, participation and involvement, negotiation and agreement, manipulation and co-optation, and the use of coercion.

Finally, managers have to be aware that some theories of change—for example, organizational ecology, life-cycle theory, dialectical theory, and evolutionary theory—limit the role of managers in initiating and controlling the change processes of organizations.

DISCUSSION QUESTIONS ■ ■ ■ ■ ■ ■ ■

1. Why is organization change so prevalent throughout the world? What has caused the rate of change to accelerate in the past two decades?
2. What role does culture play in either promoting or creating barriers to change?
3. Why is it important for managers to understand and apply sophisticated theories of change?
4. Do you think that resistance to change is as prevalent as the text claim it is? If so, based on your experience, why do people respond to change the way they do?
5. What can a manager do if the ways to overcome resistance to change fail to work?
6. In your view, is it possible for managers to succeed in implementing planned organization change?
7. What are some of the unanticipated outcomes of planned change? How can they be managed?
8. In your view, are organizations changing in ways that will reduce the contribution of specific national cultures in shaping their organizations?
9. Describe a planned change in an organization in which you participate. What was the change? How was it implemented? What were the results?

INTERNET SITES ■ ■ ■ ■ ■ ■ ■

Selected Companies in the Chapter

AT & T (www.att.com)
Deutsche Telekom AG (www.telekom3.de)

Organizational Change Sites

Total Quality Management (www.gslis.utexas.edu/~rpollock /tqm.html). This Web page has information on Total Quality Management and links to a variety of interesting sites throughout the world.

Howard Aldrich (www.unc.edu/~healdric). This site is the Homepage of Howard Aldrich, a professor of sociology at the University of North Carolina and author of *Organizations Evolving*. The page provides access to Aldrich's recent working papers on organization change.

Stephen Jay Gould (www.stephenjaygould.org). This site is devoted to the work of Stephen Jay Gould, whose concept of punctuated equilibrium was developed to explain biological evolution and has been widely used to explain organization change. In *The Structure of Evolutionary*

Theory (Harvard University Press 2002), Gould discusses uses of his theory to explain organization change beginning on page 957.

Kurt Lewin (http://fates.cns.muskingum.edu/~psych/psycweb/history/lewin.htm). This site provides biographical information on Kurt Lewin as well as a discussion of his social psychological theories of change and applications of them.

REFERENCES

Aldrich, H. E. (1999). *Organizations Evolving.* Thousand Oaks, CA: Sage.

Amado, G., Faucheux, C., and Laurent, A. (1991). "Organizational Change and Cultural Realities: Franco-American Contrasts," *International Studies of Management and Organization*, 21(3), 62–95.

Barley, S. (1986). "Technology as an Occasion for Structuring: Evidence from Observations of CT Scanners and the Social Order of Radiology Departments," *Administrative Science Quarterly*, 31, 78–108.

Beer, M., Eisenstat, R., and Spector, B. (1990). "Why Change Programs Don't Produce Change," *Harvard Business Review,* Nov–Dec, 158–66.

Burke, W. W. (1982). *Organization Development: Principles and Practices.* Boston: Little, Brown.

—— (2002). *Organization Change: Theory and Practice.* Thousand Oaks, CA: Sage.

Carroll, G. R. and Hannan M. T. (eds) (1995). *Organizations in Industry: Strategy, Structure and Selection.* New York: Oxford University Press.

Cole, R. (1990). "U.S. Quality Improvement in the Auto Industry: Close But No Cigar," *California Management Review,* 32(4), 71–85.

DiMaggio, P. (2001). *The Twenty-First-Century Firm: Changing Economic Organization in International Perspective.* Princeton, NJ: Princeton University Press.

Eakin, H. (2003). "Deutsche Telekom Posts Biggest Loss in Europe's History," *New York Times,* March 11, w1.

Gersick, C. J. G. (1988). "Time and Transition in Work Teams: Toward a New Model of Group Development," *Academy of Management Journal*, 31, 9–41.

—— (1991). "Revolutionary Change Theories: A Multilevel Exploration of the Punctuated Equilibrium Paradigm," *Academy of Management Review*, 16, 10–36.

Gold, B. A. and Miles, M, B. (1981). *Whose School Is It, Anyway?* New York: Praeger.

—— (1999). "Punctuated Legitimacy: A Theory of Educational Change," *Teachers College Record*, 101(2), 192–219.

Golembiewski, R. (1987). "Is OD Narrowly Culture-bound? Prominent Features of 100 Third-World Applications," *Organization Development Journal*, 5, 20–9.

Guillén, M. F. (2001). *The Limits of Convergence: Globalization, and Organizational Change in Argentina, South Korea, and Spain.* Princeton, NJ: Princeton University Press.

Hamel, G. (2000). *Leading the Revolution.* Boston, MA: Harvard Business School Press.

Hannan, M. T. and Freeman, J. (1989). *Organizational Ecology.* Cambridge, MA: Harvard University Press.

Harzing, A. and Hofstede, G. (1996). "Planned Change in Organizations: The Influence of National Culture." In Bamberger, P. and Erez, M. (eds.) *Research in The Sociology of Organizations: Cross-Cultural Analysis of Organizations.* Greenwich, CT: JAI Press.

Hofstede, G. (2001). *Culture's Consequences: Comparing Vaules, Behaviors, Instititions, and Organizations Across Nations.* 2d Ed. Thousand Oaks, CA: Sage.

Hunter, M. (1996). "Europe's Reborn Right," *New York Times Magazine*, April 21, 38–43.

Inglehart, R. and Baker, W. E. (2000). "Modernization, Cultural Change, and the Persistence of Traditional Values," *American Sociological Review*, 65, 19–51.

Kahn, J. (1995). "Chinese Corporations Bulk Up to Take On the World: Business Giants Believe Their Great Size Is the Key to Competing," *Wall Street Journal*, July 5, A6.

Kanter, R. M. (2001). *Evolve! Succeeding in the Digital Culture of Tomorrow.* Boston, MA: Harvard Business School Press.

Kim, C. (1992). *The Culture of Korean Industry: An Ethnography of Poongsan Corporation.* Tucson, AZ: University of Arizona Press.

Kogut, B. (2003). *The Global Internet Economy.* Cambridge, MA: The MIT Press.

Kotter, J. and Schlesinger, L. (1979). "Choosing Strategies for Change," *Harvard Business Review*, 57, 106–14.

Lewin, K. (1951). *Field Theory in Social Science.* New York: Harper and Row.

Merton, R. K. (1936). "The Unanticipated Consequences of Purposive Social Action," *American Sociological Review*, 1, 894–904.

Nicholson, N. (1998). "How Hardwired is Human Behavior?" *Harvard Business Review*, July–August, 135–47.

Nisbet, R. (1980). *History of the Idea of Progress.* New York: Basic Books.

Pettigrew, A. and Fenton, E. (2000). *The Innovating Organization.* Thousand Oaks, CA: Sage.

Poblador, N. (1992). "Change and Adaptation." In Westwood, R. (ed.) *Organizational Behaviour: Southeast Asian Perspectives.* Hong Kong: Longman.

Reich, R. (1991). *The Work of Nations: Preparing Ourselves for 21st-Century Capitalism.* New York: Knopf.

Romanelli, E. and Tushman, M. (1994). "Organizational Transformation as Punctuated Equilibrium: An Empirical Test," *Academy of Management Journal,* 37, 1141–66.

Sarason, S. B. (1996). *Revisiting "The Culture of The School and The Problem of Change."* New York: Teachers College Press.

Scott, R. (1995). *Institutions and Organizations.* Newbury Park, CA: Sage.

Sieber, S. D. (1981). *Fatal Remedies: The Ironies of Social Intervention.* New York: Plenum.

Steinmetz, G. (1995). "Customer-Service Era Is Reaching Germany Late, Hurting Business," *Wall Street Journal,* June 1, 1 & A8.

Tang, J. and Ward, A. (2003). *The Changing Face of Chinese Management.* New York: Routledge.

Tichy, N. (1983). *Managing Strategic Change: Technical, Political and Cultural Dynamics.* New York: Wiley.

—— and Sherman, S. (1993). *Control Your Own Destiny or Someone Else Will: How Jack Welch Is Making General Electric the World's Most Competitive Company.* New York: Doubleday.

Trompenaars, F. and Hampden-Turner, C. (1998). *Riding the Waves of Culture: Understanding Cultural Diversity in Global Business.* 2d Ed. New York: McGraw Hill.

Tuckman, B and Jensen, M. (1977). "Stages of Small Group Development Revisited," *Group and Organization Studies,* 2, 419–27.

Vallas, S. (2003). "Why Teamwork Fails: Obstacles to Workplace Change in Four Manufacturing Plants," *American Sociological Review,* 68, 223–50.

Van de Ven, A. and Poole, M. (1995). "Explaining Development and Change in Organizations," *Academy of Management Review,* 20, 510–40.

Weick, K. (1987). "Perspectives on Action in Organizations." In Lorsch, J. (ed.) *Handbook of OrganizationalBehavior.* Upper Saddle River, NJ: Prentice Hall.

Zuboff, S. (1985). "Automate/Informate: The Two Faces of Intelligent Technology," *Organization Dynamics,* 39–54.

■ ■ ■ ■ ■ ■ ■ ■ ■ ■ C A S E S ■ ■ ■ ■ ■ ■ ■ ■ ■ ■

Case 1   A Cultural Clash in the Entertainment Industry

Anne Marie Francesco
Barry Allen Gold

Culture and Ideology

"We're going to ruin your culture just like we ruined our own!" Jay Leno's humorous promotion for his Tonight Show on the European NBA Super Channel sounded like a threat to French Minister of Culture Jacques Toubon. In Toubon's opinion, the United States entertainment industry wants to dominate the world by any means. Toubon's opinion is shared by many of the French. For instance, French film producer Marin Karmitz, whose credits include the critically acclaimed *Blue*, sees a battle developing. According to Karmitz,

> Of course the U.S. movie industry is a big business, but behind the industrial aspect, there is also an ideological one. Sound and pictures have always been used for propaganda, and the real battle at the moment is over who is going to be allowed to control the world's images, and so sell a certain lifestyle, a certain culture, certain products and certain ideas. With the globalization of satellite and cable systems, that is what is at stake. (Stevenson 1994)

The view from the Continent is that Hollywood is the enemy—trying to standardize world entertainment tastes and bring levels down to the lowest common denominator. As writer/philosopher Regis Debray sees it, "The American empire will pass, like the others. Let's at least make sure it does not leave irreparable damage to our creative abilities behind it" (Cohen 1994). Daniel Toscan du Plantier, president of Unifrance, the French government–funded marketing and publicity association, sees the distinction between the French and Americans differently. He sees the United States as a market that reasons in terms of profit, compared with France, where the people are often driven by intangible values. The result is French films that explore emotion, ideas, passion, and existential dilemmas compared with an American cinema that is obsessed with sex, violence, and fast action.

From the American viewpoint, Jack Valenti, president of the Motion Picture Association of America (MPAA) accused the European Union of "flagrant protectionism." American movie makers viewed the French attitude as "little more than a mask for inept film making—weak scripts, slow narrative, sloppy characterization and an overarching dullness that can be stupefying" (Cohen 1994). The pragmatic American approach, despite producing some "art films" or serious movies such as *Schindler's List*, is to view movies and other entertainment as commodities. The objective is to create a product, market and distribute it, and make as much money as possible.

If the approaches to movie making are so different, why are the French worried about the American influence on their cinema? Shouldn't French moviegoers prefer their own movies rather than the "crass" American products?

Providing a graphic illustration of what troubled the French during the GATT talks, France's greatest living film actor makes a fool of himself on water skis in *My Father, the Hero*. In this latest example of that all-American art form known as 'le re-make,' Gerard Depardieu also wears loud shirts, cavorts on a Jet Ski, lets American teen-agers get the better of him, and imitates Maurice Chevalier singing "Thank Heaven for Little Girls." Many words could describe what he does here, but "hero" is not one of them (Maslin 1994). Despite the

295

cultural differences, some American artists are well received in France. In addition to the acting of Jerry Lewis, films directed by Woody Allen and Robert Altman are popular. An interesting example is the American novelist Paul Auster. Auster's symbol-laden novels sell about 20,000 copies a year in the United States and are purchased mainly by intellectuals. In France his novels sell 50,000 copies annually, and he is recognized on the street as a celebrity. It can be argued, however, that these artists are a small minority and have achieved acclaim in France because they capture European sensibilities in their work.

Culture and Politics

In France, culture is also often very closely linked to politics. A recent example was the appointment of a music director for the Paris National Opera. With great expectations, Argentine-born Daniel Barenboim was appointed music director under a conservative government. He was summarily dismissed before the debut of the new opera house when the socialists returned to power in 1988. His successor, South Korean-born Myung-Whun Chung, met a similar fate. He was dismissed in August 1994 after the conservatives won parliamentary elections.

However, in an interview unrelated to these events, Cultural Minister Toubon emphasized that "the foreigner does not understand that the cultural politics of the left and the right are the same in France. Here culture transcends political differences. It is a part of the national consensus" (Suleiman 1993).

In the United States, appointments to similar posts are usually unaffected by national politics; the board of a cultural institution appoints artistic directors according to aesthetic preferences, not the ideology of a national political party.

General Agreement on Tariffs and Trade

The views that met head on in the 1993 General Agreement on Tariffs and Trade (GATT) talks were based on extreme interpretations of each country's culture and strategy. As a result, after seven years of negotiations, the GATT agreement was almost derailed.

France spearheaded the group of European countries that fought to have audiovisual products excluded from the GATT as part of a "cultural exception." American President Bill Clinton insisted that audiovisual services must be included in the agreement and that there be no "unacceptable restrictions" on these products.

At the time, the French government was spending $350 million to subsidize the French film industry, the largest in Europe. The United States objected to the subsidies as well as French taxes and quotas on American-made movies, television programs, and music recordings, which were used to support the French film industry. In practical terms, the American movie product that the French patron paid to see was taxed, with the benefit going to the French movie makers.

In the final days of the negotiation, chief U.S. trade negotiator Mickey Kantor feared that the entire agreement would be lost if the United States did not drop the demand for a completely open European market. Consequently, when the agreement was signed by 117 countries in December 1993, films and television were entirely excluded. The French won out in their desire to protect their industry and to preserve what they viewed as their cultural identity.

Economic Realities

How will this exclusion of television and film from the GATT impact the American entertainment industry? American movie makers now have a huge percentage of the Western European market (more than 80%) and more than half of the French market (57%). France is the third largest foreign market for American movies after Japan and Germany. The U.S. movie industry makes more than half of its money from distributing films outside the United States, and this percentage has been increasing yearly.

In contrast, foreign language films in the United States capture less than 2% of box office receipts, with the French getting about half of that. In dollar terms, in 1992, the value of audiovisual exports to Europe was US$3.66 billion compared with European exports to the United States valued at US$288 million.

In 1993, of the 100 most-attended films worldwide, 88 were American, with the highest ranking non-American entry, the French *Les Visiteurs*, only at number 27.

A Uni-Culture?

The cultural relationships between the two countries have become more complex recently. For instance, Disney has formed a unit to dub, market, and distribute French films in the United States. In part, this is an attempt to lessen tensions with the French and reduce their opposition to Disney releases. Another aspect of this decision is that Disney, a partner in the EuroDisney theme park, which many Europeans criticize, needs to improve its image in France.

Many Hollywood studios have remade French films, such as *Three Men and a Baby* and *The Vanishing*, that have either never been released in the United States or that have very limited distribution. The studios believe that American actors—and the absence of dubbing—are more attractive to U.S. audiences. At the same time, however, Hollywood is casting more foreign actors in made-for-America movies. At work here is a business philosophy that argues, "Why cast an American actor when Gerard Depardieu can make them laugh in at least two languages?" (Natale 1994)

Just as foreign actors are becoming more sought after for American films, the European filmmakers are no longer filming solely in their native lands. For example, one of Frenchman Betrand Tavernier's recent films was bilingual (English and French), starring Dirk Bogarde. Polish filmmaker Krszystof Kieslowski made two recent films in France, and Italian Bernardo Bertolucci and German Win Wenders have made films on many different continents.

At one point in time, there was a clear distinction: Films from Europe were "art," whereas those from Hollywood were merely entertainment. More recently this distinction is not so clear. With American remakes of European films and a strong Hollywood influence on directors such as Jean-Jacques Beineix (*Diva*) and Luc Besson (*Nikita*), the two approaches appear to be moving toward a common direction. And as for Jack Valenti, who was so opposed to the cultural exception in the GATT talks, his advice to the French is, "Invade the American market!" (Woodrow and Valenti 1994)

Post-Gatt Culture

Woody Allen, in his 2002 movie "*Hollywood Ending*," plays a director, who on the first day on the set of a $60 million film that must be a hit to salvage his once illustrious career, finds himself suddenly blind. In his bumbling, yet astutely self-reflective, tragi-comical way, Allen succeeds in directing the film while keeping his blindness a secret.

When the movie is finished, American critics are hostile to its abysmal plot, vapid acting, blurred cinematography, and of course, inept direction. Allen, who has since recovered his eyesight because the blindness was psychosomatic, appears to be doomed to a failed career as a director. But the punchline of this one joke movie is that the French rave over his film. Allen's character exudes, "Thank God for the French, they like Jerry Lewis and me!"

Despite the enmity between the French and Americans over the meaning of culture, there appear to be steps toward softening French cultural exclusivity. For instance, James Lipton, the creator and host of "Inside the Actors Studio," who interviews American actors and directors on American Public Television, is regarded seriously by the French who view his program with French subtitles. In fact, because the French admire Lipton's no-nonsense approach to actors and directors they invited him to interview the leading French actresses Juliette Binoche and Jeanne Moreau.

But fear of American cultural dominance is always near the surface. In February 2003, the French and Canadians, with the support of "representatives of cultural organizations from 35 countries met at the Louvre to campaign for preservation of the cultural exception and to promote adoption of a global convention on cultural diversity by Unesco as a way to remove culture from the World Trade Organization" (Riding 2003, p. E3). President Jacques Chirac of France warned, "With the opening of a round of international trade negotiations, the champions of unlimited trade liberalization are once again lining up against those who believe that creative works cannot be reduced to the rank of ordinary merchandise" (Riding 2003, p. E3). ■

SOURCE: "A Cultural Clash in the Entertainment Industry" by Anne Marie Francesco and Barry Allen Gold. Reprinted by permission of the authors. The situations depicted in this case are intended to stimulate classroom discussion rather than suggest administrative solutions to the issues raised.

REFERENCES

ANDREWS, N. (1993). "Identity Crisis in the Euro-movies—Nigel Andrews Explains Why it is Becoming More and More Difficult to Tell European and Hollywood Films Apart," *Financial Times*, December 18.

BEGLEY, A. (1992). "Case of the Brooklyn Symbolist." *The New York Times Magazine*, August 30. "Clinton Rejects French Bid for GATT Concession" (1993). *The Reuter European Community Report*, October 15.

COHEN, R. (1994). "Aux Armes! France Rallies to Battle Sly and T. Rex," *The New York Times*, (Arts and Leisure Section), January 2.

FRODON, J-M. (1993). "World Commercial Negotiations and Their Repercussions in France" *(Les Negociations sur le Commerce Mondial et Leurs Repercussions en France), Le Monde*, December 10.

HOFSTEDE, G. (1980). *Culture's Consequences: International Differences in World Related Values.* Beverly Hills, CA: Sage.

KAPLAN, D. (1993). "How GATT Wrote an Unhappy Ending for Hollywood," *The Gazette* (Montreal), December 17.

KING, T. (1994). "Disney's Miramax to Form Unit to Dub, Market, Distribute French Films in U.S.," *The Wall Street Journal*, October 10.

MASLIN, J. (1994). "Depardieu's Bahamian Vacation," *The New York Times*, February 4.

NATALE, R. (1994). "Hollywood Dit Willkommen, Bienvenido," *The New York Times*, (Arts and Leisure Section), February 20.

Riding, A. (2003). "Filmmakers Seek Protection from U.S. Dominance," *The New York Times*, February 5.

STEVENSON, R. (1994). "Lights! Camera! Europe!" *The New York Times*, (Business Section), February 6.

SULEIMAN, E. (1993). "GATT Debate: Why America Has so Little Interest in France," *(Debats GATT: Pourqoi la France Interesse si peu l'Amerique), Le Monde*, December 8.

THOMAS, A. (1993). "The Audiovisual Negotiations Seen by the French Negotiator: First, an Internal Fight for Europe," *(Les Negociations sur l'Audiovisuel Vues par le Neogociateur Francais: D'Abord une Bataille Interne a l'Europe), Agence France Presse*, December 19.

WOODROW, A. and VALENTI, J. (1994). "An Interview with the Patron of American Studios Jack Valenti: 'Competition promotes quality,'" *(Un Entretien avec le Patron des Studios Americains Jack Valenti: "La concurrence stimule la Qualite"), Le Monde*, February 15.

YOUNG, J. (1994). "The Best French Films You'll Never See," *The New York Times*, (Arts and Leisure Section), October 30.

Case 2　Conscience or the Competitive Edge? (A)

Kate Button
Christopher K. Bart

The plane touched down at Bombay airport on time. Olivia Jones made her way through the usual immigration bureaucracy without incident and was finally ushered into a waiting limousine, complete with uniformed chauffeur and soft black leather seats. Her already considerable excitement at being in India for the first time was mounting. As she cruised the dark city streets, she asked her chauffeur why so few cars had their headlights on at night. The driver responded that most drivers believed that headlights use too much petrol! Finally, she arrived at her hotel, a black marble monolith, grandiose and decadent in its splendour, towering above the bay.

The goal of her four-day trip was to sample and select swatches of woven cotton from the mills in and around Bombay, to be used in the following season's youthwear collection of shirts, trousers, and underwear. She was thus treated with the utmost deference by her hosts, who were invariably Indian factory owners, or British agents for Indian mills. For three days she was ferried from one air-conditioned office to another, sipping iced tea or chilled lemonade, poring over leather-bound swatch catalogs, which featured every type of stripe and design possible. On the fourth day, Jones made a request that she knew would cause some anxiety in the camp. "I want to see a factory," she declared.

After much consultation and several attempts at dissuasion, she was once again ushered into a limousine and driven through a part of the city she had not previously seen. Gradually, the hotel and the western shops dissolved into the background and Jones entered downtown Bombay. All around was a sprawling shanty-town, constructed from sheets of corrugated iron and panels of cardboard boxes.

Dust flew in spirals everywhere among the dirt roads and open drains. The car crawled along the unsealed roads behind carts hauled by man and beast alike, laden to overflowing with straw or city refuse—the treasure of the ghetto. More than once the limousine had to halt and wait while a lumbering white bull crossed the road.

Finally, in the very heart of the ghetto, the car came to a stop. "Are you sure you want to do this?" asked her host. Determined not to be faint-hearted, Jones got out of the car.

White-skinned, blue-eyed, and blond, clad in a city suit and stiletto-heeled shoes, and carrying a briefcase, Jones was indeed conspicuous. It was hardly surprising that the inhabitants of the area found her an interesting and amusing subject, as she teetered along the dusty street and stepped gingerly over the open sewers.

Her host led her down an alley, between the shacks and open doors and inky black interiors. Some shelters, Jones was told, were restaurants, where at lunchtime people would gather on the rush mat floors and eat rice together. In the doorway of one shack there was a table which served as a counter, laden with ancient cans of baked beans, sardines, and rusted tins of a fluorescent green substance that might have been peas. The eyes of the young man behind the counter were smiling and proud as he beckoned her forward to view his wares.

As Jones turned another corner, she saw an old man in the middle of the street, clad in a waist cloth, sitting in a large tin bucket. He had a tin can in his hand with which he poured water from the bucket over his head and shoulders. Beside him two little girls played in brilliant white nylon dresses, bedecked with ribbons and lace. They posed for her with smiling faces, delighted at having their photograph taken in their best frocks. The men and women moved around her with great dignity and grace, Jones thought.

Finally, her host led her up a precarious wooden ladder to a floor above the street. At the top Jones was warned not to stand straight as the ceiling was just 5 feet high. There, in a room not 20 feet by 40 feet, twenty men were sitting at treadle sewing machines, bent over yards of white cloth. Between them on the floor were rush mats, some occupied by sleeping workers awaiting their next shift. Jones learned that these men were on a 24-hour rotation, 12 hours on and 12 hours off, every day for 6 months of the year. For the remaining 6 months they returned to their families in the country-side to work the land, planting and building with the money they had earned in the city. The shirts they were working on were for an order she had placed 4 weeks earlier in London, an order of which she had been par-ticularly proud because of the low price she had suc-ceeded in negotiating. Jones reflected that this sight was the most humbling experience of her life. When she questioned her host about these conditions, she was told that they were typical for her industry—and for most of the third world, as well.

Eventually, she left the heat, dust, and din of the little shirt factory and returned to the protected, air-conditioned world of the limousine.

"What I've experienced today and the role I've played in creating that living hell will stay with me forever," she thought. Later in the day, she asked herself whether what she had seen was an inevitable consequence of pricing policies that enabled the British customer to purchase shirts at £12.99 instead of £13.99 and at the same time allowed the company to make its mandatory 56% profit margin? Were her negotiating skills—the result of many years of train-ing—an indirect cause of the terrible conditions she had seen?

When Jones returned to the U.K., she consid-ered her position and the options open to her as a buyer for a large, publicly traded, retail chain operating in a highly competitive environment. Her dilemma was twofold: Can an ambitious employee afford to exercise a social conscience in his or her career? And can career-minded individ-uals truly make a difference without jeopardizing their future?

Conscience or the Competitive Edge? (B)

Olivia Jones described her subsequent decision as follows:

"The alternatives for me were perfectly clear, if somewhat unrealistic: I could stipulate a standard of working conditions to be enforced at any factory employed, and offer to pay an inflated price for merchandise in an effort to fund the necessary improvements. This would mean having to increase the margins in other sections of the range and explain-ing to my controller exactly why prices had risen.

"There was, of course, no guarantee that the extra cash would make its way safely into the hands of the worker or improve his working conditions. Even exercising my greatest faith in human nature, I could see the wealthy factory owner getting increasingly fatter and some other keen and able buyer being pro-moted into my highly coveted position!

"I could refuse to buy from India. This would mean I would have to find alternative sources at equally low prices to justify my action. There was always Macau, where I knew conditions were worse if anything, or Hong Kong, where conditions were certainly better, from what I had seen, but prices were much higher. I had to ask myself if I would

truly be improving the plight of the workers by denying them the enormous orders that I usually put through their factories. Or would I simply be salving my own conscience by righteously congratulating myself at not dealing in slave labour? Doubtless my production schedule would be snapped up eagerly by the next buyer who was hungry for cheap labour and fast turnaround.

"I could consider speaking to the powers that be and ask their advice. After all, the group was proud of its philanthropic reputation and had promoted its charity work and sponsorship of various causes, including Wimbledon Football Club and Miss World. This in mind, I approached my line manager, who laughed at my idealistic naivety and made it quite clear that I should hold my tongue if I knew what was good for me.

"It seemed I had but two choices. Either I quit the company and look for an employer which would be more responsible in its attitude towards sourcing merchandise, or I could continue to buy as before, but aware of the consequences and exercising a con-science wherever possible. I won't bother to list my excuses for opting for the latter choice.

"I believe that there is no solution, no generalization which can be used as a precedent in this type of scenario. I don't know to this day what action I could have taken to improve the lives of those individuals whom I felt I had compromised.

"Every day, in various work situations, employees, and specifically managers, come up against questions of conscience versus the status quo. It may be that you are encouraged to show prejudice against an individual or group of employees due to their race, colour or clique; maybe your boss asked you to lie to camouflage an embarrassing error and insinuate that the fault lies with someone else; maybe your employer's policy requires you to screw a client or a supplier to close a deal and maintain the bottom line.

"Each case is different and demands its own evaluation. Each man and woman must draw their own set of rules and regulations to suit their own situation and conscience.

"It takes brave individuals to jeopardize their careers for a cause but it is thanks to those who do take a stand that great feats of humanitarian work are successfully undertaken and completed. We should all evaluate the choices that are open to use and be true to ourselves. Let your conscience be your guide within the realms of reality.

"The most important lesson that I learned from the episode was that, above all, you have to learn to live with the choices that you make." ▪

SOURCE: "Conscience or the Competitive Edge?" by Kate Button and Christopher Bart from *The Case Research Journal*, 1993. Reprinted by permission of the North American Case Research Association. This case was written solely for the purpose of stimulating student discussion. All events and individuals are real, but names have been disguised at the request of the principals involved.

Case 3   The Careless Collaborators

Sara L. Keck
Anne Marie Francesco

As my flight from Milan to Chicago took off, I sat wondering whether I was really as insensitive to the cultural differences of colleagues as I felt. Despite the best of plans and intentions to accommodate, facilitate, and negotiate, the week's meeting in Milan had been another disaster in terms of reestablishing rapport with other team members and accomplishing productive joint research. Doubting the value of my continued membership in the group both to myself and to the team, once again I had to decide whether continued work on the international research project was worth the resources dedicated to it. The long flight home in the business class seats might be a physically comfortable one, but one likely to be fraught with meditation over the right thing to do for the team and for myself. What should I do now? Drop out of the project or continue on? If I continued, I had to find a way to address my problems in the group.

Susan's Background

Susan was a professor of management at a large state university with a growing international reputation when the invitation was first extended to join a relatively small but prestigious research group. She had received her doctorate from Columbia University after spending several years as a management consultant.

Susan's background was very broad in international experience, teaching, and research. She had been married to an Iranian for many years, had lived with her husband's family in Iran, and had taught English as a second language in Iran. After completing her doctorate, she had visited universities and/or guest-lectured in several countries, including Germany, Great Britain, the Czech Republic, Italy, France, and Belgium.

Most recently, her university had chosen her to teach in a faculty development program at the University of Indonesia because the directors of the program recognized her expertise and experience abroad.

Thoughts About Business and Academia

Work on the academic project was not that different from work on business teams. Susan had extensive experience working on teams as a consultant. She had been both a team member and leader for several projects during her time as a management consultant. Her familiarity with teams in both business and academia led her to draw multiple parallels between such teams. First, teams are often drawn from offices across geographic areas such as the project she worked on in Boise, Idaho. The members on that project came from Denver, San Francisco, Los Angeles, and Dallas. Coordination efforts were extremely important and difficult on that project, as well. Firms also form teams across national boundaries. Susan remembered a software development project on which she had worked as a consultant to design and program a system that served the needs of a multinational corporation with multiple national accounting systems.

Second, the interaction with the academic team could facilitate or damage team performance just as it could for business teams. Smoothly operating teams of any kind can lead to superior performance. Unaddressed conflicts, unclear or unacceptable roles, unbalanced power relationships, or weak members can become problems on any type of team. There was one unfortunate team problem when Susan worked on a client project: An unaddressed conflict between two team leaders who had opposing views about how best to solve a design problem led to endless bickering and a near failure to complete the project on time.

Third, both academic and business teams have a mission to accomplish and performance requirements against which to benchmark. Susan remembered well all the performance requirements from the consulting teams. On the whole, the research team's mission and execution did not seem that different from those of business teams'.

302

The Team's Background

The group, International Strategy Research Group (ISRG), had formed itself with the purpose of conducting scholarly research over national boundaries with members from multiple nations. The first project had been directed toward the managerial effects of the 1992 European Integration. Although the second project never quite got off the ground, the third project, the current one, was to be a very important one because it was funded by the European Union (EU) and because it addressed some controversial theoretical issues: the stability of transnational strategies in certain industries of importance to EU countries, for example.

The book from the first project had been well received by both scholars and managers throughout continental Europe and the United Kingdom. Despite variation in English language skills on the team (the book was written in English) and fighting among some members, the first book was of high quality and was completed on time. This first project included a group of eight professors from France, Germany, Italy, Britain, and Sweden. This original group considered themselves to be a very closely knit cohort of researchers who had personal as well as professional ties.

The second project was just getting started when Susan met Professor Kent Peters at an international conference on managing the global economy. Kent had spearheaded the final writing and completion of the first book on European Integration. Kent and Susan met at several subsequent conferences. During a trip to Britain in January 1992, they met again, and in the course of conversation, Susan mentioned that she would be traveling to the Czech Republic (then Czechoslovakia). Kent considered this a golden opportunity for the ISRG group to have interviews conducted for the second project on organizational change in Eastern and Central Europe.

Susan's Experience

I was absolutely delighted to have been asked to join the prestigious group with a controversial research agenda, and I considered the invitation evidence of the recognition of my scholarly research as well as my ability to interact well across cultures. I made preparations and conducted the Czech interviews. Unfortunately, that project never got off the ground because the European members were unable to obtain funding.

The ISRG group seemed to be signaling their continued respect for my work by asking me to join the third project, which did receive generous funding from the European Commission. While the grant would not cover expenses incurred outside the EU by Americans and funding would have to obtained elsewhere, I was still enthusiastic about participation because the study was interesting, and it was an opportunity to work in a very unusual multinational group of diverse scholars from multiple perspectives, including comparative management, strategy, and organizational behavior.

Indeed, it was a group that was diverse on multiple dimensions. There was, of course, diversity of national backgrounds. But beyond this was diversity of type of institution, individual age and academic experience, and academic discipline. I had noticed that there were only three other women in the group of 15 people, and none of these women, including myself, were of senior academic rank.

The First Meeting: Lyon, France

The first meeting for the third project took place in June 1993 in Lyon, France. Because the French team had obtained the EU funding, the French members hosted the first meeting and set the team in motion. The third project was to be conducted by representatives of Sweden, France, Germany, Italy, Portugal, Spain, Britain, Belgium, and the United States. Canada was to be included if someone could be recruited to carry out the work. This broad representation of countries and universities was new for the team. This is the first time the ISRG group had been so large and unwieldy, but the project was broad in intention within the EU grant. The monetary value of the EU grant was very high, and consequently, the size of the group was justified both from the work load and from the approval of the EU.

Each member was sent a preliminary copy of the questionnaire and asked by the project coordinator to conduct at least one pilot interview in her or his respective country. Not everyone was as fast out of the blocks as Kent and Susan. Kent, representing the British team, and Susan, being the only American member, had conducted interviews in Britain and the United States before this meeting. No one else conducted any pilot interviews.

Susan's Experience in Lyon

I planned for this first meeting in Lyon with the level of enthusiasm normally reserved for sabbatical leaves. I took a course in French, conducted pilot interviews, and rearranged my other summer obligations to avoid conflict with other responsibilities. I even convinced a friend to take my dog for the summer so that I could combine the travel to the Lyon meeting with my travel to Indonesia to minimize costs my own university would have to pay.

I began to wonder whether I was communicating well with my colleagues from the very first day in Lyon. The meetings were to begin on Monday. Despite arriving in Lyon on Saturday so that I could completely adjust to the time change, I did not see a single one of my colleagues until late on Monday afternoon. Had I misunderstood? Well, perhaps. The Monday start date meant that each would travel to Lyon on that day. The meetings would actually begin on Tuesday morning. Monday evening was spent in groups of colleagues who went out to dinner in casual restaurants in the historic part of Lyon. On the whole, the first day was unproductive but jolly good fun!

I had a strong theoretical as well as statistical training in my doctoral program at Columbia University, so each step of the research process was of interest to me as well as something to which I could contribute. Though I was disappointed that I was not part of the original theory building and felt a little like a "free loader," I was not overly concerned because I knew I could contribute to the empirical steps of the project. In addition, the team had expressed an interest in publishing the results in American journals, something of which the other members had done very little. I felt I could carry my weight as a team member by also contributing what I knew about the publication values and process of American journals.

But, I was to be surprised once again that week. Had I misunderstood once again? Had I been insensitive? Had I communicated inadequately? The team seemed not to accept descriptions of the review process, forecasts of needs for positioning of articles to maximize likelihood of publication, and so on. My suggestions about statistical rigor, methods for sample selection, and choice of sample size were all rejected as irrelevant or even wrong.

The week ended in disappointment. I had not carried my weight in the prestigious group and apparently had not used my academic knowledge and personal style to be accepted into the group. If the work was to be aimed at American publications but without American conventions, how successful would this project be? Kent assured me that the project would still be very valuable with or without statistical rigor and urged me to stay on the team despite the initial disappointment.

The evening activities in Lyon continued to be friendly, but the meetings during the day were a bit strained. The groups tended to break into national groupings. The Swedish dined together, the French went to their homes each evening, and the British and I formed a clique. The Italians and Germans preferred to go their own way.

I left Lyon, headed to Indonesia, with a sense of dread. If I could not adapt to my colleagues who shared a common historical and cultural background, how could I possibly survive a summer in Jakarta? The cross-cultural techniques I had learned did not seem to be helping, and the little French I knew helped only with taxi drivers and waiters.

Susan's New Position

In the months that followed, Susan moved to a new position at another university that equally valued international research and the development of its international reputation. Because the research and contacts seemed to be valued at the university, she decided to forge on with less than perfect enthusiasm.

Perhaps it was just as well that the project was not the first priority for her. The French team had continued on without her, failing to mail out important updates in the questionnaire, notification that industries had been chosen, and an announcement that interviews were to proceed in the first industry. When Susan learned from Kent that the other project members were receiving instructions, she became very uncomfortable with her role on the team. The planning had proceeded without her, although she had performed the detailed analyses assigned for each member at the end of the Lyon meeting and had sent the results to the French coordinator. Susan decided to call Kent in Great Britain to seek his opinion and advice. Susan was convinced that she had done something wrong. Kent's response was that everything was fine and that Susan should prepare for their next meeting.

The Second Meeting: Estoril, Portugal

Plans were in place to attend the July 1994 meeting in Estoril, outside Lisbon, Portugal. Again, no one appeared until late afternoon on Monday. Professor Pierre Simone, the senior professor of the French contingency, adjourned Monday's meeting. He preferred to have a swim. "Tomorrow, then, at 8:30 A.M." were his dismissive words. A night of revelry was to begin the proceedings once again.

This rough beginning was fortuitous of events to come. A whole series of unfortunate interactions occurred as the week progressed.

Susan's Experience

At least at this meeting, if the meetings were dismal, there would be the beach!

Tuesday morning, I left the meeting for a few minutes and returned to witness a pubic dressing down of a senior German professor by the junior French professor who was the project administrator. "Are you not capable of completing your interviews? Do you need help? We need for you to get moving," Antoine said to Professor Ditmar Schwartz as I entered the room. Academic rank notwithstanding, the senior German professor had been publicly reprimanded.

The second incident also occurred on Tuesday, when Kent asked who would be responsible for editing the book. "The book is to be written in English, so it makes sense that a native speaker of English should edit it. We have some very capable scholars in our group, but their written English skills vary widely. The editor cannot be just anyone," Kent emphasized. "What are you suggesting, Kent?" Pierre Simone countered. "Are you suggesting that we cannot speak English well? Why do you always think the English speakers are the best in the group? Look around this group and you will see that is not the case!"

"Pierre, you misunderstand my intention," Kent responded defensively. "I am merely suggesting that we avoid the disaster we faced last time when the Italians' chapter had to be rewritten at the last minute because the English was incomprehensible!"

"No, Kent, you intend to take all the royalties for yourself again as you did last time for doing nothing but merely editing the book. No, you will not selfishly take all profits this time!"

In uncharacteristic directness, Kent threatened, "Then you go ahead and try to sell this book, something you will be unsuccessful in. But, do not come to me at the last minute for help for you surely will not get it from me."

Stunned, the room sat silently. When I finally got my breath back, I mumbled under my breath, "I thought only Americans argued in this way publicly."

Tuesday evening was spent, as usual, in small groups looking for the quintessential memorable meal and entertainment. This time though, palpable resentment hung in the air, at least between the French and the British/American group. The French were not asked to join us nor did they extend an invitation. The new Spanish members went out with the French. The German professor had his meal in the hotel, claiming he wanted to watch the football match on television.

Shockingly, Wednesday turned out to be worse than Tuesday. I unwittingly became the lightening rod by suggesting the team make plans for presentations of the theoretical ideas and preliminary results. I already knew where Pierre stood on the issue because I had corresponded with him via fax regarding a deadline the previous March for a very prestigious conference. In a salty response which began with "Mrs. Hepburn, I will decide where and when this material will be presented, not you," Pierre made his position perfectly clear. I thought it rather insulting that Pierre had not used my professional title of "professor" or "doctor" in the correspondence and wondered whether it reflected a gender bias toward me as a woman. At a minimum, it seemed a friendly first name might have been appropriate.

Despite Pierre's response, it seemed that the decision should not be a unilateral one but a joint, team-level one. So, I thought it was appropriate to bring it up again before the whole group. Kent actually brought it up, and the French members were immediately against it. The Swedish, British, and Italian members favored it. The Spanish and Portuguese were rather silent on the matter. The conversation around this topic was as unpleasant as the previous day's. Personal insults were hurled. Pierre suggested in sum that the only people who were in a hurry were the young, inexperienced members who could not be trusted to conduct an acceptable presentation. So, he proposed a compromise under the following restrictions: Nontenured professors could present as long as (1) they restricted their contents to industry facts and (2) they were accompanied by a senior professor from the group. Needless to say, feathers were ruffled on all sides. Having presented multiple times at the most visible of national meetings in the field, I did not feel I needed to be chaperoned by senior faculty. The other nontenured professors shared my feelings of indignity.

"I was not treated like this when I was a student," I fumed indignantly to Kent. "I certainly do not have to stand for this now. This project is not worth this insult! Let them get someone else to do the American interviews, if they can. I challenge them to find a qualified faculty member in the United States who will put up with this nonsense. Am I this incompetent? Perhaps this is pure male chauvinism. No matter what the reason, I will not be back for another ISRG meeting," I vowed as we assessed our positions in the group. Apparently, I had spoken for the entire group of nontenured faculty on the project. Interestingly, this nontenured group was composed of all women.

Feelings of failure again dominated my thoughts as I packed to head for home. "This is a waste of scarce research time and money," I thought as I assessed the lack of achievements during the week. "I have several other projects I neglected in favor of ISRG. I will just get back to those. I will call Kent on Monday and tell him that I am withdrawing from the team."

Upon hearing of my decision, Kent immediately apologized on behalf of the whole team and urged continued participation in the project. "This will be very good for your career when it is complete," he said. "Please reconsider and don't make any decisions to leave the team without consulting me. I don't understand what is going on in the minds of the French. We need you on the team for the North American comparison."

Kent's words appealed to my analytical as well as emotional side. I knew it was good for me to remain on the team but doubted the cost, and I shared this with Kent. "If it will help, I can do two things for you," Kent volunteered. "First, I will send you all the material I receive from the French so that you need not rely upon them. Second, I will pay for

your expenses from my budget so that you will not have to cover your expenses which are higher than most of ours anyway." This conversation helped address several concerns. After thinking about Kent's generous offer, I decided to renew my interest in the project but to work on it only after completing several others that had high potential for early completion. The enthusiasm was not to return, however.

The Third Meeting: Milan, Italy

In December 1994, Susan received funding from her university and had time to conduct some of the interviews. Apparently Susan was not the only team member who lacked total commitment. Each team was to have completed 30 interviews by the third meeting, which took place in January 1995 in Milan. Only the British and German teams accomplished the task as set out in Estoril. The other teams, including the French team, seemed to have completed only about half of the intended interviews. The Milan meeting promised to be another difficult one.

The French were on time this meeting, but several other teams were missing on Monday afternoon. Despite the 3:00 P.M. scheduled start time, only the British and French had arrived at the hotel. Susan had brought a laptop and some papers to review so that she would have something to do while waiting at the hotel for the rest of the members.

After a very brief meeting lasting only minutes, the assembled group was dismissed and asked to meet promptly at 8:30 A.M. on Tuesday morning. The meeting was adjourned to the hotel lobby for casual conversation until dinner time. Predictions of doom issued from Susan and each of the British members.

Susan's Experience

Then, Tuesday morning offered another surprise from the French for me. A professor from a Canadian university, Frederick Wise, had arrived at the meeting. Not introduced nor explained, I wondered what was up. Anthony, the French professor responsible for acquiring the EU grant, addressed requests for interviews with specific American firms to Frederick who was smoothly noncommittal. "I will look into it," he responded often.

That evening at the hotel bar over Spumante, I was decidedly American in my directness toward Frederick. "So, Frederick, have you been asked to do the American interviews?"

"Well, that is what I wanted to talk to you about, Susan. How would you feel about my doing some interviews in the United States?"

This lack of finesse and diplomacy on the part of the French was revealing. "I have no problem with your doing any of them, Frederick. I would prefer that you not do any interviews in firms I have already contacted and planned on. But, the more disturbing issue is that the French have left this to you and me to work out. Why have they done this?"

Frederick responded, "Of course, I would not want to interfere in any way with your role. Perhaps, I could do interviews in Canada just across the border. I have made no commitment. We will see how the week progresses."

"How could I have come so far from my original role in this group? Is it something I have done? Is it because I am a woman? Is it because I was introduced by Kent?" I wondered after Frederick had gone. So much for the honor of participating in such a prestigious group.

Susan's Decision

In the year I had been in the group, I had the opportunity to have my professional pride wounded. But, just as seriously, I wondered whether the situation had arisen from a lack of cultural sensitivity and understanding. I also wondered whether I was qualified to teach others about cross-cultural issues, much less participate in a sophisticated multinational research project.

But, how should I decide whether to continue with the group? Certainly I had to consider whether the project could actually be executed given the requirements of the team leaders and the effort needed to complete the project. And, if I spent the time needed on this project, how would it affect my other work? I really needed to weigh the potential benefits of continuing versus the costs of quitting. How would my professional reputation be affected if I left the group? What impact would it have on my career? Would I be disappointed with myself for quitting or would it be a relief?

I resolved to speak with other colleagues about this when I arrived home. In the meantime, I reclined my spacious seat to enjoy the trip home.

Appendix

Researchers of culture have provided different frameworks for viewing average behavior or values of different cultures. Although these frameworks do not describe every individual within a particular culture, they do provide an indication of what an average person might be like. They can be used as a good starting point for understanding what to expect from someone from a particular culture. We give a summary of how three cultural researchers categorize people from the United States, France, and England here. To gain a greater understanding of these theories, it is recommended that the reader refer to the works cited in this discussion.

Gannon's Metaphors

Martin Gannon from the United States used a metaphor to describe each of 17 cultures. In his book (Gannon 1994), he describes in detail how the metaphor can be used to explain and understand the behavior of each culture. The following summary provides the metaphor and a brief description of the culture as explained by Gannon.

The United States. The metaphor for the United States is American football. Within the game we see some of the major cultural characteristics of Americans: movement, speed, aggressiveness, and competitive specialization. Although Americans are highly individualistic, the "huddling" behavior of football can be used as a metaphor to show how they function within groups. The huddling or group behavior is a societal mechanism for coordinating activities; thus Americans can be intensely committed to a group for a short time in order to accomplish certain goals. They then move on.

Americans are also very numbers oriented and use standardized rankings for judging performance. Some other cultural characteristics that are manifest in the football metaphor include time-obsessed, monochronic, nationalistic, ethnocentric, and religious. People from the United States generally value profits, fame, glory, equal opportunity, independence, individual initiative, and self-reliance.

France. The metaphor used to describe the French is French wine. The process of wine making is a complex one, a blending of science and art that has evolved over the centuries. Gannon uses this process of wine making to explain the complex, sometimes seemingly contradictory, French people. The French believe in their own cultural superiority and in their very pure and proud country. Just as there is a hierarchy of wines, so too is there a hierarchy of society, a centralized social structure. The person at the top of the hierarchy is the most important and has the power to make most, if not all, decisions.

The French have a need to control and refine life. This is manifest in bureaucratic institutions where risk taking is not encouraged. French people are hard working, argumentative, individualistic, and honorable. They enjoy life and nurture relationships but are wary of outsiders.

England. The traditional British house is the metaphor Gannon selects for the British. Both the house and the people are raised in the one "right way": to be properly British. The house is built as the people behave—in a traditional manner. There is a firmness and a respect and strong desire for privacy. We would also expect a certain orderliness. Some of the other British characteristics include resourcefulness, diplomacy, leadership, good graces, unexcitability, reserve, and patience.

Hofstede's Dimensions of Cultural Values

Dutch researcher Geert Hofstede (1980) undertook to compare work-related values of employees of IBM in more than 40 countries. Using his studies, he constructed four dimensions of cultural values that could be used to describe the preferences of people in the various cultures he studied. The first of these dimensions was power distance (PD), the degree to which people accept inequalities in power distribution. A high score indicates that people accept the fact that power is not equal among individuals. The second dimension, uncertainty avoidance (UA), is the degree to which people in a society are accepting of ambiguity and risk taking behavior. A country with a high UA score has people who seek security and try to avoid risky situations. The third dimension is individualism/

collectivism (I/C). In an individualistic society each person is expected to be self-reliant and does things on his or her own; a collective society is group oriented. People do things as expected by the society or by the clan. The fourth dimension, masculinity/femininity (M/F), describes what things people value. A masculine society is "tough" and values money, status, and things. A feminine society is "tender," and values quality of life and the nature of relationships.

The following chart indicates where the United States, France, and England scored on Hofstede's four dimensions:

	PD	UA	I/C	M/F
United States	Low	Low	I	M
France	High	High	I	F
England	Low	Low	I	M

Trompenaars' Dimensions

Fons Trompenaars (1993), also from the Netherlands, developed a set of dimensions to describe cultural values. His studies were based on surveys of thousands of managers in 28 countries over a 10-year period. The dimensions that he developed were based on the work of American anthropologists Kluckhohn and Strodtbeck (1961). Five of his dimensions are particularly relevant to business situations (Hoecklin 1995).

The first dimension, universalism versus particularism (U/P), indicates how a society applies rules of morals and ethics. In a universal society, rules and contracts are developed that can apply in any situation. A particularist culture, in contrast, looks at relationships and circumstances in a particular case to decide what is right. The second dimension, individualism versus collectivism (I/C), is similar to Hofstede's. The third dimension is neutral versus affective relationships (N/A). In neutral cultures, expression of emotion is more restrained; certain emotions are considered to be improper to exhibit in certain situations. In an affective culture, emotions are expressed more naturally.

Trompenaars' fourth dimension is specific versus diffuse relationships (S/D). In a specific society, people generally have larger public spaces (or lives), and the access to these is very open. Their private spaces are smaller and more difficult to access. In a diffuse culture, public spaces are relatively smaller, whereas private spaces are relatively larger. It is more difficult to access the public space but once one does, access to the private space often comes along with it.

The fifth dimension is achievement versus ascription (Ac/As). In an achievement culture, status and power are derived from what an individual has done. In an ascription society, the emphasis is on who the person is.

The following chart gives the relative scores of the United States, France, and England on Trompenaars' dimensions.

	U/P	I/C	N/A	S/D	Ac/As
United States	U	I	N/A	S	Ac
France	U/P	C	N/A	S	Ac/As
England	U	I	N	S	Ac

Note: When both ends of the dimension have been given, it indicates a score that is approximately in the middle.

Source: Based on dimensional scoring given in Hoecklin, L. (1995). *Managing Cultural Differences: Strategies for Competitive Advantage.* Reading, MA: Addison-Wesley. ▮

SOURCE: Copyright ©1996 Sara L. Keck and Anne Marie Francesco. Reprinted by permission of the authors. The situations depicted in this case are intended to stimulate discussion and not to suggest administrative solutions. The events reported in this case actually occurred, but the group and member names have been disguised for confidentiality.

REFERENCES

GANNON, M. J. (1994). *Understanding Global Cultures.* Thousand Oaks, CA: Sage Publications.

HOECKLIN, L. (1995). *Managing Cultural Differences: Strategies for Competitive Advantage.* Reading, MA: Addison-Wesley.

HOFSTEDE, G. (1980). *Culture's Consequences: International Differences in Work-Related Values.* Newbury Park, CA: Sage Publications.

KLUCKHOHN, S. H. and STRODTBECK, F. L. (1961). *Variations in Value Orientation.* Evanston, IL: Row, Peterson.

TROMPENAARS, F. (1993). *Riding the Waves of Culture: Understanding Diversity in Global Business.* London: The Economist Books.

Case 4   Portrait of a Young Russian Capitalist

Barry Allen Gold

"I want to make profit, not a salary"—Max Levin

In the Beginning

Beginning with the collapse of communism in 1988 and accelerating with the breakup of the Soviet Union in 1992, Russia has experienced dramatic changes. In May 1988, as part of *Perestroika*, Mikhail Gorbachev passed the Law of Cooperation. For the first time since the 1917 Revolution—excluding 1922 to 1929—this law permitted Soviet citizens to form private partnerships. In 1992, with the breakup of the USSR, Russia's parliament, under the guidance of President Boris Yeltsin, passed the State Privatization Program, which was intended to increase privatization and assist the transition to a market economy.

But, the road to capitalism has been rocky. The October 11, 1994, *New York Times* began a front page article:

> The ruble is crashing amid mounting fears of renewed inflation, and the fledgling stock market is still smarting from its first big downturn. Bankers and entrepreneurs are being gunned down in the streets. There is little financial regulation and considerable fraud.

But for American and other foreign investors, those unpleasant realities are becoming far less important than their growing sense that Russia presents a business opportunity so big that they can no longer afford to hold back.

A Capitalist's Background

Family

Maxim "Max" Levin is a 25-year-old Moscovite. His family is Jewish. Under communism they never experienced overt discrimination; religion was simply not discussed. In postcommunist Russia, Max claims, "I can be proud to be a Jew," but considers himself assimilated into Russian society and does not practice any religion.

Max describes his family's economic status under the communist regime and in 1994 as upper-middle class; for many years they have had a high, steady, secure income. Before *Perestroika*, Max's father was an upper-level manager at a state-owned petroleum refinery and then became a high-ranking government official at the Ministry of Petroleum Refining. In 1989, he became a manager at a Soviet–German joint venture refinery in Moscow. As a result of these positions, he developed many personal connections with government officials and private businesspeople. Yet, even with the liberalized political climate, he remained very concerned with which individuals and groups possessed power and control in government and industry.

Max's mother is a physician. Under communism, she earned a high salary compared with other occupations and worked in a state hospital. Soviet physicians—who never had the high status and generous salaries of medical doctors in the United States—still earn comparatively modest salaries under privatization. Beginning in 1991 Dr. Levin worked in a public clinic in Moscow.

Education

In September 1987, after secondary school, Max enrolled in the Moscow Finance Institute—renamed the State Finance Academy in 1992—to study for a degree in finance. In June 1988 he entered the Soviet Army for two years as then required by Soviet law for all 18-year-old men. His army duty was reduced to 14 months when the law was changed. Max views himself as fortunate: Because of the change he avoided duty in the USSR's war with Afghanistan. Overall, his

310

assessment of his military experience is positive; he learned discipline and matured rapidly.

Work

When he returned to school after the military in September 1989, business opportunities were beginning to open as a result of economic policies designed to create private enterprise and markets. In October 1989, with the aid of his father's business connections, Max took a part-time job in Moscow at Neftechimbank.

When Max joined Neftechimbank in 1989, it was small and mainly provided services to state-owned industries. However, as a result of privatization and the resultant growth of the petroleum industry—the bank's major client and shareholder—within a few months the bank experienced rapid growth. A year later, it was one of the largest banks in Russia. Because of the remarkable growth, work at the bank offered many opportunities and valuable experiences. For instance, as part of his training, Max was rotated among the various divisions and got an overview of banking. In addition, substantial customer growth provided Max with many personal connections with people starting businesses.

While working part-time at Neftechimbank, Max attended classes full-time in finance, accounting, and auditing. As in Russian society generally, change was occurring quickly at the Academy. For example, Price Waterhouse, one of the "Big Six" world accounting firms, presented seminars on Western accounting practices to the Academy's students. This immersion into capitalist techniques was unthinkable a year earlier.

Company Founding—1991

Capitalism was spreading. In 1991 Max left the bank. He and Sergey Kamaroff, a fellow student, formed a partnership with Vladimir Smirov, a friend and student at the Moscow State Technical Institute, with the intention of starting a business. They had no particular business in mind and no capital (there were no requirements for shareholders' capital at the time). According to Max, "In 1991 everyone tried to do *something* in business. They wanted to take advantage of opportunities." For many people a major enticement was greed: *the opportunity to get rich quick*. Max and his partners

knew people who, by setting up trading companies, became millionaires in a short time. This was comparatively easy to do in 1991, at the beginning of privatization, because there were few government regulations concerning private businesses. However, there was considerable risk: State control over the economy was still strong, and many of the new entrepreneurs violated the state monopoly on foreign trade with the prospect and, in some cases, the actuality of arrest.

Six months passed and the new corporation was inactive. The partners, who were among the first Academy students to form a corporation, still had no specific business in mind and almost no models to emulate. It slowly became clear to them that they wanted to blend "theory and practice"—to use what they were learning in school as a basis of their business.

The partners decided to translate into Russian a 50-page pamphlet written in English on how to read American corporate financial statements. They sold the translation to a small publishing company and now had some capital. Considering the success of the pamphlet, their training, and banking experience, they decided to open an accounting firm. They envisioned a growing market as companies formed, the government required more standardized financial reporting, and American and European companies began to do business in Russia, because Russian and Western accounting principles were not the same.

In March 1992 the company leased a small office in an unfashionable part of Moscow. They selected the name Marillion Accounting Firm after the novelist Tolkien to symbolize "truth." At this time they had one computer and two small business clients.

Company Growth—1992

In May 1992, Max's father suggested that they contact a Soviet–Italian joint venture company—the general manager was his college classmate. This was their first major client. The task was to set up an accounting system for the company that had been operating for two years. Because it was a sizable job, they hired two fellow students to work for them. (One of the new employees, Ilya Popov, became a partner a short time later.) All of them worked at the joint venture company for a month;

it was difficult to straighten out the books which had been neglected for the past two years. The fees they earned went to pay salaries and rent.

In December 1992, because of a growing staff, they required more space and relocated to a hotel in Moscow. Also, more elaborate, presentable offices were needed to meet with current and potential clients. At this time, they had six employees and six clients, and every quarter showed modest revenue growth.

A few weeks after moving into the hotel, members of the Russian Mafia "visited" them. Although they made threats, the firm's small size and limited operations were of no interest to the Mafia. They never returned.

Another significant early client was a watch manufacturing firm. Ilya had good relationships with the manager of the company, which was a state enterprise. After several months of negotiations, Marillion won the account. Ilya, a talented accountant, personally managed the watch company account. Eventually, Ilya and several new accountants relocated to the watch firm's offices, while Max and Vladimir worked on other accounts and sought new business.

The Insurance Industry

At this time, the three principals reorganized the company into a limited partnership with no outside shareholders. Shortly after, in summer 1992, the firm's emphasis shifted from general accounting to auditing joint ventures and limited partnerships. Also at this time, there was a change in the structure of the Russian insurance industry. Like every other industry, insurance in the Soviet Union was a state monopoly. In 1992 it was privatized, and no regulations governing insurance or standard accounting practices for insurers existed. The State Insurance Supervisory Service was formed at this time to regulate the insurance industry. The three partners viewed this as a strategic niche and decided to make insurance auditing a specialty because of their background and the emerging opportunities. It was particularly attractive because there were few competitors.

They met with several executives of the State Insurance Company, Rosgosstrackh. The discussion focused on the services they had developed and anticipated changes in government oversight of insurance companies. Marillion signed an agreement with Rosgosstrackh and got an approval from the State Insurance Supervisory Service for developing a Chart of Accounts. This was a formal mandate to set up accounting systems for insurance companies.

At this time, in addition to changes in the insurance industry, there were also changes in the Russian accounting system intended to make it more like Western accounting. Few accountants in Russia knew much about the new procedures. This enhanced the opportunity for Max and his partners. In August 1992 they began work on the Chart, which would incorporate Western accounting principles.

By December 1992 the system Marillion developed was approved and implemented. It was the first accounting system of its type in Russia and became a model for other insurance firms. Max and his partners published a pamphlet describing how to set up an accounting system for the insurance industry. They sold the book to a private publisher before the government officially printed it. This publication made the company well known and generated new business. Eventually, these guidelines were adopted by the State Insurance Supervisory Service and were codified in an official policy manual.

By December 1992, revenues were sufficient for the business to pay salaries to the principals and retain modest earnings.

In January 1993, under a new set of government regulations, every insurance company was required to adopt the new accounting practices. Marillion acquired more insurance companies as clients; Max and Sergey were now responsible for the insurance business. Ilya continued to supervise the work with the watch company, the joint ventures, and several small accounts. By April 1993 they had 10 insurance companies and 20 firms in other industries as clients.

In May 1993 Marillion moved to a larger office in a more desirable location. At this time they attracted another large client: a holding company that managed trading companies, a bank, and an insurance company.

The Company—1994

By 1994 the firm had a staff of 20 with 40 clients and was continuing to grow. Revenue was at a record high. In addition to drawing salaries, the partners split a substantial profit. In July 1994, they moved to a larger office opposite the Kremlin. This office was closer to the holding company that was their largest client. However, despite rapid growth, they were still a small company compared with the Big Six auditing firms that opened in Russia in 1992. Nevertheless, they had certain competitive advantages. In one case, Marillion was in competition with KPMG and won the account because they knew more about Russian companies. In addition, KPMG charged very high fees by Russian standards. Also, Marillion had developed a good reputation.

In September 1993, after graduating from the Moscow State Finance Academy, Max decided that it would be an advantage to know more about American business practices, particularly accounting and finance. He enrolled in an MBA program in the United States. After beginning graduate studies Max returned to Moscow to manage the company actively during the summer but otherwise limited his involvement to an investor.

In February 1994 Max incorporated a branch office of Marillion in New York City. By February 1995 the branch had one client to which it consulted regarding investments in Russian businesses.

The Future

The partners developed short- and long-range plans to develop the business. For the short term, Marillion hired a computer programmer to develop software for insurance companies. They also started to consult with foreign companies in Russia. Long-term plans included involvement in the Russian stock market as consultants for companies that wanted to obtain a listing or invest in the stock market. Finally, they planned to merge Marillion with other small companies to become more competitive with the Big Six.

Taxes

In 1994 the Russian tax rate, which is progressive, was 60% on personal income and 35% for corporate revenue. There was a 23% VAT (value-added tax) and many other taxes on specific goods and services. These high rates were part of a program to stem hyper-inflation. But high taxes have adverse effects on entrepreneurial activity. As a result, rather than not enter business or pay the tax, Russian businesspeople looked for ways to avoid taxes. For example, many entrepreneurs were paid in U.S. dollars "off-the-books" to avoid taxes and reduce the effects of hyper-inflation. In 1995, the Russian government began to close tax law loopholes.

The Mafia

In the mid–1990s the Mafia was a real problem for Russian businesses. As noted previously, when Marillion moved to its second location in a hotel in Moscow, the Mafia visited Max and his partners. Though nothing happened, the Mafia was a genuine concern. Mafia killings of businesspeople were frequent. Despite the fact that they were well publicized, they increased and the government did little to prevent Mafia activities. Citizens, Max among them, viewed the government as colluding with the Mafia and benefiting from their activities. Ironically, Max viewed the Mafia as contributing to the maintenance of order in Russian society, which became fragmented and lawless after the collapse of Communism.

For a Russian businessperson, as a practical matter to prevent drawing attention, it was not wise to purchase a Mercedes or otherwise display wealth. The Mafia was attracted to success, which increased the likelihood that a business would be infiltrated. According to Max, if you were successful and advertised it, "before too long you would be the employee and the Mafia would be your boss." Or worse. In early October 1994 an executive of the insurance company that gave Max's firm one of their first major insurance accounts was shot dead by the Mafia on a Moscow street.

Reflection and Action

In February 1995 Max's optimism of five years earlier was tinged with the realization that conducting business in the new Russian economy was not as easy as it had first appeared. In addition to the Mafia, domestic political the economic instability created uncertainty.

Russian culture also posed threats to the development of a new economic order. On April 11, 1995, the New York Times printed an article with the headline, "Latest Films for $2: Video Piracy Booms in Russia." The story recounted how Russian merchants sold counterfit copies of Academy Award-winning films such as Pulp Fiction and Forrest Gump. Svetlana Abromovna, a senior researcher at the Institute of Civil Law in Moscow, who has studied intellectual property rights for 30 years said: 'There is a law against this kind of theft. But there are many laws in Russia that nobody takes seriously. There are no penalties.' Ms. Abromovna continued. 'Private property–whether it is land, a car or somebody else's idea–is still the hardest thing for Russians today to understand. In principle everyone is for it. But in fact., nothing is harder than convincing a Russian to leave other people's property alone.'

Max, who maintained frequent contact with his partners in Russia, now also had a view of events in Russia from abroad. This complicated his decision making. He would receive his MBA from an American university in May 1995. He wondered: "Should I stay in the United States and be a consultant with American firms interested in doing business in Russia, or should I return to Russia and rejoin my partners to develop Marillion?" ■

SOURCE: Copyright © 1997 Barry Allen Gold. Reprinted by permission of Barry Allen Gold. Presented at the 1996 annual meeting of the North American Case Research Association.

Case 5   Yutaka Nakamura: A Foreigner in His Native Land

J. Stewart Black

As he neared the top of the stairs that would lead him to the subway train and his hour and a half commute to his office, Yutaka Nakamura hesitated and then quickly moved aside to allow the mass of morning commuters to push their way down to the most punctual and safe mass transit system in the world. As he stood there at the top of the stairs watching the mass of humanity before him, he reflected on the past six months since he and his family had returned to Japan from their overseas assignment in the United States. Once again, this morning his wife had cried and asked him to request another transfer overseas. After listening to his wife, Yutaka pushed back the carefully prepared breakfast his wife had made. Like most mornings lately, he left for work without eating much and with a throbbing headache left over from the previous night's drinking and socializing. As he stood there knowing that he needed to hurry down the stairs in order to catch the train that would put him into Tokyo and at his office precisely ten minutes before nine o'clock, Yutaka wondered what direction his life should take.

Background

Yutaka, 44, prior to being sent to a key subsidiary in California four years ago, was in the sales department in a large electronics firm. He was hired directly after graduating from Tokyo University, the most prestigious university in all of Japan. His wife Chizuru, 40, was a graduate of Sofia University and the daughter of a former parliament member of Japan's Lower House. Yutaka and Chizuru met when they were both employees in the same department of the electronics firm. After they were married, they waited a few years to have their first child, Kenichi, now 14 and a very bright and outgoing teenager. Three years after Kenichi was born, they had their daughter, Yukimi. Yutaka felt he had a fairly typical middle-class

Japanese life. Given that he worked in one of the largest electronics firms in the world, with operations in over 100 different countries, it was not surprising that Yutaka was asked to fill an overseas position in the marketing and sales department in southern California. He was given the position of co-vice president of marketing. Although it took some effort, Yutaka adjusted to living and working in southern California with its much more leisurely paced life and work style compared to Tokyo.

At first Chizuru had trouble adjusting to living in the United States. It took her several months before her English was sufficiently proficient for her to go grocery shopping, driving, and otherwise to take care of various family needs. Chizuru's English was much more labored than that of the other family members, but she eventually reached the point where she felt comfortable talking with the various neighbors who lived around them.

The children, on the other hand, quickly adjusted to the California lifestyle. In particular, Kenichi enjoyed whatever time he could at the beach, where he learned how to surf. Both children did extremely well in school and after their first year were completely age-proficient in English. The children attended normal American schools during the weekday, but on weekends spent one and a half days in a special Japanese school. Chizuru also had correspondence work sent from Japan and spent weekends helping the children with math, science, and Japanese reading and writing.

In general, the Nakamuras enjoyed their new lifestyle, the three-bedroom, 2,600 sq. ft. house, the two cars, the weekends of picnics, museums, and camping, the evenings spent together barbecuing in the backyard, and the yearly holiday back to Japan.

Despite enjoying their life in America, when it came time to return to Japan, all of the family

315

members were excited to return. Other than checking on schools back in Tokyo, little thought was given to preparing for the re-entry and readjustment back to Japan. After all, they were going home.

Problems Since Return

Unfortunately, things had not gone as smoothly as they had anticipated since their return to Japan. The kids, Chizuru, and Yutaka had their own particular problems in adjusting to life back in Japan.

The Children

Although Kenichi and Yukimi had spent weekends in a special Japanese school while they were overseas, when they returned, it became very clear they were somewhat behind in several key areas. In particular, they were behind in math, science, and written Japanese. As a consequence, Chizuru hired a special private tutor to help the children with these subjects. She was most concerned that Kenichi was not adequately prepared for the upcoming high school exam. She hoped he would be able to enter an "escalator" high school (i.e., those particularly well-known for facilitating their graduates in entering a prestigious Japanese university). However, soon after their return, Chizuru began to get phone calls from the children's teachers and school administrators. In particular, Kenichi's teacher commented that he asked too many questions during class, and that his memorization skills seemed to be quite poor. Kenichi also seemed unwilling to accept facts as stated by the teacher, and constantly wanted to know the logic behind various statements.

Yukimi adjusted somewhat more easily than Kenichi to school. However, not long after they returned to Japan, she complained that her classmates were calling her *Gaijin*, which translated means foreigner.

Both children commented that their peers ridiculed some of their clothes, which they had purchased while they were in California. Some of their teachers commented that both Yukimi and Kenichi were not as proficient as they should be in the variations of their speech needed when speaking to individuals of differing status. Kenichi also complained several times that he didn't get jokes told at school because he did not understand the particular slang expression that was being used. Chizuru was disappointed to find that the children's

English ability actually worked against them in their English classes. In particular, Kenichi had difficulty because he felt his English teacher had terrible pronunciation. A couple of times Kenichi offered a correct pronunciation, only to be ridiculed by his teacher and his classmates. Eventually, Kenichi had to consciously try to forget correct English pronunciation, and pronounce English words with a strong Japanese accent.

One Sunday morning, before going off to a special weekend class at a nearby *Juku*, or cram school, Kenichi asked his mother if his father would play catch with him with the half hour he had before he needed to go. Chizuru replied that his father was asleep and tired from the long hours of work. At this Kenichi exploded and burst out that his father was never around. They used to go to museums and the park and camping when they lived in the United States, now it was clear his father loved his job more than he loved his children. In tears, Kenichi ran out of the house and off to his cram session.

Above all these developments, one of the most disturbing had only recently emerged. Chizuru knew that both of the children had enjoyed much of their experience in the United States; however, lately she found them criticizing California and the United States to their friends. In fact, one day she overheard Yukimi telling a classmate that she hated America; she hated Americans; and she hated her parents for making her live in that foreign country. This 180-degree turn in attitude seriously troubled Chizuru, but she didn't know what to do about it or what it meant.

Chizuru Nakamura

Chizuru had her own difficulties adjusting to Japan. It had taken her about a year to begin to feel comfortable in the United States, but she now missed many things about their life in California. One of the most interesting aspects of life in the United States was the parties she and Yutaka attended and hosted together. When they hosted parties at their California home, her role was quite different than back in Japan. In the United States when they hosted a party, both she and Yutaka would plan the event and then greet the guests at the door. Throughout the night guests would comment to Chizuru how lovely her home was, how wonderful the dinner was, and how beautiful she looked. These compliments were, at first, somewhat strange to her, but over time became a very important source of pride and satisfaction. In addition, during dinners, as was customary, Chizuru rarely sat by her husband. Instead she was often placed next to other spouses as well as other executives and clients with whom her husband associated. Many of these guests commented directly and indirectly about Chizuru's intelligent insights concerning international affairs. After some time, Chizuru found that she quite enjoyed both attending and hosting these social interactions. Instead of simply being relegated to the kitchen and bringing in various dishes for the guests only to quickly disappear again as was the custom in Japan, Chizuru found she played an important role in the social standing of her husband, and that she had an importance in her own right.

When she returned to Japan, of course, these social interactions were completely out of the question. Yutaka rarely brought friends home, and when he did, he brought them without their wives. Her role was not that of hostess as much as it was that of waitress. Chizuru longed for her life back in the U.S. On top of losing her broader role in life, Chizuru felt she lost her husband upon returning to Japan. During their time in the United States, Chizuru had felt that she had rediscovered the man she had fallen in love with and married over 17 years ago. Many times they would talk together at night or take walks in their quiet suburban neighborhood. Especially during the last two years of their overseas assignment, Chizuru and Yutaka would often go out for dinner, see a show, or attend a cultural event. Unfortunately, those times were long gone now.

When Chizuru had first returned to Japan, she tried to re-establish relationships with some of her friends. However, whenever she tried to tell them of her experiences in the U.S., they quickly seemed disinterested and on some occasions actually accused her of showing off. This hurt Chizuru deeply. In her heart, she was simply trying to share something that was very important to her with her friends in order to reconnect with them after the long absence.

In addition to these social difficulties, Chizuru often found herself depressed because of the difficulties the children were having at school. Chizuru had prided herself on the fact that she had kept the children involved in Japanese curriculum during their stay in the United States through correspondence work and the weekend Japanese classes. She was very disappointed and frustrated to find that

once they had returned, the children were still somewhat behind in critical areas. Also, despite her best efforts, the children had not yet adjusted well to the new schools, and it was becoming increasingly doubtful that Kenichi would be able to pass the test and enter one of the more prestigious high schools. She was convinced that women in her neighborhood were talking about what a poor mother she was, and the disservice she had brought upon her children by not keeping them up-to-date in their schoolwork while overseas.

Chizuru had also found many other points of frustration during the six months since they had returned to Japan. Although she was unaware of it at first, many of the Western clothes she had purchased while in California had brighter colors than those in Japan. It had first occurred to her that her style of dress had changed when she had visited the market the first week after their return. As she was in the market buying fruits and vegetables for dinner that evening, she overheard one of her neighbors whisper to another that she must think herself better than the Japanese. After all, she was not wearing a traditional apron that all the women in that neighborhood wore when visiting the market.

The daily visits to the market were by themselves another irritant to Chizuru. In America, she had been able to shop once a week, or once every two weeks, because the refrigerator she had was large enough to store plenty of food. Going to the grocery store only once every week or two reduced the time she spent shopping and gave her more time to enjoy various activities. Now she had to spend two hours every day grocery shopping and had to spend nearly twice as much money on food because of its high cost in Japan. The high cost caused her to change the family's diet. For example, Yutaka, as well as the children, had come to like steak and other meats, but they were so expensive in Japan that Chizuru had to cut back dramatically on their purchase.

Another frustration concerned Chizuru's English language ability. In an effort to keep her language ability that she had worked so hard to achieve from declining, Chizuru joined an English class a month or so after returning to Japan. She very much enjoyed the classes until one day her sister-in-law commented that it was perhaps her attending English classes that was contributing to her children's difficulty in school. The fact that her sister-in-law would think such a thing made Chizuru wonder if she really was at the heart of her children's difficulties at school.

Her sister-in-law was not the only one with whom Chizuru had had difficulties since her return. Recently Chizuru's mother-in-law had asked her to come over. Although the request had seemed rather innocent at the time and her mother-in-law wanted nothing more than to chat, Chizuru discovered that it was a test of her loyalty. Her delay in going to visit her mother-in-law caused serious problems for a period of about two weeks. Yutaka had strongly criticized her for being so self-centered and not visiting his mother until the day after she called.

The cumulative effect of all these incidents was almost more than Chizuru could bear. One night after her husband arrived home at about 11:30 p.m., Chizuru in tears complained that she felt like Cinderella in reverse. All the wonderful things that she had come to enjoy were suddenly taken away from her, including her Prince Charming. When Yutaka replied that there was nothing that could be done, she begged him to seek another international assignment.

Yutaka Nakamura

Incidents big and small had taken their toll on Yutaka since his return to Japan. Often he had difficulty sleeping, and most mornings he headed to work with a throbbing headache. His wife was also worried because of his poor appetite. Yet, by many standards these were the typical ailments of a Japanese salaryman. Still, Chizuru encouraged Yutaka to take better care of himself. Yutaka was a little resentful of her concern and complaints. It seemed to him that on Sundays, his only free day at home, when he wanted to sleep, all he received was complaints from the family about his unwillingness to spend time with them. No matter what he did, someone was complaining.

Complaints also showed up rather frequently at work. For example, not long after he had returned home to Japan, he was reading a *Newsweek* on the train into work, just as he had often done before his assignment to America. However, once he got in his office, several of his peers chided him for showing off his language skills and reading an English news magazine instead of reading one of the more traditional Japanese news magazines. Surprised and hurt by this, Yutaka decided that from then on, even though he

would continue to read *Newsweek* in order to pass the time on the train, he would hide it before entering the office so as not to offend his peers.

He was also frustrated about the slow decision-making process in Japan. In the United States it had been uncomfortable at first to make important decisions on his own, but he soon grew to enjoy the autonomy and responsibility. Back in Japan, even simple decisions, such as approving a minor promotion budget, required him to talk to dozens of people. In fact, the more people he talked to, the more people that were suggested for him to talk to. Often the people who were suggested seemed totally unrelated to the issue on which Yutaka was working. However, he was reminded that in Japan, relationships are what makes businesses function. As a consequence, even though someone's opinion may not always directly bear on a particular project, it was important to stay connected with that person and for that person to feel that their opinion would be considered.

This emphasis on relationships also required after-hours socializing at least three nights a week until approximately 11:30 or 12 midnight. This socializing was particularly difficult for Yutaka to readjust to. The frequency was nothing short of exhausting. Twice he had fallen asleep on the train and had to stay in a hotel at the end of the line until he could take an early train home the next morning.

The commute in Japan was a far cry from his 20-minute commute in his comfortable car in California. Although he resented the complaints of his family about the time he spent at work, Yutaka was also frustrated with the long hours he spent away from his family. In fact, some days it felt as though he were wasting his entire life traveling on cram-packed, noisy trains.

Some days the train was so crowded that Yutaka could doze off without any worry of falling over. Some days after the long commute to or from work, life back in California seemed like a fading dream. Memories of going to museums, going to the beach, camping, and barbecues on the back patio were harder to recall. Now, it seemed to him that he was stuck in "no man's land." He no longer had the love and companionship of his family, and he also didn't feel completely accepted by his Japanese coworkers. It seemed to him that whatever direction he turned, any effort to try to please one group would alienate and displease another group. It was like being caught in an ever-tightening vice and there was no way out.

He felt frustrated almost on a daily basis at work because the marketing and negotiation skills that he had worked so hard to develop in the United States were going virtually unutilized back in Japan. Yutaka had gained great knowledge and insights into methods of integrating promotion print media and electronic media into unified marketing strategies. Unfortunately, in the general affairs department, these skills were not needed. Yutaka had also gained a great knowledge of how to negotiate effectively with Americans. He had mentioned his insights in this area several times to various people throughout the organization, but the only time he was allowed to utilize these skills was simply as a translator in a high-level meeting between a potential American supplier and the purchasing department. Yutaka thought to himself that he had not worked so hard at understanding Americans' negotiation tactics and thinking simply to translate words, but to formulate negotiation strategy.

Yutaka was rudely awakened from these reflections as someone crashed into him in their hurry down the steps to the subway. Unavoidably, Yutaka found himself running down the steps in order not to lose his balance. As he paid for his ticket and headed through the turnstile toward the tracks, he couldn't help but feel isolated and alone, despite being surrounded by 120 million Japanese.

Suddenly over the loudspeaker came the announcement that the train was arriving. As Yutaka looked down the track he saw the solitary beam of the approaching train. He wondered to himself how he should resolve these feelings he felt inside.

Should he ask for a transfer to another overseas assignment? If he did, he might become a permanent international assignee, rotating from one international assignment to another. This would virtually lock him out of any major advancement. Also, if he ever chose to return to Japan, it would probably be much more difficult the next time. Each time away would likely contribute to a deeper chasm between him and his home country and coworkers. Also, if the children went away again, this time it would be impossible for them to pass the entrance exams and get into a prestigious Japanese university. This would virtually guarantee that they would have to enter a foreign university. However, even if they went to a prestigious foreign university, such as Oxford, Harvard, or one of the grand ecoles in France, Yutaka doubted that they would ever be able to work for a large Japanese corporation. If they were given such a job, he doubted if they would ever be able to reach a position of any significance.

Yutaka worried that another overseas assignment would take his children away from both sets of grandparents. He had already heard enough from his mother about the pain she had suffered while the children were away. On the other hand, an international transfer could bring back the lifestyle and time together he and his wife and children had once enjoyed.

Part of him wanted to request a transfer, but another part of him deep inside recalled various stories he heard as a youth in Japan—a story of a 40-year-old son who dressed in a diaper and crawled across the floor so his parents would not feel old, a story of a son who laid naked beside his parents so that the mosquitoes would only attack him. These and other stories of self-sacrifice—for many the essence of the Japanese spirit—caused him to think about the responsibility he had to simply *gammon* or "hang in there."

As the train grew near, its flickering light sparked another alternative that would free him from disappointing someone no matter what choice he made. Yutaka flirted with this image longer than he had ever done before. ∎

SOURCE: "Yutaka Nakamura: A Foreigner in His Native Land" by J. Stewart Black from *International Management: Text and Cases* 3rd. ed. Paul Beamish, Allen Morrison, Phillip Rosenweig (eds.), Illinois: Irwin. Copyright © 1997 by J. Stewart Black. Reprinted by permission of the author.

IVEY Case 6   Ellen Moore (A): Living and Working in Bahrain

Richard Ivey School of Business
The University of Western Ontario

*Gail Ellement and
Martha Maznevski*

"The General Manager had offered me a choice of two positions in the Operations area. I had considered the matter carefully, and was about to meet with him to tell him I would accept the Accounts Control position. The job was much more challenging than the Customer Services post, but I knew I could learn the systems and procedures quickly and I would have a great opportunity to contribute to the success of the Operations area."

It was November 1989, and Ellen Moore was just completing her second year as an expatriate manager at the offices of a large American financial institution in Manama, Bahrain. After graduating with an MBA from a leading business school, Ellen had joined her husband, who was working as an expatriate manager at an offshore bank in Bahrain. Being highly qualified and capable, she had easily found a demanding position and had worked on increasingly complex projects since she had begun at the company. She was looking forward to the challenges of the Accounts Control position.

Ellen Moore

Ellen graduated as the top female from her high school when she was 16, and immediately began working full time for the main branch of one of the largest banks in the country. By the end of four years, she had become a corporate accounts officer and managed over twenty large accounts.

"I remember I was always making everything into a game, a challenge. One of my first jobs was filing checks. I started having a competition with the woman at the adjacent desk who had been filing for years, except she didn't know I was competing with her. When she realized it, we both started competing in

earnest. Before long, people used to come over just to watch us fly through these stacks of checks. When I moved to the next job, I used to see how fast I could add up columns of numbers while handling phone conversations. I always had to do something to keep myself challenged."

While working full time at the bank, Ellen achieved a Fellowship in the Institute of Bankers after completing demanding courses and exams. She went on to work in banking and insurance with one of her former corporate clients from the bank. When she was subsequently promoted to manage their financial reporting department, she was both the first female and the youngest person the company had ever had in that position.

Since she had begun working full time, Ellen had been taking courses towards a bachelor's degree at night in one of the city's universities. In 1983 she decided to stop working for two years to complete her Bachelor's Degree. After she graduated with a major in accounting and minors in marketing and management, she entered the MBA program.

"I decided to go straight into the MBA program for several reasons. First, I wanted to update myself. I had taken my undergraduate courses over ten years ago and wanted to obtain knowledge on contemporary views. Second, I wanted to tie some pieces together—my night school degree left my ideas somewhat fragmented. Third, I wasn't impressed with the interviews I had after I finished the Bachelor's degree, and fourth I was out of work anyway. Finally, my father had already told everyone that I had my MBA, and I decided I really couldn't disappoint him."

Just after Ellen had begun the two year MBA program, her husband was offered a position with an affiliate of his bank, posted in Bahrain beginning the next spring. They sat down and examined potential opportunities that would be available for Ellen once she completed her MBA. They discovered that women could work and assume positions of responsibility in Bahrain, and decided they could both benefit from the move. Her husband moved to Bahrain in March, while Ellen remained to complete her masters. Ellen followed, with MBA in hand, 18 months later.

Bahrain

Bahrain is an archipelago of 33 islands located in the Persian Gulf (see Figure C6-1). The main island, Bahrain, comprises 85% of the almost 700 square kilometers of the country, and is the location of the capital city, Manama. Several of the islands are joined by causeways, and in 1987 the 25 kilometer King Fahad Causeway linked the principal island to the mainland of Saudi Arabia, marking the end of island isolation for the country. In 1971, Bahrain gained full independence from Britain, ending a relationship that had lasted for almost a century. Of the population of over 400,000 people, about one third were foreigners.

Bahrain has had a prosperous history. Historically, it has been sought after by many countries for its lush vegetation, fresh water, and pearls. Many traditional crafts and industries were still practiced, including pottery, basket-making, fabric-weaving, pearl-diving, dhow (fishing boat) building, and fishing. Bahrain was the pearl capital of the world for many centuries. Fortunately, just as the pearl industry collapsed with the advent of cultured pearls from Japan, Bahrain struck its first oil.

Since the 1930's, the oil industry had been the largest contributor to Bahrain's Gross National Product. The country was the first in the Persian Gulf to have an oil industry, established with a discovery in 1932. Production at that time was 9,600 barrels a day. Eventually, crude output had reached over 40,000 barrels a day. Bahrain's oil products included crude oil, natural gas, methanol and ammonia, and refined products like gasoline, jet fuels, kerosene, and asphalts.

The Bahraini government had been aware for several years that the oil reserves were being seriously depleted. It was determined to diversify the country's economy away from a dependence on one resource. Industries established since 1971 included aluminum processing, shipbuilding, iron and steel processing, and furniture and door manufacturing. Offshore banking began in 1975. Since Bahraini nationals did not have the expertise to develop these industries alone, expatriates from around the world, particularly from Western Europe and North America, were invited to conduct business in Bahrain. By the late 1980s, the country was a major business and financial center, housing many Middle East branch offices of international firms.

Expatriates in Bahrain

Since Bahrain was an attractive base from which to conduct business, it was a temporary home to many expatriates. Housing compounds, schools, services, shopping and leisure activities all catered to many international cultures. Expatriates lived under residence permits, gained only on the basis of recruitment for a specialist position which could not be filled by a qualified and available Bahraini citizen.

To Ellen, one of the most interesting roles of expatriate managers was that of teacher. The Arab nations had been industrialized for little more than two decades, and had suddenly found themselves needing to compete in a global market. Ellen believed that one of her main reasons for working in Bahrain was to train its nationals eventually to take over her job.

Usually the teaching part was very interesting. "When I first arrived in the office, I was amazed to see many staff members with microcomputers on their desks, yet they did not know the first thing about operating the equipment. When I inquired about the availability of computer courses, I was informed by a British expatriate manager that 'as these were personal computers, any person should be able to use them, and as such, courses aren't necessary.' It was clear to me that courses were very necessary when the computer knowledge of most employees consisted of little more than knowing where the on/off switch was located on a microcomputer.

Although it was outside of office policy, I held 'Ellen's Introduction to Computers' after office hours, just to get people comfortable with the machines and to teach them a few basics. Sometimes the amount of energy you had to put into the teaching was frustrating in that results were not immediately evident. I often worked jointly with one of the Bahraini managers who really didn't know how to develop projects and prepare reports. Although I wasn't responsible for him, I spent a great deal of time with him, helping him improve his work. Initially there was resistance on his part, because he was not prepared to subordinate himself to an expatriate, let alone a woman. But eventually he came around and we achieved some great results working together."

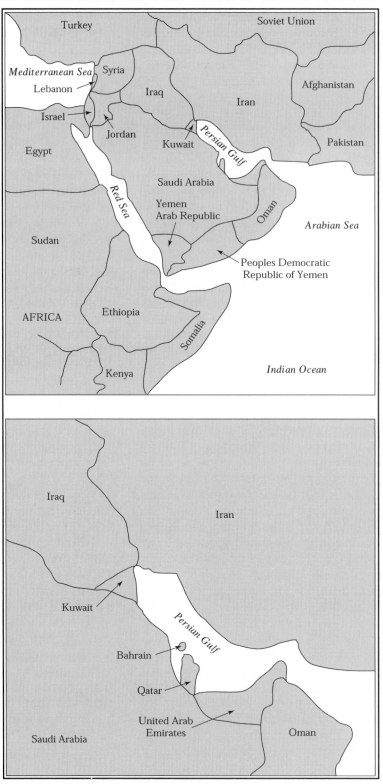

Resident in Bahrain, Volume 1, (1987) Gulf Daily News, pp. 61–63.

The range of cultures represented in Bahrain was vast. Expatriate managers interacted not only with Arabic nationals, but also with managers from other parts of the world, and with workers from developing countries who provided a large part of the unskilled labor force.

"The inequality among nationalities was one issue I found very difficult to deal with during my stay in Bahrain. The third world immigrants were considered to be the lowest level possible in the pecking order, just slightly lower than nationals from countries outside the Gulf. Gulf Arabs, being of Bedouin origin, maintained a suspicious attitude towards 'citified' Arabs. Europeans and North Americans were regarded much more highly. These inequalities had a major impact on daily life, including the availability of jobs and what relations would develop or not develop between supervisors and subordinates. Although I was well acquainted with the racial problems in North America, I haven't seen anything compared to the situation in Bahrain. It wasn't unusual for someone to be exploited and discarded, as any expendable and easily replaceable resource would be, because of their nationality."

Although many expatriates and their families spent their time in Bahrain immersed in their own cultural compounds, social groups, and activities, Ellen believed that her interaction with the various cultures was one of the most valuable elements of her international experience.

Managing in Bahrain

Several aspects of the Middle Eastern culture had tremendous impact on the way business was managed, even in Western firms located in Bahrain. It seemed to Ellen, for example, that "truth" to a Bahraini employee was subject to an Arab interpretation, which was formed over hundreds of years of cultural evolution. What Western managers considered to be "proof" of an argument or "factual" evidence could be flatly denied by a Bahraini: if something was not believed it did not exist. As well, it seemed that the concept of "time" differed between Middle Eastern and Western cultures. Schedules and deadlines, while sacred to Western managers, commanded little respect from Bahraini employees. The two areas that had the most impact on Ellen's managing in a company in Bahrain were the Islamic religion and the traditional attitude towards women.

Islam

Most Bahrainis are practicing Muslims. According to the Muslim faith, the universe was created by Allah who prescribed a code of life called Islam and the Qur'an is the literal, unchanged World of Allah preserved exactly as transcribed by Muhammad. Muhammad's own acts as a prophet form the basis for Islamic law, and are second in authority only to the Qur'an. The five Pillars of Islam are belief, prayer, fasting, almsgiving, and pilgrimage. Muslims pray five times a day. During Ramadan, the ninth month of the Islamic calendar, Muslims must fast from food, drink, smoking, and sexual activity from dawn until dusk, in order to master the urges which sustain and procreate life. All Muslims are obliged to give a certain proportion of their wealth in alms for charitable purposes; the Qur'an stresses that the poor have a just claim on the wealth of the prosperous. Finally, if possible, all Muslims should make a pilgrimage to Mecca during their lives, in a spirit of total sacrifice of personal comforts, acquisition of wealth, and other matters of worldly significance.

"Certainly the Muslim religion had a tremendous impact on my daily working life. The first time I walked into the women's washroom at work I noticed a tap about three inches off the floor over a drain. I found this rather puzzling; I wondered if it was for the cleaning crew. When a woman came in, I asked her about the tap, and she explained that before going to the prayer room, everyone had to wash all uncovered parts of their bodies. The tap was for washing their feet and legs.

One time I was looking for one of my employees, Mohammed, who had a report due to me that afternoon. I searched for him at his desk and other likely spots throughout the office, but to no avail, he just wasn't around. I had had difficulties with Mohammed's work before, when he would submit documents long after deadlines, and I was certain he was attempting to slack off once again. I bumped into one of Mohammed's friends, and asked if he knew Mohammed's whereabouts. When he informed me that Mohammed was in the prayer room, I wasn't sure how to respond. I didn't know if this prayer room activity was very personal and if I could ask questions, such as the length of time one generally spends in prayer. But I needed to know how long Mohammed would be away from his desk. Throwing caution to the wind, I asked the employee how long Mohammed was likely to be in prayers and he told me it usually takes about ten minutes. It wasn't that I felt I didn't have the right to know where my employee was or how long he would be away, I just wasn't certain my authority as a manager allowed me the right to ask questions about such a personal activity as praying.

During Ramadan, the hours of business are shortened by law. It is absolutely illegal for any Muslim to work past two o'clock in the afternoon, unless special permits are obtained from the Ministry of Labor. Unfortunately, business coming in to an American firm does not stop at two, and a majority of the non-Muslim workers are required to take up the slack."

Unlike religion in Western civilization, Islam permeates every function of human endeavour. There does not exist a separation of church, state, and judiciary. Indeed, in purist circles, the question does not arise. The hybrid systems existing in certain Arab countries are considered aberrations created by Western colonial influences. Accordingly, to function successfully, the expatriate must understand and learn to accept a very different structuring of society.

Women in Bahrain

Bahrain tended to be more progressive than many Middle Eastern countries in its attitude towards women. Although traditions were strong, Bahraini women had some freedom. For example, all women could work outside the home, although the hours they could work were restricted both by convention and by the labor laws. They could only work if their husbands, fathers, or brothers permitted them, and could not take potential employment away from men. Work outside the home was to be conducted in addition to, not instead of, duties performed inside the home, such as child-rearing and cooking. Most women who worked held secretarial or clerical positions; very few worked in management.

Bahraini women were permitted to wear a variety of outfits, from the conservative full length black robe with head scarf which covers the head and hair, to below-the-knee skirts and dresses without head covering.

"Arabic women who sincerely want change and more decision-making power over their own lives face an almost impossible task, as the male influence is perpetuated not only by men, but also by women who are afraid to alter views they understand and with which they have been brought up all their lives. I once asked a female co-worker the reason why one of the women in the office, who had previously been "uncovered," was now sporting a scarf over her head. The response was that this woman had just been married, and although her husband did not request that she become "covered," she personally did not feel as though she was a married woman without the head scarf. So she simply asked her husband to demand that she wear a scarf on her head. It was a really interesting situation: some of the more liberal Bahraini women were very upset that she had asked her husband to make this demand. They saw it as negating many of the progressive steps the women's movement had made in recent years."

Although Bahrainis had been exposed to Western cultures for the two decades of industrial expansion, they were still uncomfortable with Western notions of gender equality and less traditional roles for women.

"One day a taxi driver leaned back against his seat and, while keeping one eye on the road ahead, turned to ask me, 'How many sons do you have?' I replied that I didn't have any children. His heartfelt response of 'I'm so sorry' and the way he shook his head in sympathy were something my North American upbringing didn't prepare me for. My taxi driver's response typifies the attitude projected towards women, whether they are expatriates from Europe or North America, or are Bahrainis. Women are meant to have children, preferably sons. Although Bahrain is progressive in many ways, attitudes on the role of women in society run long and deep, and it is quite unlikely these sentiments will alter in the near, or even distant, future.

Another time I was greeted with gales of laughter when I revealed to the women in the office that my husband performed most of the culinary chores in our household. They assumed I was telling a joke, and when I insisted that he really did most of the cooking, they sat in silent disbelief. Finally, one woman spoke up and informed the group that she didn't think her husband even knew where the kitchen was in their house, let alone would ever be caught touching a cooking utensil. The group nodded in agreement. Although these women have successful business careers—as clerks, but in the workforce nonetheless—they believe women should perform all household tasks without the assistance of their husbands. The discovery that this belief holds true in Bahrain is not remarkable as I know many North American and European businesswomen who believe the same to be true. What is pertinent is these women allow themselves to be completely dominated by the men in their lives.

"The one concept I faced daily but never accepted was that my husband was regarded as the sole decision maker in our household. He and I view our marriage as a partnership in which we participate equally in all decisions. But when the maintenance manager for our housing compound came by, repairs were completed efficiently only if I preceded my request with 'my husband wants the following to be completed.' It's a phrase I hated to use as it went against every rational thought I possess, but I frequently had to resort to it."

These attitudes also affected how Ellen was treated as a manager by Bahraini managers:

"One manager, I'll call him Fahad, believed that women were only capable of fulfilling secretarial and coffee serving functions. One day I was sitting at my desk, concentrating on some documents. I didn't notice Fahad having a discussion with another male manager nearby. When I looked up from my papers, Fahad noticed me and immediately began talking in French to the other manager. Although my French was a bit rusty, my comprehension was still quite serviceable. I waited for a few moments and then broke into their discussion in French. Fahad was completely dismayed. Over the next few years, Fahad and I worked together on several projects. At first, he was pompous and wouldn't listen to anything I presented. It was a difficult situation, but I was determined to remain above his negative comments. I ignored his obvious prejudice towards me, remained outwardly calm when he disregarded my ideas, and proceeded to prove myself with my work. It took a lot of effort and patience but, in time, Fahad and I not only worked out our differences, but worked as a successful team on a number of major projects. Although this situation had a happy ending, I really would have preferred to have directed all that energy and effort towards more productive issues."

Bahraini nationals were not the only ones who perpetuated the traditional roles of women in society. Many of the expatriates, particularly those from Commonwealth countries, tended to view their roles as 'the colonial charged with the responsibility to look after the developing country.' This was reflected in an official publication for new expatriates that stated: 'Wives of overseas employees are normally sponsored by their husbands' employers, and their Residence Permits are processed at the same time. . . .' However, wives were not permitted to work unless they could obtain a work permit for themselves.

"The first question I was often asked at business receptions was 'What company is your husband with?' When I replied that I worked as well, I received the glazed over look as they assumed I occupied myself with coffee mornings, beach, tennis, and other leisure activities as did the majority of expatriate wives.

Social gatherings were always risky. At typical business and social receptions, the men served themselves first, after which the women selected their food. Then women and men positioned themselves on opposite sides of the room. The women discussed 'feminine' topics, such as babies and recipes, while the men discussed the fall (or rise) of the dollar and the big deal of the day. At one Bahraini business gathering, I hesitated in choosing sides: should I conform and remain with the women? But most of these women did not work outside their homes, and, consequently, they spoke and understood very little English. I joined the men. Contrary to what I expected, I was given a gracious welcome.

However, on another occasion, I was bored with the female conversation, so I ventured over to the forbidden male side to join a group of bankers discussing correspondent banking courses. When I entered the discussion, a British bank general manager turned his nose up at me. He motioned towards the other side of the room, and told me I should join the women. He implied that their discussion was obviously over my head. I quickly informed him that although I personally had found the banking courses difficult to complete while holding a full time banking position, I not only managed to complete the program and obtain my Fellowship, but at the time was the youngest employee of my bank ever to be awarded the diploma. The man did a quick turnabout, was thoroughly embarrassed, and apologized profusely. Although it was nice to turn the tables on the man, I was more than a little frustrated with the feeling that I almost had to wear my resume on my sleeve to get any form of respect from the men, whether European, North American, or Arab."

A small percentage of Bahraini women had completed university degrees in North America and Europe. While residing in these Western cultures, they were permitted to function as did their Western counterparts. For example, they could visit or phone friends when they wished without first obtaining permission. After completing their education, many of these women were qualified for management positions; however, upon returning to Bahrain they were required to resume their traditional female roles.

"The notion of pink MBA diplomas for women and blue for men is very real. Although any MBA graduate in North America, male or female, is generally considered to have attained a certain level of business sense, I had to constantly 'prove' myself to some individuals who appeared to believe that women attended a special segregated section of the university with appropriately tailored courses."

Ellen discovered that, despite being a woman, she was accepted by Bahrainis as a manager as a result of her Western nationality, her education, and her management position in the company.

"Many of my male Arabic peers accepted me as they would any expatriate manager. For example, when a male employee returned from a holiday, he would typically visit each department, calling upon the other male employees with a greeting and a handshake. Although he might greet a female co-worker, he would never shake her hand. However, because of my management position in the company and my status as a Western expatriate, male staff members gave me the same enthusiastic greeting and handshake normally reserved for their male counterparts."

Ellen also found herself facilitating Bahraini women's positions in the workplace.

"As I was the only female in a senior management position in our office, I was often asked by the female employees to speak to their male superiors about problems and issues they experienced in their departments. I also had to provide a role model for the women because there were no female Bahraini managers. Some of them came to me not just to discuss career issues but to discuss life issues. There was just no one else in a similar position for them to talk to. On the other hand, male managers would ask me to discuss sensitive issues, such as hygiene, with their female staff members."

The government of Bahrain introduced legislation that restricted the amount of overtime hours women could work. Although the move was being praised by the (female) Director of Social Development as recognition of the contribution women were making to Bahraini industry, Ellen saw it as further discriminatory treatment restricting the choices of women in Bahrain. Her published letter to the editor of the *Gulf Daily News* read:

". . . How the discriminatory treatment of women in this regulation can be seen as recognition of the immense contribution women make to the Bahrain workforce is beyond comprehension. Discrimination of any portion of the population in the labor legislation does not recognize anything but the obvious prejudice. If the working women in Bahrain want to receive acknowledgement of their indispensable impact on the Bahrain economy, it should be through an increase in the number of management positions available to qualified women, not through regulations limiting the hours they work. All this regulation means is that women are still regarded as second class citizens who need the strong arm tactics of the government to help them settle disputes over working hours. Government officials could really show appreciation to the working women in Bahrain by making sure that companies hire and promote based on skill rather than gender. But there is little likelihood of that occurring."

The letter was signed with a pseudonym, but the day it was published one of Ellen's female employees showed her the letter and claimed "if I didn't know better, Ellen, I'd think you wrote this letter."

Career Decisions

When Ellen first arrived in Bahrain, she had great expectations that she would work somewhere where she could make a difference. She received several offers for positions and turned down, among others, a university and a high profile brokerage house. She decided to take a position as a Special Projects Coordinator at a large American financial institution.

"In fact, the records will show I was actually hired as a 'Financial Analyst,' but this title was given solely because at that time, the government had decided that expatriate women shouldn't be allowed to take potential positions away from Bahrain nationals. The expertise required as a Financial Analyst enabled the company to obtain a work permit for me as I had the required experience and academic credentials, although I performed few duties as an analyst."

In her special projects role, Ellen learned a great deal about international finance. She conducted efficiency studies on various operating departments. She used her systems expertise to investigate and improve the company's micro computer usage, and developed a payroll program which was subsequently integrated into the company's international systems. She was a member of the Strategic Review Committee and produced a report outlining the long term goals for the Middle East market, which she then presented to the Senior Vice President of Europe, Middle East, and Africa.

After one year, Ellen was rewarded for her achievements with a promotion to Manager of Business Planning and Development, a position which reported directly to the Vice President and General Manager. She designed the role herself, and was able to be creative and quite influential in the company. During her year in this role, she was involved in a diverse range of activities. She managed the Quality Assurance department, coordinated a product launch, developed and managed a senior management information system, was an active participant in all senior management meetings, and launched an employee newsletter.

At the end of her second year in Bahrain, Ellen was informed that two positions in Operations would soon be available, and the General Manager, a European expatriate, asked if she would be interested in joining the area. She had previously only worked in staff positions, and quickly decided to accept the challenge and learning experience of a line post. Both positions were in senior management, and both had responsibility for approximately thirty employees.

The first position was for Manager of Accounts Control, which covered the Credit, Collection, and Authorization departments. The manager's role was to ensure that appropriate information was used to authorize spending by clients, to compile results of client payment, and to inform management of non-payment issues. The manager also supervised in-house staff and representatives in other Gulf countries for the collection of withheld payments.

The second post was Manager of Customer Services, New Accounts, and Establishment Services. The manager's role was to ensure that new clients were worthy and that international quality standards were met in all Customer Service activity. The manager also worked with two other departments: with Marketing to ensure that budgets were met, and with Sales to manage relationships with the many affiliate outlets of the service.

After speaking with the two current managers and considering the options carefully, Ellen decided that she would prefer working in the Accounts Control area. The job was more oriented to financial information, the manager had more influence on operations at the company, and she would have the opportunity to travel to other countries to supervise staff. Although she was not familiar with the systems and procedures, she knew she could learn them quickly. Ellen went into her meeting with the General Manager excited about the new challenges.

Ellen Meets with the General Manager

Ellen told the General Manager she had decided to take the Accounts Control position, and outlined her reasons. Then she waited for his affirmation and for the details of when she would begin.

"I'm afraid I've reconsidered the offer," the General Manager announced. "Although I know you would probably do a terrific job in the Accounts Control position, I can't offer it to you. It involves periodic travel into Saudi Arabia, and women are not allowed to travel there alone." He went on to tell Ellen how she would be subject to discriminatory practices, would not be able to gain the respect of the company's Saudi Arabian clients, and would experience difficulty traveling there.

Ellen was astonished. She quickly pointed out to him that many businesswomen were representatives of American firms in Saudi Arabia. She described one woman she knew of who was the sole representative of a large American bank in the Eastern Province of Saudi Arabia who frequently traveled there alone. She explained that other women's experiences in Saudi Arabia showed professional men there treated professional women as neither male nor female, but as businesspeople. Besides, she continued, there were no other candidates in the company for either position. She reminded the General Manager of the pride the company took in its quality standards and how senior management salaries were in part determined by assuring quality in their departments. Although the company was an equal opportunity employer in its home country, the United States, she believed the spirit of the policy should extend to all international offices.

The General Manager informed her that his decision reflected his desire to address the interests of both herself and the company. He was worried, he said, that Ellen would have trouble obtaining entry visas to allow her to conduct business in Saudi Arabia, and that the customers would not accept her. Also, if there were ever any hostile outbreaks, he believed she would be in danger, and he could not have lived with that possibility.

Ellen stated that as a woman, she believed she was at lower risk of danger than her Western male counterparts since in the event of hostility, the Saudi Arabians would most likely secure her safety. There was much greater probability that a male representative of the firm would be held as a hostage.

The General Manager was adamant. Regardless of her wishes, the company needed Ellen in the Customer Service position. New Accounts had only recently been added to the department, and the bottom line responsibility was thus doubled from what it had been in the past. The General Manager said he wanted someone he could trust and depend upon to handle the pressure of New Accounts, which had a high international profile.

Ellen was offered the Customer Service position, then dismissed from the meeting. In frustration, she began to consider her options.

Take the Customer Services Position   The General Manager obviously expected her to take the position. It would mean increased responsibility and challenge. Except for a position in high school where she managed a force of sixty student police, Ellen had not yet supervised more than four employees at any time in her professional career. On the other hand, it went against her values to accept the post since it had been offered as a result of gender roles when all consideration should have been placed on competence. She knew she had the abilities and qualifications for the position. She viewed the entire situation as yet another example of how the business community in Bahrain had difficulty accept-

ing and acknowledging the contributions of women to international management, and didn't want to abandon her values by accepting the position.

Fight Back   There were two approaches which would permit Ellen to take the matter further. She could go to the General Manager's superior, the Senior Vice President of Europe, Middle East, and Africa. She had had several dealings with him, and had once presented a report to him with which he was very impressed. But she wasn't sure she could count on his sympathy regarding her traveling to Saudi Arabia as his knowledge of the region was limited, and he generally relied on local management's decisions on such issues. She could consider filing a grievance against the company. There were provisions in Bahraini Labor Law that would have permitted this option in her case. However, she understood that the Labor Tribunals, unlike those held in Western countries, did not try cases based on precedents or rules of evidence. In other words, the judge would apply a hodgepodge of his own subjective criteria to reach a decision.

Stay in the Business Planning and Development Job
Although the General Manager had not mentioned it as an option, Ellen could request that she remain in her current position. It would mean not giving in to the General Manager's prejudices. Since she had been considering the two Operations positions, though, she had been looking forward to moving on to something new.

Leave the Company   Ellen knew she was qualified for many positions in the financial center of Bahrain and could likely obtain work with another company. She was not sure, though, whether leaving her present company under these circumstances would jeopardize her chances of finding work elsewhere. Furthermore, to obtain a post at a new company would require a letter of permission from her current employer, who, as her sponsor in Bahrain, had to sanction her move to a new employer who would become her new sponsor. She was not sure that she would be able to make those arrangements considering the situation.

"I always tell my employees, 'If you wake up one morning and discover you don't like your job, come to see me immediately. If the problem is with the tasks of the job, I'll see if I can modify your tasks. If the problem is with the department or you want a change, I'll assist you in getting another position in the company. If the problem is with the company, then I'll help you write your resume.' I have stated this credo to all my employees in every post I've held. Generally, they don't believe that their manager would actually assist with resume writing, but when the opportunity arises, and it has, and I do come through as promised, the impact on the remaining employees is priceless. Employees will provide much more effort towards a cause that is supported by someone looking out for their personal welfare."

Ellen's superior did not have the same attitude towards his employees. As she considered her options, Ellen realized that no move could be made without a compromise either in her career or her values. Which choice was she most willing to make?

Ellen Moore (B): Living and Working in Bahrain

What decision did you make and why? "I accepted the Customer Services position because I was looking for a win-win situation. The Customer Services post was, despite everything, a promotion. Fighting back was not really an option. I would never have received the Accounts Control position, no matter how hard I fought. There was no doubt of this at all. The General Manager had already made up his mind. Any effort I might have made to fight for the Accounts Control post would have compromised my effectiveness in the company, as I would be perceived as someone unwilling to accept senior management decisions.

I could have left the company, but that action would have placed me in a difficult situation, as my husband still had one year remaining on his contract and I wanted to continue working in Bahrain. I could have looked for a post with another company in Bahrain, but the economic situation had changed, and a number of companies were closing, so there was a limited number of available jobs.

When I was making the decision regarding the position I would prefer, the discussion involved three people: the General Manager, the Director of Operations, and me. No one else was aware of this discussion. If the issue had been in the public forum, and if everyone knew I had unsuccessfully requested the Accounts Control position, I would have been perceived to have lost face. It would have been difficult, if not impossible, to work there afterwards and to maintain the level of respect I had in the company. If everyone had known about the situation, I probably would have had to fight the General

Manager's decision. One reason which allowed me to work so effectively was that people had a high degree of respect for me. They felt that I had approval, tremendous approval, from senior management. If they saw that I wanted this particular position and that senior management disagreed, for whatever reason, they would assume that senior management no longer held me in the same regard.

I actually did receive a portion of the Accounts Control area because one segment, New Accounts, had been moved from Accounts Control to the area which was under my responsibility. Management had been reviewing the move during this decision process. I also received a high degree of international exposure from my Customer Service post. My reports and documents, and the statistics from my group, went to all international centers, so it was a high profile post. Interestingly, the majority of my clients were from Saudi Arabia, and I dealt with them personally when they occasionally visited our center, and when they called by phone. I didn't experience any problems when I personally handled their accounts. In fact, as I was the Senior Manager, these clients actually were pleased when I would take the time to deal with them directly. They understood that they were receiving professional attention.

"I left the job and the company after three months in the Customer Service post. I was working seven days a week, seventeen hours a day when I woke up one morning and realized that I didn't want to go to work. I recognized the signal I had always asked my employees to be aware of. I tried to salvage the situation. I phoned the Senior Vice President in Europe to see if there might be an available post in the United Kingdom. I knew him because I had made a successful presentation to him. He was keen, very enthusiastic. He found a post in London which was exactly what I was looking for at the time, but the company couldn't get the required work permit. He was very embarrassed. By this time, the people in the Bahrain unit found out I was looking and I could no longer remain with the company. I did some private consulting for about six months, assisting a company to obtain research on the Bahrain market, as well as designing the office layout and systems."

How did you decide which job to take? "I really did not have a choice. I had to accept the Customer Service post or leave the company. I could not stay where I was, as this option had not been offered. Basically, I sat down and thought about what was important to me. I said okay, it is a line position, and I want a line position; tick one in the "pro" column. Is there an appropriate number of staff reporting to me? Tick another in the "pro" column, and so on. I didn't actually make a list, but I reviewed the pro's and con's of accepting the Customer Service post, and made what I felt was a slight compromise of my values at the time. That was how I came to accept the decision."

Did you compromise your values? "I don't really think so, because I was looking for a senior management position, and this post provided that opportunity. There were times, however, when I would sit back and think, perhaps I did compromise. But, it's all relative. If that situation had occurred in North America, then, yes, it would definitely be a compromise. But given that same situation and in Bahrain, I don't believe I compromised my values. I was just incredibly fortunate to get the positions I did receive.

I have been asked if I have any regrets regarding my move to Bahrain or with my decision to take the Customer Service post. In both cases, I believe the experiences have been generally positive influences on my career. I am not looking for easy ways out or quick jumps up the corporate ladder. I expect to work hard and hope that my efforts will be recognized. When situations arise where I must compromise slightly, I evaluate my decision carefully, and once satisfied that I am not compromising more than is appropriate, I accept the situation and move on from there."

What was your experience when you returned to North America? "My husband remained in Bahrain when I returned to North America to look for a new post, rent a house, and get us settled. We were moving to Toronto, a city where I had not lived before. Everyone seemed so cold and unfriendly. I really was not prepared for this atmosphere, and it took a while for me to get used to it. And although I am a Canadian, when I returned I didn't really feel the same attachment towards Canada. I felt more like a citizen of the world. That is how both my husband and I feel right now. We're not really attached to Bahrain, although our hearts are still there with our friends. Our hearts are also here in Canada with our parents, families and friends, but we don't feel the same nationalistic ties that we felt before.

Also, someone recently commented to me about how much easier it would be to be accepted in a similar professional role in North America. My response was 'Don't be so sure. Think again!' I've been a guinea pig in most places where I have worked. I'm the youngest to do, or the first to be, or the only female ever. I'm always breaking new ground, and it's very, very difficult. In fact, I believe I was accepted more readily as a professional in Bahrain by the Arab men because I had education and experience, and I was in a senior position. Here, having an MBA isn't necessarily a ticket towards acceptance. Also, I am now working in the railroad industry and in Information Systems, both fields typically dominated by men. I have had to prove myself here once again."

How do women get international experience? "In my opinion, there are two ways that you can get a position in international business. The first is that you can enter a country on a visitor's visa, which is usually valid for several weeks for most countries. During your stay, you should go to recruitment agencies and companies. This method allows you to see what the country is like in terms of both lifestyle and working environment. You may find out that, although the country appears to be exactly what you want and looks great in a movie, it may not meet your expectations. The other route is to seek work in your own country from a company which has a large international operation. Over time, you may obtain a post within its international system. This option is much more difficult these days, particularly as firms tighten their expenses, and, therefore, limit the number of available international posts."

Do you think that if you had worked for this company in the United States, it would have transferred you to Bahrain?   "Probably not. We had a small percentage of people who were placed on international assignment. The company doesn't normally hire through its international posting system for the level of position at which I was hired. It is very expensive to transfer employees internationally, they generally attempt to hire locally. I was, therefore, a local hire for that company."

What tips would you have for women about being effective in management positions?   "I believe that it is very important not to become complacent once you attain the next level on the way up the ladder. Never assume that you will be automatically given the respect normally accorded to your position. For example, when I am introduced to someone in business as 'Here is Ellen,' I immediately stick my hand out and say, 'Hello my name is Ellen Moore, I'm the Manager of X Group for Company Y.' If I am introduced as 'here's Ellen' by one of my employees, I'll add 'and X (the staff member) is a member of my team working on your project.' You have to eliminate any ambiguity in such situations.

I strongly believe that women can obtain recognition for their efforts by understanding that they are employees first, and women second. While I was in Bahrain, I was generally regarded by Arab males as a professional, not as a female. I work very hard to ensure that I am professional at all times. I believe that treating people, at any level, from any background, with respect will usually create a positive atmosphere.

Although I am normally very professional, I will play the stereotypical feminine role when required. If I must state to the housing compound manager that 'my husband would like this repair,' I'll do that. I am very pragmatic, and recognize that sometimes I must resort to play-acting to get something accomplished, without being totally ridiculous about it. However, I'm not about to 'sell my soul to the devil.'

Do you have any ideas about how men can help women in international business? Or have you worked with any men who have been particularly helpful?   "Yes, but I think it's not just in international business, I think it's anywhere. Men often talk about the mentors they have had in their careers who have assisted them in their progress up the ladder. Women very rarely have that source of assistance. There are few women in senior positions at this time; therefore, there are few role models. In my current position, I am often regarded as a role model by female employees at lower levels. I am very cognizant of this fact and strive to maintain a positive image. For example, although I may be frustrated by some aspects of my work, I will portray a positive outlook to my employees. I believe that employees can become disconcerted by negative views expressed by management. That is not to say that I hide reality, but there's a difference between communicating a realistic and pessimistic view. I take my responsibility as a role model very seriously.

It is very difficult for most men in senior positions to become a mentor for a woman. Constant justifications of the relationship are necessary because many people perceive it as being something entirely different. As a result, the majority of men don't enter into these situations. But, while I was in Bahrain, a director of another area reporting to the General Manager often discussed business tactics with me. He and I talked about our views on management styles, as well as the future direction of the company. He was there for me when I needed assistance, and when I wanted to bounce an idea off someone. I think that a coach is what most women don't have, a person with whom they can discuss their ideas, someone who has been there before and who is willing to share his knowledge and expertise."

What is your feeling about imposing your value system or your beliefs regarding women's roles in a culture like that in Bahrain? For example, why did you write the letter to the editor of the local newspaper?   I wrote that letter because I felt very strongly about the interpretation made by the Director of Social Development. She believed that the inclusion of women in this labour legislation indicated that their contributions to the workforce were being recognized. I didn't write the letter in an effort to influence anyone's views regarding the legislation itself; that would have been a completely unrealistic purpose. I wrote the letter in order to provide an alternative viewpoint. I had often seen in Bahrain that individuals would accept the views of others without thoroughly understanding or examining all the issues, and I wanted to do my part to prevent that from occurring with this situation.

I am generally a very enthusiastic person, and people tend to follow my lead. I have to be very careful with that side of myself. I would like to believe that I have made some positive changes within my small group of colleagues. But one has to recognize that, at the same time, there is a limited amount of change possible, particularly changes for Bahraini women.

As a North American woman I was generally accorded a high degree of professional respect by Arab males in Bahrain. I have been asked if I believe the same respect would be shown to women with an Arab background who were born in North America. My response is that I don't believe they would be treated equally. Their Arab background would be considered primarily, and as Arab women, their role in society would be set forth by long standing traditional values. There are numerous changes I would like to see for Arab women, but I am realistic at the same time.

As well, individuals from Western countries often incorrectly perceive that a country such as Bahrain is similar to any Western country because of the presence of office buildings and Western firms. They don't understand that as a guest in someone's country, you must respect the cultural values of the host country. I recently read of a North American woman working in Bahrain who said that, although she knew the custom was to wear more conservative clothing, she insisted on wearing shorts in public and didn't care that people stared at her. One Bahraini woman confided in me that when a woman wears such clothing in public, it is the same as if she were walking up to all the people she meets and slapping them across the face. I wonder if that woman would feel as comfortable wearing her shorts if she took the time to understand the impact of her attire on the people she met on the street. This blatant disrespect for cultural values, while indicating a lack of acceptance for local customs, also demonstrates why many individuals from the West fail to succeed in foreign countries."

You said you were generally respected as a professional by the Arab men. Yet we hear of situations where, for example, a female bank manager working in North America is not invited by Arab male clients to attend a meeting. What are your views on this issue? "Although there could be other factors involved here, my understanding of this type of situation is that the Arab clients are not concerned with the fact that she is a woman. Instead, they most likely believe that her position in the bank is a low level post with limited decision-making power. In Bahrain, for example, the leaders of the country are fairly accessible to the people. Given that one can meet with the leader of a country, within a business environment one should be permitted to meet with the president of a given firm. In business I have found most Arab men would like to ensure that they are accorded respect by North American firms, which generally means they wish to meet with senior management who have the authority to make decisions. Individuals from Western countries may interpret these requests incorrectly."

You said that there were no Americans in this American company, you were the token North American? "Yes. Well, I'm Canadian. Most of the executives were European or from other countries in the Middle East, a situation which is not unusual for large multinational firms. The remaining staff were locally hired in Bahrain."

How about your personal relationship? "When we first met over fifteen years ago, my husband and I decided that our relationship was a partnership, and as partners that we would make decisions jointly. And, we recognized early on that we would both have very demanding careers. We sat down and tried to determine, believe it or not it actually took months to accomplish this, what criteria we would use to choose a city, if that situation occurred during our careers. How would we decide if we were offered posts in different cities.

We first thought we should base our decision on salary, with the highest paying job determining the city. But we quickly eliminated that factor as a determinant as I might have a job that pays more today, but if the post is a dead end with no promise of a future, it isn't worth a high investment. We finally decided the position which offered the most long term growth opportunity would be our primary decision criterion. And, that is how we have handled these situations. We actually sit down and say: Well, this is what I've been presented with by this recruitment agency or by this company, and your job is currently at this level. We evaluate the pro's and con's of each posting, and the long term benefits. As well, another key determinant is that good posts would have to be available for both my husband and me in whatever city we select. We seem to go through this decision process fairly often. In fact, we're going through it again. My husband just left for England to be Vice President for an American bank. He is going on a short term contract, but we will be evaluating our alternatives shortly when we have more information on the scope of his post.

My husband and I have a partnership in which each of us respects and assists the other person at all times. For example, he does all the cleaning, dusting, washing the dishes, buying the groceries and the cooking. At one point, a few years ago, I was cooking our dinners about three or four times a week, but I recently haven't had the time as my job has become much more demanding. We know that sometimes my job is more demanding, and sometimes his job requires more of his time. And we share the work in the house based on demands made on our time by our current work situation. We joke about who is the better cook; for example, there are some recipes which I usually prepared and he had his specialty dishes. It happened a few times that he prepared one of my dishes and would say 'I think I make it better than you,' and I would say, 'Really? I guess that one should be your dish from now on.' So, little by little, I started giving him a few more recipes, but he loves it. He is not cooking our dinners and hating it, he really likes contributing to our relationship in this way.

I think that both people in a relationship have to be flexible, and be willing to make compromises. They have to recognize the needs of each other and understand that these needs will change as time goes on. We often go out for dinner, just so we have special time together, to talk about everything, with no interruptions or television to take us away from each other. We don't fight like most couples I know. We talk about issues, and generally attempt to make decisions based on the 'us' rather than the 'you' or 'I.' For example, this Christmas I would like to go to a beach for a holiday. have not had a holiday for so long, and just need a holiday where I can completely relax. He, on the other hand, would like me to go to London to be with him. We have decided to compromise. I am going to London, and will relax and do nothing much while he is at work during the days. Then, we are planning to take a beach holiday sometime in February or March.

We have also made a conscious decision not to have children. I guess I have had a lot of time to think about this decision. I remember when I was in elementary school some of my friends had mothers who worked, and these friends would come home from school and no one would be there. I would come home, and my mother was there to hear about my day at school, and her presence was very special. This comparison was always at the back of my mind.

On the other hand, I recognized that in order to be truly successful at anything, you have to devote a fair amount of time to that effort. For example, someone training to be the best at a certain sport will have to give up something else, like being a great pianist. Both goals would require more time than is ever available. Alternatively, someone could choose to be adequate at the sport and to have average skills playing the piano, and that would be perfectly alright as long as the person recognized, and accepted, the fact that he or she would not be the best at either the sport or the piano. I view having children in a similar fashion. Although I agree that you can have children and also work, you have to recognize that you simply can't be the best at both. For example, an out-of-town business trip may come up on the day that the child has a school recital. Time is required to be the best at anything, and, I determined I couldn't be the best in work and the best with children. Together, my husband and I decided to choose each other and our career accomplishments.

However, you could decide to compromise, to go half way for both career and children. You could say I don't necessarily want to be the best in my career, half way is fine. But then you still have to say it's half way for the children as well. So you have to realize that you certainly can't be the best at both, but you could choose to have both. If you choose to accept that you won't be the best at both that's fine. I personally don't know how anyone who is raising children could consciously choose this route." ■

SOURCE: This case was prepared by Gail Ellement and Martha Maznevski of the Richard Ivey School of Business. Copyright ©1990 by Ivey Management Services. This material is not covered under authorization from CanCopy or any reproduction rights organization. Any form of reproduction, storage, or transmittal of this material is prohibited without written permission from Ivey Management Services, Richard Ivey School of Business, The University of Western Ontario, London, Canada N6A 3K7. Reprinted with permission, Ivey Management Services.

Case 7   Managing a Diverse Work Force in Indonesia

John E. Walsh, Jr.

Indonesian Enterprises

Paul Korsvald, the general manager of a large Norwegian paper company's subsidiary, Indonesian Enterprises, had several decisions to make before the day was over. His first decision was whether to build a small mosque next to his corrugated carton plant near Jakarta, Java. Among the Indonesian Enterprise workers, 34 were Chinese and were primarily Confucians and Buddists, 4 were Javanese Christians, and 2 of Indian extraction were Hindus. The other 352 plant workers and supervisors and the 48 office managers, and workers under him said they were Muslims (see Appendix). Many, however, were not strict followers. They practiced an Islam that had been blended with Hindu, Buddhist, and other beliefs. Jim Sterba (*The Wall Street Journal*, September 29, 1987) observes:

"Islam is different in the world's largest Moslem nation, Indonesia. It has a sense of humor. It doesn't seem so stern and insistent. It is more tolerant than Islam elsewhere."

This toleration was attributed by scholars to Indonesia's vast diverse land and population. The country, comprising 13,677 islands of which 6,000 are populated and covering 3,200 miles, has a population of more than 180 million people of 366 different ethnic groups. Although 250 different languages are spoken, Bhasa Indonesia is the official language taught in the schools. Half of the population was Javanese and two thirds of all Indonesians lived in Java, which constituted 7% of the land mass.

Friday is the holiest day of the week for Muslims, and the company was required by custom to permit workers, especially the men, to attend noon prayers and collective recitals of the Koran. Although government offices closed at 11:00 A.M. on Fridays, Indonesian Enterprises' policy was to close the plant and offices from 11:30 A.M. until 2:30 A.M. only. Paul Korsvald observed that typically fewer than 20 Muslim factory and office workers returned to work on Friday. Many excuses were given by the others, such as it was impossible to catch a bus or services were longer than expected.

Actually, after services was a time for workers to visit with friends to gossip and learn what had taken place during the week. It was also a time to bargain, barter, and buy a variety of goods and food sold near the mosque.

What bothered Paul Korsvald most was the loss in production output and paying people for not working. The average monthly salary for factory workers was approximately US$100; for office workers, it was US$150 for a six-day work week. The day began at 7:00 A.M. and ended at 3:30 P.M. including an hour-and-a-half for lunch.

How could he meet the religious needs of the Muslims and non-Muslims without losing production output and keeping costs down? To build a mosque would cost about US$30,000. Four thousand dollars of this would be spent to purchase and transport sacred stones from Mecca. If Korsvald decided to buy the mosque, he would then have to obtain the services of the local hadji (one who had made the pilgrimage to Mecca) for US$15 to bless the ground before construction began. In addition, he would be required to purchase a goat for sacrifice for about US$20. The goat's head would be buried near the mosque; the remainder given to the workers for a feast. He would also have to provide onions and green peppers to be placed on a stick to keep the rains away on the opening day of the mosque.

If he decided not to build the mosque, Paul Korsvald could also continue the current practice or he could rent seven buses for three hours, at a cost of US$50 per bus. While the buses would probably arrive on time to take the employees to the mosque, Korsvald was unsure if employees would return to the factory on the buses.

334

The Possible Purchase of Call or Prayer Call Clocks

Korsvald was faced with another dilemma as well: whether to buy from Maruem Murakemi and Company, Ltd. either ten semi-automatic prayer call clocks or fully automatic prayer call clocks, or some combination of the two. Good Muslims are required to pray five times a day, first in the morning when they arise, before lunch, mid-afternoon, after sunset and before retiring. This schedule did not have to be followed to the letter, for according to the Koran, "When ye journey about the earth, it is no crime to you that you come short in prayer if you fear that those that disbelieve will set upon you." Typically, employees would pray whenever they had spare time. However, by not praying at the prescribed times, some of the reward was lost. According to Muslim tradition, every corner of Allah's universe was equally pure, so the employees would spread their prayer rugs wherever they were when they decided to pray. Standing erect with their hands on either side of their face and their thumbs touching the lobes of their ears, they would begin, "God is most great." Still standing, they would continue with the opening Ayat (passage from the holy Koran):

Praise belongs to God, Lord of the Worlds,
The Compassionate, the Merciful.
King of the day of Judgment.
Tis thee we worship and thee we ask for help.
Guide us in the straight path.
The path of those whom thou hast favored.
Not the path of those who incur thine anger
Nor of those who go astray.

Unfortunately for Paul Korsvald, the prayers continued from noon to afternoon, because each Muslim employee would wait until he or she had spare time. If Paul Korsvald bought the semi-automatic clocks for US$30 and the fully automatic for US$35 and placed them in prominent locations throughout the plant and office, the clocks could be synchronized to proclaim an Azan (prayer call) ten minutes before noon and at 2:40 in the afternoon.

Another option existed. He could eliminate the lunch hour, the practice of the Dutch-owned companies, and end the working day at 2:00 P.M. Rather than buy the clocks, he would make it known through supervisors that plant operations would cease ten minutes before noon for prayers.

The Need to Increase Productivity During Ramadan

A third decision confronting Korsvald dealt with solving the problem of low productivity of employees during Ramadan, the holy month of fasting and the ninth month in the Arabian calendar. In this month, Muhammed, according to Muslim tradition, received the holy Koran from God as guidance for his people and made his hyiria from Mecca to Medina. From dawn to dusk, during this period, Muslims abstain from food and drink. Among those automatically exempted were the sick, the very old, very young, pregnant and nursing women, soldiers in war, and persons on long trips. Although no one in Indonesia is legally compelled to fast, many Muslim employees did.

When Ramadan fell during the hottest season, fasting took its toll. Employees, observing tradition, were noticeably nervous, excitable, and prone to flare-ups of temper. Korsvald estimated that productivity in the plant and office declined 20–30%. Korsvald had identified three options to address this issue and suspected there were others. First, he could start the plant at 3:30 in the afternoon and end at midnight. Second, he could close the plant for two weeks and require employees to take their vacations during this time. Third, he could require only those Muslim employees who were fasting to take vacations.

Selecting the Manager of the Accounting Department

A fourth decision had nothing to do with religion. He had to decide whether Mr. Abukar, a native Javan, or Mr. James Lee, an Indonesian of Chinese nationality, should be appointed to the position of manager of the accounting department. In Norway, promotion decisions were primarily based upon employee's prior work performance. However, discussions with other Western general managers operating in Java and researchers from *Business International* revealed a consensus that decisions on promotions in Indonesia placed more importance on ethnic background, personalities, and individual circumstances. Thus, managers in Indonesia had to consider whether a prospective manager was Javanese, an outer islander, Chinese, or Indian. Although Indonesia's motto is "Unity in Diversity," it made a difference, for instance, if a prospective manager was Javanese, Sumatran, or Moluccan.

The Javanese are considered an agrarian-based conservative people proud of their traditions and strong family ties. They value harmony and sensitivity to others, characteristics that historians attribute to feudal influences. Additionally, they are reluctant to convey information that could displease business associations or cause conflicts.

The outer Islanders, the Bataks of Sumatra and the Moluccans, are more prone to say what they think. The Dutch set up large tobacco, rubber, and palm oil estates in Northern Sumatra, so modern agricultural developments were concentrated there. Because these products were produced primarily for export in contrast to rice production in Java, which is consumed locally, natives possessed greater experience in international trade. The straightforwardness of the outer islanders complemented the style of Western managers, resulting in a disproportionate number of outer islanders holding key positions in foreign companies in Java.

While the Chinese accounted for less than 2% of the population, they played a key role in business and owned, according to reliable sources, more than 50% of the nation's private capital. Despite high levels of education and administrative experience, they were excluded from the bureaucracy and the military, which was dominated by the Javanese.

The official ideology of the Indonesian government was Pancasila, which consisted of five principles affirming belief in one God, humanitarianism, national unity, democracy, and social justice. A balance between national unity and social justice proved difficult. Any foreign company having too many Chinese executives would be vulnerable to resentment from indigenous Indonesians (pribumi) workers, and the Indonesian government might intervene and press for social justice. While Indians were also vulnerable to resentment, they were too small a group to constitute a threat.

Paul Korsvald had many issues to consider. James Lee was older, and age was important to Indonesians. He was unquestionably the best qualified of the two, technically and in managerial experience. He had more years of work experience with the company. Lee, fearing a backlash from the pribumi staff, might fail to give them firm orders to take disciplinary actions when needed.

On the other hand, Mr. Abukar was reasonably competent technically, pleasant to all employees and well-liked by the Indonesian accounting staff. He came from a respectable family, with several relatives working as lower level executives in the government. Further, the promotion would help him financially, because he had a large family to support. In the past, he had been extremely loyal to the company. He had been reluctant, however, to assume authority, make decisions, and work overtime. Due to a dearth of pribumi managers, it would not be difficult for Mr. Abukar to find another job at a higher salary.

Korsvald could seek a consensus (mufakat) of his key executives through tedious consultation (muskawarah). Whatever choice this consensus brought about, he risked shaming the candidate (malu) in front of others if he did not handle the promotion well. Under no circumstances did he want to create malu.

The Need to Formulate Policies

His last decision was how to formulate a policy covering responsibilities of his employees to achieve results, to reduce kickbacks, and to determine under what circumstances loans would be made to employees.

The frequent cases of stomach ulcers and heart attacks among European and American managers in Indonesia, he thought, resulted from their failure to counteract djamkeret ("dj" pronounced like "j") or rubber time. He observed that Indonesians could not be rushed and would leave an employer who tried to make them move faster or work harder. When asked, "When will the job be finished," adherents to djamkeret would simply reply, "sometime during the next few days." Modern plants with international commitments could not operate this way. So, he needed a policy that could dampen the excuses of djamkeret.

European companies operating in Asia have been offering bribes and kickbacks since the 1600s when the British East India Company won duty-free treatment for its exports by giving Mongol rulers expensive gifts including rare paintings and carvings. Korsvald, however, had difficulty adjusting to the succession of kickbacks and payoffs necessary to conduct business in Indonesia. On one occasion, his sales manager had to send twelve bottles of scotch for a party given by a purchasing agent of a large corporate customer. On another, he had to give

US$10,000 to the large corporate customer's local director. In the latter case, he was surprised to receive a silver tray as a gift from the local director. Last year on Christmas morning, he awoke to find a Christmas tree brightly lit and heavy with gleaming ornaments. On it was a card from another company's director to whom he had been forced to make kickbacks for years. "Muslim economics require that the wealth of her people be widely shared," he mused, "it insists that acquisitions and competitiveness be balanced by fair play and compassion."

In addition to kickbacks to customers, many foreign businessmen in Indonesia felt it was necessary to place someone in power in the Indonesian government associated with their company. It was rumored the family of the president of Indonesia owned shares in 15 companies including a hotel, a flour mill, and two cement factories. The president's brother strongly denied any favoritism and added that several charitable foundations were set up with business earnings.

Trading on influence was not considered corrupt unless it involved excesses. To maintain a low profile, distant relatives of top military and government officials were placed as heads or directors of companies rather than members of their immediate families.

Korsvald observed that the Chinese were adaptable. If they had to give gifts to generals or make deposits to an official's Singapore bank account and become friends for life, they did so. According to Barry Newman in *The Wall Street Journal*, April 14, 1978):

"The strategy of gift giving has been perfected by Cukongs of Indonesia, about 30 moneyed Chinese who have made fortunes for themselves and, as it happens, for the country's ruling elite. 'We don't worry,' says a manager in one of their many companies. 'We have information first hand. We know what's going on.' Occasionally, when there is money to be made, a Cukong will take a fellow Chinese for a ride on his coattails."

Korsvald wondered if kickbacks and payoffs to high officials known as the "untouchables" should be continued by his company. Frequently, he had trouble determining whether middlemen who received bribes from the company to give to his ranking officials still had influence. He was never sure how much to pay or if he was paying the right person. His experience in Indonesia convinced him that establishing good personal relations and trust did not always entail a payoff.

Lower-level civil servants continually practiced the ancient Indonesian form of social commerce called the "sticky handshake." Traditionally, funds acquired through extortion were called "smooth money," "lubricating money," or "rule 2000" (it will cost you 2,000 rupiahs). More recently, they have been labeled "illegal levies" and were required for everything from processing a passport to exporting corrugated boxes. It would be almost impossible to stop "illegal levies," because low-level civil servants needed them to live. Nevertheless, the National Command for the Restoration of Security and Order, a government body, was, at present, trying to ban illegal levies. The response was a combination of outrage and jealousy from civil servants who believed that the higher-ups were taking more and not spreading it around. Although Indonesian Enterprises' workers were better paid than civil servants, they, too, sought ways to increase their incomes. Any items the company had in stock that could be sold easily, like glue and starch, had to be closely monitored and physically secured, or they would be stolen.

Korsvald knew compassion was necessary and could produce practical results each morning. He provided free bottles of "vitasoy," soy bean milk processed in Indonesia by the Hong Kong Soy Bean Products Company of Hong Kong, to mitigate the effects on his employees of malnutrition and tuberculosis, both common ailments in Indonesia. The result was an increase in worker productivity.

Sometimes, though, his compassion created problems. He gave 25 corrugated boxes to one employee who said he wanted the boxes for moving to a new home. Later, he discovered that the boxes were sold to a woman going to Pakistan. When Korsvald confronted the employee, the employee became nervous and started to cry. "My wife was sick and I needed the money," the employee sobbed, "I'm not a criminal." Korsvald knew it would be difficult to fire the employee because of strict Indonesian labor laws, so he returned the money to the woman and treated the payment as an advance loan to the employee. Later, the employee sent flowers to Korsvald.

He wondered about what other policies he should prepare for purchasing and advancing loans.

Should his purchasing agent be responsible for all purchases up to a certain amount, say $300 in Indonesian rupiahs? Should the purchasing agent be able to further delegate authority to other departments? Should he let a policy on advance loans be made by the comptroller? Weren't there inherent dangers?

In one Western company in Jakarta, when loan policies were delegated to a pribumi comptroller, salary advances had more than quadrupled. The chief executive called in the comptroller to find out if the report was in error. It was not.

The comptroller said that, rather than follow the policy blindly, cases were judged individually. The company's new chief engineer needed a large sum of money to pay three years' rent advance for the house he had just leased and such advances were normal in Jakarta. A one-year advance in pay was made to an older employee who was making his pilgrimage to Mecca (Haj), which every devout Muslim was required to do at least once in his or her life. While the comptroller gave explanations for each advance in salary, the chief executive noticed a loan of four months' salary to a recently hired factory worker. When the comptroller was questioned about this advance he said, "The man is my brother-in-law, and my wife would be embarrassed if I didn't grant him this favor."

Korsvald wanted policies that would prevent such a problem from occurring in Indonesian Enterprises.

Appendix: Islam and the Koran

The word *Islam* literally means submission to the will of anybody, but in a religious sense it is properly defined as acceptance of what has been ordered or commanded by God via a man named Muhammed. The principles that regulate the life of Muslims in their relationship with God are called the Five Pillars of Islam. The first pillar is Islam's creed, "There is no God but Allah and Muhammed is his prophet." The second pillar is prayer and Muslims are required to be constant in prayer which under normal conditions means praying five times a day. The third pillar of Islam is charity. Those with money should help those who are less fortunate. The fourth pillar is the observance of Ramadan, the ninth month of the Arabian Calendar. Ramadan commemorates God's making Muhammed a prophet and ten years later Muhammed's Hijiah flight from Mecca to Medina. The fifth pillar of Islam is pilgrimage. Once during a lifetime a Muslim is expected to visit Mecca.

The word *Koran* literally means "that which is read," but to Muslims it is the sacred book that contains the word of God as revealed to Muhammed. The book consists of 114 chapters, 6,000 verses, and over 80,000 words. There is no specific order except the shorter chapters are at the beginning. It contains information pertaining to prophets and the people to whom they were sent. It also contains laws, dogmas, and ethical ideas. In addition, it is considered by Muslims as a first-rate piece of literature. Many Muslim writers copy its style, which they consider a miracle of eloquence. In many parts it is rhymed and unlike ordinary prose, it is chanted rather than read. During daily prayers, Muslims usually recite the opening chapter of the Koran and any other part they like. ▪

SOURCE: "Managing a Diverse Work Force in Indonesia" by John E. Walsh, Jr. from *International Business Case Studies*, ed. Robert T. Moran, David O. Braaten, and John E. Walsh, Jr. Copyright © 1994 by Gulf Publishing Company. Used with permission. All rights reserved.

Case 8   Shell Oil in Nigeria

Anne T. Lawrence

On November 10, 1995, Nigerian novelist and environmental activist Ken Saro-Wiwa was executed by hanging in a Port Harcourt prison. Just eight days earlier, he had been convicted by a military tribunal on what many observers considered trumped-up charges that he had ordered the murders of political opponents. Protests by many world leaders and human rights organizations had failed to prevent the Nigerian military regime form carrying out the death sentence.

Saro-Wiwa's execution provoked a profound crisis for the Royal Dutch/Shell Group of Companies. In its wake, some environmentalists and political leaders called for an international boycott of Shell's gasoline and other products. The World Bank announced it would not provide funding for Shell's liquefied natural gas project in Nigeria. Several groups, including the London Royal Geographic Society, voted to reject the company's charitable contributions. In Canada, the Toronto provincial government refused a $900,000 gasoline contract to Shell Canada, despite its low bid. Some even called for the oil company to pull out of Nigeria altogether. Alan Detheridge, Shell's coordinator for West Africa, told a reporter in February 1996, "Saro-Wiwa's execution was a disaster for us."

Just what was the connection between Saro-Wiwa's execution and Shell Oil? Why did the company find itself suddenly, in the words of the *New York Times*, "on trial in the court of Public opinion?" Had the company done anything wrong? And what, if anything, could or should it do in the face of an escalating chorus of international criticism?

"The Group"

The Royal Dutch/Shell Group was the world's largest fully integrated petroleum company. "Upstream," the conglomerate controlled oil gas exploration and production; "midstream," the pipelines and tankers that carried oil and gas; and "downstream," the refining, marketing, and distribution of the final product. The company also had interests in coal mining, metal mining, forestry, solar energy, and biotechnology. In all,

the Anglo-Dutch conglomerate comprised over 2,000 separate entities, with exploration and production operations in dozens of countries, refineries in 34, and marketing in over one hundred. Royal Dutch/Shell was, in both its ownership and scope, perhaps the world's most truly transnational corporation.

In 1994, Royal Dutch/Shell made more money than any other company in the world, reporting astonishing annual profits of $6.2 billion. The same year, the Anglo-Dutch conglomerate reported revenues of $94.9 billion, placing it tenth on Fortune's Global 500 list. Assets were reported at $108.3 billion, and stockholders' equity at $56.4 billion. With 106,000 employees worldwide, it had the largest work force of any oil company in the world.

The highly successful global corporation traced its history back more than a century and a half.[1] In the 1830s, British entrepreneur Marcus Samuel founded a trading company to export manufactured goods from England and to import products, including polished seashells (hence, the name *Shell*) from the Orient. In the early 1890s, Samuel's sons steered the company into the kerosene business, assembling a fleet of tankers—each named for a different shell—to ply the fuel through the Suez Canal to Far Eastern ports. At about the same time, a group of Dutch businessmen launched the Royal Dutch Company to drill for oil in the Dutch East Indies, sold under the "Crown" brand name. In 1907, Royal Dutch and Shell merged their properties in order to survive competitive pressures from Rockefeller's Standard Oil. Royal

---

[1] This account of the history of Royal Dutch/Shell is based on Hoover's Company Profile Database [On-line], "Royal Dutch/Shell Group," in *World Companies*, Austin, TX: The Reference Press, 1995; *Fortune*, "Introduction to Fortune's Global 500: The World's Largest Corporations," August 7, 1995, pp. 130–136; Jones, Geoffrey, "Royal Dutch Petroleum Company; The Shell Transport and Trading Company P.L.C.," pp. 530–532 in Adele Hast, ed., *International Directory of Company Histories*, v. 4, Chicago: St. James Press, 1991; Moody's International Manual, "Royal Dutch Petroleum Co.," 1995; and Yergin, Daniel, *The Prize: The Epic Quest for Oil, Money, and Power*, New York: Simon and Schuster, 1991.

Dutch retained a 60 percent interest; Shell, 40 percent. The resulting organization; came to be known as the Royal Dutch/Shell Group of Companies or, sometimes, simply "the Group."[2]

In the 1950s and 1960s, the company diversified, increasing its holdings in chemical manufacturing, coal mining, and metal mining. By the 1990s, however, like many large conglomerates, the Group had begun to refocus on its core competencies in oil and gas. A 1995 internal strategy memo expressed the view that the contribution of fossil fuels to the world energy supply would continue to grow until around 2030, after which fossil fuels would give way gradually to solar, wind, hydro power, and biomass, as these alternative energy sources became relatively cheaper. "It is not up to us . . . to choose the 'winning' technologies," the company concluded. "But . . . our first attention will now be devoted to the robust maintenance of our core business . . . the market for fossil fuels."[3]

Over the years, Royal Dutch/Shell had developed a highly decentralized management style, with its far-flung subsidiaries exercising considerable autonomy. The company believed that vesting authority in nationally based, integrated operating companies—each with its own distinctive identify—gave it the strategic flexibility to respond swiftly to local opportunities and conditions.[4]

The corporation was governed by a six-person board of managing directors. Reflecting its dual parentage, the Group maintained headquarters in both London and The Hague. The chairmanship rotated periodically between the president of Shell and the president of Royal Dutch. In 1995, the chairmanship was held by the Dutch president, Cornelius A.J. Herkstroter, an accountant and economist who had held positions in the company in Asia and Europe. Decision making was by consensus, with no dominant personality. Few, if any, Royal Dutch/Shell executives were well known outside the company. The company cultivated a style that was both conservative and low profile. One senior executive commented, "If you want to get ahead at BP [British Petroleum, a long-time rival], you've got to get your name in the paper, but that's the best way to get fired at Shell."

Shell Nigeria

The Shell Petroleum and Development Company of Nigeria—usually called Shell Nigeria—stated its corporate objective simply. It was "to find, produce, and deliver hydrocarbons safely, responsibly, and economically for the benefit of our stakeholders."

The Royal Dutch/Shell Group had begun exploring for oil in West Africa in the 1930s, but it was not until 1956 that oil was discovered in the Niger delta in southeastern Nigeria. In 1958, two years before Nigeria's independence from Britain, Shell was the first of the major oil companies to commence operations there. Nigerian oil was of very high quality by world standards; in the industry, it was referred to as "sweet crude," meaning that only minimal refining was required to turn it into gasoline and other products.

In 1995, Shell Nigeria was the largest oil company in the country. The company itself was actually a joint venture with the Nigerian federal government, which—in the form of the state-owned Nigerian National Petroleum Corporation (NNPC)—owned a 55 percent stake. Royal Dutch/Shell owned a 30 percent stake in the joint venture; the remaining 15 percent was owned by two European oil companies strategically aligned with Shell: Elf (French; 10 percent) and Agip (Italian; 5 percent).

Although the Nigerian government was the majority owner in the joint venture, its role was confined mainly to providing mineral rights; Shell built and managed the lion's share of the oil operations on the ground. Other players in the Nigerian oil industry, including Mobil and Chevron, mainly operated offshore. Of all the multinational oil companies in Nigeria, Shell had by far the most visibility.

Shell Nigeria's operations were huge, not only by Nigerian standards, but even by those of the parent firm. In 1995, Shell Nigeria produced an average of almost one million barrels of crude oil a day—about half of Nigeria's total output—in 94 separate fields spread over 31,000 square kilometers. It owned

---

[2]Shell Oil Company U.S., the firm that operates the familiar gas stations with the red and yellow seashell logo, is the United States operating company in the Royal Dutch/Shell Group. It was founded by Royal Dutch/Shell in 1912 and in 1985 became wholly owned by the parent firm. In 1995, Shell Oil Company U.S. did not have any direct operations, employees, or investments in Nigeria.

[3]NRC Handelsblad, "Shell: Rapid Introduction of Alternative Energy," January 25, 1995 [translation from the original Dutch by Francis de Winter]. [On-line]. Available: http://www.ecotopia.com/hubbert/debate/hubshell.htm.

[4]Jones, Geoffrey, *op. cit.*, p. 532.

6,200 kilometers of pipelines and flow lines, much of it running through swamps and flood zones in the Niger delta. In addition, the company operated two coastal export terminals, at Bonny and Forcados. By its own assessment, Shell's operation in Nigeria was "arguably [the company's] largest and most complex exploration and production venture" anywhere in the world outside North America. The Nigerian operation provided about 14 percent of Royal Dutch/Shell's total world oil production—and probably a larger share of its profits, although financial data for Shell's subsidiaries were not separately reported. Its significance to the parent firm was indicated by the fact that several chief executives of Shell Nigeria had risen to become managing directors of Royal Dutch/Shell itself.

Shell Nigeria employed about 2,000 people. Ninety-four percent of all employees, and about half of senior managers, were Nigerian. Few employees, however, were drawn from the impoverished delta communities where most oil facilities were located; for example, by one estimate, less than 2 percent of Shell Nigeria's employees were Ogoni—the ethnic group from the Niger delta of which Saro-Wiwa was a member. The percentage of local people was higher—20 to 50 percent—on Shell's seismic crews, which did the dirty and dangerous work of drilling and blasting during oil exploration.[5]

Shell's financial arrangements with the Nigerian government dated from the 1970s, when world oil markets had been restructured by the emergence of newly assertive oil-producing regions—first Libya and later OPEC, of which Nigeria was a member. The arrangements were highly beneficial to the Nigerian government. For every barrel of oil sold by Shell Nigeria, ninety percent of net revenues (after expenses) went to the federal government in the form of taxes and royalties. Shell, Elf, and Agip split the remaining ten percent.

Although Shell and the Nigerian government worked hand in glove in the oil industry, relations between the two were often strained. Although usually unwilling to comment publicly, Shell seemed to resent the Nigerian government's large take and was frustrated by its frequent failure to pay revenues due its corporate partners. Endemic corruption in Nigerian society was also a frequent irritant. Brian Anderson, Shell Nigeria's managing director (chief executive), once in a moment of apparent candor, complained bitterly to journalists of the "black hole of corruption acting like a gravity . . . pulling us down all the time."[6]

The "Giant of West Africa"

Nigeria, the Group's at times troublesome partner, had been called the "giant of West Africa." Located on the North Atlantic coast between Benin and Cameroon, Nigeria was slightly more than twice the size of California, and—with 98 million people—the most populous country on the continent. Nigeria's gross domestic product of around $95 billion placed its economy second, smaller only than South Africa's. The economy was heavily dependent on petroleum: oil and natural gas sales produced 80 percent of the federal government's revenue and over 90 percent of the country's foreign exchange. Thirty-seven percent of all exports—and 50 percent of oil exports—went to the United States, more than to any other single country.

Nigeria was a land of stark socioeconomic contrasts. The nation's military and business elites had grown wealthy from oil revenues. Yet, most Nigerians lived in poverty. The annual per capita income was $250, less than that of Haiti or China, and in the mid-1990s, economic distress in many parts of Nigeria was deepening.

A legacy of colonialism, in Nigeria as elsewhere in Africa, was the formation of states that had little historical basis other than common colonial governance. In the Nigerian case, the modern nation was formed from what had been no less than 250 disparate ethnic groups in traditional society, many with little by way of cultural or linguistic ties. The nation was comprised of three main ethnic groups: in the north, the Hausa-Fulani; in the southwest, the Yoruba; and in the southeast, the Ibo. Together, these three groups made up 65 percent of the population; the remaining 35 percent was made up of scores of smaller ethnic groups, including the Ogoni. The military in Nigeria—and, not coincidentally, the federal government—had always been dominated by the Hausa-Fulani.

In 1967, the Ibo and their allies in oil-rich southeastern Nigeria attempted to secede as the

[5]World Bank, "Defining an Environmental Development Strategy for the Niger Delta," vol. 1, Report 14266-UNI, May 30, 1995, p. 84.

[6]Quoted in Rowell, Andy, "Sleeping with the Enemy: Worldwide Protests Can't Stop Shell Snuggling Up to Nigeria's Military," *Village Voice*, January 23, 1996.

independent state of Biafra. The resulting civil war, which lasted three years, was eventually won by federal forces. A major outcome of the Biafran conflict was the emergence of a powerful federal government with weak states' rights and a deep mistrust of any move towards regional autonomy.

Since its independence from Britain in 1960, Nigeria had been ruled by military governments for all but nine years. Several efforts—all eventually unsuccessful—had been made to effect a transition to permanent civilian rule. In June 1993, then-military dictator Ibrahim Babangida annulled the presidential election, suspended the newly created national assembly, and outlawed two fledgling political parties. In his memoirs, Saro-Wiwa likened Nigeria's halting attempts to democratize to "a truck [that is] completely rusty, without a roadworthiness certificate or an insurance policy; its license has expired. Yet its driver insists on taking it out on an endless journey."[7]

In November 1993, yet another military man, General Sani Abacha, took power in a coup. The Abacha regime has been called "indisputably the cruelest and most corrupt" government in Nigeria since independence.[8] A specialist in African politics summarized the situation in Nigeria in testimony before the Senate Foreign Relations Committee in 1995:

> [The] current government appears indifferent to international standards of conduct, while dragging the country into a downward spiral of disarray, economic stagnation, and ethnic animosity . . . [It] has curtailed political and civil rights to an unprecedented degree in Nigerian history, magnified corruption and malfeasance in an endemically corrupt system, and substantially abandoned responsible economic management . . . [F]ormal lapses in macro-economic management have been accompanied by an upsurge in illicit activities, including oil smuggling, narcotics trafficking, and a prodigious cottage industry engaged in international commercial fraud.[9]

In 1993, inflation was running close to 60 percent annually, foreign debt was growing, and the country's balance of payments was worsening.

Nigeria in 1995 was by many accounts the most corrupt nation in Africa, arguably, in the world. Fabulous oil wealth and a lack of democratic accountability combined to create a society where almost everyone was on the take. General Abacha himself was reputedly a billionaire. The state-owned oil company, the NNPC—incredibly—did not publish annual accounts; by one estimate, as much as $2.7 billion was illegally siphoned from NNPC coffers annually.[10] White elephant projects—like a multibillion dollar project to develop a steel industry in a country that had neither high-grade coal nor iron ore, and a new Brazilia-like capital built from the ground up in Abuja in central Nigeria—drained public monies while enriching those lucky enough to receive government contracts. Local officials tried to get their cut. By one observer's account:

> [Traveling in Nigeria, one] is assailed with requests for payments for everything from getting through the airport to being given directions in a government ministry to having somebody talk to you . . . And it has been aggravated at the level of petty corruption by the situation of economic decline . . . and the plummeting real wages of many Nigerians, so that people simply have no alternative but to take these sorts of inducements in order to get by.[11]

Corruption was so rampant in Nigeria, *The Economist* concluded in an editorial, that "the parasite . . . has almost eaten the host."

The Ogoni People

Saro-Wiwa's people, the Ogoni, were in many ways victims both of oil development and of the Hausa-Fulani dominated federal government. Ogoniland was a small area—a mere 12 by 32 miles—that had the misfortune to be located in the Niger delta, right on top of one of the world's greatest oil reserves. A distinctive ethnic group, numbering about half

[7]Saro-Wiwa, Ken, *A Month and A Day: A Detention Diary*, New York: Penguin Books, 1995, pp. 112–133.
[8]Robinson, Randall, TransAfrica, quoted on p. 31, U.S. Committee on Foreign Relations, "The Situation in Nigeria," Hearing before the Subcommittee on African Affairs, July 20, 1995, Washington DC: U.S. Government Printing Office, 1995.
[9]Lewis, Peter M., American University School of International Service, quoted on pp. 18–19, U.S. Committee on Foreign Relations, *op. cit.*

[10]MacDonald, Scott B., Jane E. Hughes, and David Leith Crum, "Nigeria," pp. 215–241, in *New Tigers and Old Elephants: The Development Game in the 1990s and Beyond*, New Brunswick, NJ: Transaction Publishers, 1995, p. 229.
[11]Lewis, Peter M., *op. cit.*

a million in the mid-1990s, the Ogoni spoke four related languages and shared a common animistic religion. Prior to the arrival of the British in 1901, a stable Ogoni society based on fishing and farming had existed in the delta for centuries.

Ogoniland was the site of tremendous mineral wealth; and yet, over the years, the Ogoni had received virtually no revenue from its development. Somewhere on the order of $30 billion worth of oil was extracted from Ogoni-land's five major oil fields between 1958 and 1994. Yet, under revenue-sharing arrangements between the Nigerian federal government and the states, only 1.5 percent of oil taxes and royalties was returned to the delta communities for economic development—and most of this went to line the pockets of local officials.[12]

The Rivers State, that included Oganiland, was among the poorest in Nigeria. No modern sanitation systems were in place, even in the provincial capital of Port Harcourt. Raw sewage was simply buried or discharged into rivers or lakes. Drinking water was often contaminated, and water-related diseases such as cholera, malaria, and gastroenteritis were common.

Ogoniland's population density of 1,500 per square mile was among the highest of any rural area in the world—and much higher than the Nigerian national average of 300 per square mile. Housing there was typically constructed with corrugated tin roofs and cement or, more commonly, dirt floors. Only one-fifth of rural housing was considered by authorities to be "physically sound." Approximately 30–40 percent of delta children attended primary school, compared with about three-quarters in Nigeria as a whole; three-quarters of adults were illiterate. Unemployment was estimated at 30 percent. A British

engineer who later returned to the delta village where oil was first discovered in Nigeria commented, "I have explored for oil in Venezuela, I have explored for oil in Kuwait, [but] I have never seen an oil-rich town as completely impoverished as Olobiri."[13]

In 1992, in response to pressure from the Ogoni and other delta peoples, the Nigerian government established an Oil Mineral Producing Areas Development Commission (OMPADC), funded with 3 percent of oil revenues. These funds—double the prior allocation—were earmarked for infrastructure development in the oil-producing regions, mainly the delta. In 1993, the group spent $94 million, with about 40 percent going to the Rivers State. Although some projects were initiated, the World Bank later criticized OMPADC for "poor dialogue with other institution and communities" and "no environmentally sustainable development emphasis."[14]

Shell Nigeria gave some direct assistance to the oil-producing regions. In 1995, the company's community development program in Nigeria spent about $20 million. Projects included building classrooms and community hospitals, paying teacher salaries, funding scholarships for Nigerian youth, and operating an agricultural station. According to one study, however, almost two-thirds of the community development budget was allocated to building and maintaining roads to and from oil installations. Although open to the public, these roads were of little use to most delta residents, who did not own cars. Moreover, Shell made little effort to involve local residents in determining how its community development funds would be spent. The World Bank concluded that "[in] spite of . . . large investments, the impact of . . . oil company investments on improving the quality of life in the delta has been minimal."[15]

Ken Saro-Wiwa: Writer and Activist

Ken Saro-Wiwa, leader of the Ogoni insurgency, was in many respects an unlikely activist. A businessman who later became a highly successful writer and television producer, he had a taste for gourmet food, fine literature, sophisticated humor, and international travel. Yet, in the final years of his life he

---

[12]The revenue-sharing arrangements in place in Nigeria had their origins in the system of land rights in pre-colonial Africa. In traditional societies, such as the Ogoni prior to colonization, families and communities had held land rights collectively, with elaborate norms governing use. Elements of this system of land ownership remained in modern Nigeria, where all mineral rights were vested in the federal government, with residents continuing to enjoy the right to use land for farming, fishing, and the like. Accordingly, under Nigerian law, oil companies that expropriated land for exploration or drilling were required to compensate residents for loss of their use of the land (for example, for the value of lost crops) but not for the value of oil or natural gas extracted. Thus, unlike—say—the United States, where discovery of a "gusher" on a farmer's land might make him an overnight millionaire, the discovery of oil in Nigeria had the consequence of enriching the government, not individual residents of the Niger delta where oil was found. World Bank, *op. cit.*, p. 4.

[13]Rowell, Andy, "Shell Shocked: Did the Shell Petroleum Company Silence Nigerian Environmentalist Ken Saro-Wiwa?" *Village Voice*, November 21, 1995.
[14]World Bank, *op. cit.*, p. 82.
[15]*Ibid.*, p. 84.

emerged as a world-renowned advocate for sustainable development and for the rights of indigenous peoples, and he was honored with a Noble peace prize nomination and receipt of the Goldman Environmental Prize.

The British novelist William Boyd, a close friend, described Saro-Wiwa this way:

> Ken was a small man, probably no more than five feet two or three. He was stocky and energetic—in fact, brim full of energy—and had a big, wide smile. He smoked a pipe with a curved stem. I learnt later that the pipe was virtually a logo: in Nigeria people recognized him by it.[16]

Saro-Wiwa was born in 1941 in Bori, an Ogani village in the delta area east of Port Harcourt, into a large, supportive family. A brilliant student, he was educated first at Methodist mission schools in Bori and later, with the aid of government scholarships, at Government College, Umuahia, and the University of Ibadan, where he studied literature with the intention of becoming an academic.

When the Biafran civil war broke out in 1967, Saro-Wiwa, then a graduate student and lecturer at the University of Nigeria, declared his support for the federal government. As one of the few educated Ogoni to side with federal forces, he became part of what he later called "a sort of Cabinet of a government-in-exile" for the delta region, then under Biafran control. After federal forces had recaptured the delta, Saro-Wiwa was appointed civil administrator for the oil port of Bonny. His position during the Biafran conflict—that ethnic minorities in Nigeria, like the Ogoni, would do better by seeking full democratic rights in a federal state than through secession—prefigured his later views.

In 1973, then 32, Saro-Wiwa left government service to launch his own business. After four years as a successful grocer and trader, he took the proceeds and began investing in real estate—buying office buildings, shops, and homes. In 1983, having acquired sufficient property to live comfortably, Saro-Wiwa turned to what he called his "first love," writing and publishing. He proved to be a gifted and prolific writer, producing in short order a critically-acclaimed novel, *Sozaboy: A Novel in Rotten English;* a volume of poetry; and a collection of short stories.

In 1985, Saro-Wiwa was approached by a university friend who had become program director for the state-run Nigerian television authority to develop a comedy series. The result, a show titled *Basi & Co.*, ran for five years and became the most widely watched television show in Africa. Reflecting Saro-Wiwa's political views, the program satirized Nigerians' desire to get rich with little effort. The show's comic protagonist was Basi, "a witty rogue [who] hustled on the streets of Lagos and was willing to do anything to make money, short of working for it."[17]

By the late 1980s, Saro-Wiwa had became a wealthy and internationally known novelist and television scriptwriter. His wife, Hauwa, and four children moved to London, where his children enrolled in top British private schools. Saro-Wiwa joined his family often, making many friends in the London literary community who would later work doggedly, although unsuccessfully, for his release.

In 1988, Saro-Wiwa undertook a nonfiction study of the Nigerian civil war, later published under the title *On A Darkling Plain*. The work reawakened his interest in politics and in the plight of his own Ogoni people. In a speech at the Nigerian Institute of International Affairs in Lagos in March 1990, marking the book's publication, Saro-Wiwa used the subject of his historical study to lay out a theme that was to became central to the rest of his life's work:

> Oil was very much at the centre of the [Biafran] war ... Twenty years [later], ... the system of revenue allocation, the development policies of successive Federal administrations and the insensitivity of the Nigerian elite have turned the delta and its environs into an ecological disaster and dehumanized its inhabitants. The notion that the oil-bearing areas can provide the revenue of the country and yet be denied a proper share of that revenue because it is perceived that the inhabitants of the area are few in number is unjust, immoral, unnatural and ungodly ... The peoples of Rivers and Bendel States, in particular, sit very heavy on the conscience of Nigeria.[18]

---

[16]Boyd, William, "*Introduction*," in Ken Saro-Wiwa, *A Month and a Day: A Detention Diary*, New York: Penguin Books, 1995, pp. vii–viii.

[17]Bridgland, Fred, "Ken Saro-Wiwa Has Become Another Tragic Chapter in Nigeria's Sad History," *The Scotsman*, November 11, 1995.

[18]Saro-Wiwa, Ken, *op. cit.*, p. 64.

On A Darkling Plain, not surprisingly, ignited a storm of controversy in Nigeria, and *Basi & Co.* was canceled shortly after its publication, as was a column Saro-Wiwa had been writing for the government-owned weekly *Sunday times.*

Movement for the Survival of the Ogoni People

While working on his book on the civil war, Saro-Wiwa experienced a vision in which he was visited by the Spirit of the Ogoni, a fetish god in traditional society. He later described this experience:

> I received a call to put myself, my abilities, my resources, so carefully nurtured over the years, at the feet of the Ogoni people and similar dispossessed, dispirited and disappearing peoples in Nigeria and elsewhere. The Voice spoke to me, directing me what to do and assuring me of success in my lifetime and thereafter. I was adequately warned of the difficulties which this call to service would entail and the grave risks I would be running.[19]

The cancellation of his TV series and newspaper column seemed to propel Saro-Wiwa further into political activism. In August 1990, he met with a group of Ogoni tribal chiefs and intellectuals in Bori, where they drafted and signed an Ogoni Bill of Rights. This document, while reaffirming the Ogoni people's desire to remain part of Nigeria, called for political autonomy; cultural, religious, and linguistic freedom; the right to control a "fair proportion" of the region's economic resources; and higher standards of environmental protection for the Ogoni people. The document was addressed to the president of the Federal Republic and to the members of the Armed Forces Ruling Council.

Shortly thereafter, drafters of the bill of rights met to form an organization to press their demands. The group chose the name Movement for the Survival of the Ogoni People (MOSOP). Although Saro-Wiwa was the main organizer, he felt that he would be most effective as a writer and press coordinator, so he was named "spokesman." Garrick Leton, a tribal chief and former cabinet minister, was named president.

From its inception, MOSOP adopted a philosophy of nonviolent mass mobilization. In a speech in December 1990, Saro-Wiwa spelled out the organization's strategy:

> Some, looking at the enormity of the task, must ask, "Can we do it?" The answer, unequivocally, is YES . . . The next task is to mobilize every Ogoni man, woman and child on the nature and necessity of our cause so that everyone knows and believes in that cause and holds it as a religion, refusing to be bullied or bribed therefrom . . . This is not, I repeat NOT, a call to violent action. We have a moral claim over Nigeria . . . Our strength derives from this moral advantage and that is what we have to press home.[20]

MOSOP's earliest organizational efforts focused on educational work and appeals to the military government and to the oil companies. The organization published the Ogoni Bill of Rights and organized a speaking tour of the region to present it to the Ogoni. Saro-Wiwa traveled abroad—to the United States, Switzerland, England, the Netherlands, and Russia—where he met with human rights and environmentalist groups and government officials to build support for the Ogoni cause. MOSOP also issued a propagandistic "demand notice" calling on Shell and the NNPC to pay "damages" of $4 billion for "destroying the environment" and $6 billion in "unpaid rents and royalties" to the Ogoni people.

Environmental Issues

A central plank in the MOSOP platform was that the oil companies—particularly Shell—were responsible for serious environmental degradation. In a speech given in 1992 to the Unrepresented Nations and Peoples Organization (UNPO), Saro-Wiwa stated MOSOP's case:

> Oil exploration has turned Ogoni into a waste land: lands, streams, and creeks are totally and continually polluted; the atmosphere has been poisoned, charged as it is with hydrocarbon vapours, methane, carbon monoxide, carbon dioxide and soot emitted by gas which has been flared twenty-four hours a day for thirty-three years in very close proximity to human habitation. Acid

---

[19]McGreal, Chris, *op. cit.*

[20]Saro-Wiwa, Ken, *op. cit.*, p. 75.

rain, oil spillages and oil blowouts have devastated Ogoni territory. High pressure oil pipelines crisscross the surface of Ogoni farmlands and villages dangerously.

The results of such unchecked environmental pollution and degradation include the complete destruction of the ecosystem. Mangrove forests have fallen to the toxicity of oil and are being replaced by noxious nypa palms; the rain forest has fallen to the axe of the multinational oil companies, all wildlife is dead, marine life is gone, the farmlands have been rendered infertile by acid rain and the once beautiful Ogoni countryside is no longer a source of fresh air and green vegetation. All one sees and feels around is death.[21]

Shell disputed these charges. In a comment on "environmental issues" posted on the Internet, the company stated:

We have never denied that there are some environmental problems connected with our operation and we are committed to dealing with them. However, we totally reject accusations of devastating Oganiland or the Niger delta. This has been dramatized out of all proportion.[22]

Shell argued that the land it had acquired for operations comprised only 0.3 percent of the Niger delta; and that the region's environmental problems had been caused mainly by rising population, overfarming, and poor sanitation practices by local residents. Moreover, Shell charged, many of the oil spills in the area had been caused by sabotage, for which they could not be held responsible.

The Niger delta was one of the world's largest wetlands, a vast floodplain built up by sedimentary deposits at the mouths of the Niger and Benue Rivers. It was an ecologically complex area composed of four zones; coastal barrier islands, mangroves, freshwater swamp forests, and lowland rainforest. In a comprehensive study of environmental conditions in the Niger delta completed in 1995, the World Bank found evidence of significant environmental problems, including land degradation, overfishing, deforestation, loss of biodiversity, and water contamination. Most of these problems, however, were the result not of oil pollution but rather of overpopulation coupled with poverty and weak environmental regulation.

The World Bank did find significant evidence of air pollution from refineries and petrochemical facilities and also of oil spills and poor waste management practices at and around pipelines, terminals, and offshore platforms. It concluded, however, that "oil pollution . . . is only of moderate priority when compared with the full spectrum of environmental problems in the Niger Delta."[23]

Of the environmental problems associated with the oil industry, the World Bank reported, the worst was gas flaring. Natural gas is often produced as a by-product of oil drilling. In most oil-producing regions of the world, this ancillary gas is captured and sold. In Nigeria, however, gas was routinely simply burned off, or "flared," in the production fields. In 1991, over three-quarters of natural gas production in Nigeria was flared—compared with, say, less than one percent in the United States or a world average of less than five percent. In 1993, Nigeria flared more natural gas than any other nation on earth.

Gas flaring had several adverse environmental consequences. The flares produced large amounts of carbon dioxide and methane, both greenhouse gases and contributors to global warming. Residents in the immediate vicinity of the flares experienced constant noise, heat, and soot contamination. The flares, which burned continuously, lit up the night sky in much of the delta with an eerie orange glow. One British environmentalist commented poignantly after a fact-finding visit to the delta that "some children have never known a dark night, even though they have no electricity."[24]

During the early 1990s, Shell Nigeria was involved in a joint venture known as the Nigeria Liquefied Natural Gas project. The aim of this scheme, in which Shell was a 24 percent shareholder, was to pipe natural gas to ocean terminals, liquefy it, and ship it abroad in special ships at supercooled temperatures. In late 1995, the fate of this venture was still unclear.

Contrary to charges made by some of Shell's critics, Nigeria did have some environmental regulations in place. In 1988, the federal government had promulgated the Federal Environmental Protection Agency Decree and, in 1991, had followed with a set of

[21]*Ibid.*, pp. 95–96.
[22]Shell Petroleum Development Company of Nigeria, "Execution of Ken Saro-Wiwa and His Co-defendants," [Online]. Available: http://www.shellnigeria.com/news/pr14.html.

[23]World Bank, *op. cit.*, p. 108.
[24]Rowell, Andy, November 21, 1995, *op. cit.*.

National Environmental Protection Regulations. These laws, which were enforced by the Federal Department of Petroleum Resources, requires industry to install pollution abatement devices, restricted toxic discharges, required permits for handling toxic wastes, and mandated environmental impact studies for major industrial developments.[25]

Civil Disturbances in Ogoniland

During the early 1990s, civil disturbances in Ogoniland and nearby delta communities, many directed at Shell, escalated. Shell later posted on the Internet descriptions of some of these incidents. Three examples of Shell's posted accounts follow.[26]

Umuechem, 1 November 1990
[This] incident happened when armed youths invaded and occupied a rig location and nearby flowstation, chasing off staff who were not given the opportunity to make the location safe. The youths demanded N100 million [naira, the Nigeria currency, at that time worth about $12.5 million], a new road, and a water scheme. Attempts to talk with the youths, who were armed with guns and machetes, failed.

In response, Shell staff called the Nigerian police, which sent in mobile police units. In the ensuing riot, at least one policemen and seven civilians in the village of Umuechem were killed. Shell concluded its posting, "The Shell response to the threatening situation was made with the best intentions and what happened was a shock to staff, many of whom had friends at Umuechem."

Ahia, 7 March 1992
A gang of youths . . . stormed . . . a drilling rig in the Ahia oil field . . . looting and vandalizing the facility and rig camp. Rig workers were held hostage for most of the first day while property worth $6 million was destroyed or stolen. The rig was shut down for 10 days and the Ahia flow-station was also shut down . . . [A protest leader] raised the issue of the 1.5 percent derivation of oil revenues to the oil-producing communities by the government, the need for a new road, and rumours of bribery by Shell of a paramount chief . . .

In this incident as well, Shell called the police; this time, no injuries resulted.

Nembe Creek, 4 December 1993
A gang of armed youths attacked Nembe production camp as staff slept at 4 a.m., ransacking and looting offices, a workshop, stores, switchboard, mess, kitchen, and recreation block—and attacking and beating up staff. Eight staff were assaulted and wounded. The gang also shut down five swamp flow-stations and invaded a nearby drilling rig and oil service barge. Among the demands the youths made were that Shell should take over the construction of a stalled road project being built by the government, provide electricity, employ [local] people as managers and directors of Shell, and sandfill an area of cleared swamp.

Again, Shell called the police. The incident was resolved without injuries. The cost of Shell was estimated at $3 million, and production was shut down for five days.

Most of the civil disturbances followed a similar pattern, as these examples suggest. A group of young men, armed with whatever weapons were readily available, would attack one of the many far-flung oil installations in the delta. Employees would be attacked; equipment would be sabotaged; and the group would make demands. The demands would be denied; and the company would call in police. Violence against civilians sometimes followed.

Shell's summary data on patterns of community disturbances in the Niger delta, shown in Table C8-1,

TABLE C8-1 Community Disruptions in Shell's Niger Delta Operations

	Numbers	*Days Lost*
1989	34	28
1990	95	28
1991	102	243
1992	85	407
1993	169	1,432
1994	84	1,316

▮▮▮▮▮▮▮▮

Source: "Community Disturbances," [On-line]. Available: http://www.shellus.com/news/nigeria.html.

[25]World Bank, *op. cit.*, p. 55.
[26]These account are drawn from Shell Petroleum Development Company of Nigeria, "Community Disturbances," [On-line]. Available: http://www.shellus.com/news/nigeria.html.

reveal a pattern of escalating violence throughout the early 1990s, peaking in 1993.

Shell estimated that the company sustained $42 million in damage to its installations in Oganiland between 1993 and the end of 1995, as a direct result of sabotage.

The relationship between these incidents and MOSOP was complex. Saro-Wiwa's group explicitly rejected violence and repeatedly disavowed vigilante attacks on Shell or other companies; Saro-Wiwa himself frequently toured Ogoniland to restore calm. Yet, publication of the Bill of Rights and MOSOP campaigns focusing attention on injustices suffered by the Ogoni clearly had the effect of escalating expectations within Ogoni society. In this context, many young unemployed Ogoni men simply took matters into their own hands. In a democratic society, demands for electricity, roads, jobs, and piped water would find political expression. In Nigeria—where the state was run by the military and no parliamentary process existed—these demands became directed against business.

On January 3, 1993, MOSOP held a massive regional rally to mark the start of the Year of the Indigenous Peoples. The rally, held at successive locations across Ogoniland, was attended by as many as 300,000 people—three-fifths of the Ogoni population. Protesters carried twigs, a symbol of environmental regeneration.

Two weeks later, Shell abruptly announced that if would withdraw from Ogoniland. It evacuated all employees and shut down its operations. Company officials gave a terse explanation: "There is no question of our staff working in areas where their safety may be at risk."

The "Militarization of Commerce"

As civil unrest escalated in Ogoniland, Shell by some accounts began to work more and more closely with the Nigerian police, especially with mobile police units known as the supernumerary police. Shell defended this practice:

It is normal practice in Nigeria among leading commercial businesses for supernumerary police, trained by the Nigeria Police Force, to be assigned to protect staff and facilities. Violent crime is a daily occurrence in Nigeria. Over the last two years there have been more than 600 criminal

incidents against SPDC's [the Shell Petroleum Development Corporation of Nigeria] staff and operations. One in 10 of these included the use of weapons. The problem of ensuring maximum protection for its staff and facilities remains a matter of grave concern to SPDC.[27]

Shell also provided material and logistical support to police protecting its facilities. The company publicly acknowledged that it provided firearms to mobile police units. The company explained:

[Shell Nigeria] does not own any firearms. However, it does purchase side arms on behalf of the Nigerian police force for police personnel who guard the company's facilities against general crime. This is a requirement of the police force and it applies to all oil companies and other business sectors that require police protection against the high rate of violent crime in the country . . . [28]

Several human rights organizations claimed that Shell provided more than handguns to the police. A representative of the Nigerian Civil Liberties Organization reported that Shell-owned cars, buses, speedboats, and helicopters were regularly used to transport police and military personnel to the site of civil disturbances. Human Rights Watch reported that Shell was meeting regularly with representatives of the Rivers State police to plan security operations.[29]

After General Abacha took power in November 1993, he apparently decided to take a hard line with the Ogoni insurgency in an effort to induce Shell to resume operations. One of his first acts as chief of state was to assemble a special Internet Security Task Force, comprised of selected personnel from the army, navy, air force, and police and headed by Maj. Paul Okuntimo, to restore order in Ogoniland. According to internal memos, later revealed, between Okuntimo and the military governor of Rivers State, the purpose of the task force was to ensure that those "carrying out business

[27]Shell Petroleum Development Company of Nigeria, "Shell and the Supernumerary Police in Nigeria," [On-line]. Available: http://www. shellnigeria.com/news/prl13.html.
[28]Shell Petroleum Development Company of Nigeria, "Firearms: The Shell Positions," [On-line]. Available: http:// www.shellnigeria.com/news/prl12.html.
[29]Rowell, Andy, November 21, 1995, *op. cit.*

ventures in Ogoni land are not molested."[30] A memo dated May 12, 1994, read in part: "Shell operations still impossible unless ruthless military operations are undertaken for smooth economic activities to commence." Under the subheading "Financial Implication," Okuntimo advised the governor to put "pressure on oil companies for prompt regular inputs as discussed." Shell later denied giving any support to Okuntimo's operation.

In May and June, 1994, intense violence erupted in Ogoniland. Amnesty International, which collected eyewitness accounts, reported that Okuntimo's paramilitary force entered Ogoniland, where it "instigated and assisted" inter-ethnic clashes between previously peaceful neighboring groups. The units then "followed the attackers into Ogoni villages, destroying houses and detaining people." In May and June, Ukuntimo's force attacked 30 towns and villages, where its members, "fired at random, destroyed and set fires to homes, killing, assaulting, and raping, and looting and extorting money, live-stock, and food," according to the Amnesty International report. As many as 2,000 civilians may have been killed. In August, Okuntimo held a press conference where he "boasted openly of his proficiency in killing people and of payments made to himself and his men by Shell to protect oil installations" and "justified the use of terror . . . to force the Ogoni into submission."[31]

In 1995, Okuntimo's efforts notwithstanding, Shell had still not returned to Ogoniland. All its other oil production operations in the Niger delta were being conducted under round-the-clock military protection. Claude Ake, a well-known Nigerian political economist, described the situation in a chilling phrase: "This is a process," he wrote," of the militarization of commerce."[32]

Divisions within Mosop

In 1992 and early 1993, failure of MOSOP's efforts to win voluntary concessions from the military government or from Shell and deepening civil unrest in Ogoniland precipitated a split in the organization's leadership. MOSOP president Garrick Leton and his supporters favored a conciliatory approach,

working with military authorities to suppress violence in exchange for various favors from the regime. Saro-Wiwa and his followers, while not condoning violence, were opposed to any cooperation with the military. In the early months of 1993, Saro-Wiwa sought to build an "alternative power base" for his position. He organized the National Youth Council of the Ogoni People (NYCOP), " to give discipline and direction to militant young Ogonis," as well as other groups for women, teachers, religious leaders, students, and professionals. Leton bitterly resented this move, saying, "This is where the trouble started, with these parallel organizations. He [Saro-Wiwa] was doing things all on his own. He didn't want us elders any longer."[33]

The split came to a head over the presidential elections of June 1993—which were later annulled by Babandiga. Leton's faction favored participation; Saro-Wiwa's, a boycott. The matter was put to a vote, and Saro-Wiwa's followers won. Leton and his supporters—who included Edward Kobani, of whose murder Saro-Wiwa was later accused— resigned from MOSOP. Saro-Wiwa was elected president.

In late 1993, an anonymous leaflet appeared in Ogoniland. It accused Shell of offering a multimillion dollar reward to any "vultures" who could destroy MOSOP and Ken Saro-Wiwa. The term "vulture" was often used by militant youth to describe conservative leaders suspected of collusion with the military government. No one ever claimed responsibility for the leaflet.

The Arrest, Trial, and Execution of a Martyr

On May 21, 1994—just a little over a week after Okitumo's "smooth operations" memo—Saro-Wiwa was en route to a MOSOP rally, where he was scheduled to speak. On the way, his car was stopped at a military roadblock, and he was ordered to return to his home in Port Harcourt. He never attended the rally.

Later the same day, a group of Ogoni chiefs, who were allied with Leton's faction, met at one of their homes, a concrete block bungalow in the Gokana district. Their meeting was interrupted by a young man outside revving his motorcycle. One of

[30]*Ibid.*

[31]Amnesty International, "Nigeria: Military Crackdown on Opposition," November 11, 1994, AFR 44/13/94, pp. 6–7.

[32]Rowell, Andy, January 23, 1996, *op. cit.*

[33]McGreal, Chris, *op. cit.*

the chiefs, Edward Kobani, went outside to see what he wanted. According to testimony at Saro-Wiwa's trial, the young man on the motorcycle said, "So it's true the vultures are meeting . . . Ken . . . said that the vultures are sharing out money from Shell and the government."

Within an hour, the young man had returned with several hundred youths. The youths denounced the "vultures" and demanded that they come out. Albert Badey, Samuel Orage, Theophilus Orage, and Edward Kobani emerged. They were promptly assaulted and bludgeoned to death. Edward's brother, Mohammed, ran out the back door, across the garden, and into a shrine for the Spirit of the Ogoni. Mohammed, who later testified at the trial, reported:

> I am an Ogoni man, and I know churches are just window dressing. If I had gone into a church or mosque they would have killed me there. But, because of their fetish belief, they were afraid if they [went] into the shrine . . . the repercussions would be on their families for generations.[34]

In the nick of time, the police arrived and drove off the mob; Mohammed Kobani survived the attack.

The following day, May 22, Saro-Wiwa and several other leaders of MOSOP were arrested. In a televised press conference, the military governor of Rivers State blamed the MOSOP leaders for the murders. Saro-Wiwa and his colleagues were detained in a secret military camp outside Port Harcourt, where they were chained in leg irons and denied access to medical care. It would be eight months before they were formally charged.

During Saro-Wiwa's imprisonment, his brother, Owens Wiwa, met on three occasions with Shell Nigeria's managing director Brain Anderson to seek his help in securing Ken's release. Wiwa later gave an account of these meetings that was posted on the Internet. Anderson told him, Wiwa reported, that it would be "difficult but not impossible" to get his brother out of prison. Anderson allegedly said, "if [MOSOP] can stop the campaign [against Shell] we might be able to do something." Wiwa refused. Wiwa also reported that he had asked Anderson if the company had made payments to Okintumo. "The answer he gave is that 'I [emphasis added]

have never approved payment to Okuntimo.' He did not deny that Shall was paying Okuntimo. I think he knew about it, and the people in London knew about it."[35]

While later acknowledging that meetings between Anderson and Wiwa had taken place as part of an effort at "quiet diplomacy," Shell denied Wiwa's specific allegations as "false and reprehensible."

In November, General Abacha appointed a Civil Disturbances Speical Tribunal to try the case of the MOSOP leaders. Established by special decree, this tribunal was empowered to impose the death penalty for previously noncapital offenses in cases involving civil disturbances. The decision of the court could be confirmed or disallowed by the military government, but defendants had no right of judicial appeal. Amnesty International and many other human rights organizations denounced the tribunal for violating standards of due process guaranteed by Nigeria's own constitution and by international treaties.

Saro-Wiwa's trial for murder began in February 1995. Government witnesses testified that Saro-Wiwa had relayed a message to his youthful supporters, after the roadblock incident, that "the vultures who connived with the security forces to stop me from addressing you are now meeting . . . [to share] money sent them by the federal government . . . Go to the meeting place and deal with the vultures."

Saro-Wiwa's defense attorneys countered that Saro-Wiwa had been at home at the time and had had nothing to do with the killings. The defense team also presented evidence that two key prosecution witnesses had been bribed by the government with Shell contracts and cash in exchange for their statements implicating Saro-Wiwa. Shell later adamantly denied bribing witnesses, saying, "We have not paid cash, awarded contracts or used any other means to try to influence events surrounding the cases before the Tribunal."

In June, Saro-Wiwa's defense team withdrew from the case in protest after repeated rulings by the presiding judge favorable to the prosecution and after being denied access to the defendants in custody. Saro-Wiwa refused to cooperate with attorneys appointed by the court to replace them.

---

[34] *Ibid.*

[35] Rowell, Andy, January 23, 1996, *op. cit.*

Trial observers reported that from this point on, Saro-Wiwa appeared to view the proceedings as a "farce" and took little interest in them, "skim[ming] a newspaper or star[ing] blankly ahead as through he were a mere bystander at the performance around him."[36]

On November 2, the tribunal found Saro-Wiwa and eight other MOSOP leaders guilty of murder and sentenced them to death. Six defendants were acquitted. On November 8, Shell issued this statement, in response to international appeals that it seek a commutation of the sentence:

> *We believe that to interfere in the processes, either political or legal, here in Nigeria would be wrong. A large multinational company such as Shell cannot and must not interfere with the affairs of any sovereign state.*[37]

Two days later, Saro-Wiwa and eight MOSOP associates were hanged at Port Harcourt prison. His last words on the gallows were: "Lord, take my soul, but the struggle continues."

"With Deep Regret"

Shell issued a statement on the executions that read, in part:

> *It is with deep regret that we hear this news. From the violence that led to the murder of the four Ogoni leaders in May last year through to the death penalty having been carried out, the human cost has been too high.*[38]

Shell told reporters that it had approached the government privately after Saro-Wiwa's conviction to appeal for clemency on "humanitarian grounds." It would have been inappropriate, however, the company said, to have intervened in the criminal trial. The company also declined to comment further regarding human rights in Nigeria. A spokesperson stated:

> *We can't issue a bold statement about human rights because . . . it could be considered*

> *treasonous by the regime and the employees could come under attack. It would only inflame the issues.*[39]

The company also defended its actions in the months leading up to Saro-Wiwa's execution. Shell representatives stated that it would have been wrong to have sought to influence over government policy on environmental protection, Ogoni autonomy, or other issues of concern to MOSOP. With respect to the actions of the Nigerian police, the company argued that it would have been improper to provide its own armed security. An executive told the news media, "Our responsibility is very clear. We pay taxes and [abide by] regulation. We don't run the government."[40]

Shell also vigorously resisted calls by some human rights activists and environmentalists that the company withdraw from Nigeria. If it left, the company argued, whatever organization took over its operations would probably operate with lower environmental and safety standards, and the jobs of its Nigerian employees would be imperiled.

Whether or not Shell's position was justified, its public disclaimers did little to slow down the public controversy swirling around the company. By mid-1996, the company was facing a growing international boycott, the possibility that it would have to abandon plans to proceed with its liquefied natural gas project, and persistent demands that it withdraw from Nigeria altogether. The crisis threatened the company's shareholders, employers, franchisees, and customers—not only in Nigeria, but throughout the world. ∎

SOURCE: This case was written from public sources, including those provided by the Shell Petroleum Development Company of Nigeria on the Internet, solely for the purpose of stimulating student discussion. All events and individuals are real. Research was supported by the San Jose State University College of Business. This case was presented at the 1996 annual meeting of the North American Case Research Association. All rights reserved jointly to the author and the North American Case Research Association (NACRA). Copyright© 1997 by the *Case Research Journal* and Anne T. Lawrence.

[36]McGreal, Chris, *op. cit.*
[37]Fielding, Nick, and Jason Lewis, "We Are Sorry, We Cannot Interfere, Shell Insists," *Mail on Sunday*, November 12, 1995.
[38]Guardian, "Bloody Deeds Raised Against A People's Struggle To Control Their Resources," November 11, 1995.

[39]Bielski, Vince, "Shell's Game," *Sierra*, v. 81, #2, March, 1996.
[40]Barber, Ben, "Oil Firm Walks Fine Line Criticizing Nigeria," *Wahsington Times*, February 22, 1996.

REFERENCES

Amnesty International, "Nigeria: Military Crackdown on Opposition," November 11, 1994, AFR 44/13/94.

Amnesty International, "Nigeria: The Ogoni Trials and Detentions," September 15, 1995, AFR 44/20/95.

Amnesty International, "Nigeria: A Travesty of Justice: Secret Treason Trials and Other Concerns," October 1995, AFR 44/23/95.

Amnesty International, "Nigeria: A Summary of Human Rights Concerns," March, 1996, AFR 44/03/96.

Barber, Ben, "Oil Firm Walks Fine Line Criticizing Nigeria," *Washington Times*, February 22, 1996.

Beckket, Paul, "Shell Walks New Public Relations Tightrope in Nigeria," *The Wall Street Journal*, November 28, 1995 [reprinted in the *Houston Chronicle*].

Bielski, Vince, "Shell's Game," *Sierra*, v. 81, #2, March, 1996.

Boyd, William, "Introduction," pp. vii–xv in Ken Saro-Wiwa. *A Month and a Day: A Detention Diary*, New York: Penguin Books, 1995.

Bridgland, Fred, "Ken Saro-Wiwa Has Become Another Tragic Chapter in Nigeria's Sad History." *The Scotsman*, November 11, 1995.

The Economist, "The General In His Not So Solitude," April 6, 1996, pp. 43–44.

The Economist, "Nigeria Foaming," November 18, 1995, p. 15.

Field, Graham, "Nigerian National Petroleum Corporation," pp. 472–474 in Adele Hast, ed., *International Directory of Company Histories*, v. 4. Chicago: St. James Press, 1991.

Fielding, Nick, and Jason Lewis, "We Are Sorry, We Cannot Interfere, Shell Insists," *Mail on Sunday*, November 12, 1995.

Fortune, "Introduction to Fortune's Global 500: The World's Largest Corporations," August 7, 1995, pp. 130–136.

Greenpeace, "Nigeria Statement by Dr. Owens Wiwa," February 1, 1996.

Guardian, "Bloody Deeds Raised Against A People's Struggle To Control Their Resources," November 11, 1995.

Hammer, Joshua, "Nigeria Crude," *Harper's Magazine*, June 1996.

Hoover's Company Profile Database [On-line], "Royal Dutch/Shell Group," in *World Companies*. Austin, TX: The Reference Press, 1995.

Hunter, Brian, ed., "Nigeria," in *The Statesman's Yearbook: Statistical and Historical Annual of the States of the World for the Year 1995–1996*. New York: St Martin's Press, 1996.

Iloegbunam, Chuks, "Death of a Writer, Ken Saro-Wiwa [obituary]," *The Guardian*, November 11, 1995.

Jones, Geoffrey, "Royal Dutch Petroleum Company: The Shell Transport and Trading Company P.L.C.," pp. 530–532 in Adele Hast, ed., *International Directory of Company Histories*, v. 4. Chicago: St. James Press, 1991.

Lewis, Paul, "Nigeria's Deadly Oil War: Shell Defends Its Record," *New York Times*, February 13, 1996, pp. A1, A4.

MacDonald, Scott B., Jane E. Hughes, and David Leith Crum, "Nigeria," pp. 215–241 in *New Tigers and Old Elephants: The Development Game in the 1990s and Beyond*, New Brunswick, NJ: Transaction Publishers, 1995.

Mattera, Philip, "Royal Dutch/Shell Group," pp. 574–582 in *World Class Business: A Guide to the 100 Most Powerful Global Corporations*, New York: Henry Holt and Co., 1992.

McGreal, Chris, "A Tainted Hero," *The Guardian*, March 23, 1996.

Moody's International Manual, "Royal Dutch Petroleum Co.," 1995.

New York Times, "Surveys Rate Nigeria as Most Corrupt Nation for Business," June 3, 1996.

"Nigeria," [On-line]. Available: http://www.odci.gov/cia/publications/nsolo/factbook/ni.htm.

NRC Handelsblad, "Shell: Rapid Introduction of Alternative Energy," January 25, 1995 [translation from the original Dutch by Francis de Winter], [On-line]. Available: http://www.ecotopia.com/hubbert/debate/hubshell.htm.

Orr, Dacid, "Inside Nigeria: Only a Trickle of the Country's Oil Wealth is Reaching the People of the Niger Delta," *The Independent*, December 1, 1995.

Rowell, Andy, "Environment: Trouble Flares in the Delta of Death," *The Guardian*, November 8, 1995, p. 6.

Rowell, Andy, *Green Backlash*. London: Routledge: 1996 forthcoming.

Rowell, Andy, "Shell Shocked: Did the Shell Petroleum Company Silence Nigerian Environmentalist Ken Saro-Wiwa?" *Village Voice*, November 21, 1995.

Rowell, Andy, "Sleeping with the Enemy: Worldwide Protests Can't Stop Shell Snuggling Up to Nigeria's Military," *Village Voice*, January 23, 1996.

Sachs, Aaron, "Dying for Oil: Killing the Land Means Killing the People," *World Watch*, May/June, 1996, pp. 10–21.

Sampson, Anthony, *The Seven Sisters: The Great Oil Companies and the World They Made*. New York: Viking, 1975.

Saro-Wiwa, Ken, *A Month and a Day: A Detention Diary*, New York: Penguin Books, 1995.

Shell Oil Company, "About Shell," [On-line]. Available: http://www.sopc.com/aboutshell/.

Shell Petroleum Development Company of Nigeria, "Clear Thinking in Troubled Times," [On-line]. Available: http://www.shellnigeria.com/news/ prl2.html.

Shell Petroleum Development Company of Nigeria, "Community Disturbances," [On-line]. Available: http://www.shellus.com/news/nigeria.html.

Shell Petroleum Development Company of Nigeria, "Execution of Ken Saro-Wiwa and His Co-defendants," [On-line]. Available: http://www.shellnigeria.com/news/ prl4.html.

Shell Petroleum Development Company of Nigeria, "Firearms: The Shell Position," [On-line]. Available: http://www.shellnigeria.com/news/prl12.html.

Shell Petroleum Development Company of Nigeria, "Issues Background," [On-line]. Available: http://www.shellnigeria,com/issues/issback.html.

Shell Petroleum Development Company of Nigeria, "Response Statement: Verdict on Mr. Ken Saro-Wiwa and Others," [On-line]. Available: http://www.shellnigeria.com/news/prl8.html.

Shell Petroleum Development Company of Nigeria, "Shell and the Supernumerary Police in Nigeria," [On-line]. Available: http://www.shellnigeria.com/new/ prl13.html.

Shell Petroleum Development Company of Nigeria, "Shell in Nigeria," [On-line]. Available: http://www.shellnigeria.com/issues/facsum.html.

U.S. Committee on Foreign Relations, "The Situation in Nigeria," Hearing before the Sub-committee on African Affairs, July 20, 1995, Washington DC: U.S. Government Printing Office, 1995.

World Bank, "Defining an Environmental Development Strategy for the Niger Delta," v. I–II, Report No. 14266-UNI, May 30, 1995.

Yergin, Daniel, *The Prize: The Epic Quest for Oil, Money, and Power*. New York: Simon and Schuster, 1991.

Case 9 Argentina Suites (II): 1996 to 1998

Demian Hodari and Timothy R. Hinkin

Introduction

Max Sinclair had learned that running a family business was far more challenging than he had ever imagined. In the early 1990s Max had worked in various departments of his father Abraham's hotel, the Argentina Suites, in Buenos Aires, Argentina. Abraham is an Argentine physician who had made his fortune in the United States and invested much of his wealth in real estate in Buenos Aires. In 1994 Max left Argentina to pursue his Masters Degree in Hotel Administration in the United States. Upon graduation in 1996, the 27-year-old Max returned to Buenos Aires to assume the position of General Manager. Over the next few years some of the projects he had undertaken had succeeded while others had not. In March of 1999 he faced a major decision that could impact the future of the Argentina Suites.

Background

Argentina has a history of political instability but in 1983 its constitution was reinstated and since then it has operated as a democracy similar to that of the United States. Juan Peron created labor laws in the 1950s that are still in effect today that offer strong protection for the worker. Unions are a very powerful, and sometimes corrupt force. Argentina's culture has been greatly affected by its immigrant population, mostly European. Invasion by the Spanish conquistadores led to the demise of pre-Columbian cultures, resulting in the lack of a dominant indigenous population. Other European immigrant groups each adopted different roles. The Basque and Irish controlled sheep rearing, the Germans and Italians established farms, and the British invested in developing the country's infra-structure. The universal language of Argentina is Spanish, but many natives and immigrants keep their mother tongues as a matter of pride and consider themselves European rather than South American. More than one-third of the country's 32 million people live in Buenos Aires, the capital.[1] The economy is dominated by agriculture, but manufacturing is becoming increasingly important. Rampant inflation in the 1970s and early 1980s rapidly depreciated the value of the peso. By 1990 the economy had stabilized and Argentina's balance of trade was strongly favorable.[2]

The Hotel

The Argentina Suites hotel consists of 160 guestroom units and a 120-seat restaurant. It had never obtained the legal status of a hotel due to several physical irregularities and was technically an apartment building that leased its apartments on a short term (often one night) basis. In addition, due to this status, each service (such as apartment rental, laundry, food and beverage, parking) were separate entities that, on paper, were owned by some of Max's relatives, but in reality were all owned by Abraham. (see Appendix A for a list of characters in the case). Max's sister Natalie managed the hotel from April of 1987 until August of 1991. She resigned at age 29 and was replaced by her then 70-year-old uncle, Geraldo. At that time, average occupancy was 73%, most of which was business travellers. For the next several years the hotel essentially operated without a General Manager. Geraldo's role was more of a figurehead, which kept Maria, the Head of Marketing, and Monica, the Head of Administration, from battling for the official leadership position and office. Maria, Monica, and Coqui, Head of Personnel, ran the hotel, each overseeing different aspects of the operation, and making the major decisions that were communicated to Geraldo for his authorization. It was a comfortable place for them since they essentially had no supervision, and no one critiqued their work except for their uncle Abraham on his bimonthly visits. They were paid much more than they could have earned in any

---

[1]www.geographia.com/argentina/history.htm
[2]www.shadow.net/~giorgio/argentina.html

other company, worked the hours they wanted, made all the decisions, and had 100 employees doing what they told them to do.

During the early 1990s the city's hotel market changed considerably as the first new hotels in 20 years were built. Numerous international companies were looking for new markets, and Buenos Aires, a city of ten million, was attractive to many of them as it was both a tourist destination and a business center. Two Spanish companies, Sol Melia and NH had recently opened hotels. Several four star properties, including a Radisson, a Howard Johnson, and a five-hundred room Hilton Hotel, were also under construction and the 800 room Sheraton Hotel, built in 1973, had undergone a major renovation as well as being expanded to include an additional 200-room luxury tower. In addition, Marriott and Holiday Inn had taken over management contracts at other well-established upscale hotels. All of these companies had sophisticated reservations and property management systems. This development was accompanied by an infusion of expatriate talent with expertise in management, marketing, and information technology. At the same time there was an increase in international business travellers, and service quality was becoming a major competitive issue. From 1992 to 1994 the hotel experienced an Average Daily Rate (ADR) of US $92 and 77% occupancy. During 1994, the economic crisis in Mexico (known as the Tequila effect), greatly impacted the Latin American economy and occupancy dropped by around 15% by the end of 1994, and was still in decline when Max arrived in June of 1996. Total revenue for the hotel was $5.6 million in 1995.

1996: Initial Changes

Sales & Marketing

Max knew that all of the hotel's operating departments had problems, and that the Marketing Department would need substantial revamping. But he was hesitant to start his change program with this area even though he believed what a professor had once told him:

> If your sales are okay, you can solve the rest of the problems. But when sales are poor, you will have trouble focusing on other areas. It all comes down to money, the money that's coming in, and the money that's leaving. Deal with the money first.

He was afraid because he really didn't have much experience with sales and if he tampered with the area and it backfired he would lose the confidence of his managers and staff. He did, however, make a couple of small requests from the department regarding their procedures.

First, he insisted that the department put all its records into a computer database, as he was worried that too much information about the clients was simply in the heads of the sales agents. Second, since most accounts resulted from sales calls that the agents made to companies, he had them write a summary report for each visit. His cousin Maria could then review the reports each week and develop plans for follow-up. He was not sure that these changes would have an impact on sales, but at least it would make his employees aware that he was keeping tabs on their work. Other than this, he pretty much left the area alone for the first six months. He decided to focus his initial changes in a less risky area.

Housekeeping

Max started the changes at the Argentina Suites with the Housekeeping Department. He figured it was an area that was sufficiently poorly operated to merit attention, and it was not as complicated to analyze, understand, and improve as the Front Office or Administration departments. In addition, if he made major mistakes they would not affect the rest of the hotel as drastically. It was a good place for him and his staff to begin to make changes.

Even before taking over the hotel, Max hired a 20-year-old, Spanish speaking American university student as a six-month (June to December) intern. Sylvia had recently completed her junior year in a Hotel Management program. Her mission was to learn everything she could about how the housekeeping department operated, and to then propose an action plan on how to improve the department's operations with regard to cost, productivity, and quality.

Three weeks after she began, Sylvia broke down in tears in his office, overwhelmed.

> These women are driving me crazy. Each one of them cleans their rooms in a different way.

Half the time they are cleaning, they are just chatting away at me, complaining about the hotel, the other maids, your family, and even about you, though of course, I'm not supposed to mention that. I ask them why they do things the way they do, and they say because it's comfortable, or because it makes the most sense. And when I try to understand further, they shut up. I think they have never thought about how to clean or how to work. Even with all the different methods, no one cleans a room in less than 45 minutes, and most of the time, when they leave, there is still dirt or things out of place. The rooms never look the same twice.

Max asked what Noemi, the Head Housekeeper, had to say. Sylvia responded:

When I asked her to show me the correct approach, she told me that there really wasn't one standard. She prefers to allow each of her girls to work however she sees fit. As long as the final product is acceptable, then that is fine with her.

Apparently, this had been the practice ever since the hotel had opened 10 years before with Max's sister, Natalie, as General Manager. Since Noemi was still the Executive Housekeeper, and since 13 of the 16 maids had been there since the beginning, this policy had never changed. Noemi even warned Sylvia that she should not suggest changing things or the maids would revolt.

Sylvia told Max that she understood about giving people decision-making rights, and how maybe this had helped keep turnover among the staff down, but everything she had studied in school and read in housekeeping manuals recommended having standard cleaning procedures. She asked Max what she should do and he responded:

I don't have the time to get very involved. I trust you. You know what's wrong, I can tell. Be confident in yourself. Write up your proposal as best you see fit, and we'll worry about implementing it later. You have my full support.

Max was pleased with himself for delegating the responsibility, empowering Sylvia, and for not interfering too much. He knew he had to manage his time wisely; there were too many issues that needed his attention. Besides, he had spoken with Noemi several weeks before and she had assured him that she was happy with the fact that he was paying attention to her area, even if it was via Sylvia. She was especially happy that he had told Coqui, the Personnel Manager, to stay out of her department.

Personnel Department

Coqui, Max's cousin, was the Head of Personnel. Shortly after arriving, Max contracted a respected labor lawyer, Senior Martin, to review the hotel's personnel situation. Local labor laws were very complicated, and considered by most companies to be one of the major expenses and risks with doing business in Argentina. Even though salaries were low compared to the United States, mistakes in hiring, suspending, and/or firing employees could be extremely difficult and expensive.[3] Senior Martin began by examining what the hotel was doing to comply with the many laws. After one day with Coqui he sat Max down for a three espresso chat. Senior Martin explained the situation:

I've been in this business for 20 years, and it has been a long, long time since I have seen a situation like this. Everything is a lie in that office. All employees are registered at the lowest pay level. On paper, your kitchen staff consists of 12 dishwashers and one cook. Your Front Office staff is registered as one receptionist and 16 bellboys. You have no managers. It would be easy for someone, perhaps a disgruntled employee, to prove your registration is false and jeopardize the future of the hotel. Employee wages are being under-reported to the government. The company reports that each employee is earning only minimum wage while most of the staff is being paid another part 'under the table.' There are employees whose health certificates have been expired for years. It's not just that there are lies and deception. Let's face it; this is quite common in Argentina. I am simply not sure if your cousin is doing these things on purpose, or if he simply does not understand the job.

---

[3]Falsifying applications and resumes is commonplace, so the selection process can be very time consuming and expensive. Once employees are hired they are automatically eligible for three months of severance, paid by the company, if they are terminated. The documentation required to terminate an employee for just cause, which would result in no severance pay, is so complex and onerous that few companies even try to keep records.

The list went on and on. Max knew that in the past it was very easy to get away with breaking the laws regarding employee pay, and that this was done to reduce payroll taxes, which, on average, amounted to 50% of an employee's salary. It did not matter to most companies, including the hotel, that the full labor costs could not be expensed since a lot of sales were also not recorded or reported. In addition, other costs could be "created" by purchasing false invoices (at 7% of the face value) from other companies in order to increase deductible expenses; thereby reducing income taxes. For example, they could register an expense of $1,000 by paying $70 to a company who would issue them an official bill of sale for a hard-to-detect service such as maintenance repairs or a consulting service.

Max gave Senior Martin free reign to correct the situation and instructed Coqui to provide all the necessary support. He told Coqui:

Consider this your number one priority. I know there are other issues in the hotel in which you could be involved, but we will try to get by without you for now. Please focus here. I want every employee's file to be up-to date, and I want a good plan for beginning to declare (legalize) all salaries.

Coqui protested:

We've been running the hotel like this for almost 10 years and have never had a problem. We've been paying off the tax inspectors regularly during that time. Many of them have almost become friends of mine, and they assure me that there is no need to change our arrangements. All of the talk in the papers and in congress about the changes is just that; nothing will change. You don't believe it because you are a Yankee, a northerner. Doing business the way we do is probably saving your father one or two hundred thousand dollars a year. You know how he is; he hates paying taxes. You won't have an easy time convincing him about this. I won't make any changes until I receive orders from him, and I'll bet you that once he hears my point of view we'll put an end to your silliness.

Max suspected that one reason Coqui wanted to remain in control of so much cash was that he was keeping some for himself. Max would have loved to prove Coqui had been stealing, but this would be nearly impossible. Since no records were kept due to fear of a tax inspection, there was virtually no paper trail. Max also knew that his father shared his suspicions, but Abraham reasoned that even if Coqui was stealing some money, his schemes probably still saved more than they cost. Max disagreed vehemently:

Dad, you know they are stealing in payroll. And if they're stealing here, that means the Administrative Department must know, and may be stealing as well. If we let it happen in one place, then we're giving a sign that we accept this behavior. How can we expect honest behavior from the employees if the managers – your family – are cheating you? Besides, you're not here. Everything I read and discuss with lawyers, bankers, and others suggests that the country is changing faster than we realize, and while there is still going to be a lot of corruption, it's going to be tougher and more expensive to cover it up. We have to learn to be profitable and competitive based on sound hotel management rather than theft and false tax records.

Max's father gave in, albeit reluctantly. Max also had another reason for wanting to make these changes. He thought that with some restructuring of the hotel's infrastructure, it could meet international hotel chain requirements. If they were also able to get their legal situation in order, they would have an advantage over the competition when the chains looked for properties to buy. He did not have much interest in managing the hotel if the changes he could make were limited to the kind of soap the laundry used, or what color to paint the lobby. He wanted to make serious changes, to protect his father's investment for the long-term future rather than just oversee it for the short term. He had not spent two years of his life in graduate school in order to ignore what he had learned.

Front Office

While Sylvia was busy in Housekeeping and Coqui and Senior Martin were fighting it out in Personnel, Max turned his attention to the Front Office operations. There were plenty of inefficiencies here. Several amateur mystery shoppers Max had hired to evaluate the hotel's departments had confirmed all of Max's suspicions. They agreed that while the employees were very friendly and helpful, the processes were slow, tedious, and prone to error.

The complaints were as common as they were varied. For example, reservations were not taken properly and rooms were not ready on time (one guest had been checked into a room that had been occupied for over three weeks). In addition, check-out invoices were complex, prepared very slowly, and often inaccurate. Many meals that had been consumed in the hotel restaurant had not appeared on final bills. In order to fix these and other problems, Max turned to Adriana, the Administrative Department's Internal Auditor. This was someone whom he trusted. They had dated prior to Max's return to graduate school and had remained close friends.

Adriana's job for the past seven years had been to control the hotel's billing to external clients. All bills going to corporate and tour operator clients had to pass through her prior to being mailed out. This position required a lot of attention to detail and familiarity with the way the Front Office operated. She also needed to understand how the Marketing Department priced each of the 12 different kinds of rooms, how they decided the prices for each corporate client and for specific employees of those companies, and how bills were prepared and payment collected. Maria, the Director of Marketing and Max's cousin, did not believe that one company deserved one rate; as she saw it "each person is an individual and deserves a very personalized rate." Because more than 20% of bills were detected to contain errors, Adriana was well aware of the common mistakes. But, as she told Max, her job had always been to fix the mistakes rather than prevent them.

Your cousin Maria has hated me ever since I realized a few years ago that one of her employees had been stealing money for years right under her nose. She never listens to my suggestions about how we can prevent mistakes. She knows why most of them happen, but if we prevent them, then she loses influence as the Head of Marketing. She's indispensable right now because of the complicated rate system and billing procedures. Plus, only she knows how to use the computer system. It's so complicated that the front desk receptionists spend 20 minutes processing a single bill. Under the present system if they notice a mistake they have to inform her and then she comes from her office across the street and fixes it. If they can't find her, then they just let the mistake stand because they know she or I will deal with it later. I don't blame the receptionists. The guests get really upset when they have to wait.

Max decided to appoint Adriana as Front Office Manager. Moving her from the Administrative Department located across the street meant demoting Arturo, the current Front Office manager. Arturo had been with the hotel for over five years. Natalie had recruited him from the Sheraton where she found that he provided the most courteous service she had ever encountered in Argentina. Max agreed that although Arturo provided excellent service, he had no leadership ability. When asked what he would change about the Front Office, Arturo had simply remarked, "I would like to stop having nights where we are overbooked and have to walk guests.[4] I hate that."

While Max knew transferring Adriana was the right move in terms of solving the Front Office's problems, he knew this would cause problems in the department. Some of the receptionists had complained to Max about Adriana's meddling in their area, and a couple of them had asked about being promoted to Arturo's position if it ever became available. In addition, Max was worried that people would accuse him of favoritism due to his past relationship with her. But they had quit dating four years earlier, and both knew that replacing Arturo was the right decision. Max spoke with Arturo and he agreed to accept a position as front desk receptionist at the same salary as he currently received (Argentine labor laws would not permit a decrease in salary). Although Max had already decided on Adriana, he felt that he should post the job opening in the hotel. He only interviewed Ingrid, a current receptionist. She had been with the hotel since its opening and was considered efficient but overly aggressive. During her interview, when asked what changes she might make, she said she could fix most of the area's problems if Max would give her a monthly sum of money with which to motivate her employees.

A few days later Max arranged a meeting with Adriana and the Front Office employees. The meeting was scheduled between shifts in order to allow all the

---

[4]"Walking" is a hotel industry term for turning away a guest with a confirmed reservation. When this happens the hotel must pay for the guest's accommodations at another hotel. This situation often leads to an unhappy customer and can be very stressful for front desk personnel.

employees to attend. Several bellboys and receptionists showed up late because they had just finished work and had taken the time to change into their street clothes. Ingrid failed to show at all. Max had told her earlier in the day about his decision to promote Adriana and he did not think she took it well. He made his announcement regarding Adriana's new position and then left her alone with her new staff. He had told her to use the time to try and win them over. Max gave her the following advice:

I don't want you to make or even suggest any changes for a couple of months. Let them see that you are studying the area and listening to their complaints and suggestions.

Adriana responded, "But I already know most of what is wrong, I've known for years." Max replied:

Look, if you jump in and start making changes, then they will resist. Try to get them to see that the changes you want to make come from their ideas, not yours. I know they are yours, and you know it, but they don't have to. Not yet.

Adriana complained about having to wait but said she would do as he asked. "At least start looking into the computer situation," she said. "That's all I ask."

Information Technology

Max held a meeting with his department heads to discuss changing the computer system and installing a network throughout the hotel. When he asked for opinions Maria spoke up.

If we change operating systems and give more people access to the information, then it will be harder to keep people from finding out our secrets.

Max did not care. He wanted to eliminate the secrets rather than keep covering them up. When Maria finally agreed that more computers and more networking were needed, she argued that they should remain with the same IT provider as before, that they had some newer programs that could do the job.

Rather than take on the job of investigating alternative systems himself, Max formed a committee comprised of representatives from departments including Marketing, Operations, Food and Beverage, Purchasing, Engineering, and Administration. He instructed them to look into the different alternatives,

obtain estimated costs, and report back to him in one month with recommendations. He made sure that both Maria and Adriana were on the committee. He knew that Maria was upset that he had promoted Adriana. But, like he told a friend,

If they are going to kill one another, we may as well find out now. It could even make my job even easier.

Administration

Max knew that substantive change was needed in the Administration Department. Nine people were doing the work he felt four could accomplish. This was a delicate area however; mistakes made here could harm the entire company and result in both financial and legal repercussions. He also understood very little about how the department had to operate, given local constraints, and that if he decided to take charge of the area himself it would mean ignoring the rest of the hotel. Max was particularly confused about the accounting system, for total revenue for 1996 was going to be less than $3.5 million. He did, however, hold meetings with the department's employees, as he had already done with all of the hotel's employees. He noticed that most of them were very cautious not to complain about their work or Monica, even though complaints of this type had been common at most of the other meetings he had held. He also knew that they were the best-paid employees in the company.

Housekeeping: Status Report

Two months after beginning her project and two weeks before she was scheduled to return to her studies in the United States, Sylvia turned in her housekeeping report. Max read it and, while he was very pleased with her work, he was even more distressed about the Housekeeping Department. Most of her proposals seemed sound, but Max disagreed about replacing Noemi. While he conceded that she was not as qualified as he would like, he found her to be agreeable to change. Firing or demoting her could have major negative repercussions throughout the company. "If people associate our analysis of departments with firing people, then we are going to face even more resistance then we currently are," Max said. Sylvia responded:

But she will not be able to implement these changes. She won't want to; she's terrified. I know she tells you differently, but you are not up there on the floors with us. She often tells me she'll be right back and disappears for hours at a time to get away from me. She thinks of me as a spy.

Max replied:

Even more reason to keep her on. If we can get her to realize that the changes you want to make will make her department work better, make her life easier, then that will spread throughout the hotel and we'll find future change to be even easier. Remember that she's been here since before the hotel opened. The maids, while they may not respect her, do love her. She's an institution here. She organizes parties, remembers everyone's birthday, and keeps people smiling. We need her.

Sylvia responded:

But how are you going to get her to make the changes? I showed her a draft of the report. She doesn't understand most of it, things like productivity and standardization. She doesn't have the character to make people do things they don't want to, or to try new things. I think she's afraid of her employees. Some of them can't even read that well; how are they going to understand the manual I've made?

"But *you* understand." Max convinced Sylvia to stay on for another six months to implement the changes in housekeeping and to help out later on with some ideas he had for marketing. He told her to take a 10-day vacation over the Christmas and New Year's holiday, and they would start with the changes when she returned during the slower summer months. Besides thinking that Sylvia needed a vacation, he wanted to give Noemi a break and get her ready to start reorganizing her department. He liked the idea of starting the New Year with change; the symbolism was easy to grasp.

1997: Changes

Housekeeping

Late in January, on the morning on which the new housekeeping procedures were to be implemented, Max greeted the department with a breakfast of fresh croissants, coffee, and juice. The maids were surprised (some of them even cried) as this was the first time they had ever been given a free meal at the hotel. Max made a speech about how he was sure that their new operating procedures were going to be very successful and how he was counting on all their help. He congratulated Sylvia and Noemi for their hard work and wished them well.

Noemi thanked him and spoke about how this was going to be challenging for everyone, but how her girls were pleased that Max was trying to respond to many of the needs they had identified during Sylvia's research. Changes such as ensuring that their hall closets had enough supplies and linens and scheduling consecutive days off for the staff were important.

A few hours later Adriana barged into Max's office. "You had better come to the reservation office," she said.

"I'm in a meeting," Max said, pointing out the obvious.

"Well, I thought you'd want to know Noemi is on the floor screaming, pulling out her hair."

Max started to get up and then stopped. "Where's Sylvia?" he asked.

"She left the building after Noemi threw a clipboard at her."

Noemi took a few days off to relax before returning to work. It was a long few days for both Max and Sylvia for they were sure that Max's family members were secretly happy with his first real failure. Max met with Noemi upon her return and accepted the fact that having Sylvia alongside her all day may have been too much. He had simply wanted Sylvia to help Noemi teach the maids the new procedures and to help out with the coordination with the other departments.

"I know she's trying to help," Noemi said, "but if I am going to be in charge, then I need to learn how to do this myself. Give me a chance."

They finally agreed on a regular, end-of-the-day meeting between Noemi and Sylvia, with a weekly written report submitted to Max on Fridays. Sylvia, meanwhile, would help him analyze some past purchasing records that troubled him.

Personnel

Following several months of research and meetings with his labor lawyer, Max decided to completely reorganize the Personnel Department. He began by adding the Human Resource Manager position which would focus on all the non-financial decisions, such as recruitment, selection, and training. Rather than recruit from outside the company for this position, Max promoted a concierge with a degree in psychology. This concierge, Juan, had been with the hotel for almost 10 years, all of it in the same position. Max believed this was too long for someone with Juan's intelligence to spend in the same position and that his recent sub-par performance as a concierge was largely related to his boredom rather than his ability. He also knew that Juan was liked and trusted by most of the hotel employees. Max believed promoting Juan to this important position would show the other employees he was serious about improving the working conditions for dedicated employees. Coqui was not happy with the decision.

Are you crazy promoting Juan? Now all the employees will want to be promoted if they work well. I've been doing this job for years, and one thing I have learned is that when employees are good at something, you should keep them in that position because you might not ever find someone else to do it as well. Promoting Juan to my level means you are taking away all of my authority. First you tell me to stay out of the operating departments even though I've been involved in them for years. Then you take away a lot of my personnel responsibility and hire a stupid lawyer to control me. So now I'm just an administrator in charge of paying people. This is not the way to treat a manager or your cousin.

Max wanted to fire Coqui right then and there, but he couldn't. Instead, he offered him a deal. "Do what our lawyer suggests regarding organizing our paperwork to conform with the law, and when this is done we can add some new responsibilities to your job description."

Front Office

Adriana's work with the Front Office was commendable. She instituted a series of check-in procedures that eliminated much of the arbitrary decision making that the receptionists had previously undertaken, such as when to offer rate reductions and to whom one should offer upgrades. In addition, the entire rate system was modified in order to simplify administrative tasks. Companies now had one rate that varied by room type, rather than by person. Max's idea was to reposition the hotel as an extended-stay facility because of its large rooms with kitchens and sitting areas. There were no hotels like this in Buenos

Aires, while in the United States they seemed very popular. A system was established whereby rates decreased the longer a guest stayed in the hotel. This proved to be very popular with corporate clients who were relocating employees to the city.

A major change that Max insisted upon was that neither Marketing nor Administration were to have any direct authority in this area any longer. For instance, Marketing could suggest or ask for special offers to important clients but could no longer impose room rates on Front Office employees. Similarly, the Administration staff could no longer change rates or offer refunds that were not authorized by the Front Office. Neither Monica nor Maria liked these changes, and both women complained vehemently that Max was undermining their authority. He told them that he wanted a clear division of duties between the areas. Marketing was there to sell rooms, the Front Office to process the guests, and Administration to pay and collect bills.

Within a few weeks Adriana came to see Max.

On paper your ideas are great, but in reality they are not working. Monica is having her employees call me 20 times a day with questions about each account. They are asking things like 'Can I send out this bill?' or 'Is it all right if I correct the spelling of this client's name?' or 'Should I send the credit today or wait until tomorrow?' They know what to do but are being ridiculous. Maria comes to my office after every client meeting she has to ask my permission to give them a certain rate. She's smiling and acting nice, but I don't trust her.

"They are having a tough time adjusting," Max said, though he suspected it was more than that.

Information Technology

The committee looked into Maria's suggested upgrades but rejected them as being very complicated to use and not offering enough options. Rather, they decided on an alternative program that was being used in some other hotels owned by a company with which Max had friendly relations. These hotels included the Argentina Towers, which was located across the street. Adriana and another committee member told him privately that Maria had said that they would change the computer system "over her dead body." Max wondered if it would come to that.

The computer system they chose linked, for the first time, the hotel's Reservation, Front Office, and Administrative departments. Information flowed more smoothly among the departments, errors during check-in and checkout were reduced, and bills were produced faster and more accurately. Employees were generally very happy with the new system and able, they said, to work more independently of Monica. Guests complimented the staff on greatly reducing their waiting time. Monica was quick to point out that the printers often jammed because the bills were processed too quickly. Max immediately purchased some new high-speed printers.

Administration

Perhaps due to the new computer system, or the new Front Office procedures, or simplified accounting practices, the Administrative Department started to work more efficiently even without Max getting too involved. Monica would not, however, accept the fact that Max wanted to professionalize the hotel and not just keep operating it with a short-term vision. He told her he wanted to reduce administrative costs by 30 percent and she replied, "Fine, but I will not let you reduce my staff." He asked her to have her employees propose 10 new ideas on how to cut costs and improve efficiency. She did not want to do this because it might create the impression that she did not know how to manage her department. Because Monica was reluctant to take any initiative, Max met with her employees to discuss improvements. He found the majority of them spoke much more openly than they had the last time he had met with them. Most of their ideas centered on allowing each employee to take responsibility for his/her work rather than having everything approved by Monica. They also thought that they could organize themselves into teams, rather than having everyone work alone and being connected only through Monica. Max decided that he would initiate these changes.

April 1998

The hotel operated quite smoothly for the rest of the year and into 1999, and Max began to focus on some other issues. The president of one of Abraham's companies involved in managing the Argentina Suites was Patricia, Max's cousin and Coqui's sister. She was also a physician and served as the company doctor. According to the law, when an employee calls in sick, the doctor is supposed to visit them not only to attend to them, but also to confirm for the company that the employee is too sick to work and not simply faking.

Several months ago Max had calculated what Patricia cost the company in salary, benefits, vacation and expenses. He realized it was five times what he would pay if he outsourced the service to a professional medical firm that specialized in this kind of service. He had also been told by his labor lawyer that if an employee was denied medical leave for some reason, the employee could sue the hotel since the president of the firm was also the physician and thus perhaps not objective.

Max showed Patricia the numbers, and then told her that he could no longer pay her the salary she wanted. He offered her several alternatives: A) She could accept a reduction in half of her salary and benefits and keep her job; B) she could keep the same salary but work full-time for the company in another capacity; and C) she could get a job, at nearly two-thirds her current salary, with another company he had made contact with.

Patricia said she earned her salary because of the financial and legal risks she incurred as president, risks she didn't like taking and only did as a favor to his father. Max thanked her for her generosity and told her that he could relieve her of her burden and have her replaced before the next fiscal quarter. She said not to do anything until she had an opportunity to speak with his father when he came to town the next time.

A few weeks later Max had a similarly difficult discussion with Coqui, for he had decided to make some major changes involving several of his relatives. Max had recently hired a new F&B Assistant Manager, Ricardo, to assist Maria's husband, Nicolas, the current F&B Manager. Ricardo had performed extremely well, and Max wanted to promote him to F&B Manager. In addition, Max had decided to transfer Nicolas from the restaurant into Human Resources to work with Juan. He would then transfer Coqui from Human Resources to a new department, Security. This transfer would include moving him into a basement office where he could monitor the security personnel and cameras. This office used to be the employee dining room before Max arrived, and when Max asked why the employees were made to eat in a dark, windowless basement room, Coqui had responded that all employees had to make sacrifices for the good of the company. Max wondered if Coqui would now complain about his new office. Several weeks earlier Max had confirmed with Nicolas that he would accept his new assignment. Now, a few days before planning to discuss this change with Coqui, Max learned that he had already heard rumors and was not happy with the idea of his transfer. Coqui screamed at Max:

> I have been Personnel Manager for ten years now, and there is no way that you are going to take that away from me. I have worked hard to keep this hotel running smoothly, and it did long before you arrived. No matter what people say, including you, I have never stolen a peso from your father or the employees. And if you think for a minute that I am going to move into that basement, you had better be prepared for a big surprise.

Around this time a front office receptionist who had been given a few days off to deal with a family emergency called Adriana to tell her that she would be taking a few more days. Adriana explained that she could not approve additional days off because many employees were on summer vacation, and that when her leave of absence had been granted it was under the condition that it would not and could not

be extended. Nevertheless the employee did not return to wok the following day and Adriana asked that she be suspended, which entailed Coqui preparing a legal telegram and his sister Patricia signing it.

Coqui refused to prepare the document, "Have your HR manager do it," he told Max. Patricia refused to talk with Max on the telephone, "Go to hell," her husband told him. Max had no choice but to have Maria, the company's official Vice-President, sign the telegram even though the signature could be contested in court.

That night, as Max looked back at his accomplishments over the past two years, he was both pleased and frustrated. He had arrived with such ambitious plans for the hotel. The property was physically in much better condition as guestrooms had been standardized and upgraded, the management information systems had integrated the various departments, and many important legal issues had been resolved. Occupancy and guest satisfaction continued to improve (See Appendix B). While the hotel was much better positioned to compete and/or join forces with the international hotel companies that had entered the market, Max still had some major misgivings about the future. He thought about calling his father. ∎

▬▬▬▬▬▬▬ Appendix A ▬▬▬▬▬▬▬

Abraham Sinclair: Argentina Suites owner

Max Sinclair: General Manager and Abraham's son

Maria: Director of Marketing and Abraham's niece
Vice-President of the apartment rental company

Monica: Director of Administration and Abraham's niece

Coqui: Personnel Manager and Abraham's nephew
Owner of the laundry company

Sylvia: American student intern

Noemi: Head of Housekeeping

Senior Martin: Consulting attorney

Adriana: New Front Office Manager, former girl-friend of Max

Arturo: Former Front Office Manager

Juan: Human Resources Manager

Patricia: Company Doctor and Abraham's niece
President and co-owner of the apartment rental company

Nicolas: Former Food and Beverage Manager and Maria's husband

President and co-owner of the restaurant

Ricardo: New Food and Beverage Manager

▮▮▮▮▮▮▮ **Appendix B** ▮▮▮▮▮▮▮

Argentina Suites
Income Statement
1996–1999

	1996		1997		1998		1999	
Revenue								
Rooms	2,755,020	84.7%	3,370,848	83.2%	3,902,405	82.0%	3,500,496	84.3%
F & B	266,135	8.4%	391,524	10.1%	497.947	11.0%	296,667	7.5%
Telephone	155,245	4.9%	170,565	4.4%	212,759	4.7%	233,378	5.9%
Other Operated Depts	38,019	1.2%	50,394	1.3%	63.375	1.4%	47.467	1.2%
Other Income	25,346	0.8%	38,765	1.0%	40,741	0.9%	43,511	1.1%
Total Revenue	**3,239,766**	**100.0%**	**4,022,096**	**100.0%**	**4,717,228**	**100.0%**	**4,121,519**	**100.0%**
Operated Dept. Expenses								
Rooms	1,266,748	39.1%	1,182,496	29.4%	1,283,086	27.2%	1,186,997	28.8%
F & B	414,690	12.8%	442,431	11.0%	457.571	9.7%	432,759	10.5%
Telephone	132,830	4.1%	128,707	3.2%	155,669	3.3%	131,889	3.2%
Other Operated Depts	97,193	3.0%	96,530	2.4%	99.062	2.1%	119.524	2.9%
Other Income	-	0.0%	-	0.0%	-	0.0%	-	0.0%
Total Oper. Dept. Expenses	**1,911,462**	**59.0%**	**1,850,164**	**46.0%**	**1,995,387**	**42.3%**	**1,871,170**	**45.4%**
Operated Dept. Profit								
Rooms	1,488,272	45.9%	2,188,352	67.5%	2,619,319	80.8%	2,313,499	71.4%
F & B	-148,555	-4.6%	-50,907	-1.6%	40,376	1.2%	-136,092	-4.2%
Telephone	22,415	0.7%	41,858	1.3%	57,091	1.8%	-101,489	3.1%
Other Operated Depts	-59,174	-1.8%	-46,136	-1.4%	-35,687	-1.1%	-72,057	2.2%
Other Income	25,346	0.8%	38,765	1.2%	40,741	1.3%	43,511	1.3%
Total Oper. Dept. Profit	**1,328,304**	**41.0%**	**2,171,932**	**67.0%**	**1,995,387**	**84.0%**	**2,250,349**	**69.5%**
Undistributed Expenses								
Administration	453,567	14.0%	361,989	9.0%	330,206	7.0%	377,378	8.0%
Marketing	161,988	5.0%	402,210	10.0%	377,378	8.0%	283,034	6.0%
Energy Costs	161,988	5.0%	281,547	7.0%	306,620	6.5%	330,206	7.0%
Maintenance	291,579	9.0%	522,872	13.0%	518,895	11.0%	504,743	10.7%
Total Undistributed Expense	**1,069,123**	**33.0%**	**1,568,617**	**39.0%**	**1,533,099**	**32.5%**	**1,495,361**	**36.3%**
Gross Operating Profit	**259,181**	**8.0%**	**603,314**	**15.0%**	**1,188,741**	**25.2%**	**754,988**	**18.3%**
Fixed Charges								
Extraordinary Charges	17,000	0.5%	12,000	0.3%	12,000	0.3%	12,000	0.3%
Rent, Tax, Insurance, Interest	50,000	1.5%	50,000	1.2%	50,000	1.1%	50,000	1.2%
Deprecation & Amortization	75,000	2.3%	75,000	1.9%	75,000	1.6%	75,000	1.8%
Total Fixed Charges	**142,000**	**4.4%**	**137,000**	**3.4%**	**137,000**	**2.9%**	**137,000**	**3.3%**
Net Operating Profit	**117,181**	**3.6%**	**466,314**	**11,6%**	**1,051,741**	**22.3%**	**617,988**	**15.0%**
Occupancy Percentage	68%		79%		84%		80%	
Average Daily Rate	75 U$S		80 U$S		86 U$S		81 U$S	

SOURCE: "Argentina Suites (II) 1996 to 1998" by Demian Hodari and Timothy R. Hinkin in Case Research Journal, September 2003.

Case 10 Aung Sein: An Entrepreneur in Myanmar

Robert W. Hornaday

Aung Sein,[1] a citizen of Myanmar,[2] an ethnic Chinese and an entrepreneur, was having difficulty with his disposable glove business. Using a machine of his own design, Aung Sein believed he could produce enough disposable gloves to satisfy the demand in Myanmar. Many workers in Myanmar were being needlessly exposed to injury and infection because of the shortage of disposable gloves. But the Ministry of Trade (the agency that makes all major purchases for the Myanmar government) would not buy his gloves. Aung Sein decided to evaluate the costs, benefits, and risks of attempting to induce the Ministry of Trade to buy his gloves.

Until he found a way to market his disposable gloves, Aung Sein concentrated his efforts on the management of a travel agency he owned with 13 other Myanmar citizens of Chinese ancestry. In addition to organizing group tours for foreigners, his agency had contracted with a gold mining venture owned by Singaporeans. Aung Sein's agency arranged logistics support (transportation, lodging, food, and laborers) for the construction and operation of a new mine in northern Myanmar. The travel agency provided Aung Sein and his partners opportunities to earn foreign exchange; revenues from the disposable glove business would be in local currency only.

Aung Sein came from an entrepreneurial family. His father walked to Myanmar through the rugged mountain ranges from China when he was 15 years old. He arrived in Myanmar not speaking the language and owning only the clothes he wore. Aung Sein's father married a Burmese girl and raised a family. He and his wife eventually owned a grocery store in Scott Market, the main shopping place for foreigners and the well-to-do in Yangon.[3] In the 1960s, the Myanmar government took over the Scott Market store. Aung Sein's parents moved to the smaller city of Nyaunglebin, some 100 miles south of Yangon. With their savings they were able to send all of their children to college.

Aung Sein, the third of eight children, always had a desire to succeed. "My father expected me to become a physician. I enrolled in the Rangoon Medical Institute after graduating from the university with honors. When I became a physician in 1987, I entered private practice instead of joining the government health service. I operated a clinic in partnership with a pediatrics professor from the Health Institute. I was an owner, manager, and practicing physician." The conflict between his role as a business manager and his responsibilities to his patients bothered Aung Sein. "Many people who needed medical attention had no money. We tried to treat as many as we could, but the clinic could not survive without making money." Finally, Aung Sein decided that he would pursue his entrepreneurial instincts. He quit the clinic and stopped practicing medicine.

Aung Sein's measure of success was to own a large house in downtown Yangon and to employ enough people so that he could devote his time to planning entrepreneurial ventures. Others would attend to the operational details. He was always on the alert for entrepreneurial opportunities.

Aung Sein developed two guiding principles: (1) "Search for what the people want." (2) "Sell those things to them at minimum investment for maximum profit." Aung Sein did not consider these principles to be heartless capitalism. Instead, he described a win-win situation where both he and his customers would become better off through his efforts. In addition, he hoped to provide employment to many people and to train them so that they could compete in the world market. He had ideas for solar energy sources for remote villages and the production of ballpoint pens and electrical fixtures.

[1] A pseudonym.
[2] Formerly named *Burma*.
[3] Formerly named *Rangoon*, the capital city.

The Disposable Glove Business

One of Aung Sein's first ventures was the production of disposable gloves. These items were not produced in Myanmar and had to be imported—an expensive process requiring scarce foreign exchange. Because of the expense, many workers who should have used disposable gloves did not. These gloves are of the type often worn by cafeteria workers in the United States. They are not surgically sterile, which greatly lowers the cost.

Medical personnel such as midwives, paramedics, and laboratory workers should regularly wear disposable gloves to prevent infection from patients, laboratory specimens, autopsy procedures, and blood used for transfusions. The spread of AIDS in Myanmar increased the need for cheap disposable gloves that fit either hand and had a sensitive touch and feel. Other workers who regularly handle caustic materials (lead-acid batteries, insecticides, and herbicides) could also benefit from wearing disposable gloves.

The Myanmar Ministry of Trade was importing about 100,000 disposable gloves monthly from companies in the United Kingdom, the United States, Japan, and India at a price of $5 per 100 gloves. An unknown number of gloves were also being smuggled across the border from China at a price of $3.50 per 100 gloves. Midwives and laboratory workers used about 30 and 25 percent, respectively, of the imported gloves. The supply of gloves was clearly not meeting demand. Workers in Myanmar needed about 50,000 disposable gloves per day, or about 1.5 million gloves per month.

Seeing this unmet demand as an opportunity, Aung Sein built his disposable glove machine. The first model was hand-operated using plastic pellets as raw material. "My wife and I made the gloves and packaged them at home. I hooked up an electric motor to the glove-making machine to speed things up."

Financing

Aung Sein's total investment in his machinery was kyat[4] 37,000 (about US $350). "To you Americans this doesn't sound like much, but in Myanmar, this is a lot of money. I had to borrow from a money lender at rates of 5 to 10 percent per month," said Aung Sein.

---

[4]The Myanmar currency, pronounced "chawt."

Aung Sein priced his gloves at kyat 50 per box of 50 gloves—about one-fifth the price of imported gloves. The cost of electricity was negligible, because Aung Sein surreptitiously hooked up his machine to his inexpensive household electric line, avoiding the major expense of installing a commercial electric line.

"The Ministry of Trade wouldn't buy my gloves, but I sold about 1,000 boxes to private physicians," recalled Aung Sein. This provided a small profit of kyat 27,000 (about US $250) to Aung Sein and his wife. To make his glove operation self-sufficient by hiring production and marketing personnel, Aung Sein estimated that he would need an operating profit of $1,000 per month (see Exhibit C10-1).

Marketing Difficulties

Aung Sein focused his marketing efforts on the Ministry of Trade, the governmental agency with contracting authority. "They will not buy. No sale. My gloves have been approved by the Ministry of Health and my friends in the medical profession have tested the gloves. They all think my gloves are good. When I visit the Ministry of Trade, everybody is polite. They agree my gloves meet their needs and they say they will contact me with an order, but nothing ever happens."

Aung Sein suspected that the reason that Ministry of Trade bureaucrats were not interested was because they kept a percentage of the foreign exchange dollars that flowed through their hands on purchases of disposable gloves from foreign sources. If they bought his gloves using kyats, they would suffer personal financial losses. In addition, if purchasing agents secured disposable gloves within

EXHIBIT C10-1 Disposable Glove Operations—First Year 1994/1995		
	Per Unit	*Total (1,000 boxes)*
Selling Price	Kyat 50	Kyat 50,000
Raw Materials	Kyat 14	Kyat 14,000
Packaging	Kyat 5	Kyat 5,000
Total Cost	Kyat 19	Kyat 19,000
Operating Profit	Kyat 31	Kyat 31,000
Debt Principle and Interest		Kyat 4,000
Total Profit (Loss)		Kyat 27,000

Myanmar, they might be pressured to procure other disposable medical supplies within Myanmar, further cutting the foreign exchange dollars that flowed through the Ministry of Trade.

To sell disposable gloves to the Ministry of Trade, Aung Sein concluded that he would be forced to arrange payments to government officials. Payoffs could take the form of outright cash payments, gifts of expensive items such as automobiles or household appliances, or the deposit of foreign exchange in foreign banks in Bangkok or Singapore for the use of government officials when they or their families traveled outside Myanmar.

Aung Sein believed that his glove business would be good for Myanmar. "My countrymen need these gloves," he said. "Maybe I could provide some jobs." The only way to sell large quantities of gloves, however, was through the Ministry of Trade. To get officials to buy his gloves, Aung Sein felt that he would have to offer them the same inducements they were receiving from smugglers. He sat down to estimate how much Ministry of Trade officials received from smuggled gloves and whether he could still make a profit by offering similar payoffs.

Appendix: A Note on Myanmar Background

Rich in natural and agricultural resources, Myanmar was once the wealthiest country in Southeast Asia and the world's largest rice exporter. During the last days of British colonial rule before World War II, Myanmar had the highest literacy rate of any nation between Suez and Japan. The country is bisected by the Irawaddy River system, which provides a rich source of hydroelectric power, water for irrigation, and over 1,000 miles of inland navigation from the Indian Ocean on the south to the Chinese border on the north.

But Myanmar did not produce economic development and growth to match its fast-growing neighbors in Southeast Asia such as Thailand, Malaysia, and Singapore. In 1987, the United Nations General Assembly classified Myanmar as a "least developed nation" along with Chad, Ethiopia, Nepal, and Bangladesh. The U.S. State Department in 1996 estimated the gross domestic product per person in Myanmar to be somewhere between 200 and 300 U.S. dollars.

In common with most of Southeast Asia, Myanmar's economic system suffered from serious problems of corruption and smuggling. For those doing business with governments in this region, conventional wisdom pegged the "normal" payoff to bureaucrats at between 10 and 20 percent of the contract price.

Maintenance of law and order has always been a major issue in Myanmar. The Burmese are the dominant ethnic group, but they comprise only about 68 percent of the population. Over the centuries, other ethnic groups have fiercely attempted to maintain their autonomy. A small but vigorous Chinese minority has controlled most of the private sector economy. Ethnic Chinese also have usually held many key positions in government and education.

Experts agreed that political problems caused Myanmar's economic malaise. The multiparty governmental system adopted after independence from the British in 1947 could neither maintain internal order nor sustain economic development. Finally, in 1962, the army took direct control under General Ne Win, who remained a virtual dictator for 25 years. Ne Win declared that Myanmar would follow a strange mixture of European-style socialism and populist isolationism that appealed to the xenophobic strain among Burmese farmers.

The most striking aspect of this "Burmese Way to Socialism" was isolation from the rest of the world. Ne Win abruptly canceled foreign aid projects, including international exchange agreements such as the Fulbright program. Tourism was severely curtailed, and citizens of Myanmar had great difficulty getting permission to travel abroad for any reason. Ne Win built a wall around Myanmar.

Political and economic turmoil ensued. The standard of living of most people dropped below that of the prewar colonial period. Prices for gasoline and electricity skyrocketed. Black markets proliferated, and influential individuals became wealthy amid widespread economic decline and poverty.

Ne Win's policies exacerbated the situation. Private companies were nationalized. English was banned from the schools (it was returned in the 1970s). The national currency (kyat) was pegged at an artificially high level. Strong currency controls cut the flow of foreign exchange. The result was economic disaster. The lack of foreign exchange, the inflated value of the kyat, and an overgrown, corrupt bureaucracy combined to create formidable obstacles to any entrepreneurial activity.

In 1988, serious civil disturbances broke out. Police were unable to restore order. Regular army units, fresh from border combat with insurgent groups, shot down hundreds (perhaps thousands) in several major urban areas. Ne Win stepped down and a group of generals staged a coup. Ruling through the State Law and Order Restoration Committee (SLORC), the army leaders promised elections in 1990. An opposition coalition defeated the SLORC party in the 1990 election. SLORC, however, refused to turn over power and continued to govern Myanmar by decree, bypassing regular legal and political institutions, placing opposition leader Ang San Suu Kyi under house arrest.

Foreign governments began to abandon aid projects in Myanmar in the wake of the 1988 riots. The suppression of dissident groups and the inability or unwillingness of the Myanmar government to control the opium trade on the border with Thailand led to the departure of most foreign donors, including the Asian Development Bank, the United States Agency for International Development (USAID), and Japanese aid agencies. The United States withdrew its ambassador. Private foreign companies, while not forbidden to do business with Myanmar, received no assistance from governmental sources such as the World Bank, the International Monetary Fund, or the U.S. Export Import Bank. The departure of foreign donors was a major blow. Myanmar was more isolated than ever.

Recognizing the economic reasons behind the 1988 disturbances, SLORC abandoned the command economy of the Burmese way to Socialism and moved towards a market economy. The government eased visa restrictions on those entering and leaving Myanmar. Regulations were changed to encourage foreign investment, including provisions for foreign ownership of Myanmar corporations. Many of these reforms were aimed at encouraging foreign donors to return. Whether Myanmar's leaders could foster economic growth without further bloodshed was unclear.

The Foreign Exchange Problem

All businesses in Myanmar were vexed by the exchange rate problem in the 1990s. The Myanmar kyat was a restricted currency that could not be traded outside Myanmar. The Myanmar government maintained the kyat at a greatly inflated exchange rate—about six kyat to one U.S. dollar in 1996. The government required Myanmar citizens to deposit their money in kyat accounts at the official exchange rate in one of seven banks authorized to handle foreign exchange. The purpose of these restrictions was to keep foreign exchange capital from fleeing the country.

The tourist industry is usually a major source of foreign exchange for developing countries. Myanmar fits this profile. The country has world-class tourist destinations such as towering pagodas, ancient temple complexes, scenic lakes and mountains, and the Irawaddy River. In the 1990s, however, Myanmar's transportation infrastructure was practically nonexistent. Roads, airlines, hotels, and restaurants needed to be drastically improved before large numbers of tourists chose Myanmar as a vacation destination.

To encourage tourism, the Myanmar government sold dollar-denominated foreign exchange certificates (FEC) at par for U.S. dollars. The FECs could be converted to kyat at a legal "parallel market" rate of 120 kyat to the dollar that closely followed the black market exchange rate. Most facilities (hotels, airlines, shops, and restaurants) that catered to foreign tourists in Myanmar preferred payment in FECs, not kyat. Of course, there was also a brisk black market in U.S. currency. The U.S. State Department reported that $100 bills were in great demand and commanded a premium price when exchanged for kyat, in some instances 140 kyat to the U.S. dollar in mid-1996.

Myanmar citizens who maintained foreign exchange accounts could withdraw their money in FECs only for specific purchases, such as the purchase of airline tickets, or for commodities sold at special retail outlets. Any other withdrawals had to be in kyat at the rate of six to the dollar. This enabled the Myanmar government, in effect, to confiscate foreign exchange earnings from its citizens and use that foreign exchange for governmental international transactions.

The government forced citizens to sell their dollars for kyat at the official exchange rate, but converting kyat back into dollars was a different proposition. The government severely limited the amount of foreign exchange it would sell at six kyats to the dollar. Myanmar citizens could not export foreign exchange. For instance, as of mid-1996, a citizen of Myanmar desiring to travel outside the country could convert only US $65 using kyat at the official exchange rate. Businesses that desired to convert kyat back into dollars faced similar restrictions. The Myanmar government's currency policies provided ample opportunity for individuals and businesses to get around official restrictions through smuggling, bribery, and the flourishing black market.

The most popular way to get around currency restrictions is to overbill or underbill on goods and services purchased or sold on foreign markets. To keep foreign exchange from coming into a country with currency restrictions, a firm might underbill. For example, a tourist business might make a group tour deal with an agent in Bangkok for $100,000, asking the Bangkok agent to make out the invoice for $80,000 to show to Myanmar authorities and deposit the remaining $20,000 in a Bangkok bank account owned by the Myanmar tourist business.

Conversely, to get foreign exchange out, a Myanmar business would overbill a purchase made from foreigners. Assume the same tourist business buys tour buses from a Japanese firm for $80,000. The Myanmar business might ask the Japanese to state the price on the invoice as $100,000. The Myanmar firm would send $100,000 in foreign exchange. The Japanese firm would take $80,000 as payment and deposit the extra $20,000 in a Bangkok bank account for the Myanmar business.

It is important to note that overbilling and underbilling practices are not unique to developing countries. For example, kickbacks to suppliers are a frequent source of ethical and legal problems in the United States. ▪

This case is intended as a basis for classroom discussion rather than to illustrate effective or ineffective handling of an administrative situation.

"Aung Sein: An Enterpreneur in Myanmar" by Robert W. Hornaday from Case Research Journal, 2000, pp. 117–123. All rights reserved jointly to the author and the North American Case Research Association (NACRA).

Case 11 Fuqima Washing Machine Corporation

Haihong Xu

On a sunny day in January 2001, Mr. Ho Dong, CEO of Fuqima Washing Machine Corporation (FWM), was sitting in his office reading the reports from different departments. He was quite disappointed at the company's poor performance during 2000 and he was trying to find out what real problems the company was facing.

Operation in Late 1980s

FWM was formed by Mr. Ho Dong and Mr. Wang Ling in 1987. Mr. Ho was an engineer in a machinery plant at that time. He believed that there was a large market for washing machines in China as the country, with its 1.2 billion consumers, was pacing its own way towards modernization. He discussed his idea with his best friend, Mr. Wang, who was a machinist at that time. Soon they planned to start a new company.

With investment from the Foshan No.1 Machinery Works and the local government, Mr. Ho and Mr. Wang started a collectively owned company, Fuqima Washing Machine Corporation in Foshan, Guangdong province. Their first model, HDT-100, was launched in 1988. Important features were its very stable performance and low price (about 50 percent lower than similar imported models), both of which ensured that the HDT-100 was immediately accepted by the market. Distributors from all over the country waited in long queues outside the sales department to place orders. By the end of 1989, all the projected production for 1990 had already being booked.

Manufacturing

Mr. Ho became the general manager of FWM and was in charge of manufacturing while Mr. Wang was in charge of all the other functions, including procurement, sales, and financing. "At that time, it was really easy to do business. You sat in the office and you did not even need to have a phone because all the

distributors were waiting for you with checks in their hands...." Mr. Wang said, "All we needed to do was to produce, produce, and produce." Because production capacity meant the profit of the plant, Mr. Ho led his production team, working day and night, on expanding the production capacity of FWM.

In 1991, FWM bought another production line from Japan, which increased Fuqima's production capacity (two shifts) to 200,000 units annually. Moreover, this production line gave FWM the ability to produce three different models simultaneously.

In 1993, Fuqima built a new plant in Shunde, another town that is about 50 kilometers away from its old plant. The new plant was designed to produce 300,000 units (one shift) each year. In 1996, Fuqima became a public company with its shares listed on the Hong Kong stock exchange. With this new investment, FWM in 1999 acquired two local washing machine companies, one in Shenyang and the other in Chongqing. These two acquisitions increased FWM's production capacity to 1.5 million units (one shift) annually.

Sales Organization

The "old good days" did not last very long. In 1995 some strong local competitors like Little Swan and Little Duck emerged and foreign washing machine giants like Siemens and National also started local operations with their joint venture partners in China. While Mr. Ho was busy with the expansion of production, Mr. Wang made huge efforts in building up a national sales network. In 1991, Fuqima opened its sales office in Guangzhou, the capital of Guangdong Province. In 1992, Fuqima built up another five offices in Shanghai, Beijing, Chongqing, Shenyang, the capital of Liaoning Province, and Zhengzhou, the capital of Henan Province.

By the end of 1997, Mr. Wang's sales team included 235 sales representatives, 18 provincial sales managers, and 5 regional sales managers, each of whom was in charge of coordinating the sales and promotion activities in three to five provinces. Mr. Wang spent a lot of his time traveling across the country, talking with big distributors, and managing the sales of each sales representative office.

"He was a really tough boss," Mr. Shen, sales manager of the South China Region said. "When I was the sales manager of Henan Province. Mr. Wang used to come without notice. Every time he came, he would check every single penny I had used and collected. He would review all the contracts that I had signed on behalf of the company and asked me a lot of detailed questions. He tended to work long hours in the day and drank a lot with major customers at night. . . . Although it was not clearly stated in the company's regulation, it was widely believed that all the advertising budget should be approved by Mr. Wang."

Products

FWM's "flagship" was the HDT series. When FWM launched its HDT-800 in 1997, it was also a success. It had a more powerful engine and could wash more clothes. Clothes washed by HDT-800 were much cleaner, after being washed for the same amount of time, than those by other washing machines. "Compared with our domestic competitors, we have a leading edge in terms of technology and our products are very cheap when compared with imported products," Mr. Wang said.

Post Sales Service (PSS)

Post sales service was critical in the household appliance industry. For a long time, FWM outsourced its PSS to local service suppliers. Before 1999, it was the sales department's responsibility to identify the local PSS suppliers and to provide PSS. However, as Chinese consumers were increasingly concerned with PSS, FWM established its own PSS department at the end of 1999. Mr. Jiang, who used to be a regional sales manager, was promoted to be the head of the PSS department.

In the first half of 2000, Mr. Jiang recruited and identified 15 young managers from the sales department and manufacturing plants and gave them intensive training on PSS management. He also traveled a lot to talk with existing local PSS suppliers and tried to figure out how to establish the PSS network. In August 2000, Mr. Jiang proposed a 30-page plan to establish a national

PSS network. It required an initial investment of 2.5 million RMB,[1] including spare parts. However, this plan was postponed due to the company's poor performance in 2000.

Research and Development Department

New product design used to be done by a team of engineers in FWM. The R&D department was formed in 1997 when FWM felt strong pressure from its competitors. Ms. Ping, a post-Ph.D. from Qinghua University, headed it. Starting from day one, Ms. Ping led her team on work on FWM's new product, HDT-2000. Mainly imitating a Japanese model, the main features of the HDT-2000 were a small wash room, low energy consumption, and low noise level. "We must think out of the box," she always told her subordinates. "Do not let the old designs limit your thinking, your ways of design, and your personality as well."

Another important task that Ms. Ping worked on was designing a completely new model, the GDT-100. The GDT series would potentially target the high-end market. It would be one hundred percent auto-control and hands-free. The GDT-100 was supposed to be launched in May 2001. Ms. Ping wanted it to be "the best of the best." In order to improve the new model design, she visited a Japanese washing machine designing center several times and sent some of her designers to that center for training. She also proposed to Mr. Ho that FWM should outsource its product design to some international washing machine designing institutes.

Incentives and Salary

"To reward the diligent and punish the lazy" is the principle of FWM's incentive system. Based on that principle, FWM has three different incentive systems:

1. Each sales manager had his or her annual sales quota. Their income was closely related to their performance in fulfilling the quota. Each of them had a "nominal salary" of 120,000 annually and their real income was the percentage of quota fulfillment multiplied by the "nominal salary."
2. Production assembly workers' income was largely based on how many units they produced.

---

[1] Renminbi (RMB), literally "the people's money," is China's official currency. The exchange rate at the writing of this case was approximately 1 US$ = 8.3 RMB.

3. All other departments earned a fixed salary with an annual bonus based on individual performance and evaluation.

Failure of HDT-2000

On January 1st 2000, FWM launched HDT-2000. It was much smaller and lighter than any of the previous HDT models, it could save up to 20 percent on water used when compared with other washing machines, and it had an integrated drying system which enabled users in humid areas to dry their clothes very quickly. However, the sales were much lower than expected. Due to the additional drying function, the price of HDT-2000 was 25 percent higher than other products of the same capacity. Distributors and retailers were reluctant to sell the HDT-2000. Moreover, one of FWM's competitors launched a similar model in February 2000 and claimed that its product had an improved drying system, and it was much cheaper than the HDT-2000.

Fuqima planned to launch a second-round of promotion in early March. But Mr. Wang was in a traffic accident while traveling to a major customer and his doctor said that he would be in hospital for at least three months. Both the advertiser and the provincial sales manager knew that without Mr. Wang's approval, nothing could be finalized. Because FWM's other models were not new to the market, the staggering of HDT-2000's sales led to a sharp decrease in FWM's market share.

Some provincial sales managers were thinking about leaving the company because their salary was too low. "I only fulfilled 55 percent of my quota, consequently I only got 55 percent of my nominal salary," said Mr. Zou, sales manager of Guizhou Province, "I want to sell more but our products are not competitive. The company should not treat us like this." Others started to complain about the R&D department. "I really do not know what our R&D department is doing. They never ask us for opinions and they only believe what the Japanese told them. Besides the high price, HDT-2000's plastic cover looks so thin that it is very difficult for me to convince the customers that it is a high quality product."

However, Ms. Ping had a different opinion. "I agree that the plastic cover looks a little bit thin. But I think it is those sales managers' responsibility to explain to our customers why it is thinner than usual and what is the benefit. Actually, we have spent quite a few weeks in designing this cover. It is thin in order to save costs and make the washing machine light. According to our tests, our cover can last as long as those thick ones. Besides, although I did not have any experience in sales, I did sell five HDT-2000 models in a department store in two hours in Zhejiang. If they have a network that is large enough, they should have no problem in selling this model. Customers can be educated if you are patient and you know about your product."

Mr. Xiao, the manager of manufacturing and production planning, was also not satisfied with the sales department. "I do not think those sales people work hard enough. In terms of technology and quality, our HDT-2000 was much better that our competitors . . . Due to their (Sales Department's) fault, our first-line assemblers' income was also significantly decreased."

Conflict of Three Plants

2000 was also a tough year for Mr. Ho. Originally, he planned to use the Shenyang plant to support the North China market and the Chongqing plant to support the West China market. But things were not as easy as expected. The Shenyang and Chongqing plants, each of which has an annual production capacity of 500,000 units, were so large that over 30 percent of the workers could be laid-off if those plants just supported the targeted markets. But if Mr. Ho let those two plants produce more, he had to reduce the production volume of the Shunde plant. Consequently, this would reduce the income of production line workers at Shunde and worsen their morale.

Mr. Ho was also puzzled by the question, "Who should produce what?" If all three plants produced the same models, FWM had to invest heavily in duplicating molds for the three plants. Moreover, FWM also needed to find suppliers who were able to supply all three plants. If the three plants produced different models, all the plants had to have the ability to support the national market. How to balance production volumes between different models would also be a problem, as all three plants would like to produce the "best-selling" models.

Problems in the Sales Department

As the director of the sales department and senior vice president of FWM, Mr. Wang was also worried about the sales of FWM. First, Mr. Wang was worried about his customers. "They are too strong and have too much bargaining power." As more than 75 percent of the total sales were taken by only 14 distributors, these distributors were very powerful negotiators. "I really want to get rid of all of them. But, if any of them go to Little Swan or Haier, it will mean a 5 percent drop in my sales and a 5 percent rise in their sales. What can I do?"

Second, he was worried about the "cross-province selling." Due to the incentive system, some provincial managers tried to sell their products outside their own territory via the distributors. From his experience, Mr. Wang knew that those problems tended to be solved automatically if the sales were good. However, those conflicts would be extremely fierce in the case of a bad year. From the most recent reports he had, he knew that some nationwide distributors were even approaching different provincial managers for a lower wholesale price and better advertising support. Although the company had set the minimum price, some provincial managers tried to play some tricks to break the rule.

Third, he was also worried about the relationship between the sales department and the R&D department. Ms. Ping asked him many times for detailed market information and competitor product analysis. Mr. Wang was not quite sure whether he should provide this information or not as some of the information was collected from industrial spies and was very expensive and sensitive. "I once visited their laboratory and I noticed that lots of their junior managers could get highly confidential files. If this is the truth, it will be fatal for me to give my information to her. I even guess some of our HDT-2000 design was stolen by our competitors due to this. Industrial spies are everywhere."

Mr. Wang was also not satisfied with Ms. Ping's explanation about the thin cover. "The customer is God. They want a thick cover and we must give it to them. Many of Ms. Ping's words did not make much sense. The provincial sales managers are not happy these months due to the low sales volume. Most of them have reported to me and to Ms. Ping several times about the thin cover. But up to now, nothing has happened. We are soldiers fighting on the front line and we need good weapons."

The proposed GDT-100 was also a big challenge for him. From his experience, Mr. Wang understood that the GDT-100 was targeted at a completely different segment, which meant completely different distribution channels and different promotion campaigns. "If the GDT-100 really comes to the market, should I establish a new sales organization? Besides, it might change the image of our product and company as well. I really do not know whether we should do this or not."

Fourth, Mr. Wang was thinking about separating the marketing function from the sales function. "Nowadays, my managers are focusing too much on the selling side due to the incentive system. They like to spend days and nights drinking with the big distributors and wholesalers and do not pay much attention to the small ones. I think we should establish a marketing department that would work on long-term branding and customer development."

Finally, Mr. Wang was also not happy with Mr. Ho's recent decision to postpone the plan for building up the national post sales service (PSS) network. "I understand that the profitability of this year was not good and the investors have a long face with us. But the PSS network was so important. All the emerging companies like Haier have this kind of network."

Both Mr. Ho and Mr. Wang were thinking of hiring a consultant to help them solve the problems that FWM was facing. ∎

This case prepared by MBA 2000 student Haihong Xu under the supervision of Professor Juan Antonio Fernandez at CEIBS. The case was prepared as the basis for class discussion rather than to illustrate either effective or ineffective handling of an administrative situation. Certain names and other identifying information may have been disguised to protect confidentiality.

SOURCE: Case "Fuqima Washing Machine Corporation" by student Haihong Xu under the supervision of Professor Juan Antonio Fernandez at China International Business School, 2002. All rights reserved. Printed in UK and USA.

EXHIBIT C11-1 Financial and Operation Data

	1988	*1991*	*1994*	*1997*	*2000*
Sales Volume (Thousand Unit)	1.38	155	550	1,764	1,075
Sales Volume of HDT series (Thousand unit)	1.38	154	540	1,650	878
Gross Profit (Million RMB)	0.69	62	165	265	129
Net Profit (Million RMB)	0.08	7.5	35.8	85	28

EXHIBIT C11-2 Organization Structure

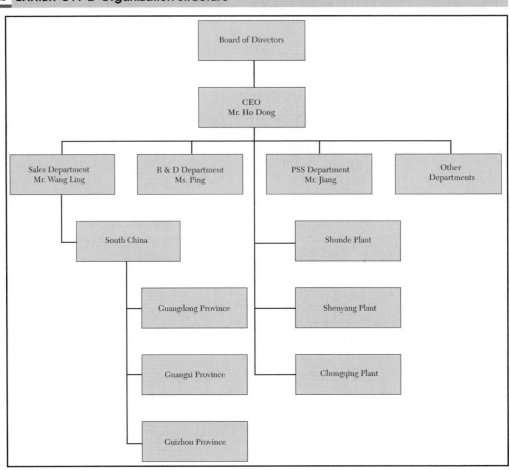

EXHIBIT C11-3 Selected Internal Memorandum

COMPANY CONFIDENTIAL

MEMORANDUM

To: Mr. Ho Dong, CEO

Cc: Ms. Ping, Director of R&D Dept.

From: Mr. Wang Ling, SVP and Director of Sales Dept.

Date: April 2, 2000

Subject: Sales of First Quarter

Dear Mr. Ho Dong,

The sales of the first quarter are not as good as expected. The HDT-2000 seemed to be too expensive for our traditional customers and one major problem with the design was identified.

The plastic cover of the HDT-2000 looks too thin. Haier uses a stainless steel sheet as a cover, which gives consumers a good impression about the quality of their products. I wonder if we could apply the same design on our products.

Besides, the doctor suggested that I stay in hospital for another two weeks and I cannot come back to work until April 16. Consequently, the promotion campaign will be postponed for some time.

Regards,

Wang Ling

COMPANY CONFIDENTIAL

MEMORANDUM

To: Mr. Ho Dong, CEO

Cc: Mr. Wang Ling, SVP and Director of Sales Dept.

From: Jiang Dawei, Director of PSS Dept.

Date: August 10, 2000

Subject: Post-Sales-Service Network

Dear Mr. Ho,

Please find the attached plan for building up the nationwide post-sales-service network. The key points of the plan are as follows:

- We will build up a PSS network covering 20 major provinces in China.
- Each of the provinces will have 1–3 customer service centers. For Shanghai, Beijing, Chengdu, Guangzhou, and Qingdao there will be four major regional customer service centers.
- There will be one PSS manager for each province and each center will have 3–5 repairing engineers and a limited inventory of spare parts.
- Each provincial customer service center will be responsible for providing technical support to local contracted PSS service suppliers, solving the problems that they are facing, and providing necessary training and spare parts.
- Each regional customer service center will have an inventory of all spare parts and some transportation vehicles. Each regional customer service center will be responsible for providing technical support, training, and spare parts to local centers.

To do that, we need an initial investment of 2.5 million yuan.

Regards,

Jiang Dawei

(Continued)

EXHIBIT C11-3 Continued

COMPANY CONFIDENTIAL

MEMORANDUM

To: Mr. Ho Dong, CEO

Cc: Mr. Wang Ling, SVP and Director of Sales Dept.

From: Board of Directors

Date. October 10, 2000

Subject: Performance in First Three Quarters

Dear Mr. Ho,

The company has suffered slight losses for three consecutive quarters. We have become increasingly worried about the performance of the company. We hope you could take immediate action to ensure the company regains its competitive advantage. We, as the major investors to the company, do not want to see the red ink on the bottom line for the fourth quarter.

Steering Committee

EXHIBIT C11-4 Map of China

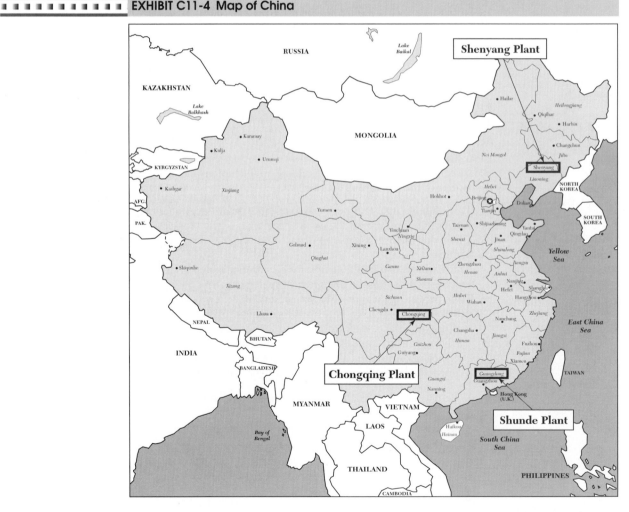

Case 12   Wellcome Israel (A)

Wellcome in Flux

As Ofra Sherman was explaining to the interior designer how much space she and her team would need in the new building, she thought to herself how this whole meeting might be a waste of time. She was having trouble concentrating on the carpet samples being put under her nose. She knew that by the time the new building would be completed her team might no longer be there to occupy their newly designed offices.

As the paint samples came onto the desk, she smiled as she realized how ironic it was that only fifteen minutes earlier she was in a meeting with the general manager of Promedico discussing the possible departure of herself and her team from the company. It was now April of 1995. It would take some months to resolve the issues arising from Glaxo's acquisition of Wellcome, which had just occurred in March. What was she to do in the interim? How would she manage her team? Keep them motivated? What did the future hold for her?

Sherman was the general manager of Wellcome Israel, a company that technically did not exist. It was perhaps more accurate to say that she was the general manager of the U.K.-based pharmaceutical company Wellcome's operations in Israel. And now Wellcome itself was being taken over by arch-rival Glaxo.

Under the best of circumstances, the uncertainty caused by take-overs disrupts the operation of an organization. But this situation was complicated by the involvement of a third company, Promedico. Promedico was the official Israeli representative for several drug companies, including Wellcome, whose personnel were based in Promedico's offices. And although Sherman and her team actually received their salaries from Wellcome, for historical reasons, their pay checks were issued by Promedico. Legally, were they employees of Wellcome or Promedico? The status had always been unclear, and there had never been any motivation to clarify it.

Sherman did not have the answers to any of the questions which she knew she would have to face shortly. As the merger unfolded, would she and her team be fired? Kept on? Within Glaxo? Within Promedico? What should she tell her staff to keep them motivated? For that matter, what should she tell her customers? The only thing she knew with certainty at that moment was that she did not want her office painted the awful shade of yellow she was being shown. If only the rest of her decisions over the coming tumultuous months would be so easy.

As the interior designer left her office, she thought about how she would manage her team during this transitional phase. On a personal level, she wondered what would happen to herself and her team in the wake of the acquisition and what the future would hold for the business she had just spent five years of her life building.

Wellcome PLC

Wellcome PLC was one of the main competitors in the international pharmaceutical industry. In recent years, Wellcome had ranked between tenth and twentieth world-wide in revenue. Its main operations were in the U.S. and U.K., and its headquarters were located next to Euston Station in London. It developed, manufactured, and marketed human health care products world-wide, with subsidiaries in 33 countries. In 1994, it had 17,182 employees and revenues of £2.6 billion, with a profit margin of just over 33 percent. Its products could be divided into two categories, prescription and non-prescription (over the counter) medicines, with the former representing over 85% of total revenues.

Wellcome had become known in the pharmaceutical industry as a specialist in anti-viral drugs (although it also had several other specialties, including antibiotics and medicines targeted at the central nervous system). Viruses were complex microorganisms, often not well-understood by medical science, that were responsible for a variety of diseases, from colds to AIDS. Wellcome's stable of products covered the range, from cold and allergy medicines such as Actifed and Sudafed (sold over-the-counter) to

Retrovir, one of the most widely prescribed treatments for AIDS. The firm's biggest revenue-producing drug for several years had been Zovirax, a treatment for herpes. Zovirax had also been approved in some countries as an over-the-counter medicine for cold sores.

Developing drugs to treat viruses was a tortuous process of theory, experimentation, publication, clinical trial, and application for regulatory approval. The total cost of launching a drug could easily exceed £100 million, and this number was also the informal hurdle for annual sales Wellcome and other companies used to determine which drugs had "made it" in the marketplace. There was usually a limited window in which such returns could be reaped, however, since competition in the industry was fierce from both new product development (meaning successful drugs could be replaced by better ones) and generics (which could take away substantial market share as soon as a drug came off patent). Zovirax patents around the world were just beginning to expire, which posed a medium-term threat to Wellcome's earnings.

In order to balance the high-risk, high-return research and development in new prescription drugs, the company had taken two other major steps: In 1994, it entered a partnership with U.S.-based Warner-Lambert, called Warner-Wellcome, to market all the two firms' over-the-counter medicines world-wide. The partnership was expected both to save costs and to expand revenues in this part of the business, which had always been a "poor cousin" to Wellcome's prescription drugs. Also, it had entered into a set of licensing agreements, region-by-region, to fill out its portfolio of offerings with complementary drugs from other companies and vice-versa. Again, this provided added revenues and greater economies of scale at relatively low cost.

Wellcome in Israel

Although Wellcome products had been sold in Israel for over forty years, strictly speaking, Wellcome Israel did not exist. For political reasons (Wellcome was very active in Arab countries) Israel was never mentioned in any Wellcome literature. For many years Israel was referred to as Greenland, and then it was put under Wellcome Hellas SA (see Wellcome Hellas organizational chart in Exhibit C12-1). This political sensitivity led to a unique organizational structure existing in Israel, one in which reporting lines were less than clear.

Promedico Limited was an Israeli company that represented the products of several drug companies in Israel. It handled distribution, marketing, and medical registration for companies such as Pfizer and Zima (see Exhibit C12-2 for a corporate organization chart). In the case of Wellcome, Promedico handled only distribution and medical registration. Marketing was the responsibility of Ofra Sherman and her team (see Exhibit C12-3), whose salaries and expenses were paid by Wellcome Hellas, not Promedico. In the Promedico structure the Wellcome team were part of the Pharmaceutical and Diagnostics division.

Although the costs of the Wellcome team (as they were known within Promedico) were born by

■ ■ ■ ■ ■ ■ ■ ■ ■ ■ ■ ■ **EXHIBIT C12-1 Wellcome Hellas SA**

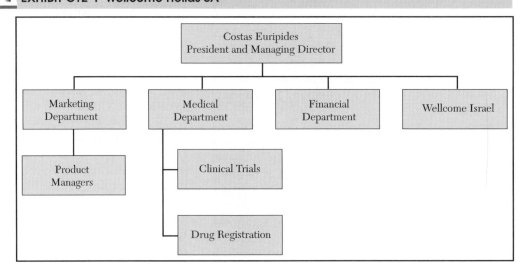

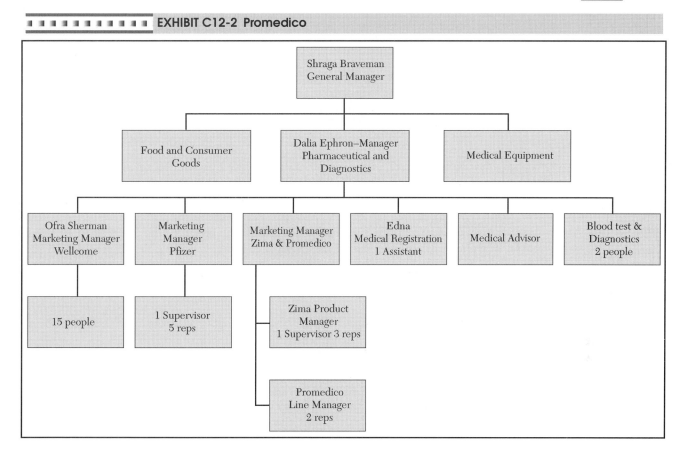

Wellcome Hellas, Promedico issued the actual pay checks every month. Promedico thus acted as a mechanism through which Wellcome could pay its people in Israel without having to put a formal structure in place.

Promedico was well paid for its services, purchasing pharmaceuticals from Wellcome and marking them up by as much as 100% to the end customer. Margins were high, because the cost of selling Wellcome products was limited of distribution and medical registration, since the Wellcome team was paid by Wellcome Hellas.

This strange organizational structure had served the purposes of both parties for some years. But as the size of the Wellcome team within Promedico grew, and with it the proportion of Promedico's total revenue which Wellcome accounted for, tensions began to grow as well.

There were tensions between Sherman and Promedico's management, as well as between the Wellcome team and members of other product teams within Promedico. In revenue and profit terms, the Wellcome team consistently outper-

formed other teams at the company. In 1994, Wellcome products accounted for approximately 50% of the Pharmaceutical and Diagnostics divisions' revenues. The fact that they were so successful and had more autonomy than other groups in the company (since they were paid by Wellcome Hellas) made them the focus of some jealousy.

To complicate matters, there had never been a written agreement between Wellcome PLC and Promedico which outlined the terms and conditions of their relationship. It had never been clear what Wellcome would decide to do if, as had become a real possibility in the last few years, the growth in its sales in Israel began to outstrip the size of its distributor. It certainly was not clear now what role Promedico would play in the shake-out that was likely to follow the acquisition.

Ofra Sherman

Ofra Sherman was the Manager of Wellcome Israel, where she had worked for the past five years. She had completed her Bachelors Degree in Biology at

▪▪▪▪▪▪▪▪▪▪▪ **EXHIBIT C12-3 Wellcome Israel**

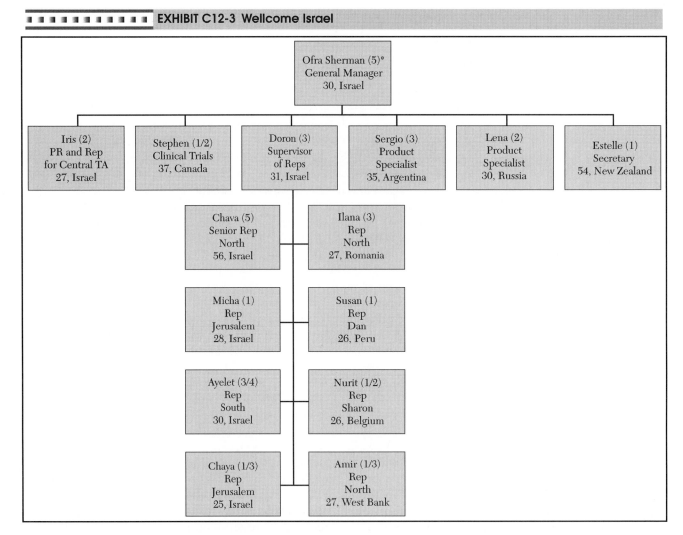

the age of 25 and began working for the Wellcome Team at Promedico as a Medical Representative. At that time the team consisted of Sherman, her boss, and two medical representatives. Sherman became Wellcome team leader after one year, as the group started to expand, and Manager in 1993.

At the age of 30, Sherman was one of the youngest managing directors within Wellcome and was considered a rising star within its international division. Her team, now consisting of 15 people, had sustained tremendous growth. It generated more than two-thirds as much revenue (US$ 7 million) as Wellcome Hellas did with 60 people (US$ 10 million).

Sherman was involved in every aspect of the operation of Wellcome Israel, from how a drug should be positioned in the marketplace, to how the invitations to a medical conference should look. Her position was similar to that of an owner/manger in the sense that she had created and built the team and also controlled every aspect of its operation.

She divided her time among five activities:

1. Managing Director – Together with her manager in Athens she would develop medium- and long-term market entry and maintenance strategies for Wellcome Israel.
2. Product Manager for Zovirax – Sherman would give training courses about this product (one of Wellcome's biggest and most profitable) and keep up-to-date on all the latest clinical literature.
3. Sales and Marketing Director – Sherman would plan all promotional activities for the different drugs, including medical congresses,

meetings with doctors, and the activities of the Wellcome sales representatives.

4. Training Manager – Most of the Wellcome team were relatively new in their jobs, so Sherman found herself spending much of her time on training activities. The senior members of the team were trained on a one-to-one basis. Almost every time she would meet with each of them, there was some training component to the interaction. The sales representatives, by contrast, were trained in group sessions which concentrated, for example, on how to have a meeting with a doctor and how to present new clinical findings. Sherman ran most of these sessions.

5. Motivator – Sherman was also the team cheerleader. Since there was little contact with the outside Wellcome organization, and since relations with Promedico had recently been under some strain, the Wellcome Israel team sometimes felt a lack of confirmation of its mission and credit for its success. This was a need Sherman conscientiously filled, celebrating every success the team and its members had, no matter how small.

Sherman and Her Team

The Senior Team met with Sherman once a week to discuss ongoing issues. She would also meet at least once a week individually with each member of the team to discuss individual problems and prospects. The atmosphere was relaxed, and team members enjoyed working together.

The Senior Team had six members (see Exhibit C12-3 for names, tenure, titles, ages, and origin). Doron, the senior member of the team, was 31 and had worked with Sherman for three years. For 2 1/2 of those years he had worked as a sales representative. Recently he had been promoted to the position of Supervisor, and he now managed the team of 10 representatives. Doron and Sherman had a close relationship; they were good friends as well as co-workers.

Iris, 27, had been with the team for two years. She was a representative responsible for central Tel Aviv and had recently been given the additional responsibility of coordinating all promotional activities. This involved organizing medical conferences to promote Wellcome's products and developing concepts for promotional gifts, which were commonly distributed to doctors. Sherman and Iris saw each other socially and were close friends.

Doron and Iris were in Sherman's inner circle. She confided in them more than in the others about Wellcome/Promedico issues and relied on them more than the others. The third member of Sherman's inner circle was Stephen, Coordinator of Clinical Trials. Stephen was 37 and had recently immigrated to Israel from Canada. Although he had only been with the team for 6 months, Sherman had started confiding in him early on, sensing in him high levels of maturity and judgment.

The last two members of the senior team were Sergio and Lena, both Product Specialists. They had both started as representatives. They were the experts on their respective products and responsible for training the representatives on specific drugs and making sure they had the latest clinical information. Both had been with the team between two and three years.

There was great camaraderie among the whole Wellcome team. Most days the team would have lunch together in the lunchroom. Sherman would use this opportunity to discuss and resolve many work-related issues. It was also an opportunity for Sherman to build team spirit and find out what was going on in the field.

Sherman's office was the nerve center of the Wellcome Team. It served as file room, storage room, and meeting room. Drug samples, promotional gifts for doctors, and product files cluttered the office. It was relatively small to begin with, and the clutter made it even more so. Sherman's staff would walk in and out of the office all day, sometimes to pick something up, other times to talk to her.

So informal was the atmosphere among the team that they would come in whether the door was open or closed (although it was rarely closed). The office sometimes seemed like a whirlwind, with four or five people doing different things at the same time.

Promedico Limited

Promedico had been established in 1946 as a distribution company. It had distributed pharmaceuticals since the beginning and over the years added medical supplies and food and consumer products.

In 1992 new management came in and implemented a major reorganization. During 1993 and 1994 Promedico went from 70 to 200 employees (including the Wellcome Team). Of these, 68% were in marketing and sales, 19% in logistics and warehousing, and 13% in administration. In the same period, sales had grown only 33%, from US $31 million to US $40 million. Of this amount, 45% was from pharmaceuticals and diagnostics, 30% from food and consumer products, and 25% from medical supplies.

By the end of 1994, Promedico was a company in trouble. It had recently lost three very important lines: two consumer products and one medical supply product. The Wellcome team (only 15 people) was generating roughly 50% of the Pharmaceutical and Diagnostics division's revenues and a similarly disproportionate proportion of profit. In view of Glaxo's recent acquisition of Wellcome, and the fact that Glaxo already had a representative in Israel (called CTS) with distribution and medical registration capabilities, it was likely that Promedico would lose the Wellcome line. Management at Promedico were understandably doing everything in their power to prevent this eventuality.

Ofra Sherman and Promedico Management

Officially, Sherman had a manager at Promedico: She was Dalia Ephron, Manager of the Pharmaceutical and Diagnostics division. Ephron was Sherman's manager in name only, however, because Sherman took her orders from Costas Euripides, Manager of Wellcome Hellas in Greece. Within the Promedico hierarchy, Sherman's position was Marketing Manager of the Wellcome Team. Sherman's peers at Promedico envied her, partly for her success and partly for her autonomy.

Sherman did not rely on Promedico management in carrying out her day-to-day duties. She did, however, receive information from them about what was happening within Promedico and would tell them what she wanted them to know about the Wellcome team, although not directly. She knew that whatever she told them would get back to the Promedico MD. The following conversation was an example of this indirect communication:

As the Vice President of Consumer Products was passing her office door, Sherman called him in and asked him about the loss of the Nestlé line (that week Promedico had lost the representation of Nestlé products). From there, the conversation turned to pharmaceuticals:

VP: Things do not look good for Promedico.
OS: Both of us know what is going on but cannot say.
VP: Given that both of us know, what do you think will happen?
OS: I think you know what will happen.

The VP smiled and left the office.

Sherman had wanted to make it clear to him that Wellcome would probably leave Promedico and to see that the message would get to the MD.

The location of Sherman's office was also significant. It was between the Managing Director and the Manager of the Pharmaceuticals and Diagnostics division. Sherman believed that she had been given this office because of her team's importance to Promedico. The location also served as a constant reminder that she was between two companies and had to continually balance the needs of her group with the needs of Promedico.

The Acquisition

Before 1986, Wellcome had been a privately held, not-for-profit enterprise. Its shares were held by the Wellcome Trust, a charitable organization set up by philanthropist Henry Wellcome nearly a century earlier. For decades, the firm operated as a charitable rather than a commercial enterprise, with the advantages of a strong public service mentality and the disadvantages of a somewhat bloated payroll and low flexibility. After the creation of Wellcome PLC and an initial public share flotation of 20%, the Wellcome Trust (which had remained separate) had sold several further tranches of stock in the public markets. However, it had continued to hold 40% of the firm's shares and had made representation to the company's management that the holding was secure and would not be sold off, at least not without lengthy discussions with management beforehand. The secure status of the Trust's holding made Wellcome management and employees feel more secure than many other companies in the pharmaceutical industry, which was going through a period of consolidation that had seen many takeovers and mergers and was expecting to see many more.

It thus came as a complete surprise in January of 1995 when Glaxo announced that it was making a hostile bid for control of Wellcome, which would create the world's largest pharmaceutical company, and had the support of the Wellcome Trust for the sale of its 40% stake. Wellcome management had heard nothing of the offer and felt that they had been betrayed. CEO John Robb asked for and received permission from the Trust to seek an alternative acquirer, but Wellcome was unable to better Glaxo's price (approximately a 2/3 premium over the prior share value) and gave up the fight in early March.

Robb had agreed to stay on to help smooth the merger but resigned as soon as he had gained assurances from Glaxo's CEO, Sir Richard Sykes, that Wellcome managers would play a substantial role in merging the two companies and would have a fair chance at getting the best jobs within it.

Before the acquisition, Ofra Sherman had usually spent 50% of her time out of the office visiting key doctors. Since the announcement, she had been spending most of her time in the office. This was necessary because several times a day she had conversations about the reorganization with someone at Wellcome Hellas or Promedico. In addition to discussions with Shraga Braverman, general manager of Promedico, and Costas Euripides, Sherman was also making use of her internal and external networks to find out as much as possible about events at Wellcome, Glaxo, and within Promedico.

When asked about the situation she was in, Sherman commented:

"I have no boss, I am in the middle of nowhere."

On one side was Wellcome Hellas; on the other was Promedico. Hovering somewhere in the distance, but closing, were Glaxo and its Israeli distributor, CTS. Complicating matters was the question of whether under Israeli law, even though Wellcome Hellas was paying their salaries, the Wellcome Team were considered Wellcome Hellas or Promedico employees.

Shraga Braverman had told Sherman not to give any information about her team's operations to anyone at Glaxo. He also told her that he would decide whether the reorganization with Glaxo would go smoothly or not and, finally, that Euripides was certain to be removed from his position at Wellcome Hellas and as a result she should no longer listen to him, taking orders only from Braverman.

Ofra Sherman was shaken by the General Manager's threats. She immediately placed a call to Costas Euripides. Although she had heard from another contact at Wellcome that Euripides would be removed after the reorganization, she still needed him to help her keep Braverman from taking complete control of the situation. It was not until the next day that Euripides returned her call. She told him what Braverman had said. Furious, he told Sherman that he was her boss and that she should do nothing without his permission.

At the same time, Sherman had told her team to gather as much information about Glaxo's operations in Israel as possible. She needed to start developing a strategy for integrating her team with the Glaxo group in the event that her team did move to Glaxo.

Should she confront the Promedico management and tell them she was planning to take her team to Glaxo? Should she go to speak to the general manager of Glaxo Israel and disregard the orders of both Braverman and Euripides? Would these actions get her fired? If only she knew what Glaxo and Wellcome were planning for her and her team. But it was clear that nothing had yet been decided and that she would either have to wait or to act on very little information other then her own intuition.

All Sherman could really do at this point was develop a series of "What if?" scenarios. She needed to make sure that whatever the outcome was, she would be ready for it. What if the team stayed at Promedico? What if the team had to be integrated with Glaxo? What kind of a job would Glaxo offer her? What if they had no job for her at all? She tried to decide how she would handle each of these possibilities and what actions she would have to take.

Finding a Way Forward

This was the first time in Sherman's career that she had been involved in a situation where she had virtually no direct control over the outcome. She knew that she could do little to affect decisions that might decide her own and her team's future. The situation was very uncertain. The only certainty was that the Glaxo and Wellcome organizations were merging in all countries where they both had a presence, and Israel would be no exception.

The other variable in the equation was Promedico. The managing director of Promedico had told her that he would do everything in his power to keep the Wellcome line. And, in the event that Promedico lost the line, he claimed he would not permit Sherman or any member of her team to go to Glaxo.

To complicate matters, the former managing director of Promedico (who had been removed two years previously during the reorganization but remained as a consultant) had told Sherman the exact opposite, that she should take her team and leave Promedico immediately. Sherman suspected the former MD wanted her to do this so that he could make the current MD look bad and take control of the company again, but he had also made some good arguments. On their own, the Wellcome team might have more power–and be able to attract more support and higher pay–than at Promedico. They were more efficient than Glaxo in Israel, making half the revenue with only 1/3 the people. Without Promedico in the picture, they might be able to make their own deal with Glaxo, or even approach other drug companies.

Glaxo had set 1 June as the deadline for finalizing the reorganization plans in the different countries. In theory by that date, even if Sherman did nothing, the situation would be resolved.

The result of all these events was that Ofra Sherman no longer had a clear, long-term agenda and that her short-term agenda was focused primarily on the reorganization. At the same time, she had to try to keep herself and her team motivated. The situation was particularly difficult for Sherman because she had no one to discuss it with. She could not discuss it with her subordinates or with her peers at Promedico. Although she informed her people when developments occurred, she could not discuss her personal situation with them. The one person she had thought she could confide in, the former managing director, she now felt might be biased because of his own interests. She was truly alone.

As she played with the carpet samples the interior designer had left in her office, Sherman wondered again about what she should do. Should she be patient and wait for the situation to be resolved by the respective managements? Should she be pro-active and do what she felt would be in the best interests of her team? Or should she do what might be in her own best interest: not wait for the outcome, but start looking for another job now?

Wellcome Israel (B)

Uncertainty at Wellcome

"Because we were not an important area, we were the last one anyone contacted. All over Europe, Wellcome and Glaxo people were making decisions about who would stay, who would leave, who would move, etc. In Israel, nobody came."

Ofra Sherman, General Manager of Wellcome Israel, was remembering the long months between the announcement of Wellcome's purchase by arch-rival Glaxo and the resolution of the local situation in Israel, where both companies were represented by third parties. From March through the summer of 1995 the big question had been, what would happen to the Wellcome Israel team? Would they all be fired? Would some of them be kept on? In what kind of positions? Would Glaxo or its representative, CTS, find places for all of them?

Sherman's team of 15 were funded by and reported to Wellcome Hellas, the firm's Greek subsidiary. However, their pay checks were cut by Promedico Limited, the Israeli company in whose Tel Aviv offices they were based and which was responsible for distribution and medical registration of Wellcome's products in Israel. It had never been quite clear whether the Wellcome team, who handled marketing and sales, were legally employed by Wellcome Israel or Promedico.

Waiting for a Resolution

Although she had considered taking some kind of action to resolve the uncertainty of the team's situation following the announcement of the merger, Sherman had elected to wait. With both the new Glaxo-Wellcome and Promedico having designs on the group, she felt stuck. It was clear that both had claims on them and that, were she to try to resolve the conflict in favor of one or the other, she might only get herself fired. Instead, Sherman kept her eyes and ears open, hoping to glean some information that might help her prepare for the resolution to the conflict before it finally came.

One rumor that Sherman had heard through her Wellcome network was that Wellcome Hellas would be merged into the existing Glaxo organization in Greece and that Costas Euripides, her boss, would lose his job. This worried her, because he had always been her main connection to the world-wide firm, the anchor that allowed her to stand up to Promedico management when necessary. When she first heard the rumor, she had asked Euripides about it, and he had responded angrily. While not denying that he might be leaving, he insisted that she continue to take orders from him.

Negotiating a Place

The three months without official word from Glaxo-Wellcome seemed an eternity. Finally, in late June, Costas Euripides was removed from his post, and Greece and Israel were separated. It began to become clear that Wellcome Israel would have to work things out directly with Glaxo's Israeli representative, CTS.

"There was a disconnection," Sherman recalled. "I was left completely alone because my manager in Wellcome Hellas was fired. It was a total change. We didn't know what was going to happen."

Sherman started negotiations with the General Manager of Glaxo in Israel, who, in a similar fashion to Sherman at Promedico, reported to the General Manager of CTS. While he was negotiating with Sherman about jobs for the Wellcome team, he was also negotiating with Promedico about the total picture, including registration, licensing, and distribution. Promedico had earlier told Sherman they were determined not to lose the Wellcome line, although she had tried to let them know that the choice might not be theirs, or hers, to make.

"Within the negotiations between us, we really started to move forward," Sherman recounted. "But between Promedico and Glaxo there were a lot of problems. There was a period in which the Glaxo manager left the negotiations with us, left us hanging. Then I figured out Promedico and he were having difficulties reaching agreement."

Israel was the only place in the world that Wellcome was not an independent company and neither was Glaxo. The situation was therefore unique: The two distributors were fighting each other for control of the Israeli business. Before the merger, Glaxo had had around 45 people to Wellcome's 15. But their revenues were only twice as high as Wellcome's. Sherman felt Glaxo should have had much more. By comparison, Wellcome was really a very profitable company in Israel. The two firms competed in the same segments: Glaxo's antibiotics were broadly parallel to Wellcome's anti-virals. In some product lines they were not in competition, but broadly speaking they still sold to the same groups of doctors.

It was not a long battle. As Sherman had predicted months earlier, the decision lay far beyond Israel's borders. Despite Promedico's successful record (at least, in representing Wellcome) and its protestations, Glaxo-Wellcome finally determined that CTS would be its sole representative. In the end, the Glaxo Israel GM offered a job at CTS to every person on the Wellcome Israel team. Only five of the fifteen members accepted.

Sherman's Choice

Ofra Sherman was not one of them. Glaxo, conscious of her success record, had tried hard to build a place for her and offered her the leadership of a functional department, reporting to the General Manager. Sherman, however, felt she would not be satisfied with the position or the company. She had some concerns about the atmosphere, which she saw as more directive than Wellcome. She felt the norms of behavior there were more aggressive and less cooperative than those at Wellcome. But even if she had seen it as a highly autonomous, empowering firm with a talented team and great potential to grow, at Glaxo Sherman would no longer be in charge. Having built Wellcome Israel and been its General Manager, how could she settle for less, especially at a company that had been a rival and whose performance her own team had already bested?

In developing her career options during the long months of waiting for a resolution, Sherman had done her homework. She had considered doing an MBA at a top European business school, but put the possibility aside for the moment because of the cost. She had thought hard about joining Glaxo, where five of her team had gone. She also thought about working elsewhere within Promedico, like three of her reps who moved over to the Pfizer group within the company. (Five others, however, had turned down Glaxo's offer and were still looking for work.)

In the end, it was Sherman's relationships within Promedico that landed her new position: General Manager of Cure Medical, a medical equipment company combining three different divisions—heart valves, pacemakers, and dialysis equipment (in all of which Cure represented foreign manufacturers). Cure was located in the same building as Promedico. The man who had built the company had become the General Manager of Promedico, but had given up control of Cure in exchange for shares in both companies. Promedico and Cure were now closely held by the same owner.

The previous General Manager of Cure Medical had been relieved of his duties about the same time that Wellcome had been bought by Glaxo. As it gradually became clear to Promedico's GM and owner that they would lose the Wellcome business, they decided they didn't want to lose Sherman as well, so they offered her the job. She started her new position on September 15. As she described it:

"We are different companies sitting in the same building, but with a very close relationship. Promedico has the ability and willingness to help Cure with operational problems when necessary. But ultimately Cure is not really part of Promedico, or any of the companies Promedico represents. We have our own stationery and full company status, unlike Wellcome Israel. Wellcome Israel wasn't independent. Basically, I was promoted."

Reflections on Change

Having landed on her feet, Sherman looked back on her experience of the past few months:

"For me it was something new. You know, you can think that you are a bad manger and think that you may go down or get fired, but you never take into consideration that internationally your company will be taken over, and that locally it will be even more complicated. Your performance is excellent, but you have to leave anyway. It doesn't depend on you at all; it's completely out of your control.

"It's something that I won't be able to forget for the rest of my life. An experience like that at the age of thirty you don't expect. It's a once in a lifetime experience. But I still ask, 'Why me?' After I had already built up Wellcome Israel into a very good, successful company, built a team, got everything all organized, then suddenly a storm came and took everything away.

"After so many years in Wellcome I feel that everything I built is just going away, and it's not easy. Especially if you are not the one who caused it or was even related to it. Gone. Just like that." ▪

This case was prepared by MBA student Daniel Mueller under the supervision of Maury A. Peiperl, Assistant Professor of Organisational Behaviour and Director of the Careers Research Initiative at the Centre for Organisational Research, London Business School.

"Wellcome Israel (A)" by Daniel Mueller and Maury A. Peiperl from *The European Case Clearing House*. All rights reserved. Printed in UK and USA. Web Site: *http//www.eech.cmnfield.ac.uk*.

Case 13   Conoco's Decision: The First Annual President's Award for Business Ethics

J. Brooke Hamilton, III
Mark Smith
Steve L. Scheck

On a December Friday in 1999, Steve L. Scheck, general auditor for Conoco Inc., directed the other members of the award selection team toward lunch in the corporate dining room. They had spent the morning reviewing all the nominees for Conoco's first annual President's Award in Business Ethics. The heavy lifting would take place that afternoon. The team was charged with deciding who should receive the award and how the process should be improved for next year.

As they walked through the corridors of the headquarters campus in Houston, Steve reflected on the events that had brought this group together. He recalled the meeting with Archie Dunham, Conoco's president, chairman, and CEO, when the idea first surfaced. In their discussion, Dunham had indicated that he wanted to initiate a "President's Award for Business Ethics." "We have a president's award for the other core values of safety and health, environmental stewardship, and valuing all people," he stated. "Why don't we have an award for business ethics?" Steve had agreed to get started on the project right away. Now a year later and after a great deal of planning, the process was coming to fruition. The award recipient or recipients would be presented with a trophy at the company's honors banquet and featured in an awards video circulated internally and externally. All the nominees would receive a note of congratulations from the president, chairman, and CEO that certainly would provide some carryover in their annual performance evaluations. After the discussion of the candidates that morning, Steve had his own preliminary judgments on who should be selected. He was curious to see what the other members of the selection team thought.

Background and History of the Company

In 1999, Conoco was a large integrated oil company. The firm traced its origins back to the Continental Oil and Transportation Company first incorporated in Utah in 1875. At the time of the case, it was a global firm operating in more than 40 countries in the oil exploration, transportation, refining, and marketing sectors of the industry. The company had approximately 16,700 employees plus contractors and joint venture partners.

The firm's history had not been without difficulties. During the oil shocks of the early 1980s, the company lost its independence. In 1981, DuPont acquired Conoco in order to insure adequate feed stocks for DuPont's chemical business. In 1992, the international oil analyst Schroder and Co. rated Conoco last in overall exploration results among the 14 firms it surveyed.

As the oil crisis abated, the need to secure feed stocks seemed less important to DuPont. Wall Street was pressuring the company to improve its performance. DuPont's response was to streamline its operations. In the early 1990s, Conoco's new president, Archie Dunham, began a program of rationalizing Conoco's assets and developing new sources of supply. The company was successfully spun off from DuPont in a complex public offering and stock swap in 1999. In 1999, the Schroder survey ranked the firm number 1 in exploration efficiency among the major oil companies.

The newly independent company had the task of reintroducing itself to the stock market and establishing its own identity. While retaining its decades old retailing identity as "The Hottest Brand Going!"

Conoco's new corporate identity campaign centered on Domino, the fast cat, emphasizing that in the new global energy environment, speed and agility matter more than size. Internally, the company emphasized a culture based on Conoco's core values of safety, environmental stewardship, valuing all people, and business ethics. The company developed compensation plans that closely align employees' interests with those of their shareholders. Under these plans, a portion of an employee's pay was tied to the total shareholder return, as well as other performance objectives, including upholding Conoco's core values. Conoco maintained that upholding these core values provided a powerful advantage for a company intent on global growth and that they were one of the reasons Conoco was welcomed around the world by customers, partners, governments, and communities.

The management believed this values focus was particularly important for a global oil producer. The nature of the product, business, and technology required that the company have a big footprint. The firm must go where the oil is, move it, refine it, and sell it where it is needed. Conoco employees are natives of many countries and expatriates in many countries. They deal with governments, suppliers, joint venture partners, contractors, workers, and civilian populations in many places in the world. All of this means dealing with the environmental and moral hazards of the world community. The oil industry has a bad press, some of it, possibly, well deserved. However, the world economy depends on the flow of oil, and the industry is not going away any time soon.

Conoco was proud to have avoided major disasters, such as the *Exxon Valdez* oil spill. In 1998, it was the first of the major oil companies to have converted completely to double-hulled tankers, a full 17 years before the U.S. government's deadline in 2015. It promoted this and other safety and environmental accomplishments prominently in its annual report. One of the ways it did this was by having awards and contests in these areas. The winners received a letter from the president, and their accomplishments and pictures were published in the annual report.

Development of the Award

Conoco had formal programs throughout the company to insure that employees understood and put into practice the company's core values of safety

and occupational health, care for the environment, valuing all people, and business ethics. (The 1999 Annual Report is shown in Exhibit C13-1.) The ethics program included a formal ethics policy, procedures for insuring integrity and compliance with laws and ethics, and a 24-hour ethics action line for employees to seek guidance and report possible violations. In developing the business ethics award to complement this program, Steve had decided to work with a team of managers who were interested in the ethics process and who represented areas in which ethics questions would be a part of daily business. Debbie Tellez, assistant general counsel, Business Development; L. Cathy Wining, general manager, Materials and Services; and Barbara Govan, human resources generalist, formed the core team, which was completed by several key persons around the world to insure inclusion of global perspectives. The team met over a period of several months, with a number of drafts circulated and revised, to design a process for soliciting and judging nominees for the award. (The award guidelines are shown in Exhibit C13-2.)

Award Guidelines

The purpose of the award was to "support and recognize ethics as one of Conoco's four core values," to recognize "extraordinary examples" of "leadership" that demonstrate "excellence" in "conduct" and to provide "role models whose behavior embodies what Conoco stands for" (Exhibit C13-2). Rather than simply stating that the award was to be given for ethical conduct, the guidelines made a number of distinctions. The award was to reward individuals or groups for good conduct and to inspire it in the actions, attitudes, and opinions of others. It sought to reward both individuals and groups, to recognize both significant and sustainable activities, to include both business and personal conduct, to be concerned with both ethics and law, and to represent Conoco's values both internally and externally. Conoco's business conduct guide, *Doing the Right Thing,* set the standards with which every employee was expected to comply. The ethics award was to recognize individuals who had gone beyond compliance.

Instead of simply assuming that good conduct is worthwhile, the award guidelines spelled out why

▪ ▪ ▪ ▪ ▪ ▪ ▪ ▪ ▪ ▪   EXHIBIT C13-1   ▪ ▪ ▪ ▪ ▪ ▪ ▪ ▪ ▪ ▪

Think Big, Move Fast: Delivering on Our Promises

Our vision is to be recognized around the world as a truly great, integrated, international energy company that gets to the future first. Conoco operates in more than 40 countries worldwide and at year-end 1999 had approximately 16,700 employees. Conoco is active in both the upstream and downstream segments of the global petroleum industry.

DISTINCTIVE CORPORATE CULTURE DEFINES CONOCO—PAST, PRESENT, AND FUTURE

CORE VALUES—AN UNWAVERING COMMITMENT

Safety and Health: Conoco is dedicated to protecting the safety and health of our employees, who maintained an outstanding safety performance in 1999. The total recordable injury rate of 0.36 per 100 full-time employees was just slightly above the previous year's record low. During the past 5 years, employee safety performance has improved more than 60 percent. Conoco has achieved these outstanding results through the company's efforts to continuously improve safety systems and processes, and because employees take personal responsibility for their safety and the safety of their coworkers. This sense of shared concern was reflected in the safety performance of the thousands of contractors who work at Conoco facilities. Contractor safety performance improved 17 percent in 1999, and 64 percent during the last 5 years.

Environmental Stewardship: Conoco is working to minimize the impact of the company's activities on the environment. The number of significant environmental incidents was reduced to zero in 1998, with one occurring in 1999. "Significant" incidents are major releases or spills with the potential to affect our neighbors. Over the past 5 years, emissions of volatile organic compounds (which contribute to smog) have been reduced by an estimated one-third,

while Conoco's global refining operations have continued to reduce flaring and sulfur emissions. Ernst & Young, a global accounting and auditing firm, is conducting an independent evaluation of Conoco's worldwide reporting processes for future data on safety, health, and environmental performance. This audit will help us better measure the company's progress in these areas. In the communities where Conoco operates major facilities, we maintain a flow of information to local residents through Citizens Advisory Councils, which bring together community representatives and Conoco managers.

Valuing All People: Conoco operates in more than 40 countries and has a diverse global workforce. We draw on the different perspectives and cultures of our employees, along with their combined experience, knowledge, and creativity, to gain a powerful business advantage around the world. Throughout the company, we strive to create an inclusive work environment that treats all people with dignity and respect. In such an environment, employees are recognized and valued for their experience, intellect, and leadership.

Business Ethics: Conducting business with the highest ethical standards is critical to Conoco's continuing success. As Conoco becomes more global, the company is subject to an ever-widening variety of laws, customs, and regulations. This requires us to be flexible and innovative in our business dealings, while at the same time resolute about doing what's right, both legally and ethically. Adherence to the highest ethical standards is a condition of employment at Conoco. The company has a formal ethics policy and procedures for conducting business with integrity and in compliance with all applicable laws. Employees are required to review the policies and procedures regularly and complete an annual certificate of compliance. A 24-hour telephone hot line also provides employees a way to seek guidance or report possible conflicts.

Source: Conoco 1999 Annual Report, pp. 22–24.

▪ ▪ ▪ ▪ ▪ ▪ ▪ ▪ ▪

■■■■■■■■■■ **EXHIBIT C13-2** ■■■■■■■■■■

Guidelines: President's Award for Business Ethics

PURPOSE

The **President's Award for Business Ethics** was created to support and recognize this as one of Conoco's four core values. This award recognizes individuals or groups that make significant and sustainable contributions to this core value.

The award is designed to inspire others by recognizing extraordinary examples of individual and/or group leadership that demonstrates on an ongoing basis, sustainable excellence in personal and business conduct. The people recognized are role models whose behavior embodies what Conoco stands for both internally and externally.

DEFINITION/JUDGING CRITERIA

Living up to Conoco's core values in everything we do, individually and as a company, is fundamental to Conoco's success. Conoco must conduct its business with the highest ethical standards. As our activities grow and extend into new areas of the world, we are subject to an ever-widening variety of laws, customs, and regulations. We need to be flexible and innovative, and at the same time absolutely unwavering in doing what is right, ethically and legally, so that we may enhance our corporate image, and still gain competitive advantage and increase shareholder value.

Conoco's business conduct guide, *Doing the Right Thing,* provides a summary of the company's policies and standards, and of significant laws relating to our business. Every employee is personally responsible for compliance with those laws and standards. However, this award is designed to recognize those individuals who go beyond simply complying with company policies or the applicable laws.

It is designed to recognize those individuals who seek to change the actions, attitudes, or opinions of others with regard to what constitutes ethical behavior, both internally and externally. This may be done through the role modeling of a significantly higher standard of ethical conduct; through the implementation of policies and practices that drive our actions, or the actions of others externally, beyond the minimally acceptable standard or customary behavior; or through decision making that demonstrates that "doing the right thing" from an ethical perspective increases shareholder value.

Nominations should represent extraordinary behavior and will be judged according to specific criteria described here.

1. The significance of the achievement, effort, or behavior. Significant improvement above the minimum required for ethical conduct; linkage to business objectives and implementation of policy and standards; and/or successful performance in spite of difficult and challenging circumstances such as location, language, culture, and/or alignment with and cooperation between Conoco and an external party.

2. The degree of innovation/creativity displayed. Proactive assessment of and response to a need; implementation of new approaches to address ethical business conduct.

3. The degree or extent of employee involvement or support with respect to the higher standard or expectation role modeled or implemented. A work environment exists that encourages employees to conduct themselves ethically at all levels; employees recognize the value of strong ethical behavior and are accountable for their conduct; employees are actively involved in the administration of company standards and training others; and/or rewards and recognition programs reinforce the desired behavior at all levels across the company.

4. The leadership qualities exhibited in challenging norms or customary practices. Persistence in implementing improvement programs or new approaches that lead to outstanding ethical performance.

5. The impact on the company's image/value; internally (with employees) and/or externally (with stakeholders such as partners, governments, suppliers, customers, and communities) in a way that creates shareholder value over time.

(Continued)

(*Continued*)

ELIGIBILITY

Nominees for this award may be an individual employee (regular or temporary), a team, an entire work unit, or retiree of Conoco, for leadership or conduct while in Conoco service in the year of nomination. Contractors may be included in team or work unit awards. There may be multiple recipients each year, dependent upon the number and quality of nominations received. An organization's size or a person's position within the company is not a deciding factor.

THE AWARD

The President's Award for Business Ethics will be presented annually to award recipients or their representatives at a special recognition ceremony. This award will reflect a unique and globally symbolic representation of ethics and will be consistent in stature with that of other President's Awards. The award will remain with the group or individual. Any additional forms of recognition will be left to the discretion of the business units.

SELECTION TEAM

Conoco Leadership Center–Legal and Finance are jointly responsible for coordinating the selection process to determine award recipients. Input on selection team membership will be solicited from multiple sources, with final selection of the team made by the president and CEO. The selection team will be vested with the power to select a winner(s) and other finalists. The team's decision will be reviewed and endorsed by the president and CEO.

The selection team will consist of employees who are recognized as credible role models and able to provide an objective assessment. Team makeup will reflect a broad and global cross-section of the organization. Diversity of thinking styles, beliefs, cultures, and backgrounds will be represented, as well as different salary grades, genders, and ethnic and business perspectives.

Source: Conoco Inc., 1999.

To insure new perspective while maintaining continuity, we expect about one-third of the team's membership to transition in any given year. About one-third of the team will be comprised of former recipients of the award.

In addition to employees, global external resources will be invited to participate on the team to provide additional perspectives.

NOMINATION

Each year, Conoco's president and CEO will send a communication to all employees inviting nominations. The communications will be combined with nomination requests for the other three Conoco core values.

Nominations shall be submitted using *this on-line form,* or follow the format described here:

- The name, address, phone number, and e-mail of the person submitting the nomination and responsible for providing any additional information if necessary.
- The name of the individual(s) being nominated. Indicate the name of the nominated team of work group if applicable.
- **Reasons/Results**—Briefly describe WHAT was accomplished. Include details of any measures or impact of the behavior or activity involved to the extent possible, the drivers, and the significance of the accomplishment.
- **Strategy and Tactics**—Briefly describe HOW the results were achieved. What obstacles had to be overcome? What new or innovative tools or processes were used?
- **People**—Describe WHO was involved in this achievement and why they made a difference. Describe the leadership criteria exhibited and the degree of teamwork and networking that was necessary.

Nominations should consist of no more than three pages, including a brief introductory summary. Clear and concise nominations are encouraged. The selection team will make judgments based upon "substance" of the achievement, not form or length of the nomination.

this and the other core values were important to Conoco:

> Living up to Conoco's core values in everything we do, individually and as a company, is fundamental to Conoco's continuing success. Conoco must conduct its business with the highest ethical standards. As our activities grow and extend into new areas of the world, we are subject to an ever-widening variety of laws, customs, and regulations. We need to be flexible and innovative, and at the same time absolutely unwavering in doing what is right, ethically and legally, so that we may enhance our corporate image, and still gain competitive advantage and increase shareholder value (Exhibit C13-2).

According to the guidelines, the specific criteria for judging the award candidates were:

1. Significance of the achievement
2. Degree of innovation/creativity
3. Degree of employee involvement
4. Leadership qualities exhibited
5. Impact on Conoco's image/value

The form on which all employees were invited to submit nominations asked for a description of:

1. The reason for the nomination, in terms of the results that were accompanied
2. Strategy and tactics, describing how the results were achieved, including obstacles and innovations
3. People involved and why they made a difference, including aspects of leadership and teamwork

Those eligible for the award included individual employees (regular or temporary), a team, an entire work unit, or retiree of Conoco, for leadership or conduct while in Conoco service in the year of nomination. Contractors could be included in work units. Multiple recipients were possible. The award winner(s) were to be decided by a selection team representing diverse constituencies, and confirmed by Archie Dunham, the president, CEO, and chairman. Persons outside the company (global external resources) were asked to participate in order to provide additional perspectives. For new perspective and continuity, one-third of the team was expected to change each year, and about one-third was to be made up of former recipients of the award (Exhibit C13-2).

The Selection Process

The selection team met at Conoco's corporate campus in Houston in December 1999. The team had been chosen by the president, after input from a variety of sources. After introductions, the team members heard comments on the importance of the process by one of the champions of the Ethics Award and a member of the president's top management team, Bob Goldman, senior vice president for finance and CFO. The meeting facilitator then presented the ground rules for the deliberations, and the discussion began. A Conoco employee selector, called a *validator,* had been assigned by the team chair to do a work-up of each nominee before the meeting. Each validator gave a 10-minute summary of this background information on his or her nominee to the group. The validator then placed that nominee into one of three categories: outstanding, good, or weak. The "outstanding" nominees were to constitute an initial short list of potential award winners, though other candidates could be added to this list by the committee. After each validator's presentation, the selectors asked questions and discussed the nominee, but no comparative rankings were made by the committee at this phase of the discussion.

Presentation of the Nominees by the Validators

Twelve nomination forms had been submitted by employees, with one nominee receiving two separate nominations. After each nominee was described to the committee by a validator, committee members were allowed to ask for clarifications regarding the facts presented or to add facts that not been mentioned. Then the validator was asked to rank the nomination as "outstanding," "average," or "weak," in order to develop a short list for discussion of the relative strengths of the nominees.

(1) Patrick R. Defoe, Asset Manager, Grand Isle, Louisiana

The first nomination presented was Patrick R. Defoe, asset manager, Grand Isle, Gulf Coast and Mid-Continent Business Unit, Lafayette, Louisiana. "Patrick Defoe is an example of ethical leadership in a very unexciting business unit," his validator began. "The Grand Isle asset (50+ platforms and associated pipelines situated in the Gulf of Mexico) was a mature field, destined to be sold off within several years. The reservoir was depleting, making the property no longer internally competitive for development funding. That information gets around, and the tendency is for everyone involved, from the bottom to the top, to become lax on dotting the i's and crossing the t's. Everyone is worried about his or her own future with the company. Especially toward the end, as people begin transferring out or retiring, it's difficult to uphold the value of the asset for sale. Patrick would not let that happen. He let people know that there was work to be done and that it would be done according to Conoco standards. His persistent and sustained leadership approach over a 6-year period turned around the performance of Grand Isle in every respect. He introduced new programs in vendor convergence, alliance contracting, and proactive maintenance, and began to actively manage the unit's relationships with regulatory bodies such as Minerals Management Service.

"He would not tolerate ethical or other core value lapses from employees or from contractors. When computer equipment on some of the platforms was missing, phones were stolen, and employees' cars were vandalized, he followed up with a thorough investigation rather than looking the other way. These could have been considered minor incidents because the monetary value was small, and the unit would soon be sold. Patrick felt business ethics involved the small things as well as the big things. When there were allegations of environmental misconduct and unethical behavior involving documents, he called in legal/security and gave them a free hand to investigate no matter who was involved. As it turned out, both allegations were essentially unfounded, but he implemented the minor changes recommended by the investigators.

"Pat Defoe motivated his people to deliver, and they did in terms of costs per barrel, safety, and environmental stewardship. As the description on the nomination form indicates, platform fires decreased from 17 in 1996 to none in 1999, and incidents of regulatory noncompliance dropped from 42 to 2 in the last year. The continuous improvement in the asset's performance was crucial to the successful sale, which realized some $47M for the company's bottom line."

"How did he keep his employees motivated when they knew the property was up for sale?" one selector asked. "Usually employees just want to retire or get transferred out and leave the problems to someone else."

"He took it upon himself to actively network for other employment opportunities throughout Conoco," replied the validator. "Although getting rid of an asset of this size inevitably results in some layoffs, he found places throughout Conoco (in Downstream, Natural Gas and Gas Pipelines, in Venezuela, Dubai, Indonesia and U.S. Upstream) for high-performing individuals, while at the same time maintaining the quality of work at Grand Isle. He carved out several 'win-win' solutions for Conoco. I can close by saying that this is a strong nomination. Because of his good work, Pat has been put in charge of assimilating an acquisition in Canada."

"A good example of the fact than no good deed goes unpunished!" one of the outside selectors noted.

(2) Georgian LPG Terminal Project Team, Georgia and Russia

The next nomination presented was the Georgian LPG Terminal Project Team. The team members included David Huber, lead, Conoco Energy Ventures, Istanbul and Batumi; Roy Mills, finance, London and Batumi; Harry Crofton, development engineering, London; Mikhail Gordin, supply logistics, Moscow; Asuman Yazici, marketing manager, Istanbul; Fiona Braid, legal, London; and Pat Cook, human resources, London. "This nomination represents ethical conduct in very difficult circumstances by employees some of whom were fairly new in their positions with Conoco," the validator began. "It is an Indiana Jones story. You arrive at the airport in an exotic regional capital with a briefcase full of $100 bills, and you have to open a bank account, find a hotel room, and start doing business there.

"Conoco saw an opportunity to become the first Western oil company to establish offices and a hydrocarbon operation in Batumi by refurbishing a liquefied petroleum gas terminal there for transshipment and sale of LPG gas in Turkey and the eastern Mediterranean. The idea was to buy the product in Russia and ship it by rail to the terminal. This was Conoco's first venture into the area, so it was critical that the team set the proper ethical tone for future business and that all employees, expatriate and native, uphold the Conoco values. The target was to have the first train load of gas arrive at the terminal just as the repairs were completed. They were financing the remedial work on the terminal; purchasing the LPG; arranging for transportation through customs in Russia, Azerbaijan, and Georgia; making terminal arrangements in Adjaria; and reselling the product in Turkey. Roy Mills was overseeing the transfer of funds that had to be coordinated with the rebuilding of the terminal by a Turkish contractor based on engineering work monitored by Harry Crofton. Mikhail Gordin, who at that time was based in Moscow, was scouring the country to secure a supply of natural gas and negotiating a transportation agreement with both a freight forwarder and the local refinery management. There were many setbacks at both ends, frequently created by pressure to sweeten deals and alter scheduled work plans. Though bribes and kickbacks are illegal in these areas, many companies who operate there accept them as distasteful necessities because the legal infrastructure is often insufficient to stop such practices. There was a lot pressure on the team members to go along with these types of payments in order to keep the project on schedule. By their refusal to make any 'extraordinary' payments and their constant reminder to local employees, suppliers, and local customs and tax officials that business would have to be done according to Conoco standards or not at all, the project now operates successfully without constant harassment for such payments.

"David Huber, the team lead, used his persistence and experience of working in Russia to convince the local government of Adjaria that LPG terminaling and transportation via Batumi would be an attractive business opportunity." The nominator points out that through his vision setting and understanding of the cultural differences and language barriers, David was able to assemble a multinational, multilingual team capable of working across all of the countries involved: Mikhail, who was responsible for finding the gas and transporting it through customs in Russia, Azerbaijan, and Georgia; David and Harry, who made the terminal arrangements workable in Adjaria; and resale of the product in Turkey by Asuman. It is also important to mention the financial, legal, and human resource services provided by Roy, Fiona, and Pat.

"There was one other positive aspect of this story. In order for governments and businesses to understand the Conoco way of doing business, it was crucial to hire local employees who would adhere to Conoco

values that ran contrary to some local practices. In an area where personal references are practically worthless, human resources, through Pat Cook, checked all references and used a special interview process to vet all new hires. Integrity was a prime concern and a killer factor in hiring. Team members reinforce this concern through advice regarding expected behavior, auditing, and recognition. In addition, in order to assure that good conduct was rewarded by salary schedules appropriate to the region, the team sought salary advice from the United Nations Development Program, a first for an energy company. The UNDP praised the company's treatment of employees in the region. Overall, I think this a strong nomination."

"What worries me about this situation is that we would be rewarding employees for doing what was expected of them," objected a selector. "The company policy is clear about not paying bribes. These guys did what they were supposed to do."

"Were there any extra pressures from within the company, other than the usual concern to meet targets with a profitable project?" asked one of the outside selectors. "That might make their behavior extraordinary. Remember, the guidelines talk about 'overcoming obstacles.'" (see Exhibit C13-3)

"Well, these employees were relatively new in these particular jobs and new to that area, so even a failure caused by a conflict of Conoco's ethical practices with local practices could have been perceived as more serious than for a more experienced person. In a company like ours that really stands behind its values, failure on those grounds would have been accepted as the right way to do business, but the perception of danger might still be there for newer employees. From a business standpoint, however, there were no more than the usual pressures to succeed."

"There was no pressure directing them to violate the company's ethical standards, but there was extra pressure," another selector said. "Remember that our primary project in the region had already gone under, so the LPG terminal was our only active effort. We needed the terminal to succeed in order to have a platform from which to launch other projects. The team members knew that if they failed, Conoco would likely pull out of the region entirely."

(3) Eric Johnson, Excel Paralubes, Lake Charles, Louisiana

"This may not be as dramatic a story," began the validator, "But it represents behavior that deserves

▮▮▮▮▮▮▮▮▮▮▮ **EXHIBIT C13-3** ▮▮▮▮▮▮▮▮▮▮

Organizational Structures That Block Ethical Action

ARE ILLEGAL AND UNETHICAL ACTIVITIES COMMON IN THE WORKPLACE?

The 2000 National Business Ethics Survey (hereafter NBES'00), conducted by the Ethics Resource Center, showed that in comparison to their 1994 survey data, companies are doing more in terms of their ethics programs—more have written standards, ethics training programs, and means for employees to get ethics advice. Many ethics indicators have improved, and a majority of employees are positive about ethics in their organizations. Many employees believe that their supervisors and organizational leaders talk about and model ethical behavior at work. Interestingly, there are relatively few differences in the ethics perceptions of employees in the government, for-profit, and nonprofit sectors.

In a 1997 survey (hereafter "EOAS'97") conducted by the Ethics Officer Association and the American Society of Chartered Life Underwriters and Chartered Financial Consultants, 48 percent of American workers admitted to illegal or unethical actions in the past year.

The NBES'00 reported that 33 percent of American workers observed behaviors that violated either their organization's ethics standards or the law. [This report was based on a nationally representative telephone survey of 1,500 U.S. employees conducted between November 1999 and February 2000.]

A 1999 survey (hereafter KPMGS'99) conducted by KPMG LLP, a professional services firm, indicated that greater than 75 percent of U.S. workers surveyed had observed violations of the law or company standards in the previous 12 months. Nearly 50 percent said their company "would significantly lose public trust" if the observed infraction had been reported by the news media. [This report is based on questionnaires sent to the homes of 3,075 randomly selected U.S. working adults in October and November 1999. 2,390 completed questionnaires were returned for a response rate of 78 percent.]

WHAT ARE THE MOST COMMON ILLEGAL AND UNETHICAL ACTIVITIES?

The top five types of unethical/illegal activities in the EOAS'97 were:

1. Cutting corners on quality control
2. Covering up incidents
3. Abusing or lying about sick days
4. Deceiving or lying to customers
5. Putting inappropriate pressure on others

Others mentioned included cheating on an expense account, discriminating against coworkers, paying or accepting kickbacks, secretly forging signatures, trading sex for sales, and ignoring violations of environmental laws.

The five types of misconduct observed most frequently according to the NBES'00 were:

1. Lying
2. Withholding needed information
3. Abusive or intimidating behavior toward employees
4. Misreporting actual time or hours worked
5. Discrimination

Common infractions cited in the KPMGS'99 were sexual harassment and employment discrimination; other offenses mentioned included deceptive sales practices, unsafe working conditions, and environmental breaches.

WHAT ARE THE FACTORS THAT LEAD TO ILLEGAL AND UNETHICAL ACTIVITIES IN THE WORKPLACE?

The top 10 factors that workers reported in EOAS'97 as triggering their unethical activities are:

1. balancing work and family
2. poor internal communications
3. poor leadership
4. work hours and workload

(Continued)

(*Continued*)

5. lack of managementsupport
6. need to meet sales, budget, or profit goals
7. little or no recognition of achievements
8. company politics
9. personal financial worries
10. insufficient resources

Midlevel managers most often reported a high level of pressure to act unethically or illegally (20 percent). Employees of large companies cited such pressure more often than those at small businesses (21 percent versus 14 percent). High levels of pressure were reported more often by high school graduates than by college graduates (21 percent versus 13 percent).

The NBES'00 indicated that one in eight employees feels pressure to compromise their organizations' ethics standards. Almost two-thirds who feel this pressure attribute it to internal sources—supervisor, top management, and coworkers. Employees with longer tenure in their organizations feel more pressure to compromise their organizations' ethics standards. Employees who feel this pressure to compromise observe more misconduct in the workplace.

The KPMGS'99 reported that nearly three-fourths of the respondents blamed cynicism and low morale as the reason for employee misconduct. Fifty-five percent of respondents said their CEO was unapproachable if an employee needed to deliver bad news. Sixty-one percent thought their company would not discipline individuals guilty of an ethical infraction.

AN ORGANIZATIONAL FOCUS IS AS IMPORTANT FOR UNDERSTANDING ETHICAL BEHAVIOR AS AN INDIVIDUAL FOCUS

Because many of the causes cited as triggering unethical behavior are organizational factors, organizational focus is as important as an individual focus for understanding the obstacles to ethical behavior. By focusing on structure, it is possible to identify certain common features of business organizations that act as organizational blocks to ethical behavior. These ways of organizing business activity can make it difficult for individuals to act in an ethical way, even if the corporation's ethics code requires ethical behavior. James A. Waters ("Catch 22: Corporate Morality as an Organizational Phenomenon," *Organizational Dynamics,* Spring 1978. Reprinted in Donaldson and Werhane, *Ethical Issue in Business* 3rd Edition, 1988) identifies seven such blocks to ethical action.

1. Strong role models who follow unethical practices make it difficult for new employees trained by them to imagine how the assigned tasks could be done without unethical practices. Corporations must pay careful attention to the messages that new employees get during their training about the importance of following the firm's ethics code.

2. The strict line of command followed in many organizations makes it difficult for individuals down the chain to resist an immediate supervisor's order to do something unethical. The employee must assume that the order has come from higher up the chain and represents company policy. If there are no channels of communication for questioning the ethics of an action without going to the higher ups who presumably originated the order, the employee is unlikely to risk retribution by going above his or her supervisor's head. Thus, compliance in unethical activities can often be enforced by lower-level supervisors without the higher company officials ever knowing about it.

3. The separation of policy decisions from implementation can be a strong block to ethical action. In most organizations, policy is set by upper management without discussion with lower-level employees. Lower level employees may then be forced to resort to unethical activities in order to carry out unreasonable policies or goals set by the top management or risk losing their jobs.

4. The division of work necessary to accomplish the goals of large organizations also makes reporting unethical activities difficult. Employees in one channel do not see it as their responsibility to report wrongdoing in other channels nor do they usually have enough information about what is going on throughout the organization to be certain that the activities are unethical.

(*Continued*)

(Continued)

5.   Task group cohesiveness can frustrate even well-structured internal reporting procedures. Members of a work group who are engaged in unethical activities will exert strong pressure on every member to be loyal to the group rather than report the activities to the company.

6.   Loyalty to the company can lead to protection from outside intervention by the law or adverse public opinion. Employees can avoid investigating reported unethical activities for fear that word will get out that wrongdoing has occurred.

7.   Another organizational block is constituted by ambiguity about priorities. Corporate ethics codes may not make it clear to employees how conflicts between performance criteria and ethical criteria

should be resolved. Companies may reward employees only on the basis of the "hard" measurable criteria of meeting sales goals or profit projections with no consideration given to the means used to achieve these ends.

Two further blocks that Waters does not mention are time pressure, which may make unethical shortcuts seem like the most expedient solution to a workload that cannot be completed in the time permitted, and inadequate resources to complete the job with ethical means. Overcoming these organizational blocks in meeting the expected standards of behavior would qualify as "extraordinary" and worthy of recognition.

Note: This exhibit is not a Conoco document but is included by the authors to facilitate case discussion.

▪▪▪▪▪▪▪▪▪

recognition just as well. It involves day-to-day ethical leadership that set the tone for the employees of one of our joint ventures. EXCEL Paralubes is an effort to leverage technology and personnel from Conoco and Pennzoil in the creation of a product and profits that neither organization could realize alone. Conoco is the managing partner in the venture, which is sited next to the Conoco facility in Lake Charles.

"The nomination came from a Conoco manager working as the organizational development coordinator for Petrozuata Upgrader, another joint venture in Venezuela. The nominator had been part of the EXCEL start-up and knew that EXCEL had developed innovative work processes that had contributed to the success of EXCEL and would be readily adaptable to help with organizational development in Petrozuata. He asked Eric to share them with Petrozuata. Eric responded that he would be happy to help but that certain of these processes represented a competitive advantage to the EXCEL joint venture. Though these processes would certainly add to the bottom line at Conoco through its Venezuela venture, they could not be given out in fairness to the joint venture partner, Pennzoil. This response from a loyal Conoco employee who was conscious of his ethical and legal obligations to his joint venture so impressed

the nominator that he submitted Eric for the award. The nominator also stated that, following Eric Johnson's leadership in this area, he has conveyed this standard of conduct to his peers at Petrozuata so that they are aware of their obligation to protect not only Conoco's interests but those of their joint venture partners as well.

"As I looked into Eric's activities at EXCEL, I was more and more impressed that this was not an isolated incident and that Eric was modeling ethical conduct crucial to the success of Conoco joint ventures. If we are the managing partner in the venture, the other partner needs to be confident that the Conoco employees in charge will not show any favoritism to Conoco in cost sharing. To hear tell from the EXCEL and Conoco people on the site, Eric is fair to a fault. The EXCEL operation is right next to the Conoco plant in Lake Charles, Louisiana, and the two plants jointly use some of the facility. Eric has gotten flak from his counterparts at the Conoco plant for not cutting them any slack on sharing costs for these joint facilities. They would rather not have these costs show up in their budgets, but he reminds them that he is wearing his EXCEL hat and needs to look out for the interests of EXCEL. On one occasion, for example, he made Conoco pay for its share of grading the road that borders both plant sites. Although that may seem unimportant, it sets a tone for all of the Conoco employees lent to the venture and has given Pennzoil such confidence in the fairness of the operation that they are planning additional ventures with Conoco. I think this nomination is another strong one."

"But again, isn't this conduct that we expect of all employees? Does it rise to an award level?" asked a selector.

"Well, you need to realize that his long-term career is with Conoco and that most managers after several years with the joint venture return to work with their parent company. By upholding these standards he is risking burning some bridges with managers at Conoco that he might be working for or with in the future," replied the validator.

"We also have to consider that joint ventures of this kind are important to a company the size of Conoco, and we haven't been doing them for that long. We need models for how to make those ventures work, and an award might help to get the message out as to our company's expectations," another selector added.

(4) Terry Beene, Retail Marketing, Houston, Texas

"When Conoco, for competitive reasons, elected to include convenience stores in our retail stations," the validator began, "the company found itself with a whole new kind of employee. Instead of the salaried engineers, managers, and support staff who make up most of the work force, we were responsible for recruiting, training, motivating, and monitoring a group of not very highly paid hourly workers who were our retail face to the public. In addition, these not very highly paid workers were surrounded by all kinds temptations in the form of merchandise and cash, in a situation where direct supervision was too costly. Looking at this problem, Terry decided that there were two main options. One was to assume that a small percentage of employees were going to steal and concentrate on catching and punishing them. The other was to assume that the great majority of employees were honest and that a program that spent time and money recognizing their honesty in the face of temptation would motivate them to continue their good conduct. Such a program could convert or drive out the bad actors as well.

"Terry decided to emphasize 'keeping honest people honest.' The program was designed to catch people being honest and reward them for it. The first step was a strong training program for new employees that began with a unit that explained all the ways that employees could steal from a convenience store. Employees who expect to steal were thereby warned that the company knew all of their methods, and most of the dropouts occurred in this early phase of the training. Honest employees understood what the temptations were and were taught how to avoid them. They understood that the company uses extensive control measures and that one of the purposes of these was to 'catch them doing something right.' Once on the job, the employees were continually motivated to be honest with visits by mystery shoppers who rewarded them on the spot for good behavior and reported on store procedures to management.

"A second phase of the program involved systemized operational practices designed to decrease the opportunity for theft to occur. There are extensive control measures to manage inventory and track sales through scanning technology and regular and surprise audits. Security cameras have been installed in virtually all stores within the last 2 years. Honest employees were encouraged to be honest by knowing that dishonest behavior would be caught and punished. However, the emphasis even in the audits was to reward people whose inventory and cash are all properly accounted for rather than focusing on the threat that controls pose to those who do wrong. The desire to accurately measure inventory and control losses was the catalyst in the decision to employ new and innovative scanning technology. The data resulting from this loss control program has also proved valuable in the development of trend reports and standardized operations reports that can highlight loss control problems before they become critical.

"The results of this approach to managing retail sales have been significant. Although the standard rate of losses in the industry is 2 percent to 4 percent of gross revenue per year, Conoco's loss percentage has averaged 1.13 percent over the past 3 years. This difference translates into additional revenues of $1.5M and $2.5M per annum over the past 2 years. The turnover rate for employees is also significantly lower than the industry average, which contributes to lower recruitment and training costs.

"In his position as director of security in retail operations, Terry was the sole employee in the retail sector assigned to loss control. His work designing and selling this program throughout the sector resulted in a function-wide commitment to the retail loss control program at all levels. Because of his efforts, loss control focused not on fixing problems by firing dishonest employees but on training personnel to recognize the importance of honesty and on implementing sustainable processes to prevent problems from occurring. All in all I think this nomination warrants serious consideration."

(5) Raymond S. Marchand, Upstream Aame, Damascus, Syria

"Raymond Marchand is a unique individual. Born a French-Algerian, Raymond has translated his dual nationality into a unique understanding of how to preserve Conoco values in some of the most complex and challenging business cultures in the world. As a young man, he fought the Algerians as a member of the French foreign legion's Blackfoot brigade, a group that planned to parachute into Paris to assassinate French President DeGaul for granting Algerian independence. After his military service, Raymond began working for Conoco as a laborer in the 1960s and quickly advanced into management responsibility. He has been in charge of the company's operations in Chad, Egypt, The Congo, Somalia, Angola, and Nigeria, and is now heading operations in Syria. His leadership in doing business the Conoco way or not doing business at all involved relationships both outside and inside the company. By his own example, he established a clear policy of integrity in all dealings with government officials and contractors, and taught both native and expatriate employees that requests for 'exceptional' payments could be refused continually without insulting the person making the request.

"Raymond is most masterful in difficult business environments. In Somalia, the U.S. government employed his experience in negotiating in a corrupt environment without compromising his standards. As the situation there deteriorated, Raymond was forced to leave the country to the sound of gunfire. In Nigeria, his high ethical standards and personal negotiating style changed the paradigm of what was acceptable business conduct for Conoco's Nigerian employees, our Nigerian indigenous partners, and our Nigerian government contacts. His approach took the risk of losing business opportunities. The respect he garnered for his way of operating, however, gained opportunities for Conoco, especially as a new government under President Obasanjo made the ideal of integrity fashionable in that country.

"Nigeria was a particularly challenging environment because 95 percent of the Conoco workforce was native born and had grown up in an atmosphere in which companies bought their way into whatever situation they wanted to be in. Marchand taught the whole organization from top to bottom that business could be conducted without such payments. His alternative to bribes was establishing relationships based on trust and dependability, an approach that requires spending the time to build personal relationships. Actions speak louder than words in establishing trust, and as his nominator put it, 'You can see his heart behind everything he says and does.' With the company's indigenous partners, he was successful in resolving contractual problems and educating them about Conoco's core values, especially ethical behavior. In doing so, he earned not only their respect but a wider recognition within the business community and the government that Conoco's integrity is second to none in Nigeria.

"Because of his leadership, many of our operating costs have been lowered by newly empowered, bright young native Nigerian employees. Throughout Nigeria, I am told, all the Conoco employees respond to requests for 'extraordinary' payments with Marchand's characteristic smile, two raised and waving hands, and the phrase 'No can do!' delivered in a loud friendly voice. This behavior has become so standard that most people do not even request payments from Conoco employees.

"Inside the company, Marchand has shown an equally high level of integrity. Whenever accusations have surfaced about irregularities in his operations, he has immediately requested a full company investigation of the matter and has insured the full cooperation of all employees in his shop. When notified that he was being posted to Syria, he requested a meeting with a management committee from auditing and legal affairs to map out strategies for dealing with the business environment in that country. I think his career achievements set a standard against which future award nominations can be measured."

"That mention of career achievement raises some interesting points regarding the award criteria," observed an outside selector. "Should the President's Ethics Award recognize only heroic ethical conduct that goes beyond the standard expected of every employee or should employees be rewarded for meeting the expected standards? If employees are recognized for meeting the expected standard, should this be only for consistent behavior over time (a lifetime of ethical action) or for behavior in difficult circumstances (pressures to meet other performance criteria)? Or would the company's objectives be furthered in giving awards sometimes for behavior that shows how the standards can be followed in ordinary circumstances (a good example, or 'Charlie Brown' award)?"

"It seems that we have examples of all of these possibilities in this group of nominees," another selector said. "In giving this first award, the company will be setting some kind of a standard for future nominations, though an evolution of the standards is certainly possible. However, I think it is important to keep in mind that our decision may encourage some and discourage other types of nominations from being submitted in the future."

"We might want to consider giving more than one award this first year, because we are reviewing conduct from several prior years rather than one prior year," one selector said.

"It is interesting," another selector noted, "that we have some real diversity among the nominees. We have overseas and domestic. We have upstream (exploration and production), midstream (transportation and refining), and downstream (retailing). We have career nominations and specific project nominations, and we have individuals and

a team. The only kind of nomination missing is for a single action that was unique enough, had such important consequences, or was done under such difficult circumstances that it was significant enough for a nomination."

Making the Decision

The morning passed quickly as the nominees were presented. "These five nominees have made the short list based on the validators' evaluations," the facilitator said as she stood up to indicate that the descriptive phase of the work was concluded. "But any of the others can be considered as we begin to make judgments this afternoon. Archie (President Dunham) considers this award to be important for Conoco. We have a real task ahead of us. Steve has promised us an excellent lunch before we decide whom to recommend for the first President's Award for Business Ethics." ■

In addition to company documents and other sources cited, the case is based on the personal experiences of two of the authors as members of the selection team. Dialogue is meant to represent the substance of the discussion and is not a transcription of the meeting. The author's notes did not allow attribution of remarks to individual committee members. Some material from the nomination forms is included in the dialogue. Conoco Phillips had generously granted permission to use the company materials presented in this case.

Case 14   West Indies Yacht Club Resort: When Cultures Collide

Jeffrey P. Shay

In early December 1994, Patrick Dowd, a 30-year-old management consultant, stared out his office window at the snowy Ithaca, New York, landscape. Dowd reflected on his recent phone conversation with Jim Johnson, general manager of the 95-room West Indies Yacht Club Resort (WIYCR), located in the British Virgin Islands. Johnson sounded desperate to pull the resort out of its apparent tailspin and noted three primary areas of concern. First, expatriate manager turnover was beginning to become problematic. In the past 2 years, the resort had hired and then failed to retain three expatriate waterfront directors and three expatriate food and beverage directors. Second, although the resort had not initiated a formal guest feedback program, Johnson estimated that guest complaints had increased from 10 per week to more than 30 per week over the past 2 years. The complaints were usually given by guests to staff at the front desk, written down, and passed on to Johnson; usually, they were centered on the deteriorating level of service provided by local British Virgin Islands' employees. Many repeat guests claimed, "The staff just doesn't seem as motivated as it used to be." Third, there appeared to be an increasing level of tension between expatriate and local staff members. In the past, expatriates and locals seemingly found it natural to work side by side; now a noticeable gap between these groups appeared to be growing.

Johnson had come to know Dowd and his reputation for being one of the few expatriate management consultants in the region who seemed to have a real grasp on what it took to manage effectively in the Caribbean. The two had become better acquainted in 1993 when the world-renowned sailing school that Dowd was working for, Tradewind Ventures, was contracted to develop new family-focused programs to be offered by the resort. Through this experience, Dowd gained in-depth knowledge of the resort. Dowd's reputation and knowledge of the resort prompted Johnson's call to see if Dowd would be interested in working as a participant observer at the resort to determine the underlying reasons behind his three major concerns. Johnson requested that Dowd work at the resort during three Christmas holiday weeks to observe resort staff during the peak season. Dowd would then present an analysis of his observations and make recommendations regarding what actions could be taken to improve the situation. Although Dowd had never provided consulting in this specific area (i.e., an analysis of the cultural influences on the behavior of workers in the Caribbean), he gladly accepted the challenge: It coincided with his personal experience in the region and recent courses on cross-cultural management that he had taken at Cornell University. Dowd moved over to his bookcase and pulled books, brochures, and other information off the shelf and began reading. He was departing for the British Virgin Islands in 1 week and wanted to get a head start on his background research.

British Virgin Islands' Tourism Market

Thirty-six islands, 16 of which are inhabited, comprise the 59-square-mile chain of British Virgin Islands (BVIs) (Exhibit C14-1). Unlike the neighboring islands of St. Thomas and St. Croix, which underwent extensive tourism development during the 1970s and 1980s, the BVI government carefully planned and restricted growth. The result was a carefully carved niche in the Caribbean market—positioning the island chain in the exclusive/ecotourism market segment.

From 1950 to 1970, the BVIs hosted the traveling elite. During the early 1970s, the introduction and rapid growth of bareboat chartering [boats ranging from 28 feet to 50 feet, which chartered (rented) to tourists qualified to take the boats out without the assistance of a licensed captain] made the small island chain affordable for tourists with moderate budgets as well. Bareboat charters offered a unique vacation opportunity—one that connected tourists with the islands' rich natural beauty and intriguing history by allowing tourists to visit quiet harbors and

401

▪▪▪▪▪▪▪▪▪▪▪▪ **EXHIBIT C14-1 Map of the British Virgin Islands and Location of Luxury Hotels and Resorts**

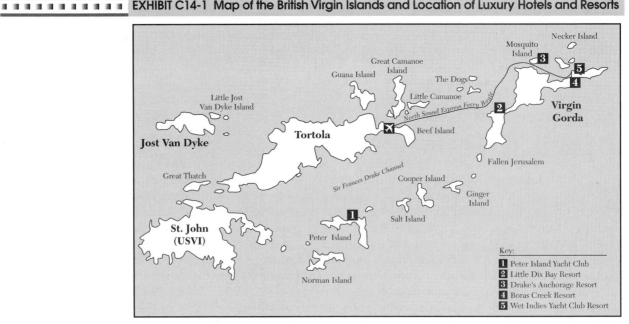

villages that were void of larger cruise ships and large hotels. The BVI's calm waters and steady trade winds were soon filled with charter boats as the chain of islands quickly became known as the premier chartering location in the world. By the early 1990s, there were more than 500 charter boats available in the Virgin Islands, with the largest company, The Moorings, managing more than 190 charter boats in the BVIs alone. Although charter industry growth in the BVIs drew the attention of major developers, the combination of strict government regulations constraining the size of new hotels and resorts along with limited access provided by the small Beef Island Airport kept these developers and mass tourism out. As a result, smaller mid-scale to upscale hotels and resorts were developed in the BVIs.

Upscale Hotels in the British Virgin Islands

Although several mid-scale hotels were developed and operating in the BVIs by the mid-1980s, there were only four truly upscale hotels in the island chain in addition to WIYCR (Exhibit C14-1). Each of these hotels provided three meals per day (not including alcoholic drinks) and access to activities (e.g., water sports equipment) as part of the price for the room. Biras Creek was an independent resort located adjacent to WIYCR's property and overlooked North Sound of Virgin Gorda (Exhibit C14-2). This resort featured 34 rooms, one restaurant, three tennis courts, a private beach with a bar, a small marina, and several miles of nature trails. Peak season double occupancy rates in 1994 for Biras Creek ranged from $395 to $695 per night and, similar to WIYCR, this resort was only accessible by sea. After facing high turnover of expatriate resort managers and expatriate assistant managers for the past 5 years, Biras Creek implemented a policy of hiring individuals for these positions for 3-year contracts. After the contract was completed, managers were required to seek employment elsewhere. The owners felt that most managers became less effective after 3 years because they suffered from burnout.

Drake's Anchorage was an independent resort located on the 125-acre Mosquito Island, an island situated at the northern entrance to North Sound (Exhibit C14-2). This small resort offered 12 rooms, a beachfront restaurant, a protected anchorage for charter boats, a picturesque hiking trail, and four secluded sandy beaches. Peak season double occupancy rates in 1994 ranged from $400 to $600 per night. Expatriate managers oversaw operations at this resort as well. Guests staying at this resort were primarily interested in a relaxing, secluded vacation with limited activities.

Little Dix Bay Resort opened in 1964 as part of the Rockefeller Resort chain. In 1993, after a multimillion-dollar renovation project, Rosewood Hotels and Resorts, a Dallas-based company, acquired the management contract for the resort. This resort offered 98 rooms ranging in price from $480 to $1,000 per night in 1994 during peak season for a double occupancy room. This resort was located on the north-western shore of Virgin Gorda and overlooked the Sir Francis Drake Channel, a channel cutting through the heart of the BVI chain (Exhibit C14-2). In addition to a fine dining restaurant, the resort offered small boats (i.e., Sunfish, Lasers, and Whalers), water skiing, and day excursions to snorkeling and diving sites for guests. These amenities made Little Dix the WIYCR's strongest local competitor. Under the management of Rosewood Hotels and Resorts, expatriate managers often rotated every 2 to 3 years from one Rosewood property to another. Its prices and impeccable service attracted some of the most affluent tourists visiting the region.

Located on Peter Island, the Peter Island Yacht Club was operated by JVA Enterprises, a Michigan-based firm that acquired the resort in the early 1970s (see Exhibit C14-1). The resort had 50 rooms, a fine-dining restaurant, a marina, and a beautiful secluded beach. Peak season double occupancy rates ranged from $395 to $525 per night in 1994. This resort was also managed by expatriates and had been recently remodeled after being struck by two hurricanes in the early 1990s. Similar to Drake's Anchorage, this resort primarily attracted guests looking for a secluded island vacation with limited activity.

BVI Labor Market Laws and Regulations

All hotels operating in the BVIs faced a number of challenges beyond the strict regulations on development. Perhaps the most significant challenge was dealing with local labor market laws and regulations. Despite the restricted growth in tourism, the supply of qualified service employees severely lagged demand. Four general government restrictions and policies exacerbated the challenge of hiring and managing staff. First, organizations were granted only a limited number of work permits to attract more experienced service employees from foreign countries. Expatriate work permits were granted based on the total number of employees working at a resort (i.e., the more employees a resort had, the more expatriates it could hire) and the availability of locals who possessed the skills

---

¡¡¡¡¡¡¡¡¡¡¡¡ **EXHIBIT C14-2 Virgin Gorda and Its Luxury Hotels**

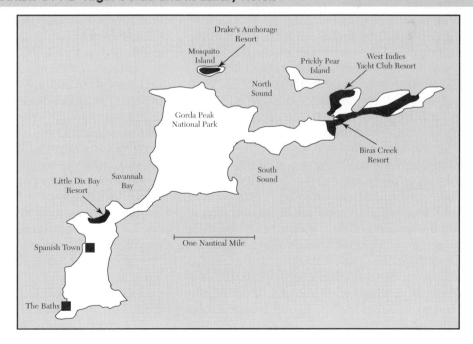

requisite for the position. The latter meant that resorts had to post positions in local newspapers for at least 1 month before requesting a permit for an expatriate.

Second, organizations were not permitted to lay off staff during slow seasons. This created significant challenges for resorts like WIYCR that ran at nearly 100 percent occupancy during the peak season (December through May) and as low as 40 percent during the off season (June through November). Especially hurt by this were luxury resorts that required high staffing levels to provide the services that guests expected during the peak months but were then left overstaffed during the off-season periods.

Third, policies restricting the conditions under which an employee could be fired severely limited an organization's ability to retain only the best workers. For example, one hotel manager claimed, "It is hard to fire a local employee even if he steals from us. We are often required to file documents with the government and then attend a formal hearing on why we dismissed an employee. Because it is so difficult to fire someone who steals, imagine how difficult it is to fire someone who doesn't work hard, is always late, or forgets to come to work! Our hands are really tied by these regulations."

Finally, organizations were under extreme pressure to promote BVI locals into management positions whenever possible. As noted earlier, before hiring an expatriate manager a resort had to advertise the position for at least a month. In addition, if a local approached the resort with minimal requisite skills for the job but was enthusiastic and willing to learn, the resort found it difficult in the current environment to overlook the local and hire the expatriate. As a result of these restrictions and policies, managers often found themselves overstaffed with under qualified workers.

Mangers overcame these dilemmas in a number of ways. To combat regulations on foreign employees, organizations often paid foreign staff through their offshore corporate headquarters and limited the amount of time they actually spent at the resort, hotel, or other service site. In response to restrictions on laying off staff, organizations offered attractive vacation components to their employment contracts. This allowed the organization to pay lower wages and to decrease excess labor during off seasons. Managers, forced to retain staff regardless of their productivity levels, rationalized that excess labor costs were offset by lower wages in the region, avoidance of costs associated with training a new employee, and the need for extra staff during peak season.

Hotels and resorts also realized that although many entry-level employees could continue to be trained on the job, locals seeking managerial positions would require more formalized training. Unfortunately, neither the BVI nor the U.S. Virgin Islands had developed hospitality management training programs because there was no critical mass of local managers required to start such programs. Instead, hotels and resorts sent promising young staff to service training programs in the Bahamas and Bermuda in an effort to prepare them for management positions.

The West Indies Yacht Club Resort

In 1964, the Kimball family sailed into the North Sound of Virgin Gorda (Exhibits C14-2 and C14-3). The sound's natural beauty captivated the family, and they knew it was a place to which the family would soon return. Nestled on the mountainside of the innermost point, the Kimballs found a shorefront pub and five cottages known as The West Indies Resort. The cottages were rustic, with only cold water running in the bathrooms. It was at the resort's pub that Joe Kimball met Armin Dubois, the property's eccentric owner. Dubois had been a pioneer Virgin Islands yachtsman who had found paradise on these shores and never left.

Under Dubois' management, an old diesel generator supplied lighting, and water was collected on the roofs and stored in cisterns that doubled as cottage foundations. The pub and restaurant served mariners when Dubois felt like it. Dubois established his own protocol. Mariners blew foghorns just off the main dock, and Dubois responded as to whether or not he was open for business. Even after being invited ashore, guests were unsure as to how long the hospitality would last. Dubois was notorious for turning off the generator to let guests know they had outstayed their welcome.

By early 1973, after several visits to North Sound, Kimball asked Dubois if he would sell or lease property so that he could build a family cottage. Dubois replied several months later that he wasn't interested in selling or leasing a small piece of property but

Fast Tacks Weeks. Initial efforts to fill slow season periods centered on leveraging the resort's competitive advantage. Fitch developed the Fast Tacks Program, which targeted specific sailing groups and utilized the resort's vast sailing resources. These groups ranged from racing to cruising, from families to couples, from senior citizens to young adults. During certain weeks in the historically slow fall season, sailing celebrities were invited and gave specialized seminars to guests. Perhaps the most widely noted week is the ProAm week, in which guests are assigned to teams with some of the top match racing skippers in the world. In addition to becoming a major source of income to the resort, the weeks have become a key free advertising vehicle. Articles in sailing magazines have served not only to promote the weeks themselves but have also increased reader awareness of the sailing experience that the resort can offer.

Family Weeks. To change the resort's image, Fitch marketed special programs during traditional school break periods to families. These weeks provided special services, including instructional and recreational programs, for children and young adults. By providing a fun yet safe environment for children, parents were free to spend time alone enjoying activities designed for their tastes (e.g., harbor sunset cruises). In addition, there were several family excursions planned throughout the week that offered an opportunity to enjoy exploring reefs and other islands together.

Capturing the Market Earlier. In addition to the family weeks and Fast Tacks weeks, marketers realized that there was another market that they had been ignoring that could significantly reduce some of its occupancy cycle troubles. Instead of waiting until a couple had established themselves or started a family, why not get them when they were tying the knot? After all, the resort provided one of the most romantic atmospheres in the Carribbean. Moreover, the majority of weddings in North America, the primary market for the resort, occur during the slow periods of summer and fall. In response to this revelation, the resort began to actively market wedding and honeymoon packages. The resort that these guests would return for second, third, and fourth honeymoons and bring their children when they started their families.

---

would entertain an offer to buy out the whole property. In late 1973, Kimball did just that.

Kimball's painstaking attention to detail fostered development of the property's unique character. His vision was to provide a truly ecology-conscious and comfortable place for travelers to enjoy an environment perfect for sailing, fishing, snorkeling, diving, and combing beaches. To accomplish this, Kimball maintained many of Dubois' earlier practices. For example, the resort continued to generate its own electricity and collect and distill its own water. In addition, the resort used gray water (partially treated water) to irrigate the hillsides and used solar power wherever possible. In sharp contrast to the multistory designs used by other Caribbean developers, Kimball constructed 55 individual bungalows that were scattered along the hillside and preserved the natural beauty for which the resort was known. Kimball differentiated the resort from others in the region by acquiring the world's largest resort fleet of sailboats (e.g., J24s, JY15s, Cal 27s, Freedom 30s, Lasers, Sunfish, Rhodes 19s, Mistral sailboards) and powerboats (e.g., Boston Whalers and sport fishing boats). These carefully selected boats were easy for even inexperienced guests to handle. These acquisitions

in conjunction with the resort's sailing instruction program established the resort's reputation as one of the premier water sports resorts in the world. Subsequently, Kimball changed the resort's name to the West Indies Yacht Club Resort to leverage the distinct aquatic recreational activities that the resort offered.

In 1987, with the resort's reputation growing and business booming, Kimball acquired a 15-year renewable management contract for The Sandy Point Resort, located adjacent to his property. The additional facilities, including 40 more rooms, a second restaurant, a swimming pool, a fuel dock, and beach, gave the property the critical mass necessary to compete with local and international competitors. The resort also outsourced the provision of scuba services from the Virgin Islands Dive Company. By 1990, the property had become a fully operational, water-sports–oriented, ecology-conscious resort that encompassed more than 75 acres and a mile of beachfront.

The resort faced two major challenges: an occupancy cycle with high peaks and low valleys and changing market demographics. Resort managers estimated that occupancy rates from 1985 to 1990 had ranged from 80 percent to 100 percent during the peak season from mid-December until the end of May and 40 percent to 60 percent from June until early December. These fluctuations were thought to occur because key customer markets sought Caribbean vacations during the colder winter months but found it hard to justify a trip to the tropics during spring, summer, and fall when the weather at home was more acceptable. It wasn't until the resort was forced to carry Sandy Point's additional overhead that management realized the need to address occupancy rate fluctuations. One of the most difficult costs to manage was labor. To provide the high-end service for which the resort was known, the number of staff employed by the resort had increased substantially. According to Jim Johnson, the resort was barely able to meet its guests' needs during peak season; during the slow season, the resort was overstaffed.

Changing market demographics also posed a challenge. In the past, the resort predominantly attracted couples of all ages. However, changing market demographics severely hampered its ability to attract both new and repeat guests. Former guests who had begun to raise families of their own recalled the intimate moonlit dinners and walks on the beach but could not recall ever seeing any children and, therefore, did not identify the resort as "family friendly." The resort had never turned away families but had focused marketing efforts primarily on affluent couples without children. Changing demographics forced the resort to reexamine the message conveyed by its advertising.

As a result, the resort launched a new marketing campaign in 1990. Advertising targeted families, and the staff prepared to cater to family-specific needs. The resort created sailing instruction programs for children and a host of activities designed to keep children busy while their parents enjoyed quiet time together. Family excursions onboard some of the resort's larger yachts provided the opportunity for families to sail together and explore some of the less inhabited islands. In addition, the resort added special Christmas, Easter, and Thanksgiving family programs that offered an entertaining atmosphere for the whole family. The resort changed, and the market was responding favorably as occupancy rates began to climb, even during the difficult slow season. Tom Fitch, the director of marketing and special promotions, also implemented several additional marketing initiatives in an attempt to increase occupancy during slower periods (Exhibit C14-3).

By 1994, the resort began to see initial indications that the marketing initiatives were working. Although the resort still had some difficulty in attracting guests during the period between June and August, the resort increased its occupancy rates during the period between September and December to 70 to 80 percent. The resort was rated as one of the best tropical resorts in the world by Conde Nast Traveler and maintained a strong position in the upscale segment of the BVIs. Peak season rates for double occupancy rooms ranged from $390 to $595 per day, with meals and access to all water sports equipment included.

Despite the resort's prime location for water sports activities and strong reputation as the premier water sports resort in the Caribbean, management remained concerned about being able to match the service levels provided by their competitors. Increased availability of water sports at competing resorts threatened the resort's differentiated market position. WIYCR managers knew that some of their former guests were vacationing at nearby Little Dix Bay because that resort now offered similar water sports activities and had rates that overlapped those offered at WIYCR. Guests had been dissatisfied with the declining level of service they had experienced during their last visit to WIYCR. WIYCR managers feared that this trend might continue if changes were not implemented soon.

Fast Tacks Weeks. Initial efforts to fill slow season periods centered on leveraging the resort's competitive advantage. Fitch developed the Fast Tacks Program, which targeted specific sailing groups and utilized the resort's vast sailing resources. These groups ranged from racing to cruising, from families to couples, from senior citizens to young adults. During certain weeks in the historically slow fall season, sailing celebrities were invited and gave specialized seminars to guests. Perhaps the most widely noted week is the ProAm week, in which guests are assigned to teams with some of the top match racing skippers in the world. In addition to becoming a major source of income for the resort, the weeks have become a key free advertising vehicle. Articles in sailing magazines have served not only to promote the weeks themselves but have also increased reader awareness of the sailing experience that the resort can offer.

Family Weeks.   To change the resort's image, Fitch marketed special programs during traditional school break periods to families. These weeks provided special services, including instructional and recreational programs, for children and young adults. By providing a fun yet safe environment for children, parents were free to spend time alone enjoying activities designed for their tastes (e.g., harbor sunset cruises). In addition, there were several family excursions planned throughout the week that offered an opportunity to enjoy exploring reefs and other islands together.

Capturing the Market Earlier.   In addition to the family weeks and Fast Tacks weeks, marketers realized that there was another market that they had been ignoring that could significantly reduce some of its occupancy cycle troubles. Instead of waiting until a couple had established themselves or started a family, why not get them when they were tying the knot? After all, the resort provided one of the most romantic atmospheres in the Caribbean. Moreover, the majority of weddings in North America, the primary market for the resort, occur during the slow periods of summer and fall. In response to this revelation, the resort began to actively market wedding and honeymoon packages. The resort hoped that these guests would return for second, third, and fourth honeymoons and bring their children when they started their families.

The WIYCR Organization

Company Headquarters

Kimball insisted on managing strategic planning, finance, and reservations activities from an office in Chicago, Illinois (see Exhibit C14-4). He wanted to live in the United States and attend to other investments (none of which were in hospitality) and argued that these activities were easily separated from the day-to-day operations that took place at the resort. As the resort expanded and Kimball grew older (he was now in his 70s), he visited WIYCR less frequently and never during peak weeks. Moreover, Kimball, who once prided himself on knowing the name of each employee at the resort, knew fewer and fewer of his employees by name. As a result, when he did visit the resort the

local employees thought that Kimball seemed increasingly removed and distant.

Marketing and Special Promotions

Kimball firmly believed that marketing activities should take place close to the consumer. As a result, Tom Fitch, the 32-year-old marketing and special promotions director, managed from a small office in the southwestern corner of Connecticut. Fitch grew up as an active sailing competitor on Long Island Sound (an area that stretches from New York City to the southeastern tip of Connecticut) sailing circuit and was well connected within the sailing industry. Fitch's strong sailing background coupled with being centrally located within the largest sailing community in the United States afforded great opportunities for promoting the resort with its target market. Unlike Kimball, Fitch was always on property during the high season and special promotions weeks. Fitch believed that it was important during these weeks for him to tend to the special needs of guests he had attracted to the resort. Local employees often underestimated the work required to plan and market these programs. Seeing him socialize with guests while on property, local employees questioned whether his job was really full-time once he left the resort and returned to the states. After all, they only saw him periodically when he came in for a few weeks, threw large parties, and frantically tried to assure that the guests' needs were met.

Jim Johnson, General Manager

In the WIYCR organization, the general manger traditionally oversaw all functional areas of the hotel and played an important role in strategic planning. Jim Johnson, the 48-year-old expatriate general manager originally from the United States, was hired in 1990 based on his extensive hospitality experience and academic training. His experience included several years as assistant manager of Little Dix Bay Resort and a master's degree in hospitality management from Cornell University. Johnson worked from his home in Miami, Florida, most of the time in order to spend more time with his family, provide his children with stronger educational opportunities than those offered in the BVIs, and to reduce the number of expatriate permits that the resort required. Johnson averaged approximately 2 weeks at the resort per month, staying for longer periods of time during the high season and shorter

▪▪▪▪▪▪▪▪▪▪ **EXHIBIT C14-4 West Indies Yacht Club Resort Organizational Chart**

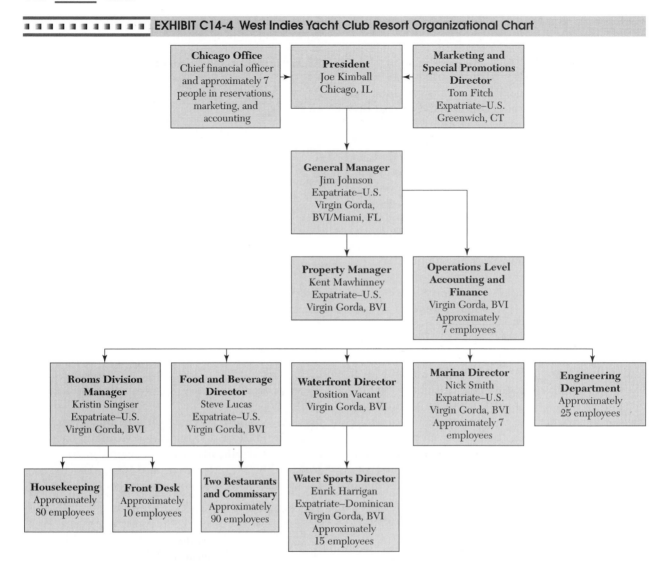

periods of time during the low season. Johnson spent most of the time while at the resort in his office and in meetings with the heads of the various departments. Local employees often referred to him as a "behind the scenes" manager; he provided detailed goals, objectives, and actions for his staff but was not present for the execution of plans. Johnson generally felt confident in his management team, especially his property manager whom he personally recruited and hired.

Kent Mawhinney, Property Manager

The property manager was generally the second in command at the WIYCR and was responsible for implementing the general manager's plans and moni-

toring the results. Kent Mawhinney, the 40-year-old property manager from the United States, was hired by Johnson in 1992 and had an impressive background that included working on the management staff for 6 years at Caneel Bay, a Rockefeller Resort located on nearby St. John (in the U.S. Virgin Islands). Mawhinney was a hands-on manager who believed that "management by walking around" was needed in the Caribbean. Resort employees knew Mawhinney as a manager who was willing to get his hands dirty, and they greatly appreciated this attitude.

Kristin Singiser, Rooms Division Manager

The rooms division manager was responsible for two departments at the WIYCR: housekeeping and the front desk. To many guests, it seemed like Singiser had been at the resort forever. In fact, Singiser had been hired in 1985 as part of the front desk staff and was now 35 years old. She was born and raised in the midwestern United States. She came to the resort with little hotel industry experience, had only been to the Caribbean as a tourist prior to taking the job, and proceeded to work her way up in the WIYCR organization to her current position. She was well respected by the guests and local staff because of her never-ending energy and constant smile. However, after 11 years at the property, Singiser was beginning to get more frustrated with problems she faced over and over again. Her staff knew how Singiser felt but also knew that the issues were mainly between her and the Chicago office.

Steve Lucas, Food and Beverage Director

The food and beverage director was responsible for two restaurants, a commissary, an employee dining facility, and three bars that were located on the WIYCR property. The resort had experienced high turnover in this position, with three food and beverage directors resigning to return to the United States within the past 2 years alone. Steve Lucas, 28 years old with recent experience working as the food and beverage director for an exclusive California resort, was currently filling this position. Lucas was from the United States and had an impressive restaurant industry track record. He was hired by the resort in the middle of November 1994 and arrived at the property during the first week of December. Lucas had no previous experience working outside the United States.

Nick Smith, Marina Director

The marina director was responsible for the resort's growing marina operations, run largely out of the Davy Jones marina. This marina included dock space for up to 35 boats, a fuel and water dock, and yacht maintenance services. The marina attracted yachting enthusiasts who were seeking a short stay in a resort environment. Nick Smith was promoted 8 years ago to his current position as marina director. Smith, now 45 years old, was originally from the United States and had been working at the resort for nearly 15 years. He lived on the property along with his wife and their 6-year-old daughter.

Waterfront Director

The waterfront director's position was created to assign responsibility to oversee the growing waterfront activities at the resort. The director's responsibilities included overseeing the water sports department and its director (as well as the resort's fleet of day excursion boats), planning and promoting day excursions, and developing and maintaining relationships with the sites that day excursions visited. The resort had hired several expatriates for the waterfront director position. For a variety of reasons, these expatriates had not worked out. Two had become alcoholics, and one had mysteriously packed his belongings and departed in the middle of the night. This position was currently vacant, with most responsibilities assumed by Nick Smith and Enrik Harrigan.

Enrik Harrigan, Water Sports Director

The water sports director was primarily responsible for the resort's fleet of small- to medium-sized boats and its windsurfing program. From 1986 until 1992, the water sports department had been under the leadership of Bill Jones, a Canadian who fell in love with the resort while staying there as a guest. His easygoing management style was well respected by a staff that would seemingly do anything for him. Unfortunately for the resort, Bill returned to Canada in 1992. The next most senior member of the water sports staff was 27-year-old Enrik Harrigan, a windsurfing guru from Dominica (part of the Windward Island chain located in the southern Caribbean Sea) who had been working at the resort for about 5 years. Harrigan assumed the responsibilities as water sports director and was well respected by the staff but found he had difficulty assigning tasks and managing the operation.

Dowd Arrives in the British Virgin Islands

On December 15, 1994, Dowd arrived at WIYCR. He found it hard to imagine the imminent transformation of the serene British Virgin Islands into an environment overwhelmed by a frenzy of holiday tourist activity. Within a few days, thousands of tourists would invade the BVIs, stretching its natural, human, and capital resources to their limits. The natural beauty that the islands offered was a familiar sight for Dowd, who had spent 10 years working as a management consultant for small- to medium-sized hotels in the Caribbean. Tradewind Ventures, a world-renowned sailing school, introduced him to the British Virgin Islands through summer employment as a skipper and operations director in 1986. For the next 6 years, Dowd worked year-round for Tradewind Ventures as a management consultant during the winter months and operations director during the summer. During his tenure with Tradewind Ventures, Dowd added the Cabarete Beach Hotel (Cabarete, Dominican Republic) and the West Indies Yacht Club Resort (Virgin Gorda, British Virgin Islands) to his client base. In addition, Dowd had completed his bachelor of science and masters in business administration at Babson College. The primary point of differentiation between Dowd's consulting service and those offered by the larger consulting companies rested in his understanding of the Caribbean market and, most importantly, its people. His understanding had evolved through interactions both professionally and socially with local nationals from the region. Mike McClane, manager of a nearby charter boat company, respected Dowd's ability to understand the local nationals, saying, "You really must understand my employees. Heck, Small Craft (employee's nickname) considers you a friend, and I'm the only other outsider I know to accomplish that. It took me 5 years; you've done it in two summers!"

Driven largely by his desire to study the challenges associated with expatriate management assignments, Dowd had entered the doctoral program in hotel administration at Cornell University in September 1994. Dowd hoped that his understanding of the local culture would be enhanced by what he had learned over the past semester in the classroom at Cornell. His first semester introduced him to theoretical explanations for differences in behaviors across cultures. He wondered whether these tools would be helpful for interpreting behaviors and then communicating what they meant to Johnson and his managers.

Dowd's Observations of Operations

Night had fallen on the Caribbean and as the North Sound Express [a ferry that takes passengers from the Beef Island Airport on Tortola to various resort locations on Virgin Gorda (Exhibit C14-1)] approached the main dock at WIYCR, Dowd noticed the familiar stride of a former colleague from

Tradewind Ventures. Dave Pickering, a 22-year-old Cleveland native, had been working in the water sports department for nearly a month and was looking forward to Dowd's arrival. Pickering had worked with Dowd for the past three summers as a skipper and program director at Tradewind Ventures. Although Pickering had worked in the Caribbean for these three summers, his interactions had been primarily with the expatriate staff that Tradewind Ventures brought down each summer. Working side by side with the locals was a much different experience. Pickering had been hired by WIYCR in early December 1994 as part of the water sports staff. He was primarily responsible for teaching sailing lessons, taking guests out on the larger boats, and signing out water sports equipment to guests.

Pickering extended an enthusiastic and firm handshake as Dowd got off the ferry. "Welcome to The Rock," he said. "The Rock" was the term coined by expatriates to describe living at the secluded resort. The two walked up the dock, and Pickering paused for a minute. "Looks like someone forgot to come out and greet the guests again. It will take me a few minutes to give the briefing, so go along to the front desk if you want. I'm sure you're familiar with the routine. We're going out to Saba Rock (a small island about 300 feet off the resort's north beach) in about a half-hour, so why don't you drop your stuff in your room and meet me at the dinghy dock." Dowd nodded and headed for the front desk.

Kristin Singiser met Dowd at the front desk, and they exchanged greetings. Suddenly, Singiser looked confused. "Who met you down on the docks?" she asked.

"Dave was down there and is giving the guest briefing," he replied.

"That's odd. Dave is supposed to be off tonight. I wonder who was supposed to meet you down there?" Singiser said with a disturbed look on her face. She assigned Dowd to his room, picked up the radio microphone, and called one of the golf cart chauffeurs to come for him. As Dowd walked out of the lobby, he thought, "What would have happened if nobody showed up to greet us? Sure, I'm working here, but those people who were on the boat with me are paying thousands of dollars to be here. What would they think?"

Although Dowd knew that he had an 8:00 A.M. meeting with Johnson, he could not help but enjoy the company of his island friends. Saba Rock was the only real hideout for expatriates and local national employees from WIYCR. A few tourists managed to find a dinghy ride out to the small pub on the half-acre island, but they were usually the more adventurous types and were always welcome.

Pickering always had such a positive disposition; however, tonight a hint of irritability seemed to come across in his voice. "You know why I am here . . . right?" Dowd asked.

"Yes, I think so. Kent Mawhinney told me something about you coming down here to observe operations and make some suggestions for improvements. Boy, do I have some suggestions. How about firing everyone and bringing down our old staff from Tradewind Ventures?" he candidly replied. Dowd couldn't help but inquire further. Pickering said that when he arrived a few weeks earlier, the employees really welcomed him aboard. This seemed normal; Pickering had always been considered one of the more affable members of the Tradewind Ventures staff. Pickering said that each day coworkers in the water sports department distanced themselves more and more. Pickering said, "The harder I work, the greater the distance between us becomes."

"I don't understand," Pickering continued. "I've even tried to do some of their work to get back in good favor with them, but nothing seems to work. It's gotten to the point where I think some of these guys don't like me at all."

As Pickering continued, he questioned whether the resort's compensation system could ever work. Employees were paid an hourly rate based on their tenure at the resort. As Pickering understood the resort's compensation system, each year resort employees were given a raise without any performance review. Dowd asked Pickering for some concrete examples of why the system wasn't working. Pickering explained, "Even some of the most senior guys in the water sports department hide from work. These senior employees know that they will get raises even if they don't do a good job . . . excuse me, these guys get raises even if they don't do their job at all."

Pickering did not understand why the locals weren't taking advantage of the opportunity to get tips. Pickering was making $50 to $100 extra per day on tips alone; when he told his fellow employees this, they laughed and said it wasn't worth that much to them to have to work so hard. Dowd asked if Pickering had discussed his concerns with any of the managers. Pickering replied that he'd had a few conversations with Mawhinney about it but hadn't been able to find an opportunity to speak with Johnson. The discussion continued until Dowd's eyes began to grow heavy. He climbed in a dinghy and headed back to the resort.

Johnson arrived at the Clubhouse Restaurant just a few minutes past 8 A.M. Dowd had already found his way to the breakfast buffet and sat with a plate full of local fruits and pastries. Johnson seemed rushed and told Dowd that he would have to keep the meeting short. Johnson told Dowd that he did not want to influence Dowd's observations by explaining what he thought were the problem areas at the resort. Instead, Johnson would point out departments generating complaints and let Dowd observe without any biases. Dowd realized that this would be difficult because he knew so many of the employees, but it was a role in which Dowd had been successful in the past. Dowd found that getting to the bottom of problems in organizations in the Caribbean often required gaining acceptance by the group, a status that was achieved only through gaining local employees' trust and establishing friendships. It was only then that employees would open up. Johnson wanted Dowd to focus on front desk, food and beverage, and water sports services and indicated that the resort's staff was at Dowd's service in terms of discussing operations. Johnson finished his coffee, wished Dowd's luck, and left. As he watched Johnson walk out the door, Dowd thought, "It's always so easy to pick out the expatriate down here . . . we always seem in such a hurry."

Dowd finished his breakfast and made his way down the shoreline to meet with Mawhinney, the property manager. He was greeted by Mawhinney at the top of the spiral staircase leading to the administrative offices. Mawhinney told Dowd that he was leaving on his daily rounds and asked Dowd to join him. Mawhinney had extensive experience working in the Caribbean, and Dowd knew he would be a rich resource. As they walked off to their first stop, Dowd bluntly asked Mawhinney what he thought the main problems were at the resort. Mawhinney replied that the most basic problem was getting plans implemented. When Mawhinney managed in the United States, his employees had been concerned with the opportunity for advancement and really worked hard to prove themselves. In the Caribbean, things were different. Local employment laws almost guaranteed jobs, and employees knew this. As a result, employees were more concerned with fitting in with their coworkers than with making a good impression. The resort had provided opportunities for some of the locals to be promoted, but few seemed interested. In his opinion, locals did not want the added responsibility, even if it meant more money. In some cases, the resort thought that rewarding the best employees with a title and some authority would help management gain more control over their employees. The result was an employee with a title who was unwilling to take on any of the job's responsibilities. "If the employees only realized what they could have if they worked a little harder and took these positions seriously, they could move up in the organization," Mawhinney commented.

The property tour took about an hour. Mawhinney visited each department head, a mix of local nationals and expatriates (see Exhibit C14-4). His conversations instilled a sense of urgency to get the resort in shape for the coming week. In each case, he offered assistance in any way necessary to ensure reaching the resort's desired goals and objectives. Dowd was particularly impressed by the amount of detail that Mawhinney recalled regarding each manager's immediate challenges. Mawhinney pointed out to Dowd that one of the main differences between managing in the United States and managing in the Caribbean is how managers have to communicate with employees. Because there is a 70 percent functional illiteracy rate on the property, he could not rely on memos as he had in the States. Instead, he managed by physically demonstrating to his staff what had to be done. For example, Mawhinney's maintenance staff had been told several times that garbage was to be placed in a specific storage area. The staff continued storing the trash in the wrong place until Mawhinney physically showed them where and how it was to be stored.

By 10:30 A.M., Mawhinney and Dowd had completed the tour of the resort with the exception of the restaurants. As the two approached the clubhouse dining area, Dowd noticed a man in his early 30s arguing with a local cook who looked to be in his 50s. (Later, Dowd would find out that this was the head chef, who had worked at the resort for more than 20 years.)

"Why didn't you tell me that you couldn't get the ingredients for cheesecake? The menus have already been printed, and now we're going to look like fools! What is wrong with you people?" the man asked the cook.

Mawhinney interrupted, "Steve, what seems to be the problem?"

"Well, once again they failed to tell me that something was wrong," Lucas replied.

Mawhinney looked at the cook and asked if he could have a moment alone with Lucas. The cook welcomed the opportunity to leave the tense situation. Mawhinney calmed Lucas down and said that it was just part of the challenge of working in paradise. Mawhinney guided Lucas back over to Dowd, introduced the two, and informed Dowd that he had to get back to his office for a conference call with the resort's head office in Chicago.

Lucas and Dowd exchanged stories about their backgrounds. Lucas had been hired 2 weeks ago because the former food and beverage director had quit. When Dowd asked him whether he liked his new job, Lucas replied:

It's a bit early to tell. One thing is for sure . . . it's a lot more challenging than I ever imagined! I know the staff has been here for a while, but I don't know how they ever managed. They seem to work as a "seat of your pants" type operation. No planning, no commitment, no enthusiasm. It's surprising, because I have heard that this resort is one of the best places for people down here to work. I guess the biggest challenge is the fact that I know the people in Chicago expect big things from me, and I plan to deliver . . . no matter what it takes. I just wish I had more time to train these people properly before we are hit with the big rush next week. Did you know that The Clubhouse and The Carvery are expected to serve 1,000 dinners on New Year's Eve? After dinner, we expect that another 500 to 800 charter boat tourists will be coming ashore for the entertainment at the bar. Meanwhile, my staff is accustomed to our average nightly seating of about 100 for the rest of the year. This will be a big test for them . . . and, I guess for me, as well.

Dowd asked Lucas how he was adjusting to the local culture. "I am having a great time so far. It's so much fun hanging out with a different group of guests every week. I am not looking forward to the slow season around here though. Then, who will I have to hang around with? I haven't made very many local friends and that's mostly because I want to keep business and pleasure separate anyway."

Their conversation went on for another 20 minutes. Finally, Lucas looked eager to get back to overseeing the preparations for tonight's meal, so Dowd closed the conversation and moved on. As Dowd walked away, he stopped to glance back at Lucas. Lucas was hovering over one of his staff, checking to make sure that each ingredient was properly measured before being added to the pot. "What a way to have to manage," Dowd thought.

Singiser entered the restaurant with an apologetic look on her face. "Sorry I am so late. Glad you found yourself a piña colada to keep you occupied," she said.

"So, what took you so long?" Dowd asked jokingly.

Singiser explained that it had been a long day. The Chicago office had over-booked the resort by 20 percent for the coming week without telling the guests that there might be some inconveniences. Therefore, it was her job to greet guests on the dock and tell some of them that they would have to stay on board one of the resort's larger charter boats for a few nights until rooms became available. Meanwhile, other families were told that the children and parents would be staying at opposite ends of the resort. As if dealing with understandably irate guests was not enough, her staff had made several disturbing remarks.

"They asked me, 'Why is everyone always coming down on us about providing good service when Chicago pulls a stunt like this?' I just don't know how to reply. My staff faces angry guests all day as a result of this fiasco. How can I expect them to be courteous when the guests are so mad and the staff had no influence on the situation? The worst part is that Chicago has done this to us for the past 3 years. Each time, I tell my staff to just manage this time and I'll try to make sure it doesn't happen again. I go to bat for them but seem to strike out every time."

Over a lobster dinner, the two discussed many other challenges that Singiser had faced over the years. Much of the locals' behavior she had become accustomed to, but some things were still frustrating, "Sometimes you feel like the only way you can manage these people is to bash them over the head with it," she commented. Apparently, her style was to demonstrate exactly what she expected of her front desk staff, knowing that some of then would get it

right and others would continue to do it their own way. When they continued to do it their own way, it was time for "bashing them over the head with it." Despite all of her frustrations, Singiser was probably the most respected expatriate on the WIYCR staff. Over her long tenure, she had adapted to the local culture, made close friends with the locals, and recognized what it took to get things done. However, she still felt challenged when trying to motivate her staff. "Money, opportunity for advancement, all of the normal incentives—they all don't seem to make any impact," she said.

In previous conversations with Singiser's staff, Dowd had solicited their opinions. Most staff said that Singiser was different. She had a sincere interest in them and was involved with the local culture. She frequently took trips with her staff to the neighboring islands and invited employees to her bungalow for dinner on occasion. Sure, she was tough, but her staff felt that managers had to be that way sometimes.

As they finished their meals and enjoyed an after-dinner drink, Singiser suggested that Dowd spend at least a day working alongside the staff at water sports. That would give him an inside look at a department critical to the resort's success. After all, water sports were the main reason that guests chose the resort for their vacation.

Walking down the path to the water sports shack, Dowd knew that he had an interesting day ahead of him. He had extensive water sports experience but had only observed WIYCR's operations from a guest's perspective. Throughout the day, Dowd took mental notes on how the department operated and how the locals worked (or didn't work). Harrigan was behind the desk at the shack most of the day; his assistant Mitchell (a 25-year-old local Virgin Gordan) raced about the harbor on a 15-foot Whaler (a small powerboat) taking guests out to boats. It was surprising that Harrigan allowed some of his senior staff to avoid work. Fergus and Muhammad (both in their late 20s and from Virgin Gorda), for example, conveniently wandered off during the peak morning rush. Guests were left standing in line for 15 minutes because the desk was short-staffed. With Fergus' and Muhammad's help at the desk, Dowd thought that the wait could be reduced to 5 minutes. The daylight sun was waning, and guests wanted to get out on the water. When some of the senior staff did interact with guests, they were reserved and not overly courteous. Guests asked questions, and the staff mumbled incoherent responses. However, one group of guests did have an advantage: guests who had bought several rounds of drinks for the staff the previous evening. When these guests arrived at the desk, the senior staff would jump to their feet and greet them like these guests were part of the local family. Dowd jokingly referred to this as "pre-service tipping."

Working at the water sports department, Dowd found himself hustling the whole day, thinking that maybe some of it would rub off on his fellow workers. He had a slight advantage over Pickering's socialization into the group because Dowd had worked alongside the local staff during the three previous Thanksgiving vacations as part of a joint project between WIYCR and Tradewind Ventures. The group had accepted him long ago. He thought, "Maybe if they see me working hard, they will think its OK." By the end of his first day, Dowd had earned $100 in tips. He told the local staff, and they didn't believe him until he laid the money on the counter. He explained how they could easily do the same thing and make a killing this week. They reluctantly replied, "Yeah, right, like we could do that."

At the end of the day, Dowd, Fergus, and Muhammad stopped for a beer at the commissary (a small snack bar). Dowd asked them how they thought things were going in the water sports department. Fergus replied, "Things went more smoothly when Bill (Jones) was around. He gave us clear directions regarding what we had to do for the day, and we did it. Things are different with Enrik (Harrigan). He's really laid back, and we often don't know what we're supposed to be doing." Dowd also inquired about how they felt about the expatriates that worked at the resort, and Muhammad's comments summarized the discussion. "We have so many managers from the States, and they don't stay here very long. Many of them think they can just come in here, and we'll instantly be their friends. I'm tired of making friends just to have them leave a year later. The worst part is that they think we want to become managers like them. Managing people takes too much effort. I'm just not interested in leaving my friends behind just to make a little more money."

When Dowd was not speaking with the resort's management or its employees, he spent his time with the guests. The following quotes summarized the comments made by guests regarding guest interactions with resort's staff: There was nothing for us to do at

night from December 23 until December 26. I know that the staff has to celebrate Christmas, but it would have been nice for us to have something to do.

I was waiting in line for almost 10 minutes at the bar. They only had two bartenders on, and they moved so slowly. Plus, all the guests are getting their own drinks. Why do they have five waitresses? They just stood there. Can't they work behind the bar, too?

We were out on the Almond Walk (a terrace area attached to the resort's main restaurant) and thought that a waiter would come by. When we asked one of the waitresses, she said that she was assigned to the dining room. The dining room had served its last guest an hour before and was located about 25 feet from the Almond Walk. Someone should tell them that it's OK to go out onto the walk and serve other guests.

I asked the restaurant manager to call a waiter over for me, but I'll never do that again. He went over to his wait staff and told them that they were incompetent. I felt so bad. I think that the staff purposely avoided our table for the rest of the night because they were afraid of getting into trouble again.

I was looking forward to being greeted at the docks by someone who would help me with my bags. After all, I'd just finished a 10-hour trip and am paying a lot of money to be here. When I asked the front desk staff, they apologized and said that someone must have forgotten. It's surprising that I am paying this much money for people to forget. What's that about first impressions being the most important?

Reading the brochure, I really thought that the programs for the kids sounded great. However, the first few days my kids said that the staff weren't very interested in making them have a good time. They seemed like they were more interested in when they got off work than with making my kids have a good time. Then they had Dave. What a difference! The kids came back excited about everything they did that day. He was so energetic and interested in my kids.

I told the front desk that they should really spray for bugs out on the terrace or get one of those bug lamps. There are so many mosquitoes out there in the evening. The staff doesn't seem to be too interested in responding though.

We called maintenance the other day to tell them that our rooms are not fully operational in terms of things like showers, screens, and faucets working. It's kind of surprising to be at a resort like this without at least the basics. They said they would send someone by today, but that was 3 days ago. I think I will go to one of the other managers next.

Today I went to the beach at around 10 A.M., and they were already out of towels again. The beach attendant said that he would bring some back as soon as he found them. I guess he didn't find any because it's been 3 hours, although I did see him standing around at the other end of the resort talking with some friends. Do you think he even looked for them?

Listening to these comments, Dowd wondered which problems related to poor management relations with local staff, which related to simply poor work by the local staff, and which related to poor managing by the expatriates. One thing was sure—issues in all of these areas were beginning to affect the guests.

Making Sense of It All

Dowd had been at the resort for just 1 week, and the information from interviews with managers, local employees, and resort guests along with personal observations filled his head as he began to prepare for his meeting with Johnson the following morning. It was clear that there needed to be

some changes at the resort if Johnson was going to resolve the issues concerning expatriate turnover, increasing guest complaints, and the level of tension between some of the expatriate managers and the local employees. The first wave of peak season guests, those coming for the Christmas holiday, would arrive tomorrow and stretch the resort's resources to their limits. Dowd wondered how he could best use the information gathered to analyze the current situation and provide some course of action for Johnson that would address his concerns. Dowd sat at his table and began to organize his thoughts. ■

This case was prepared as a basis for class discussion rather than to illustrate either effective or ineffective management. All individuals and events are real but the name of the company and its managers and staff have been disguised at the request of the organization. The case benefited from the suggestions of several anonymous reviewers from the Case Research Journal. The author also wishes to acknowledge the company's management for their assistance in gathering data for the case.

"West Indies Yacht Club Resort: When Cultures Collide" by Jeffrey P. Shay from Case Research Journal, 2001, pp. 109–127. Copyright © 2001 by the Case Research Journal and Jeffrey P. Shay.

Case 15   Ireka Construction Berhad: A Chinese Family Business Goes Public

Anne Marie Francesco

Lai Siew Wah, the managing director of Ireka Construction Berhad, put down his paper. It was October 1997 and the newspaper was filled with more bad news about the Malaysian economy and the economies of the neighboring countries. After 30 years in business, Mr. Lai had seen a lot. The company certainly had come a long way from those early days when he was more or less on his own. Ireka was a public listed company with big plans for the future, but, with the worsening economic situation, did the company need to change all those plans?

Company History

Ireka Construction Berhad was founded by Lai Siew Wah[1] in Kuala Lumpur, Malaysia in 1967. Mr. Lai's company specialized in earthmoving contract work for tin mines, factory sites, housing lots, and roadwork construction. The company was established as a sole proprietorship and run as a family business. Chan Kay Chong, Lai Siew Wah's brother-in-law, joined the company in 1975, and Mr. Lai's brother, Lai Foot Kong, who had been helping out informally, began working full time with him in 1977.

In the mid-1970s, the Malaysian government started to upgrade the road system, and this provided an opportunity for the small family business to expand. The business changed from a sole proprietorship (Syarikat Lai Siew Wah) to a private limited company (Lai Siew Wah Sdn. Bhd.) at the end of 1975. The company took work as a subcontractor initially but later was able to become a registered government contractor.

As the management gained experience, they were able to take on more complex engineering construction projects, many for the government. From roadworks, they moved on to bridges and flyovers

(overpasses), and infrastructure projects became a major strength.

However, in 1984 and 1985, Malaysia experienced a recession. The country had a negative GNP, and there were difficult times for all. Many companies went out of business. However, Lai Siew Wah Sdn. Bhd. was able to keep going with the tin mining work that was available. Throughout this difficult period, the company did not lay off any staff, and there were no reductions in salary. In return, the staff developed a strong loyalty to the company and the family.

By 1986, the market started to come back. Because the company was known as a performing contractor, it was able to obtain work on three packages of the new 900 kilometer North-South Highway in peninsular Malaysia.

At this time, Lai Siew Wah also began to consider expansion and bringing in non-family members and decided that having the company bear his own name was too personalized. So the name of the company was changed to Ireka Construction Sdn. Bhd. The name Ireka comes from the Malay word *reka* meaning "create" with an English word "I" in front to make it more meaningful: "I create."

In the late 1980s and early 1990s, the Malaysian government encouraged companies to go public, and a second stock exchange was established in Kuala Lumpur. As construction jobs were getting larger, it was also becoming more important to have access to larger amounts of funding. Consequently, on June 12, 1992, Ireka Construction Sdn Bhd. became a public company known as Ireka Construction Bhd, and in July 1993 they were listed on the second board of the Kuala Lumpur Stock Exchange.

During this period, Ireka's business was also becoming more diversified. In 1988, almost half the business came from public sector related construction work, but by 1993 that type of business represented less than five percent of the total. Instead, most contracts were with private corporations. The

---

[1]Malaysian Chinese generally put their surnames first.

416

company became a Malaysian government registered "Class A" contractor, meaning that it could bid for and undertake construction projects of unlimited value. Because of the company's status as a listed company, Ireka now had greater visibility within Malaysia and also the ability to raise significant amounts of capital to fund these large projects.

Ireka's construction activities included water supply and treatment plants, steel structural work, buildings, golf courses, and turnkey/design and build construction projects that made use of special construction techniques such as the Indonesian *sorsobahu* (thousand shoulders), which minimizes traffic disruption while building overpasses in congested areas, and the French *autopont* (highway bridge), a fast-track pre-fabricated steel overpass construction system.

In the mid-90s, Ireka diversified into hotel and property development. In its most ambitious undertaking to date, the company began in 1994 to acquire land and to make plans to build a five star luxury hotel at a prime site in downtown Kuala Lumpur. Ireka took total responsibility for the project as developer, architect, and contractor, and in 1996, the company signed a management agreement with Westin Hotel Company to operate the hotel as Westin's first Kuala Lumpur property. They hoped that the hotel would be ready for a gala millennium New Year's Eve opening on December 31, 1999.

In 1996 Ireka had its first successes outside Malaysia. An Ireka led consortium signed a memorandum of understanding with the Philippine National Construction Corporation to finance, design, and construct a section of an elevated highway system in Manila, Philippines. In 1997, the company was actively pursuing possible projects in Myanmar, India, the Philippines, and China.

In 1997, Ireka employed over 500 people and had an after-tax profit of RM7,584,000 on turnover of RM171,169,000.[2] It also owned and operated one of the largest fleets of civil engineering plants and machinery in Malaysia. The Ireka vision was

To play a prominent role in **nation-building** and to consolidate and improve on our position as one of the country's **most progressive** and **reputable** construction-based companies through strong emphasis on **timely completion** of our

projects and **quality** of construction made possible by cohesive **teamwork** and strength in management.

Our motto is to serve, to build and not to yield.

The Lai Family and Ireka Corporate Strategy

Although Ireka became a public company in 1992, over half the shares in 1997 were still owned by Lai Siew Wah and his family or companies that were wholly controlled by them. The Lai family also took an active role in running day to day operations. Lai Siew Wah was the managing director; his brother, Lai Foot Kong, the deputy managing director; their sister, Lai Man Moi, the director (finance), and her husband, Chan Kay Chong, the director (administration). Members of the second generation also held important positions. Lai Siew Wah's oldest son, Lai Voon Hon, was the director/group general manager, and Lai Siew Wah's daughter, Monica Lai, was the financial controller.

The board of directors also had some non-family members. These were highly qualified professionals including two retired corporate lawyers and a mining engineer.

The Family's Vision of the Future

According to Mr. Lai Foot Kong, going public meant the company had to be prepared to accept new ideas. He felt that the modern way of doing business would be beneficial for the growth of the company. "We can not blindly adopt Western systems. The management systems must be adapted to the needs of the region. Fine tuning is needed, and we must adapt to the mentality and culture of the locals."

In the future, the directors planned to place more emphasis on qualification in selecting people for management positions within the company. Their idea was to reduce the family business image by making sure that whoever was in a position had the training and experience necessary to do the job. They wanted equal opportunities for both family members and others to take control with the decision based on who was best qualified.

Although two of Lai Siew Wah's children held important positions in the company, both had relevant education and experience before they took their jobs. Lai Voon Hon had both a degree in architecture

---

[2]On December 31, 1997, the exchange rate was US$1 = RM3.87.

and an MBA from well-known universities in England and had worked as a design architect and a project architect for leading architectural firms in London, Hong Kong, and Kuala Lumpur. Monica Lai had also been educated in the U.K. and was a qualified chartered accountant. She too had worked in London and Hong Kong for top international accounting firms.

Interestingly, many of the more senior management positions that were not held by family members had been filled after the company went public or immediately before. That group of managers included mostly young, well-qualified professionals, hired through executive search firms or through the directors' client/associate network.

Mr. Chan Kay Chong believed that Ireka needed to continue to recruit more educated people and that they would need new management to lead the company. The future leaders of the company would be those who were best suited for the positions, not just family members. His nephew, Voon Hon, and his niece, Monica, had both the qualifications and the interest to work for Ireka, but he himself had no intention of bringing his own children into the business. Mr. Chan felt that the company needed to expand and diversify and that they could not remain in one business all the time. So, the company was always looking for new ideas.

In fact, as a means of getting outside opinions, when Lai Voon Hon was doing his MBA, he worked with a consultant from his university to study the future strategic direction of Ireka. The report had been very influential in shaping the future of the company and setting a general path for transition and growth. It also gave Voon Hon a very good idea of what he would encounter when he took up his position with Ireka a year later. In the three years that he had been with the company, 80 percent of the recommendations from his report had been implemented.

Many of the engineers and senior staff working in Ireka had been with the company for a long time. In the "old days," the management style was very "hands on." The directors had frequent contact with everyone and followed the work progress very closely. There was still a feeling of closeness among the staff, almost like a family unit themselves, and Lai Siew Wah had a great deal of contact with operations where people felt free to openly discuss their problems with him. However, with a workforce of 500 spread out among many different work sites, it was now difficult to have the same level of contact with everyone as before.

The directors wanted to maintain the feeling of closeness among staff as they grew, but the many new people often posed a threat to the older staff. As Ireka diversified and became involved in more sophisticated types of projects, the need for well qualified professional employees kept increasing. Although the management was proud of its history of retaining staff, even when times were tough, they were not willing to promote people based only on loyalty or seniority. As a result, some older, more senior people left the company because they didn't see any future. Many of those who started their own businesses returned as subcontractors for Ireka. Some joined the competition.

For Lai Voon Hon, a major challenge was how to keep existing staff happy and bring in new people. He felt the company would fare better in the long run if they could maintain the feelings of family and togetherness. Ireka needed to find a way to bring the two groups of people together so that all could contribute.

Some of the key things the management was trying to focus on to meet this challenge included:

1. *Developing a clear organizational structure.* Ireka had developed formal job descriptions in 1997 and had revised the organization structure twice within the year to respond to changes and growth in operations. The purpose was to make sure that each person was clear what his or her responsibilities were and what career paths might be open.

2. *Improving communications.* Since the company was growing rapidly, the managing director could not have the opportunity to talk to all the employees all the time. But, it was still important that people talked to each other to find out what both management and staff were doing. Particularly, with employees working at many different project sites, it was important that both headquarters and the sites knew what was going on.

Ireka also wanted to improve communications to promote a positive working climate and maintain the feelings of family. The directors wanted people to feel comfortable working together so they tried to provide both formal and informal opportunities for people to meet and exchange information.

In 1994, Ireka started a company Sports and Recreation Club. The club organized team sports and outings for the employees and their families. In 1996, the Club was formally recognized by the Malaysian government Registrar of Societies, and Ireka pledged RM25,000 as an initial fund for the operation of the club.

There was also a newsletter distributed to all staff produced by the human resources department. The *Ireka Newsletter* came out on a bimonthly basis and included company and staff news with lots of pictures and staff contributions.

Another means for improving communication was the formation of the Projects Operations Supervisory Board (POSB). The POSB included the three project directors and the managing director. These were the most senior level managers responsible for actual operations. By having a formal communication channel through the POSB, the senior people were better informed about the status of ongoing projects and they were able to share or transfer resources when needed.

In mid-1996, the company had also established a Head of Divisions Forum that included the various division heads and the board of directors. The group of about 20 met after work about once a month to discuss strategic issues and current and future plans for the company. Although it seemed at the beginning to be all one way communication (with the directors doing all the talking), over time the division heads began to express themselves more. The division heads were sometimes reluctant to speak up as they were concerned that top management would not listen to them and that it was not appropriate to criticize those in more senior positions.

3. *Setting a clear corporate vision.* The third thing Ireka needed to do was to explicitly state where they planned to go and how they would get there. They had set a corporate vision and planned to review it every four years for relevance. It was imbued in everything they had to do. But, many employees were still unclear about how they could contribute to the vision. Management kept reminding them but they left people on their own.

The Employee Stock Option Scheme (ESOS)

Another way the directors hoped to encourage a sense of belonging and commitment from the staff was through the introduction of the Employee Stock Option Scheme (ESOS). The directors' intention was to give employees stock options with the idea that when the employees owned a part of the company through the stock, this would give them a greater sense of shared responsibility. The ESOS was approved by the Registrar of Companies in 1996.

When the ESOS was first implemented, many employees who took the options sold the shares right away. Instead of holding the shares and seeing themselves as part owners of the company, most employees just saw the ESOS as another cash benefit. However, not long after the ESOS was started, share prices began to fall and many of the employees who had not sold their options saw the value of their investment diminished on paper. The fall was due to the declining economic situation in Malaysia that eventually became part of the more serious Asian financial crisis in late 1997 rather than any specific problems with the company, but the impact on employees was still negative.

The Human Resources Department

The directors also felt that it was important for future growth to coordinate all human resource (HR) functions and align them with the strategic direction of the company. Previously, HR activities were carried out by the individual heads of divisions and nothing was coordinated. Therefore, standards and procedures for basic HR were not consistent across the company.

In 1995, Mrs. Lee Poh Yoke, an HR professional, was brought in to set up a formal HR department. She needed to build HR systems in virtually every area, including recruitment and selection, training, performance appraisal, compensation and benefits, disciplinary procedures, etc.

Although changes were made slowly and a mechanism was set up to get feedback before implementation, there was a lot of resistance to the development of professional HR systems. Many people had a traditional view of HR as a "dumping ground" for people problems. If employees had a performance problem, some managers expected HR to fire those people for them. Some managers also thought HR should handle any interpersonal problems or conflicts that came up in their departments. Anything that had to do with people management seemed to be seen as the responsibility of HR.

There were also conflicts over how the new HR systems should be set up. The HR Committee, which included directors and many department heads, was asked to give input on a wide variety of proposed systems. Managers did not want to lose control, but often did not have any professional HR experience on which to base their suggestions. Poh Yoke found herself having to implement HR systems that she herself did not believe were suitable. The result was that some HR systems had to be changed after implementation because they did not work well. Further, the many changes and later revisions of changes caused some people to have a bad impression of the HR Department.

The Employees' View

The general view from many employees was that the company was going in the right direction. The directors were making improvements and trying to change. Working in a large listed company was seen as positive, and the expansion helped to boost the confidence of the staff. The level of satisfaction seemed to be reasonably high, as reflected by some of the comments from employees: "The staff get along well together." "It's a good company; the family members are nice people."

There were also a lot of positive reactions to the changes that had been implemented. "There was good planning of the system. The directors described the changes, introduced them slowly, and they are working well." "The new system works well. It is much better managed and more systematic." "The new structure is good." "People are receiving the changes comfortably." "People are adapting well."

Some of the attempts to change organizational communication were also well received. "Younger managers are more motivated because their views are listened to; there is the Forum to discuss ideas." "The Forum helps managers to communicate and resolve issues." "Top managers treat managers equally. Whether you are a family member or not, you can still give comments." "Younger managers are now more open with their views." "The new performance appraisal system is good. It provides a chance to discuss the work situation."

But there were also many concerns expressed. Many people believed that even though it was a publicly listed company, it was still a family run business. Ireka was described as "still conservative, tightly controlled. It's not opening up and growing as fast as possible." Many employees also felt that decision making was slow.

Another concern was that there was too much interference and involvement from the top. "Managers follow requests out of respect even if they think it's not right." There was also a feeling that there was some overlapping of responsibilities.

Another criticism expressed was that there needed to be more transparency. Employees wanted more information about the directions and goals of the company as they were feeling uncertain about their future.

Tying together performance and rewards was also suggested as a need. Some people felt that since the new performance appraisal system was not linked to the bonus or other outcomes, that it wasn't very useful. To them, the purpose of the performance appraisal system was not clear. Also, some employees thought that it was important to give rewards and recognition when objectives were accomplished and that the company was not doing that.

Many employees also commented that their workload was becoming heavier, busier, or more complicated than it had been in the past. Some were even too busy to join the Sports and Recreation Club activities.

All in all, the employees knew that the human issues were not so simple and that the directors still needed to make some improvements in control and management systems.

The Road Ahead

It was clear that the Lai family had set into motion a plan to diversify and expand their business and to make it more professional. Many changes had taken place in the company including the big step of going public. In the future, the directors hoped to continue down this road and to eventually upgrade their stock listing to the main board of the Kuala Lumpur Stock Exchange. Although they were qualified for the main board in 1997, they still felt the need to further diversify and move into new areas. They were thinking about further hotel and real estate development, new construction methods, special niche markets, doing more international work, or perhaps construction-related manufacturing.

However, all of this would only be possible if they could successfully manage the transition. All of the directors agreed that there were still many problems, particularly with people, that still needed to be worked out. So, considering the financial crisis that was affecting all of Asia in 1997, could they move ahead? ▪

SOURCE: "Ireka Construction Berjad: A Chinese Family Business Goes Public" by Anne Marie Francesco. Copyright © 1999 Ann Marie Francesco. Reprinted by permission of the author.

Case 16 Malaysian-German Chamber of Commerce and Industry

H. Richard Eisenbeis and Martin Schmidt

In July 1994, Wilhelm Berg became General Manager of the Malaysian-German Chamber of Commerce and Industry (MGCC) in Kuala Lumpur, Malaysia. Upon his arrival in Kuala Lumpur and after being shown his temporary quarters, he went immediately to the Chamber office and called a meeting of the permanent staff. After ushering the staff to their seats around the conference table, he briefly introduced himself and made a speech that included the following statements:

"As a result of my work at the headquarters of the Association of the German Chambers of Commerce and Industry in Germany, I am well aware of the problems faced by the Malaysian Chamber at this moment. Although MGCC has been operating in Malaysia for eight years, it has yet to show a profit and still remains heavily dependent on subsidies provided by our German Chamber and the German Government. In fact, the Chamber's losses are such that unless it shows a profit within the next year, it is doubtful whether MGCC will survive for another year.

"As if this is not bad enough, I understand that Dr. Fong, head of the Trade Fair Department, has quit the Chamber and taken some valuable survey data with him that we have little hope of recovering. However, we should not let this discourage us. I have some ideas how we can turn the Malaysian Chamber into a profitable enterprise within a very short time. I'm certain that the Chamber Board will approve of my recommendations as soon as I have the opportunity to present them. As for the staff of the Chamber, if we all cooperate and pull in the same direction, I'm certain we'll become profitable within a year's time."

He then added, "I wish to thank Mrs. Giesela Abe for doing a great job and holding the Chamber together since my predecessor, Dr. von Bonin, left three months ago. It is evident that she has done an excellent job." He paused and then added, "Although some reshuffling of positions will be forthcoming, Mrs. Abe's is not one of them. I am asking her to continue as Assistant General Manager."

After this very brief speech he quickly dismissed the group and returned to his office.

The Malaysian-German Chamber of Commerce and Industry

MGCC was founded in 1986 for the purpose of providing information to German companies that were searching for trading and investment opportunities in Malaysia's rapidly expanding economy. In 1990, negotiations were completed between the Association of German Chambers of Commerce and Industry and the Malaysian government to give the organization the status of a bilateral Chamber of Commerce servicing both Germany and Malaysia. The mission of this newly formed organization was to promote and increase business opportunities for both Malaysian and German firms by providing them with timely and relevant information about business, trade, investment, and political and legal issues.

Since its inception in 1986, the Chamber had been supported by subsidies from the German Chamber of Commerce and Industry which in turn received financial support from the German Government. It was originally envisioned that the Malaysian-German Chamber would become self-supporting and profitable in one or two years after its formation by charging Malaysian and German firms for the information and services they received. After the cooperative agreement was reached between the German Chamber and the Malaysian government in 1990, the Malaysian-German Chamber was incorporated into an independent organization (MGCC) that reported to a Board of Directors comprised of eight German and eight Malaysian owners and managers of business firms operating in Malaysia. During its four years

421

EXHIBIT C16-1 Services Offered by the Malaysian-German Chamber of Commerce and Industry

- Members' meetings, functions, newsletters, circulars, and Handbook.
- Compiling lists of manufacturers, exporters, importers, and representatives.
- Facilitating trade introductions, nominating lawyers, auditors, consultants, and other specialists.
- Undertaking market research and producing market studies.
- Providing information and assistance on Customs and immigration matters.
- German VAT Refund Service.
- Establishing joint ventures, technology transfer, and license arrangements.
- Initiating and assisting trade missions to both Malaysia and Germany.
- Assisting members in their day-to-day operations by conducting surveys on services such as power supply and telecommunications, and placing the findings with the appropriate government authority.
- Representing German trade fair and exhibition companies as to bookings for both exhibitors and visitors. The Chamber currently represents major trade fair organizers in Berlin, Cologne, Dusseldorf, Frankfurt, Hannover, and Munich.

under the direction of Dr. von Bonin, MGCC was never able to approach the breakeven point let alone show a profit. Because the Board of Directors believed that under Dr. von Bonin's management the Chamber would never show a profit, the Board elected to terminate his employment with the organization in April 1994. When Mr. Berg assumed control of MGCC in July 1994, the organization was structured as shown in Exhibit C16-1.

MGCC derived its revenues from fees paid by businesses for information gathered, analyzed, and interpreted by the Marketing and Fair Trade Departments. Its customers were basically small to medium-sized companies who, unlike large firms and multinational corporations, could not afford to do extensive independent research in Malaysia. In order to serve these smaller companies, most of which had limited budgets for exploring potential for doing business with either Malaysian or German firms, the Chamber charged lower fees for these services than large independent consulting firms. It also charged German firms more for its services than Malaysian firms. Exhibit C16-2 compares differences in fees charged to German and Malaysian firms for various services.

A third source of revenue was derived from the annual membership fees collected from approximately 150 companies registered with MGCC. In exchange for these annual fees, member firms received free services and a monthly bulletin containing up-to-date information concerning economic, political, and legal happenings in Malaysia and Germany.

Wilhelm Berg

Wilhelm Berg, age 40, had earned a master's degree in Business Geography at a German university and, after graduation and before coming to MGCC, had worked as a salesman for a large German corporation. He was hired by MGCC in 1989 as an administrator and remained in that position for five years before being offered the position of General Manager of MGCC in Kuala Lumpur. He accepted the position without hesitation and immediately made preparations to move his wife and ten-year-old daughter to Malaysia. The salary that went along with his promotion and the spacious residence he was to occupy in Kuala Lumpur left no doubt in the minds of his colleagues that he had made a major career move upward in the German Chamber's organizational hierarchy.

Mrs. Giesela Abe

Independently wealthy and divorced from a Chinese business man, by age 55 Giesela Abe had been living in Malaysia for 33 years. She and her two grown daughters resided in a wealthy neighborhood in Kuala Lumpur. She was one of the original employees hired when MGCC opened its doors in 1986. Abe spoke fluent Malay, English, and German and

EXHIBIT C16-2 Malaysian-German Chamber of Commerce and Industry's Board of Directors 1994

Datuk Muhammad Feisol Hassan, President Chairman, Wembly Rubber Products (M) Sdn Bhd
Herbert Weiler, Vice President Managing Director, OE Design Sdn Bhd
Berhard S. Konken, Treasurer Managing Director, Behn Meyer & Company (M) Sdn Bhd
John Chong, Managing Director, Festo Sdn Bhd
Dato' G. S. Gill, Chairman, G. S. Gill Sdn Bhd
Dato' Lau Foo-Sun, Managing Director, LP consultant Sdn Bhd
Knut Herzer, Managing Director, Bayer (Malaysia) Sdn Bhd
Dr. Willy Janowski, Technical Managing Director, Robert Borsch (Malaysia) Sdn Bhd
Mike Krishman, Director, Burgmann (Malaysia) Sdn Bhd
Manfred Lewandrowski, Managing Director, Staedtler (Malaysia) Sdn Bhd
Benno Reischel, Managing Director, Gerling Service Asia Sdn Bhd
Raja Aznin Raja Hj Ahmad, Managing Director, Syarikat Jaya Raya
Sit Hin Kin, Executive Director, Mannesmann Steel & Pipe Sdn Bhd
Victor Szechenyi, Managing Director, BASF (Malaysia) Sdn Bhd
Teh Lam Sam, Managing Director, Boehringer Mannheim (Malaysia) Sdn Bhd
Thomas A. Veriohr, General Manager, Deutsche Bank AG Kuala Lumpur

was highly committed to the welfare of Malaysia and its people. She felt an intense loyalty toward the MGCC and was highly respected and well-liked by her fellow employees and the Board. Although Abe had no formal business training, she was considered to be a major contributor within the organization. And, she was considered especially valuable because of her ready access to most of the Malaysian authorities and the executives of many of the prominent firms doing business in Malaysia. It was no secret that she wanted the General Manager's position after the dismissal of Dr. von Bonin. But, it was rumored by those outside of the Chamber that she was not given the position because of her provincial views and lack of vision for the organization.

Transition

In the weeks that followed, Berg met frequently with the three most influential members of the Board of Directors to outline his goals, plans, and strategies for increasing revenues and making the Chamber profitable. The three Directors included the President of the Board, a Malaysian businessman; the Vice-President of the Board, a German owner of a large jewelry company in Malaysia; and the Treasurer, a German manager of a large German trading company doing business in Malaysia. Berg asked for approval to expand MGCC's services by (1) offering (individually tailored) customized solutions to firms requiring the types of information MGCC provided, (2) providing workshops, seminars, and in-house presentations for firms operating in the same industry, and (3) consulting with and charging all participants who attended these workshops, seminars, etc. separately instead of collectively. The President, Vice-President, and Treasurer gave preliminary approval to Berg's ideas and asked him to work out a detailed business plan to present to a full meeting of the Board.

After receiving approval from the entire Board to proceed with his ideas, Berg consulted with Mrs. Abe and explained the proposals he had made to the three Board members. Although Abe had reservations about the feasibility of Berg's ideas, she was impressed by his enthusiasm and strong convictions. In spite of these reservations, she agreed that his proposals were worth pursuing and assured him of her full support.

In the two months that followed, the staff seldom saw Berg. He typically came to the office very early in the morning and would work with his door closed until late in the evening. The few times he did appear for reasons other than the weekly Monday morning staff meeting, he either could be found discussing the financial state of the Chamber with the chief accountant or meeting with selected Board members to discuss future operations and his new ideas on how to improve the long-term profitability of the Chamber. He also spent time with a freelance journalist, employed part time by the Chamber, discussing how to upgrade the bulletin distributed monthly to Chamber customers.

The staff meetings typically lasted from two to three hours and were characterized by long monologues by Berg expounding upon his ideas. There was little or no opportunity for staff members to provide feedback or otherwise engage in meaningful dialogue. All decisions were made unilaterally by Berg or by Berg after consultation with the Board. Staff members were allowed no opportunity for input into the decision-making process.

German firms comprised most of the Chamber's clients and to better serve them, Berg insisted that the staff improve their language skills to enable them to interact more effectively with their German clients. He hired a teacher from the German Goethe Institute in Kuala Lumpur to instruct the staff in conversational German for two hours every morning. While the staff were not pleased with this arrangement, all passed the first examination after two and one-half months of instruction.

During the first several months, Berg made no attempt to restructure the Chamber. However, because he had some experience with trade fairs, he assumed the administrative responsibilities of Dr. Fong, the previous head of the Trade Fair Department who had left the Chamber before Berg arrived. The two experienced employees who had reported to Dr. Fong were now to report directly to him. Whereas previously these two employees had some decision making responsibilities, Berg made it clear to them that from then on he would make all the decisions for the unit no matter how trivial.

As a result of his first trade fair initiative, Berg convinced ten German companies to send representatives to Kuala Lumpur to meet with Malaysian businessmen and to familiarize them with the services provided by the Chamber. Should the event be successful, the Chamber would realize substantially more revenue from this one organized event than could be generated by offering many of its standard services to a large number of firms. As it turned out, the event was a financial success and most of the participants were pleased with the results. Most of these companies indicated that they would contract for the Chamber's services in the immediate future.

Disharmony in the Ranks

While on the surface it appeared that preparations had gone smoothly for the visit of the representatives of German companies to Kuala Lumpur, the staff of the marketing and trade fair departments felt otherwise. They complained to Abe of the extreme amount of effort that went into organizing this event and the overtime required. In order to prepare properly for the visit, all members of both departments had to suspend their normal activities of providing information and services to their regular clientele. After listening to their complaints, Abe decided to discuss the matter with Berg.

Abe went to Berg's office and upon entering, began the conversation by saying:

"Mr. Berg, the staff are pleased that the visit of the representatives from the German companies was successful and that they and our Board of Directors are pleased with our efforts. But, I must tell you that in preparing for the event we exceeded our present work capacity. The marketing and trade fair staff were producing at their maximum capabilities before we began organizing the event. I believe it is accurate to say that they are most upset. During the planning stages they had no time to work on their normal tasks and requests have piled up on everyone's desk. We are already receiving complaints from customers waiting for information."

Berg replied, "I understand that this may have imposed some hardships for the staff, but remember this was a first for this kind of an undertaking for the Chamber. I'm certain that things will go more smoothly as we gain more experience in organizing these types of functions. I've already planned three more even bigger functions at the Hilton within the next two months. I'm sure you'll appreciate that this will substantially improve our profits.

He continued, "Don't worry about the staff being over-worked. Once they develop a routine for organizing these types of functions, everything will go just fine."

Abe pondered the situation in light of Berg's reply.

"Maybe you're right," she said. "But, I am worried about putting all of our effort into these new activities at the risk of neglecting other customers.

I believe that we should seriously consider hiring more people."

Berg leaned back in his chair and said, "The Board will not give us money to hire new personnel. We must first show that our new strategy will really increase profits. You just take care of the marketing staff and let me take care of bringing in new business."

It was a disturbed Mrs. Abe that left Berg's office that afternoon. She felt her resentment of Berg beginning to grow.

Over the next month, the situation grew worse, complaints from staff to Abe (suddenly a sympathetic listener) increased, and morale began to deteriorate. Customers continued to complain about the long delays in filling requests for information. Although the staff had not yet acquired the desired level of proficiency in German to routinely provide the level of service desired by German clients, because of time constraints, German classes were discontinued. In order to prepare adequately for the three upcoming promotional events, it became necessary for the staff to put in many hours of overtime. The two Trade Fair Department staff were able to do nothing else. Incoming requests to this department from an increasing number of firms were processed by two new inexperienced unsupervised German trainees. In addition, Chamber efficiency was hampered by potential customers who visited MGCC and requested guided tours. It was also during this time that redundancies began to surface between the Trade Fair and Marketing Departments because of Berg's unwillingness to share information with Abe and the Marketing Department.

Tension began to surface among various staff members. The Chinese staff suddenly became annoying to other staff and a conflict erupted between Indian staff members and staff members of Chinese decent. Abe believed that this occurred because they stopped interacting with one another unless absolutely necessary. The fact that members of the various departments began conversing only in their native languages only added to the tension. Requests for information continued to pile up, some for as much as three months. Believing that things would only deteriorate further without Berg being made aware of the situation and receiving his permission to hire more employees, Abe again approached him with her assessment of the situation.

"Mr. Berg, "she said," we have a serious personnel problem. Our employees are very unhappy with the current state of affairs. They believe they cannot continue to both organize these promotional events and still meet customer demands if you don't hire more people with experience to lighten the load. We desperately need more staff to handle the work load in a timely fashion. If we continue operating as we are, we'll not only lose more of our best clients but some of our more experienced personnel as well."

Berg again rejected Abe's recommendations again citing the major reason as being the unlikelihood of Board approval and the lack of money. Abe did not attempt to press the issue and left Berg's office angry and frustrated feeling that he had once again brushed her off without attempting to come up with some reasonable solution to the problem. Her resentment of Berg and his methods continued to grow.

The next day the two German trainees form the Marketing Department complained to Berg of the outdated computing capabilities and blamed the bureaucratic structure of the Chamber as being a major cause of the inability of the unit to work efficiently and to complete tasks on time. They were especially annoyed that members of the Trade Fair Department were not able to make even the simplest decisions without his stamp of approval. They identified other barriers to efficiency as being that all outgoing faxes had to be hand-written and recorded into two ledgers, that all phone calls to German customers could only be made from the desk of Berg's secretary and that the subject of the conversation of the phone calls had to be hand written as well. By way of a solution the trainees suggested that: (1) Berg give members of the Trade Fair Department some decision-making responsibilities, (2) he upgrade the computers to handle e-mail, (3) he allow phone calls to German clients be made from outlets other than his secretary's desk, and (4) he hire more people to handle the increased work load. Once more, as he had told others in the past, he would first have to obtain approval from the Board of Directors before enacting these recommendations.

A week later, Berg gave Abe permission to hire several inexperienced Malaysian students as temporary staff at the minimum wage. The Malaysian students were of little help because the staff had little time available to train them properly. No changes were forthcoming concerning computer upgrades, faxes, e-mail, or phone calls, and the reporting structure of the Trade Fair Department was not changed. This lack of positive action on the majority of the trainee's recommendations was perceived by the Chamber staff as a lack of trust on the part of Berg and the Board. Nevertheless, the three promotional functions scheduled by Berg were all successful and highly profitable. Dissatisfaction among Chamber personnel reached an all-time high.

In December 1994 and January 1995, the two experienced and highly qualified staff members in the Trade Fair Department resigned from the Chamber and as a result many important activities in the Chamber were brought to a standstill. Alarmed at the loss of two of the Chamber's most valuable employees, the Board began to pay closer attention to Chamber operations and its internal structure. As a result, the Board gave Berg permission to hire four experienced full-time employees (three Chinese women and one Malaysian man). Upon their arrival at the Chamber in March 1995, Berg combined the Trade Fair and Marketing Departments and removed Abe from the chain of command. In essence, all members of the Chamber now reported directly to him and he insisted on retaining total decision-making responsibility within the organization.

Moreover, he rewrote job descriptions for all personnel so that each member of the merged departments was responsible for performing all tasks including organizing trade fairs and handling requests from specific industry sectors. Under the new structure, Abe was placed in a position where she was to function solely as an assistant to Berg. Her new responsibilities included (1) assisting Berg in identifying German firms who were willing to participate in the promotional events organized by MGCC in Malaysia, (2) maintaining a steady stream of correspondence with these firms, and (3) recruiting new member organizations for MGCC. Abe's resentment of Berg reached the boiling point.

Within the next few weeks, Berg began to realize that most of his time under the new structure was now consumed in assisting employees in performing their daily tasks. Because no two customer requests were

the same and because he insisted that employees consult with him before taking action, he found little free time to devote to the larger issues facing the Chamber. Even after he realized that he needed to delegate and he told the Marketing personnel to make decisions on their own, he would take pains to review those decisions and give additional instructions on how requests should be processed. It was especially disturbing to staff that he would take it upon himself to issue detailed instructions in areas in which he had little or no expertise. The motivation and productivity of the Chamber staff declined to its lowest level ever.

The low morale and lower productivity did not seem to bother Berg. He continued to plan for more and more promotional functions without attempting to acquire additional resources or upgrade computer capabilities. A major setback occurred in April 1995 when a seminar addressing issues associated with environmental technology drew over 200 participants, after the seminar it was found that the company for whom MGCC had organized the seminar was without sufficient funds to pay for it. Because the Chamber had financed the event in advance of payment by the company, the Chamber sustained a loss of 30,000 Deutsche Marks. Also during this period, customer complaints citing poor service and long turn-around times for requests for information reached new highs.

Finally, Giesela Abe could tolerate it no longer. Not only had she been removed from the chain of command, there was no longer anyone with any influence to run interference for the staff. Her beloved Chamber was on the brink of disaster. Abe believed that it was her responsibility to do something to salvage the organization she helped build. After all, she was not without her own sources of influence.

In the months that followed, Chamber staff noticed a steady stream of Board members entering and leaving Abe's office. On December 1, 1995, Berg was asked to submit his letter of resignation to the Chamber's Board of Directors. ▪

SOURCE: "Malaysian-German Chamber of Commerce and Industry" by H. Richard Eisenbeis, Ph. D. and Martin Schmidt, Hasan School of Business, Colorado State University-Pueblo. Reprinted by permission.

Case 17 A Candidate for Saudi Arabia

Lotte Kragelund and Mikael Søndergaard

Introduction

Mrs. Svendson, the Human Relations Manager of Natural Thirst Killer, a Danish soft drink producer, looked out the window and wondered whom to choose for the job of Sales Manager for the rapidly growing Saudi Arabian drink market. The resumes of ten candidates with sales experience were on her desk this Friday afternoon in October 2001. The candidates were almost equally qualified in terms of experience in the soft drink market. Most of them had never been expatriated before and they had very different personalities.

First-Hand Impression

Mrs. Svendson wondered what personal traits would do well in the Saudi Arabian business world. The Sales Manager job meant expatriation to Saudi Arabia to set up the business. It was a very attractive position and all the candidates were high performers in their present positions.

Mrs. Svendson had gone on a business trip to Saudi Arabia a few weeks ago, which was sponsored by the Danish company Dan Cookies. This company had been in business in the country for 19 years. They enjoyed a very good relationship with a Saudi Arabian prince who was Dan Cookies' sponsor.

Initially, Mrs. Svendson did not realize the importance of sponsorship in Saudi Arabia. She contacted the Danish Embassy in Riyadh and asked the Commercial Department for information about doing business in Saudi Arabia. She was told that every company that wanted to do business in the country had to have a local partner. Otherwise, it would be impossible to enter the market due to extremely high taxes and lack of local knowledge. She then realized the importance of the sponsor relationship. Before establishing a business in Saudi Arabia, Natural Thirst Killer needed to find a sponsor. Additionally, the sponsor had to provide guarantees for the financial as well as the legal matters of the company.

Doing Business in Saudi Arabia

While in Saudi Arabia Mrs. Svendson realized the importance of the relations with the sponsor when she talked to Peter, a Danish expatriate. Peter had encountered difficulties because the company he worked for wanted to switch sponsors. The decision caused a lot of trouble. Peter explained to Mrs. Svendson that it was illegal to start working with a new sponsor without first leaving the country and concluding an agreement with the old sponsor. When Peter's sponsor realized that Peter's company was about to switch to another sponsor, he told him that he would make sure that Peter went to jail if his company tried to dump him.

Peter did not understand that the sponsor was serious but did when the police came to his house and told him the same story. After this, Peter drove to the airport to get his wife out of the country. Then, he left his house and did not return for six months. In the meantime, he lived in different places until his company and the old sponsor finally found a solution. Peter said, "That's not too much fun. I haven't seen my wife since. I've talked to her on the phone, and she doesn't want to go back to Saudi now, so I have to stay here alone."

The Market

Mrs. Svendson had information indicating that European products are popular among Saudi Arabian consumers. Since Saudi Arabia is a multiracial country with an affluent customer base and different ethnic tastes, specific food consumption patterns have emerged. Special attention is given to selection and price, which is why products come from all over the world.

The three consumer categories in Saudi Arabia include: Saudi Arabian consumers, expatriates from third world countries, and other expatriates (Westerners and other Arabs). Saudi Arabian people have an annual per capita income of US$6,700, and their major expense is food. The Saudi Arabian average family includes a mother, a father, and 6 or 7 children. Dining at fast food restaurants like Mc Donald's, Pizza Hut, and KFC, and shopping at modern malls and supermarkets have become very popular and are a major form of entertainment for the Saudi Arabian family.

The beverage market is valued about US$1 billion. The carbonated soft drink sector accounts for at least 50% of the output. Concentrates for other beverages (fruit juice, diluted drinks, and powdered juice) are also in demand.

The Population

With an estimated total population of 21 million people, Saudi Arabians make up two-thirds of the total. The rest are expatriates, with the majority from third world countries. The demographic profile of the national population is changing. More than 50% of the Saudis are under the age of 17, and the population growth rate is 3.5% per annum.

The Saudi Arabian consumer is becoming more educated as to quality, nutritious value, price, and packaging. In-store promotions and television and print media advertising are keenly observed by the Saudi Arabian consumers. Saudi Arabian consumers have become more price conscious and seek good value for money but are willing to pay extra for premium quality products. Products from the West are viewed favorably and generally considered of premium quality.

The per capita income for most nationalities, with the exception of Europeans and Americans, is substantially lower than for the Saudi Arabians. The changing structure of the expatriate population, which accounts for a sizeable portion of the domestic food market, household goods, consumer products, and services, will change spending patterns as the number of expatriate families of non-American and non-European nationality increases. These families have a higher percentage of children born in Saudi Arabia than before.

Living in Saudi Arabia

Mrs. Svendson thought about all the conversations she'd recently had with Danes living in Saudi Arabia. She was aware that recruiting the wrong candidate could turn out to be a very expensive failure. That was a part of the reason why she had been sent to the site for which the applicant was to be recruited. She had interviewed 27 Danish expatriates.

The Human Relations Manager from the Dan Cookies Company, which she visited in Saudi Arabia, told her that the last time he tried to hire a person for the job as Sales Manager in Saudi Arabia, he had chosen the wrong candidate, and the company had faced problems in their relationship with their Saudi Arabian customers. After the Sales Manager left, Dan Cookies received faxes from several customers threatening to cancel their contracts due to a detail in delivery terms. Dan Cookie's Human Relations Manager told Mrs. Svendson:

We had to hurry hiring a new Sales Manager with a personality that's suitable for the company, the country, and our customers. The new Sales Manager had to be able to establish and maintain the future relationships with Saudi Arabian customers. It was an unusually expensive move which was motivated by the high risks of failure for the company. But, we managed to find the right person and we didn't lose any of our customers.

While thinking of all the interviews with the Danish expatriates, she tried to figure out what kind of personality the new Sales Manager would need in order to be able to work effectively in the Saudi Arabian market.

During Mrs. Svendson's visit to Saudi Arabia, Danish expatriates had told her that living and working in Saudi Arabia requires a lot of different personal traits. Additionally, the family must understand and accept the fact that living and working in Saudi Arabia is different from Danish conditions.

The females have to be aware that they have to accept wearing a long black dress called an "Abayya" and a black headscarf. This is part of the Sharia, the Islamic law based on the Koran. Additionally, women do not have the same opportunities to work as in Denmark. In Saudi Arabia, women are only allowed to work in the health care service or as teachers for female students. Furthermore, women are not allowed to drive, which makes getting around difficult.

During Mrs. Svendson's visit, she had realized that wearing the "Abayya" and the black headscarf was not a big deal. Everyone else was doing it and after a few days in the country, she did not even think about it. It was like putting on a jacket when leaving the house. However, one of the expatriates who had tried to hire candidates for jobs in Saudi Arabia said to Mrs. Svendson:

I've seen many Danish having difficulties getting used to their new life in Saudi Arabia. It's sad to see a family split up because of the difficulties for women here. A Danish woman who is used to having a job and wants to continue her career just does not fit here.

She clearly remembered one of the expatriates who had been living in Saudi Arabia with his family for six years saying:

The couples who manage to live here without difficulties are often couples with small children or couples having no children or grown-up children. Those who have teenage children have to choose either to send the children to boarding school in another country or leave the country.

The restrictions in the country make for very different living conditions for a Danish family. One restriction is that the Sharia forbids alcohol which makes it difficult or very expensive to buy wine and beer. An expatriate told Mrs. Svendson that some people made wine and beer in their homes.

Mrs. Svendson was sure that it demanded a lot from every member of the family to leave a country like Denmark and make a living in Saudi Arabia. She thought of the whole family because she had realized that living alone was not a good idea for an expatriate in a country like Saudi Arabia. She had talked to four men who were living alone either because they were bachelors, their wives and children had gone home because they did not like living in the country, or because their children were too old to go to school in Saudi Arabia. Foreign students cannot get any kind of education in Saudi Arabia after they turn 16.

However, she was sure that living in Saudi Arabia could be very comfortable. From the viewpoint of a young wife with small children, she could imagine that being able to be a housewife, for example, having enough time to take care of the children, would be much more fun than experiencing stress all day to get the children to kindergarten and commute to work. One of the Danish expatriates told Mrs. Svendson:

Actually, I think living here with your wife and your children can be very pleasant because your

wife has plenty of time to take care of the kids. In Denmark it is necessary for both parents to work. Otherwise it is hard to make a living.

Besides the importance of the family feeling comfortable, Mrs. Svendson thought of one of the personality traits mentioned by a Danish expatriate. Common among the ones who were doing well in Saudi Arabia was a warm and relaxed personality. It seemed like the expatriates with a good sense of humour and a friendly attitude were doing the best job and felt the most comfortable in Saudi Arabia. They all thought that a part of their personality was to joke and have time enough to talk to their Saudi Arabian business partners whom they often called their friends and often invited for dinner.

Doing business with Saudi Arabs seemed to be a matter of building strong friendships.

One of the expatriates who had been dealing with Saudi Arabs for 15 years told Mrs. Svendson that he had met many Westerners who attempted to cooperate with a Saudi Arabian partner, but failed when they tried to hasten or exert pressure to get an agreement or contract. One expatriate found:

Trust building with a Saudi Arabian partner takes time. If you want to establish and maintain a relationship with Saudi Arabians you have to be patient and wait until they feel that they can trust you.

Mrs. Svendson also talked to a very disappointed Sales Manager during her visit to Saudi Arabia. The Sales Manager had been working in the country for six months. He told her that he wanted to go back to Denmark, because he did not like dealing with Arabs. He did not like the waiting time—for example, he did not want to wait a month for a simple contract. Every time he tried to deal with Saudi Arabians, he could not relax. He wanted to go back to Denmark to concentrate on the European market. He said, "This is my first time in the Middle East, and I'll never return."

An expatriate who had been Sales Manager in Saudi Arabia for four years told Mrs. Svendson:

I don't know why, but I've always had a very warm relationship with Arabs. What I mean is that your business relation has to be like a friendship. A lot of Danes never get along with Arabs. It's not because I look like an Arab or act like them. But I know that it is very important to be patient. Being impatient and too serious just makes the relation complicated. When you are working here you have to accept the unwritten rules of how to negotiate. Being patient and making the Arabs feel that you like them and respect them are very important if you want to succeed in this part of the world.

Being able to work with people from different cultures was another important skill. Mrs. Svendson remembered an expatriate who had been working in Saudi Arabia for three years. He felt that it was very important to understand the people he was working with. He told her about one of his employees, a Sudanese worker. One day the Sudanese was standing outside the building at four o'clock ready to go home. The Dane asked him if he was not feeling well. The Sudanese told him that he was hungry, so he wanted to go home. The Dane told him that he was paid to stay until five o'clock. The Sudanese answered: "That's right but I'm hungry anyway!" he turned around and went back to work. Later the Dane told him that he should bring a sandwich instead of getting hungry and then wanting to go home for lunch. The Sudanese thanked him for the information. The Danish expatriate was sure the Sudanese was used to leaving his workplace when he was hungry. It seemed that being able to tell the employees, who were from many different cultures, what to do instead of what not to do was an important skill.

A Danish expatriate who had been working in Asia, Kuwait, and the United Arab Emirates said to Mrs. Svendson:

Sometimes you just have to think that the most simple thing to do, just isn't the simplest thing to do for other people. That is what I've experienced by working with many different people from many different cultures.

He pointed at his experience with other cultures by saying:

At least I know that there is always a difference between my own culture and the one I am living in right now. Sometimes I don't understand what's going on because of the differences, but I'll just have to accept the differences. If you can't accept the differences, you shouldn't apply for a job in Saudi Arabia.

In order to be able to accept the differences, Mrs. Svendson figured that it must be important for the future Sales Manager to have experiences with cultures that differ from the Danish or other European cultures.

The Candidates

Being able to work and feel comfortable in Saudi Arabia required many different personal traits. Mrs. Svendson looked at the applications one more time trying to find the right person for the job:

Mr. Nielsen is 35 years old. He has a lot of experience with soft drinks, he is married to a nurse and they have three children who are two, four, and six years old. He has a master's degree in business and ten years of experience with the Danish soft drink market, but no experience with travelling or with the Middle East. During the interview he seemed to like joking and was very friendly and open minded regardless of the type of question.

Mr. Olsen is 30 years old. He is a bachelor and does not have any plans for getting married right away. He has two years of international experience with fast moving consumer goods. He has a Ph.D. in International Management. During the job interview, Mr. Olsen said that he was convinced that he would like to work and live in Saudi Arabia. He seemed very positive and very talented according to his academic achievements. He said he liked going to parties and socializing with other people.

Mr. Salih was born in Kuwait in 1962, but moved to Denmark in 1978. He got married to a Danish woman in 1989 and is a Danish citizen. They have no children, but would like some soon. He speaks Arabic, English, and Danish fluently and has a degree in business from the University of Copenhagen. He told Mrs. Svendson that he is Muslim, but does not feel like one. He said, "I'm not applying for this job because I want to go to Mecca. I don't even pray every day."

His wife is Christian and works as an English teacher at The American International School in Copenhagen. She likes her job very much and would like to stay in Denmark, but if her husband gets the job, she is willing to go to Saudi Arabia.

Mr. Hansen is 30 years old. He is married to a 28-year-old Malay woman, and they have a two-year-old daughter. He does not have any specific experience with soft drinks. He moved to America where he graduated from high school and got a B.A. in Business at the University of California. He has experience with fast moving consumer goods in markets in Asia, Malaysia, and Europe. His wife would like to spend more time with their daughter. She is tired of getting up early to take the daughter to kindergarten. They have heard about life in Saudi Arabia from another Danish family living in Saudi Arabia. They both seem to know what it takes to live there. Mr. Hansen said, "I really like working with people from different cultures. It makes my day much more interesting, and I think it is a wonderful challenge."

Mr. Steensen is 61 years old. He is married to a 57-year-old nurse. He has 37 years of experience with different cultures in the Middle East, primarily the Gulf countries. They have grown-up children and would like to go to Saudi Arabia because they were expatriates in Saudi 13 years ago and liked it a lot. They left the Gulf countries because they wanted their children to go to high school in Denmark.

Mrs. Jensen is 40 years old and married to a 45-year-old lawyer. They have two children in high school. She has 20 years experience with soft drinks and has been in touch with many companies in the Middle East. She has tried to negotiate with Arabs and thinks it is a great challenge. She and her husband have both been travelling extensively and now they would very much like to live in another country. If she gets the job, her husband will quit his job. He enjoys playing golf and has heard of the great possibilities of playing golf in Saudi Arabia. The children will stay in Denmark and go to a boarding school. They both seem very friendly and open-minded.

Mr. Andersen was divorced six months ago. He is 47 years old and does not want to remarry. He told Mrs. Svendson that , "The best thing that has happened to me was getting that divorce. Now I really can concentrate on my job. I love my job and I'm hoping to get a job that makes me work all the time. I do not want time to socialize."

Mr. Andersen has 15 years of experience, mostly with selling cookies.

Mr. Jorgensen is 38 years old. He is married to a Spanish woman. They have two children who are 10 and 12 years old. They would both like to go to Saudi Arabia for a few years until the children have to go to high school. Mr. Jorgensen told Mrs. Svendson, "My wife misses the warm weather and would very much like to go to a warmer place. And I'm sure that Saudi Arabia is the right place."

He has a lot of experience dealing with the Spanish, Italian, and French markets. He is used to travelling around 100 days a year.

Mr. Jacobsen is 30 years old. He just got married to a 25-year-old woman who graduated from a university last summer. They would like to have children soon and think that life in Saudi Arabia would be the perfect place to do that. In Saudi Arabia they would have plenty of time to take care of their children. Mr. Jacobsen sells computers, but would like to try to work with fast moving consumer goods abroad. He likes to talk to people and is very open-minded.

Mr. Davidsen is 55 years old. He is married to an anthropologist who has been studying Egyptians for 15 years and would like to go to Saudi Arabia to study the Saudis and their culture. Mr. Davidsen has heard a lot about the Middle East from his wife. He would like to experience the region himself. He likes to talk and work with people from different cultures. He is a very experienced Sales Manager from another soft drink company. He would like to stay in the same business because he is knowledgeable. They have three children who are in high school and at the university. Two children are still living at home.

Mrs. Svendson is scheduled to meet with the CEO on Monday morning to decide on the candidate to run operation in Saudi Arabia. She has the weekend to put the candidates in order of priority.

The weather outside was windy and rainy. She fantasized about going to Saudi Arabia herself. It was going to be a long weekend. ▪

SOURCE: Case "A Candidate for Saudi Arabia" by Lotte Kragelund and Mikael Sondergaard. This case was written by Lotte Kragelund and Mikael Sondergaard, associate professor of the University of Aarhus, on leave from the University of Southern Denmark as a basis for classroom discussion.

■ ■ ■ ■ ■ ■ ■ ■ ■ ■ **EXERCISES** ■ ■ ■ ■ ■ ■ ■ ■ ■ ■ ■

IVEY Exercise 1 Where Have You Been?

Richard Ivey School of Business
The University of Western Ontario

An Exercise to Assess Your Exposure to the Rest of the World's Peoples

Paul Beamish

Instructions

1. Go to the lists of countries. For each, note the total number and names of those countries you have visited, and the corresponding percentage of world population which each country represents. Sum the relevant regional totals in the summary.
2. If used as part of a group analysis, estimate the grand total for the entire group. Then consider the following questions:

- Why is there such a high variability in individual profiles (i.e., high exposure vs. low exposure)?
- What are the implications of each profile for one's career?
- What would it take to get you to personally change your profile?

Lists of Countries

Region: Africa

Country	2000 Population (in millions)	% of World Total
1) NIGERIA	126.9	2.1
2) ETHIOPIA	64.2	1.1
3) EGYPT	63.9	1.1
4) CONGO (DEM. REP)	50.9	0.8
5) SOUTH AFRICA	42.8	0.7
6) TANZANIA	33.6	0.6
7) SUDAN	31.0	0.5
8) ALGERIA	30.3	0.5
9) KENYA	30.0	0.5
10) MOROCCO	28.7	0.5
11) UGANDA	22.2	0.4
12) GHANA	19.3	0.3
13) MOZAMBIQUE	17.6	0.3
14) CÔTE d'IVOIRE	16.0	0.3
15) MADAGASCAR	15.5	0.3
16) CAMEROON	14.8	0.2
17) ANGOLA	13.1	0.2
18) ZIMBABWE	12.6	0.2
19) BURKINA FASO	11.2	0.2
20) MALI	10.8	0.2

(Continued)

Country	2000 Population (in millions)	% of World Total
21) NIGER	10.8	0.2
22) MALAWI	10.3	0.2
23) ZAMBIA	9.8	0.2
24) SENEGAL	9.5	0.2
25) TUNISIA	9.5	0.2
26) SOMALIA	8.7	0.1
27) RWANDA	8.5	0.1
28) CHAD	7.6	0.1
Subtotal	730.1	

Source of all Statistics, except for Taiwan: 2002 World Bank World Development Indicators

Country	2000 Population (in millions)	% of World Total
29) GUINEA	7.4	0.1
30) BURUNDI	6.8	0.1
31) BENIN	6.2	0.1
32) LIBYA	5.2	0.1
33) SIERRA LEONE	5.0	0.1
34) TOGO	4.5	0.1
35) ERITREA	4.0	0.1
36) CENTRAL AFRICAN REPUBLIC	3.7	0.1
37) LIBERIA	3.1	0.1
38) CONGO, REP.	3.0	0.0
39) MAURITANIA	2.6	0.0
40) LESOTHO	2.0	0.0
41) NAMIBIA	1.7	0.0
42) BOTSWANA	1.6	0.0
43) GAMBIA, THE	1.3	0.0
44) GABON	1.2	0.0
45) MAURITIUS	1.1	0.0
46) GUINEA-BISSAU	1.1	0.0
47) SWAZILAND	1.0	0.0
48) DJIBOUTI	0.6	0.0
49) COMOROS	0.5	0.0
50) EQUATORIAL GUINEA	0.4	0.0
51) CAPE VERDE	0.4	0.0
52) SAO TOM and PRINCIPE	0.1	0.0
53) MAYOTTE (FR)	0.1	0.0
54) SEYCHELLES	0.1	0.0
Subtotal	794.8	13.2

Source of all Statistics, except for Taiwan: 2001 World Bank Atlas

Region: North America and Caribbean

Country	2002 Population (in millions)	% of World Total
1) USA	281.5	4.7
2) MEXICO	97.9	1.6
3) CANADA	30.7	0.5
4) GUATEMALA	11.3	0.2
5) CUBA	11.1	0.2
6) DOMINICAN REPUBLIC	8.3	0.1
7) HAITI	7.9	0.1
8) HONDURAS	6.4	0.1
9) EL SALVADOR	6.2	0.1
10) NICARAGUA	5.0	0.1
11) PUERTO RICO (U.S.)	3.9	0.1
12) COSTA RICA	3.8	0.1
13) PANAMA	2.8	0.0
14) JAMAICA	2.6	0.0
15) TRINIDAD AND TOBAGO	1.3	0.0
16) BAHAMAS	0.3	0.0
17) BARBADOS	0.2	0.0
18) BELIZE	0.2	0.0
19) NETHERLANDS ANTILLES	0.2	0.0
20) ST. LUCIA	0.1	0.0
21) VIRGIN ISLANDS (U.S.)	0.1	0.0
22) ST. VINCENT & THE GRENADINES	0.1	0.0
23) GRENADA	0.1	0.0
24) ARUBA (NETH.)	0.1	0.0
25) DOMINICA	0.1	0.0
26) ANTIGUA AND BARBUDA	0.1	0.0
27) BERMUDA (U.K.)	0.1	0.0
28) ST. KITTS AND NEVIS	0.1	0.0
29) CAYMAN ISLANDS	0.1	0.0
Subtotal	482.6	8.0

Region: South America

Country	2000 Population (in millions)	% of World Total
1) BRAZIL	170.4	2.8
2) COLOMBIA	42.2	0.7
3) AGRENTINA	37.0	0.6
4) PERU	25.6	0.4
5) VENEZUELA	24.1	0.4

(Continued)

Country	2000 Population (in millions)	% of World Total
6) CHILE	15.2	0.3
7) ECUADOR	12.6	0.2
8) BOLIVIA	8.3	0.1
9) PARAGUAY	5.4	0.1
10) URUGUAY	3.3	0.1
11) GUYANA	0.7	0.0
12) SURINAME	0.4	0.0
Subtotal	345.2	5.7

Region: Western Europe

Country	2000 Population (in millions)	% of World Total
1) GERMANY	82.1	1.4
2) UNITED KINGDOM	59.7	1.0
3) FRANCE	58.8	1.0
4) ITALY	57.6	1.0
5) SPAIN	39.4	0.7
6) NETHERLANDS	15.9	0.3
7) GREECE	0.5	0.2
8) BELGIUM	0.2	0.2
9) PORTUGAL	0.0	0.2
10) SWEDEN	8.8	0.1
11) AUSTRIA	8.1	0.1
12) SWITZERLAND	7.1	0.1
13) DENMARK	5.3	0.1
14) FINLAND	5.1	0.1
15) NORWAY	4.4	0.1
16) IRELAND	3.7	0.1
17) LUXEMBOURG	0.4	0.0
18) MALTA	0.3	0.0
19) ICELAND	0.3	0.0
20) CHANNEL ISLANDS (U.K.)	0.1	0.0
21) ISLE OF MAN	0.1	0.0
22) ANDORRA	0.1	0.0
23) GREENLAND (DEN.)	0.1	0.0
24) FAEROE ISLANDS (DEN.)	0.1	0.0
25) MONACO	0.1	0.0
26) LIECHTENSTEIN	0.1	0.0
27) SAN MARINO	0.1	0.0
Subtotal	388.4	6.4

Region: Eastern Europe

Country	2000 Population (in millions)	% of World Total
1) RUSSIAN FEDERATION	145.5	2.4
2) UKRAINE	49.5	0.8
3) POLAND	38.6	0.6
4) ROMANIA	22.4	0.4
5) YUGOSLAVIA, F.R. (SERB. & MONT.)	0.6	0.2
6) CZECH REPUBLIC	0.2	0.2
7) BELARUS	0.0	0.2
8) HUNGARY	0.0	0.2
9) BULGARIA	8.1	0.1
10) SLOVAK REPUBLIC	5.4	0.1
11) CROATIA	4.3	0.1
12) MOLDOVA	4.2	0.1
13) BOSNIA and HERZEGOVINA	3.9	0.1
14) LITHUANIA	3.6	0.1
15) ALBANIA	3.4	0.1
16) LATVIA	2.3	0.0
17) MACEDONIA, FYR	2.0	0.0
18) SLOVENIA	1.9	0.0
19) ESTONIA	1.3	0.0
Subtotal	337.2	5.6

Region: Central Asia and Indian Subcontinent

Country	2000 Population (in millions)	% of World Total
1) INDIA	1,015.9	16.8
2) PAKISTAN	138.0	2.3
3) BANGLADESH	131.0	2.2
4) AFGHANISTAN	26.5	0.4
5) UZBEKISTAN	24.7	0.4
6) NEPAL	23.0	0.4
7) SRI LANKA	19.3	0.3
8) KAZAKHSTAN	14.8	0.2
9) AZERBAIJAN	8.0	0.1
10) TAJIKISTAN	6.1	0.1
11) GEORGIA	5.0	0.1
12) KYRGYZ REPUBLIC	4.9	0.1
13) TURKMENISTAN	5.1	0.1
14) ARMENIA	3.8	0.1
15) MONGOLIA	2.3	0.0
16) BHUTAN	0.8	0.0
17) MALDIVES	0.2	0.0
Subtotal	1,429.4	23.6

Region: Central Middle East

Country	2000 Population (in millions)	% of World Total
1) TURKEY	65.2	1.1
2) IRAN	63.6	1.1
3) IRAQ	23.2	0.4
4) SAUDI ARABIA	20.7	0.3
5) YEMEN	17.5	0.3
6) SYRIAN ARAB REPUBLIC	16.1	0.3
7) ISRAEL	6.2	0.1
8) JORDAN	4.8	0.1
9) LEBANON	4.3	0.1
10) UNITED ARAB EMIRATES	2.9	0.0
11) WEST BANK AND GAZA	2.9	0.0
12) OMAN	2.3	0.0
13) KUWAIT	1.9	0.0
14) CYPRUS	0.7	0.0
15) QATAR	0.5	0.0
16) BAHRAIN	0.6	0.0
Subtotal	233.4	3.9

Region: Asia Pacific

Country	2000 Population (in millions)	% of World Total
1) CHINA (EXCL. HK & MACAO)	1,262.4	20.9
2) INDONESIA	210.4	3.5
3) JAPAN	126.8	2.1
4) VIETNAM	78.5	1.3
5) PHILIPPINES	75.5	1.2
6) THAILAND	60.7	1.0
7) MYANMAR	47.7	0.8
8) SOUTH KOREA	47.2	0.8
9) MALAYSIA	23.2	0.4
10) TAIWAN	22.4	0.4
11) NORTH KOREA	22.2	0.4
12) AUSTRALIA	19.1	0.3
13) CAMBODIA	12.0	0.2
14) HONG KONG (SAR – CHINA)	6.7	0.1
15) LAO PDR	5.2	0.1
16) PAPUA NEW GUINEA	5.1	0.1

(Continued)

Country	2000 Population (in millions)	% of World Total
17) SINGAPORE	4.0	0.1
18) NEW ZEALAND	3.8	0.1
19) FIJI	0.8	0.0
20) MACAO (SAR – CHINA)	0.4	0.0
21) SOLOMON ISLANDS	0.4	0.0
22) BRUNEI	0.3	0.0
23) SAMOA	0.2	0.0
24) FRENCH POLYNESIA (FR.)	0.2	0.0
25) NEW CALEDONIA (FR.)	0.2	0.0
26) VANUATU	0.1	0.0
27) GUAM (U.S.)	0.1	0.0
28) MICRONESIA, FED. STS.	0.1	0.0
29) TONGA	0.1	0.0
30) AMERICAN SAMOA (U.S.)	0.1	0.0
31) KIRIBATI	0.1	0.0
32) MARSHALL ISLANDS	0.1	0.0
33) NORTHERN MARIANA ISLANDS	0.1	0.0
34) PALAU	0.1	0.0
Subtotal	2,036	33.7

Summary

Region	# of Countries	Which You Have Visited	2000 Population (in millions)	Region's % of World Population	% of Population You Have Been Exposed To
AFRICA	54	—	794.8	13.2	—
NORTH AMERICA and CARIBBEAN	29	—	482.6	8.0	—
SOUTH AMERICA	12	—	345.2	5.7	—
WESTERN EUROPE	27	—	388.4	6.4	—
EASTERN EUROPE	19	—	337.2	5.5	—
CENTRAL ASIA and INDIAN SUBCONTINENT	17	—	1,429.4	23.6	—
MIDDLE EAST	16	—	233.4	3.9	—
ASIA PACIFIC	34	—	2,036.2	33.7	—
GRAND TOTAL	208	—	6,047.2	100.0	—

Exercise 2   Selected Intercultural Incidents

S. Paul Verluyten

Directions: Your instructor will assign you one or more of the scenarios. Discuss the behavior described in the scenario using non-pejorative, non-judgmental language. After discussing the scenarios, your instructor will give you further information and ask you to discuss the question(s) at the end of the segment and to describe what it tells you about your own cultural beliefs.

1. I spent three months in the USA. For two weeks, I was recovering from cultural shock as it was my first time in an English speaking country and it was really hard for me to say something in English.

An incident happened to me after a few weeks. We went out for a party. The house where the party took place was in a side street. After some time we discovered (two other Czechs and me) that there was a student standing in front of the house who was acting as a guard. They told us that he was watching people not to go on the street with a glass of beer or wine in their hand. As soon as someone tried to leave the house and walk in the street with a drink, he immediately ran after them and explained that it is forbidden to drink any alcohol on the street.

Later on, we found out that there are many other strange prohibitions in the U.S., such as prohibitions to drink a beer in a park or a picnic area, and many more . . .

(Mariana L., Slovakia, on her first visit to the U.S.)

How do you feel about drinking beer, wine, and liquor? If you drink, do you do so in order to get drunk or for the taste of it?

2. In the summer of 1984 I was on holiday in Bulgaria with my father. We lived with a Bulgarian family and once in the evening we invited them to go out and have a cup of coffee with us. They replied *da* ('yes'), but turned their head from the left side to the right side, as if they were saying 'no'.

We were really surprised because we did not understand what they meant. We didn't know whether our invitation was accepted or not . . .

(Natalia B., Czechoslovakia, on a visit in Bulgaria)

How would you say 'yes' or 'no' when in Greece?

3. Kei, a Chinese friend I met in England, announced that she was coming over to Spain for a visit, and I wanted to introduce her to my parents also. I liked the idea of her visit but I was worried about the behavior she might exhibit in front of my—fairly conservative—parents.

After her arrival she had her first meal with me alone, and again she did not mind burping or farting in front of me, and even if she used to say 'excuse me' I found it terribly rude.

Thinking of a polite way to express my dissatisfaction without hurting her, I started shaking my legs like one does when one is nervous or upset. Kei said: 'Ana, don't shake your legs like that, don't you know this is really impolite?'

(Ana S., Spain, with a Chinese friend)

Would you tolerate Kei's behavior or would you try to change it?

4. If you go to a swimming pool in the Czech republic, there is always a sign that says: 'After bathing, please take off your swimsuit and wash yourself with soap.' If someone did keep his swimsuit on, Czechs would consider this strange as well as unhygienic.

Having this notice in mind, I went to a public swimming pool in England and naively took off my swimsuit when taking a shower afterwards. The British women around me were petrified.

(Andrea K., Czech Republic, in England)

Would you take your swimsuit off for the shower on your first visit to a swimming pool in Prague?

5. In the summer of 1992, I was in Agadir, Morocco, with a friend of mine, who is born in Belgium but has a Moroccan father.

We were invited to have dinner with some of his relatives. He told me in advance that we would have to eat with our hands.

At one point, I could feel I did something terribly wrong. As soon as my friend noticed that I was using my left hand at the table, he told me (in Dutch) to stop doing so. After that, everything proceeded smoothly and the dinner went fine.

(Koen C., Belgium, in Morocco)

Could you finish a meal while using only the tips of three fingers?

Were you told that a handshake should always be done with your right hand? What about other functions, such as handing something to someone?

Why is the left hand also (albeit much less strongly) taboo in Europe and the U.S.? Is it for the same reasons as in the Muslim world, or for entirely different reasons?

6. In Italy it is quite common among males to kiss each other on both cheeks, especially on birthdays or other celebrations and when we meet again after a long time.

   While in England, I wanted to wish an English friend a merry Christmas and approached in order to kiss him. He backed off horrified.

(Ignazio M., Italy, in England)

Is there any situation where two males might hug each other in public in your country? (In Northern Europe, they do after they score a goal at a soccer game, for instance: Why is it acceptable then?)

Would you accept Ignazio's hug, or would you back off as the English male did?

7. In 1991, I was a student at a university in Pennsylvania, USA. I lived on campus and I shared a room with a girl from India.

   Many times at night, while we were studying, she asked me: 'Petra, do you feel like drinking a Coke?' And I replied 'yes' or 'no.' But invariably, her next question always was: 'Could you get me one?' So whether I wanted something from the vending machine or not, I went four floors downstairs, and brought her what she wanted. It didn't bother me, it just surprised me that someone would ask for this on regular basis instead of helping herself.

   Later I realized that my Indian friend came from a wealthy Indian family living in Nepal. Their house was full of young Nepali girls and boys who lived with them as servants. And now she was in America, on her own, doing her own laundry, tidying up her room, so at least she found someone to bring her a can of Coke—to keep a trace of her old living standard.

   As for me, I spent the first twenty years of my life in Czechoslovakia, under a socialist regime, and 'servant' was a word that in my mind belonged to the last century.

(Petra K., Czech Republic, with a friend from India)

How would you react if you were in Petra's place?

8. Edinburgh, Scotland, August 1990. I was there for three weeks with my cousin Paola and my friend Valentina to study English.

   Once, Valentina and I went looking for my cousin Paola on campus where she was taking her classes. There we met Yuko and a Japanese friend of hers. As Yuko lived in the same house as Paola and they were also in the same class, I asked her whether she had recently seen Paola. After her negative reply, I gently asked her to say to Paola that we were looking for her, if she happened to meet her.

   I noticed that after this request Yuko and her friend stood there instead of continuing their walk, but I did not pay much attention and walked away.

   After fifteen minutes we came back the same way. From afar, I noticed that Yuko and her friend were still standing exactly in the same place as before. They were still waiting for Paola! We decided to hide and to wait for them to go away, in order not to embarrass them. After some ten more minutes, it was clear that they would not leave unless we did something. So I went to them and gently told them that 'it was OK, now Valentina and I would wait for Paola' and thanked them for their patience. They thanked us profusely (for releasing them from their duty, I suppose) and then they walked away.

(Raffaella P., Italy, with a Japanese friend)

How could you tell Yuko that you only want her to inform Paola if she happens to run in to her, not to look for her actively, even less wait for her to pass by? Notice that if you say literally that this is what you want, as Raffaella did in the story, Yuko may think that you want more, as the Japanese are used to stating less than what is really requested.

9. I had the opportunity to spend two weeks in Pretoria and Cape Town, South Africa. I went there with Aldo, an older Italian man who does not speak English.

   Aldo told me that for the 25th anniversary of his marriage he was going to buy a diamond for his wife in South Africa, and he suggested that I be the interpreter between him and the seller.

   Buying a diamond is not easy. You have to know a lot of characteristics: the size, the purity, and so on.

   We spend several hours inspecting many different diamonds. After three hours Aldo was close to selecting among those the diamond he wanted to buy, but he still wanted to know everything about its characteristics in detail. For me and Aldo, the buying process up to then had been proceeding very naturally.

Suddenly the South African seller told us that he was very busy and had other business to do—when we were on the verge of concluding the deal for this expensive stone. In Italy, it sometimes took me the same length of time (a couple of hours) to buy a pair of trousers!

Aldo got upset and we left the store without buying. Then Aldo told me that he had been reluctant to buy the diamond from that seller for other reasons also: the seller did not look him directly into the eyes and had not shaken his hand vigorously . . .

(Mario P., Italy, in South Africa)

How would you react if the salesperson got impatient with you when you were buying something?

How do you feel when, during a conversation, your interlocutor avoids eye contact?

10. When my friends and I first arrived in Maastricht we had not had any sleep for almost 48 hours. But we were all starving, so three of my friends and I headed for a pizzeria in a busy area of town.

After deciphering the menu with some difficulty, we were ready to order; but there was no waiter to be found. About fifteen minutes later we were greeted and our order was taken.

Already very impatient at this point, we waited for another 20–25 minutes before we got our food. In addition, I did not receive exactly what I ordered. (In this situation, in the U.S., a manager would have visited the table, apologized profusely and possibly taken money off the bill.) All I got was a quick, 'I am sorry.'

After we had finished eating, we waited impatiently for the bill, but they never brought it to our table. We had to ask the waiter specifically for the bill, and only then did he oblige.

My reaction to the situation was that, as obvious American tourists, we weren't important to the waiter or restaurant and were therefore disregarded.

(Catherine P., U.S., in the Netherlands)

Describe what eating out in a restaurant means to you. Explain what you expect from a waiter in a restaurant: constant care? discretion?

11. My mother and I arrived in Bad Breisig, Germany, to spend a few days visiting with her relatives. I was very excited to meet these people as I had not seen them since the age of seven. Upon arrival,

my mother and I jumped out of the car and emotionally ran to her aunt and uncle with outstretched arms. Instantly I noticed that they did not reciprocate our emotion as they stood with their arms at their sides and an indifferent expression. This bothered me as I interpreted it as a rude gesture—distant and unwelcoming. Looking back now I realize I misinterpreted their behavior. I know this now because as we continued our visit with them I marked a change in their treatment of us: more touching, smiling, and an overall greater sense of warmth!

(Greta P., U.S., in Germany)

Would you adapt your behavior to the German customs and refrain from smiling, etc. or not?

12. One of my first nights in Maastricht I attended a movie with a few other American students. We were excited to find out that the movies here were in English.

As soon as I had gotten comfortable in my seat and was in to the movie an usher from the movie theater angrily came to me and motioned that I was to remove my feet from the seat in front of me.

(Caroline C., U.S., in the Netherlands)

Try to identify other 'typically American' behavioral traits that may be considered rude in other countries.

13. I was born and raised in Singapore and I went to Taiwan for a visit last year, when I was twenty-three years old. I saw flowered wreaths at a shop. I thought that somebody had passed away, but I then discovered that it was really the Grand Opening of the business. In Singapore, flowered wreaths are only used for funeral ceremonies.

(John C., Singapore, in Taiwan)

Identify regional cultural differences within your own country. Avoid trivia and stereotypes, such as 'there is more sunshine in the South (or the West, or . . .), therefore people are more laid back, etc.'

14. I traveled with Stephanie throughout Europe for twenty days before classes started. In Italy, we were lost in a town and could not find our hostel. A nun offered to help though she spoke very little English. She had a motion that was foreign to us and we interpreted it to mean go away. In reality, it now seems that the nun was begging us to follow.

(Jennifer M., U.S., in Italy)

Which other gestures do you commonly make, and which codified meaning do they convey? How certain are you that those gestures will be correctly interpreted in other countries? How could you find out?

15. In my class there are some thirty Americans, and four Indonesians including me.

When the professor asks questions in class, none of the Indonesians will raise their hands and volunteer for an answer, even if they know it. Typically, only the Americans participate in the classroom discussion.

The professor called one of us one day and asked why we were not participating in the discussions. He attributed our passiveness to a lack of interest in the subject.

In fact, in Indonesia, raising our hands and participating in a class discussion is not out custom. However, we are more than willing to answer questions when the teacher points to us or calls our name in class.

(Omar H., Indonesia, in the Netherlands)

What could be the respective merits of the two teaching styles described above?

16. A businessman from the former Czechoslovakia went to the United Arab Emirates to discuss a deal. The meeting with his counterpart, an Arab businessman, was to take place in the Arab's house, as is apparently common there.

As he was invited to a dinner in someone's house, the Czech businessman decided to bring flowers for his host's wife, as he would have done at home. He was sure the wife would be pleased and her husband would appreciate the attention the visitor paid to them. The talks would start in a positive atmosphere.

The Czech man brought the flowers and expected at least a good welcome, but in fact he was not even allowed to enter the house.

(Petra T., Czech Republic, in the U.A.E.)

What are the respective roles of males and females in your culture? Do people expect the same behavior from both groups, or not?

17. Last summer, my friends and I were traveling by car through various Middle Eastern countries and at one time we stopped at a gas station in a remote area in the south of Turkey.

After we filled our tank we went to the toilet. Surprisingly, there was one there and it was clean as well. With relief we started to wash our hands and faces.

Suddenly two old Turkish farmers in very dirty clothes pushed us aside and started using the wash basins, primarily to wash their feet, their nose and ears, etc.

We felt that these two Turks were very rude, and also, we found it rather bizarre that they would want to wash their feet and some other specific parts of their body such as their nose and ears, while their working clothes were (and remained) incredibly dirty. We stood there rather embarrassed and perplexed and could not understand what was going on there, in a public bathroom.

(Michael F., U.K., in Turkey)

Write down everything you know about Islam, and then check your knowledge on accuracy and comprehensiveness.

18. A few years ago I shared a flat in London with two people from Korea. They were very decent and nice to talk to, but it was nearly impossible for me to share dinner with them. When they were eating, they always made loud smacking noises that I found truly disgusting.

Things got worse when they got a cold and their noses were stuffed. Then they would sit in front of the TV for hours constantly sniffing, without ever blowing their nose.

(Robert K., U.K., with Korean friends)

Would you accept the Koreans' behavior or ask them politely to change?

Make a short inventory of behavioral traits that you would qualify as polite or impolite, concentrating on those where you are most likely to find cultural differences.

19. Last summer I worked in Seattle, USA for four months, as a painter on a ship. On one occasion I was painting the main walkway on the deck of the ship. This is a very popular part of the boat as everybody must pass this area in order to enter or leave the vessel, which makes the painting job less monotonous.

On this particular day the hours passed rather quickly, until I was suddenly shaken from my ladder onto the deck three feet below. A Mexican worker was furiously shouting at me and clearly close to physically assaulting me.

He said that I was 'sneaking him out' and that every time he passed by me, I was staring at him in a threatening way as if to look for a fight. I didn't have a clue what he was talking about.

Other Mexican workers eventually managed to calm him down and convince him that I had absolutely no hostile intentions with respect to him.

(Garret B., U.K., with a Mexican co-worker)

In which situations is eye contact appropriate or inappropriate in your culture? What does the presence or absence of eye contact convey to you when someone is talking to you?

20. A few years ago I spent the summer traveling through Turkey with some friends. We stopped in a small town where Ali, a Turkish guy, probably a little bit older than we, appeared and started to offer us ice-cream. At first we found the asking price incredibly high, but then we started bargaining about it and eventually we discovered that the ice-cream would not cost us any more here than elsewhere.

We started to enjoy this bargaining business we were not used to, so as a game we went on bargaining with Ali about the prices of the different kinds of ice-cream and soft drinks that were on offer.

Then someone as a joke offered Ali the option of getting married with the blond girl from our group against the totality of the ice cream and soft drinks that Ali carried with him. To our surprise, rather than continuing this amusing game, Ali immediately agreed, which is against standard Turkish buying practice. We still thought, though, that he had a good sense of black humor and we continued to work out the specifics of our agreement: the girl against his goods.

However, as our whole group (including the girl) got ready to get into our cars and leave, things got a bit out of hand. Ali tried to prevent us from leaving with the girl, and started offering to us other, more valuable things against the girl. Ali now quickly became rather angry, and we felt it was best to get into our cars as quickly as possible and leave the place without any further ado.

(Jiri P., Czech Republic, in Turkey)

What was the best way to get out of this embarrassing situation?

How much of a say do the parents and the family have in your culture when it comes to the marriage of the children?

21. In a seaside resort in Spain, I approached an African vendor who was trying to sell 'African art' (or so he claimed) to the tourists. There was an inexpensive wooden giraffe I liked and wanted to buy (while I was well aware, of course, that it did not deserve to be qualified as artwork). The African seller asked 1500 pesetas for it (approx. US$ 10.00), so I just opened my wallet and took out the money to pay him.

The African looked rather astonished at what I did, and did not take my money. Rather, he turned to another African nearby and they started a discussion in their native language. After a while, the vendor turned back to me and made it clear that he refused to sell me the giraffe.

(An V.D., Belgium, with an African vendor)

There may be more than one possible explanation for what happened (as there often is). Have you ever bargained for the price in your own country or elsewhere? Is it customary to bargain in your culture, and if so, for which goods is it appropriate/inappropriate (food? clothing? a hotel room? a new or used car? a house? etc.)?

What are the underlying mechanisms of the bargaining process?

22. I am on my university's swimming team, and in 1997 I received a scholarship to participate in a two-week training program in the United States, together with my friend Griet.

We were surprised to be offered to stay for two weeks in the house of Patsy, our American coach, whom we had never met before. For two weeks, we spent virtually our whole day in the company of Patsy, as she was our coach in the training program (we spent eight hours a day with her at the swimming pool) as well as our host (we went home together, did our shopping, and cooked dinner together, watched television together in the evenings). We felt we were getting rather intimate with her, as she was telling us in detail about her recent divorce and other aspects of her private life.

Back in Belgium, we called Patsy a couple of times in order to stay in touch. The next year, Patsy told us on the phone that she had been asked by another Belgian swimming team to set up a training program for them, and that she would be in Belgium for ten days. We were delighted: at last a chance to see each other again!

But Patsy never called. Months later, we discovered that she had indeed come to Belgium for ten days, but she had gone back home without attempting to get in touch with us. We have not heard anything from her ever since.

(Barbara M., Belgium, with an American 'friend')

Do you feel that Patsy's behavior was normal and appropriate, or not?

Define what 'friend' means to you. Which other terms/categories of acquaintances would you want to distinguish? Describe friendship structures in your culture.

23. In the summer of 1997 I spent my vacation in Thailand. I visited a Buddhist temple where everyone was sitting on the ground in front of this immense statue of Buddha, so I did the same. But a temple guard came to me and explained that I had to sit in another position. In fact, I had my legs stretched out in front of me and the soles of my shoes were pointing towards the Buddha: this is totally inappropriate.

Then I left the temple, but again the guard felt the need to intervene. I simply walked towards the entrance door located opposite the Buddha statue, but in that way I was showing my back to the Buddha. I should have moved away from the Buddha walking backwards in order to avoid showing my back to him.

(Filip L., Belgium, in Thailand)

Is there any taboo attached to showing feet or any other part of the body in your culture (of course there is!)? Please explain!

24. A man from Morocco had made an appointment in a hospital in Antwerp, Belgium, for a chest X-ray of his twelve-year old daughter. As he came to the hospital in the morning with her, he discovered that the radiologist was male, and there was no female radiologist available. He refused to let the male radiologist take the X-ray of his daughter and left.

That same afternoon, an orthodox Jewish man came to the same radiology department for an X-ray. Now the team of doctors had changed, and the only radiologist present was a woman. The Jewish man refused to be approached by her and returned home without undergoing the examination.

(Erwin M., Belgium)

In a city where there is a traditional Muslim and/or orthodox Jewish community (or any other community with special needs or taboos), should hospitals ensure that there are always two doctors, one male and one female, on duty in every department? Or should they specify the sex of each doctor when advertising days and hours of consultation? Or should they expect minorities to drop (some of) their taboos and adapt to 'mainstream' culture? Or is it preferable to encourage such minorities to set up their own hospitals and other services (schools, banks, . . .)?

25. For several years in a row we spent our vacation in Mauritius, that beautiful island in the Indian Ocean to the East of Madagascar and Africa. One day, after attending mass at the Catholic Church, a family invited us to have dinner at their home that evening. We were obviously delighted and honored by the invitation which showed that the local people really started to accept our presence among them.

As is common in Belgium, we bought a small present that we brought with us to our hosts' house that evening. We were warmly welcomed, but to our surprise our hosts turned down the gift we had brought, and when we insisted they seemed to become upset rather than anything else. We eventually returned home with our own gift, plus with food and gifts that the hosts had given to *us* at the end of the evening.

Some time later, we were able to clear things out with them and both parties discovered that the etiquette regulating invitations is very different in Mauritius and in Belgium.

(Jan V., Belgium, in Mauritius)

Describe the 'dinner invitation rituals' in your culture: how do you invite someone, do you bring a gift and if so which gifts are appropriate, etc.

SOURCE: "Selected Intercultural Incidents" by S. Paul Verluyten. Reprinted by permission of S. Paul Verluyten. Antwerp, Belgium, pverluy@ruca.us.ac.be

Exercise 3   The Owl: Cross-Cultural Sensitivity

Theodore Gochenour

Purpose

To experience and understand how cultural values influence behavior and relationships.

Group Size

Any number of groups of five to seven members.

Time Required

50 minutes or more.

Preparation Required

In a previous class session, your instructor will assign you to take the role of X-ian, American/Westerner, or observer. You will be given a role sheet to prepare for the exercise. X-ians must meet for about an hour prior to class to prepare for the role-playing. Americans/Westerners meet for no more than 15 minutes before the role-play begins.

Room Arrangement Requirements

Circles of five chairs set up in various places around the room.

Exercise 4   The East–West Game
(Emperor's Pot)

Donald Batchelder

Purpose

To explore dynamics of cross-cultural interactions when one group wants something from the other.

Group Size

An even number of groups with 10 to 19 people in each group.

Time Required

One class period of 90 minutes, or two class periods of 50 minutes each.

Exercise Schedule

	Unit Time	Total Time
1. Groups form Students are assigned a group, either "West" or "East." If the class is large enough to have more than one East/West group, each East group is paired with a West group. Within each group, role assignments are made. Participants within each group decide who will play which role.	**5 min**	**5 min**
2. Groups prepare Groups discuss what their culture and behaviors will be like and they practice various interactions. This part may be done the class before, or assigned as a group project for outside class.	**30+ min**	**35 min**
3. Role play A delegation from the East visits the West group, while simultaneously a delegation from the West visits the East group.	**20 min**	**55 min**
4. Debrief The instructor leads a discussion on what occurred.	**20+ min**	**75 min**

Exercise 5   Race from Outer Space

An Awareness Activity

Dorothy Goler Cash

Goals

1. To compare qualities and skills needed to lead a single racial group and those needed to lead a mixed racial group.
2. To increase awareness of social values and how these may differ among people and groups.

Group Size

Twelve to fifteen members (preferably both male and female).

Time Required

One and one-half to two hours.

Materials

1. Newsprint and felt-tipped markers for each group and for the facilitator.
2. Masking tape for each group.

Physical Setting

A room large enough for three small groups to meet privately, with a place to hang newsprint.

Process

1. The facilitator divides the participants into three groups of four to five members each (extra members become observers):
   a. People from Alpha
   b. People from Beta
   c. People from Gamma
   The facilitator gives three sheets of newsprint, markers, and tape to each group.

2. The facilitator explains that each group is a race of creatures from one of three planets. On each planet all creatures are alike—they look alike, their religion and social class are alike; the only difference is that some are male and some are female. Each group will have fifteen minutes to develop a profile of its race on newsprint by responding to the following items (the facilitator posts the guidelines and reads them aloud):
   a. Describe your physical appearance.
   b. Briefly describe your religion or spiritual/moral beliefs.
   c. Describe the physical environment in which you live.
   d. Describe the socio-economic structure of your society.
   e. What is expected of females in your society?
   f. What is expected of males in your society?

3. At the end of fifteen minutes, each group is directed to choose one of its race to present a profile report to the other groups. (Three minutes per group.)

4. Following the three groups' reports, the facilitator initiates a discussion of similarities and differences among the three races. (Ten minutes.)

5. Next, each race is given ten minutes to list the five most important personal qualities and the five most important skills needed to become a leader of that race. These characteristics are listed on newsprint by each group.

6. The races compare their lists, and characteristics are tallied. For example:

Qualities	A	B	G	Skills	A	B	G
1. Strong	X			1. Communicates	X	X	
2. Brave	X	X		2. Listens			X
3. (etc.)				3. (etc.)			
4.				4.			
5.				5.			

7. The facilitator explains that a war of the planets will destroy Alpha, Beta, and Gamma and that the races must take their possessions and leave to pioneer a new planet that is uninhabited, on which they can all live together. The facilitator redivides the participants into three groups with approximately equal numbers of people from Alpha, Beta, and Gamma in each group. They are given ten minutes to get acquainted and reiterate their similarities and differences.

8. The group must then decide which qualities and skills on the tally sheets they must have available in order to lead this racially mixed group. (One-half hour.)

9. Each group reports on its discussion, then the facilitator leads a general discussion of leadership demands in the new situation and how these might differ from the previous situation. (Twenty minutes.)

Variations

1. Two or three characteristics (step 2) can be provided for each group by the facilitator.

2. The male–female aspect can be eliminated to establish the races as unisex.

3. Each group can select a group leader who best represents the posted qualities and skills, after step 8.

4. Additional questions concerning education, politics, families, etc., can be added to the profile.

Exercise 6   How Many Things do You Like to do at Once? An Introduction to Monochronic and Polychronic Time

Allen C. Bluedorn

Carol Felker Kaufman

Paul M. Lane

Right now you are reading this article in one of two fundamentally different ways. You may be reading and deliberately doing nothing else, or you may be reading and watching television or eating or conducting a conversation or perhaps doing all of these while you read. The former approach, focusing entirely on one task, is the *monochronic* approach to life: do one thing at a time. The latter approaches, simultaneously being actively involved in two or more activities, are termed *polychronic* approaches. And as is implied by the word "approaches," there are degrees of polychronicity, ranging from people who tend to be very monochronic to those who are extremely polychronic.[1]

A question that often arises about the idea of polychronicity concerns the meaning of "simultaneously" and "at once." For example, is working on three different projects during a one-hour period an example of polychronic of monochronic behavior? Are they actually carried out at the same time, or are the parts of one activity interspersed or "dovetailed" with the others? Actually, both patterns are considered to be polychronic time use.

If three projects are dealt with completely and in sequence—A is begun and completed before B is started, B is begun and started before C, and C is begun and completed before any other project is started—the behavior is clearly monochronic, extremely monochronic. However, if the following intermittent pattern occurs—resume A from a previous time, stop A and begin B, stop B and return to A, stop A and begin C, stop C and return to B, etc., always making progress on each task, albeit slowly—a much more polychronic behavior pattern is being followed. Even more polychronic would be someone who is writing a letter, talking on the phone, eating an apple, and listening to the *War of 1812 Overture* simultaneously.

In addition to the directly observable patterning of your activities, your subjective reactions to events are also indicators of polychronicity. Compare, for example, two managers who are both planning to write a report in the morning. Both begin writing, and after thirty minutes, both managers receive a phone call. Manager A regards the phone call as an interruption and attempts to reschedule the call for a time later in the day. Manager B answers the phone, has a complete conversation with the caller, and returns to work on the report after the call. Manager A is relatively monochronic because unplanned, unscheduled events are considered interruptions that should be minimized and not allowed to interfere with scheduled activities. Manger B is relatively polychronic because the unscheduled event was handled as a normal part of life, of equal or greater importance than planned activities (i.e., writing the report).

Thus, we need not consider the concept of "simultaneous," of "at the same time" as an absolute. Were we to do so, we would not be able to speak of degrees of polychronicity and would be forced to classify people as being either polychronic or monochronic. Instead, we can identify time use behavior more accurately along the monochronic/polychronic continuum presented in Figure E6-1.

"How many things do you like to do at once? An introduction of monochronic and polychronic time" by Allen C. Bluedorn, Carol Felker Kaufman, and Paul M. Lane from Academy of Management Executive, 1992, Vol. 6, No. 4. Reprinted by permission of Academy of Management.

449

▪ ▪ ▪ ▪ ▪ ▪ ▪ ▪ ▪ ▪ ▪ **FIGURE E6-1** Monochronic/Polychronic Time Use Continuum

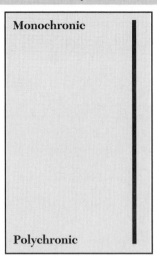

Individuals vary in their orientation along this continuum as do organizations and entire cultures. You will soon be able to identify your own orientation along this continuum as well as recognize how monochronic or polychronic the cultures of your employing organization and department are.[2]

Many of these fundamental variations are so subtle that they often go unrecognized because they exist beneath the level of conscious awareness. Differences in patterns related to time horizon, pace, and punctuality can be found as well as tendencies to use time monochronically or polychronically. However, individuals are sometimes unaware of the particular aspects of their "time personalities," although they can readily report actual time use preferences and behaviors. Furthermore, polychronicity is important, not only because it is a fundamental distinction in and of itself, but because pioneering research indicates that it is related to many of our other important behaviors and attitudes.

Anthropologist Edward Hall has observed that differences in space utilization and the priorities given to human relationships over task accomplishment vary with monochronic and polychronic cultural orientations[3]. His observations indicate that people with a monochronic orientation are task-oriented, emphasize promptness and a concern for others' privacy, stick to their plans, seldom borrow or lend private property, and are accustomed to short-term relationships with other people.

Conversely, people with a polychronic orientation tend to change plans, borrow and lend things frequently, emphasize relationships rather than tasks and privacy, and build long-term relationships with family members, friends, and business partners. Because of these relationships and polychronicity's stature as a core defining characteristic of temporal attitudes and behaviors, an understanding of monochronic and polychronic orientations is vital to understanding our own behaviors, the ability to manage in the international arena, and the ability to manage in an increasingly culturally diverse workplace.

How Polychronic Are You?

Researchers Carol Kaufman, Paul Lane, and Jay Lindquist conducted an extensive survey of polychronic time use in which they examined individuals' tendencies to use time either polychronically or monochronically. They developed a scale, the Polychronic Attitude Index (PAI), which attempted to capture the respondent's general attitude toward performing more than one activity at a time.[4] Respondents were also requested to report the likelihood of their participation in some specific types of activity combinations. As anticipated, several activity combinations were found to be significantly correlated with the PAI. Thus, one's score on the PAI provides a preliminary indication of whether an individual has the

▪▪▪▪▪▪▪▪▪▪▪▪ FIGURE E6-2 Polychronic Attitude Index

Please consider how you feel about the following statements.
Circle your choice on the scale provided: strongly agree,
agree, neutral, disagree, or strongly disagree.

I do not like to juggle several activities at the same time.	Strongly Disagree 5 pts	Somewhat Disagree 4 pts	Neutral 3 pts	Neutral Agree 2 pts	Strongly Agree 1 pt
People should not try to do many things at once.	Strongly Disagree 5 pts	Somewhat Disagree 4 pts	Neutral 3 pts	Neutral Agree 2 pts	Strongly Agree 1 pt
When I sit down at my desk, I work on one project at a time.	Strongly Disagree 5 pts	Somewhat Disagree 4 pts	Neutral 3 pts	Neutral Agree 2 pts	Strongly Agree 1 pt
I am comfortable doing several things at the same time.	Strongly Disagree 1 pt	Somewhat Disagree 2 pts	Neutral 3 pts	Neutral Agree 4 pts	Strongly Agree 5 pts

Add up your points, and divide the total by 4.
Then plot your score on the scale below.

1.0	1.5	2.0	2.5	3.0	3.5	4.0	4.5	5.0

Monochronic   Polychronic

The lower the score (below 3.0) the more monochronic your
organization or department; and the higher the score, (above 3.0)
the more polychronic.

potential and desire to combine activities in the same block of time. In contrast, prior research on polychronicity has been primarily qualitative and observational.

Kaufman, Lane, and Lindquist's work produced the four-item scale presented in Figure E6-2. We suggest that you complete the four-item scale right now and then score yourself. By completing this scale you will gain a better understanding of the monochronic/polychronic continuum and learn about an element of your own personality most people do not know about themselves.

Kaufman et al.'s survey was completed by 310 employed adults in southern New Jersey. Their sample is fairly representative of the general U.S. population and provides the only existing baseline against which your response may be compared.

The mean score in their sample was 3.128, which you can use as a point of comparison for your own score. Kaufman et al. found that polychronic time use was negatively correlated with role overload (the more polychronic the individual, the less role overload the individual tended to experience), and positively correlated with education (the higher the education level, the more polychronic the respondent tended to be), working more than 40 hours per week (the more polychronic tended to work more than 40 hours per week), and social group and club membership (the more polychronic were more likely to belong to social groups and clubs). Polychronic time use was not, however, correlated with gender (contrary to Hall's suggestion), age, income, or marital status.

How Polychronic Are Your Department and Organization?

After Kaufman et al. had completed the first phases of their work, Bluedorn built upon it to develop a five-item scale for measuring the monochronic/polychronic continuum as a component of organizational culture.[5]

Unlike Kaufman et al.'s original scale, his scale asks respondents to report on the general time use orientations they perceive in their departments and organizations rather than about their own individual orientations. This scale, tested in a sample of 205 employees drawn from a medium-size bank in Missouri, is presented in Figure E6-3. We suggest that

▪ ▪ ▪ ▪ ▪ ▪ ▪ ▪ ▪ ▪ ▪ ▪ **FIGURE E6-3** Monochronic/Polychronic Orientation Scale

Please use the following scale to indicate the extent to which you agree or disagree that each statement is true about 1) your organization and 2) your department.

		Strongly Disagree	Somewhat Disagree	Slightly Disagree	Neutral	Slightly Agree	Somewhat Agree	Strongly Agree
We like to juggle several activities at the same time.	Organization	1 pt	2 pts	3 pts	4 pts	5 pts	6 pts	7 pts
	Department	1 pt	2 pts	3 pts	4 pts	5 pts	6 pts	7 pts
		Strongly Disagree	Somewhat Disagree	Slightly Disagree	Neutral	Slightly Agree	Somewhat Agree	Strongly Agree
We would rather complete an entire project every day than complete parts of several projects.	Organization	7 pts	6 pts	5 pts	4 pts	3 pts	2 pts	1 pt
	Department	7 pts	6 pts	5 pts	4 pts	3 pts	2 pts	1 pt
		Strongly Disagree	Somewhat Disagree	Slightly Disagree	Neutral	Slightly Agree	Somewhat Agree	Strongly Agree
We believe people should try to do many things at once.	Organization	1 pt	2 pts	3 pts	4 pts	5 pts	6 pts	7 pts
	Department	1 pt	2 pts	3 pts	4 pts	5 pts	6 pts	7 pts
		Strongly Disagree	Somewhat Disagree	Slightly Disagree	Neutral	Slightly Agree	Somewhat Agree	Strongly Agree
When we work by ourselves, we usually work on one project at a time.	Organization	7 pts	6 pts	5 pts	4 pts	3 pts	2 pts	1 pt
	Department	7 pts	6 pts	5 pts	4 pts	3 pts	2 pts	1 pt
		Strongly Disagree	Somewhat Disagree	Slightly Disagree	Neutral	Slightly Agree	Somewhat Agree	Strongly Agree
We prefer to do one thing at a time.	Organization	7 pts	6 pts	5 pts	4 pts	3 pts	2 pts	1 pt
	Department	7 pts	6 pts	5 pts	4 pts	3 pts	2 pts	1 pt

Add up your points, for your organization, and your department. Divide each total by 5. Then plot both scores on the scale below.

1.0	1.5	2.0	2.5	3.0	3.5	4.0	4.5	5.0	5.5	6.0	6.5	7.0

Monochronic   Polychronic

The lower the score (below 4.0) the more monochronic your organization or department; and the higher the score, (above 4.0) the more polychronic.

you complete the scale in Figure E6-3 for both your department and your entire organization at this time. Then follow the instructions to score your department and organization.

The results in Figure E6-3 reveal your perceptions of your department's and organization's location on the monochronic/polychronic continuum (they will not necessarily be at the same place on the continuum). To determine the "real" locations of your department and organization on the continuum, a survey drawn from a large sample of your department and organization would be necessary. However, your perception by itself is still useful because you can now use it to compare to your own orientation, as measured by the scale in Figure E6-2, to your perceptions of your department and organization in Figure E6-3. We suggest that you now plot your results from Figure E6-2 and Figure E6-3 on the scales in Figure E6-4, which will allow you to compare your personal time use orientation with that which you perceive in your department and organization.[6]

The more polychronic the department, the more externally focused it tended to be. The more polychronic departments also tended to have longer time horizons. These results, which should be considered preliminary findings, may indicate that more polychronic individuals would also havebetter matches with departments that have longer time horizons and more of an external orientation.

Managerial Implications

Although the monochronic-polychronic distinction creates as many potential implications for behavior and action as there are people, three behavioral domains are particularly prominent: individual time management, supervision/coordination, and cultural diversity.

Individual Time Management

Much of traditional prescriptive time management emphasizes a monochronic orientation. To wit: In

▪ ▪ ▪ ▪ ▪ ▪ ▪ ▪ ▪ ▪ ▪ **FIGURE E6-4 Orientation Comparison**

To compare your individual Monochronic/Polychronic orientation with your department and organization, copy your score from the three scales onto this chart.

Individual

1.0	1.5	2.0	2.5	3.0	3.5	4.0	4.5	5.0

Monochronic   Polychronic

Department

1.0	1.5	2.0	2.5	3.0	3.5	4.0	4.5	5.0	5.5	6.0	6.5	7.0

Monochronic   Polychronic

Organization

1.0	1.5	2.0	2.5	3.0	3.5	4.0	4.5	5.0	5.5	6.0	6.5	7.0

Monochronic   Polychronic

To interpret the score, rather than using exact numerical values, use general comparisons such as "middle of the scale" or "clearly above" or "clearly below" the midpoint.

an orderly fashion carefully plan your day by organizing a schedule based on your priorities with a specific allotment of time allocated for each activity. Kaufman et al. have suggested that more polychronically oriented consumers may be more successfully marketed to by learning which types of activities they would like to have combined with others. For example, many people may like to drive and conduct business at the same time (cars and cellular phones) or watch the news and a ball game at the same time (picture-in-picture televisions). Their idea of identifying activities whose combination is attractive to customers can readily be extended to the personal time management enterprise through a series of questions.

- Which activities require your undivided attention?
- Which activities do you prefer to do in combination with other tasks?
- Which activities do you prefer to have grouped together?
- Which activities would you prefer not to be grouped together?

Candid answers to these questions and their corollaries can lead to a more sophisticated approach to time management by moving beyond the general use of priorities to establish schedules. Using this approach in addition to priorities establishes multiple criteria for deciding what things you plan to do when. By identifying which types of things seem to go together and which do not, a self-managed process of job enrichment can accompany the more traditional time management task.

The closer your individual preference score is to that of your organization or department, the closer your "fit" or "match" in terms of the monochronic/polychronic orientation, but the closeness of the match may indicate more than just a fit or misfit with the monochronic/polychronic continuum alone. Bluedorn's bank study revealed some very large correlations between a department's polychronicity and the extent to which it emphasizes an external focus (on customers, suppliers, changing technologies, etc.) rather than an internal focus (interpersonal relations and development, rules, procedures, etc.).

Your own orientation—relatively monochronic or relatively polychronic—will naturally make some of the preceding questions and issues easier to deal with than others, and it will also lead you to different ways to deal with them.[7]

If you are relatively polychronic, you may find it more difficult giving an activity your undivided attention than will your monochronic counterpart. Conversely, if you are relatively monochronic, you may have more difficulty than your polychronic colleague grouping certain tasks together to be performed during the same time period; and the more diverse the activities, the more difficulty you are likely to have grouping them together.

Earlier in this article we discussed behaviors associated with monochronic and polychronic orientations, one of which was the individual's degree of flexibility in regard to plans and schedules. The time management fundamental of the daily To-Do list that identifies your activities and assigns priorities to them is a plan and a schedule. Given the association of polychronic orientations with greater flexibility toward plans and schedules, polychronic individuals may be more flexible in their approach to the To-Do list.

First, they are likely to be less precise in scheduling completion times for tasks, if they even use them at all. Second, they should be more likely to modify the items on their lists (add, postpone, delete) as well as alter item priorities as the day proceeds; but this flexibility is neither a universal advantage nor a disadvantage. Flexibility in one situation may lead to the exploitation of an unanticipated opportunity, but in other situations it may lead to unproductive dithering. Third, the practice of using priorities to say no to lower priority requests, especially when the requested activities involve interaction with other people, should be more difficult for more polychronic people too.

Supervision and Coordination

Regardless of whether you are a first-line supervisor managing a single work group or a CEO managing multiple divisions or departments, the polychronicity issues described for individual time management have direct analogues at these higher levels. Which tasks and assignments do your people seem to be able to handle simultaneously (e.g., selling computers and teaching customers how to use them), and which do they have trouble handling if assigned together (e.g., selling computers and repairing them)? Which tasks do they like to handle simultaneously and which ones are better if given one at a time (e.g., taking inventory)? And which tasks might the organization be able to *learn* to handle simultaneously (e.g., designing new computers and repairing current models), giving it competitive advantages in any environment where time-based competition exists?

All of these issues imply the universal management activity of *delegation*, an act that can be influenced by your own monochronic/polychronic orientation as well as that of your subordinate.

Or consider the very monochronic boss. He is so insistent on a tightly planned schedule—everything has its time and only one thing at a time is scheduled—that he delegates almost everything to ensure his ability to be working on only one task at a time. The resulting avalanche of delegated tasks may overwhelm the constantly inundated subordinate, especially if the subordinate has a relatively monochronic orientation too. The subordinate in this case will gain very little in terms of skill enhancement from the delegated tasks and will probably feel continuously overwhelmed and miserable.

Although similarity between delegator's and subordinate's degree of polychronicity would seem to be the obvious route to harmony and successful delegation outcomes, the issue may be more complex than it appears at first glance. For example, an extremely polychronic boss may so enjoy the stimulation of multiple activities carried out simultaneously or in a short period that she fails to delegate enough tasks to subordinates. Not only would polychronic subordinates be potentially experiencing a too-monochronic environment for their own work satisfaction, but they would not be developing skills in a variety of activities, which is a major benefit and purpose of delegation.

Overall, you need to recognize your own orientation and that of your subordinate because you must take *both* into account to successfully delegate over the long term. If you and your subordinates

differ in orientation, do not consider such differences impediments. Such differences may actually be complementary and provide opportunities to improve the results of delegation in your department.

Cultural Diversity

" . . . when people or groups with different [temporal] perspectives interact, conflicts often arise. Misunderstandings occur when intention and action are judged, by different participants, on different temporal scales. Values are attached to these scales. *The differences in temporal perspective often go unrecognized by the participants.* [Emphasis added] But the differing temporal scales have values associated with them nonetheless, and the temporally divergent actions lead to value inferences by the participants about each other."[8] Thus has James Jones succinctly described the *raison d'etre* for understanding temporal concepts such as monochronic/polychronic orientation when working with culturally diverse groups. To illustrate the problems that may occur if you do not understand these temporal differences, put yourself into the following situation.

You are a sales representative for a U.S-based company that is attempting to expand into overseas markets. As part of the expansion effort, you are traveling around the world to call on several potential customers. Your itinerary includes appointments in New York, Paris, Berlin, Tunis, and Seoul. You want to make a good impression on your firm's prospective clients in each location, but you are far from an expert on France and Germany, let alone Tunisia and South Korea. Thus, you are quite anxious about how people in these different cultures will react to your behavior, and you are equally concerned about your own abilities to attribute the correct meanings to the treatment you will receive from the French, Germans, Tunisians, and Koreans.

That there will be language differences is obvious, but you were recently briefed that some of the greatest non-language difficulties in cross-cultural interactions are those arising from differences in beliefs, values, and behaviors concerning time. For example, what does it mean when a French manager keeps you waiting for thirty minutes after your scheduled appointment time? Does it mean the same thing that it means when an American or a Korean manager keeps you waiting? Similarly, should you end your appointment at the scheduled time if you have not covered everything you want to discuss, or should you attempt to continue your meeting even if you would be going beyond your scheduled time allotment? And should you try to keep going in Tunis, but not in Berlin?

Although you may not know the exact answers to the questions raised in the scenario, you have a competitive advantage over anyone who does not even know that there are questions, that there may be a difference in these matters between cultures, and that these differences are often crucial differences.

It is hackneyed now to expound on the increasingly diverse nature of the American workforce, let alone the greater diversity of the global economy. But if, as analysts such as Hall and Jones assert, the temporal components of culture are the most fundamental, recognizing and understanding those components, and hence the differences among cultures concerning them, becomes essential for productive cross-cultural management and interaction.

For example, when a relatively monochronic North American interacts with a more polychronic Latin American, misinterpretations and misattributions of behavior, if not friction and conflict, are likely to occur unless some attention has been paid to identifying and learning such differences in temporal behavior and norms. The situation may be even more complex in interactions with the Japanese who tend to be monochronic in their use of technology and in dealing with non-Japanese, but who are very polychronic in respect to most other matters. Similarly, misunderstandings may occur among major subcultures within the United States.[9] And monochronic/polychronic time use, however important, is but one of many ways cultures may differ temporally. If people coming from different cultures and traditions understand these differences, or even that there may be differences, conflicts related to polychronicity and other temporal differences can be managed more effectively.

Conclusion

The more polychronically oriented among you have not only finished this article, but have also finished lunch or are about to change the subject of your conversation; the more monochronically oriented

are about to begin lunch or will now make that phone call. Either way, you have learned about one of the subtler yet more profound ways individuals can differ from one another.

As we have seen, an understanding of the monochronic/polychronic continuum can lead to better self-management as well as better management of our organizations and our relationships with people from different cultures and traditions. Given the increasingly international nature of business and management, the strategic competitive advantages will be held by the individuals, companies, and nations who learn how to successfully manage cultural diversity. And temporal differences such as monochronic/polychronic orientations are among the most basic cultural differences to manage.

ENDNOTES

1. Edward T. Hall developed the concepts of monochronic and polychronic time and presented them most extensively in his book, *The Dance of Life: The Other Dimension of Time*, which was published in 1983 by Anchor Press. Additional material is provided in *Understanding Cultural Differences* by Edward T. Hall and Mildred Reed Hall, published in 1990 by Intercultural Press.
2. Some time writers (not all) such as James W. Gentry, Gary Ko, and Jeffrey J. Stoltman in "Measures of Personal Time Orientation," in Jean-Charles Chebat and Van Venkatesan (eds), *Time and Consumer Behavior* (Val Motin, Quebec, Canada: Universite du Quebec a Montreal, 1990), reserve the use of the word "orientation" to refer to an individual's relative emphasis on the past, present, or future. Throughout this article we have used "orientation" in its more traditional, more generic sense of establishing a location or position with respect to some phenomenon.
3. See Hall and Hall, Endnote 1.
4. Kaufman, Lane, and Lindquist's research is reported in their article, "Exploring More Than 24 Hours a Day: A Preliminary Investigation of Polychronic Time Use," *Journal of Consumer Research*, 18, 1991, 392–401. The scale presented in Figure E6-2 produced an alpha reliability coefficient of 0.67 in their study.
5. Allen Bluedorn's study is reported in the working paper, "Time and the Competing Values Model of Culture: Adding the Fourth Dimension," which is available from him at the University of Missouri-Columbia. The scale in Figure E6-3 produced an alpha reliability coefficient of 0.74 in the bank sample, and he is currently involved in research on a large insurance company to see if his results will replicate.

6. Carol Kaufman, Paul Lane, and Jay Lindquist provide a much more extensive discussion of matching individual and organizational time styles and orientations in their article, "Time Congruity in the Organization: A Proposed/Quality of Life Framework," which is forthcoming in *The Journal of Business and Psychology.*

7. We would like to thank the following individuals who suggested some of the implications of MP orientation for individual time management: Kevin Adam, Barbara Braungardt, Greg Boivin, Steven Briggs, James Dawes, Matthew Harper, Mary Hass, Mike Ondracek, and Julie Witte.

8. The quotation is from page 27 of James M. Jones' article, "Cultural Differences in Temporal Perspectives," in J. E. McGrath (ed), *The Social Psychology of Time*, (Newbury Park, CA: Sage Publications, 1988).

9. The relative orientations of North and Latin Americans are taken from Hall, *The Dance of Life.* The description of the Japanese is from Edward T. Hall and Mildred Reed Hall, *Hidden Differences: Doing Business With the Japanese*, which was published in 1987 by Anchor Press/Doubleday.

SOURCE: From *Academy of Management Executive* by Allen Bluedorn et al. Copyright © 1992 by Academy of Management. Reproduced with permission of Academy of Management in the format Other Book via Copyright Clearance Center.

Exercise 7 Double-Loop Thinking: Seeing Two Perspectives

Anne B. Pedersen

Objective

To analyze a cross-cultural encounter from at least two perspectives, that is, from the viewpoints *of both* those involved.

Participants

1–30.

Materials

Handouts, paper and pencil/flip chart or chalkboard.

Setting

No special requirements.

Time

50–70 minutes.

Rationale

The incident provided below describes a cross-cultural encounter between two students, one the participant identifies with and the second, "the other."

The situation is examined first from "your" perspective and then from the perspective of "the other," with a distinction being made between the facts of the encounter and the inferences about it made by each. What you learn during this exercise is a way to see the incident, your role in it, and the values governing your behavior more accurately from the perspective of the other person.

Procedure

Your instructor will provide materials and instructions.

"Double-Loop Thinking: Seeing Two Perspectives" by Anne B. Pederson from Experiential Activities for Intercultural Learning, ed. by H. Seelye. Reprinted by permission of Intercultural Press, Inc., Yarmouth, ME.

Exercise 8   Bribery in International Business

Dorothy Marcic

Purpose

To discuss issues related to ethical behavior in international business dealings.

Group Size

Any number of groups of 4–6 members.

Time Required

One class period.

Preparation Required

Students read mini-cases and decide what action should be taken in each one.

Cases

1. You are driving to a nearby country from your job as a manager of a foreign subsidiary. In your car are a number of rather expensive gifts for family and friends in the country you are visiting. When you cross the border, the customs official tells you the duty will be equivalent to $200. Then he smiles, however, hands back your passport and quietly suggests you put a smaller sum, say $20, in the passport and hand it back to him.

What do you do?

2. You have been hired as an independent consultant on a United States development grant. Part of your job involves working with the Ministry of Health in a developing country. Your assignment is to help standardize some procedures to test for various diseases in the population. After two weeks on the job, a higher-level manager complains to you that money donated by the World Health Organization to the ministry for purchasing vaccines has actually been used to buy expensive computers for top-ranking officials.

What do you do?

3. You have been trying for several months to privatize what was formerly a state-owned business.

The company has been doing well and will likely do better in private hands. Unfortunately, the paperwork is slow and it may take many more months to finish. An official who can help suggests that if you pay expenses for him and his family to visit the parent company in the United States (plus a two-week vacation at Disney World and in New York City), the paperwork can be completed within one week.

What do you do?

4. One of your top managers in a Middle Eastern country has been kidnapped by a terrorist group that has demanded a ransom of $2 million, plus food assistance for refugees in a specified camp. If the ransom is not paid, they threaten to kill him.

What do you do?

5. On a business trip to a developing country, you see a nice leather briefcase (which you badly need) for a reasonable price in the local currency (the equivalent of $200 on the standard exchange rate). In this country, however, it is difficult for the locals to get U.S. dollars or other hard currency. The shop clerk offers you the briefcase for $100 if you pay in U.S. dollars.

What do you do?

6. You are the manager of a foreign subsidiary and have brought your car with you from the U.S. Because it is a foreign-purchased car, you must go through a complicated web of lines and bureaucracy (and you yourself must do it—no one can do it for you), which takes anywhere from 20 to 40 hours during business hours. One official tells you, however, that he can "help" if you "loan" him $100 and buy him some good U.S. bourbon.

What do you do?

7. Your company has been trying to get foreign contracts in this developing country for several months. Yesterday, the brother-in-law of the Finance

Minister offered to work as a consultant to help you secure contracts. He charges one and one-half times more than anyone else in a similar situation.

What do you do?

8. You have been working as the director of a foreign subsidiary for several months. This week, you learned several valued employees have part-time businesses that they run while on the job. One of them exchanges foreign currency for employees and visitors. Another rents a few cars to visitors. And so on. You are told this has been acceptable behavior for years.

What do you do?

9. As manager of a foreign subsidiary, you recently discovered your chief of operations has authorized a very convoluted accounting system, most likely to hide many costs that go to his pocket. Right now, you have no real proof, but rumors are circulating to that effect as well. This chief, however, has close ties to officials in the government who can make or break your company in this country.

What do you do?

10. You have been hired to do some management training in a developing country. The costs of the program are almost entirely covered by a U.S. government agency. The people responsible for setting up one of the programs in a large company tell you they want the program to be held in a resort hotel (which is not much more expensive than any other) in a beautiful part of the country. Further, because they are so busy with all the changes in their country, they cannot come to a five-day program, which is what has been funded. Could you please make it a little longer each day and shorten it to three days? You would get paid the same.

What do you do?

11. You have been hired by an investment firm funded by U.S. dollars. Your job is to fund companies in several former communist countries. If you do not meet your quota for each of three months, you will lose your job, or at least have your salary severely cut back. One of the countries is still run by communists,

though they have changed the name of their political party. They want you to fund three companies that would still be tightly controlled by the state. You know they would hire their relatives to run those companies. Yet, if you don't fund them, no other opportunities will exist for you in this country.

What do you do?

12. Your new job is to secure contracts with foreign governments in several developing countries. One of your colleagues takes you aside one day to give you "tips" on how to make sure you get the contracts you are after. He tells you what each nationality likes to hear, to soothe their egos or other psychological needs. For example, people in one country like to be told they will have a better image with the U.S. government if they contract with your company (of course, this is not true). If you tell them these things, he says, they will most definitely give you the contracts. If not, someone in another company will tell them similar things and they will get the contracts.

What do you do?

13. You have been asked to be on the board of directors of a large telecommunications company about to be privatized. The two main organizers of the project, former government officials, have asked that their names not be used until after all the governmental approval is set, as they are concerned with being accused of using undue influence in other privatization projects.

What do you do?

14. You are the manager of a foreign company in a country where bribery is common. You have been told an important shipment has arrived but it will take up to six months to clear the paperwork. However, you were informed casually that a "tip" of $200 would cut the time to three days.

What do you do?

From *International Management, Cases and Exercises 1st edition* by Marcic/Puffer. © 1994. Reprinted with permission of South Western, a division of Thomson Learning, www.thomsonrights.com. Fax 800 730 2215. Management International.

Exercise 9 Babel: Interpersonal Communication

Phillip M. Ericson

Goals

1. To examine language barriers, which contribute to breakdowns in communication.
2. To demonstrate the anxieties and frustrations that may be felt when communicating under difficult circumstances.
3. To illustrate the impact of nonverbal communication when verbal communication is ineffective and/or restricted.

Group Size

An unlimited number of equal-sized groups of four, six, or eight members each.

Time Required

Approximately two hours.

Physical Setting

A room large enough for the groups to meet comfortably.

Materials

1. A pencil and paper for each participant.
2. A blindfold for each group member.

Process

1. The facilitator divides the large group into subgroups.
2. When the groups have assembled, the facilitator announces that each group is to create a language of its own. This language must be significantly different from English and must include the following:
   1. a greeting
   2. description of some object, person, or event
   3. an evaluative statement about an object or a person
   4. a farewell

Group members must be able to "speak" their group's language at the end of this step. (Forty-five minutes.)

3. Within each language group, members number themselves sequentially, i.e., 1, 2, 3, 4, etc. The facilitator announces the location of a new group to be composed of all participants numbered 1. He likewise forms new groups of participants numbered 2, 3, 4, and so on.
4. The facilitator directs members to pair off in the new groups. Each member must teach his new language to his partner without using English or any other recognized language. (Twenty minutes).
5. The facilitator distributes a blindfold to each group. A blindfolded volunteer from each group teaches his language to the group. A second volunteer repeats this task. (Twenty minutes.)
6. The facilitator distributes blindfolds to all remaining participants. Participants are told to stand in their second groups, and all chairs are moved aside. Participants blindfold themselves and are instructed to find their original groups without the use of any conventional language or people's names.
7. When the original groups have been reformed, the facilitator instructs them to discuss the activity and to answer the following questions:
   1. What did this experience illustrate about communication?
   2. How did you feel during the experience?
   3. What did you learn about yourself from it?
8. The facilitator leads a general discussion on the problems faced by people who do not understand a language and on the difficulties that blind people may have in communicating.

Variations

1. The requirements for the new vocabulary can be changed to make the task more difficult or less difficult.
2. All participants can be blindfolded for step 5.
3. Real language can be used. The phrases can be preset.

"Babel: Interpersonal Communication" by Philip M. Ericson from *A Handbook of Structured Experiences for Human Relations Training*, Vol. V. pp. 16–17. Copyright © 1975 by Pfeiffer, an imprint of Jossey-Bass Inc., Publishers.

Exercise 10   Ugli Orange Case

Robert J. House

Purpose

To practice negotiation skills in a conflict situation.

Group Size

Any number of groups with three members.

Time Required

40 minutes

Related Topics

Interpersonal Communication

Exercise Schedule

	Unit Time	Total Time
1. **Groups form** Form groups of three members. One person will be Dr. Roland, one will be Dr. Jones, and the third will be an observer.	5 min	5 min
2. **Read roles** Roland and Jones read only their own roles, while the observer reads both.	5 min	10 min
3. **Role-play** Your instructor will give you more information to begin the role-play.	10 min	20 min
4. **Observers report** Observers report the solutions reached. Groups describe decision-making process used.	10 + min	30 min
5. **Class discussion** The instructor will lead a discussion on the exercise.	10 min	40 min

SOURCE: "Ugli Orange Case" by Robert J. House from *Organizational Behavior*, 4e by Marcic. Copyright (copyright symbol) 1995 by Dr. Robert J. House. Reprinted by permission of the author.

Exercise 11   Work Values Exercise

Carol Wolf

Objectives

- To get people to think and talk about their own values and life histories as they relate to work, including the cultural patterns embodied therein.
- To explore the ways in which the group or organization reflects or stimulates conflict with the values of individual members of subgroups.
- To engage in values clarification (individual and group).

Setting

Sufficient space for large- and small-group discussions.

Participants

Individual, small groups (3–5), or large group.

Time

1 hour.

Materials

Flip chart, markers. Participants need pen and paper. Handouts 1 and 2.

Rationale

Diverse groups of people often have very different ideas about the meaning and purpose of work. Some of these differences are culturally based, others may stem from different life experiences. Quite often, these differences are unspoken, or even outside of awareness—yet they are often the root of assumptions, judgments, and conflicts in the workplace. Understanding personal and organizational value systems is a critical component in the development of diversity awareness and the bringing about of organizational change. Highlighting core organizational values, or uncovering what may be unspoken or hidden values, can help groups and individuals to better understand what enables (or disables) teamwork and effective organizational alignment. The "Work Values Exercise" helps participants take the first steps in building a foundation based on the valuing of diverse

perspectives and skills. (Note: The group must be at a point in their development where open dialogue about differences is acceptable.)

Procedure

1. Have participants break into small groups (3–4 members each). Ask them to respond to and discuss their answers to each of the questions listed in Handout 1. (Approximately 20 minutes. Facilitator should make sure they don't get stuck on the first subject.) In the meantime, put the definition of "value" on a flip chart and post the list of work values.

2. Distribute Handout 2. Based on their previous discussions, ask participants to pick their three most important values from Handout 2 and, continuing in their groups, do all or some of the following:
   a. Talk about the values they chose, why they picked them, and what they mean for them.
   b. Discuss how they believe their values differ from the values of their group (organization) as a whole.
   c. Talk about what needs to change in order for them to feel more comfortable with/committed to the group.

Outcomes

Information gleaned from this exercise can be used as lead-in to a variety of areas, including improving reward and motivation policies, evaluating employee performance, improving team building, diagnosing work conflicts, or clarifying group identity.

Handout 1

Questions

1. When was the first time in your life that you worked? Describe what you did. How did you know it was work?

464

2. What was positive about this experience? What was negative?
3. What did you learn from this and subsequent experiences about yourself and work? (For example, why you work, what you need in order to work well.)
4. What messages or lessons did you get from your family about work? Who taught you? How?

Examples

"I learned that I can't stand tedious jobs" (work value: variety).

"I learned that the people I work with are important" (work value: relationships).

Handout 2

Definition of "Value"

A principle or quality intrinsically valuable or desirable (Webster's Ninth New Collegiate Dictionary).

Work Values

Respect
Communication
Clear purpose
Relationships—working with others
Individual achievement
Challenging work
Contribution to goals/sense of accomplishment
Recognition
Rewards
Security
Chance to develop/improve
Efficiency
Good pay/benefits
Variety of work
Control over work
Environment/surroundings
Others:

"Work Values Exercise" by Carol Wolf from *Experiential Activities for International Learning*. Reprinted by permission of Intercultural Press, Inc., Yarmouth, ME.

Exercise 12 Japanese Decision-Making Exercise (Ringi/Nemawashi)

William Van Buskirk

Goals

To give students the opportunity to work through a meaningful task in the manner of Japanese consensual decision making.

   To compare their own experiences of group decision making with the Japanese approach.

Preparation (optional)

Background reading: Chapter 3 of *The False Promise of the Japanese Miracle*, by P. Sethi, N. Namiki, and C. Swanson.

Exercise Schedule

	Unit Time	Total Time
1. Introduction Instructor explains the processes of Ringi and Nemawashi and sets up the structure of the exercise. Group composition includes group leaders (Kacho) and student manager (Bucho).	**5 min**	**5 min**
2. Primary groups meet Groups of four to six members design a final exam format that is likely to be a valuable learning tool and basis of evaluation.	**20 min**	**25 min**
3. Secondary groups meet New groups of four to six members continue with assignment as above, using what was discussed in primary groups as a basis. These are called secondary groups (Kacho). After this session, groups can meet in whatever way they want. The professor will give guidance during one or two open ended class sessions. Outside class meetings occur at the instigation of the group leaders and the student manager.	**20 min**	**45 min**
4. Whole class decides Generation of a Ringi document specifying the content of the exam. Document must be signed by all students in the class. Instructor discusses what problems, if any, this document might cause with university administration.	**30 min** **(new class)**	
5. Evaluation Evaluation of the exercise. How much did it resemble the descriptions of Ringi and Nemawashi found in the literature? What difficulties did we encounter? Were those difficulties likely to be present in the Japanese context? If so, how would they likely be managed? This evaluation may be done in the context of class discussions and as part of the final exam.	**15 min**	**45 min**

Exercise 13   Dimensions of National Culture and Effective Leadership Patterns: Hofstede Revisited

Peter Dorfman

Purpose

To measure value systems.

Group Size

Any number.

Time Required

20 minutes.

Exercise Schedule

	Unit Time	Total Time
1. Preparation Complete inventory.		
2. Class discussion	**20+ min**	**20+ min**

Instructor leads a discussion on Hofstede's value system:

In the questionnaire that follows, please indicate the extent to which you agree or disagree with each statement. For example, if you strongly agree with a particular statement, circle the 5 next to the statement.

1 = strongly disagree
2 = disagree
3 = neither agree nor disagree
4 = agree
5 = strongly agree

Questionnaire

	strongly disagree			strongly agree	
It is important to have job instructions spelled out in detail so that employees always know what they are expected to do.	1	2	3	4	5
Managers expect employees to closely follow instructions and procedures.	1	2	3	4	5
Rules and regulations are important because they inform employees what the organization expects of them.	1	2	3	4	5
Standard operating procedures are helpful to employees on the job.	1	2	3	4	5
Instructions for operations are important for employees on the job.	1	2	3	4	5
Group welfare is more important than individual rewards.	1	2	3	4	5

Group success is more important than individual success.	1	2	3	4	5
Being accepted by the members of your work group is very important.	1	2	3	4	5
Employees should pursue their own goals only after considering the welfare of the group.	1	2	3	4	5
Managers should encourage group loyalty even if individual goals suffer.	1	2	3	4	5
Individuals may be expected to give up their goals in order to benefit group success.	1	2	3	4	5
Managers should make most decisions without consulting subordinates.	1	2	3	4	5
Managers should frequently use authority and power when dealing with subordinates.	1	2	3	4	5
Managers should seldom ask for the opinions of employees.	1	2	3	4	5
Managers should avoid off-the-job social contacts with employees.	1	2	3	4	5
Employees should not disagree with management decisions.	1	2	3	4	5
Managers should not delegate important tasks to employees.	1	2	3	4	5
Managers should help employees with their family problems.	1	2	3	4	5
Managers should see to it that employees are adequately clothed and fed.	1	2	3	4	5
A manager should help employees solve their personal problems.	1	2	3	4	5
Management should see that all employees receive health care.	1	2	3	4	5
Management should see that children of employees have an adequate education.	1	2	3	4	5
Management should provide legal assistance for employees who get into trouble with the law.	1	2	3	4	5
Managers should take care of their employees as they would their children.	1	2	3	4	5
Meetings are usually run more effectively when they are chaired by a man.	1	2	3	4	5
It is more important for men to have a professional career than it is for women to have a professional career.	1	2	3	4	5
Men usually solve problems with logical analysis; women usually solve problems with intuition.	1	2	3	4	5
Solving organizational problems usually requires an active, forcible approach, which is typical of men.	1	2	3	4	5
It is preferable to have a man, rather than a woman, in a high-level position.	1	2	3	4	5

Background Work Values

Geert Hofstede examined international differences in work-related values and came up with the four dimensions: power distance, uncertainty avoidance, individualism, and masculinity. Below are brief definitions of each of the four dimensions.

Power Distance (PD) measures human inequality in organizations, looking at the boss's decision-making style, employees' fear of disagreeing with the superior, and how subordinates prefer a boss to make decisions. Power distance assesses the interpersonal power or influence between lower- and higher-ranking employees, as perceived by the less powerful one. Essentially, it looks at how less powerful people validate the power structure. Cultures with a low score tend to respect individuals, strive for equality, and value happiness. Those with a high score look to servitude and tact of lesser individuals, while allowing great privileges to those with influence. Other characteristics of low-scored cultures are that managers tend to consult subordinates when making decisions, perceived work ethic is stronger, close supervision is evaluated negatively by subordinates, and employees are cooperative. High scorers are less likely to have managers consult subordinates, and employees are reluctant to trust each other.

Uncertainty Avoidance (UA) explains each society's Search for Truth and the anxiety people feel in a situation with conflicting values or unstructured outcomes. Cultures with high uncertainty avoidance try to minimize the anxiety with a thorough set of strict laws and behavior norms. To ease the discomfort on the philosophical level, there is a belief in One Truth, the One Way. Low uncertainty avoidance cultures tend to have fewer rules and more acceptance of diversity of thought and behavior. Organizations, too, try to avoid uncertainty by creating rules, rituals, and technology that give the illusion of predictability. Even group decision-making, however, is a means for avoiding risk because no one is held accountable. Countries that have low UA tend to have less emotional resistance to change, a stronger achievement motivation, a preference for managerial careers over specialist fields, and hope for success. On the other hand, countries with high UA tend to have more emotional resistance to change, weaker achievement motivation, a preference for specialist careers over managerial, and a fear of failure.

Individualism (I) looks at the degree to which people are part of groups or on their own. In collective societies, everyone is born into a strong clan of uncles, aunts, and cousins (even third and fourth) who are part of one unit. Each person contributes to the group and at some time receives care from the group. Loyalties are to the group above everything else. In more individualistic societies, people are more or less on their own and are expected to take care of themselves and their immediate family. In collective countries (with a low I score), there is often an emotional dependence on the company, managers aspire to conformity and orderliness, group decisions are considered better than individual ones, and managers value security in their work.

In societies with a high I score, though, there is more emotional independence from the company; managers aspire to leadership and variety; managers seek input from others, but individual decisions are still seen as better, and managers value autonomy in their work.

Masculinity (M) versus its opposite, femininity, examines how roles are distributed between the sexes. The predominant pattern of socialization worldwide is for men to be more assertive and women to be more nurturing. In countries with high M scores, the successful manager is seen as more male—aggressive, competitive, just, and tough—and not as feminine—soft, yielding, intuitive, and emotional (as the stereotypes define it). In countries with high M scores, earnings, recognition, and advancement are important to employees, work is more central to people's lives, achievement is defined in terms of wealth and professional success, people prefer more salary rather than fewer working hours. "Theory X" gets some acceptance, and there is higher job stress. In societies with low M scores, on the other hand, co-operation and security are valued by employees, work is less central to people's lives, achievement is defined in terms of human interactions, people prefer fewer working hours rather than more salary, "Theory X" is less accepted, and there is lower job stress.

TABLE S13-1 Cultural Dimension Scores for Ten Countries

	PD	*ID*	*MA*	*UA*	*LT*
USA	40L	91H	62H	46L	29L
Germany	35L	67H	66H	65M	31M
Japan	54M	46M	95H	92H	80H
France	68H	71H	43M	86H	30*L
Netherlands	38L	80H	14L	53M	44M
Hong Kong	68H	25L	57H	29L	96H
Indonesia	78H	14L	46M	48L	25*L
West Africa	77H	20L	46M	54M	16L
Russia	95**H	50**M	40*L	90**H	10**L
China	80**H	20**L	50**M	60**M	118H

PD = Power Distance; ID = Individualism; MA = Masculinity; UA = Uncertainty Avoidance; LT = Long-Term Orientation; H = top third, M = medium third, L = bottom third (among 53 countries and regions for the first four dimensions; among 23 countries for the fifth)
*Excerpted from Geert Hofstede (1993), *Academy of Management Executive*, 7(1), 81–94.
Used with permission.
**estimated

Exercise 14   Royal Flush: A Cross-Cultural Simulation

Jessica Robinson, Tamu Lewars, La Shanda Perryman, Torla Crichlow, Kimberly Smith, John Vignoe,
Current and Former Students, Emory University, Atlanta, Georgia

Background

Corporations need to adopt a global mindset to stay competitive. As a result, cultural sensitivity can contribute as much to the bottom line as does technical proficiency. More and more, the employee population of many corporations reflects the diverse demographics of its environment. Additionally, there is an increasing need for interaction and partnerships between U.S. and foreign corporations. Moreover, companies are realizing that in order to successfully achieve company objectives; managers need to adjust negotiation and interpersonal skills to accommodate cultural differences and distinctions.

The Simulation

The class will be divided into four cultures. Each team will receive 16 cards. Each of these cards is worth a certain number of points depending on the culture. You can divide these cards within your culture however you want. You can work as individuals, small groups of 2 or 3, or a collective in order to achieve your culture's goal. There are three phases to Royal Flush: the Deal, the Shuffle, and Poker.

Objective

In order to be successful, you must achieve two goals. First, using the cultural skills learned in class, you are to observe the characteristics of the other cultures and attempt to successfully adapt or flex to the culture. Second, achieve the goal set for you by the CEO of your culture.

Task

Your CEO is in dire need of 320 points. The CEO needs these points so that your culture can complete the research for the cure of CULTURITUS, a deadly disease in your land. Your country can start treatment for this deadly disease if you receive only 190 points and can achieve a cure with 320 points. Therefore, your culture/company needs a minimum of 190 points and a maximum of 320 points. You do not have to reveal how many points you need to the other cultures, but you can reveal your purpose for trying to trade for points. All cultures (Jack, King, Queen, and Ace) share the common goal of researching a cure for CULTURITUS.

Getting Your Points

The other cultures combined have the ability to give you the points you need. In order to get those points, you must adapt to their culture, interact with them in that culture, and ask for the card that you need. If the opposite culture does not feel that you have adapted, they may choose to give you a different card from the one you want. It is up to you to let the other culture know what card you need and what cards will be acceptable. The culture that approaches or initiates conversation must be the culture that adapts, but it is also the culture that can receive cards.

The Deal (10–15 minutes)

You are divided into 4 groups, ACE Culture, KING Culture, QUEEN Culture, and JACK Culture. Use this time to read through a description of your cultures and get to know yourself. Also, decide how you are going to work for your points. You can work as individuals, pairs, or a collective; it's up to you.

The Shuffle: (5–10 minutes)

You are in a social setting interacting with your culture. Take this time to observe the other cultures, while interacting only with your culture.

Poker: 10–20 minutes

Play the game. The key is to interact. You can return to your respective cultures as many times as you want to discuss different strategies or see if you have maximized your points. Remember that for every card you get, you must give up one card. At the end of the poker phase, your culture can only hold 16 cards.

SOURCE: "Royal Flush: A Cross Cultural Simulation" by Jessica Robinson, Tamu Lewars, La Shanda Perryman, Torla Crichlow, Kimberly Smith, John Vignoe, Current and Former Students, Emory University, Atlanta, Georgia, published in Business Communication Quarterly, Dec., 2000, Vol. 63, Issue 4.

Exercise 15 Management in the Year 2200

Hiroaki Izumi

Purpose

To explore issues in management in other cultures.

Group Size

Any number of groups of four to six people.

Time Required

50 minutes.

Exercise Schedule

1. Pre-class

Read background and answer questions.

	Unit Time	Total Time
2. Group discussions	**20 min**	**20 min**
Groups of four to six answer questions.		
3. Class discussion	**30 min**	**50 min**

Groups report results and instructor leads discussion on issues of "cross-cultural" management.

Background

The year is 2200 A.D. During the past two centuries, Earth has achieved interstellar travel at faster-than-light warp speed. Because of overcrowding and depletion of resources on Earth during the second half of the 22nd century, we began to colonize other planets in other star systems. People were sent out to assist in civilizing uninhabited planets and to extract their resources for shipping back to the industries in our home solar system. About 100 years ago, a major political upheaval on Earth put most of the colonies out of touch with us for about 75 years. They no longer were able to ship resources to Earth so they began interstellar commerce amongst themselves. They

"Management in the Year 2200" by Hiroaki Izumi.
Reprinted by permission of City University of Hong Kong.

continued to extract resources but they also began some limited industrialization themselves. The level of development on these colonies could be compared to that of LDCs on Earth during the 20th century, but at a much higher level of technological sophistication.

Recently, about the year 2175, when contact was re-established with the Earth colonies, interstellar trade with them was also re-established. Earth is trying to regain the lost commercial trade that existed prior to the political problems and loss of contact. But the situation has changed. The colonies no longer act as colonies, but more like nations on their own. They have tariff barriers, their own commercial laws and codes based on the old common law ideas, political parties and full governments, their own corporations and business infrastructures, their own educational systems, and their own market structures. In fact, during almost one generation of separation from Earth, each of the colonies began to develop their own human subcultures based on the conditions that existed on their planet.

One planet that recently regained contact with Earth is in the Orion constellation of stars. It is the only colony in that area, so the colony is known as the Orion colony and the people on the planet as Orions.

The Orion colony is rather strange by Earth standards. The planet is relatively new in geological terms and still has Ice Age conditions. The climate is very harsh due to the cold weather. It is, however, rich in certain rare elements trapped in pockets in the ice. Before losing contact with Earth, the Orions traded in the rare elements that they extracted from the ice by mechanical means. The equipment is highly sophisticated and fully automated. Unfortunately, even automated equipment must be maintained and serviced. Furthermore, the ice must be prospected using labor-intensive methods in which individuals must go out on the ice and run specialized sensing equipment, which has a very limited life-span.

> Earth, surprisingly, has not changed much in how we do business, our diversity of political parties and ideologies, our lifestyles, our mores and norms; and our knowledge of how to deal with strange cultures. We still tend to be slightly xenophobic, too concerned with making money, living for the short term with emphasis on quick return on investments (though there is some improvement in favoring long-term investments among some groups), and we haven't improved our production and marketing skills much. We've only improved our production methodologies.

Because of the cold weather and great physical endurance needed for prospecting and servicing and maintaining the equipment, most of the field workers are women who are much better suited to the work. Women's better physical heat retention, smaller size, greater manual dexterity, and greater muscle endurance provide them with physiological advantages that cannot be matched by men. Having recognized these qualities early on, Orion women were better technically educated than Orion men. Because of their technical expertise and educational advantages, they also quickly took over control of much of the organizational management positions, with women generally being the top executives. The men were relegated to lower-level positions in the large mining organizations, the small-business market system, lower level education system, clerical work, or househusbands. In fact, one could say that the traditional Earth-type sex relationships were reversed on the Orion colony.

This has led to some interesting conditions concerning the Orion culture. First, a strong feminist culture exists. Women like to be seen as individualistic, independent, and stoic, but at the same time very feminine in appearance. The frontier mentality of individualism and independence runs strong in both the female and the male population. Small nuclear families that often stay together for many years are the norm.

The language is the same as the Interlingua used on Earth, so they have no real communication problem. People from Earth do find the common usage of the language a little strange. Instead of the subject-verb-object sentence structure used on Earth, Orions tend to leave out the subject and start sentences with verbs. A linguist from Earth might consider this a sign of a high level of action orientation in the society. Orions say it is because they generally know who they are talking to during a conversation.

Everyone is literate and highly educated through the education system based on lesson transmission to children at home. Children receive their lessons on the three-dimensional holographic, interactive television network, which is the same system used for entertainment in the home and communication with those outside. Because education is free and widely available, it could be depreciated. But survival on the ice, work, and independence depends on good education, so it is appreciated and even valued. With its wide availability, everyone has achieved a high level of education for a colony in the boondocks.

> The Orions spend much of their free time trying to achieve higher self-actualization through greater education. You might even say they have a thirst for exploration of new territories, new ideas, new levels of understanding, and their own minds.

They live in underground family dwellings that are connected to others by 3-D holographic video-telephone, computerized delivery systems connected to all major stores and services, and computerized pneumatic shuttle service—like individualized train compartments. Dwellings are grouped in sets of three called a module. These sets of three dwellings are, in turn, connected to a more widely spaced grouping of three other family modules. These sets of three modules are called blocks. Nine blocks make up a district. Some districts are made up on strictly commercial units, also structured in the modular system of modules-blocks-districts. An indeterminate number of districts make up one Orion city. Everything in these cities is underground, but the high-technology infrastructure allows for rapid communication, transport, and intra-city commerce. Unfortunately, this superb infrastructure tends to break down in intercity commerce. While communication over the ice is no problem most of the time, transportation across it is often interrupted by icestorms, shifting ice and icequakes, electromagnetic storms, and static-electricity storms.

The nuclear families of a dwelling module is the core of the culture, and each modular group of families tries to be as self-sufficient as possible because they could easily be cut off from the rest of the district or city by a major disaster. The people in each module are so close that they often share child-care duties, work duties, religions, and sometimes even spouses.

In terms of the old Hofstede culture analysis, the module dwellers would be described as moderate in Individualism, low in Power Distance, low in Uncertainty Avoidance, and high in Femininity. This means that they have slight collectivist tendencies based on the modular dwelling system. The low Power Distance characteristic arises from the individualistic and equalizing tendencies of the frontier culture; out on the ice, your status doesn't matter. They have to have low Uncertainty Avoidance. It's a risky life in the colonies, especially on the Orion ice. High Uncertainty Avoidance people wouldn't last. The high Femininity level results from the frontier mentality also. Because they have to always look out for each other when people are working on the ice, they tend to be greatly concerned for others and their own quality of life. They also emphasize relationships over acquisition of money and material goods because they have most of what they need. They also have learned that being too assertive on the ice can be fatal.

As for other value dimensions, they believe in harmony with nature (especially the ice), have a "present" Time Orientation (they really don't have much of a past and they don't know what is going to happen in the future), and a "doing" Activity Orientation (they like to work and accomplish things). Living on the ice with a high Femininity Behavior Orientation, they have come to believe that people are generally good. They have a slight Group Orientation in their belief concerning people's relationship with others due to their modular dwelling system. The modular dwelling system has also contributed to their "mixed" Conception of Space. In one module, there is really little private space. But with those outside, they tend to stress privacy.

The tendency for family modules to be somewhat private towards other modules or strangers allows them to hold many different philosophical beliefs without conflict between philosophies.

Their religions are generally electric and very individualized. There is no real common system of religions. The only consistent religious factor is that families in one module tend to hold similar religious or philosophical beliefs. In general, people from one module will not ask people from another module about their private lives, but will accept people on face value. A cultural norm, though, is that if you are visiting another module where the values differ from your own, you will accept the values, beliefs, and behaviors of that module as your own as long as you are a guest in that module. Thus the beliefs and values of the people must allow for adaptability and tolerance. You cannot visit another module and push your values and behaviors on them, nor can you use them yourself. Such behavior would constitute a gross violation of social norms. You would no longer be welcome in that module.

The demographics of Orion colony show that the mean age of the people is about 50 Earth years and they have a life span of about 150. So the population pattern tends to be tulip shaped. They normally don't start families until at least 40 Earth years. Starting families is not a problem because the sexes are almost evenly balanced. The tulip-shaped demographics and equal number of sexes resulted from the Orions' belief in birth control to regulate population and sex of children.

The government of Orion colony is based on a modular structure of city-states. Each Orion city-state has its own separate form of democratic government, but they all send representatives to a planetary council in the largest city of Intbus.

Within each city-state, the exact form of government can vary, but they are generally democratic structures based on representation by districts. Districts usually have no need for government, per se, but they usually do have ad hoc working committees to get things done on a group basis. These ad hoc committees spring up and then disband on a need basis. The lack of a strong governmental tendency at the district level can be attributed to the Orions' general dislike of extensive government interference. Modules like to be left alone, as do districts. If anything needs to be done on a group basis, the people would rather solve the problem on an ad hoc consensus and involvement basis. So committees for special projects are always springing up and then disappearing. They can work in an ad hoc manner because of the highly accommodative nature, low Power Distance, high Femininity Behavior Orientation, present Time Orientation, slight Group Orientation, and "doing" Activity Orientation of the Orions.

> Their business systems also tend to be highly modular. Even the large firms are based on a modular structure, with each module handling a function, production, or geographic area.

These business modules are highly flexible in that a single functional module from the support core could be transplanted into another business organization without much trouble. Production modules, which constitute the technical core of industrial organizations, could be easily assigned to produce different products if they were provided with the correct equipment. Geographic business modules of the marketing function could easily be reassigned responsibility for a different geographic region without too much trouble. Thus Orion business organizations are highly flexible and loosely connected.

Each major business organization is made up of a central core module that coordinates the work of all other modules; functional, production, and geographic modules; and sourcing modules. Within these modules, the workers generally work in teams with very little hierarchy. The modules can be said to have lean, flat structures with little bureaucracy. Usually everyone is on the same level and the leadership works in a facilitative rather than directive manner.

The functional modules are normally production, marketing, finance, and accounting. The only type of function that they really lack is the Research and Development (R&D) function. Businesses in the Orion colony do not conduct R&D because they have not yet produced significant technological research expertise. The sourcing modules are closely interlinked modules that supply resources and materials to the technical core of the main organization. Each of these sourcing modules are smaller organizations in their own right. They are linked with the major business organization through a commonality in organizational missions, philosophies, goals, and objectives. These smaller sourcing modules are, however, expendable to the major business organization.

If they are no longer needed because the major business organization has changed its business or its organizational mission, the services of the sourcing modules may be sold to another major business or they may be left on their own.

Production systems in businesses tend to be highly modular. The production equipment is fashioned to take advantage of the flexible manufacturing systems technology. One piece of equipment can often be used for manufacturing several different items. All of this equipment is fully automated. The work of production team members is to service, maintain, control, and modify the equipment to obtain the best performance from the equipment.

The Orion economy is dominated by the major conglomerate businesses that extract rare elements. Using mining as their cash cow, these businesses have diversified into industrial goods production, consumer goods production, and services. Surrounding these major conglomerates are many medium-sized sourcing modules. Servicing these sourcing modules are small-sized independent firms. Other specialized services and goods are provided by other small independent firms. For consumer retailing, boutiques or small shops are the norm. The only exception is food, which is centrally produced and distributed directly to homes. Most of these businesses can be considered relatively young, except for the major conglomerates, which got their start when the planet was colonized.

People shop when they have to. Foodstuffs are delivered to their homes, so weekly grocery shopping is unnecessary. Clothing and other household goods are bought at the small boutiques in the shopping districts. Purchases are made on an electronic credit transfer system through the central city computer. Purchases are usually made by males, who often stay home and raise children. Open hours of the stores differ by district, and at least one shopping district is open at any time of the day since being underground means there is no night or day.

> Research of the Orion colony has shown that they have a desire to trade with Earth for new Earth clothing fashions, educational material, fresh Earth foods brought to Orion in stasis chambers that keep them fresh forever, the latest industrial equipment, the latest consumer technology, and the latest transportation technology.

Industrial goods are purchased by firms directly from other firms using the electronic credit transfer system of the central city computer. Supply contracts are usually not used. Deals are often consummated by a simple shake of hands. These agreements are generally renegotiated every six Earth months. Distribution of industrial goods occurs through a separate underground transportation network than is used by commuters or retail goods. The transportation system is fully automated, very efficient, and reliable.

Shipping bulk goods to Orion colony takes two Earth months, but small packages and people can get there in two Earth weeks. Communication with Earth is even quicker. Electronic messages sent by subspace radio can reach Earth in two days. This does not indicate, though, a lag in communication—it is not instantaneous.

Question

You are a middle-level manager in a large conglomerate based on Earth. You have been given responsibility for the exploitation of an ex-colony in the Orion star cluster. The top management directive to your department is to develop a strategy for the commercial exploitation of the Orion colony. They want you to tell them how to go about benefiting from Earth's recent contact with this planet; how should they invest their time and money? What kinds of problems are they likely to face in dealing with these people? And what can you do to overcome these problems? Remember, you'll have to come up with some hypotheses concerning how Orions do business. You'll have to make some intelligent and supportable guesses at how they structure and carry out various business functions.

SOURCE: "Management in the year 2200" by Hiroaki Izumi.

Glossary

achievement society A society that emphasizes attainment of position and influence. Competence determines who occupies a particular position. People in more powerful positions hold them because of their skills, knowledge, and talents.

activity orientation The categorization of a culture according to whether it is a doing, being, or containing/controlling culture.

affective autonomy Individuals independently pursue positive experiences that make them feel good, and value is put on pleasure and an exciting and varied life.

affective commitment When employees identify and become involved with the organization and feel an emotional attachment to it.

affective communication style The verbal communication style in which the speaker is process oriented and receiver focused.

affective culture A culture that believes expressing emotions is natural and appropriate. Not to express emotions may be considered dishonest.

affective-intuitive conflict style A style for handling conflict that is more common in high-context cultures. This approach uses circumlocution or flowery speech to make an emotional appeal, and ambiguity and understatement to diffuse conflict.

affirmative action An attempt to make up for past systematic discrimination against women and minorities through a quota employment system.

agreement In the negotiation process, the parties come to a mutually acceptable solution.

ambivalent leadership A leadership style that a culture with contradictory norms and values produces. Alternating between opposite values and behaviors is not the product of inadequate understanding of human nature, but rather consists of difficulty acting in a consistent, coherent way in response to the diverse, sometimes conflicting, values of a complex, heterogeneous, society.

artifacts The most visible and observable elements of organizational culture; the concrete aspects of an organization that symbolizes its culture. These include material aspects of the organization such as its architecture, physical layout, and decoration.

A second type of artifact is slogans, organizational stories, myths, corporate heroes, rites, rituals, and ceremonies.

ascriptive culture A culture that believes people are born into influence. Those in power naturally have the right to be there because of their personal characteristics.

autonomy cultures People see individuals as autonomous, bounded entities who find meaning in their own uniqueness.

axiomatic-deductive conflict style A style of handling conflict that reasons from the general to the specific, going from basic ideas to their implications.

barriers to change Those factors that prevent an organization from appropriately modifying to new conditions. Rigidity that can stifle and eventually kill an organization.

basic assumptions The foundations of a culture: shared ideas and beliefs about the world and society as a whole that guide people's thoughts and actions.

basic human nature Analysis of a culture based on the assessment of that culture's belief in people as good, evil, or neutral/mixed.

basic underlying assumptions Unconscious beliefs and values that structure feelings, perceptions, thoughts, and actions that members of a culture view as the only correct understanding of life.

behavioral diversity Differences among team members in language and norms of behavior.

being culture A culture that emphasizes enjoying life and working for the moment; people work to live rather than live to work.

bicultural group A group in which two or more members from each of two distinct cultures come together.

boundaryless organization Breaks the traditional demarcations of authority, political, communication, and task specialization found in bureaucracies and other organizational structures. Features of a boundaryless organization include a widespread use of project teams, interfunctional teams, networks, and similar structural mechanisms, thus reducing boundaries that typically separate organizational functions and hierarchical levels.

brownouts Expatriates who finish their assignments but do so ineffectively.

bureaucracy In this type of organization, each position has fixed official duties. Conduct is governed by impersonal rules and regulations. Effort is coordinated through a hierarchy of levels of authority. Order and reliability are maintained through written communication and files. Employment is a full-time occupation for members of the organization. Appointment to office is made by superiors. Promotion is based upon merit.

centralization When decisions are made by a few people—usually those at the top—an organization is centralized.

Chinese family business A family business structure, usually one of two types. The first type is small businesses that include only family members. The second type is controlled by family members but also employs nonfamily members and operates as a clan or extended family, which permits it to grow considerably larger than businesses that restrict themselves to family members.

chromatics Communication through colors.

chronemics The use of time in a culture. Two dominant patterns are characteristic: monochronic time schedule and polychronic time schedule.

code of ethics Although these are not laws, they codify behavior that is unacceptable under certain conditions. Organizations expect their members to adhere to them or suffer penalties.

codetermination Worker representatives hold decision-making roles on corporate boards. Popular in Germany, it has permitted German industry to adjust effectively and peacefully to economic change.

cognitive diversity The differences in how team members perceive the team's challenges and opportunities.

collectivist society A society that values the overall good of the group. The expectation is that people subordinate their individual interests and needs for the benefit of the group. Because being part of the group is so important, it is very clear how people in the group should behave.

communication The process of transmitting thoughts or ideas from one person to another. Central to groups because it is the major mechanism for achieving their goals. Culture affects communication in groups by shaping roles and statuses and the interactions among them.

communitarian A society that emphasizes group membership, social responsibility, harmonious relationships, and cooperation.

comparative method A technique for the systematic study of behavior in multiple cultures whose aim is to reduce reliance on a single set of values.

compensation and benefits Develops and administers the salary system and other forms of remuneration such as vacation and sick pay, health insurance, and pension funds.

compensatory model Suggests that dissatisfaction in one domain can be made up in the other.

complexity The extent to which an organization has subparts. Three important components of complexity are horizontal differentiation, vertical or hierarchical differentiation, and spatial dispersion.

compromise In negotiations, the requirement that all parties give up something in order to reach a decision.

conceptual approach to ethics Focuses on the meaning of key ideas in ethics such as obligation, justice, virtue, and responsibility. The emphasis is to refine definitions of important ethical concepts through philosophical analysis.

confrontation strategy The degree of directness in communication is a concern. With a direct strategy, the negotiator will clearly verbalize concerns to the other party, whereas an indirect strategy either hints at similar concerns or expresses them nonverbally.

Confucian work dynamism Organizations that have concern with the future. They consider how their current actions could influence future generations, for example, value is placed on thrift and persistence.

containing/controlling culture A culture that emphasizes rationality and logic. People restrain their desires to try to achieve a mind/body balance.

content theories Motivation theories that focus on the "what," identifying factors that cause people to put effort into work.

context Hall developed the concept of context to explain differences in communication styles among cultures. He defined context as the information that surrounds an event, and is therefore inextricably bound up with the meaning of that event. Cultures can be categorized on a scale from high to low context.

context dependent Approaches are only effective in certain countries or companies.

context free Practices that apply to any country or company.

context specific Practices apply in companies or countries that are similar.

contextual style A verbal communication style that focuses on the "role" of the speaker, and meanings are expressed for the purpose of emphasizing certain role relationships.

contingency theories The view that there are multiple causes of behavior.

continuance commitment Employees feel attached to an organization because they realize that they will lose something if they leave.

conversational overlaps This occurs when more than one person speaks at the same time.

core group Consists of several employees from different cultural backgrounds who meet regularly. The group members discuss their attitudes, feelings, and beliefs about cultural differences and how they influence work behavior.

corporate social responsibility theory This theory holds that the obligation of business is to maximize profits for the company's stakeholders, such as suppliers, customers, employees, stockholders, and the local community.

cross-cultural communication Occurs when people from more than one culture communicate with each other. Noise develops due to differences in language, values, and attitudes, among other factors.

cross-cultural negotiations Occurs when members of different cultures negotiate with each other.

cross-cultural training (CCT) Prepares an expatriate to live and work in a different culture because coping with a new environment can be much more challenging than dealing with a new job. An organization can choose an appropriate CCT method using three situational factors of the expatriate's assignment: culture novelty, degree of interaction with host country nationals, and job novelty.

cultural ethical relativism The doctrine that what is right or wrong, good or bad, depends on one's culture. If the values of a society support certain acts as ethical and morally correct, then they are acceptable behavior for that society.

cultural determinism The position that all behavior is the product of culture. Ignores economic, political, technological, and biological factors as plausible explanations.

culture The way of life of a group of people.

culture-free approach It states that because of technology, policies, rules, organizational structure, and other variables that contribute to efficiency and effectiveness, the role of national culture in shaping organizational behavior, and therefore the need to understand it, is irrelevant for management.

culture shock An adverse or confused reaction to behavior in other cultures, challenges understandings between ourselves and others. What is "normal" behavior becomes problematic.

decode In the communication process, the receiver interprets the meaning of the symbols used by the sender to understand or comprehend the meaning of the message.

descriptive approach to ethics The study of ethics using the methods and theories of social science. Researchers study the ethics of a particular society or corporation and explain their effect on behavior without making judgments regarding their correctness.

descriptive organization theories An attempt to portray organizations realistically.

determinist organization theories Through logical argument, inductive and deductive theories, and empirical research, management scholars and sociologists have argued that one variable explains more of the structural aspects of organizations than others.

Dialectical Theory An approach to understanding development and change in organizations. The balance of power between opposing entities determines stability or change. If the struggles and accommodations continually taking place between these parties are maintaining the balance of power, stability reigns. If one side gains enough power to tip the scales and engage the status quo, change occurs.

diffuse cultures Cultures where the focus is on conceptual wholeness and relationships of all kinds are valued. People in diffuse cultures maintain a relatively smaller and more carefully guarded public space in their personal relationships.

direct communication style The speaker tries to convey true feelings through the choice of words.

distributive justice The issue of how rewards can be distributed in a fair manner: (1) An outcome to input ratio should be relatively equal for every employee; (2) an equality norm in which each employee receives the same outcomes regardless of inputs; and (3) a need norm suggests each employee be given outcomes according to his or her need.

distributive outcome The idea that the amount of resources available for negotiators to divide is fixed, which is consistent with a win-lose or lose-lose solution.

diversity A range of differences, including gender, race, ethnicity, and age—characteristics that might be apparent from looking at someone. It also includes differences that are not visible, such as education, professional background, functional area of expertise, sexual preference, and religion. All of these differences are important because they affect how individuals behave within an organization.

diversity training The major focus of this training is raising levels of awareness and sensitivity to diversity issues. The time required for the program varies from a few hours to a few days.

doing culture A culture in which the emphasis is on action, achievement, and working.

dysfunction A negative outcome of an organization.

efficiency perspective The key concept is corporate social responsibility—argues that the obligation of business is to maximize profits for shareholders.

Eiffel Tower culture A classic bureaucratic structure that emphasizes a division of labor and coordination through a hierarchy of authority, and relies on planning to accomplish its goals.

egalitarianism society A society where people generally think of each other as moral equals sharing basic human interests.

elaborate communication style In communication, the quantity of talk is relatively high, description includes great detail, and there is often repetition. The use of metaphors, similes, and proverbs is frequent, many adjectives modify the same noun, and verbal elaboration and exaggeration are typical.

embedded society A society where people view others as inherently part of collectives. Meaning in life comes from social relationships, identification with the group, and participation in the group's shared way of life and goals.

encode In the communication process, a message is expressed in an understandable format for the receiver.

enculturation A non-intentional process that includes all of the learning available as the result of what is in an environment to be learned.

entitlement norm The rights of individuals in society to seek out, obtain, and maintain gainful employment. Every individual has the right to work and be an active participant in his or her employment.

equal employment opportunity Prohibition of discrimination on the basis of such variables as race, gender, ethnicity, religion, color, age, disability, pregnancy, national origin, and citizenship status.

equality norm Each employee receives the same outcomes regardless of inputs.

equity norm Defined by Equity Theory that an outcome to input ratio should be relatively equal for every employee.

Equity Theory The basic premise of this theory is that people try to balance their inputs and outcomes in relation to others.

espoused values The public values and principles that the organization's leaders announce it intends to achieve. They include mission statements, goals, and ideals.

ethical universalism Maintains that there are universal and objective ethical rules located deep within a culture that also apply across societies.

ethics Moral standards, not governed by law, that focus on the human consequences of actions. Ethics often require behavior that meets higher standards than that established by law, including selfless behavior rather than calculated action intended to produce a tangible benefit.

ethnocentrism The belief that the group to which one belongs is the primary group, and all other groups are rated according to how they compare to the primary group.

Evolutionary Theory Borrows key ideas from biological evolutionary theory and views change as a continuous cycle of variation, selection, and retention. The creation of new forms of organizations emerge by blind or random change. The evolutionary selection of organizations occurs through the competition for scarce resources, and external forces select entities that best fit the resource base of an environmental niche.

exacting communication style A communication style in which the emphasis is on precision and using the right amount of words to convey the desired meaning.

expatriate failures Those who do not remain abroad for the duration of their assignment.

expatriates Employees who work outside their home countries.

Expectancy Theory A theory of motivation that rests on important assumptions about people's behavior. (1) Behavior is a result of personal and environmental factors. (2) People's decisions about whether to belong to an organization and how much effort to put into performing influence their behavior in organizations. (3) Because of different needs, people seek different rewards from the organization. (4) People decide how to behave on the basis of beliefs about what leads to the most desirable outcomes.

experience In organizations, it is a factor that can cause barriers to arise due to differences in life events between two individuals. When two people are from different cultures, it is likely that their life experiences have varied in many ways. Lacking a common body of experience is likely to make communication more difficult.

expressed values level Represents how people in the culture explain the manifest level of their culture.

expressive-oriented In high-context cultures, people do not separate person from issue in conflicts.

external culture The multiple national and local cultures that influence internal organizational culture.

external-oriented society The society tries to harmonize with the environment and have more focus on the "other."

external sources of change Events in the environment that are usually beyond the organization's control. They can affect the organization immediately, influence other elements in its environment that then affect it, or make their impact in the future.

face Usually identified as exclusively part of Asian culture, it is found in many cultures. Face is an ethical concept that is part of the general culture and internalized rather than an institutionalized code of ethics. Saving one's face and that of other group members is of central importance in highly integrated and authoritarian cultures. A behavior that protects harmony, tolerance, and solidarity.

facial gazing Looking at the counterpart's face. Eye contact is one of the most intense forms of facial gazing.

factual-inductive conflict style A style used to handle conflict that focuses on relevant facts and moves toward a conclusion using an inductive approach.

family organizational culture An organization that emphasizes personal, face-to-face relationships. It is hierarchical with an authority structure based on power differentials commonly experienced between parents and children.

feedback In the communication process, the reversal of the initial sender/receiver roles to let the sender know if his or her message was received and understood.

feminine culture A culture that places importance on "tender" values such as personal relationships, care for others, the quality of life, and service. Gender roles are less distinct and often equal.

Five-Stage Group Development Model Theory of group development that views groups as experiencing five distinct phases: (1) Forming, (2) Storming, (3) Norming, (4) Performing, (5) Adjourning.

followers Group members who do not have leadership roles.

formal group This type of group reflects the idea that pooling resources for decision making is superior to individual effort. In most instances management appoints a leader, membership is mandatory, and rules govern behavior.

formalization The extent that rules, policies, and procedures govern organization members' behavior. The more extensive the documentation of appropriate behavior, the more formalized the organization.

future-oriented society A society that emphasizes the long term. Uses the past and present to gain future advantage.

geographical location A situational factor for negotiators in deciding where to hold a negotiation.

global company A centralized company that follows a strategy built on global-scale cost advantage.

globalization The transcendence of previous geographic, economic, political, and cultural boundaries towards a new world order. Increasing awareness of activities in other parts of the world.

goal setting theory A theory of motivation that involves the effect that goal setting has on performance. Based on the idea that people are motivated by intentions to work toward a goal.

group A number of people who are in contact with one another and who are aware of some significant commonality.

group culture The basis can be membership in a formal or informal group, an occupation, union membership, ethnic or religious background, or membership in a department that provides common experiences.

The groups maintain themselves just as subcultures do through shared symbols, ceremonies, rituals, and values, which become a means for establishing a group's identity that differentiates itself from other groups.

group decisions Groups pool the skills, talents, and experiences of many people instead of relying on one decision maker. Group decision making, the active participation of many people, increases the likelihood of decision implementation.

group-oriented society A society in which a positive relationship to the collective is important.

group structure The patterns of interaction among members. Elements that compose structures are rules, norms, roles, and statuses. These concepts are useful for understanding groups in all cultures.

groupthink A group decision-making process that occurs when members of a highly cohesive group are unable to evaluate each other's inputs critically.

guest workers In Germany, after World War II when there was a shortage of men, industry recruited workers from abroad with the intention that these workers would eventually go back to their homeland. The foreign worker population has increased dramatically since that time.

guided missile culture An egalitarian culture that is impersonal and task oriented. This culture is egalitarian because it employs experts in technical fields. Experts work on projects together rather than take directives from superiors. Technical expertise reduces emotional elements in the culture, producing a bureaucratic culture based on knowledge rather than position or on emotional ties.

habit Regular, stable patterns of events over time that are taken for granted and become mindless actions. All organizations engage in habitual behaviors.

haptics Communication through the use of bodily contact.

harmony A factor when analyzing cultures and their relation to nature. A culture that is in harmony with nature attempts to orient behavior to coexist with nature.

hierarchical society A society that values group relationships, but emphasizes the relative rankings of groups within an organization or society as a whole, making them more class conscious than group societies.

hierarchy A culture that uses a social system with clearly defined roles to make sure people behave responsibly.

Herzberg's Motivation-Hygiene Theory Developed in the 1950s and 1960s and built on Maslow's theory, the premise of Herzberg's theory is that satisfaction and dissatisfaction are two dimensions rather than opposite ends of a single dimension.

heterarchy A form of multinational organization that utilizes aspects of markets and hierarchies.

heterogeneity Diversity in the workforce.

high-contact culture High-contact cultures usually are in warmer climates, have a greater interpersonal orientation, and are seen as interpersonally "warm."

high-context communication One type of communication in which most of the information is either in the physical context or internalized in the person, while very little is in the coded, explicit, transmitted part of the message.

home culture consensus Values widely shared by the home culture and therefore are maintained in an ethical decision.

homogeneous Cultures and groups that contain members who have the same backgrounds and generally understand events and the world in general more similarly than other types.

horizontal differentiation The way that tasks performed by the organization are divided.

hygiene factors Also called extrinsic or context factors, are factors outside the job itself that influence the worker.

immediate environment Forces in an organization with which it is continually in contact and that can create pressures for change. Some examples of these forces are domestic competition, population trends, social trends, governmental actions.

incubator culture It attempts to minimize organizational structure and culture and develops with this mind-set: "If organizations are to be tolerated at all, they should be there to serve as incubators for self-expression and self-fulfillment." Minimal organizational structure facilitates a culture that is egalitarian, personal, and highly creative. In most cases, incubator cultures are in knowledge and science industries.

indirect communication style The speaker selects words to hide his or her real feelings.

individual change When the behavior of a person is different as a result of new information, training, experience, or rearrangement of an organization's structure.

individual ethical relativism The view that there is no absolute principle of right and wrong, good or bad, in any social situation. The individuals in a particular situation determine what is right and wrong. In its extreme form, ethics are a personal judgment independent of societal norms and values.

individualistic society The people in this type of society relate to each other through personal characteristics and achievements. People have concern for themselves and their families, rather than others. The individual is important, and each person's rights are valued. The society structures laws and rules to preserve the rights of the individual and to allow individual development and achievement.

influence strategy Reflects the negotiator's use of power.

informal groups Evolve naturally in organizations, often without the awareness of management. People who work together in a functional area, across specializations, or as a result of frequent contact can form relationships based on similar experiences, common interests, and friendship. Informal groups vary in their contribution to an organization's goals.

information exchange The stage in the negotiation process when each party states an initial position, usually in a presentation, followed by questions, answers, and discussion.

information strategy What information is disclosed and how it is conveyed.

ingroup member Someone with whom a person has an affective relationship, usually a family member, friend, colleague, neighbor, or classmate.

initial offer In negotiation, the beginning statement of intent made by each party, is influenced by culture.

inner-directed culture A society where people conceive of virtue as being inside the individual and believe that conscience and convictions are internal.

inputs In Equity Theory, these are what someone brings to a situation. An employee's inputs include education, previous work experience, personality, and personal characteristics.

institutional theory A theory that views the primary source of change as external and beyond the control of management.

instrumental orientation The orientation of people in low-context cultures who view conflict in the world in analytic, linear logic terms, and separate issues from people.

instrumental style The verbal communication style in which the sender uses goal-oriented, sender-focused language.

integrative agreement Negotiators must transform fixed resources into something valued differently by each party, and then distribute the resources to the party that values them most.

integrative solution The outcome of a win-win agreement; all parties achieve their objectives.

intellectual autonomy People follow their own ideas and value curiosity, creativity, and open-mindedness.

interactional justice An aspect of procedural justice that considers the interpersonal relations.

intercultural negotiation When members of different cultures negotiate with each other.

interests These reflect the underlying need or reason for a negotiator's position.

internal change factors An organization's technical production system, political processes, and culture. At times these factors exert strong and direct pressures for change. At other times, when the organization is in equilibrium, internal factors maintain organizational stability but retain the potential for creating change.

internal organizational culture Artifacts, values, and basic assumptions that create meaning for organizational insiders and present it to those outside the organization.

internal-oriented culture A culture that believes nature is controllable. The individual or his or her group is in control of a situation.

international contingency model of leadership The reasoning supporting the model, which provides general guidelines for international managers, not a scientific theory, is that different leadership styles fit various national cultures.

international firm A firm that develops products and innovations in their domestic market and then transports them to foreign affiliates.

international human resource management (IHRM) Includes three major areas: (1) The management of human resources in global corporations; (2) the management of expatriate employees; and (3) the comparison of human resource management (HRM) practices in a variety of different countries. Includes recruiting and selecting employees, providing orientation and training, evaluating performance, administering a compensation system, and handling other aspects of labor relations.

international organizational behavior The study of behavior in organizations around the world.

interpersonal characteristics Considers whether the way the organization treats employees conveys respect and supports positive social relationships among organizational members.

interpretive scheme A way to make sense of the arrangements of positions and activities in an organization. It acts as a perceptual filter, embodied in stories and myths, that creates meaning out of routine, frequently experienced events, as well as unique situations.

intimate zone A distance of less than 18 inches (46 cm) that is used by very close friends.

intracultural negotiation Members of one culture negotiate with each other.

Islamic work ethic The view that life without work is meaningless and work is an obligation, can enhance organizational commitment.

job enrichment Application of Herzberg's Motivation-Hygiene Theory, to motivate workers, a job must include many motivation factors.

kinesic behavior Communication through body movements, including facial expression, gestures, and posture.

labor relations Identifies and defines the roles of management and workers in the workplace.

laws Imposing mandatory compliance accompanied by formal punitive sanctions.

leadership Leadership is a management style that focuses on creativity, vision, and long-term organizational development, rather than routine operations.

Learned Needs Theory McClelland proposed that three major needs influence people's behavior. These needs are not instinctive desires, but learned. The learned needs, which help explain individual differences in motivation, are need for achievement, need for power, and need for affiliation.

Life-Cycle Theory A development theory that borrows concepts from fields as diverse as biology, child development, and moral development. The central view of life-cycle theory is that the developing organization has within it an underlying form, logic, program, or code that regulates change and moves the group from a given point of departure toward an end that is prefigured in the present state.

long-term oriented Societies that have concern with the future. Values are thrift and persistence.

lose-lose solution In negotiation, all parties must give up something. A compromise is a lose-lose solution.

low-contact cultures People in these cultures prefer to stand farther apart and touch infrequently. These cultures are often in cooler climate zones, and people there are task oriented and interpersonally "cool."

low-context communication Communication in which the mass of the information is vested in the explicit, coded, transmitted part of the message rather than in the physical context.

macro-level change typology A theory that provides a larger framework for understanding the processes of organizational change. These theories identify processes that create change independent of national culture and, to some extent, managerial action.

manifest culture Easily observable elements of a culture, such as behaviors, language, music, food, and technology.

maquiladoras International manufacturing and processing facilities in Mexico.

masculine society The "tough" values such as success, money, assertiveness, and competition are dominant in such societies, and there are often significant differences between men's and women's roles.

Maslow's Hierarchy of Needs A theory of general motivation developed by Maslow that theorized an individual would try to satisfy one category of needs at a time and that the hierarchical order of needs is the same for everyone.

mastery culture A culture that attempts to change aspects of the environment through technology when necessary or desirable.

matrix organization A type of organic structure. Instead of a bureaucratic authority structure with employees accountable to one supervisor, an employee reports to more than one supervisor.

mechanistic organization A centralized organization that is highly formalized and specialized with a micro division of labor.

micro division of tasks A type of job specialization by breaking jobs into their smallest components that individuals can perform well with low levels of education and training.

mixed orientation A society with a tendency to believe people are basically good, however, in some situations they do behave in an evil manner.

mixed society In space orientation, this society's views on space fall somewhere between public and private societies, with a combination of public and private spaces.

monochronic time schedule A culture where things are done in a linear fashion one activity at a time. Time schedules are important, and an appointment is treated seriously. Time is seen as something that can be controlled or wasted by people.

monolithic organization An organization that is predominately homogeneous. People who are different from the majority often work only in a limited number of positions or departments. Because people with different backgrounds do not hold positions throughout the organization, to survive minority group members usually follow the organizational norms set by the majority. Intergroup conflict is relatively low because the organization is so homogeneous; however, discrimination and prejudice are common.

motivation The amount of effort that an individual puts into doing something.

motivation factors Also called intrinsic or content factors, these are aspects of the job itself, including achievement, recognition, interesting work, responsibility, advancement, and growth. The presence or absence of these factors influences the satisfaction and motivation of workers.

motivation strategy Expresses the interests of the parties.

multicultural groups Groups that contain members of three or more ethnic backgrounds.

multicultural teams Groups that contain workers from different cultural groups who learn how to maximize their effectiveness by taking full advantage of their differences.

multinational firm A firm whose focus is on a strategy that is primarily country oriented and locally responsive. Their structures are decentralized.

multiple structures Complex structures that contain both bureaucratic administration and more organic structures. In addition to requiring more coordination, these types of organizations often experience conflict as a result of the coexistence of different structures.

need norm Each employee receives outcomes according to personal need.

negotiation The process of bargaining between two or more parties to reach a solution that is mutually acceptable.

neutral culture People in this type of culture try to control emotion so as not to interfere with judgment. Expressing emotion at a culturally inappropriate time may be considered irrational.

neutral orientation A cautious approach toward people in general in order to protect yourself, because although the belief is that people are mostly good, they can act in evil ways.

noise Factors responsible for distortion and interruption that enter the communication process.

nonrational elements of culture A theory about how much leaders can manage organizational culture holds that these nonrational elements are behaviors not grounded in empirical data or distorted to serve a particular group's interests. These include destructive or negative emotions, erroneous beliefs, and idiosyncratic interpretations of the organization's past, present, and future. Leaders are unable to control these aspects of organizational culture.

nonverbal communication The part of the message other than the words, such as facial expressions, gestures, and tone of voice. Nonverbal meanings in different cultures vary tremendously.

nonverbal tactics Negotiating behaviors other than the words used, for example, tone of voice, facial expressions, gestures, and body position.

normative approach to ethics This approach constructs arguments in defense of basic moral positions and prescribing correct ethical behavior. These arguments may rely on social science studies and conceptual clarification, but they focus primarily on the rationale for a particular position, often on the basis of logic as much as empirical evidence.

normative commitment People feel a sense of obligation to remain with a firm and believe that employees should be loyal to their employer.

normative organizational theories These theories attempt to formulate the way organizations ought to function.

norms Guides of behavior and beliefs that are informal, usually unstated, and taken for granted by group members. Groups generate their own norms rather than have norms forced upon them.

norms of justice Behaviors the society accepts as fair.

obligation norm A belief that holds all individuals in society have a duty with respect to working. This norm includes the notion that everyone has a duty to contribute to society by working, a duty to save for their own future, and the duty to value one's work, whatever its nature.

observable attributes Visible characteristics of an individual such as race, ethnic background, age, and gender.

oculesics Communication through eye contact and gaze.

open systems Organizations interact with their environment rather than exist independently of surrounding influences. Organizations continuously require inputs from the environment in the form of raw materials, human resources, finance, and ideas. After the inputs are transformed through a variety of processes, an organization returns output to the environment in the form of products, services, and knowledge.

organic structure Decentralized organizations that have low formalization and specialization based on depth of knowledge. Flexible and change oriented, creativity is fostered. Knowledge and ability determine participation in decision making and problem solving rather than position titles. Decision making is decentralized, and there is an attempt to involve lower-level participants in decision making whenever possible. Communication channels operate vertically and horizontally.

organization development (OD) The application of social science research and theories to create more "rational" organizations. OD involves attempting to improve organizational efficiency and effectiveness, create organizational "health," and build capacity to change continuously.

organization structure change The deliberate rearrangement of the positions, departments, or other major units of an organization.

organizational behavior modification The application of Reinforcement Theory to motivate workers in organizations. A four step process: (1) Ensure workers know the behaviors they are expected to carry out as part of the job; (2) train observers and have them record the workers' correct and incorrect behaviors; (3) reinforce workers who practice correct behaviors and provide corrective feedback; and (4) evaluate the effects of the program on behavior.

organizational change The reconfiguration of the components of an organization to increase efficiency and effectiveness. Change can occur at the level of the individual, group, or organizational structure.

organizational citizenship behavior (OCB) Things that an employee does for the organization that are not formally part of the job.

organizational commitment An employee's attachment to a particular organization.

organizational culture The basic assumptions of an organization as it learns to cope with problems of external adaptation and internal integration. These assumptions work well enough to be considered valid and, therefore, to be taught to new members as the correct way to perceive, think, and feel in relation to those problems. To the members of the organization, it is the "natural" way of understanding the business world and taking action.

organizational justice Perceptions of fair treatment within an organization.

organizational structure The arrangement of positions in an organization. Positions, or roles, are intentionally structured to accomplish the goals of the organization. The basic components of structure are complexity, centralization, and formalization.

outcomes In Equity Theory, what one takes from a situation—for example, pay, benefits, working conditions, coworker relationships, and training opportunities.

outer-directed A culture where people believe virtue is outside the person and located in nature and relationships. Individuals from outer-directed cultures are flexible and try to harmonize with the environment and focus on the "other."

outgroup member A person with whom there is no recognized relationship, often a stranger.

particularist society A society that is more contingency oriented, believing circumstances and relationships are more important in deciding what is right or good.

past-oriented culture A culture that emphasizes tradition and uses time-honored approaches. Tradition and history are important.

path-goal model of leadership This model attempts to explain how the behavior of a leader influences the satisfaction and performance of subordinates dependent on aspects of a situation. The task of leadership is to strengthen subordinates' perception of the ties among effort, performance, and desired outcomes. To do this a leader should adapt her style to various situations. The four leadership behaviors follow: (1) directive leadership, (2) supportive leadership, (3) participative leadership, and (4) achievement-oriented leadership.

perception An individual's personal view of the world. Whether it is correct or not, it is a person's definition of reality.

performance evaluation The systematic appraisal of employees' performance within the organization. Its purposes are to provide information for organizational decisions such as promotions and salary increases and to give feedback to employees to help them develop and improve.

personal communication style A verbal communication style that focuses on the speaker.

personal zone The distance from 18 inches to about 4 feet (46 cm to 1.22 m), used for close working situations or to give instructions.

persuasion In the negotiation process, the parties try to convince their counterparts to accept their proposals. This might involve the parties consciously trying to work toward a mutually acceptable solution or one party using persuasive arguments to influence the other.

plural organization A type of organization that includes a wider variety of people, and management makes a greater effort to include people who differ from the majority.

polychronic time schedule People tend to do several things at the same time. In a P-time culture, schedules are subordinate to personal relationships.

population ecology A theory that views the primary source of change as external and beyond the control of management. For example, similar to natural selection in biology, population ecology views the environment as selecting those types of organizational forms that survive. Organizations do not adapt; instead, certain types fail and are replaced with different types.

power distance The extent to which less powerful members of organizations accept that power is unequally distributed. It ranges from small to large. Suggests that national cultures low on power distance—those most likely to question the leader's actions—would be the least supportive followers, whereas cultures high on power distance would be the most supportive of a group leader's efforts.

practical approach to ethics A variant of the normative perspective, involves developing a set of normative guidelines for resolving conflicts of interest to improve societal well-being.

preparation stage Negotiators plan how to approach the actual negotiation and try to learn as much as possible about their negotiating partner. This stage typically takes place at the home office before the face-to-face meeting. The negotiators must understand their own positions and anticipate the positions of the other party through considering each party's objectives, needs, and interests.

present-oriented culture A culture that focuses on the short term—what is going on now, including activities and relationships.

primary socialization The specific culture that one learns while growing up. A complex, nonexplicit, prolonged process of learning appropriate age, gender, ethnic, and social class behavior from families, friends, schools, religious institutions, and media.

priorities Indicate the importance of different alternatives.

private society In this type of society, it is important for each person to have his or her own space.

procedural justice Examines the fairness of processes for making organizational decisions about outcomes.

process motivation theories These theories focus on the "how," the steps an individual takes in putting forth effort.

Project GLOBE (Global Leadership and Organizational Behavior Effectivness) A long-term, multiphase, multimethod project to study cross-cultural leadership differences and similarities among countries.

proxemics The use of space, either personal or office, to communicate.

public society In this type of society, space belongs to all.

public zone Distances over 12 feet (over 3.66 m), used infrequently for formal occasions such as for a speech.

punctuated equilibrium model A theory of group development. The first meeting is important for the group because it sets the climate for the group and establishes its leadership. This is followed by a period of equilibrium, which is routine group functioning that changes abruptly at the midpoint of the group's allotted time. This equilibrium is disrupted by recognition that the task must be completed and creates a revolutionary change in the group's arrangements. The new arrangements shift to a task orientation that results in project completion.

receiver The person who is the recipient of the sender's message in the communication process.

recruitment The process through which an organization takes in new members. Involves attracting a pool of qualified applicants for the positions available.

Reinforcement or Learning Theory The premise of this theory is that the environment determines people's behavior. As people grow from children into adults, what they learn is a result of the outcomes of their behavior. If individuals receive a reward for what they do, it is likely they will repeat it.

relation to nature Kluckhohn and Strodtbeck's concept to analyze a culture as to how it relates to nature either through subjugation to it, harmony with it, or mastery of it.

relational characteristics Considers whether the way the organization treats employees conveys respect and supports positive social relationships among organizational members.

relationship-building stage The negotiating parties begin their discussion, typically at one of their offices or at a mutually acceptable neutral location. The objective is for the parties to get to know one another.

resource limitations Societies and organizations within them have varying levels of scarce resources—human, financial, intellectual.

retributive justice Perceptions of the fairness of punishments given to those who do wrong.

reverse culture shock The disorientation experienced by a returning expatriate.

ringisei A Japanese term that means participation in group decision making.

role conflict Within an organization, group members often occupy multiple roles with different statuses. When the demands of the various roles are incompatible, role conflict occurs.

roles Sets of norms that define what behavior is appropriate for and expected of various positions within a group.

room arrangements A situational factor for negotiations that includes the physical setup of the place for the negotiations.

rules Guidelines for expected behavior that the organization imposes on group members and can formally sanction for disobedience.

secondary socialization Occurs after primary socialization and usually equips people with the knowledge, skills, and behavior to achieve adult roles successfully, particularly occupational roles.

secular-rational values A society that emphasizes individualistic striving.

selection Process through which an organization takes in new members. Requires choosing from the recruitment pool the candidate whose qualifications most closely match the job requirements.

selection of negotiators Involves choosing the number of people and exactly who will represent a team. The number chosen often reflects the organization's national culture.

self-expression values culture A culture where people are trusting and tolerant of others, politically active, happy, and put priority on self-expression and quality of life.

sender The person who initiates the communication process.

sequential culture Cultures in which people do one thing at a time, make appointments and arrive on time, and generally stick to schedules.

short-term oriented A society's values are toward the immediate past and present. There is respect for tradition and fulfilling social obligations, but the here and now is most important.

silence In negotiating, a period of nonresponsiveness, used to reflect on what has been said, what should be said, or if a problem arises. The Japanese consider this a normal part of conversation.

simple organizational structure There is little need for elaborate coordination because the organization is not complex; top management supervises through direct supervision. There is also centralization in top management with employees exerting little independent decision making or influence. The organization's goals are those of its top manager, who is frequently also its owner.

social control mechanism Through culture—particularly a strong, effective culture—the organization defines the reality that organization members experience. It socializes new members into a particular way of doing things and periodically resocializes its long-term members. For example, organizational rites and ceremonies reward and reinforce desired behavior as well as demonstrate and legitimate the organizational power structure.

social power Authority or the ability to have others follow directives without question.

social zone A distance of 4 to 12 feet (1.22 to 3.66 m), used in most American business situations.

socioemotional leader Also known as the relationship or maintenance leader, focuses on the emotional and social aspects of a group. They encourage and praise others, resolve conflicts, and engage in behavior that facilitates the group's work. This leader role focuses on constructing and maintaining group cohesion.

space orientation A method of looking at differences in culture by indicating how people relate to the ownership of space, either public, private, or mixed.

spatial dispersion A variable of organizational structure that is a component of complexity. The activities of an organization can be in one place or in different locations on either the basis of power centers, that is, hierarchy or specialization.

specific cultures Cultures that tend to be objective and atomistic because they break things down into small parts. In their relationships, people usually have large public spaces and relatively smaller private spaces with the separation between spaces rigidly maintained.

spillover model Suggests that satisfaction at work spills over into satisfaction at home and conversely dissatisfaction at work can create problems at home.

status The rank of the role in the hierarchy of the group.

status-value approach People make comparisons to "everybody" or "people in general," or they may compare themselves to groups who are dissimilar in order to judge fairness.

stereotyping A shortcut to "understanding" someone by categorizing him or her as a member of a particular group, and then assigning him or her the characteristics of that group. Stereotyped characteristics may be based on data learned from other sources.

strategy The overall approach to negotiation that establishes the set of behaviors that the negotiator believes will lead to goal accomplishment.

structural characteristics Focus on whether the rules and policies of the organization lead to fair evaluation.

structuralism The view that organizational structures influence organizational values.

subculture A separate set of cultural norms that set a group apart from the larger group. Contributing to subculture formation are age, gender, race, ethnic background, religion, and national culture. Subcultures contain their own rituals and ceremonies that have distinct meaning for their members and create ingroup identification.

subjugation orientation A society's tendency for people to do several activities simultaneously, the time for appointments is approximate, and interpersonal relationships are more important than schedules.

succinct communication style A communication style in which people are comfortable with a relatively low quantity of talk. Understatements, pauses, and silence convey meaning.

survival society One that puts priority on economic and physical security over self-expression and quality of life, are intolerant of homosexuality, and describe themselves as unhappy.

symbolic meaning system Selective interpretations of societal and organizational traditions, customs, rituals, and artifacts that contribute to organizational culture. The leader interprets and shapes the larger culture to the needs of the organization. Its products are particular ways of doing things in organizations in different cultures and a distinctive organizational identity.

task leader Also called the initiating leader, focuses the group on goal achievement. Task leaders clarify the goals, present information, ask other members for information, and evaluate the group's progress toward making a decision. The task leader's efforts aim toward specific outcomes.

team A type of group that uses self-management techniques to achieve goals to which its members express high commitment. Teams have more cohesiveness and responsibility and use member talents more effectively than do other groups.

Teleological Organizational Theory This theory relies on the philosophical doctrine that a purpose or goal is the final cause for guiding the movement of an organization. Emphasis is on goal achievement, and it underlies much managerial and organizational behavior theory.

temporal distribution The ability of virtual teams to cross the boundaries of time.

time limits The real or presumed deadlines under which negotiating parties operate. The expected time for a negotiation varies with culture.

time orientation A society's focus on the past, present, or future.

token group A group that consists of members with the same background with the exception of one member who is different in some significant way. The

token member probably interprets things differently from the other group members.

tradition A preference for acting based on custom and precedent. The most compelling reason for adherence to tradition is that the practices it prescribes have worked sufficiently well to warrant continuing them.

traditional orientation toward authority People have values that reflect preindustrial society and the centrality of the family.

training and development Planned individual learning, organization development, and career development. It is a recognized professional field known as human resource development.

transformational leadership A more commonly found type of leadership than charisma, especially in contemporary business organizations in which a leader acts as a teacher, role model, and inspirational figure to create conditions under which subordinates enthusiastically contribute to the organization. It also includes a focus on the nonroutine aspects of an organization, including establishing a vision for the organization's future, making decisions with long-term consequences, creating an organizational culture, and initiating and managing change.

transmit In the communication process, the message is sent via a medium such as voice, fax, memo, or e-mail.

transnational firm A firm that avoids dichotomous structures such as product based or geography based, centralized or decentralized, independent or dependent. It attempts to achieve solutions tailored to specific situations, and differentiated structures replace systemwide structures. This type of firm creates high levels of interdependence among countries and cultures.

Two-Factor Theory The premise for Herzberg's Motivation-Hygiene Theory that satisfaction and dissatisfaction are two dimensions rather than opposite ends of a single dimension.

uncertainty avoidance A measure that indicates a culture's preferred amount of structure, ranging from strong to weak. Strong uncertainty avoidance cultures prefer more structure, resulting in explicit rules of behavior, either written or unwritten. Weak uncertainty avoidance cultures favor unstructured situations. The culture is more flexible and easygoing.

underlying attributes Not directly observable characteristics of an individual such as education, technical abilities, tenure in the organization, socioeconomic background, personality characteristics, and values.

union density The percentage of all employed people in a country who belong to a union.

universal culture In this type of culture, people believe the definition of goodness or truth applies to every situation. Judgments are made without regard to circumstance.

urgency A factor that determines which course of action will be used to resolve ethical conflicts. The more urgent the need for resolution, the more likely actions such as avoidance, forcing, or accommodation will be chosen because infiltration, education, negotiation, and collaboration take extended time.

value judgments Culturally biased assessments of behavior.

values orientations Indicators of how different societies cope with various issues or problems.

variations In the Kluckhohn and Strodtbeck framework, a culture favors one or more of the approaches associated with a particular values orientation.

verbal negotiation tactics Spoken negotiating behaviors such as initial offer made, promises, threats, and recommendations.

vertical differentiation The number of levels in an organization. A measure of this is the number of levels between the highest and lowest position in an orga-

nization. The assumption is that the higher the level, the greater the authority of the position.

virtual teams Groups of geographically and/or organizationally dispersed coworkers who use a combination of telecommunication and information technologies to accomplish an organizational task.

voice An opportunity for employees to express their opinions.

win-lose solution In negotiation, one party receives all it wants by forcing or demanding the other to concede defeat.

win-win solution In negotiation, all parties are able to achieve their objectives.

work-family conflict Activities in one domain interfere with those in the other.

work-family facilitation Experience, skills, and opportunities from one domain make it easier to participate in the other.

work-family interface How aspects of life at work and at home influence each other and the impact of that influence on the individual.

Index

Conscience or the Competitive Edge? (B), 300–301
Cultural Clash in the Entertainment Industry, A, 295–298
Ellen Moore (A): Living and Working in Bahrain, 320–329
Ellen Moore (B): Living and Working in Bahrain, 329–333
Fuqima Washing Machine Corporation, 370–376
Ireka Construction Berhad: A Chinese Family Business Goes Public, 416–420
Malaysian-German Chamber of Commerce and Industry, 421–426
Managing a Diverse Work Force in Indonesia, 334–338
Portrait of a Young Russian Capitalist, 310–314
Shell Oil in Nigeria, 339–351
Wellcome Israel (A), 377–384
Wellcome Israel (B), 384–386
West Indies Yacht Club Resort: When Cultures Collide, 401–415
Yutaka Nakamura: A Foreigner in His Native Land, 315–319
Centrality of values, 63
Centralization, 237, 239
Champoux, J.E, 182, 189
Chandler, A.D., 6, 239
Chaney, L.H., 78, 85
Chang, A., 108, 123
Change agent, 286
Charismatic authority, 221
Charles, K.R., 136, 143
Chase-Dunn, C., 2
Chatterjee, S.R., 141, 143
Chen, C.C., 179, 184, 185, 189, 199, 245
Chen, M., 90, 93, 94, 99, 102, 211
Chen, Z.X., 39, 43, 189
Cheng, B.S., 178, 189
Child, J., 239
Chinese family business (CFBs), 245–246
Chinese Value Survey, 26–27
Chiou, E.F., 144, 185
Chiou, W.C.K., 189
Chiu, R.K., 98, 102
Choi, J., 184, 185, 189
Chowanee, G.D., 167, 170
Christakopoulou, S., 91, 102
Christensen, S.L., 206, 207, 212
Chromatics, 79
Chronemics, 79
Chu, P., 160, 170
Claes, M.T., 203, 211
Clugston, M., 177, 190
Co-determination, 110
Codes of ethics, 61–62
Cognitive diversity, 117
Cohen, B.P., 179, 189, 295
Cole, R., 256, 292
Collaboration-problem solving, 63
Collectivism, 23–24
Collins, G., 238

Communication
barriers to cross-cultural communication, 79–81
chromatics, 79
chronemics, 79
cross-cultural communication, 72
defined, 71
direct *versus* indirect style, 74
elaborate *versus* succinct style, 74
emotions, expression of, 76–77
enhancing cross-cultural communication, 82
instrumental *versus* affective style, 76
kinesic behavior, 77–78
language usage, 72–74
nonverbal communication, 76, 77, 78
personal *versus* contextual style, 75, 76
process of, 71
proxemics, 78
verbal communication styles, 74, 75
virtual cross-cultural communication, 81–82
Communitarian society, 31
Comparative method, 9
Comparative perspective, 9–13
Compensation, 164–166
Compensatory model, 182
Competitive advantage, role of, 5
Complexity, 237, 238
Compromise, 88
Conaway, W.A., 79, 85
Confrontation strategy, 91
Conoco's Decision: The First Annual President's Award for Business Ethics, 387–400
Conscience or the Competitive Edge? (A), 299–300
Conscience or the Competitive Edge? (B), 300–301
Containing/controlling culture, 22
Content theories, 126
Context dependent, 157
Context-free practices, 157
Context specific, 157
Contextual style, 75
Contingency theories, 239
Continuance commitment, 173
Convergence, role of, 13
Conversational overlaps, 94
Coombs, T., 131, 144
Coon, H.M., 24, 44
Cooper, C.L., 256
Cooper, M.L., 182, 190
Core groups, use of, 206
Cornfield, D.B., 4
Corporate social responsibility, 51–53
Couto, D.L., 270
Cox, T., 111, 123, 198, 202, 206, 207, 209, 211
Cox's model of the multicultural organization, 202–204
Coyle, W., 162, 170
Cross-cultural adjustment, 162–163
Cross-cultural communication, 72. *See also* Communication
Cross-cultural ethical issues, 56–57, 58–59, 60

Cross-cultural negotiations, 96, 99–100
Cross-cultural trade, acceleration of, 2
Cross-cultural training (CCT), 161–162
Cross-cultural typology, 266–267
Crystal, D., 72, 85
Cullen, J.B., 41, 43
Cultural Clash in the Entertainment Industry, A, 295–298
Cultural determinism, 7–8
Cultural differences, role of, 195–196
Cultural ethical relativism, 51
Cultural influences, 90, 91–92, 97–98
Cultural metaphors, 36–37
Cultural values in the 21st century, 11–12
Culture
achieved status *versus* ascribed status, 32
activity orientation, 22
basic assumptions, 19
basic human nature, 22
being culture, 22
Chinese Value Survey, 26–27
collectivism, and, 23–24
Confucian word dynamism, 26
containing/controlling culture, 22
cultural metaphors, 36–37
defined, 18
doing culture, 22
embeddedness *versus* autonomy, 30
enculturation, 19
expressed values level, 19
future-oriented culture, 22
group-oriented society, 23
Hall's cultural framework, 32–33
hierarchical societies, 23
hierarchy *versus* egalitarianism, 30
Hofstede's dimensions of cultural values, 23, 24, 25
individualism, and, 23–24
individualism *versus* communitarianism, 31
individualistic societies, 22
inner direction *versus* outer direction, 32
Kluckhorn and Strodtbeck's variations, 20–21
levels of, 18–19
manifest culture, 18
masculinity and femininity, role of, 26
master *versus* harmony, 30
mastery cultures, 21
mixed or neutral orientation, 22
and organizational behavior, 39–40
past orientation, 22
present-oriented culture, 22
primary socialization, 19
relation to nature, 21
relationships among people, 22
Ronen and Shenkar's country clusters, 33–34
Schwartz's Value Survey, 27, 29
secondary socialization, 20
sequential time *versus* synchronous time, 32
socialization process, 20
space orientation, and, 23
specificity *versus* diffusion, 31–32